LEIBNIZ

LEIBNIZ

Determinist, Theist, Idealist

ROBERT MERRIHEW ADAMS

OXFORD UNIVERSITY PRESS
New York Oxford

Oxford University Press

Oxford New York
Athens Auckland Bangkok Bogotá Buenos Aires Calcutta
Cape Town Chennai Dar es Salaam Delhi Florence Hong Kong Istanbul
Karachi Kuala Lumpur Madrid Melbourne Mexico City Mumbai
Nairobi Paris São Paulo Singapore Taipei Tokyo Toronto Warsaw

and associated companies in
Berlin Ibadan

First published in 1994 by Oxford University Press, Inc.
198 Madison Avenue, New York, New York 10016

First issued as an Oxford University Press paperback, 1998

Library of Congress Cataloging-in-Publication Data
Adams, Robert Merrihew.
Leibniz : determinist, theist, idealist / Robert Merrihew Adams.
p. cm.
Includes bibliographical references and indexes.
ISBN 0–19–508460–8
ISBN 0–19–512649–1 (pbk.)
1. Leibniz, Gottfried Wilhelm, 1646–1716.
I. Title.

1 3 5 7 9 8 6 4 2

Printed in the United States of America
on acid-free paper

For my mother,
Margaret Baker Adams,
the historian of our family

Preface

I did not set out to write a book on Leibniz. Through more than twenty years I have taught graduate and undergraduate courses on the philosophy of Leibniz—once at the University of Michigan, and more times than I can now enumerate at UCLA, usually at intervals of two or three years. My debt to the students, and sometimes colleagues, who attended those classes is enormous, and no longer specifiable in detail. About fifteen years ago I began to publish articles on Leibniz. Eventually, at the suggestion of colleagues, I began to think about publishing a collection of papers on Leibniz, and set out to write a couple of new ones to complete the collection. These grew, and the older pieces were thoroughly revised, and in large part reorganized and rewritten, and all the pieces acquired multiple cross-references to each other. The result is a book, and no longer a collection of papers.

The majority of the material is new. Chapter 1 is a reworking of "Leibniz's Theories of Contingency," *Rice University Studies*, 63, No. 4 (Fall 1977), pp. 1–41. Chapter 2 and much of Chapter 3 are a reworking of "Predication, Truth, and Trans-World Identity in Leibniz," which was published in *How Things Are: Studies in Predication and the History and Philosophy of Science*, edited by James Bogen and James E. McGuire (Dordrecht: Reidel, 1985), pp. 235–83. Some material in Chapter 8 comes from "Presumption and the Necessary Existence of God," *Noûs* 22 (1988): 19–32. Chapters 9 and 10 contain much material from "Phenomenalism and Corporeal Substance in Leibniz," *Midwest Studies in Philosophy* 8 (1983): 217–57. A German version (not in all parts exactly a translation) of much of the material of Chapter 11 is forthcoming in *Studia Leibnitiana*, vol. 25 (1993), under the title, "Form und Materie bei Leibniz: die mittleren Jahre." I am grateful to the publishers of these pieces for their permission to reprint the material here.

I am grateful also to the many scholars with whom I have discussed Leibniz and related topics, orally and in writing, over the years, particularly to Marilyn McCord Adams, Wallace Anderson, David Blumenfeld, Herbert Breger, Tyler Burge, John Carriero, Keith DeRose, John Earman, Ursula Franke, Amos Funkenstein, Daniel Garber, Glenn Hartz, Paul Hoffman, Jeremy Hyman, William Irvine, Nicholas Jolley, Marianne Kooij, Mark Kulstad, Marc Lange, Marianne Laori, Louis Loeb, J. E. McGuire, Fabrizio Mondadori, Massimo Mugnai, Alan Nelson, Derk Pereboom, Ayval Ramati, Nicholas Rescher, Marleen Rozemond, Donald Rutherford, Heinrich Schepers, Robert C. Sleigh, Jr.,

Houston Smit, Margaret Wilson, Norton Wise, and Robert Yost. John Carriero, Daniel Garber, and Paul Hoffman provided extremely valuable written comments on part of the work.

Marleen Rozemond and later Ayval Ramati gave important help as my research assistants. I have benefited from the extraordinary scholarly generosity of Heinrich Schepers and associates at the Leibniz-Forschungsstelle of the University of Münster and the late Albert Heinekamp and associates at the Leibniz Archive of the Niedersächsische Landesbibliothek in Hannover, who made the documents on which they are working available to me and other scholars. Professor Schepers was particularly helpful with advice about the dating of texts. Robert Sleigh and Massimo Mugnai were also generous in sharing texts.

I am grateful to UCLA for sabbatical support during the first writing of Chapters 9 and 10 and for funding research assistance in the later stages, but mainly for providing the environment for research and especially for teaching in which this book developed. I was inspired by generous encouragement of the project from my colleagues Alan Nelson, David Kaplan, Robert Yost, and the late Montgomery Forth. The book would be much poorer, if it would exist at all, without the stimulus of the splendid graduate students we have had in our department.

It is a pleasure to record these debts of gratitude.

Los Angeles, California R.M.A.
June 1993

Contents

LEIBNIZ

Introduction

The last twenty years or so have seen a flowering of Leibniz studies. The organizers of a recent international workshop called it "the Leibniz renaissance."[1] In the United States interest in the philosophy of Gottfried Wilhelm Leibniz (1646–1716) was enhanced in the 1970s by the excitement over modal logic and "modal metaphysics." The idea of a *possible world* was central to these developments, and that gave them an obvious connection with Leibniz. I think there was also a subtler and deeper, though perhaps more debatable, connection between Leibniz and the new work in modal metaphysics. From its beginning, partly through the influence of the Vienna Circle, analytical philosophy had been Kantian rather than Leibnizian in its methodology. By that I mean that its treatment of philosophical topics, especially in metaphysics, tended to be governed by epistemological views and subject to strict, prior epistemological constraints. It was characteristic of much early modern philosophy, and especially the critical philosophy of Kant, to assign a dominant role to epistemology. Of the great early modern philosophers, however, Leibniz was probably the least preoccupied with epistemology. He was typically willing to begin an argument with whatever seemed true to him and might seem true to his audience, without worrying too much about whether epistemology would present it as something we can really know. Much of the development of modal metaphysics in the 1970s and since has proceeded in this Leibnizian way—perhaps because of the strength of the grip that certain "intuitions" have had on many of the philosophers involved in the movement.

The Leibnizian approach to metaphysics might seem embarrassingly uncritical, and perhaps it would be if strong constraints on metaphysics could be derived from an epistemology that deserved our full confidence. If we view available epistemologies more skeptically, however, we may think that they are not generally more reliable than our "intuitions," and that we cannot usually do better than to begin our thinking with what seems right to us. Our interpretation of Leibniz need not depend on our own stance on this issue. Excellent work on his thought has been done by philosophers whose views on methodology in meta-

[1]Centro Fiorentino, *Leibniz Renaissance*. I give all references by abbreviations or by short names and titles; full details are found in the bibliography.

physics are quite opposed to his.[2] For better or worse, however, this is a point on which my own views are supportive of Leibniz.

Leibniz: Determinist, Theist, Idealist is not an introduction to Leibniz's philosophy, nor even a fully comprehensive account of his metaphysics. It is a piece of research into three areas related to the three attributes mentioned in the title.[3] The three topics are connected, as is everything in Leibniz's thought. My development of the first is presupposed in my treatment of the other two. That Leibniz was a theist is hardly debatable. How much a determinist and how much an idealist he was are more controversial; I believe he was more of both than some interpreters have thought. I am not sympathetic with his determinism, but am very much in sympathy (though not in detailed agreement) with his theism and his idealism.

The question of Leibniz's determinism has drawn much recent attention, in large part because of its connection with two theses related to modal metaphysics. One is Leibniz's doctrine that every predicate true of any substance is contained in the individual concept of that substance. The other is his closely related denial of counterfactual individual identities—his denial that Antoine Arnauld, for example, would have existed, and been the same individual, if he had married. These theses have held fascination for students interested in the relation of logic to metaphysics. The second has been seen as a rejection of what has been known in recent modal metaphysics as "transworld identity." The first has been one of the grounds for suspicion that no truths at all can be contingent for Leibniz. These issues, and others connected with them, form the subject of Part I of the book. One theme that emerges from my argument there (a theme in tune with much of the most recent Leibniz scholarship) is that Leibniz's views on these topics are less dominated by his logical doctrines than was thought by Bertrand Russell and Louis Couturat, the most influential Leibniz scholars of the early part of our century. Leibniz's view of the problems was largely shaped by his theology, and his use of logical doctrines in dealing with them cannot be understood apart from such metaphysical conceptions as that of substantial form.

The metaphysical core of Leibniz's philosophical theology has attracted less attention than its intrinsic interest deserves. In some ways it is also the core of his metaphysics. It is intricately connected with his logical doctrines and is the context for his fullest reflections about the nature of existence and of essence, and also about the most general structural relationships of the properties of things. These topics are discussed in Part II of the book, in the framework of a comprehensive study of Leibniz's treatment of the ontological argument for the existence of God, which I regard as exceptionally interesting. I do not think Leibniz's or any other version of the ontological argument is likely to convince many people of the existence of God, but a related argument, which seems to me to have more persuasive force, and perhaps to be the most promising of all a priori arguments for the existence of God, is discussed in Chapter 7. One reason for the neglect of this part of Leibniz's thought

[2]For such disagreement by fine scholars, see, e.g., Mates, *Philosophy of Leibniz*, p. 51, and C. Wilson, "Critical and Constructive Aspects of Leibniz's Monadology," p. 293.

[3]What I have to say about another major topic of Leibniz's metaphysics, the identity of indiscernibles, has been said in a much less historical context in R. Adams, "Primitive Thisness and Primitive Identity."

is that its fullest development, in most respects, came in his early years, and many of the most important texts were quite inaccessible until the relevant volume of the Academy edition of Leibniz's works (A VI,iii) was published in 1980. I have tried to give a full account of the most important texts.

Leibniz's doctrine of monads and his theory of the physical world may have been overshadowed at times by the interest in his philosophy of logic, but they can hardly be said to have been neglected. How could they be neglected? In teaching about Leibniz I have always found that students are instantly fascinated by the monads, and full of questions about them. At the same time, Russell's well-known report that he initially "felt . . . the *Monadology* was a kind of fantastic fairy tale, coherent perhaps, but wholly arbitrary,"[4] resonates with the first impressions of many students. In fact, I believe that Leibniz's theory of monads, in its essentials, though not in all its details, represents an important, permanent metaphysical alternative, one of the handful of fundamental views in this area that has a real chance of being true. I would not claim to prove that much here, but I will try to give in Part III a full account of Leibniz's view, including those of his arguments that seem to me of most permanent importance, and those aspects of his view that may commend it as preferable to other forms of idealism or phenomenalism.

I argue that throughout the mature period of his thought (1686–1716), his view is as idealistic as is implied in his statement of 1704 that "there is nothing in things except simple substances, and in them perception and appetite" (G II,270/L 537). Some interpreters have tried to find more realistic commitments in some period or strand of his mature philosophy, and some of these attempts are addressed in Part III. Particular attention is paid to interpretations that find more realistic implications in Leibniz's efforts to rehabilitate certain Aristotelian Scholastic conceptions; I argue that the Aristotelian conceptions that Leibniz undoubtedly does use are employed in the service of his idealism.

I have tried throughout to maintain a rigorously historical approach, attempting to establish as accurately as possible, and with the best evidence possible, what Leibniz actually said and meant. This is not to say that my approach is unphilosophical. I believe that historical accuracy and careful attention to the historical context are important to the philosophical as well as the historical value of work in the history of philosophy and, conversely, that philosophical argument and critique are important for historical understanding in philosophy.

One reason for the philosophical importance of patient and careful attention to the actual meaning of Leibniz's writings in their historical context is that he was indeed a great philosopher, great enough that an arbitrary interpretation of his work, more relevant to our historical context than to his, is unlikely to be as interesting philosophically in the long run as what he actually thought. Indeed, the very strangeness of his context, and of some of his thoughts, is a boon for philosophy. Progress in philosophy is more likely to consist in understanding possible alternatives than arriving at settled conclusions. And we are familiar enough with the familiar; part of what the great dead philosophers offer us is alternatives to our usual way of thinking—alternatives thought out in great

[4]Russell, *Philosophy of Leibniz*, p. xiii.

depth and with uncommon rational sensitivity. Part of what we are doing in studying the history of philosophy, moreover, is placing our own philosophizing in its largest context in a conversation that has been going on for many hundreds of years. Just as we are likely to understand better what we are doing in any discussion if we accurately remember and understand how it has gone, so we are likely to understand our own philosophizing better if our conception of its longer historical context is accurate.

As for the value that philosophical argument and critique have for historical understanding, I believe that R. G. Collingwood's view, that the proper method of history is that of rethinking past thoughts in one's own mind,[5] is largely true of the history of philosophy. The aim of the rethinking is to discover the inner rationale of the thoughts one studies. As Collingwood recognized, this method can be fruitfully applied only to thoughts (and actions) that lend themselves to understanding in terms of a rationale. It therefore may not be applicable to as much of history as Collingwood may have hoped. But if applicable anywhere, it is surely applicable in the history of philosophy, where the objects selected for study, for philosophical reasons, are always people whose thoughts are believed to have had a notable rationale. The rationale is a structure that there is a permanent possibility of recreating in thought—a point that fits nicely with Collingwood's idealism. The *historical* question in the history of philosophy is what the actual rationale was. It is a question we cannot very well answer without attaining a good *philosophical* understanding of the rationale. To do that, we must try to develop the arguments involved in the rationale, and we must subject the rationale, as we understand it, to searching criticism. For it is a piece of philosophy we are trying to understand, and argument and criticism are essential to philosophy.

This approach may sound, and my practice of it may seem, too ethereal for some historians. Other approaches may be more appropriate for other historical subjects, but I think this one is appropriate for the history of philosophy. I have tried to pay attention to the relation of Leibniz's metaphysics to its intellectual context, including the scientific and especially the religious thought of his time, and the social pressures at work in the discussions he was involved in. Yet my principal concern is with the intrinsic rationale of his thought. I have made no general application of a hermeneutics of suspicion. Not that I think (nor would Leibniz himself have thought) that he was free of hidden and unconscious motives. On some points, the project of understanding his rationale itself requires some attention to suspicions of insincerity in his statements. In the end, however, Leibniz's reasons are more interesting than his motives. He had one of the most brilliant intellects of all time, but he was not particularly impressive in the more practical aspects of his life. His writings contain a reasoned structure of thought (at least one) that has a permanent claim on the attention of philosophers, whether or not it accurately reflects all the motives that may have underlain his writing as well as his other conduct. What is most interesting about such a person is likely to be best understood by a historian whose training and interests are primarily philosophical.

[5]Collingwood, *Idea of History*, pp. 205–31.

I

Determinism: Contingency and Identity

1

Leibniz's Theories of Contingency

There is a familiar conception of Leibniz's views about the nature of necessity and contingency that portrays him as a sort of grandfather of possible worlds semantics for modal logic. According to this conception, Leibniz envisages an infinity of possible worlds, of which God (who exists necessarily) chooses and actualizes one (the best). Necessary truths are propositions that are true in all possible worlds. Contingent truths are propositions that are true in the actual world but false in at least one other possible world. Which worlds are possible, what would happen in them, and how they are related to one another as similar or dissimilar, better or worse, do not change from one world to another; therefore, all truths about what is possible are necessary. (This Leibniz is, to be precise, a grandfather of possible worlds semantics for S5, the strongest of the usual systems of modal logic.) For this reason also the property of being the best possible world belongs necessarily to the world that has it. The root of contingency is that it is not necessary but only contingent that God chooses to actualize the best. All and only those truths are contingent whose truth depends on God's free choice of the best.

We meet this Leibniz in chapter 3 of Bertrand Russell's *Critical Exposition of the Philosophy of Leibniz*. An important part of Russell's interpretation is the famous exception he makes in Leibniz's principle that in every true proposition the concept of the predicate is contained in the concept of the subject. "The assertion of existence, alone among predicates, is synthetic," Russell says, "and therefore, in Leibniz's view, contingent."[1] All other predicates are contained in the concepts of the subjects that have them; existence is not, however, except in the case of God. Therefore, truths about what any possible individual or possible world is like, or would be like if it existed or were actual, are all necessary, but truths about which possible world is actual, and therefore which possible individuals exist, are contingent.

Russell gave up these views after reading Louis Couturat. "Recent discussions," reported E. M. Curley, accurately, in 1974, "have tended in some measure to go back to Russell's original view (before Couturat) that, apart from the proposition that God exists, existential truths are not analytic."[2] I think this tendency leads backward, not only in time but also in our understanding of

[1]Russell, *Philosophy of Leibniz*, p. 27. The views discussed here belong to the first edition, however, and were retracted in the preface to the second edition.

[2]Curley, "Recent Work on 17th Century Continental Philosophy," p. 242.

Leibniz. For the familiar Leibniz described above is in large part a creature of misunderstanding, though not exactly of fiction.

A variety of conceptions of the problem of contingency, and solutions to it, can be found in Leibniz's writings. There was development in his thought on it, and he held more than one solution at once. (The two main solutions are set out in sections 1 and 2 of this chapter.) An accurate account of Leibniz's theories of contingency will therefore be rather complex. We will come toward the end of it, rather than at the beginning, to the question whether he regarded existence as a predicate contained in the concepts of things that exist.

1. *Leibniz's First Main Solution*

Even before he thought of the problem of contingency in terms of his conceptual containment theory of truth, Leibniz had "found [himself] very close to the opinion of those who hold everything to be absolutely necessary," but "was pulled back from this precipice by considering those possible things which neither are nor will be nor have been" (FC 178/L 263). Just how close he was to the cliff, we shall see in section 1.1; in sections 1.2–1.5 we shall consider the way in which he says he was rescued from it.

1.1 On the Brink of the Precipice

In May 1671 Leibniz wrote a letter to the legal scholar Magnus Wedderkopf about "the necessity of events" (A II,i,117f./L 146f.).[3] He begins by arguing that everything that happens is determined by God's decree and admitting that this is a "hard" conclusion. He then traces the cause of Pontius Pilate's damnation—from his lack of faith, to his failure to pay attention, to his failure to understand the utility of paying attention, to a lack of causes of such understanding.

> For it is necessary to analyze everything into some reason, and not to stop until we arrive at a first reason—or else it must be admitted that something can exist without a sufficient reason for its existence, and this admission destroys the demonstration of the existence of God and of many Philosophical theorems. What then is the ultimate reason of the divine will? The divine intellect. For God wills those things that he understands to be best and most harmonious, and selects them, as it were, from an infinite number of all possibles.

Leibniz goes on to state that the ultimate reason of things is found in the essences, possibilities, or ideas of things, which "coincide with God himself," are understood by God, and have no reason outside themselves. Leibniz draws a strongly necessitarian conclusion:

> Since God is the most perfect mind, however, it is impossible for him not to be affected by the most perfect harmony, and thus to be necessitated to the best by the very ideality of things. . . . Hence it follows that whatever has happened, is happening, or will happen is best and therefore necessary, but . . .

[3]All quotations in this section are from this letter, unless otherwise indicated.

with a necessity that takes nothing away from freedom because it takes nothing away from the will and the use of reason.

Three points deserve comment here.

1. Leibniz has already slipped over the edge of the precipice in this letter. He states flatly and without qualification that everything that ever happens is necessary. This is his simplest solution to the problem of contingency. If there is no contingency, there is no need to account for it or explain its nature. Leibniz did not remain content with this position, however. On his own copy of the letter to Wedderkopf he later wrote, "I have since corrected this; for it is one thing for sins to be infallibly going to happen, and another thing for them to be going to happen necessarily." He continued to ascribe necessity to all things, but only with some qualification. In 1679 he wrote, "What is actual is *in some way* necessary" [italics added] (Gr 536). Even in free actions there is allowed (in 1710) to be "hypothetical" and "moral" necessity, but not "absolute" or "metaphysical" necessity (G VI,37).

2. Leibniz was a compatibilist, maintaining to the end of his life (LC V,3) that every event is determined but some acts are nonetheless free. According to the formula of his maturity, freedom consists in intelligence (understanding the object of deliberation), spontaneity (insofar as the source of the action is within the agent), and contingency (which excludes absolute, logical, or metaphysical necessity, but not hypothetical or moral necessity) (T 288–90,302; cf. G VII,108–11). In the letter to Wedderkopf, however, we meet a more extreme compatibilism, which does not make contingency a necessary condition of freedom. In this early work voluntariness and intelligence seem to suffice for freedom: necessity "takes nothing away from freedom because it takes nothing from the will and the use of reason." The later addition of contingency as a condition of freedom is surely related to the change in Leibniz's willingness to admit without qualification the necessity of all events, but the latter development in his thought comes sooner than the former. In a work of 1673, in which he argues vigorously against the claim that sins are (unqualifiedly) necessary (A VI,iii,124ff.), he still says, "To preserve the privilege of free will, it is enough that we have been so placed at a fork in the road of life, that we can do only what we will, and can will only what we believe to be good; but can trace out, by the fullest given use of reason, what should be regarded as good" (A VI,iii,133). Similarly, in his notes on a conversation with Bishop Nicolaus Steno (Niels Stensen), 27 November 1677, he defined freedom simply as "rational spontaneity" (VE 302 = LH IV,4,3C,12–14). And in a paper from 1678–82 he opposes freedom to constraint and to ignorance, but says nothing by way of opposing it to necessity (VE 7–10 = LH I,3,5,23–24). Later, however, Leibniz distinguished a sense in which freedom is opposed to necessity and a sense in which it is opposed only to compulsion (B 121); in several texts from the years 1681–87 (Gr 299,308,229; cf. G VII,108–111; Gr 381f.) and later (Gr 421, G III,58f.) he ascribes *both* kinds of freedom to human agents—though even in his last years he could define the free as "the spontaneous with choice" (VE 1088 = LH IV,8,60–61).

3. In the letter to Wedderkopf the argument for the necessity of all events is not based on the conceptual containment theory of truth, but rather on the nature

of God and the principle of sufficient reason. This latter, more theological argument against contingency is by far the one most often addressed by Leibniz in his writings; and we shall be concerned with it in most of this chapter.

The letter to Wedderkopf is an exceptional text. It is hard to regard as merely tentative a view that Leibniz communicated to an eminent person with whom he was by no means intimate. But he may not have held the extreme necessitarian position for any length of time. It seems not to have been held in a fragment on free will written just a few months before or after the letter (A VI,i,540f.).[4]

1.2 *Things Possible in Their Own Nature*

By 1677 the necessitarian position was replaced by a theory Leibniz frequently repeated, publicly and privately, to the end of his career, which must be regarded as his principal (and most confident) solution to the problem of contingency. The basic idea of this solution is briefly stated in a comment on Spinoza from about 1678: "On the hypothesis of the divine will choosing the best, or operating most perfectly, certainly nothing but these things could have been produced; but according to the very nature of things considered in itself [*per se*], things could have been produced otherwise" (G I,149/L 204). We find it more fully stated in a paper on freedom, probably written in the early 1680s.

> But we must say that God wills the best by his own nature. Therefore he wills necessarily, you will say. I shall say with St. Augustine that that necessity is happy. But surely it follows from this that things exist necessarily. How so? Because a contradiction is implied by the nonexistence of that which God wills to exist? I deny that that proposition is absolutely true. Otherwise those things which God does not will would not be possible. For they remain possible, even if they are not chosen by God. It is possible indeed for even that to exist which God does not will to exist, because it would be able to exist of its own nature if God willed that it exist. But God cannot will that it exist. I agree; yet it remains possible in its own nature, even if it is not possible in respect to the divine will. For we have defined possible in its own nature as that which does not imply a contradiction in itself even if its coexistence with God can be said in some way to imply a contradiction.[5] . . .
>
> Therefore I say: that is possible, of which there is some essence or reality, or which can be distinctly understood. . . . If God had decreed that no real line must be found which should be incommensurable with other real lines (I call real a line that actually bounds some body), it would not therefore follow that the existence of an incommensurable line implies a contradiction, even if God, from the principle of perfection, could not fail to ordain in this way. (Gr 289f./AG 20–22)

On this view, the actual world, and the things that exist in it, are not necessary but contingent, because other worlds are possible in which those things would not exist. The possibility of those other worlds does not depend on the

[4]On the dating, see A VI,i,537 and ii,579, and Kabitz, *Die Philosophie des jungen Leibniz*, pp. 121–26.

[5]Here Grua inadvertently omits the clause, *etsi eius coexistentia cum Deo aliquo modo dici possit implicare contradictionem*. See VE 277.

possibility of God's choosing them. It is enough, for the contingency of the actual world, if the other possible worlds are "possible in their own nature" or "do not imply a contradiction in themselves," considered apart from God's choice.

Leibniz still takes this position in the *Theodicy*. He reports that Abelard agreed "that it can well be said that that man [who in fact will be damned] can be saved, in respect to the possibility of human nature, which is capable of salvation, but that it cannot be said that God can save him, in respect to God himself, because it is impossible for God to do that which he ought not to do." He comments that Abelard therefore need not have held, as he did, that "God cannot do anything but that which he does," for "the others . . . do not mean anything else when they say that God can save that man, and that he can do that which he does not do" (T 171). The possibility of the alternatives among which God chooses is internal to them, and this internal possibility of the alternatives is enough to make God's choice free.

> In a word, when one speaks of the *possibility* of a thing it is not a question of the causes that can bring about or prevent its actual existence; otherwise one would change the nature of the terms and render useless the distinction between the possible and the actual, as Abelard did. . . . That is why, when one asks if a thing is possible or necessary, and brings in the consideration of what God wills or chooses, one changes the question. For God chooses among the possibles, and for that very reason he chooses freely, and is not necessitated; there would be neither choice nor freedom if there were but one choice possible. (T 235; cf. T 44,45,228,230–32,234,367)[6]

The first problem about this theory is to understand what is meant by "possible in its own nature." If a certain world is inferior and so cannot be chosen by God, is that not by virtue of its own nature? Why, then, should we not say that it is impossible in its own nature?

The theory requires a relatively narrow understanding of the nature, essence, or concept of a thing or a world. The essence of a substance, in the narrow sense, contains information about such things as the perceptions the substance has, and perhaps the geometrical configurations and motions expressed by those perceptions, and about the substance's powers and tendencies to produce perceptions in itself—but not about other substances.[7] It is in this sense that Leibniz can say, "That is possible of which there is some essence," even if God could

[6]Robert Sleigh, in his superb book on *Leibniz and Arnauld*, pp. 82f., doubts that Leibniz still adheres to the "possible-in-its-own-nature" theory of contingency in the *Theodicy*, and offers an ingenious interpretation of T 235, where it does not imply that theory. I am not persuaded, however, because I think there are too many passages of the *Theodicy*, many of them cited here and in sections 1.4 and 1.5, that are most naturally interpreted on the basis of the "possible-in-its-own-nature" theory. There is also a letter of March 1713 to Christian Goldbach in which Leibniz gives an extended treatment of the problem of contingency, using only ideas belonging to the "possible-in-its-own-nature" theory, and identifies this as the view defended in the *Theodicy* (LG 189).

[7]This presupposes that information about a substance's perceptions and their (internal) content does not of itself contain information, in the relevant sense, about other substances—that apart from considerations of intersubstantial harmony, it does not entail the existence of the substances perceived. I believe that Leibniz was committed, on the whole, to this presupposition; there are things in his writings from 1686 and later, however, which could be taken as suggesting the opposite. See Chapter 3, section 3.

not choose to actualize it (Gr 289). Necessity as well as possibility can be viewed as internal to essences in the narrow sense; indeed, what Leibniz means by necessary existence is precisely existence that follows from the essence of a substance without consideration of the essence of any other substance (see Chapter 5, section 1). Conversely, one main sense in which things are contingent, for Leibniz, is that they depend on God's will (and power) for their existence (or nonexistence).

Of course, Leibniz famously speaks of each substance as having an individual concept in a much broader sense in which it is "complete" and contains much information about other substances—indeed, perhaps it contains all truths. This complete concept, I believe, is supposed to follow from the substance's essence in the narrower sense, but only in combination with truths that follow from the essences of other substances and their interrelations. In the *Discourse on Metaphysics* "essences" seem to be equivalent to complete concepts (DM 16), but Leibniz's use of the term 'essence' is quite fluid.

The nature of a possible world, in the narrow sense, is constructed from the essences, in the narrow sense, of the substances that would exist in it. Leibniz may indeed have thought of it as the sum of those essences. But we may think of it as containing also all sorts of relations among the substances—which are more perfect than which, how they perceive or express each other, and so forth. Thus is built up what we may call the *basic concept* of a possible world. It is to contain information about everything that happens *in* that world, but not everything that is true about its relation to God's will.

By analogy with the complete concept of an individual, we can also speak of the *complete concept* of a possible world, which is to be fuller than the basic concept and contain information about everything that is true about that possible world, including whether it is the best, or nearly the best, or far from the best, of all possible worlds, and whether God therefore chooses or rejects it.[8] We may take it to be Leibniz's position that a world is possible in its own nature if its *basic* concept contains no internal contradictions, and nothing that is incompatible with its actuality so long as certain determinants of God's choice are kept out of the picture; its *complete* concept may contain God's rejecting it, but that does not keep it from being "possible in its own nature."

Questions remain about just what is to be excluded from a world's basic concept.

1. Does it include any concepts of other possible worlds? It seems natural to exclude them, since we are trying to capture the idea of a possibility that is internal to one possible world. And by excluding them we can be certain of not including enough information to imply God's rejection of the world represented by the basic concept. On the other hand, the solution of the problem of contingency does not strictly require the exclusion of this information if the right information about God is excluded. And if rational creatures would exist in the world

[8]The distinction between basic and complete concepts of a possible world is not explicit in Leibniz. He does speak of the concept of a possible world, but without making the distinction: "this universe has a certain principal or primitive concept, of which particular events are only consequences" (LA 41).

of the basic concept, they would presumably think about alternative possibilities; so by containing their thoughts, the basic concept would contain partial concepts of alternative possible worlds. But this does not prove that the basic concept of a possible world must include *complete* concepts of other worlds. For no creature, no being other than God, according to Leibniz, conceives possible worlds in enough detail to determine which is the best.

2. Do basic concepts of possible worlds include any facts about God? Leibniz seems flatly to exclude God from the world when, in discussion with Gabriel Wagner, 3 March 1698, he rejects some of Wagner's suggestions, saying, "These things would be true, taking the word 'World' so that it includes God too. But this usage is not appropriate. By the name 'World' is normally understood the aggregate of things that are changeable or liable to imperfection" (Gr 396). Similarly, Leibniz refers to the world in 1697 as "the Aggregate of finite things" (G VII,302/L486), and in the early to mid-1680s as "the composite of all creatures" (VE 166 = LH IV,7C,70) or, with an unusual restriction, "the Aggregate of all bodies" (VE 418 = LH IV,7C,111–14).[9] If Leibniz conceives of the basic concept of a possible world as a sum of essences of (possible) substances, God's essence will be excluded from the sum. On the other hand, Leibniz speaks of the possible things that are the alternatives for God's choice as containing in their concepts certain decisions of God, considered as possible, so that God chooses among certain possible divine actions, as well as among possible creatures (C 23f.; LA 49–51; cf. G I,360). This causes no problem for the theory of contingency, provided that the divine decisions that are included in the alternatives for God's choice are noncomparative decisions concerned only with the laws or order of the world to which they belong.

What is important for Leibniz's treatment of contingency is that the basic concepts of possible worlds do not include God's choice *among* possible worlds. In order to exclude it, they must exclude some information either about God or about other possible worlds. And it is not clear that excluding information about other worlds will always be enough. If "the damnation of an innocent is . . . possible in itself," and does not "imply a contradiction in terms," as Leibniz wrote in texts dating from 1677 and the early 1680s, the basic concept of such a thing may very well have to exclude information about God's justice, for Leibniz does not seem to think one has to compare possible worlds in order to determine that a just God would not choose such a state of affairs. Indeed, the information that Leibniz invokes from outside the concept of this state to explain the way in which it is not possible is not about other possible worlds, but only about God: it cannot actually exist "because it is incompatible with the presupposed existence of God, whose perfection (from which justice follows) cannot permit such a thing" (Gr 300,271).

[9]These formulations suggest a conception of possible worlds as less complete than they are normally conceived to be today. A similarly restricted conception persisted in post-Leibnizian German philosophy. Thus "the world" is defined by Wolff (*Vernünftige Gedanken*, § 544) as a connected "series of changeable things" and by Crusius as (*Entwurf der nothwendigen Vernunft-Wahrheiten*, § 204) as "the whole aggregate of all finite things."

1.3 Hypothetical Necessity

Even if a satisfactory explanation can be given of what it is for a thing or a world to be possible in its own nature, there remains an important objection to Leibniz's use of this notion in accounting for contingency. His claim is that the actuality of this world is contingent because other worlds are still possible in their own natures even if they are not possible in relation to God's will. But in presenting this theory of contingency, in some of the earlier texts (Gr 289f.; A VI,iii,127f.), Leibniz seems to admit that it is necessary that God chooses this world. And if it is necessary that God chooses this world, and it follows necessarily from that that this world is actual, must not the actuality of this world be necessary and not contingent? As Curley puts it:

> It is an uncontroversial truth of modal logic that if *p* is necessary and entails *q*, then *q* is necessary. So if it is (absolutely) necessary that God choose the best, and if the existence of the best world is (hypothetically) necessary in relation to his choice, then it is (absolutely) necessary that the best world exist.[10]

Leibniz makes much use of the term 'hypothetically necessary', which Curley rightly brings in here. Leibniz says repeatedly (e.g., in DM 13) that contingent truths are *hypothetically* but not *absolutely* necessary. 'Hypothetical necessity' is normally, as he recognized (G III,400/AG 193), a synonym for 'necessity of the consequence'. So he seems to be using the traditional distinction between necessity of the consequence and necessity of the consequent: 'If *p* then necessarily *q*'[11] can mean either that 'If *p* then *q*' is necessary (necessity of the consequence), or that if '*p*' is true then '*q*' is necessary (necessity of the consequent). But then necessity of the consequence (hypothetical necessity) combined with necessity of the antecedent implies necessity of the consequent. If '*p*' and 'If *p* then *q*' are both necessary, then '*q*' is necessary.

Leibniz raised this very objection against himself in his "first Theodicy," written in dialogue form in 1673 as *The Philosopher's Confession*, and given to Antoine Arnauld and others.[12]

> God's existence is necessary. From it follow the sins that are contained in [this actual] series of things. What follows from the necessary is necessary. Therefore the sins are necessary. (A VI,iii,127)

The answer that Leibniz first wrote was as follows:

> I reply that it is false that whatever follows from what is necessary is necessary. From truths, to be sure, nothing follows that is not true. Yet since a particular [conclusion] can follow from purely universal [premises], as in [the

[10]Curley, "Recent Work on 17th Century Continental Philosophy," p. 243. Substantially the same objection was raised by a "Roman Catholic Theologian" whom Des Bosses consulted and quoted in a note to § 201 of his Latin translation of Leibniz's *Theodicy* (Dutens I,273).

[11]I use ordinary (single) quotation marks in place of corner quotes, since the latter are not universally understood.

[12]I owe this information, and the phrase "first Theodicy," to the introduction to Saame, 14, 16, 22. Saame's excellent edition is now superseded by A VI,iii, as a standard reference, but his introduction and notes remain extremely valuable.

> syllogistic figures] Darapti and Felapton, why not something contingent from something necessary? (A VI,iii,127)[13]

Thus baldly stated, Leibniz's answer seems simply to ignore the modal axiom to which Curley appeals. Leibniz acknowledged the axiom, however, at least by 1675, when he wrote, "Whatever is incompatible with something necessary is impossible" (A VI,iii,464). He therefore distinguished two types of necessity and impossibility. "The concept of the impossible is twofold: that which has no Essence; and that which has no Existence or which neither was nor is nor will be, which is incompatible with God or with existence or with the reason which makes things to be rather than not" (A VI,iii,463). Leibniz accordingly corrected his answer in the manuscript of *The Philosopher's Confession* (very likely about the end of 1677),[14] to incorporate such a distinction:

> I reply that it is false that whatever follows from what is necessary *through itself* is necessary *through itself.* From truths, to be sure, nothing follows that is not true. Yet since a particular [conclusion] can follow from purely universal [premises], as in [the syllogistic figures] Darapti and Felapton, why may not something contingent, *or necessary on the hypothesis of something else,* follow from something that is necessary *through itself*? (A VI,iii,127f.)[15]

He also added:

> In this place we call *necessary* only that which is necessary *through itself*—that is, which has the reason of its existence and truth within itself. Such are the Geometrical truths, and of existing things only God. The others, which follow from the supposition of this series of things—that is, from the harmony of things—or from the Existence of God, are *contingent through themselves* and only hypothetically necessary. (A VI,iii,128)[16]

Here it is clear that in spite of the traditional terminology of hypothetical necessity, the absolute or per se necessity that Leibniz denies in affirming contingency is something more than the traditional necessity of the consequent.[17] In Leibniz's conception of hypothetical necessity, the absolute necessity or contingency of the antecedent is no more important than the externality of the

[13]Here I translate the text of A VI,iii, minus Leibniz's later additions.

[14]Additions to a manuscript are hard to date, but we know that Leibniz was working on this text, and thinking along these lines, at this time. The manuscript bears marginal comments by Nicolaus Steno, in Steno's hand, and responses to them in Leibniz's hand, which surely date from the period of Steno's residence in Hannover, from late 1677 to 1680. Steno and Leibniz had a long discussion on the subject on 27 November/7 December 1677. Leibniz's record of his own views in that discussion expresses the same theory of contingency as these additions to *The Philosopher's Confession*, as I will shortly explain. On these matters, see A VI,iii,115 and the introduction to Saame, 20–23.

[15]Here I translate the full text of A VI,iii, italicizing Leibniz's principal additions.

[16]Here the italicized words were underlined by Leibniz. What Leibniz says here is important for his conception of God as a necessary being; see Chapter 5, section 1.

[17]Conversely, 'hypothetical necessity' could mean for Leibniz something stronger than it traditionally meant, something that excludes only per se necessity. Fabrizio Mondadori argues along different lines for a similar conclusion in his very thorough and illuminating study of Leibniz's treatment of this topic; see Mondadori, "Necessity ex Hypothesi," esp. pp. 196–205.

antecedent to the consequent. What follows necessarily from what is necessary through itself is certainly necessary by necessity of the consequent, in the traditional sense. It is not necessary through itself, however, but only hypothetically necessary, and contingent, in Leibniz's sense, if the antecedent from which it follows is external to it, and not contained in its own nature. The phrase Leibniz uses here, 'necessary *ex alterius hypothesi*' [necessary on the hypothesis *of something else*], expresses his meaning better than the more usual 'necessary *ex hypothesi*'.

This conception of hypothetical necessity is expressed only slightly less clearly in another early passage. In Leibniz's record of his side of his conversation on 27 November 1677 with Nicholas Steno, who read *The Philosopher's Confession* and commented on it, he says that "there is an *absolute necessity* when a thing cannot even be understood, but implies a contradiction in terms," and "there is a *hypothetical necessity* when a thing's being *some other way* can indeed be understood through itself, but it is necessarily *this way*, nonessentially [*per accidens*], on account of other things outside itself already presupposed" (Gr 270f.).

In his later writings Leibniz is usually less explicit about his interpretation of hypothetical necessity, and indeed it may be questioned whether he adhered consistently to his account of contingency in terms of things possible in their own nature. The evidence that his adherence to it was not consistent and unwavering has to do with the question whether effects that are contingent in the sense of being only hypothetically necessary must have contingent causes, and likewise whether effects that are possible in themselves must have possible causes. There are passages, both early and late, in which Leibniz says that the possibility or essence, as distinct from the actual existence, of any being depends on the possibility of a cause or reason of its existence, which seems to imply that the concepts of creatures as possible depend on the concept of God as possibly causing them.

Thus in 1676, in connection with the ontological argument for the existence of God, Leibniz wrote that a most perfect Being "cannot be unless it has a reason of existing from itself or from something else" (A VI,iii,572).[18] While it is God whose possibility Leibniz is discussing here, he is clearly relying on a general principle that would make the possibility of *any* being depend on the possibility of a reason for its existence. This threatens to undermine the distinction between internal and external possibility on which his first main theory of contingency is based.

Of course this text may well have preceded, by some months, Leibniz's full development of that theory of contingency. And by 1678 or 1679 Leibniz himself was using a distinction between internal and external possibility to criticize a Spinozistic proof that was based on an assumption very similar to his own assumption of 1676. He endorses a proof that a substance conceived through itself is possible in the sense that it "can be conceived," but with a reservation:

> But thus far it can still be doubted whether it is therefore possible in the way in which *possible* is taken in this context—that is, not for what can be con-

[18]This passage is part of an argument discussed at length in Chapter 5, section 2.3.

> ceived, but for that of which some cause, analyzable ultimately into the first cause, can be conceived. For not all of the things we can conceive can therefore be produced, on account of other, superior things with which they are incompatible. (G I,143/L 199)

Being unable to be produced (by a perfectly wise and good God) on account of incompatibility with superior things is exactly the way in which Leibniz thought that something possible in its own nature might nonetheless lack a more external sort of possibility. In 1678 or 1679 he sees that this point invalidates an existence proof that depends on inferring the possibility of a cause from the possibility of a thing in its own nature. That in 1676 he proposed (to himself, at least) a proof that depends on the converse inference from impossibility of a cause to what appears to be understood as impossibility of a thing in its own nature may be taken as suggesting that by 1676 he had not yet worked out the distinction between internal and external modalities or the theory of contingency that depends on the distinction.

Perhaps he had not. But the view expressed in 1676 recurs at intervals through Leibniz's middle and later years. There is a paper from the mid-1680s (Gr 310f.), for example, that hints, though it does not unambiguously imply, that effects that are contingent in the sense of being only hypothetically necessary must have contingent causes. Writing to Arnauld in 1686, Leibniz says that "the possibilities of individuals or of contingent truths contain in their concept the possibility of their causes, namely of the free decisions of God" (LA 51). In a letter of 1701 to Burcher De Volder, Leibniz says, "for conceiving of the essence of [a substance], the concept of a possible cause is required; for conceiving of its existence, the concept of an actual cause is required" (G II,225/L 524). Similarly, Leibniz seems to think that the possibility of an effect requires the possibility, though not the actuality, of some cause of it, when he says, in a letter of 1714 to Louis Bourguet, "Generally speaking, in order for a thing to be possible, it suffices that its efficient cause be possible; I except the supreme efficient cause, which must exist in fact" (G III,572/L 661).[19] In some of these passages it is not explicit that the possibility of a thing *in itself* is at issue; but the statement of 1701 to De Volder about essence is surely about internal possibility.

I am not persuaded by this evidence, however, that Leibniz ever abandoned the distinction between internal and external possibility, or the theory of contingency based on it. For in the *Theodicy* of 1710 he still says that considerations about what God chooses, and in general about the causes of a thing, are not relevant to the question of the thing's possibility (T 235, quoted earlier in section 1.2). And it would not be plausible to interpret Leibniz there as meaning only that the *actuality* of the causes is irrelevant, while tacitly assuming that the *possibility* of the causes is relevant. For he is explicitly attacking Abelard, whom he reads (T 171) as arguing, not merely from the nonactuality, but from the alleged impossibility of God's having chosen otherwise than God actually did. The idea that it is enough for contingency that there are a plurality of alternatives for God's choice that are possible in themselves is more clearly and

[19]Two of the passages quoted here were called to my attention by David Blumenfeld, who also pointed out the problem they cause for my interpretation.

emphatically presented in the *Theodicy* than any other well-articulated solution to the problem of contingency.[20] By the time of writing the *Theodicy*, as we shall see, Leibniz had developed a more ambitious theory of contingency that enabled him to hold that God's choice of this world to actualize is contingent, and therefore that contingent existences do have a contingent cause in God; this more ambitious theory is not clearly presented in the *Theodicy*, however.

Perhaps there is some vacillation or inconsistency in Leibniz's treatment of hypothetical necessity and the relation of a thing's possibility to the possibility of a cause of it. But we may be able to obtain a consistent reading of all (or almost all) the texts if we draw the right line between attributes of God that are, and that are not, to be taken into account in the basic concepts of possible worlds. In particular, we should consider the hypothesis that Leibniz consistently (and persistently) supposed that the internal possibility of created things depends on God's omnipotence or power to create them, but not on God's justice, by which God discriminates among the internally possible creatures.

1.4 *The Reality of Choice*

We may be tempted to object that the conception of the contingent as that which has some alternative that is possible *in itself* (if not in relation to God, or God's justice) does not really show how there can be any contingency in the Leibnizian universe, nor how God's choice among possible worlds can be free. For what is contingent in this Leibnizian sense may still be necessary by necessity of the consequent—that is, absolutely necessary—in the traditional (and twentieth-century) sense. And the choice of this world to actualize may be necessitated by God's nature as perfectly good, even if other worlds remain possible in themselves. If this is all that Leibniz has to offer in defense of contingency, his system may be thought as necessitarian as Spinoza's.

Most of what is said in this objection is right, in a way, but it overlooks the nature of Leibniz's interest in free will and contingency, along with his stated view of the difference between his determinism and Spinoza's. His interest in contingency is rooted in his interest in divine and human free will—with respect to which he is, after all, a compatibilist. We must let him define for himself what kind of compatibilist he is. At one time, as we have seen, he regarded unqualified necessity as compatible with freedom. Later his principal reason for insisting on some sort of contingency in connection with free action seems to have been to ensure the reality of choice—to ensure that what happens is really influenced by final causes and judgments of value.

This is the point that Leibniz most often insists on in distinguishing his views about necessity from Spinoza's. Spinoza held that there are no final causes in nature, that God does not act for an end, and that things are called good or bad with regard only to how they affect us, being quite indifferent to God (*Ethics*, I, Appendix). He said that actual intellect and will must be referred to God-as-an-effect [*natura naturata*] and not to God-as-a-cause [*natura naturans*] (*Ethics*, I,

[20] I still hold this view, despite Sleigh's arguments to the contrary; see Sleigh, *Leibniz and Arnauld*, pp. 82f., and note 6 above.

prop. 31), and denied that a divine intellect or will could resemble ours in anything more than name alone (*Ethics*, I, prop. 17, schol.). Indeed there is no room in Spinoza's system for God to choose, for there is nothing to be excluded by God's choice. By the necessity of the divine nature, since it is infinite in Spinoza's sense, absolutely everything possible must be actual (*Ethics*, I, prop. 16).

On all of these points Leibniz disagreed with Spinoza. Even in the most extremely necessitarian interpretation of Leibniz's system, God's choice has a real and important role to play. For even if God's choice of this world is necessary, other worlds are possible in their own nature and are not excluded without God's choice but only through (the necessity of) God's choosing this one. God's choice is an indispensable link in the chain of explanation for the actuality of this world. "The nature of things, taken without intelligence and without choice, has nothing sufficiently determining" (T 350). The comparative value of the different worlds also has a crucial explanatory role, in which Leibniz employs a notion of final cause.[21]

Leibniz emphasizes this disagreement in his discussions of Spinoza, early and late. In the period 1676–78, near the time of Spinoza's death, Leibniz commented, "But it is not at all to be thought that all things follow from God's nature without any intervention of the will" (A VI,iii,364; cf. Gr 279), and "Even if it is true that not everything happens for the sake of human beings, it still does not follow that [God] acts without will or understanding of the good" (G I,150/L 205). In the *Theodicy* he wrote:

> Spinoza . . . appears to have explicitly taught a blind necessity, having denied to the author of things understanding and will, and imagining that good and perfection relate only to us and not to him. It is true that Spinoza's opinion on this subject is somewhat obscure. . . . Nevertheless, as far as one can understand him, he acknowledges no goodness in God, properly speaking, and he teaches that all things exist by the necessity of the Divine nature, without God making any choice. We will not amuse ourselves here refuting an opinion so bad, and indeed so inexplicable. Our own is founded on the nature of the possibles—that is to say, of the things that do not imply any contradiction. (T 173; cf. T 174,371–74; RS 48–50/AG 277f.)

If we will allow Leibniz to disagree with Spinoza in his own way, rather than in some way that we might impose on him, this should be enough to show that his determinism is not properly called Spinozistic.

1.5 Moral Necessity

When Leibniz says that he opposes a "brute" or "blind" necessity (T 174,349), he means (sometimes with explicit reference to Spinoza) a necessity that denies

[21] A similar point is made by Margaret Wilson, in her interesting paper, "Leibniz's Dynamics and Contingency in Nature," pp. 284f.: "Even if one should conclude that the denial of a truth of fact *must* lead to contradiction on Leibniz's premises, there remain vast differences between his system and the necessitarianism of Spinoza. The main point can be expressed very simply: Leibniz's philosophy requires that the explanation of any existential proposition involve reference to value, purpose, perfection."

to God intelligence and choice (T 371–72). Similarly, in the *Theodicy*[22] he admits a "moral" but not a "metaphysical" necessity of God's choosing the best. Leibniz usually gives little or no explanation of this distinction, and one might be tempted to take it as a promissory note for a less strongly necessitarian theory that he was unable to provide in detail. But in fact 'morally necessary' had a precise meaning. The morally necessary is what one morally ought to do. In his early writings on jurisprudence (1671–78) Leibniz enunciated a system of moral modalities (a very rudimentary deontic logic) in terms of what is possible, impossible, necessary, or contingent (i.e., omissible or not necessary) "to be done by a good man" (A VI,i,465ff.). "I call *morally impossible* that which it is not possible to do without committing a sin" (A IV,i,471). "*Obligation* . . . is a moral necessity—that is, a necessity imposed on him who wants to keep the name of 'a good man'" (Gr 608). Similarly, "*duty* [*officium*] is whatever is necessary in the perfectly just" (C 517). Accordingly, when Leibniz says that God's choice of the best is morally necessary, we must take him to mean that it is necessary that if God did not choose the best, God would not be perfectly good. It is noteworthy that Samuel Clarke, his contemporary, did take this to be Leibniz's meaning. Clarke's examples of moral necessity are "that a *good Being*, continuing to be *Good*, cannot do *Evil*; or a *wise* Being, continuing to be *Wise*, cannot act *unwisely*; or a *veracious* Person, continuing to be *veracious*, cannot tell a Lie" (G VII,423). (Clarke also thought this a "figurative" and philosophically uninteresting sense of 'necessity'.)

It is in keeping with this conception that the *Theodicy* speaks of being "necessitated morally by wisdom" (T 237), identifies moral necessity with "the choice of the wise, worthy of his wisdom" (T pd2), and says that "it is a moral necessity that the wisest is obliged to choose the best" (T 230). In some of his discussions of moral necessity Leibniz's concern for the reality of choice comes together pretty explicitly with his idea of the contingent as that which receives necessity only from outside itself and has alternatives that are possible in themselves. He distinguishes between "metaphysical necessity, which leaves no place for any choice, presenting only one possible object, and moral necessity, which obliges the wisest to choose the best" (T 367), and says:

> But that sort of necessity which does not destroy the possibility of the contrary has that name only by analogy. It becomes effective, not by the essence of things alone, but by that which is outside them and above them, namely by the will of God. This necessity is called moral, because with the wise, what is necessary and what ought to be are equivalent things. [T aVIII (G VI,386)]

2. *Leibniz's Second Main Solution*

We have now explored the set of ideas that constitute the innermost and surest bastion of Leibniz's defenses against the denial of contingency. Even if everything actual is necessarily actualized by God on account of the divine goodness,

[22]Leibniz used the concept of moral necessity much earlier, but had applied it to God's choice of the best only since 1707, according to Grua, *Jurisprudence*, p. 235.

the things that God chooses are not necessary through themselves, but only on the hypothesis of something external to them, and they have alternatives that are possible in themselves. They are therefore in a certain sense contingent, and only hypothetically necessary. Leibniz finds contingency in this sense worth defending, because it preserves the reality of God's choice, distinguishing the "moral" necessity that he ascribes to God's action from the "brute" or "blind" necessity that he thinks belongs to it in Spinoza's system. Leibniz adhered to these views from 1677 to the end of his life.

But we have yet to examine the outer walls of his castle of contingency. In the end, Leibniz not only denied that this world, which in fact is actual, is necessary through itself; he also denied that it is necessarily actualized by God. In several papers from the 1680s we see him struggling to justify this denial and fit it into his philosophy. By 1690 he had made much progress in understanding the problem and had attained a solution that seems to have satisfied him fairly well.

2.1 The Contingency of Which World Is Best

According to Leibniz, this world, rather than any other possible world, is actual because God chooses to actualize whatever is best, and this is the best of all possible worlds. Therefore, if it is contingent that this world is actual, it must either be contingent that God chooses whatever is best or be contingent that this is the best. Which is it that is contingent? Leibniz explicitly raised this question in several papers written between 1689 and 1706; he tended to favor the answer that what is contingent is that this world is the best.

In one note from about 1695 he raises the question without answering it:

> The formal cause [of the knowability of future contingents] is the coherence of terms, or the fact that the predicate inheres in the subject, even if the cause why it inheres depends on two things, the universal bestness and God's decision to choose the best. Or is God's general decision necessary?[23] Or is it not that 'This is the best' is true, but not necessary; it is true but not demonstrable a priori. Is it not therefore contingent? (Gr 351)

Although the question is not answered here, Leibniz's inclination is clear.

It is explicit in other texts, including an important paper from 1689 or 1690, the earliest work known to me in which Leibniz defined the alternatives:[24]

> We must see whether if we suppose that this proposition is necessary: *the proposition which has the greater reason for existing exists*, it follows that the proposition which has the greater reason for existing is necessary. But the inference is rightly rejected. For if the definition of a necessary proposition is, that its truth can be demonstrated with geometrical rigor, then it can indeed

[23]Leibniz first wrote "God's general decision is necessary"—then changed it, producing a sentence that is quite awkward in the original.

[24]The date is that of Leibniz's Italian tour; the manuscript is written on Italian paper (VE 1763). The text belongs to a period when Leibniz was in comfortable possession of the infinite analysis theory of contingency, but seems still to have been working out the ideas expressed in the quoted passage. In my translation I omit the many phrases crossed out by Leibniz.

> happen that this proposition can be demonstrated: *every truth, and only a truth, has the greater reason*, or this one: *God always acts most wisely*. But it will not therefore be possible to demonstrate this proposition: *contingent proposition A has the greater reason*, or *contingent proposition A is conformed to the divine wisdom*. And therefore also it does not follow that contingent proposition A is necessary. And therefore even if it were conceded that it is necessary that God chooses the best, or that the best is necessary, still it does not follow that that which is chosen is necessary, since no demonstration that it is the best is given. (Gr 305f./AG 30)

Here Leibniz is rather careful not to assert that it is necessary that God chooses the best. But he does commit himself to the view that it is not necessary that this (which God has chosen) is the best, although it is in fact the best. Of the two ways in which the necessity of that which God has chosen could be denied, Leibniz is readier here to deny the necessity of 'This is the best' than the necessity of 'God chooses the best'.

His stance is the same in a note written in the early 1690s:

> Or does this follow: 'This proposition is necessary: God does the best. Therefore that which God does is necessary'? The inference is not valid. For the conclusion follows the weaker part. But it is not demonstrable that a certain thing is the best, nor, therefore, [can it be demonstrated] what must be done. Or shall we rather say that this proposition too, 'God does the best', is not necessary but only certain? The previous opinion appears to be best, since this proposition: A is the best, is certain, but is not necessary since it cannot be demonstrated. (Gr 336)

We do not have to deny the necessity of 'God does the best', since that which is the best is not necessarily the best.

In another text, the latest and most revealing of the series, Leibniz begins by stating again that 'This is the best' is not necessary even if 'That which is the best is chosen' is necessary. He says that he does not know whether God's not choosing the best implies a contradiction. But he asserts flatly that "This is the best," though true, "is not demonstrable by a demonstration that shows that the contrary implies a contradiction." Then he seems to change his mind and shifts to a less cautious position on the necessity of God's choosing the best:

> It is the same argument: God wills necessarily the work that is most worthy of his wisdom. I say that he wills it, but not necessarily, because although this work is the most worthy, that is not a necessary truth.[25] It is true that this proposition: God wills the work that is most worthy of him, is necessary. But it is not true that he wills it necessarily. For this proposition: This work is the most worthy, is not a necessary truth; it is indemonstrable, contingent, a truth of fact. (Gr 493)

The argument here turns on an ambiguity of 'necessarily'. Leibniz saw it as an ambiguity of scope. He accepts the 'necessarily' as "applied to the copula" (that is, to the whole proposition), but not as applied to "what is contained in the copula" (that is, as internal to the predicate). He will affirm that "God is

[25] *Vérité*. Grua, by mistake, has *suite*. Grua has also inserted quotation marks in the text of this passage.

necessarily the one who wills the best. But not the one who necessarily wills the best" (Gr 494). It is misleading, however, for Leibniz to make an issue of which verb 'necessarily' modifies. The crucial point in the ambiguity is whether the necessity applies *de re* to the object that God in fact wills. This point could be brought out by distinguishing wide from narrow scope of the definite description operator in "God necessarily wills the work that is most worthy of his wisdom." If it has wide scope, the necessity applies *de re* to the work, and the sense of the proposition is, 'The work that is most worthy of God's wisdom is such that it is necessary that God wills *it*'—which Leibniz denies. But if the definite description operator has narrow scope, the sense is rather, 'It is necessary that God wills whatever work is most worthy of God's wisdom'—which Leibniz here accepts. Of course it would be anachronistic to expect Leibniz to have made the point that way.

The date of this text deserves comment. It cannot possibly have been written before 1706, because it is a note made in reading the third volume of Pierre Bayle's *Réponses aux questions d'un provincial*, which was published at the end of the previous year.[26] This refutes Nicholas Rescher's suggestion that it was only "until the year 1686, when his mature philosophy took form" that Leibniz preferred denying the necessity of 'This is the best' to denying the necessity of 'God chooses the best'.[27]

It should also be noted that the proposition, "God wills necessarily the work that is most worthy of his wisdom," which is quoted from Bayle, is discussed again (with the same reference to Bayle) in the *Theodicy*, where it is denied (T 237). Leibniz does not make there the distinctions that he had made in the note from 1706, but only appeals to the difference between metaphysical and moral necessity. What he is denying in the *Theodicy*, however, should probably be understood in light of the earlier note.

2.2 *Necessity, Demonstrability, and Infinite Analysis*

The thesis that the property of being the best of all possible worlds belongs only contingently to the world that has it has seemed so evidently false to some recent philosophers that they have been unwilling to regard it as a part of Leibniz's mature philosophy. "That this world is the best possible world is presumably a necessary fact," according to Curley;[28] Rescher says, "it is difficult to see how what is best could avoid being determined with necessitation when the substances are conceived *sub ratione possibilitatis*."[29] That this world is the best does not depend on which world exists, or is actual, or is chosen by God. Leibniz insists that the values of things are completely independent of God's will.[30] The "bestness" of this world is rather the ground of its being chosen by God and hence actual and existent.

[26]December 1705, dated 1706. See Labrousse, *Pierre Bayle*, vol. I, p. 259, n. 88. Leibniz had seen the volume by February 1706 (G III,143).

[27]Rescher, *Philosophy of Leibniz*, pp. 69f.

[28]Curley, "Root of Contingency," p. 94.

[29]Rescher, *Philosophy of Leibniz*, pp. 69f.

[30]As pointed out in this connection by Lovejoy, *Great Chain of Being*, p. 173.

In several of his mature writings, however, Leibniz did assert that the bestness of that which is best is contingent, as we have seen, and I do not know of any text from the mature period of his philosophy in which he asserts or implies the opposite. How can he have thought what he appears to have thought? The explanation is to be sought in the idea, which occurs in all of the crucial passages, that it cannot be *demonstrated* what is best. Leibniz brings in here, implicitly, his very formal ideal of demonstration by analysis in a finite number of steps. For of all his solutions to the theological version of the problem of contingency, that which proceeds by denying the necessity of facts about which things are best is the most clearly connected with his conception of contingency in terms of infinite analysis.

This conception is indeed rather fully stated in the earliest of the papers in which we have found Leibniz saying that it is contingent what is the best.

> And here[31] is uncovered the secret distinction between Necessary and Contingent Truths, which no one will easily understand unless he has some tincture of Mathematics—namely that in necessary propositions one arrives, by an analysis continued to some point, at an identical equation (and this very thing is to demonstrate a truth in geometrical rigor); but in contingent propositions the analysis proceeds to infinity by reasons of reasons, so that indeed one never has a full demonstration, although there is always, underneath, a reason for the truth, even if[32] it is perfectly understood only by God, who alone goes through an infinite series in one act of the mind. (Gr 303/AG 28)

This is Leibniz's solution to the version of the problem of contingency that has fascinated his twentieth-century readers, the version that asks, "if the concept of having the predicate at a given time inheres in the concept of the subject, how can the subject then lack the predicate without contradiction and[33] impossibility, and without loss of its concept?" (FC 179/L 264) The solution is that a predicate can be contained in the concept of a subject without this containment being provable by analysis in a finite number of steps. Leibniz will say that in such a case the subject's lacking the predicate does not "imply a contradiction," and that its having the predicate cannot be "demonstrated" and is contingent (FC 181/L 264).[34]

An example may help us understand how such cases may arise. It may be that there is a property, ø, such that for every natural number, *n*, it can be proved that *n* has ø, but the universal generalization that every *n* has ø cannot be proved except by proving that 7 has ø, that 4 has ø, and so on until every *n* has been accounted for—a task that can never be completed. In this case it is a purely mathematical truth that every *n* has ø, but it cannot be demonstrated. And it is

[31]Grua has *Et hoc arcano* where the manuscript reads *Et hic arcanum*. See VE 1763. AG follows Grua.

[32]*Etsi*; Grua has *et*.

[33]FC's *ab* is a misreading of *atque*. See VE 1768.

[34]This text is probably from 1689 (VE 1767). For similar statements from 1686 or earlier, see C 17/MP 97; GI 74,130; and from 1715, G III,582/L 664. Note that in Gr 303/AG 28, as in C 1f./AG 98f., finite demonstrability is presented as a necessary, and not just a sufficient, condition of necessity, contrary to the claim of Castañeda, "Leibniz's View of Contingent Truth in the Late 1680's," pp. 266f.

a purely mathematical falsehood that some *n* lacks ø, but no contradiction can be derived from it in a finite number of steps. Alfred Tarski decided to say that a system of which these conditions hold, but in which 'Some natural number lacks ø' can be proved, is *consistent*, but not *ω-consistent*.[35] He thus reserved the use of 'inconsistent', without qualification, to express a proof-theoretical notion rather than the notion of mathematical falsity. Similarly, Leibniz reserves 'implies a contradiction' to express a proof-theoretical notion rather than the notion of conceptual falsity or being false purely by virtue of the relations of concepts. He thinks, of course, that the latter notion is expressed simply by 'false'.

It is not difficult to see how it would follow, from this conception of contingency, that it is contingent which possible world is the best. For one would presumably have to consider infinitely many aspects of a world in order to assign a value to it as a whole. And then one would have to compare infinitely many worlds in order to determine which is the best. It could not be determined by any finite analysis; hence, it is contingent. Several commentators have explained Leibniz's reasoning along these lines,[36] and Leibniz himself did so. In a paper on "Necessary and Contingent Truths" (Couturat's title), which contains what seems to me an early statement of his infinite analysis conception of contingency, Leibniz points out that the universe has infinitely many aspects, and adds:

> Indeed, even if one could know the whole series of the universe, one still could not give the reason for it, unless one had set up a comparison of it with all the other possible [series]. From this it is clear why no demonstration of any contingent proposition can be found, no matter how far the analysis of concepts is continued. (C 19/MP 99; cf. Gr 343 from the early 1690s)

There remain difficult questions, never resolved by Leibniz or his commentators, about just how analysis is supposed to work in the relevant cases. *Analysis*, for Leibniz and the seventeenth century, was a method of proof beginning with the conclusion to be proved and working back to the axioms from which it follows—though in an infinite analysis the axioms are never reached. The method that begins at the other end, with the axioms, was called *synthesis*.[37] In conformity with this distinction, Leibniz described finite and infinite analyses as proceeding from the proposition to be proved, by substituting definitions, or parts of definitions, for its terms (FC 181f./L 264f.). But the process of determining which is the best of all possible worlds by comparing the values of all the worlds seems likely to be a synthesis, rather than an analysis, in this sense. Indeed Leibniz gives us no idea how one would even begin an analysis, finite or infinite, to determine which world is the best possible, although it is clear that he thought the infinite number of worlds to be compared is one ground of the contingency of God's choice of this world. Perhaps something like the following form of analysis is intended. Let 'W*' be a proper name of the world that happens to be actual. An analysis of 'W* = the best of all possible worlds' will require the re-

[35]Tarski, "Einige Betrachtungen."

[36]Couturat, "On Leibniz's Metaphysics," p. 31; Rescher, *Philosophy of Leibniz*, pp. 38f.; Abraham, "Complete Concepts," p. 278; Broad, *Leibniz: An Introduction*, p. 35; cf. Curley, "Root of Contingency," p. 94.

[37]Cf. Hacking, "Infinite Analysis," pp. 127f.

placement of one or both sides of the equation by an analysans. To reduce the equation to identities by such replacement, we would need on the right-hand side an analysans including a statement of the complete (or at least the basic) concepts of all the possible worlds, but that is not finitely statable.

Another difficulty is that while it does seem that it could not be proved in a finite number of steps that a certain world is the best possible, there might perhaps be a finite proof that a certain world, or any world of a certain sort, is not the best possible. Leibniz himself seems to have thought it could be demonstrated that no world in which God damns the innocent is the best.

> The damnation of the innocent is indeed possible in itself, or something that does not imply a contradiction; but it is not possible for God. . . . For we do not need to examine the whole harmony of things in order to know whether God is going to damn someone innocent eternally. (Gr 300; cf. Gr 271)

Here Leibniz seems to be confronted with a truth, 'No one innocent will be damned eternally', which satisfies one of his criteria for contingency (its contrary is possible in itself), but not the other (it would not require an infinite analysis to prove it). Leibniz does not tell us how to resolve this conflict; indeed, I doubt that he realized its existence.

We may also be tempted to object that the infinite analysis conception of contingency represents contingency as illusory, or at best merely relative to our intellectual incapacity (as Spinoza had regarded it: *Ethics*, I, prop. 33, schol. 1). It is natural to conclude that for Leibniz, as A. O. Lovejoy put it, "though we are unable to attain an intuitive apprehension of the necessity [of a judgment which appears to us as contingent], . . . we can nevertheless be sure that the necessity is there, and is recognized by the mind of God."[38] Russell took a similar view in 1903, when he wrote, "Where an infinite analysis, which only God can perform, is required to exhibit the contradiction, the opposite will *seem* not to be contradictory"; he did not think the alternative suggestion, "that the denial of an analytic truth might not be self-contradictory," would commend itself to Leibniz.[39]

This objection rests on a fundamental misunderstanding of Leibniz's conception of necessity and contingency. The distinction between them "is drawn on logical grounds alone," as Rescher rightly points out.[40] It is not an epistemological distinction, and it is not based on a relation in which contingent propositions stand to us but not to God. It is based on a difference in the logical form of the reasons by virtue of which propositions of the two sorts are true. Contingent truths are just as contingent for God as they are for us, and God can no more demonstrate them than we can; for not even God can "see . . . the end of the analysis, since there is no end" (FC 182,184/L 265f.).[41] Leibniz does say that

[38]Lovejoy, *Great Chain of Being*, p. 175. Cf. Copleston, *History of Philosophy*, vol.4, p. 286.

[39]Russell, "Recent Work on the Philosophy of Leibniz," p. 378, n. 8.

[40]Rescher, *Philosophy of Leibniz*, p. 44, n. 24.

[41]In DM 13, and in GI 131 and perhaps GI 74, all from 1686, Leibniz seems to speak of a "demonstration" of contingent truths that is beyond the powers of finite minds to accomplish. And in an early text, probably from 1677 to 1680 (VE 115 = G VII,194) he speaks of all truths as "demonstrable." This may be due either to carelessness or, more likely, to unclarity or variation in his terminology during a formative period of his thought. Usually, at least from 1689 on (e.g., VE

God can know contingent truths a priori (that is, through their reasons), and that we cannot. But these epistemological relations are not constitutive of contingency; they are only consequences of the logical property that is constitutive of contingency.

Two initially plausible principles about (logical) necessity are that whatever is true purely by virtue of the relations of concepts is necessary, and that whatever is necessary must be logically demonstrable. Leibniz seems at first to have assumed both principles. The light that was kindled for him by the knowledge of the analysis of infinites (C 18/MP 97) was the realization that the two assumptions are incompatible because some propositions that are true solely by virtue of the relations of concepts are nonetheless not provable by anything that he would count as a demonstration. Leibniz held consistently to the second principle. His usual definition of the logically necessary is that it is that whose contrary implies a contradiction (e.g., T pd2). And we have seen that Leibniz treats 'implies a contradiction' as expressing a proof-theoretical property that does not belong to propositions whose falsity can be discovered a priori only through an infinite analysis (FC 181/L 264; cf. C 17/MP 96f.). The realization of the incompatibility of the two principles therefore enabled Leibniz with a clear conscience to give up the first principle, which had made his theory of truth seem to leave no room for contingency.

When Russell charged that the infinite analysis conception of contingency would at most yield truths that only seem to be contingent, he was explicitly and mistakenly assuming that whatever is false purely by virtue of the relations of concepts must be self-contradictory for Leibniz. Similarly, Curley seems to be assuming a conception of necessity in terms of conceptual truth, rather than in terms of demonstrability, when he says that the bestness of this world "is not rendered any the less necessary by the number of other possible worlds being infinite rather than finite."[42] For our own use, of course, we may well prefer a conceptual truth conception of necessity to a demonstrability conception. If so we will rightly conclude that Leibniz's infinite analysis theory does not give us real contingency. I believe that conclusion is substantially correct, as I think the demonstrability conception of necessity is fundamentally misguided.[43] But that presents no *internal* objection to Leibniz's system. The contingency we are demanding, he can only regard as a brute fact and a violation of the principle of sufficient reason, which he has no intention of admitting in his mature philosophy.

It is just as clear in the essay "On the Radical Origination of Things" of 23 November 1697 (G VII,302–8/L 486–91) as in the letter to Wedderkopf of May 1671 (A II,i,117f./L 146f.) that Leibniz thinks of everything in the world as determined ultimately by the divine nature, and particularly by the relations of concepts in God's intellect. From this point of view the problem of contingency is to find a difference between *ways* in which facts are determined by relations

1775f. = C 1f./AG 98f.), he is careful not to say that contingent truths have "demonstrations" though they have "proofs" a priori that are known to God.

[42]Curley, "Root of Contingency," p. 94.

[43]See R. Adams, "Divine Necessity." As indicated there, I would not exactly endorse a conceptual truth conception of necessity, either.

of concepts—a difference that is both important and plausibly related to the preanalytic notions of logical or metaphysical necessity and contingency. The difference between truths that are and are not demonstrable in a finite number of steps is Leibniz's candidate for this role.

If this looks like an attempt to solve a philosophical problem by definition, there is some evidence that that is what Leibniz meant to do. Writing in February 1698 to G. W. Molanus about what he regarded as excessively necessitarian explanations of the occurrence of sins, he said:

> But the more I consider the matter, the more manifestly I seem to myself to see that the error [*peccatum*] was not so much in realities as in formulas, on account of assumed definitions of freedom, necessity, will, and right that are not only less philosophical, and less familiar, but also less suited to edification. From them ways of speaking were bound to arise that are offensive to pious ears. By these ways of speaking, to be sure, the greatness of God is extolled, and human pride put down (which seems to have been the aim of those speaking more rigidly); but on the other hand, inadequate provision was made for celebrating God's goodness, and arousing our love toward him. What if therefore, as I am almost persuaded, by merely developing definitions all that harshness could be softened, and it is permitted to remove the controversy about which people have sounded so tragic; do you think this should be neglected? (Schrecker 84)

2.3 Contingent Connections among Possibles as Such

As a consequence of his infinite analysis theory of contingency, Leibniz accepted another thesis, which some commentators have been most reluctant to admit as part of his philosophy. Russell noted in 1903 that "the view that infinite complexity is the defining property of the contingent has the curious consequence that truths about possible substances are contingent."[44] Both C. D. Broad and Curley have claimed that Leibniz did not accept this consequence,[45] but their claim is untenable. That you exist in the best possible world is a fact about you conceived as a possible substance; its contingency follows from what Leibniz wrote in several places about the contingency of which world is best.

Indeed, the idea that there are contingent connections among things considered as possible becomes quite important to Leibniz in the *Discourse on Metaphysics* and the correspondence with Arnauld. This is to be expected, in view of Leibniz's insistence that all of the acts of any individual follow from the concept of that individual considered as possible. It is crucial to his theodicy that the connection between our natures or concepts and our sins and other evils be one that would have been there, no weaker and no stronger, even if God had not created us (cf. DM 30). So if it is important to our freedom that we be contingently connected with our actions, this following of our actions from our concepts must somehow be a contingent connection between them and us considered as possible. Accordingly, Leibniz says in § 13 of the *Discourse* that

[44] Russell, "Recent Work on the Philosophy of Leibniz," p. 374, n. 5; cf. Russell, *Philosophy of Leibniz*, p. 26.

[45] Broad, *Leibniz: An Introduction*, p. 36; Curley, "Root of Contingency," pp. 92f.

there are two sorts of connection, one absolutely necessary but the other contingent, by which different events follow from the complete concept of a created person.[46]

Arnauld was perhaps the first to find this strange. He argued that, on Leibniz's view, the connection between Adam and everything "that has happened and will happen to him and his posterity" must be necessary, "because," as Leibniz put it, "I consider the individual concept of Adam as possible," and "possible concepts in themselves do not depend on the free decisions of God" (LA 28–30,40). There are two main points in Leibniz's reply to this objection.

1. "The possibles are possible before all the actual decisions of God, but not without presupposing sometimes the same decisions taken as possible" (LA 51). This is because the complete concept of any possible thing involves (as possible) some decisions that God would make (for instance, in establishing laws of nature) if God actualized the world to which that thing belongs. Here Leibniz clings to the idea that truths involving God's decisions are contingent. But now it seems they need not depend on what God actually decides; it is enough if they involve divine decisions considered as possible. We may wonder why the merely possible divine decisions should be thought to have this relevance.

2. The connection between a created person, considered as possible, and the events of his or her possible world is "intrinsic" (LA 51) and "certain" but not "necessary," although the failure of the connection would destroy the individual concept of that person (LA 52; cf. LA 41). Here it seems clear that Leibniz's position involves contingent connections within possible worlds, and hence contingent truths that do not depend on which world is actual.[47]

The same view is expressed by Leibniz in other texts:

> It is of the nature of an individual substance that its concept be perfect and complete, and contain all its individual circumstances, even contingent ones, down to the least detail. . . . Yet these individual [circumstances] are not therefore necessary, and do not depend on the divine intellect alone, but also on decisions of the divine will, insofar as the decisions themselves are considered as possible by the divine intellect. (Gr 311)

[46]Hector-Neri Castañeda, in his interesting article on "Leibniz's View of Contingent Truth in the Late 1680's," proposes an interpretation of the two types of connection that is quite different from mine. If I understand him, he identifies the two types of connection with the existential and essential uses of the copula 'is' that Leibniz distinguishes (GI 144). Fabrizio Mondadori has pointed out to me that such a distinction was current in Leibniz's time, and can be found, for example, in Francisco Suárez's *Metaphysical Disputations*, XXXI,xii,44–45. The substance of this distinction, however, is simply that the truth of an "existential" predication depends on the actual existence of its subject and predicate terms, whereas the truth of an "essential" predication does not. Since, according to Castañeda's Leibniz, "every contingent truth" involving the existential copula "is underlain by its corresponding necessary truth" involving the essential copula (Castañeda, "Leibniz's View of Contingent Truth in the Late 1680's," p. 264), all that is contingent, intuitively, in such a case, is the *existence* of the subject and/or predicate, not the connection between them. Speaking, technically, of a different copula when the existence of the terms is implied does not, *intuitively*, make the contingency of the existence rub off on the connection. In this respect the position Castañeda ascribes to Leibniz is no more intuitive than the one I attribute to him.

[47]Mondadori, in "Leibniz and the Doctrine of Inter-World Identity," pp. 32f., takes it that what is not necessary here is the actualization of the individual; but that does not adequately explain why Leibniz should call the *connection* contingent. Cf. note 46 above.

> God decided to create a creature whose full concept involves such a series of graces and free actions, although not necessarily but by such a connection as the nature of the thing involves. (Gr 383)

These quotations are probably from the mid-1680s (VE 1105,1122). From about 1695, according to Grua, is a reading note in which Leibniz states flatly, "There are some indemonstrable truths even in possible things—namely about contingent things regarded as possible" (Gr 353).

How can the connection between an individual substance and some of the properties or events involved in its concept be contingent? Leibniz offers hints of some answers to this question, but they are by no means as clear as his best-worked-out answers to the question of how the existence of those creatures that are actual can be contingent. Three answers may be distinguished.

1. In § 13 of the *Discourse* Leibniz says that the predicate of deciding to cross the Rubicon and winning the battle of Pharsalus is contained in the concept of Julius Caesar, but that it is not "necessary in itself" that those things happen to him. This suggests that Leibniz thought of Caesar's deciding not to cross the Rubicon, or his losing at Pharsalus, as things that are possible in themselves, in something like the way that non-actual possible worlds are possible in themselves although they are impossible on the hypothesis of something else. But how can we make sense of this suggestion, if the source of the threatening necessity is in the concept of Caesar himself? That might be thought to constitute a necessity internal to Caesar's deciding and winning, since he himself is a constituent of those events.

It may be important here that Leibniz distinguishes, within an individual's complete concept, between features that are particular to the individual, and the laws of that individual's universe, which also enter into the concept of the individual. To Arnauld he says:

> Thus all human events could not fail to occur as they have actually occurred, given that the choice of Adam was made; but not so much because of the individual concept of Adam, although that concept contains them, but because of the designs of God, which also enter into that individual concept of Adam, and which determine that of that whole universe. (LA 51)

It seems clear that in the *Discourse* Leibniz is thinking of the intrinsic but not necessary connection between Caesar and his decision to cross the Rubicon as depending on laws that govern Caesar's world.

> [T]his predicate of Caesar is not so absolute as those of numbers or of geometry, but . . . it presupposes the sequence of things that God has chosen freely, and that is founded on the first free decision of God, the import of which is to do always that which is most perfect, and on the decision that God made (in consequence of the first) with regard to human nature, which is that a human being will do always (though freely) what seems the best. (DM 13)

This suggests the hypothesis that Caesar's deciding not to cross the Rubicon is viewed by Leibniz as possible in itself because it is excluded by Caesar's individual concept only in virtue of the laws of Caesar's universe, and not purely by what is particular to Caesar in Caesar's concept. This would explain the contingency of connections depending on merely possible divine decisions, if those possible decisions are identified with laws of a universe.[48]

This is a possible interpretation, but not without problems, of which the chief is that, as we shall see in Chapter 3, section 1, Leibniz's views imply that the laws of Caesar's universe are incorporated not only in Caesar's individual concept, but also, concretely, in the primitive forces that constitute Caesar's very substance. Can *Caesar's* doing something precluded by laws so incorporated in his very substance be possible in itself? An adequately informed judgment on this question must await Chapter 3, where we will explore a variety of considerations bearing on the tightness of the connection between an individual substance's primitive forces and the events that happen to it.

2. An alternative reading is possible of the statement, in § 13 of the *Discourse*, that if someone did the opposite of something that is involved in his complete concept, "he would do nothing impossible in itself, although it is impossible (*ex hypothesi*) for that to happen." Maybe just as God chooses freely because God chooses among a plurality of possible worlds, each of which is possible in itself even if it is impossible in relation to God, so a creature can act freely by choosing among a plurality of actions, each of which is possible in its own nature even if it is impossible in relation to the complete concept of the choosing creature. In 1697, at any rate, Leibniz was explicitly willing to explicate the freedom of creatures as well as of God in terms of the plurality of alternatives for choice:

> It is more exact even to say that the good actions of God, the Angels confirmed [in good], and the glorified Saints are not necessary, although they are assured; and the reason is because they are done by choice, whereas there is necessity when there is no choice to make. When there are several paths, one has the freedom to choose, and although one may be better than another, that's just what makes the choice. . . . [I]t is not indifference of equilibrium, so to speak, that constitutes freedom, but the faculty of choosing among several possibles, even though they are not all equally feasible or convenient for the one who acts. (Schrecker 97)

Leibniz here identifies one way in which he thinks the structure of creatures' choices is like that of God's choices. In both cases the agent's choice among a plurality of alternatives is an essential part of the metaphysical reason for the actuality, or the nonactuality, of each alternative. This seems to be enough to establish the reality of choice, but intuitively I would not say that it establishes the internal contingency of the alternatives for choice.

If the latter is to be established by this approach, the alternatives among which creatures choose must probably be regarded as somewhat general, rather than as completely individual, actions. Caesar's alternatives on the bank of the Rubicon, for example, must be crossing and not crossing, rather than Caesar's crossing and Caesar's not crossing. Individual concepts must be kept out of the objects of choice. This line of thought, therefore, seems not to provide an expla-

[48]For a very interesting discussion of the relation of laws and possible divine decrees to contingency, and in general a much fuller and richer account of contingent connections within a single possible world than I attempt here, see Carriero, "Leibniz on Infinite Resolution and Intra-Mundane Contingency."

nation of the contingency of *Caesar's* deciding to cross the Rubicon. But it does show us a way in which Leibniz could say that the *reality* of Caesar's choice is preserved.

3. Contingent connections between possibles can be explained in terms of the infinite analysis theory of contingency. Leibniz gives such an explanation of the contingency of 'Peter denies'. "The concept of Peter is complete, and so involves infinite things; therefore one never arrives at a perfect demonstration" (GI 74). 'Peter denies' is under discussion in this text as an existential proposition, but the argument evidently works just as well if the subject is considered only as a possible person—as Russell perceived with dismay.

There are even more difficult problems, however, about how infinite analysis is supposed to work in this case than in the case of bestness among possible worlds. Leibniz mostly ignores these difficulties, and I will not try to do much more here than point them out. The first is the problem of the Lucky Proof.[49] Even if infinitely many properties and events are contained in the complete concept of Peter, at least one of them will be proved in the first step of any analysis. Why couldn't it be Peter's denial? Why couldn't we begin to analyze Peter's concept by saying, 'Peter is a denier of Jesus and . . .'? Presumably such a Lucky Proof must be ruled out by some sort of restriction on what counts as a step in an analysis of an individual concept, but so far as I know, Leibniz does not explain how this is to be done. On the other hand, we may wonder how we can even begin an analysis of the individual concept of any person, as Leibniz seems to imply that we can. For such a concept, being complete, is not our concept but God's, and we do not seem to have a definition with which to begin to replace it.[50]

2.4 *Reasons That Incline without Necessitating*

One of the things Leibniz never tired of saying about free choices is that their causes, motives, or reasons "incline" but do not "necessitate." Lovejoy calls this "misleading if edifying phraseology" and a "verbal distinction, absolutely meaningless in the light of [Leibniz's] other doctrines."[51] One is tempted to agree with this harsh judgment, for Leibniz does not give much explanation of the difference between inclining and necessitating. But I think the distinction has a place in the interpretation of Leibniz I have been developing.

Leibniz presents the idea of reasons that incline without necessitating, sometimes in connection with the notion of a choice among alternatives that are possible *in themselves* (T 45,230; LC V,8–9), and sometimes in connection with the infinite analysis theory of contingency. In the latter connection, which seems to me the more illuminating of the two, Leibniz says, "There is the same proportion between necessity and inclination that there is in the Mathematicians' Analysis between exact equation and limits that give an approximation" (Gr 479; cf. Gr 303, T k14). This statement was written in the years around 1700 in a memorandum that also makes clear how infinity is supposed to enter into

[49] I am indebted to William Irvine for this name for it.

[50] Cf. Broad, *Leibniz: An Introduction*, p. 27.

[51] Lovejoy, *Great Chain of Being*, p. 174.

the influence of reasons on the will. The word 'incline' suggests the image of a balance that is tipped or inclined to one side or the other by the preponderance of weights; and 'balance' (noun and verb) occurs, at least figuratively, several times in the memorandum. Leibniz liked mechanical analogies of volition (T 22, G VII,304/L 488), and in particular that of the balance (cf. NE 193). He later wrote to Clarke (V,3) that "reasons in the mind of a wise being, and motives in any mind whatsoever, do that which answers to the effect produced by weights in a balance." Though not necessitating, the balance of motives determines as certainly as the balance of weights: "We always follow the direction toward which there is more inclination or disposition" (Gr 479); we never fail to do so (T 43).

The motives that play the role of weights in the scales of volition include all our perceptions, subconscious as well as conscious, according to Leibniz. "Several perceptions and inclinations contribute to the complete volition, which is the result of their conflict. Some of them are separately imperceptible; the mass of these makes an uneasiness which pushes us without the subject of it being seen" (NE 192; cf. Gr 480).

Here the infinite makes its appearance. For in Leibniz's system the mass of subconscious perceptions in a finite spirit is a confused perception of the whole universe, in all its infinite complexity. Every fact about the world is perceived, and our perception of it has some influence on our will; those perceptions of which we are not conscious are nonetheless weighed in the balance en masse, by virtue of their contribution to our feelings. Our minds, being finite, cannot completely understand the motives of our choices, because they are infinitely complex. On the same ground, the connection between a free decision and its ultimate reasons or motives will be contingent, and cannot be demonstrated, in the senses laid down in the infinite analysis theory of contingency. Much of this, including some connection between contingency and the infinity of influences, is explicit in the memorandum quoted earlier. Leibniz speaks there of our ignorance "of an infinity of little influences on us of which we are not conscious," which sometimes lets us have the illusion that the factors moving our will are equally balanced. And he immediately adds:

> That shows that it is indeed always true that our *freedom*, and that of all other intelligent substances right up to God himself, is accompanied by a certain degree of indifference or contingency, which has been defined in such a way that we and those substances are never necessitated, since the contrary of that which happens always remains possible or implies no contradiction. (Gr 480f.)

The reference to God should not be taken as suggesting that God has subconscious motives, for Leibniz's God perceives everything distinctly. But Leibniz did say that "God had infinite reasons competing with each other, which he considered when he judged this possible universe worthy to be chosen"; he offered it as an explanation of why the truth of "This series of the universe is the best" cannot be known a priori by us (Gr 343). God's reasons, like ours, incline but do not necessitate, because they are involved in a conflict of such infinite complexity that the resulting volition cannot be demonstrated (in the strict sense) from them.

Leibniz himself seems strangely to get this point wrong in a letter to Jaquelot of 1704, where he explicitly links the notion of inclining with things being too complex for us to understand them. He says that "future things are contained in the soul even less than in God, because they are in the soul distinctly only in an inclining and confused way, and not explicitly and perfectly as in the Divine ideas" (G III,472). This linkage of themes is revealing, but Leibniz has the shoe on the wrong foot in this text (even apart from the puzzling suggestion of a *confused* way of being in the soul *distinctly*). For he thinks that God, too, is only inclined, not necessitated, by reasons (T 230), although God's perceptions are in no way confused. What is essential to inclination, therefore, is not confusion, but the infinity of factors that in our finite minds gives rise to confusion.

2.5 Is 'God Chooses What Is Best' Contingent?

The contingency of 'God chooses this world' could be explained and defended by holding either that 'God chooses what is best' is contingent or that 'This world is the best' is contingent. We have seen that Leibniz prefers the latter alternative, but he explicitly rejects the other in only one of the texts we examined. More often he leaves open the possibility of holding that both are contingent. There seems to have been more vacillation and uncertainty in Leibniz's mind about whether it is necessary or contingent that God chooses what is best than about any other main issue in the problem of contingency. I shall argue, however, that the view that it is necessary is required by other features of Leibniz's philosophy.

Many passages in which Leibniz appears to address this issue yield no solid evidence on it, in view of some of the subtleties that we have already seen in his position. When he says, for example, "God's decisions about contingents certainly are not necessary" (Gr 385), the claim can be taken *de re* with respect to the contingents: for any contingent, what God decides about *it* is not necessary (because it takes an infinite analysis to determine what is best). It may not be implied, therefore, that it is not necessary that God decides to order contingent things as well as possible. Similarly, when Leibniz says that "God was infallibly led by his wisdom and goodness . . . to give [the world] the best form possible; but he was not led to it necessarily" (T k14), the expression "to it" [French *y*] does not make clear whether the denial of necessity applies *de re* to that form which is in fact the best possible for the world, or whether it applies *de dicto* to God's giving the world *whatever* form is best. We have to bear in mind Leibniz's saying that "it is a necessary proposition" that God wills the best, but that God does not will it "necessarily," because what is best is not necessarily so (Gr 493f.).

On the other hand, our present question remains equally unanswered when Leibniz says, as he often does, such things as "God cannot fail to choose the best," for Leibniz has distinguished several sorts of inability and necessity. He may mean only a moral necessity (as he says in such a context at T aVIII), whereas we are interested in logical or metaphysical necessity.

And when Leibniz says that "God wills the best by his own nature" (Gr 289), or that the reason for God's eternal free action is "the divine nature or perfection itself" (C 405), he says nothing more than is implied by his analytic theory of truth. What we want to know is whether God's voluntary optimizing is *demonstrable*—that is, whether it follows by a finite or only by an infinite analysis from the divine nature. In fact, in both the texts I have just quoted on this point, it is stated or suggested that it is not demonstrable (Gr 288, C 405).

First of all, therefore, we must seek texts in which necessity is asserted or denied, *de dicto*, of some such proposition as 'God chooses what is best', and in which the necessity is explicitly or contextually indicated as logical or metaphysical, or is stated or explained in terms of demonstrability. There are several such texts, and they speak on both sides of the question.

The most explicit texts for the indemonstrability and hence the contingency of the crucial propositions date probably from the early 1680s, when Leibniz was actively engaged in formative work on a variety of solutions to the problem of contingency. In one he denies flatly that the proposition 'God chooses the best,' or 'God wills the best,' can be demonstrated (Gr 301).[52] A contrast is introduced in a similar denial: "Thus, that God loves himself is necessary, for it is demonstrable from the definition of God. But that God does what is most perfect cannot be demonstrated, for the contrary does not imply a contradiction" (Gr 288).[53]

The contrast recurs in some later texts. In the early 1690s Leibniz noted with approval Thomas Aquinas's opinion that "God's attitude toward himself is necessary and natural, but his attitude toward other things is not necessary, nor forced, but voluntary" (Gr 333).[54] And in the *Theodicy* he says, "The love that God has for himself is essential to him; but the love of his glory, or the will to obtain it, is not essential to him at all" (T 233; cf. T 175,230). (Here God's glory is conceived as an external attribute, "the reflection of the divine perfection in created beings."[55])

The contingency of 'God chooses what is best' seems more favored in the *Theodicy* than in the private papers Leibniz wrote while preparing the book. In addition to the passage just cited, there is a list of things said to be necessary "in a certain sense," but not "logically, geometrically, or metaphysically"; among them is that "God himself chooses the best" (T 282; it would not be plausible to read this denial of logical necessity as *de re* with respect to the best). If the *Theodicy* were our only source for Leibniz's opinions, I think we would find nothing incompatible with the impression that Leibniz thinks it contingent, *de dicto*, that God chooses what is best. The general tenor of the book would leave us with that impression, although most passages in it can be interpreted otherwise in light of Leibniz's other works.

[52]Leibniz muddied the waters a little by adding "or identical" to the claim that the first of these is "a first proposition"; but the context makes clear that what he really wanted to say is that it is *like* an identical proposition in being a truth but indemonstrable. In another relevant text from more or less the same period Leibniz says that "in a certain way it is of physical necessity [here distinguished from metaphysical necessity] that God does all things as well as he can" (C 21/MP 101).

[53]This paper (quoted in section 1.2) is also an important source for the view that non-actual things remain possible in their own natures even if they are not possible in respect to the divine will. It might be quibbled whether in the quoted passage demonstrability is denied only *de re*, with respect to that which is most perfect, but I think that would be an unnatural reading of the text.

[54]The same set of notes, however, expresses the view that it is demonstrable that God cannot do evils, which I will discuss later in this chapter. The reference to Aquinas is given as *Summa contra gentiles*, I,82ff.; the correct citation would be I,80ff.

[55]Grua, *Jurisprudence*, p. 307.

Section 13 of the *Discourse on Metaphysics* gives a similar impression. Probably the most important utterance bearing on the issue there is the mention of "the first free decision of God, the import of which is to do always that which is most perfect." For if this decision is free and freedom implies contingency, it will follow that 'God decides to do what is best' is contingent.

The strongest texts on the other side are those already discussed in section 2.1 of this chapter,[56] in which Leibniz pointedly refrains from denying, and in 1706 affirms, that 'God chooses the best' is necessary in the sense of being demonstrable. Those texts date from about 1689 to 1706; but there is a note, probably from the early 1680s, in which Leibniz says, "From God's essence or supreme perfection it follows, certainly and, so to speak, by a necessary implication, that God chooses the best" (Gr 297). He goes on to explain God's freedom in terms of the plurality of alternatives possible in their own nature. The phrase "by a necessary implication" is important here. When Leibniz wrote in 1698 that "it follows from the nature of God that he prefers the most perfect" (Gr 393), he left some ambiguity. For he also said that *all* truths, even contingent ones, follow from God, who is the highest truth (Gr 347). Might God's preference for perfection follow from the divine nature by an infinite rather than a finite analysis, and therefore contingently? But what follows from God's essence "by a necessary implication" must be necessary—though the qualification "so to speak" or "if you will" [*si ita loqui placet*] still leaves a little uncertainty.

In reading notes from the 1690s Leibniz held that "the inability to do evils can be demonstrated of God" (G 333) and "rigorously, it can be said that the good Angels can sin, and that does not imply a contradiction, but in God it does imply one" (Gr 360). Leibniz held more consistently to this thesis than to the more general claim that it is demonstrable that God chooses the best. Even in one of the papers from the early 1680s in which he says flatly that 'God chooses the best' is not demonstrable, Leibniz says that damning the innocent eternally is not possible for God and is therefore one of those things "whose . . . existence implies a contradiction" (Gr 300).

The only text against this of which I am aware is in the *Theodicy*: "However it does not imply a contradiction for God to will (directly or permissively) a thing that does not imply a contradiction" (T 234). Nothing is said here explicitly about whether it is contingent, *de dicto*, that God does no evil or that God chooses the best. For the possibility that is asserted is pretty clearly *de re* with respect to the objects of God's choice: it is claimed about everything, that if it is possible in itself, considered without regard to its relation to God's will (cf. T 235), then it is also possible for God to will to actualize it. But since Leibniz thought the eternal damnation of the innocent is possible in itself (Gr 300), it does seem to follow that it is possible for God to damn the innocent eternally—which is not far removed from the conclusion that it is possible for God to do evil.

In general, however, Leibniz seems inclined to the view that it is demonstrable that God does no evil, whether or not it is demonstrable that God chooses the

[56] In another text, from 1677, Leibniz wrote that "God necessarily and yet freely chooses the most perfect" (VE 305 = LH IV,4,3C,12–14); but this seems not to be in the framework of the infinite analysis conception of contingency.

best. Indeed, even his 1706 reading note on Bayle in which he says that "God wills the work that is most worthy of him" is a necessary proposition ends with a hint that God "cannot do or will moral evil" in some sense stronger than that in which God cannot fail to create the best possible world (Gr 494).

But if Leibniz holds that it is demonstrable that God does no evil, how can he avoid the conclusion that it is demonstrable that God does not prefer the less perfect? "For as a lesser evil is a kind of good, by the same token a lesser good is a kind of evil, if it forms an obstacle to a greater good" (T 8). And in maintaining the axiom, *Minus bonum habet rationem mali* [A lesser good has the character of an evil] (T 194, DM 3, G III,33), Leibniz does not suggest that it is contingent. So he seems committed to holding that preferring the less perfect would necessarily be doing something evil.

God is more than sinless. That "God is an absolutely perfect being," morally as well as metaphysically, is virtually a definition for Leibniz (DM 1), and so far as I know he never suggests that it is contingent. If it is not true by definition, or at least demonstrable, how is he so confident that it is true at all? Surely he does not know it by experience. And he denies that it is known only by faith (T pd44). Both Rescher and Curley seem to me to err in saying that Leibniz would solve the problem of contingency by holding that God's goodness is contingent.[57]

But that is not the only way in which he could deny that it is necessary that God does what is best, for the belief that God does what is best is based on two premises: that God is "a most perfect Being," and that "the operation of a most perfect Being is most perfect" (Gr 16). Once, probably in the early 1680s, Leibniz did say that the second of these is contingent: "God's choosing a less perfect from among many perfect things does not imply an imperfection in God" (Gr 300). I agree with this statement,[58] but find it astonishingly un-Leibnizian and do not think it fits into his philosophical system.

One objection to including it in the system is inconclusive. Leibniz says it is morally necessary for God to choose the best. This means that it is necessary that a perfectly good agent in God's position would choose the best (see section 1.5 of this chapter). It follows that it is necessary that if God chooses the less perfect, God is imperfect (cf. G III,33). But the crucial question here is how strong this necessity is. Is the morally necessary only what it is *demonstrable* that a perfectly good agent would do? Or is it enough for moral necessity if the action is contained in the concept of a perfectly good agent, even though an infinite analysis would be needed to show the reason of the containment? The weaker requirement seems to me to be the one assumed in Leibniz's mature writings: he appears to regard God's choice of this world as morally necessary (cf. T pd2), but it is not demonstrable that a perfectly good agent would choose this world, since it is not demonstrable that it is the best.

Other arguments, however, show that Leibniz cannot consistently hold that it is contingent that a supremely perfect being would choose the more perfect. For suppose that is contingent. Then either it must be contingent that a supremely perfect being is perfectly good, wise, and just, or else it must be contingent that

[57]Rescher, *Philosophy of Leibniz*, p. 45; Curley, "Root of Contingency," p. 95.
[58]R. Adams, "Must God Create the Best?"

a perfectly good, wise, and just being would choose the more perfect. Neither of these is contingent for Leibniz, for the following reasons.

Leibniz regards justice as "an essential attribute of God" (Dutens IV,iii,280, where this is not asserted, but contextually implied). And since God's justice, for Leibniz, "depends on wisdom and goodness" (Dutens IV,iii,261; cf. G III,34), the latter perfections must presumably be regarded as essential to God, too.

Leibniz would have to admit that it can be demonstrated, from acceptable definitions of these perfections, that they imply a preference for the best.

> The end of goodness is the greatest good, but in order to recognize it, wisdom is needed, which is nothing other than knowledge of the good, as goodness is nothing other than the inclination to do good to all, and to prevent evil unless it is necessary for a greater good or to prevent a greater evil.[59]

Thus Leibniz seems unable to escape the conclusion that it is demonstrable, and hence logically necessary, that God, as an absolutely perfect being, does what is best.

The conflict in Leibniz's thought is reflected in divergent pronouncements about "the root of contingency." In the mid-1680s he set out, somewhat tentatively, the idea that in dealing with problems of contingency we must "have recourse to that one thing which is not essential in God, but free—namely, the decision of the will, from which alone a source of contingency in things can be sought" (Gr 311). This is not unambiguous, but seems to agree with Rescher's judgment that for Leibniz "the ultimate source of contingent truth is clearly" in God's choosing "to act in the most perfect way," rather than in the bestness of that which is chosen.[60] Elsewhere Leibniz locates the root of contingency not in the divine will, but in the objects among which God chooses. In the early 1680s he wrote, "The root of freedom in God is the possibility or contingency of things"—by which he means the plurality of alternatives possible in themselves, as the context shows (Gr 298). About 1696, likewise, he wrote notes on the views, ascribed to Scotus and Aquinas, respectively, that the root of contingency is in the will of God as free and as efficacious. Leibniz commented that the former view was circular. As to the latter, "contingency is in the nature itself of truth, or of the object, as of possibility, as of existence" (Gr 348; cf. Gr 353). Here perhaps what Leibniz has in mind is that contingent truths cannot be proved by a finite analysis.

The circle with which Leibniz charged Scotus has to do, presumably, with seeking the ultimate reason for all contingent facts in a divine decision which is itself one of the contingent facts to be explained. Often Leibniz sees an infinite regress in place of this circle, and almost always he condemns it as vicious. There is one text from the early 1680s, however, in which he accepts the infinite regress; and this acceptance assumes great importance for the interpretations of Rescher and Curley.

[59]Quoted by Grua, *Jurisprudence*, pp. 212f., from *Mittheilungen aus Leibnizens ungedruckten Schriften*, ed. by G. Mollat (Leipzig: 1883), p. 48. Grua says the text is from 1701–1705. On this subject see in general Grua, *Jurisprudence*, pp. 198–222.

[60]Rescher, *Philosophy of Leibniz*, p. 39.

> The first principle about Existences is this proposition: *God wills to choose the most perfect.* This proposition cannot be demonstrated; it is the first of all propositions of fact, or the origin of every contingent existence. . . . For if anyone asks me why God decided to create Adam, I say: because he decided to do what is most perfect. If you ask me now why he decided to do what is most perfect, . . . I answer that he willed it freely, or because he willed to. Therefore he willed because he willed to will, and so on to infinity. (Gr 301f.)

Curley says that this text presents "the only one of the various ways in which Leibniz invokes infinite processes which seems . . . to have any bearing on the problem of contingency."[61] Rescher does not cite this passage, but does propose, as Leibniz's main solution to the problem of contingency, that "God's moral perfection follows from His metaphysical perfection, but deduction would require an infinity of steps."[62] Something of this sort is required, of course, if the supposed contingency of 'God chooses what is best' is to be reconciled with Leibniz's conceptual containment theory of truth and infinite analysis theory of contingency.

Rescher's formulation deftly avoids the obvious objection that the infinite regress of reasons violates the principle of sufficient reason. Leibniz's use of the principle in proving the existence of God requires him to refuse to accept an infinite regress of reasons as itself constituting a sufficient reason. Furthermore, Leibniz had said, "it is absurd [to suppose] that a free will is an ultimate reason, since the free will itself has its requirements [*requisita*], for it is not an independent Being [*Ens a se*]" (A VI,iii,120).[63] A sufficient reason must be found in something of metaphysical necessity; the ultimate reason for the existence of all things is to be found in the divine essence and intellect. Rescher recognizes and accepts this. In his interpretation the ultimate sufficient reason is found in God's metaphysical perfection; if there is an infinite regress of volitions, it has a reason outside itself in God's nature. But in conformity with the infinite analysis theory of contingency, this reason cannot be proved by a finite analysis.

In the paper in which he accepts the regress, however, Leibniz was not as deft as Rescher, for he refused to ground the infinite regress of volitions in God's essence. "No other reason can be given why God chooses the most perfect than because he wills to. . . . And certainly he wills freely, because outside his will no other reason can be given than the will." He goes on to claim that "nothing is therefore given without a reason, but that reason is intrinsic to the will" (Gr 301). The infinite regress of reasons he describes certainly does not satisfy his principle of sufficient reason. It is noteworthy, moreover, that this rather early paper contains no explicit appeal to the infinite analysis theory of contingency. I know of no work in which Leibniz develops the infinite regress of volitions into the sort of solution that Rescher proposes for him.

[61] Curley, "Root of Contingency," p. 96.

[62] Rescher, *Philosophy of Leibniz*, p. 45.

[63] This is a response to one of Steno's comments in the manuscript of *The Philosopher's Confession*, and therefore comes probably from about the end of 1677, as explained in note 14. On Leibniz's use of *requisita* [requirements] as a term for necessary conditions, see Chapter 4, section 1.

This text, as Grua says (Gr 259), is exceptional. It is the same short paper in which Leibniz denied that choosing the less perfect would imply an imperfection in God. The infinite regress of volitions, and the whole idea of willing to will, were explicitly rejected by Leibniz at about the same time, as well as both earlier and later. In another paper probably from the early 1680s he wrote, "Indeed God cannot will voluntarily; otherwise there would be a will to will [and so on] to infinity" (Gr 289). In the letter to Wedderkopf and in *The Philosopher's Confession* he had denied, with explicit reference to God, that anyone wills what to will (A II,i,117/L 147) or wills because he wills (A VI,iii,124). In the *New Essays* Leibniz says, "We do not will to will, but we will to do; and if we willed to will, we would will to will to will, and that would go to infinity" (NE 182). Here nothing is said explicitly about God. There is an explicit reference to God in the *Theodicy*, however: "It is, in a sense, an abuse of terms to say here: one can will, one wills to will; power is related here to the actions that one wills" (T 234).

There are, it must be granted, two texts that support the idea that divine decisions, considered as possible, are part of the object of other divine decisions (C 24), or more vaguely, that "God executes all reflex acts at once and once for all" (Gr 345). Indeed, Leibniz thought of possible divine decisions as involved in the concepts of possible creatures among which God chooses, but in these texts it is not stated or suggested that God's general decision to do what is best is the object of a prior decision, nor that the regress of decisions provides the *reason* for the decision to act.

At any rate, the infinite regress of volitions is clearly not a keystone of Leibniz's position on contingency. On this and other grounds that we have reviewed, it is fair to say that the view that 'God chooses what is best' is contingent must not be regarded as a thesis of Leibniz's philosophy, much less as a basis of one of his principal solutions to the problem of contingency.

2.6 *An Exception for Existence?*

We are now in a position to deal with the question whether Leibniz meant to solve the problem of contingency by making existence an exception to the rule that the predicate of a true proposition must be contained in the concept of the subject. There are several compelling arguments for a negative answer.

1. Leibniz says something that looks very much like an explicit negative answer, in the *New Essays*:

> But when one says that a thing exists, or that it has real existence, this existence itself is the predicate—that is to say, it has a concept linked with the idea that is in question, and there is a connection between these two concepts. (NE 358)[64]

2. In many formulations of his conceptual containment theory of truth Leibniz says explicitly that the concept of the predicate is contained in the concept of the subject in contingent as well as necessary truths (FC 179/L 263f.; LA

[64]I am indebted to W. E. Abraham, "Complete Concepts," p. 278, for calling this reference to my attention.

56; C 16/MP 96; C 519/L 267f.; C 272; G VII,199f.; Gr 303/AG 28). In view of these statements, it seems perverse to suppose that Leibniz meant to explain the possibility of contingency by making an exception to the theory for those propositions that he regarded as contingent.

3. Leibniz made a number of attempts to explain how existence is contained in the concepts of those things that exist. These attempts typically involve some or all of the following claims. The predicate of existence is in some way equivalent to "entering into the most perfect series of things" (C 9) or to pleasing God (C 405).[65] The analysis of concepts would have to be carried to infinity, however, to prove the existence of any contingent thing (GI 74; cf. Gr 304f./AG 29). The underlying idea, of course, is that existence is contained in the concepts of existing things, not directly, but by virtue of the factors that determine God to create those things.

4. As Couturat pointed out, "existential propositions are not the only contingent propositions" for Leibniz.[66] Couturat chose an unfortunate example: laws of nature, which are indeed contingent, but are also existential according to Leibniz, as Curley has pointed out.[67] In sections 2.1 and 2.3 of this chapter, however, we have seen better examples of contingent propositions whose truth, according to Leibniz, does not depend on what exists—namely, the propositions asserting the bestness of this possible world[68] and the contingent connections within possible worlds.

5. The version of the problem of contingency that troubled Leibniz most persistently throughout his life does not depend on his conception of the nature of truth, and it cannot be solved by making the predicate of existence an exception to that conception. For the problem is that the existence of all actual things seems to follow not just from their own concepts, but from the concept of God, whose existence Leibniz always regarded as absolutely necessary. The principle of charity favors an interpretation according to which a problem so important for Leibniz is addressed by his theories of contingency.

Some of Leibniz's texts may seem to speak on the other side of the question, but I am not persuaded that they seriously undermine my interpretation. One is a passage near the end of a paper commonly known as "Necessary and Contingent Truths," where Leibniz says that "the possibility or Concept of a created mind does not involve existence" (C 23/MP 104). This statement, however, seems flatly inconsistent with what he asserts at the beginning of the same paper about

[65]For the former equivalence see also Gr 325; B 119f.; C 405,360,376/P 51,65f.; for the latter see also GI 73; on both see Chapter 6, section 2.

[66]Couturat, "On Leibniz's Metaphysics," p. 28.

[67]Curley, "Root of Contingency," p. 91.

[68]Objecting to the relevance of this evidence, Castañeda argues that "Leibniz may have had both a coherent and exciting metaphysical theory of contingency, and a problematic theological extension of it" (Castañeda, "Leibniz's View of Contingent Truth in the Late 1680's," p. 270). But the contingency of which world is best seems to be a straightforward consequence of Leibniz's infinite analysis theory of contingency, rather than a problematic extension of it. It does not have the characteristics of the clearly problematic theological extensions of his metaphysics that he was willing to entertain in his last years (see Chapter 10, section 5.4); he does not characterize it as "above reason" or as inaccessible to his usual philosophical approaches. Leibniz certainly did not regard the theological in general as problematic, and his metaphysics is pervasively theological.

existences, in saying that "all the knowledge of propositions that is in God, whether it be of simple understanding, about the Essences of things, or of vision about the existences of things, or middle knowledge about conditioned existences,[69] results immediately from the perfect understanding of each term that can be the subject or predicate of any proposition" (C 17/MP 96). The best consistent reading of the paper, I think, is one on which the *complete* concept of any existent thing does involve its existence, and "the possibility or Concept of a created mind" that "does not involve existence" is understood in a narrow sense, as discussed earlier in section 1.2. This reading is suggested by the theological context of the problematic statement, which is immediately preceded by the statement that God "first considers a Mind as possible, before he decides that it ought actually to exist" (C 23/MP 104). The possibility (or concept) of a created mind is here considered as an alternative for God's choice, and therefore in abstraction from those other factors in God that determine God's choice among things that are "possible in themselves." And it is by virtue of those factors in God that the existence of an existent creature follows from its concept in the wider sense—that is, from its complete concept.

This paper on "Necessary and Contingent Truths" contains important developments of the infinite analysis theory of contingency. It is undated, and its watermark has not yet been connected with any particular dates (see VE 455). But like the parts of "General Inquiries" devoted to the theory (GI 60–75,130–37; dated 1686), it seems to me to have an experimental quality not present in statements of the theory from 1689 (FC 179–85/L 264–66, Gr 303f./AG 28f.). One sign of its experimental character is the intriguing passage in which Leibniz says that "Free or intelligent Substances" have the privilege "that they are not bound to any certain subordinate Laws of the universe, but act spontaneously from their own power alone, as if by a sort of private miracle, and by looking to some final cause they interrupt the connection and course of efficient causes operating on their will" (C 20/MP 100). Underlying this statement is the thought that free choices cannot be predicted by any laws of nature that can be understood by a finite mind. This thought can be supported by reflections on infinite analysis, and connects with things Leibniz says about miracle in DM 16. But speaking of free choices as routinely interrupting the connection of efficient causes seems quite contrary to Leibniz's usual views about the pre-established harmony, in which final causes do not disturb the order of efficient causes. As early as July 1686 he writes to Arnauld about the agreement of mind and body, "each one following its laws, and the one acting freely, the other without choice," and contrasts this with the changes in "the laws of bodies" and in "the regular course of thoughts of the soul" that are involved in the occasionalist hypothesis (LA 57f.; cf. LA 74f.,93f.; E 127f./L 457f.; and, much later, G III,657). I therefore think that "Necessary and Contingent Truths" was written in a fairly early period of

[69]'Middle knowledge' signifies God's knowledge of counterfactual conditional truths. The term was originated by the sixteenth-century Jesuit theologian Luis de Molina, whose highly controversial theory on the subject, however, is inconsistent with the implications of what Leibniz asserts here. Cf. R. Adams, "Middle Knowledge and the Problem of Evil."

the development of the infinite analysis theory, not later than July 1686 and perhaps considerably earlier.[70]

It contains a passage (C 18/MP 98) in which Leibniz treats 'essential' and 'existential' as equivalent, respectively, to 'necessary' and 'contingent'. It is not the only text in which he does this, so it is possible that these texts represent a variety of views. But we must be cautious about drawing metaphysical implications from this rather conventional usage.[71] Two texts may be cited as evidence that, in speaking this way, Leibniz did not necessarily mean to imply that all contingent truths depend on which finite things actually exist. (He did of course think that no necessary truths depend on the existence of any being except God.)

"Necessary [truths] are of Essences, contingent [truths] of Existences" (Gr 354), wrote Leibniz, probably in the mid-1690s, without offering any explanation of a special sense of 'essence' or 'existence'.[72] But this is in the same set of reading notes in which he states flatly, "There are some indemonstrable truths even in possible things—namely about contingent things regarded as possible" (Gr 353). If these indemonstrable, and hence contingent, truths are "of" existences, they must presumably be "of" merely possible existences as such.

From the mid-1680s comes even clearer evidence on this point, in a text in which "essential" is equated with "necessary" and "existential" with "contingent" (Gr 311). Here these terms are used to assert that "not only essential or necessary [truths] . . . but also existential, so to speak, or contingent [truths] are contained in this complete concept of Peter [as] possible." And since "this complete concept" refers to one that Leibniz has said God understood perfectly "even before he decided that this Peter who afterwards denied ought to exist," the "existential" truths mentioned here cannot be understood as depending on the actual existence of the creatures they are about—a point perhaps partly acknowledged by the qualifier, "so to speak [*ut ita dicam*]" attached to the term "existential" here. Corresponding to this broad sense of 'existential' is a narrow sense of 'essential', and presumably also of 'essence' (cf. section 2.3 of this chapter). For only a portion of the truths contained in the complete concept of Peter are said here to be "essential." In case the narrow sense of 'essential' was not clear enough from the context, Leibniz added a qualifying clause to one of the statements I have quoted from this text: essential truths are "those, namely, that flow from incomplete or specific concepts, and therefore are demonstrated from the

[70]Heinrich Schepers proposed 1678 as its approximate date in his paper, "Zum Problem der Kontingenz bei Leibniz," pp. 344, 350n; 1686 is favored by both G.H.R. Parkinson (MP 96) and Robert Sleigh ("Truth and Sufficient Reason in the Philosophy of Leibniz," p. 210). Massimo Mugnai considers 1684–86 to be the probable period of composition ("'Necessità *ex hypothesi*' e analisi infinita in Leibniz," p. 153).

[71]The distinction between existential and essential propositions plays a central role in the interpretation offered in Benson Mates, *Philosophy of Leibniz*. I have responded to Mates's arguments in a review of his book in *Mind* 97 (1988): 299–302. The distinction is concerned, in the first instance, with actual existence as entering or not entering into the truth conditions for categorical propositions, and I cannot see that Leibniz used it to frame a theory of contingency, though it does occur in his writings. (See note 46 above.)

[72]As regards 'essential', cf. Gr 373, probably of the same period and similarly without explanation.

terms, in such a way that the contrary implies a contradiction" (Gr 311). The implication is clear that not every truth flowing from an individual's *complete* concept is necessary, or "essential" in the relevant sense.

All interpreters agree that Leibniz always believed there is at least one necessary existential truth: that God exists. But he does not normally mention this as an exception when equating existential with contingent propositions.[73] There is, I think, no reason to take these (usually rather casual) identifications more strictly in the other direction—as excluding contingent propositions that are not existential in the usual sense—given that Leibniz says there are such propositions, as we have seen, and that his most fully developed theory of contingency implies there are.

3. *Leibniz and Possible Worlds Semantics*

It has been discovered that by beginning with the idea that the possible is what is true in some possible world and the necessary is what is true in all possible worlds, and varying our assumptions about the relations of possible worlds to each other, we can obtain models that validate different systems of modal logic. This discovery has given birth to *possible worlds semantics*—the interpretation of modal notions in terms of truth and falsity in (or at) possible worlds. It has shed so much light on modal logic, and has so affected our interest in the notion of possible worlds, that it is especially natural for us to assume that Leibniz also conceived of necessity as truth in all possible worlds and contingency as truth in some but not all possible worlds. It is not at all clear that he did, however.

The closest I have seen him come to expressing this conception is in the paper on "Necessary and Contingent Truths," which I have argued in section 2.6 is not later than 1686, where he says that necessary truths, "which can be demonstrated by analysis of Terms . . . not only will obtain while the World stands, but would still have obtained if God had created the World on a different plan [*alia ratione*]" (C 18/MP 98). This is suggestive, but not conclusive, for on any reasonable interpretation Leibniz regards no world as possible in which something demonstrable is false (if we overlook the problem about the damnation of the innocent as discussed in section 2.2). What we want to know is whether he thought that all the truths that do not depend on which world God created are necessary. In "Necessary and Contingent Truths" he at least comes close to holding that they are. He says that contingent truths, which "cannot be demonstrated by any analysis . . . not only express what pertains to the possibility of things, but also what actually exists, or would exist contingently on certain conditions"[74] (C 18/MP 98).

[73]But cf. Gr 386, where an explanation of the necessity of eternal truths, "because there it is not a matter of existence, but only of Hypothetical propositions," is immediately followed by just this qualification: "Hence it must be said that no absolute [i.e., unconditional] proposition is necessary except that which follows from the nature of God. Certainly no Being exists by its own essence or necessarily except God."

[74]In this context Leibniz also says that "existential or contingent" truths "are true for a certain time," and he gives interesting reasons for thinking it would take an infinite analysis to estab-

Even in the same paper, however, Leibniz also says something inconsistent with this view; this is one sign of the experimental character of the text. For the text itself expresses the point that it would take an infinite comparison of possible worlds to determine the reason for the existence of the one that is actual (C 19/MP 99). From this one can infer, as Leibniz did in 1689 (Gr 305f./AG 30) that it is contingent that this is the best of all possible worlds. And this will be a contingent truth which "would still have obtained if God had created the World on a different plan." I have argued that Leibniz's infinite analysis theory of contingency requires there to be such truths.

The first step in dealing with this issue is to distinguish two things Leibniz may mean by 'possible world'. He may mean a world whose concept is not *demonstrably* inconsistent, or he may mean a world whose *basic* concept (as I have put it in section 1.2) does not involve, demonstrably or otherwise, a contradiction or conceptual falsehood.

The first of these interpretations fits with Leibniz's usual conception of necessity in terms of demonstrability, and indeed yields a possible worlds semantics for it. Given the plausible assumption that not all conceptual truths are demonstrable, the conceptual truth and demonstrability conceptions of necessity demand different modal logics. The strong system S5 seems to be the right modal logic for the conceptual truth conception of necessity.[75] But the characteristic axiom of S5, '~N*p*⊃N~N*p*' (if not necessarily *p*, then necessarily not necessarily *p*), is not valid on the demonstrability conception of necessity. For a proposition may be indemonstrable without being demonstrably indemonstrable. (In rejecting this axiom, it should be noted, one rejects the assumption that all truths about the possible as such are necessary.) The weaker system S4 seems to be the right system for the demonstrability conception of necessity. Its characteristic axiom, 'N*p*⊃NN*p*' (if necessarily *p*, then necessarily necessarily *p*), will be valid under that conception, for what can be demonstrated can thereby be demonstrated to be demonstrable.

By the same token, if we assume that a world w_2 is possible relative to a world w_1 if and only if nothing is true in w_2 whose falsity can be demonstrated in w_1, we obtain the result that the relation of relative possibility among possible worlds is reflexive and transitive but not symmetrical. It is reflexive, if we restrict consideration to worlds that are possible (that is, possible relative to the actual world), for Leibniz will surely hold that 'Something is true which is demonstrably false' is (in the actual world) demonstrably false, but it must be true in any world that is not possible relative to itself. The transitivity of the relation of relative possibility is proved as follows. Suppose it is not transitive. Then there must be a world w_2 which is possible relative to a world w_1, and a world w_3 which is possible relative to w_2 but not to w_1. There must be some proposition *p* which is true in w_3 but whose falsity can be demonstrated in w_1, though not in

lish what is the state of things at any given time. But surely not all contingent or existential truths have reference to a particular time. For instance, the truth that this world, as a whole, is actual, does not. The fact that no such exception is noted in this text is one more sign of its rough, experimental character.

[75]See R. Adams, "Logical Structure of Anselm's Arguments," pp. 45f., for a brief argument on this point.

w_2. But then there is a proposition (that p is not demonstrably false) which is true in w_2 but demonstrably false in w_1; its falsity is demonstrated in w_1 by demonstrating the falsity of p. So w_2 is not possible relative to w_1, contrary to the hypothesis, and the relation of relative possibility must be transitive after all. It is not symmetrical, however. For there is, as Leibniz supposes, at least one proposition p which is possible, and actually true, but not demonstrably possible. A world in which it is true that p is demonstrably false will therefore be possible relative to the actual world, but the actual world will not be possible relative to such a world.

It is known that a relation of relative possibility that is reflexive and transitive but not symmetrical is the principal feature that a system of possible worlds should have if it is to provide a semantics for S4 but not for S5.[76] Thus the possible worlds semantics based on the demonstrability conception of possible worlds seems to fit the modal logic suggested by the demonstrability conception of necessity.

But does Leibniz hold this conception of possible worlds? Certainly he does not work out an S4 semantics; he does not even raise the question of a relation of relative possibility among possible worlds. The crucial question is whether he understands 'possible' in 'possible worlds' in terms of demonstrability and indemonstrability.

He seems to imply that he does, when he says in March 1698, "There are as many possible worlds as there are series of things that can be thought up which do not imply a contradiction. This thesis is identical with me, for I call possible that which does not imply a contradiction, and so in this sense it cannot be refuted" (Gr 390). I assume that "does not imply a contradiction" expresses a proof-theoretical notion here, as it usually does in Leibniz. On this interpretation Leibniz here lets a consistent, univocal use of modal terms carry the proof-theoretical notion of possibility into his conception of possible worlds.

On the other hand, the demonstrability conception of possible worlds has some strikingly un-Leibnizian consequences. First, a possible individual will in general exist in more than one possible world. Leibniz holds that many of the properties contained in an individual's complete concept cannot be demonstrated from the concept. Worlds in which the individual lacks various of those properties will therefore not be demonstrably inconsistent. Second, each actual individual will be compossible with individuals of almost every possible sort, in the sense of coexisting in some possible world with an individual of that sort. For the coexistence of a certain actual individual with most possible sorts of individual will not be demonstrably inconsistent. Third, there will be possible worlds in which different worlds will be the best possible, for the bestness of this world is not demonstrable. Fourth, there will be possible worlds that have (with one exception) all the perfection that the actual world (considered as possible) has, and more. There will be, for example, a world as good as the actual world in other respects, from which the horrors of the Thirty Years War are absent. Leibniz surely did not think it could be demonstrated that the world would be less perfect without the Thirty Years War. The exception, the perfection that the actual

[76]Kripke, "Semantical Analysis of Modal Logic I."

world has but those worlds lack, is *conceptual consistency*, as we may call the property of not involving, not even indemonstrably, a contradiction.

Leibniz never accepts these consequences. Indeed, he explicitly rejects the idea of an individual existing in more than one possible world (T 414).[77] And for his theodicy and theory of creation he *needs* modalities quite different from those generated by the demonstrability conception of necessity. For example, he must claim that God *couldn't* have created a world as good as the actual world in other respects but lacking the horrors of the Thirty Years War. This 'couldn't' cannot be explained in terms of demonstrability. And Leibniz certainly does not mean that God was prevented by divine *goodness* from choosing such a world, having judged that the horrors of the Thirty Years War are better than conceptual inconsistency. Rather, it is not within God's *power* to create such a world, because it is not possible in its own nature.

The claim that two possible substances are *compossible*, likewise, is surely not just the claim that they are not *demonstrably* incompatible, in spite of the fact that Leibniz defined "compossible" as "that which with another does not imply a contradiction" (Gr 325). For it is the lack of compossibility that keeps additional excellent substances from existing in the actual world (G III,572f., C 534), but the addition of such substances is surely not demonstrably inconsistent with the concepts of actual things.

One may be tempted to accuse Leibniz of cheating in his theodicy by using modal terms equivocally. There is a sense in which God couldn't have created a better world than this one (it is conceptually false that there is such a world), but in that sense God also couldn't have done anything different at all (it is conceptually false that God does anything different). There is also a sense in which God could have done something different (it is not demonstrable that God does not, say, omit to create giraffes), but in this sense God could also have made something better than this world (it is not demonstrable that no possible alternative is better).

There is yet another sense of 'could' and 'couldn't' available to Leibniz, however, in which he can say, without equivocation, both of the things he wants to say. God *could* have done something different, in the sense that only the divine goodness keeps God from doing so. But God *couldn't* have created a better world than this, in the sense that it is not only God's goodness that keeps a better alternative from being possible. We could systematize these modalities (although Leibniz did not) by using 'It is possible that *p*' to mean roughly that if it were not a conceptual truth that God is perfectly good, it would not be a conceptual falsehood that *p*.[78]

Leibniz's chief use of the imagery of possible worlds is at those points in his theory of creation that require this last sort of modality. "There are several possible Universes, each collection of compossibles making one of them" (G III,573). The possible worlds are the alternatives among which God chooses, with only

[77]Our investigation of the sense in which he can have done this (and hence our account of possible worlds) will not be complete until the end of Chapter 3, however.

[78]I assume here that a counterfactual conditional with a conceptually false antecedent need not be vacuously true or vacuously false. I think this assumption could be justified within the framework of Leibniz's conceptual containment theory of truth.

the divine goodness keeping God from choosing one of the worlds that are in fact rejected. There must not be among them a world as good in other ways as the actual world but lacking the horrors of the Thirty Years War. The conception of a possible world implied by this imagery, which must therefore be reckoned Leibniz's principal conception, is not that of a world that is not demonstrably inconsistent. It is, rather, that of a world whose basic concept does not involve (demonstrably or otherwise) a contradiction or conceptual falsehood, a world whose basic concept is conceptually consistent.[79]

If we admit to the basic concepts of worlds information about everything except God's goodness and God's choice among worlds (see section 1.2), this conception of possible worlds probably yields a satisfactory semantics for 'It is possible that *p*', interpreted as meaning that if it were not a conceptual truth that God is perfectly good, it would not be a conceptual falsehood that *p*. Helpful though it would be in explaining the theory of creation, Leibniz does not really develop this interpretation, and does not usually use 'it is possible that' in this sense. His main conception of possibility is the proof-theoretical one that can be analyzed in terms of indemonstrability of falsehood. Thus Leibniz's main conception of possible worlds does not provide a possible worlds semantics for his main conception of possibility. If we put the two conceptions together, we get the result that there are propositions which are possible but are not true in any possible world. 'It would be best if there were never any wars' is such a proposition. 'Judas exists without betraying Jesus' may be another (cf. DM 30).[80]

I do not mean to suggest that Leibniz was fully aware of the diversity of sorts of modality at work in his philosophy. Had he been conscious of it, he would presumably have articulated the relevant distinctions more clearly and avoided some apparent inconsistencies. He might also have explored the relations between the different sorts of modality and the notion of a possible world. But he did not, and it is quite misleading to think of him as a grandfather of possible worlds semantics, given the bad fit between his principal conception of possible worlds and his principal modal concepts.[81]

4. On Leibniz's Sincerity

On no point has more suspicion of a cleavage between a public and a private Leibnizian philosophy arisen than on the problem of contingency. Leibniz's sincerity in the *Theodicy* has often been impugned, and often defended. The most spectacular charge of duplicity was one of the earliest, but it is not widely accepted. In 1728, twelve years after the event, and after Leibniz's death, a

[79]Cf. Schepers, "Zum Problem der Kontingenz bei Leibniz," pp. 345f.

[80]Whether it is depends on considerations, and possible further refinements in the notion of a possible world, which will be taken up at the end of Chapter 3.

[81]It should also be noted that Leibniz was not unique in his own time in using the notion of possible worlds. Nicolas Malebranche, in his *Treatise of Nature and Grace* (1680), I,13 (OM V,28), speaks of "an infinity of possible Worlds," of which God chose "the most perfect, in relation to the simplicity of the ways necessary for its production or for its conservation." I know of no evidence that Malebranche was influenced on this point by Leibniz at this early date.

Lutheran theologian, Christopher Matthäus Pfaff, published an account (but not the complete texts) of letters exchanged between him and Leibniz. He claimed that he had said he thought Leibniz was being playful in the *Theodicy*, pretending to oppose Bayle's skepticism while really confirming it, and that Leibniz replied, in a letter of 2 May 1716, "You have hit the nail on the head. And I am amazed there has been no one hitherto who has sensed that this is my game. For it is not for philosophers always to take things seriously. In framing hypotheses, as you rightly point out, they try out the force of their mental talents."[82] If we believe Pfaff's report, we may suppose (as Pfaff did not) that Leibniz was being ironic or playful with him.[83] In any event, it is hard to know what to make of Leibniz if he was not serious in his defense of the thesis that the actual world was chosen as the best possible by a perfect deity. The Leibnizian philosophy that has held the interest of posterity depends in most of its parts on that thesis, and Leibniz has not left us even a sketch of a philosophy that does not depend on it.

With regard to subtler developments of his system, however, there can still be doubts about Leibniz's sincerity, especially in the *Theodicy*. It is partly but not entirely vindicated by the results of the present investigation. It is emphatically clear in the *Theodicy*, as in the rest of his work, that Leibniz is a compatibilist and a determinist. The solution of the problem of contingency that is most clearly developed in the *Theodicy*, that nonactual things are possible in themselves even if they are not possible in relation to God's will, is one that Leibniz also held, and never abandoned, in his private papers from 1673 on. It is a solution that imposes a minimum of qualification on the necessity of all things.

The infinite analysis theory of contingency is partly stated in the *Theodicy*, in § 14 of the remarks on King:

> For one may say in a way that these two principles [of contradiction and sufficient reason] are contained in the definition of True and False. Nevertheless, when in making the analysis of the truth that has been proposed one sees it depending on truths whose contrary implies a contradiction, one may say that it is absolutely necessary. But when in pushing the analysis as far as one pleases one is never able to arrive at such elements of the given truth, one must say that it is contingent, and that it has its origin from a prevailing reason that *inclines without necessitating*. (G VI,414)

Here, as in a letter to Louis Bourguet in 1715 (G III,582/L 664), Leibniz says that necessary truths receive a finite analysis and contingent truths do not, but without stating that this is what contingency consists in, or that the concept of the predicate is contained in the concept of the subject even in contingent truths.[84]

[82]Pfaff, "Fragmentum Epistolae," p. 127

[83]As argued in Blondel, *Une énigme historique*, pp. 1–15. According to Pfaff's own account, at least one of his contemporaries took this view, and some doubted the accuracy of Pfaff's report of Leibniz's statement.

[84]Only slightly more revealing, I think, is a text written quite likely about 1710 for Leibniz's own use, in which he says that something follows "infallibly" but "not necessarily; that is, not in such a way that it could ever be demonstrated that the contrary implies a contradiction," and gives as a reason, "because the analysis goes to infinity" (RML 412).

We have seen that the view that 'God chooses what is best' is contingent, about which Leibniz was very hesitant in his private papers, seems to occur in one or two passages of the *Theodicy*. This might be due to some development of his thought, but no such explanation is plausible for the *Theodicy*'s striking omission of any mention of the view that it is contingent that this world is the best. The latter view was well worked out, affirmed, and never rejected in Leibniz's private papers; and it is plausibly inferred from his infinite analysis theory of contingency, which he clearly continued to believe when he wrote the *Theodicy*.

Moreover, the frequent and unelucidated use that the book makes of the terms 'moral necessity', 'hypothetical necessity', and 'incline without necessitating' leaves the reader with a less necessitarian impression of Leibniz's thought than these terms would leave if they were accompanied by the explanations of their meaning that are presented or suggested by his less public writings. One is not reassured about Leibniz's sincerity when one reads, in a letter from Leibniz to Bartholomew Des Bosses discussing the use of 'moral necessity' in the *Theodicy*, the comment that "in general I should prefer the words to be interpreted in such a way that nothing bad-sounding follows" (G II,419f.).[85]

The lack of candor in the *Theodicy* is evident; the motives for it, whether pedagogical or self-protective, are not. It is interesting that Leibniz had written once, probably in 1676:

> Metaphysics should be written with accurate definitions and demonstrations, but nothing should be demonstrated in it that conflicts too much with received opinions. For thus this metaphysics will be able to be received. If it is once approved, then afterwards, if any examine it more profoundly, they will draw the necessary consequences themselves. (A VI,iii,573)

One of the difficulties in the *Theodicy*, however, is that so many of Leibniz's "accurate definitions" are omitted that one must turn to other works to find the material necessary for a more profound examination.

[85]Des Bosses, a Roman Catholic, was preparing a Latin translation of Leibniz's *Theodicy*. In the Roman Catholic Church propositions could be officially censured as "bad sounding [*male sonans*]," which is weaker than condemning them as "false"; see, e.g., Denzinger, *Enchiridion*, p. 370 (following § 1340).

2

The Logic of Counterfactual Nonidentity

1. Problems of Transworld Identity

Among the theses that Leibniz sent to Antoine Arnauld in February 1686, the one that aroused Arnauld's initial objection was the following statement:

> Since the individual concept of each person contains once for all everything that will ever happen to him, one sees in it the proofs a priori or reasons for the truth of each event, or why one has occurred rather than another. (LA 12)

All the predicates of an individual substance are contained in the concept of that individual, according to Leibniz. This thesis gives rise to many questions about the relation of individuals to their predicates. Why should the predicates be contained in the *concept* of the individual, and not just in the individual itself? Why does Leibniz infer from the conceptual containment thesis, as he does (DM 14), that all the states of an individual substance are *caused* by previous states of that individual alone? We will come to these questions, in the course of this chapter and the next, but the present investigation is organized around another issue. It is an issue of counterfactual identity; Arnauld raised it in these words:

> Since it is impossible that I should not always have remained *myself*, whether I had married or lived in celibacy, the individual concept of *myself* contained neither of these two states; just as it is well to infer: this block of marble is the same whether it be at rest or be moved; therefore neither rest nor motion is contained in its individual concept. (LA 30)

Arnauld affirms transworld or counterfactual identity as a reason for rejecting Leibniz's conceptual containment thesis. He denies that his actual predicate of lifelong celibacy is contained in his individual concept, on the ground that he is the same individual as one who would, under some possible circumstances, have married. In his response, as in a number of other places in his writings, Leibniz made clear that he did not accept Arnauld's assumption of counterfactual identity. He held that no actual individual creature would have existed if anything at all had gone differently from the way things go in the actual world—that if Arnauld, for example, had married, he would not have been Arnauld [or more precisely, that anyone who got married would not have been Arnauld (cf.

Gr 358)]. Why did Leibniz hold this? That is the central question of this chapter and the next.

As it touches on an issue that is very much alive today, this aspect of Leibniz's philosophy has received much attention from recent interpreters.[1] In recent discussions the issue has been couched in terms of *transworld identity*. We ask about the identity or nonidentity of individuals in different possible worlds; this conceptual apparatus affords convenient ways of making such issues precise. Leibniz himself cast the issue in very similar terms at least once (T 414). At the same time, we should note that he normally used counterfactual conditionals to frame the issue rather than putting it in terms of possible worlds. This is important because counterfactual conditionals have a well-known relativity to context which may be lost from view in thinking in terms of possible worlds. I think we can safely use the apparatus of possible worlds in dealing with the relatively formal considerations that will occupy us in this chapter. But the more metaphysical arguments studied in Chapter 3 will lead me to conclude in the end that Leibniz is probably committed to a sweeping denial of transworld identity only under an understanding of 'possible world' that differs from our usual present understandings even more widely than I suggested in Chapter 1, section 3.

At the outset, we should note an important difference between Leibniz and present-day philosophers who are interested in transworld identity. For the latter, talk about possible worlds serves to explicate the structure, if not the basis, of logical possibility and necessity. What is possible is what is true in (or at) some possible world; what is necessary is what is true in (or at) all possible worlds. From this point of view, the denial of transworld identity seems to entail that no actual individual could possibly have had different properties from those it actually has. To say that Caesar, for example, could have turned back from the Rubicon is to say that there is a possible world in which he does, and that obviously must be a possible world in which he exists. But if there is no transworld identity, then Caesar exists only in the actual world, in which he crosses the Rubicon. So it seems to follow that he could not have turned back. Leibniz emphatically rejects this conclusion, however. Much of § 13 of his *Discourse on Metaphysics* is devoted to developing the thesis that, while the crossing of the Rubicon is contained in the individual concept of Julius Caesar, it follows "that it was reasonable and consequently assured that that would happen, but not that it is necessary in itself, nor that the contrary implies a contradiction."

David Lewis has developed his well-known "counterpart theory" as a way of rejecting transworld identity without denying that we could have had somewhat different properties from those we actually have. According to Lewis, no individual exists in more than one possible world, but there is a "counterpart relation" that obtains among sufficiently similar individuals in different possible worlds. Your counterparts are "people you might have been," so to speak. To say that it would have been possible for you to have done a certain thing that you did not do is to say that there is a possible world in which a counterpart of

[1]See Mates, "Individuals and Modality in the Philosophy of Leibniz"; Mondadori, "Leibniz and the Doctrine of Inter-World Identity," "Reference, Essentialism, and Modality in Leibniz's Metaphysics," and "Understanding Superessentialism"; M. Wilson, "Possible Gods"; Mates, *Philosophy of Leibniz*, ch. 8; Sleigh, *Leibniz and Arnauld*, ch. 4.

yours does it.[2] Several recent interpreters[3] have pointed out that Leibniz has a use of proper names that suggests something like Lewis's counterpart theory. He speaks, for example, of "possible Adams" in the plural, meaning "possible persons, different from each other, who fit" a general description consisting of a part of the predicates of the first man in the actual world (LA 41f.; cf. LA 20).

Margaret Wilson has argued convincingly,[4] however, that it is a mistake to ascribe to Leibniz a counterpart-theoretical account of possibility and necessity *de re* in terms of alternative possible Adams, alternative possible Caesars, alternative possible Arnaulds, and so forth. Leibniz never (so far as I know) gives such an account. For him to do so, as Wilson points out, would be inconsistent with his conception of God's freedom. For Leibniz holds that there are infinitely many possible worlds that God could possibly have created, and he never speaks of alternative "possible Gods" who could have created the different worlds. He seems to be committed, not only by this silence, but also by the doctrine of God's necessary existence, to the view that it would have been *the same* God that created whatever possible world was created. In other words, Leibniz seems to have accepted transworld identity for God while rejecting it for every other individual.

These apparent inconsistencies can be removed by understanding Leibnizian possible worlds as I proposed in Chapter 1. I argued there that Leibniz's principal conception of possible worlds can be captured by saying that a possible world is a world that God could have created were it not for the goodness that is part of the divine nature. This is the conception on which Leibniz depends in his theodicy and his account of creation. He is committed to the view that the choice of this world that God has actually created, and God's not creating any other possible world, are contained in the concept of God. But it is precisely because this is the world that God would find to be best, in comparing all possible worlds, that these choices follow from God's essential wisdom and goodness. One of Leibniz's main concerns in his thinking about possible worlds is to maintain the reality of God's choice. And the crux of this matter, as Leibniz perceived it, is that God (one and the same God, presumably) should have had a plurality of *internally* consistent worlds to choose from.[5] Which world God chooses is determined by the divine wisdom and goodness, in conjunction with the value of the worlds, and in that way follows from the concept of God. But the worlds are real alternatives for God in that God could have chosen any one of them were it not for the divine goodness.

This enables us to understand why Leibniz allowed God to have transworld identity. He is prepared to say that the same individual God could have been the creator of different possible worlds because the sense in which God "could" have is that were it not for God's wisdom and goodness, or were it not for those worlds' inferiority, God could have—not that God's creating them would have been perfectly consistent with the divine nature. But this very same conception of the sense

[2]Lewis, "Counterpart Theory and Quantified Modal Logic."

[3]Especially Mondadori, "Reference, Essentialism, and Modality in Leibniz's Metaphysics," pp. 94–101.

[4]M. Wilson, "Possible Gods."

[5]See Chapter 1, section 1.4.

in which God could have created a different world requires that no *creature* occur in any possible world in which something occurs which is contrary to the nature of that creature (considered apart from the reasons for God's choice among worlds). For then it would not be because of its inferiority, and God's wisdom and goodness, but because of an internal conceptual inconsistency in that world, that God could not create it. (By a "conceptually inconsistent" proposition I mean one whose negation is contained in the concept of its subject, whether or not any finite analysis or demonstration would render that containment explicit. A conceptually inconsistent proposition may therefore be possible in the Leibnizian sense, explained in Chapter 1, of not being *demonstrably* false.)

There is much more to be said about Leibniz's reasons for denying transworld or counterfactual identity to creatures. As Wilson has remarked, "we know what *use* Leibniz wants to make of" this doctrine, theologically: "He wants to use it as a basis for denying that God is responsible for a created individual's misfortunes or bad choices, since *that individual* couldn't have existed unless he made those choices and experienced whatever he in fact experiences."[6] Leibniz says that God "did not make Sextus wicked. . . . All he did was grant him existence, which his wisdom could not refuse to the world in which he is included" (T 416). Leibniz thought that this entitled him to hold that evil is not caused by God, but by the limitations inherent in the concepts of the creatures that it was best, on the whole, for God to create (DM 30, T 20). He also thought it provides an answer to complaints that individuals might be tempted to make against God: "You will insist that you can complain, why did God not give you more strength. I reply: if he had done that, you would not be, for he would have produced not you but another creature" (Gr 327; cf. A VI,iii,148).[7]

These theological motives are important for understanding Leibniz's denial of counterfactual identity, but, as Wilson suggests, he undoubtedly thought he could give other *reasons* for it. Two of them will detain us only briefly. A particularly bad argument is found in a letter that Leibniz sent to Arnauld in July 1686, but is missing (whether as a result of a later correction, I do not know) from the copy retained by Leibniz at Hannover. Responding to Arnauld's claim, as formulated by Leibniz, "I find clearly in the individual concept that I have of myself that I shall be myself whether or not I take the trip that I have planned" (LA 52), Leibniz says:

> If it is certain that *A* is *B*, whatever is not *A* is not *B* either. So if *A* signifies Me, and *B* signifies the one who will take this trip, it can be concluded that whoever will not take this trip is not me; and this conclusion can be drawn from the certitude alone of my future trip, without having to impute it to the proposition in question. (RL 39)[8]

[6]M. Wilson, "Possible Gods," p. 729. As will be clear from Chapter 3, I agree with Wilson's statement only subject to some qualifications of the sense of "couldn't" in it.

[7]I have discussed this reply at some length in R. Adams, "Existence, Self-Interest, and the Problem of Evil."

[8]The concluding "without . . ." phrase in this passage is obscure. Without imputing what to what proposition? My guess is that Leibniz's meaning was that the conclusion can be drawn on the grounds stated in this passage without imputing certainty, as a *premise*, to anything as sweeping as the predicate containment theory of truth.

Leibniz seems to be arguing here that a contradiction would be involved in counterfactual identity of an individual, on the ground that I, who am going to take a certain trip, cannot also have the property of not taking that trip. But of course the question is not whether I could *also* have the property of not taking the trip, but whether I could have had that property *instead of* my actual property of taking the trip.

A different argument is suggested by the statement, "It follows also that it would not have been our Adam, but another, if he had had other events, for nothing prevents us from saying that it would be another. Hence it is another" (LA 42). This looks like an appeal to the Principle of Sufficient Reason: there is no compelling reason to say it would be the same individual if different events happened to him; therefore, it would not be the same individual. This is a weak argument. It leaps over vast stretches of disputed territory. Arnauld was at least initially inclined to say, for example, that our ordinary conception of a person keeps us from saying it would have been another Adam if he had never sinned. One wonders, moreover, whether the argument does not cut both ways. As Wilson says, "The question presents itself insistently: what prevents us from *denying* it would be a different Adam if circumstances had been different . . . ?"[9] Would it be any easier to find a sufficient reason for denying counterfactual identity than for affirming it? Leibniz seems to assume here that presumption favors nonidentity—that identity needs to be explained in a way that distinctness does not, and hence that there is more need of reasons for affirming than for denying identity. Perhaps that is correct. I think it is not without plausibility in some cases. But not seeing how Leibniz would defend it, I will pass on to other arguments.

2. *The Conceptual Containment Theory of Truth*

It is natural to turn next to the argument that has drawn the most discussion.

> Finally [he wrote to Arnauld] I have given a decisive reason, which in my opinion ranks as a demonstration; it is that always, in every true affirmative proposition, necessary or contingent, universal or singular, the concept of the predicate is included in some way in that of the subject, *praedicatum inest subjecto* [the predicate inheres in the subject]; or else I do not know what truth is. (LA 56)

This is the argument by which Arnauld confessed himself especially impressed when he gave up the debate with Leibniz about individual concepts (LA 64). We shall consider what is the theory of truth to which Leibniz here appeals, what were his reasons for holding it, and whether it does entail his denial of trans-world or counterfactual identity.

As usually stated by Leibniz, the conceptual containment theory of truth applies to categorical propositions—that is, to propositions of subject-predicate form. He sometimes applied it to conditional propositions, holding that they are true if and only if the consequent is contained in the antecedent (e.g., C 401);

[9]M. Wilson, "Possible Gods," p. 729.

but that need not concern us here. The six traditional types of categorical proposition, with an example of each, are:

universal affirmative:	All men are married.
universal negative:	No man is married.
particular affirmative:	Some man is married.
particular negative:	Some man is not married.
singular affirmative:	Arnauld is married.
singular negative:	Arnauld is not married.

Only two of these types, the universal and singular affirmatives, are mentioned in the formulation of the theory that I have quoted (as also in C 16f.,519/MP 96, L 268). This is no accident, for Leibniz applies the theory more straightforwardly to these types than to the other four. Nevertheless, it is clear that he sometimes expresses it in a more sweeping form, claiming that in *every* true proposition, without restriction as to type, the concept of the predicate is contained in the concept of the subject (DM 8; GI 132).

The conceptual containment theory is closely associated with Leibniz's preference for what is nowadays called an "intensional" as opposed to an "extensional" interpretation of the categorical propositions. (Perhaps in some sense it *is* that preference.) Roughly, an *extensional* interpretation is one that treats the truth or falsity of propositions as depending on relations among the extensions of the terms, where the extension of a term is the class of things that satisfy it, or which it characterizes.[10] An *intensional* interpretation is one that treats the truth or falsity of propositions as depending on relations among the intensions—that is, the concepts—of their terms.

Since Leibniz's discussion partner, Arnauld, was coauthor of a famous logic text, the *Port Royal Logic*, it is of interest to note that a similar distinction is made in that book between the comprehension [*compréhension*] and the extension [*étendue* or *extension*] of an idea. The comprehension of an idea consists of "the attributes which it includes in itself, and which cannot be taken away from it without destroying it." The extension of an idea consists of "the subjects with which that idea agrees," or which contain it.[11] The extension of a general term, however, may be viewed in the *Port Royal Logic* as constituted by both the species and the individuals that fall under it. Both relations of the comprehensions of terms and relations of the extensions of terms are used in the *Port Royal Logic* in justifying the basic rules of traditional logic.[12]

Scholars have noted that Leibniz worked out quite a variety of both intensional and extensional treatments of the logic of predicates, and that he preferred the intensional approach.[13] For the sake of brevity, I will abstract somewhat from

[10]See Railli Kauppi, *Über die leibnizsche Logik*, pp. 254–56, for a comparison of Leibnizian and modern conceptions of classes.

[11]Arnauld and Nicole, *Port Royal Logic*, I,6; II.17.

[12]Arnauld and Nicole, *Port Royal Logic*, II,17–20.

[13]The interpreter to whom I owe the most on this subject is Kauppi. The whole of her excellent book, *Über die leibnizsche Logik*, is a study of the intensional and extensional approaches in Leibniz's logic. She seems to me correct in her reply (pp. 210, 251f.) to the charge of Couturat that Leibniz ought to have preferred the extensional interpretation. (See Couturat, *La logique de Leibniz*, pp. 19–32.)

this variety and discuss only the one intensional and the one extensional interpretation that are most closely related to the controversy between Leibniz and Arnauld. Leibniz did not have fixed terminology corresponding to 'intensional' and 'extensional'; so I will use these more modern terms. He distinguished the two principal types of treatment variously as in terms of ideas [*secundum ideas* or *ex ideas*] on the one hand and in terms of instances [*per exempla subjecta*] or individuals belonging to the terms [*per individuis terminorum*] on the other hand (C 300; G VII,215/P 119f.; cf. C 53/P 20). In Leibniz, unlike the *Port Royal Logic*, the extensional treatment is almost always in terms of the individuals, not the species, that fall under the general terms.[14]

The contrast between the two interpretations is easiest in the case of *universal affirmative* propositions. As an example, take the proposition, 'All gold is metal'. Extensionally interpreted, it means that the extension of 'gold' is contained in the extension of 'metal': the class of gold things is contained or included in the class of metal things. Intensionally interpreted, it means that the concept of metal is contained in the concept of gold. Extensionally, the subject is contained in the predicate in this type of proposition, if the proposition is true. Intensionally, the predicate is contained in the subject. Leibniz noted this "inversion" of the containment relation, contrasting his own intensional interpretation with the extensional interpretation of "the Schools," who

> say that metal is wider than gold, and if we wished to enumerate the individuals of gold on the one hand and the individuals of metal on the other, the latter would certainly be more than the former, which will therefore be contained in the latter as a part in the whole. (C 53/P20)

'Some metal is gold' is a *particular affirmative* proposition. Extensionally interpreted, it means that the extension of 'metal' intersects the extension of 'gold': the class of metal things and the class of gold things have at least one member in common. The intensional interpretation of particular affirmatives is less obvious. Leibniz wants to say that in these propositions, too, "the concept of the predicate is contained in some way in the concept of the subject"—but in what way? It does not seem to be true that the concept of gold is included in the concept of metal. For something can be metal without being gold.

Leibniz's solution to this problem is that "in a particular affirmative proposition it is enough that the thing should follow when something is added." He gives an example to show what sort of addition he means: "although metal does not by itself contain gold, nevertheless some metal, with an addition or specification (for example, that which makes up the greater part of a Hungarian ducat) is of such a nature as to involve the nature of gold" (C 51/P 19). This choice of an example is not a happy one. For it seems doubtful that the concept of gold is contained in the *concept* of metal that makes up the greater part of a Hungarian ducat.

Leibniz gives a better example elsewhere, suggesting that 'Some man is a laugher' could be understood as 'A laugher-man is a laugher.' Here the "addition" of the specification 'laugher' to the concept of man yields a subject con-

[14]G VII,244/P 141 seems to present an exception, as noticed by Kauppi, *Über die leibnizsche Logik*, p. 43.

cept (of laugher-man) which manifestly does contain the predicate of being a laugher. It might seem that this method of intensional interpretation has the unacceptable result that all particular affirmatives turn out to be true, since we can always "add" the predicate concept to the subject concept. But Leibniz denies that we can always make such an addition. The qualified subject concept resulting from the addition must be *consistent* in order to verify a particular affirmative proposition, on his interpretation. Thus, he says that "a laugher-stone would not be a laugher since a laugher-stone involves a contradiction" (G VII,214/P 118). Intensionally interpreted, therefore, 'Some *A* is *B*' means that the concept of *A*, with some consistent addition, includes the concept of *B*.

Different (though equivalent) treatments of the negative propositions are found in Leibniz. He says that "negative propositions merely contradict the affirmatives, and assert that they are false." A particular negative does nothing but deny a universal affirmative, and "a universal negative proposition merely contradicts a particular affirmative" (C 52/P 19f.). This treatment of the negative propositions, as negations of the affirmatives, can, of course, be applied to both the intensional and the extensional interpretations. Since the particular affirmative 'Some *A* is *B*', intensionally interpreted, means 'The concept of *A*, with *some* consistent addition, contains the concept of *B*', the universal negative, 'No *A* is *B*', will mean 'The concept of *A*, with *any* consistent addition, does *not* contain the concept of *B*'. In this treatment negative propositions are viewed as cases of exclusion rather than inclusion of concepts, and Leibniz commonly states the conceptual containment theory of truth accordingly, as applying only to affirmative propositions (e.g., LA 56; C 519/L 268; G VII,208/P 112).

A more natural and perspicuous intensional interpretation of the negative propositions results if they are formed by negating the predicate in the affirmative proposition of the same quantity, rather than by negating the opposite affirmative proposition. "In a Negative Proposition, when we deny that a predicate is in the subject in this way that I have said, by that very act we affirm that the negation of the predicate, or a term that is contradictory to the predicate, is in the subject" (C 86/AG 11). In this approach, the universal negative, 'No *A* is *B*', means 'The concept of *A* contains the concept of not-*B*'. This renders the negative proposition as a case of concept-*in*clusion rather than *ex*clusion, though the concept included is the negation of the one traditionally identified as the predicate "term" of the proposition, rather than that concept itself. In the paper from which I have cited this approach, accordingly, Leibniz crossed out the word "affirmative" from the statement that "In every affirmative proposition . . . the notion of the predicate is involved in the notion of the subject" (C 85/AG 11). An analogous treatment can be applied to the extensional interpretation.

I use the traditional square of opposition to summarize (1) the extensional and (2) the intensional interpretation of the universal and particular propositions, as follows:

All A is B.	**No A is B.**
(1) The class of *B* contains the class of *A*.	(1) The class of not-*B* contains the class of *A*.
(2) The concept of *A* contains the concept of *B*.	(2) The concept of *A* contains the concept of not-*B*.

Some A is B.
(1) The class of *B* intersects the class of *A*.
(2) The concept of *A*, with some consistent addition, contains the concept of *B*.

Some A is not B.
(1) The class of not-*B* intersects the class of *A*.
(2) The concept of *A*, with some consistent addition, contains the concept of not-*B*.

With regard to universal and particular categorical propositions at least, the intensional interpretation is substantially equivalent to the conceptual containment theory of truth.

The intensional interpretation of singular propositions, however, is both more problematic and more relevant to our present investigation. At this point it will be helpful to take up some terminology from the Leibniz-Arnauld correspondence. Arnauld agreed with Leibniz that there is a *complete concept* which God forms of every individual and which contains all of the individual's predicates—everything that will ever happen to that individual. That much clearly follows from the doctrine of divine omniscience that was common property to the two thinkers. They agreed that complete concepts of individuals are known only to God, not to us; we have to think of individuals through incomplete concepts. They also spoke of an *individual concept* of each individual, which is minimally characterized by Arnauld in the following words:

> It seems to me that I ought to regard as contained in the individual concept of *me* only what is such that I would no longer be *me* if it were not in *me*; and that everything that is on the contrary such that it could be in *me* or not be in *me*, without my ceasing to be *me*, cannot be considered as being contained in my individual concept. (LA 30f.)

Leibniz maintained that the individual concept of every created individual is its complete concept. Arnauld disputed this, at least partly on the ground that it seemed to imply the denial of counterfactual identity, for it follows from the definition of an individual concept that I could not be me if I lacked any predicate contained in my individual concept. So if my complete concept is my individual concept, it seems to follow that I could not be me if I lacked any of my actual predicates.

In this discussion Leibniz takes the subject concept of a singular proposition to be an individual concept and seems to give such propositions an intensional treatment of the same sort as universal propositions.[15] For instance, 'Arnauld is married' would mean that the concept of being married is contained in the individual concept of Arnauld, while the truth, 'Arnauld is not married', means that the concept of not being married is contained in Arnauld's individual concept.

x is F.
The individual concept of *x* contains the concept of *F*.

x is not F.
The individual concept of *x* contains the concept of not-*F*.

The question naturally arises, however, why singular propositions should not be treated in the same way as particular rather than universal propositions. Leibniz's intensional interpretation demands of particular propositions only that the concept of the subject *with some consistent addition* contain the concept of

[15]Cf. Arnauld and Nicole, *Port Royal Logic*, II,3.

the predicate (or of the predicate's negation). Why should more be demanded of singular propositions? Why shouldn't 'Arnauld is married' mean that the individual concept of Arnauld, *with some consistent addition*, contains the concept of being married? And why wouldn't Arnauld be correct in saying that the concept of *married Arnauld* is his individual concept with a *consistent* addition?

These questions appear even more pressing when we recall that for Leibniz a *negative* proposition is the contradictory of the singular affirmative (C 52/P 19f.). Now, suppose the singular affirmative is treated on the model of the *universal* affirmative and means that the individual concept of the subject contains the concept of the predicate. Then its negation will be treated as analogous to a *particular* negative, which is the contradictory of a universal affirmative, and will mean that the individual concept of the subject, *with some consistent addition*, contains the complement of the concept of the predicate. Thus 'Arnauld is not married' will mean that not the individual concept of Arnauld, but that concept with some consistent addition (say, the concept of celibate Arnauld), contains the concept of *not* being married.

Suppose, on the other hand, that the singular affirmative is treated on the model of the *particular* affirmative and means that the individual concept of the subject, with some consistent addition, contains the concept of the predicate. In that case its negation, by analogy with the *universal* negative, must mean that the individual concept of the subject, as such, contains the negation of the concept of the predicate. On this reading, 'Arnauld is not married' will mean that the individual concept of Arnauld itself contains the concept of *not* being married.

Leibnizian principles thus seem to generate a complete new square of opposition, with four types of proposition, out of the two original types of singular proposition:

x is F. The individual concept of *x* contains the concept of *F*.	**x is not F.** The individual concept of *x* contains the concept of not-*F*.
x is F. The individual concept of *x*, with some consistent addition, contains the concept of *F*.	**x is not F.** The individual concept of *x*, with some consistent addition, contains the concept of not-*F*.

In this square, as in the traditional square of universal and particular propositions, the diagonally opposite propositions are mutually contradictory. All the logical relationships of the square of opposition are reproduced.

This is a strange result. Leibniz certainly wants to have two intensional types of singular proposition instead of four. Yet any choice of only two out of the four types in the square seems to run some risk of being arbitrary. Leibniz himself seems inclined to choose the top two types in the square, the two that correspond to universal propositions. There is a serious objection to that choice, however, in that those two types are not contradictories but contraries, which can both be false together. On the other hand, if he refused to choose, he would be left with four types of singular proposition, and would have to regard the two ordinary forms of singular proposition ('*x* is *F*' and '*x* is not *F*') as ambiguous—which also seems undesirable.

We do not have to guess what Leibniz's solution to this problem would be, for a considerable part of the problem occurred to him and was discussed by him.

> Some Logical difficulties worth solving have occurred [to me]. How does it come about that opposition works in [the case of] the singular [propositions], 'The Apostle Peter is a soldier' and 'The Apostle Peter is not a soldier', whereas otherwise a universal affirmative and a particular negative are opposed? Shall we say that a singular [proposition] is equivalent to a universal and to a particular? That's right. . . . For some Apostle Peter and every Apostle Peter coincide, since the term is singular. (G VII,211/P 115)

Here Leibniz sees that there is a problem about treating the singular negative as the contradictory of the singular affirmative, and that the problem arises from the possibility of interpreting the singular propositions either as analogous to universal propositions or as analogous to particular propositions. His solution is to insist that the two interpretations of each singular proposition are equivalent, "coincide," and so collapse into one.

But how is that equivalence possible, within the framework of a Leibnizian intensional interpretation? Inspection of the apparent square of opposition for singular propositions will show that the reduction of the four types to the two desired types requires that the individual concept of x with any consistent addition be equivalent to the individual concept of x. This requirement will be satisfied if and only if there is no predicate not already contained in the individual concept of x which can consistently be added to it. What is required, in other words, is precisely that the individual concept of x be a complete concept.[16] For a complete concept, as we shall see in section 6, is one to which no new predicate can consistently be added.

3. *Actuality in the Conceptual Containment Theory*

Leibniz says that, as opposed to an extensional calculus based on relations of classes of individuals, "I have preferred to consider universal concepts, or ideas, and their combinations, because they do not depend on the existence of individuals" (C 53/P 20). I think we can guess what the advantage is that Leibniz thus claims for the intensional interpretation. There are well-known difficulties in maintaining the validity of the traditional inferences in the square of opposition, under an extensional interpretation, if the subject or the predicate concept (or one of their complements) has an empty extension, because of the way in which the truth of the propositions, extensionally interpreted, depends on the existence of individuals satisfying (or not satisfying) the concepts. Leibniz could justify all the traditional inferences, under his intensional interpretation, without assuming anything about the actual existence of individuals, but assuming only that the subject and predicate concepts (and their complements) are consistent (and hence *possibly* exemplified).

[16]The connection of this solution with the doctrine that individual concepts are complete is noted by Kauppi, *Über die leibnizsche Logik*, p. 213.

From another point of view, however, the fact that under an intensional interpretation, the truth of the categorical propositions does not depend on the existence of individuals can be seen as a serious *disadvantage*. Many of the propositions to be interpreted are normally understood to be about the universe of actually existing things in such a way that their truth or falsity *ought* to depend on the existence of individuals. From the standpoint of common sense, it may be implausible to say (as the usual extensional interpretation does) that 'All centaurs are made of metal' is true if no centaurs exist, but it is at least as implausible to say (in accordance with the intensional interpretation) that 'Some dogs are green' is true if the concept of a green dog is consistent.

Leibniz will not be speechless in the face of this problem. He had a method for dealing with it. If 'Some pious human being is poor' means that poverty of a pious human being is not just possible but actual, Leibniz will state it as 'A poor pious human being is existent', where 'existent' means existing in the actual world (C 270–73). Intensionally interpreted, this yields 'The concept of a poor pious human being, with some consistent addition, contains the concept of existing in the actual world.' Here we must think more about what is meant by 'consistent addition'. Does it mean (1) an addition that could be made without engendering a *demonstrable* inconsistency—that is, an inconsistency that could be proved by a finite analysis? Or does it mean (2) an addition that would not result in any conceptual inconsistency at all? Or perhaps (3) an addition that would not result in any conceptual inconsistency in the *basic* concept[17] of a possible world in which the amplifed concept would be exemplified? The first of these cannot be what is meant. For the interpretation is intended to apply to contingent propositions, which it would take an infinite analysis to prove or disprove (cf. C 272). Indeed, 'A poor pious human being is existent' is such a proposition. And while the third sense, invoking basic concepts of worlds, may be what is meant in some contexts, I think the second sense must be intended where 'existent' is being treated as a predicate, since one must go outside the basic concept of any possible world to determine which world is actual.

Interpreted with this sort of existential import, 'Some pious human being is poor' will be true if and only if the concept of existing in the actual world can be added to the concept of a poor pious human being without generating any conceptual inconsistency. And that will be true if and only if a poor pious human being exists in the best of all possible worlds. For given the necessary existence of a God of perfect wisdom, power, and goodness, a conceptual inconsistency is involved in the actuality of any world but the best. This interpretation is borne out by Leibniz's efforts to define 'existence' and 'existent' in terms of entering into the most perfect series of things, or being compatible with more things than anything incompatible with it is, or being pleasing to God.[18] As definitions, these are problematic, but it is clear that Leibniz's intensional interpretation of propositions intended to be about the way things actually are will work only on the assumption that the concept of existing in the actual world and the concept of existing in the best of all possible worlds can be added, without any conceptual inconsistency, to exactly the same concepts.

[17]This terminology is introduced and explained in Chapter 1, section 1.2.

[18]C 9,360,376,405/P 51,65f.; cf. Gr 325 and Chapter 6, section 2 in this volume.

Universal propositions can be treated in an analogous way. For example, if 'Every human being sins' means not that sinlessness is conceptually inconsistent with humanity, but only that sin is actually universal among human beings, it can be rendered as 'The concept of a human being that does not sin contains the concept of not existing in the actual world' (cf. C 271). As for singular propositions, 'Arnauld is (actually) celibate' can presumably be rendered as 'The concept of celibate Arnauld contains the concept of existing in the actual world'—which will be true if and only if Arnauld exists, and is celibate, in the best of all possible worlds.

4. An Anti-Semantical Theory of Truth

Leibniz held a very austere view of conceptual containment. He thought that all true propositions are either "identities" or reducible by (a perhaps infinite) analysis of terms to identities. Among categorical propositions, identities have such forms as '*A* is *A*', '*A* is not non-*A*', and '*AB* is *A*' (C 518,369/L 267, P 59). Reduction by analysis of terms proceeds by the use of definitions, or by substitution of (more complex) equivalent terms for the original terms of the proposition (see C 518,68/L 267; G VII,44). I take it from this that in truths that are not explicitly identical, conceptual containment is supposed to be based on a formal (though perhaps not finite) logical construction of the terms of the proposition out of simpler concepts. And this construction, at least insofar as it is relevant to the truth of the proposition, proceeds by the simple logical operations of conjunction and negation.

Leibniz does speak of other "*simple particles* or primitive syncategorematic terms," such as 'in' (C 358/P 49), which play a part in the composition of concepts, but conceptual containment and exclusion seem always to turn on conjunction and negation. If a predicate is contained in a subject concept, it is because they are identical or the subject concept is a conjunction one of whose conjuncts is identical with the predicate. If the subject excludes the predicate, that is because it is the negation of the predicate (or vice versa), or because the subject or predicate or both are conjunctions of concepts and one of them is, or includes as a conjunct, a concept that is the negation of the other or of one of the other's conjuncts. Leibniz's general statements of his theory of conceptual containment seem not to allow for any other relation of implication or inconsistency between concepts than these.

This may not be consistent with all his applications of the theory.[19] For instance, I have argued in section 3 that actual existence is contained in the concepts of those things that actually exist, on Leibniz's view, by virtue of their belonging to the best of all possible worlds. But is the relation of *better than* between possible worlds reducible to purely syntactical relations among concepts? Perhaps Leibniz thought so, but it's far from obvious that it is so, and he has not left us any demonstration that it is. He has left us general statements, however, that seem to imply a purely syntactical theory of truth.

[19] I am indebted to Marianne Kooij for pressing me on this point. Similar issues will arise in Chapters 5 and 6.

Leibniz may be contrasted with Descartes on this point. In his early *Rules for the Direction of the Mind*, Descartes held that we are acquainted with a number of "simple natures," which cannot be analyzed into anything simpler. In spite of their simplicity, he thought these natures may have a necessary connection with each other; one may be

> so implied in the concept of another, by some confused reason, that we cannot conceive either distinctly if we judge that they are separated from each other. It is in this way that shape is conjoined with extension, motion with duration or time, and so on, because it is impossible to conceive of a shape that has no extension at all, or a motion that has no duration at all. (AT X,421)

Descartes could not explain these implications in the way proposed by Leibniz, for Descartes maintained that shape, extension, motion, and duration are simple and explicitly denied that they can be analyzed. He could not, therefore, regard them as conjunctions of simpler properties. In other words, Descartes supposed that there are primitive necessary implications between concepts, which are not to be explained by structures of conjunction and negation within the concepts. He was less explicit about primitive inconsistencies between concepts, but he did say that the simple natures can be sorted into those that are ascribed to the intellect, those that are ascribed to bodies, and those that are ascribed to both (AT X,419). Implicit in this division, I think, is the assumption that there is some sort of necessary incompatibility between the purely intellectual and the purely material natures, even though they are simple. Knowledge and doubt, for instance, cannot have a shape.

Descartes's position is plausible. If there are any simple concepts, I should think there probably are primitive implications and inconsistencies between them. Leibniz will have none of it, however. He maintains an account of conceptual implication and inconsistency that is an ancestor of the attempt to explain all logical necessity and all logical implication in terms of analyticity. One place in his philosophy where something hangs on this is in his version of the ontological proof of the existence of God. Early and late he gives an argument (discussed in Chapters 5 and 6 in this volume) for the possibility of God's existence that presupposes that conceptual inconsistency cannot arise except by a conjunction of concepts in which one concept is a negation of the other.

The consequence of defining truth in terms of conceptual containment, so formally understood, is a radically anti-semantical theory of truth. That is, it is a theory in which the truth or falsity of a proposition does not depend at all on what objects, or even what properties, are represented by the simple concepts that enter into the proposition. Truth or falsity depends only on the logical structure of the proposition and the internal logical structure of its concepts. In this sense, truth is not a semantical but a purely syntactical property of propositions, according to Leibniz's theory.

The point is underlined by two consequences that follow from the theory, although Leibniz may not have recognized them. First, suppose, as Leibniz did, that all concepts are ultimately composed of simple concepts. It follows from Leibniz's theory that God does not need to know what simple concepts are involved in a proposition *P*, or what properties are represented by the simple concepts in *P*, in order to know whether *P* is true or false. God has only to know the logical structure of *P* in order to know whether *P* is true. Suppose, for example, that God intuits a representation of a complete analysis of *P*, in which each simple concept is represented consistently and uniquely by a symbol. God could know whether the represented proposition is true or false without knowing what the symbols stand for. Of course, Leibniz would insist that God does know what simple concepts are involved in every proposition (and what properties they represent, if that is different); but God's knowledge of the truth and falsity of propositions does not depend on that.

Second, if Leibniz's theory of truth is correct, the actual world is perfectly symmetrical with respect to simple concepts. Take any true proposition *P*. Suppose *A* is a complete analysis of *P*; perhaps *A* is infinitely complex. And let *F* and *G* be two simple concepts occurring in *A*. Now consider the proposition *Q* formed by interchanging *F* and *G* at all of their occurrences in *A*. It follows from Leibniz's theory that *Q* is true if *P* is, because, when fully analyzed, they have exactly the same logical structure, and therefore *Q*'s subject concept will contain *Q*'s predicate if and only if *P*'s subject concept contains *P*'s predicate.

This is not to say that there is no place in Leibniz's philosophy for a semantics—that is, for a theory of how thought and/or language represent things distinct from themselves. On the contrary, Leibniz believed that each of us has infinitely many thoughts that "express," and constitute "perceptions of," things outside our own minds, and he devoted a lot of attention to this relation, which is, in a broad sense, a semantical relation. It is just that in his philosophy the truth and falsity of propositions are determined independently of this semantical relation (or perhaps more accurately, prior to it). This makes it all the more difficult to answer the question to which we turn next.

5. *Why Did Leibniz Hold the Conceptual Containment Theory?*

Clearly, the conceptual containment theory of truth is an extraordinary doctrine. Why did Leibniz believe it? He saw some advantages for formal logic in an intensional interpretation of the logic of predicates, but those formal considerations are inconclusive, and Leibniz knew it.[20] Robert Sleigh has proposed "Leibniz's effort to explain possible individuals, possible worlds, and creation in terms of God and his concepts" as the source of the conceptual containment theory of truth.[21] I am sure that Leibniz's doctrine of creation is at least a major part of the source of the conceptual containment theory. Specifically, I do not believe Leibniz would have adopted the conceptual containment theory of truth had it not been for his prior adherence to a form of the Principle of Sufficient Reason that makes every truth follow, in some sense, from the necessary existence and nature of God.

In the works of the 1680s and later, Leibniz sometimes proposes a derivation of the Principle of Sufficient Reason from the conceptual containment theory

[20]See especially Kauppi, *Über die leibnizsche Logik*, pp. 247–52.

[21]Sleigh, "Truth and Sufficient Reason in the Philosophy of Leibniz," p. 236.

of truth (C 519/L 268; cf. T k14). Louis Couturat even held that Leibniz identified the principle with the theory.[22] But it is not plausible to suppose that Leibniz accepted the Principle of Sufficient Reason *because* he believed the conceptual containment theory of truth. The principle was one of his first metaphysical commitments. In his letter of 1671 to Magnus Wedderkopf and in *The Philosopher's Confession* of a year or two later we see the young Leibniz wrestling with the apparently deterministic implications of the principle, but the conceptual containment theory of truth makes no appearance there (A II,i,117f./L 146f.; A VI,iii,115–49). In the early 1670s Leibniz even wrote out a proof of the Principle of Sufficient Reason that is not based on any theory of truth, but on his conception of a "requirement [*requisitum*]":[23]

Proposition:
Nothing is without a reason,
or whatever is has a sufficient reason.

Definition 1. A *sufficient reason* is that which is such that if it is posited the thing is.

Definition 2. A *requirement* is that which is such that if it is not posited the thing is not.

Demonstration:

Whatever is, has all [its] requirements.
For if one [of them] is not posited the thing is not *by def. 2.*
If all [its] requirements are posited, the thing is.
For if it is not, it will be kept from being by the lack of something, that is, a requirement.
Therefore all the Requirements are a sufficient reason *by def. 1.*
Therefore whatever is has a sufficient reason.
Q.E.D. (A VI,ii,483)

The crucial premise of the proof is that nothing can fail to exist except for lack of a requirement (i.e., a necessary condition) of its existence. This seems to beg the question, since anyone who denies the Principle of Sufficient Reason will suppose that when all the necessary conditions of a thing's existence are given, there might still remain both a possibility of its existing and a possibility of its not existing—unless trivially necessary conditions (such as the thing's existence itself) are included here among its requirements, in which case the sum of the requirements will constitute a sufficient reason only in a very uninteresting sense of 'reason'. Leibniz clearly liked this argument, however. It is repeated in *The Philosopher's Confession* (A VI,iii,118) and seems to come to much briefer expression in 1716 in Leibniz's last letter to Samuel Clarke (LC V,18).

Thus Leibniz would have believed in the Principle of Sufficient Reason even if he had never thought of the conceptual containment theory of truth. But the theory does provide an *explanation* of *how* there is a sufficient reason for every truth. For in any true proposition the *way* in which the predicate is contained in the concept of the subject, with or without involvement of God's choice of the best, will express the reason for that truth. I think that is the point of the pas-

[22]Couturat, "On Leibniz's Metaphysics," pp. 20f.
[23]For more on this conception, see Chapter 4, section 1.

sages in which Leibniz seems to derive the Principle of Sufficient Reason from the theory.[24]

Perhaps the theory was practically forced on him by his commitment to the principle. He may have been unable to see any reason as *sufficient* that was not grounded in conceptual relations. That is not the only way in which the Principle of Sufficient Reason can be understood, but it is one way. Historically, the most important alternative, I think, is to suppose that the decision of a free will can constitute a sufficient reason for a truth that does not follow from concepts, but Leibniz firmly rejected this view when it was proposed to him by Clarke (LC III,2; IV,1–2).[25]

Leibniz presented his conceptual containment theory to Arnauld, however, not as a consequence of the Principle of Sufficient Reason, but as an analysis of the notion of truth. Apart from the theory, he says, "I do not know what truth is" (LA 56). So we still want an explanation of why he thought the theory is required for an understanding of the notion of *truth*. And the first question that will occur to most of us in this connection is, Why didn't Leibniz define the truth of propositions in terms of their *correspondence with facts*? After all, as I noted at the end of section 4, Leibniz did believe that our concepts and true beliefs express things distinct from us.

Some remarks of Michael Dummett about Frege may shed light on this aspect of Leibniz's thought:

> Frege, although a realist, did not believe in the correspondence theory of truth. . . . The truth of a (complete) sentence or of the thought which it expresses is not relational: there is no question of our having first to discover the state of affairs which the sentence is intended to describe, and then to compare the sentence with it to see whether or not it corresponds; the sentence is simply true or false without qualifications. Facts, in Frege's ontology, are not further constituents of reality, . . . alongside objects, truth-values, concepts, relations, and functions. They are, rather, to be identified with true thoughts.[26]

Much of what Dummett says here about Frege could also be said about Leibniz. Facts have no more independent a place in Leibniz's ontology than in Frege's. This world, for Leibniz, is the totality of (finite) things, not of facts. It is virtually defined as *aggregatum rerum finitarum* [the aggregate of finite things] (G VII,302/L 486). If reality is composed of things rather than of facts, it falls primarily to concepts rather than to propositions to correspond with reality, for it is concepts that express (or fail to express) things. That may be why it was natural for Leibniz to think of a proposition as a complex of concepts or terms—a conception of the proposition for which there was also precedent in medieval logic. And, given that what one is doing in framing or asserting a proposition is connecting concepts or terms in a certain way, the realist's demand that every truth should have "some foundation in the nature of things" (DM 8) naturally comes to expression as a demand that there should be "some real connection

[24]For a similar verdict, see Brody, "Leibniz's Metaphysical Logic," pp. 53f.

[25]Leibniz is responding to § 1 of Clarke's second letter and § 2 of Clarke's third letter (see G VII,359f.,363,367,371f.). Cf. Rowe, *Cosmological Argument*, Ch. 2, and R. Adams, review of Rowe.

[26]Dummett, *Frege: Philosophy of Language*, p. 442.

between" the terms of the proposition that is true (G VII,300/L 226; cf. C 518f./ L 267f., LA 56).

What has just been said is indeed important for an appreciation of the conceptual framework in which Leibniz saw the issue, but the objection that was raised in terms of a correspondence theory of truth can still be raised in these new terms. At least for propositions about actual things, we may ask, Why can't the real connection between the terms of the proposition be a containment of the predicate in the concrete thing to which the subject concept corresponds? Isn't that indeed the normal understanding of the Aristotelian formula *praedicatum inest subjecto* [the predicate inheres in the subject] to which Leibniz so often appeals? Why must the predicate be contained in the *concept* of the subject?

Precedents have been sought for Leibniz's theory. Leibniz himself in several places ascribes to Aristotle the view that the predicate of a true proposition inheres in the subject.[27] Sometimes that theoretically ambiguous claim is all that he ascribes to Aristotle (GI 16,132). But at least once he says that "Aristotle observed" that "the nature of truth universally consists in" this inherence (C 518f./L 267). And at least once he seems to ascribe to Aristotle the thought that the inherence is a conceptual containment. Contrasting Aristotle's way of stating propositions as '*B* is in *A*', instead of the ordinary '*A* is *B*', Leibniz says that "the popular way of stating [propositions] regards rather the individuals, but Aristotle's has more regard to the ideas or universals" (NE 486).

Descartes could be read as asserting the conceptual containment theory of truth when he proposes the following definition: "When we say that something is contained in the nature or concept of a thing, it is the same as if we had said that it is true of that thing or can be affirmed of it" (AT VII,162). But it seems to be the containment, rather than truth, that Descartes is defining here. And Charles Jarrett has pointed out that while Descartes is committed by his argument to the inference from conceptual containment to truth, he does not explicitly endorse the inference from truth to conceptual containment.[28]

The *Port Royal Logic*, which was largely Arnauld's work, seems to hold the view that the predicate of a true proposition is contained in the *concrete* subject, without implying that it is contained in the *concept* of the subject. It states, for example, that "it is true that lions are all animals, that is to say, that each one of the lions includes the idea of animal."[29] This statement presents an easy target for Leibniz. For how does an individual, concrete lion include the *idea* of animal? Presumably lions do not conceive or understand the idea of animal. And we who do have the idea in the sense of conceiving or understanding it are not animals *because* we conceive or understand it; we also understand the idea of lion, but are not therefore lions. If lions are animals because the *idea* of animal is contained in something, the idea or concept of lion seems to be the likeliest

[27]In their translation of NE 486, Peter Remnant and Jonathan Bennett suggest *Prior Analytics* I, 25^b32, as a possible source in Aristotle for this view. But I do not wish here to enter into any discussion of the interpretation of Aristotle.

[28]Jarrett, "Leibniz on Truth and Contingency," pp. 88f.; cited by Sleigh, "Truth and Sufficient Reason in the Philosophy of Leibniz," p. 234.

[29]Arnauld and Nicole, *Port Royal Logic*, II,17.

container. And indeed the concept of lion does in the relevant sense include the concept of animal.

But if lions are animals by virtue of *containing* something other than the *idea* of animal, what would it be? Two candidates come to mind. First, could it be the universal property, animality? Like other early modern philosophers, Leibniz was no Platonist about universals. The only universals he recognized were concepts and "possibilities in resemblances" (NE 323f.).[30] And since he thought that relations between substances exist only in the mind, he would have to say that a lion's resemblance to other animals is contained, strictly speaking, in the concept that a mind forms of lions by comparing them with other animals, rather than in the lion itself.

Second, there are, of course, concrete particular animals; and if identity can be regarded as a (degenerate) case of containment, we could say that each of the lions contains an animal—namely, itself. But Leibniz might well have thought this *too* degenerate a case of containment to satisfy his belief that predication should be explained in terms of containment. These considerations may also be some part of the explanation of Arnauld's ready approval of Leibniz's conceptual containment theory of truth.

These are technicalities, however, and we ought not to lay too much weight on them. If Leibniz had wanted to avoid the conceptual containment theory of truth, he could have said that (at least in some cases) the real connection between the terms of an affirmative proposition on which its truth depends is that its predicate corresponds with, or expresses, the concrete individual things that its subject concept corresponds with or expresses (or some of them, if the proposition is particular). Besides which, we shall in the next chapter show that the containment of predicates in concrete individual substances was not for Leibniz a rejected alternative to the conceptual containment theory of truth; there is a sense in which he would affirm it as a concomitant of the theory. In fact, I believe it was largely because of his views about the structure of concrete individual substances that he found it plausible to include all their predicates in their concepts.

6. *Conceptual Containment and Transworld Identity*

Before taking up these considerations about the structure of individual substances, however, I want to point out an important flaw in the argument against transworld identity from the conceptual containment theory of truth. Leibniz and Arnauld appear to have assumed that the denial of transworld or counterfactual identity follows from Leibniz's theory of truth. This is a natural assumption to make, but it is incorrect. The two doctrines are logically independent: neither entails the other.

Let us note first that the denial of transworld identity does not entail the full conceptual containment theory of truth. If each possible individual exists in only one possible world, I think it does follow that the concept of each possible indi-

[30]Leibniz's views about the ontology of logic are discussed more fully in Chapter 7.

vidual contains (in some relevant sense) its whole history in the one possible world in which it occurs. But it does not follow that the concept of each possible individual contains an answer to the question whether that individual (actually) exists or whether its possible world is actual. For there would be no inconsistency in denying transworld identity (in agreement with Leibniz) while holding a voluntaristic view of creation (in sharp disagreement with Leibniz). In such a voluntaristic doctrine it would be held that God could create an inferior world (indeed, any world at all) without doing anything conceptually inconsistent; and hence that no answer to the question which possible world is actual, or which possible creatures exists, is contained in any concepts. So far as I can see, that is perfectly compatible with the claim that each possible creature exists in exactly one possible world. But it is not consistent with Leibniz's conceptual containment theory of truth, which is explicitly applied to *all* propositions, including existential propositions (as I have argued in Chapter 1, section 2.6).

More important for our present purpose is the fact that the denial of transworld identity does not follow from the conceptual containment theory of truth. I shall try to establish this fact by sketching a view in which both the conceptual containment theory and the transworld identity of individuals are affirmed. This view starts with Leibniz's thesis that individual concepts are complete concepts. *Completeness* can be understood here as a purely logical property of concepts. "An individual or complete term" may be defined as one to which it is "superfluous" to add any other term whatsoever (GI 71–72).[31] A complete concept, in other words, is one to which no predicate not already contained in it can be added (without conceptual inconsistency). Or what comes to the same thing, it is a concept that contains one member of every pair of mutually contradictory predicates. Such a concept obviously will contain all the predicates of anything that satisfies it.

Completeness is a very interesting property of concepts from a logical point of view. The part of logic that concerns us here is the logic of predicates. Leibniz thought of all concepts as generated, principally by conjunction and negation, from predicates that are absolutely simple. In this generation two types of concepts are distinguished from all others: the extreme cases of simplicity and complexity. Both types are associated with distinguished features of Leibniz's metaphysics. At one extreme, he associated the absolutely simple concepts with God, identifying them with the definitive attributes of God (A VI,iii,578f./L 167f.).[32] At the other extreme are the complete concepts, which are reached by conjoining more and more predicates until no new predicate can be added without some conceptual inconsistency; these complete concepts are associated with individuals. Indeed, Leibniz uses the idea of completeness to provide a purely logical characterization of individual substance. He virtually *defines* an individual substance as a thing whose definitive concept is complete (DM 8; cf. GI 71).

What are the predicates with respect to which individual concepts are complete? That is, what are the predicates with respect to which an individual concept, according to Leibniz, contains one member of every mutually contradic-

[31]Cf. Kauppi, *Über die leibnizsche Logik*, pp. 168, 231.

[32]This point is discussed more fully in Chapter 4.

tory pair? Does the individual concept of Leibniz, for instance, contain exactly one of the predicates 'more than one meter tall' and 'not more than one meter tall'? Apparently not, for Leibniz was less than one meter tall in 1647 and more than one meter tall in 1670. For this reason, perhaps the predicates with respect to which Leibnizian individual concepts are complete must in general be indexed to times, as proposed in 1972 by Benson Mates.[33]

Mates points out, however, that we must be careful about the sort of indexing to be ascribed to Leibniz. He argues persuasively that Leibniz saw the fundamental attributes of things as temporally unqualified, and therefore would not wish to see references to times simply incorporated in the properties from which individual concepts are constructed. In a more recent treatment of the subject Mates proposes a solution that, in effect, incorporates time-references in the subject rather than the predicate. Thus, instead of saying that the complete concept of Alexander the Great contains the predicate, 'king in 335 B.C.', Mates will now have Leibniz say that "any 335 B.C.-stage of Alexander the Great . . . contains . . . the attribute King."[34] But replacing enduring substances with their momentary stages as the primary subjects of properties is as contrary to Leibniz's way of speaking as imposing a temporal qualification on the properties. I am inclined therefore to think the best solution would assign a time-index to the copula by which the predicate is attached to the subject. Neither 'A is B_t' nor 'A_t is B', but 'A is$_t$ B', would express the deep structure of a typical Leibnizian predication.

However the details are worked out, inconsistency will be avoided by saying that the individual concept of Leibniz contains in some way the predicates 'more than one meter tall' and 'not more than one meter tall', but only with respect to different times. In a way that is intended to be neutral among the different ways in which the time-index could attach to the structure of a predication, we may say that it is with respect to "time-indexed predications" that a Leibnizian individual concept is complete. And that is the important point for our present purpose. For, as Mates also points out:

> If Leibniz considered [an individual] concept as containing a time-parameter, it is hard to see why he did not also build in a parameter relating to the different possible worlds. Thus the complete individual concept of Adam would not only indicate what attributes he had at what time, but what attributes at what time (or other time-like relation) *in what world*.

In this way, Mates suggests, Leibniz could accept transworld identity

> and yet could retain the principle so important to him that every individual concept involves all that would ever happen to a corresponding individual and reflects all the other individual concepts that are compossible with it.[35]

In other words, the individual concept of an individual that exists in more than one possible world could be complete—complete with respect to *world-indexed* predications.

[33]Mates, "Individuals and Modality in the Philosophy of Leibniz," pp. 108f.
[34]Mates, *Philosophy of Leibniz*, pp. 88f.
[35]Mates, "Individuals and Modality in the Philosophy of Leibniz," p. 109.

Completeness with respect to world-indexed predications is not in itself enough for Leibniz's conceptual containment theory of truth. For if the individual concept of Arnauld contains both of the predications 'Arnauld is (at some time in some possible world) married' and 'Arnauld is (at all times in some possible world) celibate', the conceptual containment theory will require that the individual concept of Arnauld also contain an answer to the question whether the *actual* world is one in which Arnauld is sometimes married or always celibate. And the world-indexed predications do not directly tell us that. The solution to this problem would be easy for Leibniz, however. It is essentially the same as his solution to the problem of accounting for actual existence and actual nonexistence in terms of conceptual containment. On the view suggested by Mates there would be no *internal* conceptual inconsistency in a possible world in which Arnauld marries, but Leibniz could still say that there would be an external conceptual inconsistency in God's actualizing it, because it is an inferior world. The predication of *actual* marriage is therefore not contained in Arnauld's individual concept, which contains rather the predication of *actual* perpetual celibacy, because it contains a history of perpetual celibacy for Arnauld, not as the only possible history for him, not as the only history in which he would strictly be himself, but as the history that is indexed to the world that is in fact the best of all possible worlds.[36] Thus actual celibacy and actual existence would be contained in Arnauld's individual concept in exactly the same way.

Thus world-indexed predication would seem able to account for those counterfactual identities that Leibniz most clearly means to deny. Since an account of transworld or counterfactual identity in terms of world-indexed predications can satisfy the conceptual containment theory of truth in this way, the theory does not require a denial of transworld or counterfactual identity. The rejection of counterfactual identity, like the conceptual containment theory of truth itself, does not seem adequately supported by the more abstractly logical reasons that Leibniz provides.

[36]This solution does require a revision of Arnauld's definition (or partial definition) of 'individual concept' (LA 30f., quoted in section 2 of this chapter). In this solution the predication of perpetual celibacy (i.e., of *actual* perpetual celibacy) is supposed to be contained in Arnauld's individual concept, although there are possible worlds in which Arnauld would not be perpetually celibate and would still be himself. What remains true in this solution is that nothing is contained in Arnauld's individual concept, *independently of the question which world would be chosen by God as the best possible*, except predicates such that Arnauld would not be himself if they were not true of him.

3

The Metaphysics of Counterfactual Nonidentity

The richly deserved prestige of Bertrand Russell's and Louis Couturat's works on Leibniz set a fashion of trying to see his philosophy as principally derived from his logic and philosophy of logic. Much in Leibniz's own work seems to invite this approach. But the deductive order in which Leibniz presents his doctrines, especially in his writings of the 1680s, is misleading. An adequate foundation of the system—or even a fully adequate explanation of his having held it—cannot be found in his philosophy of logic. We have to turn to his less formal views, not only about God and creation, but also about causation and perception, in order to understand the motivation for his philosophy of logic, which was as much shaped by them as they by it.[1] In particular, it is clear that he found in his views about causation and perception reasons for denying transworld or counterfactual identity.

Trying to respond to the common-sense appeal of Antoine Arnauld's affirmation of counterfactual identity, Leibniz wrote:

> It seems to us indeed that this block of marble brought from Genoa would have been exactly the same if it had been left there, because our senses make us judge only superficially, but at bottom because of the connection of things the whole universe with all its[2] parts would be entirely different, and would have been another [universe] from the beginning, if the least thing in it went otherwise than it does. (LA 42)

This passage does not present a fully articulated argument. But I take it Leibniz means that if we combined our ordinary conceptions of individuality and individual identity with a correct understanding of the connections of things, we would not make the "superficial" judgments of counterfactual identity that common sense in fact makes, but would conclude that no actual individual would exist if the universe had differed from the actual world in respect of "the least thing."

If we put the matter in terms of possible worlds, we may say that Leibniz's argument finds a target in Arnauld, if Arnauld's belief that he could have been married and would still have been himself is based on the assumption that

[1]Cf. Mondadori, "Leibnizian 'Circle'."

[2]Here I correct Gerhardt's reading, *nos* (G II,42), to *ses*, in accordance with Le Roy, 109.

(1) In some possible world, *w*, there exists a man whose characteristics and history are exactly like those of Antoine Arnauld in the actual world until some time at which, in *w*, the man marries.

Leibniz seems to be denying (1) and also committing himself to

(2) There are no two possible worlds that are qualitatively identical before a certain time but different thereafter.

and

(3) No individual substances in (qualitatively) different possible worlds are exactly alike, qualitatively, during an initial portion of their histories.

Leibniz still seems to be committed to (3) twenty-four years later in the *Theodicy*, where he says that among those possible worlds that "differ from the actual world only in one particular thing and its consequences" there are worlds

> in which will be found, not exactly the same Sextus that you have seen [in the actual world] (that is impossible; he always carries with him what he will be), but similar Sextuses, who will have everything that you already know of the real Sextus, but *not everything that is already in him* without being noticed, nor consequently everything that will yet happen to him. (T 414, my italics)

It follows from (3) that an Arnauld who married, in another possible world, must have had there, from the very beginning of his existence, different characteristics from those of the actual Arnauld. Leibniz evidently thinks that those differences would be sufficient grounds for denying transworld identity. This is not the place to discuss at length whether transworld identity must indeed be denied if (3) is accepted and (1) is rejected. I think Leibniz's inference at this point is at least plausible. Our strongest intuitions of transworld identity are of individual identity in alternative possible continuations of the history of a world—that is, in alternative possible continuations of exactly the same history, of the world and of the individual, until the time at which the alternatives diverge. A convincing argument against the possibility of such alternative continuations of the same history would greatly weaken the intuitive support for transworld identity, in my opinion.

But does Leibniz have a convincing argument against that possibility? He seems to reject it "because of the connection of things." But the "connection" referred to is presumably a feature of the *actual* world—the laws or order in accordance with which every actual event has always been prefigured in its causes and will always be recorded in its effects, as Leibniz believes. Why couldn't some other *possible* world, by virtue of a difference in its laws, or by a miracle, diverge qualitatively from the actual world only after a certain time? And why wouldn't that permit transworld identity? Our task in this chapter is to investigate these questions, considering how individual substance is related to laws of nature (section 1) and to the possibility of miracle (section 2). Then, in section 3, we shall consider the extent to which the "connection of things" referred to here is to be understood in terms of perception. In the end, in section 4, I will conclude that Leibniz's philosophy supports proposition (3) only under an understanding of 'possible world' that differs more widely from present-day understandings than we saw him to differ in Chapter 1.

1. Substance and Law

To the question of why there couldn't be a possible world that is just like the actual world up to some time but diverges qualitatively thereafter due to some difference in the *laws* of that possible world, I think Leibniz would reply that any difference in the laws of the universe would imply a qualitative difference between the possible worlds from the very beginning—indeed, that it would imply a qualitative difference in every individual substance from the very beginning. This is connected with Leibniz's views about transtemporal identity. Almost immediately after the passage I have quoted about the marble from Genoa, Leibniz goes on to say:

> Since, then, one supposes . . . that it is I who subsist during the time AB and who am then in Paris, and that it is still I who subsist during the time BC and who am then in Germany, there must necessarily be a reason that makes it true to say that we endure—that is to say, that I, who have been in Paris, am now in Germany. For if there is no [reason], one would have as much right to say it is someone else. It is true that my inner experience has convinced me a posteriori of this identicalness, but there must also be a [reason] a priori. (LA 43)

The unsupported assertion that there must be a reason a priori may strike us at first as merely a question-begging assertion that the reason must be conceptual containment, but I think that is an anachronistic reading of the text. Leibniz does not usually use 'a priori' in the epistemological sense to which we have become accustomed since Kant, but in its older, original sense, in which a reason a priori is an argument from the causes rather than the effects of the fact to be proved (as explained in the appendix to this chapter). For Leibniz a proof a priori explains the fact proved; a proof a posteriori does not. That is the crucial difference between them. Here Leibniz is saying that there must be a reason that explains why different states at different times should be said to belong to the same substance. In other words, he is saying that there must be a reason that explains his own identity through time; he does not think that such identity can be an inexplicable primitive.

Its explanation is to be sought in a conceptual containment, according to Leibniz.

> Now it is not possible to find another [reason for this identicalness] except that my attributes of the preceding time and state, as well as my attributes of the following time and state, are predicates of one and the same subject, *insunt eidem subjecto* [they are in the same subject]. Now what is it to say that the predicate is in the subject, except that the concept of the predicate is included in some way in the concept of the subject? And since, from the time I began to be, it could be said truly about me that this or that would happen to me, it

> must be acknowledged that these predicates were laws included in the subject or in my complete concept which makes what is called me, which is the foundation of the connection of all my different states and which God knew perfectly from all eternity. (LA 43)[3]

We may wonder why Leibniz thought that the inclusion of earlier and later states in a single *concept* is peculiarly apt to explain a transtemporal identity. Surely he did not suppose that a concept arbitrarily framed to include parts of his own youth and the old age of Arnauld could ground the transtemporal identity of an individual as well as his own identity through time is grounded by his individual concept. What is it, then, about individual concepts that fits them to explain transtemporal identity?

The answer to this question is to be found in the claim that "these predicates were *laws* included in the subject or in my complete concept . . . which is the foundation of the connection of all my different states." I think the laws here are conceived as *causal* laws, and as founding a connection of successive states, not only in thought but also in reality. The greatest threat to our understanding of this part of Leibniz's philosophy is a prejudice that may have its historical roots in Locke and Hume—an assumption that conceptual connections cannot also be causal connections, that they impose necessity only on our thought, and cannot explain why anything occurs in reality. Leibniz certainly did not make this assumption, as is clear from his conceptual containment theory of truth and his use of it to explain the Principle of Sufficient Reason. Leibniz thought that conceptual connections are precisely what do ultimately explain the existence of all real things and the occurrence of all real events.

The coalescence of conceptual and causal connections is most marked in the notion of *substantial form* that plays a central role in Leibniz's mature philosophy. For Leibniz as for Aristotle, a substance's form is closely related to the definition or concept of the substance; we may think of the form, perhaps, as a concrete expression of the individual concept of the substance. At the same time, forms are real causes of actual effects; Leibniz identifies the substantial form with the primitive active force of the substance.[4] Leibniz brings these ideas together in the following passage from an important text that may have been written during the period of the Leibniz-Arnauld correspondence.

> For the nature of an individual substance is such that it has a complete concept, in which all the predicates of the same subject are involved. . . . But since all things have transactions [*commercium*] with other things, either directly or indirectly, it follows that the nature of every substance is such that by its force of acting and being acted on, that is by the series of its immanent operations, it expresses the whole universe. . . . And this principle of actions, or primitive force of acting, from which a series of various states follows, is the form of the substance. (G VII,316f./MP 84f.)

[3]This and the previous long quotation are from a preliminary draft of Leibniz's letter of 14 July 1686 to Arnauld. In the letter itself the argument is less fully developed on the points that most concern us here, but it is supplemented with a link to Leibniz's critique of Cartesian views about extended substance (LA 53f.; cf. Sleigh, *Leibniz and Arnauld*, p. 126f.).

[4]Leibniz's conception of substantial form is expounded much more fully in Chapter 11, section 1.

There is in each individual substance, Leibniz believes, a primitive force that he calls a substantial form, or the form of the substance. And this form is so closely connected with the individual concept of the substance that Leibniz thinks it self-evidently valid to infer from the completeness of the concept to the sufficiency of the form or force for the generation of a complete expression of the universe. There are two points calling for discussion here: the connection between form and concept and the connection of identity with form as force.

1. The connection between form and concept is signaled in § 10 of the *Discourse on Metaphysics*, where Leibniz argues that there is something right about the Aristotelian idea of substantial forms. For immediately after having introduced the doctrine of the completeness of the concept of each individual substance (DM 8), and drawn from it the consequence that "each individual substance expresses the whole universe in its own way" (DM 9), Leibniz states that ancient and medieval philosophers "had some knowledge of what we have just said, and that is what led them to introduce and maintain the substantial forms that are so much criticized today" (DM 10).[5] C. D. Broad argued that such consequences as the causal independence and expressive completeness of each substance could not follow from the conceptual containment theory of truth or the complete concept theory of substance without the addition of an independent premise to the effect that there is in the concrete actual substance what Broad called an "ontological correlate" of the concept of the substance.[6] Why didn't Leibniz see any need to articulate a separate premise of that sort? The answer probably lies in the close connection of form and concept in his mind. The substantial form is the "ontological correlate," as Broad put it, of the concept of the substance: "It will be insisted that [Julius Caesar's] nature or form corresponds to" his individual (and complete) concept. Leibniz does not reject this assumption, though he combats an objection that is based on it (DM 13). He took for granted that the definitive concept (God's concept) of a substance would represent its internal causal structure, its "nature or form," as his Aristotelian ideal of "real" and "causal" definition (DM 24; G IV,424f./L 293) would lead one to expect. For this reason, the containment of Adam's sin in Adam's individual concept is not exactly an *alternative* to the containment of the sin in Adam himself. For if Adam's individual concept represents Adam's internal causal structure, whatever follows from the one follows from the other, also.

2. There are several places in his later writings where Leibniz seems to explain the trans-temporal identity of a substance in terms of "the perpetual law which makes the sequence of perceptions that are allotted to it" and in which "its individuality consists" [T 291 (1710)]. In 1698 he wrote of "that law of the order that makes the individuality of each particular substance" (G IV,518/L 493).[7] "That there is a certain persisting law which involves the future states of that which we conceive as the same: that is what I say constitutes the same substance"

[5]The relevance of DM 10 to the conceptual containment theory has been overlooked by many interpreters. It is rightly emphasized in Garber, "Leibniz and the Foundations of Physics," pp. 60–62.

[6]Broad, *Leibniz: An Introduction* p. 24f.

[7]I owe this reference to Sleigh, *Leibniz and Arnauld*, p. 129.

[G II,264/L 535 (1704)].[8] Successive momentary states belong to the same individual substance, according to Leibniz, if and only if they are produced by the same persisting individual *law*.

Now if we think of causal laws as abstract objects, we might think that the same law could be responsible for the sequence of states of several different individual substances. But Leibniz evidently has something else in mind. As Louis Loeb has pointed out, Leibniz's criterion of trans-temporal identity depends on his denial of causal interaction between created substances.[9] The succession of states of each individual substance, or *monad*, forms an isolated causal series, so that two states occurring at different times belong to the same individual substance if and only if the earlier is a cause of the later: "Perception is the operation proper to the soul, and the nexus of perceptions, according to which subsequent ones are derived from the preceding ones, makes the unity of the perceiver" [G II,372/L 599 (1709)].

The "law" or "nexus" that constitutes the unity through time of an individual substance is for Leibniz not merely a formula that describes the series of states. It is rather a substantial form, concretely realized in the substance at every moment of its existence. As we have seen, Leibniz identified this substantial form with a "primitive force of acting." The concept of force has a central metaphysical role in Leibniz's thought. "The very substance of things consists in the force of acting and being acted on," and therefore a denial of "lasting force" to created things, reserving it to God alone, comes to the same thing as Spinoza's "doctrine of most evil repute," that "God is the very nature or substance of all things" (G IV,508f./L 502; cf. RML 421, LA 133, G IV,594). The force that constitutes the very substance of things is "primitive force," and Leibniz links it with law. Primitive forces, Leibniz wrote to Burcher De Volder in 1704 or 1705, are "internal tendencies of simple substances, by which according to a certain law of their nature they pass from perception to perception" (G II,275/AG 181). The primitive forces can even be *identified* with laws: "the primitive force is as it were the law of the series" of successive states of an enduring thing (G II,262/L 533). This "law of the series" is surely also the "persisting law" that constitutes the transtemporal identity of an individual substance (G II,264/L 535), and also the "laws included in the . . . complete concept" (LA 43). This licenses inferences from the contents of the concept of a substance to concrete forces or tendencies in the substance itself.

We began this section of our investigation with the question, Why couldn't there be a possible world that is just like the actual world up to some time but diverges qualitatively thereafter, due to some difference in the laws of that possible world? I think we are now in a position to see that Leibniz rejects an

[8]These words are part of a passage that is bracketed in Leibniz's manuscript (as I have verified on a photocopy of the manuscript), and which was presumably not sent to De Volder, probably because it dealt with a question that Leibniz preferred, on reflection, not to raise with his correspondent at this point. But the statement is not crossed out, and there are enough similar texts to remove any doubt that Leibniz did indeed hold the view expressed here. For other passages, and a good discussion, see Loeb, *From Descartes to Hume*, pp. 317-19.

[9]Loeb, *From Descartes to Hume*, pp. 317–19.

assumption that gives rise to that question. He rejects the assumption that causal laws and relations are imposed from the outside on individuals that are causally neutral in their individual natures (G IV,507,584/L 500). Causal powers or forces are primitive features of reality as Leibniz conceives of it; they are not to be analyzed in terms of causally neutral states plus extrinsic laws. Leibniz thinks that the laws are *internal* to individual substances and that they are permanent and unchanging throughout the substance's history, constituting the *form* of the substance. In a possible world that had different laws from the actual world, therefore, every individual substance affected by the difference (that is, all individual substances) must always have been constituted by a "primitive force" that is qualitatively different from that which constitutes the corresponding individual in the actual world. In that respect, the individuals of that other world differ qualitatively from their actual counterparts, from the beginning of their existence. They have different substantial forms. Leibniz could plausibly claim that so basic a difference is enough to rule out transworld identity and make them distinct possible individuals.

2. *Substance and Miracle*

Section 1 dealt with one way in which it might be supposed that two possible worlds could be qualitatively identical before a certain time but then diverge. I have argued that Leibniz may have rejected difference in the laws of the two worlds as a basis for such divergence on the ground that, in his opinion, a difference in the laws implies a qualitative difference in the individual substances of the two worlds from the very beginning of their existence—a qualitative difference in the substantial forms or primitive forces of the substances. But we must also consider why Leibniz should not have thought that two possible worlds with *the same laws* could differ qualitatively only after a certain time. Shouldn't an omnipotent God be able to suspend the operation of any law or created force and work a miracle for which there was no preparation in the previous qualitative history of the world? If so, won't there be a possible world in which such a miracle happens, and another, just like it before the miracle, in which the miracle does not happen?

Admitting that God could, by a miracle, prevent Antoine Arnauld's substantial form or primitive force from having its natural effect of lifelong celibacy would undermine the case I have been developing for denying Arnauld's counterfactual identity with a possibly married man. It is easy enough to see why Leibniz would think that a man whose substantial form was qualitatively different from the beginning of his existence would not be identical with Arnauld, but why would a *miracle* preclude counterfactual identity? Suppose there is a possible world, *w*, whose history is exactly like that of the actual world up to 1632. In *w*, of course, there is a man *a*, born in 1612, who is qualitatively identical with the actual Antoine Arnauld for the first twenty years of his life. In particular, the primitive force that *a* has in *w* is qualitatively identical with the primitive force that Arnauld has in the actual world, and would have lifelong celibacy as its natural effect. But we are to suppose that in *w*, *a* marries in 1632 as a result of a miracle that prevents *a*'s primitive force from having its natural effect. The occurrence of one such miracle does not, in itself, seem to me a plausible reason for denying that *a* could be, in *w*, numerically the same person as the actual Antoine Arnauld. Leibniz could support his rejection of transworld identity more easily if he denied that there is any such possible world as *w*. But would his commitment to divine omnipotence permit him to deny it?

The tradition of Christian Aristotelianism, to which broadly speaking Leibniz's views on causality belong, had limited, more than many moderns would, the dependence of causality on God's will. Many medieval philosophers held, for example, that God could choose to create or not create fire, but, having determined to create fire, God could not withhold the (causal) power of heating from the fire that would exist, because this power is essential to fire. These predecessors of Leibniz would generally have said, however, that once God has created a substance with certain causal powers, God could miraculously suspend or obstruct those powers, or prevent them from operating (because the actual operation of the powers is not essential to the creature), and could equally refrain from doing any such miracle. Alternatively, God could miraculously annihilate the creature.

God's miraculous powers are so important to Christian orthodoxy that it would have been difficult for Leibniz to deny them. We are not surprised to find him saying that "the laws of nature are subject to the dispensation of the Legislator" and that "God can dispense creatures from the laws that he has prescribed for them, and produce in them what their nature does not hold, in doing a *Miracle*" (T pd3). We shall have to see in what sense he can have accepted this.

This question will lead us into a fairly lengthy discussion. We will begin in section 2.1 with a feature of Leibniz's system that seems to favor interpreting miracles as somehow caused by the primitive forces inherent in creatures. We will go on in sections 2.2–2.3 to consider some of Leibniz's explicit discussions of the miraculous. In these texts, however, Leibniz mainly discusses what miracles *are*, not what they *could be*. Such texts are obviously relevant to our investigation. On any interesting interpretation, Leibniz's argument about the Genoese block of marble requires certain limits on the types of miracles that *actually* occur. The question what limits, if any, Leibniz would impose on the types of miracles that God *could* perform, which will be taken up in section 2.4, is obviously important, too, and more difficult to answer. Nonetheless, I believe we will be able eventually, in section 4, to arrive at a satisfactory interpretation.

2.1 *The Kingdom of Nature and the Kingdom of Grace*

However they happen, such miracles as actually occur in the Leibnizian universe are there to serve the aims of what Leibniz called "the kingdom of grace," in which God is related to rational creatures, not only as their architect and maker, but also, more personally, as a just and benevolent monarch (DM 36, T 247, Mon 87–90). The problem about the nature of miracles is for Leibniz a part of a more general problem about the relation of the kingdom of grace to the kingdom of nature. And he developed a solution to that more general problem, in terms of *pre-established harmony*.

His famous theory of preestablished harmony operates on several levels. At the deepest level there is a harmony between the perceptions of different monads. There is also a harmony between body and soul, which can also be seen as a harmony between diverse causal systems—between the kingdom of "efficient causes," a system of mechanical causation operating in the phenomenal, corporeal world, and the kingdom of "final causes," a system of teleological causation operating within the monads. At the highest level there is a harmony between "the Physical kingdom of Nature," comprehending the "two Natural Kingdoms" of efficient and final causes, "and the Moral kingdom of Grace, that is to say between God considered as Architect of the Machine of the universe, and God considered as Monarch of the divine city of Minds" (Mon 87).

This highest level of harmony addresses a crucial problem for Leibniz's theodicy. In the *Discourse on Metaphysics* the most general standard of perfection governing God's choice among possible worlds appears to be metaphysical: a "balance" between "simplicity of the ways of God"—that is, of laws—and "variety, richness, or abundance" in the creatures produced (DM 5). Such metaphysical perfection is of limited relevance, however, to the religious problem of evil, which is centrally concerned with God's *moral* goodness, God's goodness *to* created *persons*. For what is to guarantee that a machine of nature, producing the richest variety of beings in accordance with the simplest laws, will not just grind created persons to mincemeat, regardless of any virtue they may possess?[10]

This problem arises quite clearly in Nicolas Malebranche's *Treatise on Nature and Grace* and related works, which Leibniz certainly had in mind when writing the *Discourse*. The phrase, "the simplicity of the ways of God," which Leibniz uses in the *Discourse*, is used repeatedly by Malebranche to signify what he regards as a most important criterion of the perfection of God's action in creating and governing the world. It would be unworthy of God's wisdom, Malebranche holds, to compromise the simplicity of God's ways by making a lot of miraculous exceptions to the laws of nature to prevent particular evils. Malebranche affirmed an "order of grace" as well as an "order of nature," but insisted that God operates by universal laws, avoiding frequent miraculous exceptions to them, in *both* orders. This regard for universal laws explains God's permission of many evils. "God ought not to disturb the order and simplicity of his ways to prevent a birth defect [*un monstre*], a sterility, an injustice" (OM VI,40). More drastically still, "if God has permitted sin, and if there are so many people damned, it is not that God does not love his works [*son ouvrage*], but that, as he should, he loves his wisdom infinitely more than his works."[11] The statement that God loves his wisdom more than his works, or even explicitly "that he loves his wisdom more than his Works, more than human beings, and that he ought not to disturb the order and simplicity of his ways in order to

[10]It is perhaps worth noting here that the problem of assuring a harmony between natural and moral orders is precisely what leads to the postulation of a deity in Kant's moral theology.

[11]OM VIII,684. This text was published in 1686, the year the *Discourse* was written. All the other texts of Malebranche I cite in this paragraph were published by 1685.

provide for our needs" (OM VI,35f.), is almost a refrain in Malebranche's writings on this subject.[12]

Leibniz evidently wished to be more reassuring on this subject. Already in the *Discourse* he insisted that "it is not to be doubted that the happiness of minds is God's principal end, and that he puts it into effect as much as the general harmony permits"—and indeed that God has so ordered things that minds endure as minds forever, and that they will be perfectly happy provided only that they love God with a sincere and serious good will (DM 5,36). But in the *Discourse* Leibniz offers no very clear explanation of how this "moral" purpose of God's fits together with the more general metaphysical criterion of perfection, except that he observes that minds are capable of more perfection than other beings, and interfere less with other beings, and thus presumably contribute more to the perfection of the universe (DM 36,5)—and more still, in proportion as they are happy, since Leibniz understands pleasure and happiness as perception of perfection (DM 15).

In both the *Theodicy* and the *Monadology*, however, Leibniz holds that there is a preestablished harmony between the moral order and the metaphysical perfection of the natural order. What is important about this for our present purpose is that it implies that the best possible world is one in which the aims of the kingdom of grace are realized by the workings of the kingdom of nature, and thus by natural objects operating according to their own inherent laws, without divine interference. Thus, having introduced the harmony between the kingdoms of nature and of grace in the *Monadology*, Leibniz continues:

> This Harmony makes things lead to grace by the very ways of nature, and [brings it about] that this globe, for example, must be destroyed and repaired by natural ways at the moments when the government of minds demands it, for the punishment of some and the reward of others. (Mon 88)

And in the *Theodicy* Leibniz writes that

> there is reason to judge, following the parallelism of the two kingdoms, that of final causes and that of efficient causes, that God has established in the universe a connection between the penalty or reward and the bad or good action, in such a way that the former is always attracted by the second, and that virtue and vice get their reward and punishment in consequence of the natural course of things, which contains yet another species of pre-established harmony than that which appears in the commerce of the soul and the body. (T 74)

Similarly, Leibniz objects to Pierre Bayle's apparent belief that "God could better have attained his end in the kingdom of Grace if he were not attached to these laws [of the kingdom of nature], if he had dispensed himself more often from following them, or even if he had made others" (T 340). Bayle had written sarcastically of a God who "would prefer to let the whole human race perish rather than to suffer some atoms to go faster or slower than the general laws

[12]In addition to the texts already cited, see Malebranche's *Treatise of Nature and Grace*, I,43 (first published in 1680), the Additions to I,23,39,47,56 (1684), and §§ 23 and 26 of the third Éclaircissement (1683) (OM V,49f.,37,47f.,52f.,58–60,184–196); also Malebranche's responses to Arnauld's criticisms, OM VII,533,555f. (1685). (The Additions and third Éclaircissement are not included in Riley's translation of the *Treatise*.)

demand"; he "would not have made this opposition if he had been informed of the system of general harmony that I conceive," Leibniz says, "which implies . . . that matter is disposed in such a way that the laws of motion serve the best government of minds, and that consequently it will turn out that he has obtained the most good that is possible, provided that metaphysical, physical, and moral goods are counted together" (T 247). The concluding proviso reminds us, of course, that Leibniz does allow that the best possible world may be one in which the happiness of rational creatures is compromised to *some* degree for the sake of more physical or metaphysical goods (cf. T 118), though he does not stress this point as harshly as Malebranche did.

These statements do not absolutely exclude miracles in which God would bring something about that did not follow from the substantial forms and previous states of creatures, but they are not favorable to belief in such miracles. For the purpose of miracles is to advance the aims of the kingdom of grace, but what Leibniz says in the *Theodicy* and the *Monadology* about the general relationship between the kingdom of grace and the kingdom of nature indicates that the aims of the kingdom of grace are achieved by a pre-established harmony between the two kingdoms rather than by divine intervention that bypasses the active principles of the kingdom of nature. We must still consider, however, what Leibniz actually asserts about miracles.

2.2 *"Essence" and "Nature"*

The possibility and nature of miracles was a sensitive issue for Leibniz. It engages his attention in several sections of the *Discourse on Metaphysics*, where he explicitly asks "how it is possible for God sometimes to influence human beings or other substances by an extraordinary or miraculous concurrence, since it seems that nothing extraordinary or supernatural can happen to them, given that all their events are only consequences of their nature" (DM 16). His reply depends on a distinction between two types of law. Miracles "are always in conformity with the universal law of the general order" (DM 16), but not with certain "subordinate maxims or laws of nature" (DM 17; cf. DM 6–7). The same view, which we must now examine more closely, is stated briefly when Leibniz introduces the subject of miracles in his correspondence with Arnauld (LA 51).

The universal law of the general order is a law that governs the mutual relations of absolutely all substances and events in the universe. By definition, it is without exception; any law to which there is an exception is not universal in the relevant sense. Leibniz claimed that we can see that every possible world has an order of this sort. He appealed to geometrical examples. No matter what sort of line is drawn, he says,

> it is possible to find a concept or rule, or equation common to all the points of that line, in virtue of which [its] changes [of direction] must occur. . . . Thus it can be said that in whatever way God had created the world, it would always have been regular and in a certain general order. But God has chosen the one that is the most perfect, that is to say, the one that is at the same time the simplest in hypotheses and the richest in phenomena. (DM 6; cf. G VII,312/ MP 78f.)

Leibniz regarded it as a rather trivially necessary truth, therefore, that the universe is ordered by a universal law to which there are no exceptions—not even miraculous exceptions.

The general order of the actual world, however, cannot be comprehended by any created mind (DM 16). (How that is consistent with the preeminent simplicity of the actual general order, Leibniz does not explain, so far as I am aware.) On the other hand, "everything that is called natural depends on the less general maxims that creatures can comprehend" (DM 16; cf. NE 65, G III,353). These less general maxims include the "laws of nature" that human science can in principle discover. And there can be exceptions to them. Indeed, Leibniz holds that miracles are such exceptions. His stating the contrast in terms of what is comprehensible only to God, and not to *any* created mind, certainly suggests that Leibniz thinks of the general order as infinitely complex and of the natural laws as only finitely complex. The natural laws are only finitely *understandable*, however, not finitely *demonstrable*, for they can have exceptions, and hence are neither necessary nor demonstrable.

For our present purpose, the most important question here is how these two types of law are related to the substantial form that constitutes a created substance. If the universal law of the general order is incorporated in the substantial form of a particular substance to which a miracle is not going to happen, then that substance would have to have had a qualitatively different substantial form or primitive force if a miracle were going to happen to it, and two possible worlds could no more differ with respect to miracles than with respect to laws without differing qualitatively from the beginning. But if it is only the laws of nature that are incorporated in the substantial forms of individual substances, then two possible histories of a substance could be qualitatively the same up to a certain time, proceeding from the same substantial form or primitive force, and could then diverge by a miracle, which would require God to interfere with the operation of the primitive force in one of the histories.

So far as I know, Leibniz does not directly answer this question about substantial forms. But he does propose in the *Discourse on Metaphysics* a distinction between the "essence" and the "nature" of an individual substance, corresponding to the distinction between the two types of law.

> That could be called our essence[13] which includes all that we express, and as it expresses our union with God himself, it has no limits and nothing goes beyond it. But that which is limited in us can be called our nature or our power [*puissance*], and in this regard that which goes beyond the natures of all created substances is supernatural. (DM 16)[14]

[13]On the first draft, but not on the more finished surviving copies, Leibniz added here the words "or idea."

[14]Leibniz was not always loyal to this terminological distinction. In a draft for a letter of 8 December 1686 to Arnauld, the "concept, idea, essence," and "nature" of an individual substance are treated as equivalent and as containing "everything that is to happen to it" (LA 68f.)—a "low watermark" for the distinction, as remarked in Sleigh, *Leibniz and Arnauld*, p. 79. At NE 433 Leibniz suggests a similar (but perhaps not exactly the same) distinction between the "essential" and the "natural," but he also seems somewhat willing to use 'essential' more broadly, to cover the territory of the merely natural as well as that of the strictly exceptionless.

Two interpretations of this passage are possible. In the first, it is the "nature or power" that here corresponds to the substantial form. It is a causal force in the concrete substance, but the "essence" is only an idea in the mind of God. It is only the subordinate laws of nature that are incorporated in concrete substances. In the second interpretation, it is the "essence" that here corresponds to the substantial form. It is not only an idea in the mind of God, but also a causal force in the concrete substance, which thus incorporates the universal law of the general order. I believe the second interpretation is to be preferred, at least as an understanding of the predominant tendency of Leibniz's thought, but there is a case to be made for the first interpretation, and we will begin with it.

2.2.1 Substantial Form as "Nature"

Grounds for the first interpretation might be sought in Leibniz's insistence that later states of free creatures (Caesar's crossing the Rubicon, for example) are only contingently connected with their earlier states (DM 13; cf. Gr 384). But this hardly commits Leibniz to denying that the earlier states contain the law of the general order from which the later states follow, since he certainly thought that the complete concept of a free creature in some sense contains the laws from which its actions follow, but still maintained that the connection between the concept and the actions is contingent (DM 13). If this is understood in terms of the infinite analysis conception of contingency, there is no reason why free actions could not flow contingently from an infinitely complex law of the general order incorporated in the substantial form of the agent. Leibniz certainly thought that the concrete causal structures of created substances must be infinitely complex in order to mirror the complexity of the whole universe.

A detail in this discussion that might support the first interpretation is that Leibniz suggests it could be said in defense of Caesar's freedom that the actions contained in his complete concept "belong to him only because God knows everything." And to the counterobservation that Caesar's "nature or form corresponds to" his complete concept, Leibniz says, "I could respond by the example of future contingents, for they have no reality except in the understanding and will of God" (DM 13). This certainly would fit with the view that the "essence" that contains all of Caesar's acts is only an idea in the mind of God, and that what is concretely expressed in Caesar's substantial form is something less comprehensive. But I doubt that a heavy weight of interpretation should be laid on these arguments, for Leibniz lays them aside as not "satisfy[ing] the difficulties" (DM 13).

The strongest evidence I have found for the first interpretation is in a letter of April 1687 to Arnauld, a letter which surely must have left Arnauld thinking that Leibniz believed in miracles and helps of grace ("extraordinary concurrences of God") that are not produced by anything in creatures. In the end, I am inclined to think that Leibniz meant to be (misleadingly) noncommittal, asserting nothing about extraordinary concurrence, when he wrote in this letter, "Setting aside extraordinary concurrence, [God's] ordinary concurrence consists only in conserving the substance itself in conformity with its previous state and the changes that [that state] holds" (LA 91f.). A reader might be pardoned, however, for taking Leibniz to mean that in metaphysical rigor, God does something more than conserve a substance when it is an object of God's extraordinary concurrence. A similar implication might easily be drawn when Leibniz, in the same letter, asserting that "the actions of minds change nothing at all in the nature of bodies, nor bodies in that of minds," adds that "God changes nothing there [i.e., in their nature] on their occasion, except when he works a miracle" (LA 93). The implication that miracles involve something more than conservation of created substances seems even more strongly supported by a passage written for the letter that Leibniz did not send Arnauld, but struck out even on his own copy. There he invoked the Scholastic distinction between immanent (intrasubstantial) and transeunt (intersubstantial) causation, and "claimed that, in metaphysical rigor, transeunt causation is restricted to God's operations and comes in three forms: creation, conservative causation, and the production of miracles."[15]

What is especially striking, however, about the treatment of miracle in the letter is that Leibniz offers an explicit criterion of the miraculous:

> I admit that the authors of occasional causes will be able to give another definition of the term, but it seems that according to usage a miracle differs internally and by the substance of the act from an ordinary action, and not by an external accident of frequent repetition; and that strictly speaking God works a miracle when he does a thing that surpasses the forces that he has given to creatures and conserves in them. (LA 93)

In reading this definition, we should bear in mind that Leibniz and Arnauld both attacked occasionalism on the subject of miracles, but from quite different directions. Leibniz repeatedly accused the occasionalists of implying that all events in nature are miraculous (e.g., LA 57f.). Occasionalists would not admit this; Malebranche held that most events in nature are not miraculous because God produces them not by particular but by general volitions (for instance, not by willing that I see red on this occasion, but by willing that all human minds shall see red when their bodies are affected in a certain way, in which mine happens now to be affected). Leibniz here suggests that this leaves the occasionalists with too superficial a conception of miracle. His comments accurately reflect a fundamental difference between him and Malebranche, which is that Leibniz recognizes created substances as true causes, whereas Malebranche accepts only God as a true cause. Leibniz proposes a criterion of the miraculous that does leave Malebranche with too many miracles.

It threatens to leave Leibniz himself with too few miracles, however. This is a serious matter in his correspondence with Arnauld, who already feared that Malebranche would end up not with too many miracles, but with none or with miracles inadequately distinguished from God's ordinary activity (RML 219–22). Leibniz will end up with no miracles, by his own criterion, unless he thinks that God sometimes does to creatures things that "surpass the forces that he has given to" them. This letter clearly implies that Leibniz did think that, and it was at best disingenuous if he really thought that there is in each created substance a causal structure that produces *all* its states, miraculous as well as ordinary.

[15] I quote from the description of this passage in Sleigh, *Leibniz and Arnauld*, p. 134.

2.2.2 *Substantial Form as "Essence"*

I think there is a good case for supposing that Leibniz was disingenuous in just this way and that by 'forces', as ascribed to creatures in this letter, and 'nature or power' in DM 16, he means only a part of the primitive force or total causal structure inherent in a created substance. This is strongly suggested in DM 16:

> If we include in our nature everything that it expresses, nothing is supernatural to it, for it extends to everything, since an effect always expresses its cause and God is the true cause of substances. But as that which our nature expresses more perfectly belongs to it in a special way, since it is in that that its power consists, and since [its power] is limited, as I have just explained, there are plenty of things that surpass the forces of our nature, and even those of all limited natures. Consequently, in order to speak more clearly, I say that miracles and extraordinary concurrences of God have this peculiarity, that they cannot be foreseen by the reasoning of any created mind, however enlightened it might be, because the distinct comprehension of the general order surpasses them all.

There are three points to be noted in this passage.

1. The "effect" of which Leibniz says here that it expresses God as its cause, and therefore expresses everything, is surely not just an idea in God's mind, but a concrete structure in the substances of which "God is the true cause." This agrees with the fact that Leibniz is prepared to say, not merely of an individual *concept*, but of "each individual substance," that in expressing the whole universe "it expresses also the aforesaid miracles" (LA 40f.). The "nature" construed broadly as including everything expressed by the substance is clearly the same as "our essence, which includes all that we express" (DM 16), and it can be identified with what Leibniz calls "primitive force" or "substantial form," if this talk about created substances expressing even miracles is to be believed.

2. The "power" of our nature consists only in "that which our nature expresses more perfectly." What Leibniz has "just explained" (in DM 15) about the limited power of finite substances is that "practical" talk about such substances "acting" on each other, and thus exercising "power," can be understood in terms of differences in how well each substance "expresses" what is going on. The forms in which this recurrent Leibnizian theme[16] is developed in DM 15, however, seem to me to shed less light on DM 16 than does Leibniz's later statement that a substance is "*active* insofar as what is distinctly known in it serves to give a reason for what happens in another, and *passive* insofar as the reason for what happens in it is found in what is distinctly known in another" (Mon 52). Now if something happens in a created substance miraculously, in a way that does not agree with the laws of nature that finite minds can understand, the reason for that event will presumably be vastly less distinctly "known in" that substance (that is, it can much less easily be read off the previous states of the substance) than if it were produced in accordance with those laws of nature.

[16]The idea is not original with Leibniz, so far as I can judge. Something very close to it is found in Spinoza (*Ethics*, III, def. 2). Leibniz did not acknowledge intellectual debts to Spinoza, though he was generally eager to acknowledge such debts to predecessors (even unfashionable ones, such as the Scholastics) who were not regarded as heretics.

This will be a reason for saying that in the miraculous event the substance is neither active nor exercising any power, and that the event exceeds anything it has the "power" to produce—even though, in metaphysical rigor, the miraculous states of the substance are produced by the substance itself in accordance with the universal law of the general order that is included in the "essence" to which God has given concrete expression in the "form" of that substance.

This interpretation of DM 16 is supported by the fact that in the summary of DM 16 that Leibniz sent to Arnauld in February 1686, "our nature," whose forces are surpassed by "the extraordinary concurrence of God," is equated with "our distinct expression, which is finite and follows certain subordinate maxims" (LA 13). Similarly, when Leibniz implies to Arnauld that God sometimes "does a thing that surpasses the forces that he has given to creatures," he may have meant only that God sometimes does a thing that is not distinctly expressed (in advance) by creatures because it does not agree with the laws of nature that finite minds can grasp—though he can hardly have expected Arnauld to understand him in this sense. Thus, when Leibniz's letter carries a strong suggestion that in miracles God changes something in the "nature" of created substances, he may be thinking only of changes in (or exceptions to) the subordinate laws that are intelligible to us.

3. The inability of created minds to foresee miracles and extraordinary concurrences of God, or to understand the order on which they depend, plays a central role in this interpretation. It is a point that is often emphasized in Leibniz's discussions of miracle.[17] The reason we cannot foresee miracles is that the order on which they depend is too complex for us to grasp. Accordingly, Leibniz sometimes indicates that miracles are distinguished from nonmiraculous events by their *not* having simple explanations. In the copy he kept of his April 1687 letter to Arnauld, immediately after the definition of miracle that I have quoted, Leibniz says that if God decreed that any body swung in a circle in a sling should *always* continue in circular motion when released from the sling, "without being pushed or restrained" by any other body, this would be a miracle even though it happened regularly, "since this motion cannot be explained by something simpler" (LA 93).

The simplicity of explanations plays a particularly decisive part in the discussion of miracles in a draft Leibniz wrote in 1702 for a reply to François Lamy, an occasionalist critic of the system of pre-established harmony. Here Leibniz repeats his objection that if God is the sole cause of natural events and the events produced are natural whenever God acts according to general laws, then natural events will differ from miracles only by an external accident of frequent repetition.

> The natural and the miraculous would not differ in themselves, but only by the external denomination (*denominatione extrinsica*) taken from the antecedents and consequences. For what is preceded and followed by [events] like it would be natural, and what is not such would be a miracle.

But in going on to explain that "there is an essential difference between the natural and the miraculous," what Leibniz emphasizes is that "not every sort of rule or

[17]See RML 203 (1685), C 508 (1702–4), G III,353 (1704).

law is fit to make a law of nature." For example, if God established a rule that a planet should always move in an elliptical orbit, without any mechanical action of other bodies to keep its path elliptical,

> God would have established a perpetual miracle, and . . . it could not be said that the Planet would go that way in virtue of its nature or following natural laws, since it is not possible . . . to give a reason for such a phenomenon, which would need [to be given], however, because that [elliptical] motion is composite, hence the reason must come from simpler motions.

Whereas, if the composite motion is caused by simpler motions of other bodies, "then it will be in these simpler reasons that the nature of the thing will consist" (G IV,587f.).[18] In short, the essential, internal distinction of the miraculous from the natural seems here to depend on the simplicity of the explanations, or system of laws, in accordance with which natural events are produced. And that is certainly consistent with Leibniz's thinking that the universal law of the general order, to which even miracles conform, and which is not so simple, is concretely expressed in the substantial form of every created substance.

A similar interpretation can be given to another document which otherwise would seem to support an opposite interpretation of DM 16. Material rather similar to Leibniz's letter of April 1687 to Arnauld can be found in correspondence between Leibniz and his patroness, the Duchess (later Electress) Sophia, in 1691. She had written to him about a young prophetess in Lüneburg who claimed to receive dictation from Christ and had apparently been able to respond pertinently in German to questions presented to her in English in a sealed paper which she did not open (A I,vii,29–31). Leibniz responded that he was "thoroughly persuaded that there is nothing but [what is] natural in all that, and that there must be some embellishment in the affair of the sealed note in English." Such a person shows the surprising resources of the human mind, and should not be persecuted or reformed, but preserved as a museum piece [*piece de cabinet*], though he also thought "one would do well not to put the young lady prophetess to the test of sealed notes any more" (A I,vii,33,40). Leibniz went on to say, however, that "*the great Prophets*, that is to say, those who can teach us the details of the future, must have supernatural graces. And it is impossible that a limited mind, however penetrating, could succeed at that" because of the "infinity of causes" on which each future event depends (A I,vii,35).

Sophia did not take up these comments about the supernatural, but ended a subsequent letter about the case with the blunt and sweepingly naturalistic remark, "whatever it may be, it is always a very strange effect of nature, for I comprehend nothing that surpasses nature. I believe that everything that happens is natural, even when we do not know the cause of it" (A I,vii,44). In his next letter Leibniz commented on this statement as a "point of importance":

> That is very solid, provided it is explained correctly. It is very true, then, that everything that is done is always natural to the one that does it, or to the one that aids in doing it. Thus what a human being does with the aid of God, if it is not entirely natural to the human being, will at least be natural to God,

[18] For a very similar discussion of the miraculous, directed against occasionalism, see G IV,520f./ L 494f.

> inasmuch as he aids in it; and it cannot surpass the divine nature, nor consequently all nature in general. But popularly when Nature is spoken of, that of finite substances is understood, and in this sense it is not impossible for there to be something supernatural, which surpasses the force of every created being. It is when an event cannot be explained by the laws of movement of bodies, or by other similar rules that are noticed in finite substances. And I have shown in an earlier letter that one encounters that every time one finds a succession of true prophecies that go into detail. It is true that they are rare, like all other supernatural things. (A I,vii,46f.)

It may be harder to see Leibniz as disingenuous here than in writing to Arnauld. Sophia was a trusted friend; moreover, Leibniz would have been more in agreement with her if he had taken a less supernaturalist line here—though in the seventeenth century it was doubtless safer in general to be more orthodox (and on this point more supernaturalist) than one's patrons, rather than less so.

It is striking, however, that Leibniz echoes the language of DM 16, speaking of what "surpasses the force of every created being," and that he equates the miraculous with what is inexplicable in terms of laws "that are noticed [*se remarquent*] in finite substances." The laws that are *noticed* in creatures are presumably the simpler laws, which they express more distinctly. This suggests that the distinction between the natural and the miraculous is being drawn here in terms of the simplicity or complexity of the laws, rather than where they are expressed—which leaves open the possibility that Leibniz is indeed thinking of the complex but exceptionless law that grounds miracles as expressed in the forms or primitive forces of created substances. He may have left that unsaid with Sophia simply because he did not generally expound his subtlest metaphysical thoughts to her.

One apparent consequence of this interpretation of the difference between the natural and the miraculous is that the free actions of creatures will be miraculous. For Leibniz certainly thought that free actions "cannot be foreseen by the reasoning of any created mind" because of the complexity of the order on which they depend. Leibniz made this point himself:

> But indeed Free or intelligent Substances have something greater and more remarkable, in a certain imitation of God: that they are not bound to any certain subordinate Laws of the universe, but act spontaneously from their own power alone, as if by a sort of private miracle. . . . And this is true inasmuch as no creature is a knower of hearts that can predict with certainty what some Mind is going to choose in accordance with the laws of nature. (C 20/MP 100)

This is an exceptional text, in part because it also says that free agents "interrupt the connection and course of efficient causes operating on their will"—something that seems quite contrary to Leibniz's usual views, as expressed, for example, in his letter of April 1687 to Arnauld (LA 93f.).[19] But even aside from that, which may be just a lapse, I know of no other text in which Leibniz assimilates free actions to miracles, and it may be that the assimilation did not usually seem welcome to him.

[19]See also Chapter 1, section 2.6, where I take this point as evidence of a comparatively early date (before July 1686) for C 16–24.

Despite any problems on this point, and despite such textual evidence as we have seen on the other side, I think the tenor of Leibniz's philosophy in general favors the view that the whole universal law of the general order is incorporated in the substantial form or concrete causal structure of each created substance.[20] It is interesting in this connection that in the *Theodicy*, having suggested that though our souls preexisted our birth as human beings, it may have required a special or extraordinary operation of God to elevate them from mere sentience to rationality (T 91), Leibniz adds that "I would prefer to do without miracle in the generation of the human being, as in that of other animals," which can be done if we suppose that "those souls alone that are destined to attain one day to human nature contain the reason that will appear there one day" (T 391)—presumably implying that the effect of extraordinary divine action should have been incorporated in these souls from the beginning.

One further argument for this interpretation is the following. According to Leibniz, we—not only our concepts, but also we concretely—express the whole universe, including all the miracles that occur in it (LA 40f.). How do we express it? By virtue of our substantial form or primitive force, from which always proceed perceptions of the whole universe, the perceptions being produced by laws that express the laws by which the events perceived are produced. But if our substantial form expressed only the laws of nature and not the whole law of the general order of the universe, then perceptions of miracles, which are not produced by the laws of nature, will not follow from our substantial form. Does the divine "clock-maker" have to intervene in each of us at every instant to cause us to perceive the miracles that occur in the universe? Or does God adjust us all only once, when the miracle occurs, in which case our perceptions after the miracle do not perfectly agree or harmonize with those before? Each of these consequences would certainly be unpalatable to Leibniz.

Leibniz himself points out similar problems. Allowing to Bartholomew Des Bosses that "God could create infinitely many new Monads," Leibniz adds that "it should be thought that the old monads were already so ordered by God from the beginning, when he created them, that their phenomena corresponded formerly to the monad that was still to be created; unless we prefer God to change all the other monads by a miracle, when he creates a new one, so as to accommodate them to the new one, which is less likely" (G II,371/L 598). Another pertinent text is a curious section of the *Theodicy* where Leibniz suggests that the miracle of Cana (John 2:1–11) may have been worked "by the ministry of some invisible substances, such as the angels, as the Rev. Father de Malebranche also holds,"[21] rather than by a direct divine intervention in nature.

[20]There is a text in which Leibniz explicitly raises the question whether "precisely the futurity itself of an action . . . is an intrinsic denomination or a real affection in the will?" (Gr 387) An answer is not given unambiguously, and the text is published by Grua in a manifestly imperfect state of preservation, but I think the document predominantly supports the answer that the futurity of the action is somehow in the nature of the creature, not only in God. An interesting piece of evidence included in the text is that efficacious grace, which obviously might be regarded as a divine intervention in human lives, is here identified by Leibniz as a "created entity or reality," which is presumably a real cause *in* the concrete created person, not only in God.

[21]See Robinet, *Système et existence dans l'oeuvre de Malebranche*, p. 112, on the development of this theme in the thought of Malebranche.

> However if the changing of water into wine at Cana were a miracle of the first rank, God would have changed thereby the whole course of the universe, because of the connection of bodies; or else he would have been obliged to obstruct that connection, miraculously again, and to make the bodies not involved in the miracle to act as if no miracle had happened; and after the miracle was over, he would have had to restore everything, even in the bodies that were involved, to the state it would have reached without the miracle, after which everything would be returned to its original channel. Thus this miracle demanded more than it seemed to. (T 249)

2.3 *"Miracles of the First Rank": Creation, Conservation, Incarnation, Annihilation*

The passage just quoted is one of a group of texts from the last years of Leibniz's life, in which he speaks somewhat differently about miracles but draws the line between divine and creaturely action exactly where (in my opinion) his fundamental principles require it to be drawn. It is only "miracles of the first rank" (cf. LC V,117) that involve no causal agency of creatures. "The changing of water into wine could be a miracle of that [inferior] species" that angels might be naturally able to do. "But creation, incarnation, and some other actions of God surpass all the force of creatures, and are truly miracles, or even mysteries" (T 249; cf. T pd23).

Of the principal actions that are reserved to God on this view, creation has the largest role in Leibniz's metaphysics, and claims the most discussion here. *Creation* (understood broadly) is production of the existence of a finite being. It is a miracle in the metaphysically strong sense that no cause of the existence of any creature is to be found in that creature (since only God exists per se), or in any other creature (since the causal efficacy of created substances, according to Leibniz, is purely immanent, and does not extend beyond their own internal states). But God's causing the *existence* of creatures seems to constitute no interruption in the order of nature. So long as each creature, through its substantial form, causes all its own *states*, God's causing its existence, including the existence of its substantial form, does not contribute to any way in which an individual created substance could have existed without some of the states that its substantial form would naturally produce.

This integration of creation with the causal role of created substantial forms is too easy, however. It suggests that, given the existence of a creature with its substantial form produced by God, the creature itself causes all its own states, so that nothing more than the existence of the creature has to be supplied by God. But there are prominent texts in which Leibniz appears to reject that view. His actual views about creation are complex and subtle, difficult to discern and not easily reconciled with his belief in the causal agency of the substantial forms of creatures.

The view of Durand de St. Pourçain and others, that "the concurrence of God with the creature (I mean physical concurrence) is only general and mediate, and that God creates substances and gives them the force that they need, and that after that he lets them act, and does nothing but conserve them, without helping them in their actions" is mentioned by Leibniz only to be rejected as providing an inadequate account of the *conservation* of creatures by God (T 27).

> *God is the conserver of all things.* That is, things are not only produced by God when they begin to exist, but they also would not continue to exist unless a certain continuous action of God terminated in them, on the cessation of which they themselves would also cease. (Gr 307)

And "this dependence obtains, not only with regard to substance, but also to action" (T 27; cf. Gr 381, RML 490). "God concurs in the actions of things, insofar as there is something of perfection in the actions"; indeed, God's concurrence "is directed not only to the existence and acts of a thing, but even to the mode and qualities of existence, insofar as there is something of perfection in them" (G VI,440).

Conservation falls under the heading of creation, understood broadly, and Leibniz is prepared to speak of conservation, with suitable explanations, as "continuous [or continued] creation" (Gr 330; T 27,382–85).[22] "For the dependence being as great in the sequel as in the beginning, the extrinsic denomination, of being new or not, does not change its nature" (T 385). Alternatively, 'creation' can be understood in a narrower sense, as signifying the beginning of the divine productive activity that, in its later stages, is called "conservation" (Gr 307). If we understand creation in the narrower sense, and distinguish conservation from it, then conservation will be as much a miracle of the first rank as creation. "For the dependence [of creatures on God] being as great in the sequel as in the beginning," conservation exceeds all the force of creatures as much as (initial) creation does. Indeed, conservation is the aspect of creation (in the broad sense) that has the most implications for the relation of God's activity to that of creatures.

The thesis asserted by Leibniz that God in conserving creatures continually produces their actions as well as their substance could seem to lead to the occasionalist conclusion that God is the only agent. And if God is the only agent, then of course the whole argument tying all of a created substance's states to its identity by way of their production by its substantial form falls by the wayside. But Leibniz will not accept the occasionalist conclusion.

> I grant in some way . . . that God continually produces all that is real in creatures. But I hold that in doing it he also continually produces or conserves in us that energy or activity which according to me constitutes the nature of substance and the source of its modifications. And so I do not grant that God alone acts in substances, or alone causes their changes, and I believe that that would be to make the creatures totally futile and useless. (G IV,588f.)

The first sentence of DM 8 indicates that Leibniz wanted to find a middle way between the occasionalism of Malebranche and the rather deistic position of Durand, and that he thought it no easy task: "It is rather difficult to distinguish the actions of God from those of creatures; for there are some who believe

[22] See also DM 14, where Leibniz says that "created substances depend on God, who conserves them and who, indeed, produces them continually by a kind of emanation as we produce our thoughts." Gr 330 dates very likely from the early 1690s (VE 451).

that God does everything, [and] others imagine that he does nothing but conserve the force that he has given to creatures." Malebranche would argue that there is no middle way here, and that occasionalism follows from the conception of conservation as continued creation.[23] How did Leibniz think he could escape between the horns of this dilemma?

Robert Sleigh, in an illuminating discussion of this problem, suggests that "Leibniz's mature position" is to be found in his claim that "the perfection that is in the action of the creature comes from God, but that the limitations that are found there are a consequence of the original limitation and of the preceding limitations that have occurred in the creature" (G VI,348),[24] or in Sleigh's words, that "God produces what there is of perfection in the states of creatures; creatures produce whatever there is of limitation in their own states."[25] There is no doubt that Leibniz made this claim, and its intended function in his theodicy, as a way of avoiding the conclusion that God is the author of sins and other evils, is explicit (T 30) and obvious.

As a metaphysical middle way between occasionalism and deism, however, it seems to me less promising. Its fundamental disadvantage is that it seems to compete with Leibniz's strategy for distinguishing between activity and passivity within created substances. Leibniz classified a substance as active in any event in which it "passes to a greater degree of perfection," and passive in any event in which it "passes to a lesser degree" of perfection (DM 15). Identifying substantial form with primitive active force, and primary matter with primitive passive force, he therefore treats the former as a tendency to perfection, or distinct perception, and the latter as a tendency to imperfection or limitation, or confused perception.[26] But if God's conserving activity produces directly all the perfection in the states of creatures, in such a way that creatures produce only the imperfection of their states, the conclusion is close at hand that God's is the only *active* force and that creatures have only *passive* force. That may be enough to avoid the occasionalist conclusion that creatures are not real causes at all, but it seems quite inconsistent with Leibniz's theory of created substantial forms as active forces.

There must be something in the reasoning leading to this conclusion that is out of keeping with Leibniz's intentions in attributing all and only the perfection in creatures to the divine agency. For that attribution is followed, in the *Theodicy*, by passages implying that *all* the "accidents" or "qualities" of created substances are produced by the creatures themselves.

> The production of modifications has never been called *creation*. . . . God produces substances from nothing, and the substances produce accidents by the changes of their limits. . . . I maintain that all Souls, Entelechies or primitive forces, substantial forms, simple substances, or Monads, by whatever name

[23]Nicolas Malebranche, *Entretiens sur la Métaphysique* (1688), VII,vi–xi (OM XII,155–63).

[24]P. 390 in Huggard's English translation of the *Theodicy*.

[25]Sleigh, *Leibniz and Arnauld*, p. 185. Sleigh cites several other texts for this position. As he notes (p. 184), Thomas Aquinas takes a very similar position in his *Summa contra Gentiles*, book 3, ch. 71. I am much indebted to Sleigh's discussion, and also to the excellent discussion in Robinet, *Architectonique disjonctive*, pp. 418–42.

[26]This aspect of the theory of form and matter is discussed at length in Chapters 11–13.

> one may call them, cannot be born naturally, nor perish. And I conceive of qualities or derivative forces, or what are called accidental forms, as modifications of the primitive Entelechy, just as shapes are modifications of matter. (T 395–96)

"The primitive Entelechy" here is clearly the soul, substantial form, or primitive active force,[27] and its accidents or qualities are included, along with those of matter, among the "modifications" that do not require creation but are produced by the created substances themselves. The characterization of modifications, as such, in terms of limits and changes of limits seems intended to accommodate these claims to the thesis that creatures produce in themselves only limitation. But I confess that I still do not see how Leibniz may have thought that the latter thesis could be made wholly consistent with his characterization of substantial forms as active forces tending toward perfection.

I think that in allocating perfection and imperfection to the action of God and of creatures, respectively, Leibniz had the problems of theodicy more on his mind than those of metaphysics. More light seems to me to be shed on the latter by another line of thought developed in the *Theodicy*.

> Suppose that the creature is produced anew at each instant; grant also that the instant, being indivisible, excludes all temporal priority. But let us notice that it does not exclude priority in nature, or what is called priority *in Signo rationis*, and that that is enough. The production or action by which God produces is prior in nature to the existence of the creature that is produced; the creature taken in itself, with its nature and its necessary properties, is prior to its accidental affections and its actions; and yet all these things occur in the same moment. God produces the creature in conformity with the demand [*exigence*] of the preceding instants, following the laws of his wisdom; and the creature operates in conformity with that nature that he returns to it in creating it always. (T 388)

In one respect this passage steers uncomfortably close to the occasionalist horn of the dilemma. The last sentence could easily suggest that in relation to later states of a created substance, its earlier states are only occasional causes, to which God attends in accordance with "the laws of his wisdom." We may wonder whether this is consistent with texts in which Leibniz seems to speak of real and direct causal effects of the earlier on the later in creatures (e.g., G II,275/AG 181; G IV,532). Even in the present context, however, Leibniz does disagree with occasionalism in what he says about the order of causes within a single instant of time. God produces the whole reality of the creature in each instant, the accidental affections and the actions as well as the nature of the creature. But within what God produces there is a natural (not a temporal) order, the nature of the creature being prior to its affections and actions. What God (directly) produces, we may say, is not just the creature's nature or substantial form or *capacity* to produce, and not just the creature's nature *and* its affections and actions, but the creature's nature "operating" and thus *producing* its affections and actions.[28]

[27]Leibniz's use of his terminology in the quoted passage is somewhat imprecise, however, as hinted by the phrase "by whatever name one may call them." See Chapters 10–13.

[28]For a similar interpretation, see Robinet, *Architectonique disjonctive*, p. 440.

In thus producing the creature's producing, God's conserving activity has a direct causal relation to the creature's actions, but without excluding the productive agency of the created nature.

Other passages support this interpretion as well—for instance, the statement from 1702, quoted above, that "God continually produces all that is real in creatures. But I hold that in doing it he also continually produces or conserves in us that energy or activity which according to me constitutes the nature of substance and the source of its modifications" (G IV,588f.). Similarly, when Leibniz says that the concurrence of God is "*immediate*, since the effect depends on God, not only because its cause originated from God, but also because God's concurrence is neither less nor more remote in producing the effect itself than in producing its cause," he is clearly speaking of effects that not only have God as an immediate cause, but also have created causes, themselves produced by God.

A carefully worded statement, written in 1702 and published in 1712, presents an interesting disjunction: "For it is God who conserves and continually creates their [creatures'] forces, that is to say, a source of modifications that is in the creature, or indeed [*ou bien*] a state by which it can be judged that there will be a change of modifications" (G IV,568/L 583). In the second alternative, stated in terms of a state that grounds *predictions*, commitment to metaphysically real influence of earlier created states on later ones is carefully avoided. A metaphysically real production of creatures' modifications by forces that are in them is affirmed in the first alternative, but that may apply only to an action of the forces that is *simultaneous* with the modifications produced.

We can speculate a little further about the nature of the explanatory relation between earlier and later states of the same created substance in Leibniz's theory of conservation. Leibniz said in 1706 to Des Bosses that "there is in the active power [of creatures] a certain *demand* [*exigentia*] for action and therefore for divine concurrence for action," a demand that, though "resistible," is "founded in the laws of nature constituted by divine wisdom." Without such an active power or force in the creature, Leibniz declared, God's "ordinary concurrence" would not suffice to give rise to the action (G II,295; cf. T 388). I take it that the "demand" is envisaged here as temporally prior to the action demanded. Perhaps it was also Leibniz's view that the causally efficacious action of the forces of a created substance is always simultaneous with its effect, but that it produces the effect, in accordance with the relevant laws, *in view of* the substance's previous states.[29]

Conservation, on my interpretation of Leibniz's view, does not involve God's producing any state of a creature that does not also have a "source" in the nature or substantial form of the creature. "The creature does not concur with God to conserve itself," Leibniz agrees, but he sees "nothing that prevents it from concurring with God for the production of some other thing, and particularly of its [own] internal operation, as a thought, a volition, would be, things really distinct from the substance" (T 391). So if creation, in the broad sense, including conservation, were the only "miracle of the first rank," the only action of God

[29]This way of putting it takes rational agency as model for the action of created substances as such. That was in fact Leibniz's model, as I shall show in Chapter 11, section 1.3.

that strictly surpasses "all the force of creatures," Leibniz would not be committed to any miracle in which a creature's history departs from the pattern laid down in its substantial form. There are at least two other types of divine action, however, that Leibniz classifies as miracles of the first rank, and we must now consider them.

One of them is *incarnation*. It is a special case. Obviously, nothing would be an incarnation of God unless God participated directly in it. But incarnation is not a matter of causing states of a created substance; rather, it is a union of the divine with a human nature. There is another text in which Leibniz, proposing to account for most apparent miracles as produced through the ministry of angels, says:

> Thus there would be no absolute miracles in these things, except the creation of things and the union of God with the first creature [that is, with the human nature of Jesus Christ]; the rest would happen by laws of nature, but by laws that would fit the first creature and the angels. Furthermore, through the union God would not change the natural laws of the first creature, since he would have no need of this change. This union would therefore change nothing in the phenomena, even though the state of union differs internally from non-union. (RML 413)

It seems to follow that divine incarnation, as conceived by Leibniz, does not imply that anything occurs in the history of creatures *as such* that has no source in their substantial forms.

The other action that Leibniz says is reserved to God alone is *annihilation*. In his correspondence with Clarke, Leibniz introduces his distinction between "miracles of an inferior sort, which an angel can work," and "miracles which none but God can work . . . [o]f which kind are creating and annihilating" (LC IV,44).[30] Leibniz may have thought that God never, in fact, annihilates a created substance. In the text quoted in the previous paragraph, he says, "I prefer to say that God has not acted miraculously except in the Creation and the incarnation" (RML 413). But Leibniz certainly believed that God *can* annihilate created substances. "For we know well that the power of God can render our souls mortal, totally immaterial (or immortal by nature alone) as they may be, since he can annihilate them" (NE 67). That is the reverse of the coin of Leibniz's belief that created substances are continually conserved in existence by God. It will be important to come back to this question of the possibility of annihilation in our consideration of the modal issue that I have deferred to this point.

2.4 *The Modal Issue*

We began with the question whether there are possible worlds, or possible individual histories, that are qualitatively identical before a certain time but differ-

[30]I follow Clarke's translation here, except for punctuation. Leibniz goes on to say that mutual attraction of bodies at a distance, and continued circular motion of a body, would be "supernatural" unless there were a mechanical explanation. He could be taken here to be assigning these to the first rank of miracles, but it is at least arguable that his thought about these cases, which were very relevant to his controversy with Clarke, had more to do with the idea, discussed above, that "laws of nature" must provide explanations of a certain simplicity.

ent thereafter and, specifically, whether such a difference *could* arise by a miracle. What I think we have seen most clearly thus far about Leibniz's treatment of miracles is that he was not committed (though he may have been tempted) to the view that in miracles (or in some of them) God *does in fact* cause something to happen to a created substance that is different from what would follow from the previous states of that substance by the most comprehensive laws built into its substantial form. Even if we think, as I do, that Leibniz's philosophy is best represented by the view that the whole, exceptionless general order of the universe is built into the substantial forms of all created substances, and that they therefore have always expressed or prefigured all the miracles that actually happen to them—and even if we add to this view that that *would* have been true, no matter what miracles God had done—that does not settle the crucial modal issue. We must ask whether (1) it is only God's commitment to *harmony* that assures the prefiguring of all miracles in substantial forms, or whether (2) the nature of substance as such makes it absolutely impossible even for God to create a substance whose concrete form or nature does not perpetually express absolutely everything that ever happens to it.[31]

The second is what is required if possible worlds or histories differing qualitatively only after a certain time are to be excluded. The strongest textual evidence for ascribing this view to Leibniz may be found in the *Discourse on Metaphysics*, particularly in § 16. The question addressed in that section is

> how it is *possible* for God sometimes to have influence on human beings or on other substances by an extraordinary and miraculous concurrence, since it seems that nothing extraordinary or supernatural *can* happen to them, in view of the fact that all their events are only consequences of their nature" [italics added].

This certainly suggests that in proposing the answer that miracles happening to a created substance are a consequence of its "essence" but not of its "nature," Leibniz supposes that it is not *possible* for the miracles not to be consequences of the "essence," which I have argued is to be identified with the substantial form, or at least to be regarded as fully expressed by the substantial form.

Why would it be *impossible* for miracles to happen to a substance that are not consequences of its "essence," and hence of its substantial form? An answer in terms of the nature of causality, and indeed of the divine causality, is suggested by the statement that nothing is supernatural to our essence "since an effect always expresses its cause and God is the true cause of substances" (DM 16). But the answer suggested by the formulation of the question in DM 16, and by DM 6–9 as the background of the question, is that the nature of a substance as such requires an inherent essence or substantial form in the substance from which all of its states flow. Against the background of DM 6–9, the apparent reason for this answer is Leibniz's conceptual containment theory of truth. This is a disappointing observation, inasmuch as I have been seeking, in the present

[31]The phrase "to it" marks a restriction of the scope of the present inquiry into the modal issue. I postpone until section 3 the question (also related to the law of the general order) whether the nature of substance allows God any ability to create a substance whose concrete form fails to express something that happens *outside it.*

chapter, an alternative to the conceptual containment theory as a ground for Leibniz's rejection of transworld identity.

An alternative rationale might be sought in the nature of substance as active. The following argument has arguably Leibnizian premises:

(1) Necessarily, a created substance does not exist (at any time) unless it acts (at that time).

(2) Necessarily, a created substance does not act (at any time) unless all its states (at that time) follow from its own substantial form and its own previous states.

(3) Therefore, necessarily, a created substance does not exist (at any time) unless all its states (at that time) follow from its own substantial form and its own previous states.

This argument is formally valid; (3) does follow from (1) and (2). (1) is certainly a Leibnizian doctrine (G IV,469f./L 433); it is connected with Leibniz's argument that created things must have active powers if they are to be substances and not mere modes as Spinoza thought (LA 133; G IV,508f./L 502). The considerations about transtemporal identity presented in section 1 of this chapter might also have inclined Leibniz to accept something like (2). The most questionable point in the argument is the universal quantifier ("*all* its states") in premise (2). Without it the argument will not exclude any miracles. But one might have thought that the most that would be required for a substance to act (at all) would be that *some* of its states follow from its own substantial form and previous states. Leibniz may have accepted (2) in its full strength, however, believing that the universal quantifier there is required for the grounding of trans-temporal identity (cf. LA 43). And if the conclusion (3) can be derived in this way, it will follow that

(4) However God works miracles, it cannot be by causing something to happen to a created substance that does not follow from the creature's own substantial form and previous states, unless the creature is thereby annihilated.

The concluding qualification in (4), about annihilation (a "miracle of the first rank"), is significant. An argument based on the requirements for (continued) existence of a created substance cannot exclude the possibility of events by which the substance would cease to exist. This argument therefore does not support the thesis that it is absolutely impossible for the *annihilation* of a substance to be an event that was not caused, nor even expressed, by the substance's substantial form and previous states.

In fact, there is considerable evidence, at least in the *Theodicy*, that Leibniz recognized a sense in which God *could* at any time annihilate a created substance, no matter what its previous history might have been. He declares that "in truth, it does not follow *necessarily* from the fact that I am, that I shall be; but that still follows *naturally*, that is to say, of itself, *per se*, if nothing prevents it" (T 383).

The claim that my future existence does not follow "necessarily" from my present existence is not decisive for our present purpose, since it could just mean that the connection between them is not (finitely) demonstrable. More important is the indication that the future existence follows only "naturally" from the present, for following "naturally," in Leibniz, generally signifies a connection that depends on God's choice of a harmonious world. Similarly, it seems to be Leibniz's view that conservation, as well as (original) creation is a *voluntary* operation of God (T cd9), which should imply that the connection between present and future existence of a creature depends on God's choice, which is of course in fact the choice of a harmonious world.

Leibniz also says that "God produces the creature in conformity with the demand [*exigence*] of the preceding instants, following the laws of his wisdom" (T 388; cf. G II,295). This seems to imply that the (re)production by which God conserves any given creature in existence depends on God's wisdom and hence, certainly, on God's goodness and choice of the best. This text could be read as implying that it depends on God's goodness, not only whether the individual creature will continue to exist but also whether any continued existence it has will conform to the demands of its substantial form or inherent primitive forces. But I think this reading is not imposed on us; we can still suppose that God's causing a substance to have any state not following from its primitive forces and previous state would be counted by Leibniz as annihilation.

From these passages of the *Theodicy* taken together emerges the view that God *could* annihilate any created substance at any time, in the sense that only the divine goodness prevents God from doing that.[32] It would be difficult to ascribe to Leibniz at this point the view that if God did annihilate a substance, that annihilation must have been expressed and perceived in the substance from the very beginning of its existence, and that this requirement does not depend on God's wisdom or goodness, so that God *could* not, in the sense invoked here, annihilate a substance whose previous states do not demand it. That interpretation would hardly be consistent with Leibniz's statement that it is by "following the laws of his wisdom" that God's conserving activity agrees "with the demand of the preceding instants" (T 388). At least with respect to annihilation, Leibniz's statements in the *Theodicy* suggest a sort of possibility of alternative individual histories that differ only after a certain time.

3. *Perception and Relations*

Such a possibility is suggested even more strongly in Leibniz's thought about relations. In the case of relations, unlike that of miracles, there is no doubt of how Leibniz thinks things go in the actual world. Actually, every substance at every time completely expresses all its relations with every other substance, and every event, in the whole (actual) world. Leibniz asserts that repeatedly, in discussions of substance, of perception, of preestablished harmony, and never contradicts it. The issue here can only be whether God *could*, in some relevant sense,

[32]On the importance of this type of possibility for Leibniz's theory of creation, see Chapter 1, section 3.

have made a substance that would not have expressed all its relations, and hence whether there are possible individual histories that are perfectly alike internally but differ in some of their relations.

Issues about the possible existence of an actual substance in a world in which some of its actual relations would fail are not prominent in Leibniz's discussions of transworld or counterfactual identity, which are much more concerned with whether there are possible worlds in which actual creatures act or suffer otherwise than they do in the actual world. A focus on the latter question is easily explained by Leibniz's (and Arnauld's) religious and ethical interests. Nonetheless we can ask whether according to Leibniz there is a possible world in which Adolf Hitler, for example, does not exist, or is less malicious than in the actual world, but in which there is a man both numerically and qualitatively identical with the actual Antoine Arnauld [except, of course, for the merely "extrinsic denominations" that Arnauld actually has by virtue of his (distant) relations to Hitler].

This question can be divided into two parts: (1) Are there possible worlds in which there is a man *qualitatively* identical with the actual Antoine Arnauld, but no one qualitatively identical with the actual Adolf Hitler, except for purely relational properties of the individuals? (2) If there are such possible worlds, does at least one of them contain someone *numerically* identical with the actual Antoine Arnauld? Leibniz has little to say about the second of these questions. Our starting point in his argument about the Genoese block of marble, with its claims about *qualitative* differences, leads me to focus, for the time being, on the first question. Leibniz has a lot to say that bears on it—but some of his statements may tell in opposite directions.

The passage about the Genoese marble may suggest a negative answer. Leibniz says there not merely that the *stone* would have been qualitatively different from the beginning if *it* were going to stay in Genoa, but that "because of the connection of things the whole universe *with all its parts* would be entirely different, and would have been another [universe] from the beginning, if *the least thing in it* went otherwise than it does" (LA 42, italics added). So if Leibniz is denying that there are possible worlds in which the block of marble, or its counterpart, is qualitatively the same as in the actual world until the time of its actual transportation, but then stays in Genoa, he is equally denying that there are possible worlds in which one substance is internally different from its actual counterpart but other substances start out only relationally different from their actual counterparts. What is "the connection of things" that precludes such possible worlds? We have seen that for Leibniz the primitive force of each individual substance provides the connection that precludes (if anything does) pairs of possible individual histories that differ internally after but not before a certain time. Is there something in Leibniz's conception of things that might play an analogous role in precluding pairs of possible individual histories that differ relationally but not individually?

The obvious candidate for this role is *perception*. Leibniz held that each substance always perceives everything that ever occurs in the whole universe. Throughout his life, Antoine Arnauld, for instance, perceived the existence of Adolf Hitler, and every detail of Hitler's career, though of course Arnauld was not conscious of these perceptions. It seems to follow that if a possible world in which Hitler did not exist contained a man who is internally just like the actual Arnauld, that man would, in that world, "perceive" some things that do not exist. Perhaps this inference could be resisted by holding that any sufficiently complex internal state of a perceiving substance could be placed in one-to-one correspondence with *any* sufficiently complex possible world, with or without Hitler, and would therefore constitute an accurate perception of whatever world the substance existed in. Leibniz does often explain perception in terms of one-to-one correspondence, but he could hardly afford to accept this trivialization of his concept of perception and the consequent trivialization of his pre-established harmony.

If he does not accept it, his alternatives are to admit that there are possible worlds in which some substance fails to perceive the whole world just as it is (fails to perceive it as not containing Hitler, for instance), or to deny that there are possible worlds that differ qualitatively with respect to the existence or internal properties of some but not all of their substances. There is much to incline Leibniz to the second alternative. He thought that it follows from the nature of truth that there are no purely extrinsic denominations, and hence that every substance perceives the whole universe (C 520/L 268f.). Perhaps he thought that this precludes possible worlds in which any substance fails to perceive the whole world just as it is. (Of course, he recognized that there are false beliefs, but he thought that the beings that have them also, unconsciously, perceive the world exactly as it is.) On this view, the whole general order of the universe, including its relational aspects, would be incorporated in the concrete substance as it is included in the substance's complete individual concept, and not merely by virtue of God's wise choice of a most harmonious world. The relational laws of the general order would be incorporated in the substance's perceptions as the laws of intrasubstantial causation are incorporated in its primitive force. And all of the substance's states and relations would follow from the force and the perceptions it has at any given time, so that there would be no possibility of a predicate's being contained in the individual concept and not being contained in the concrete substance.

This has the very important advantage for Leibniz of providing a nontrivial sense in which possible individuals can fail to be "*compossible*" with each other. In thinking about the problem of evil in more or less Leibnizian terms, it is natural to ask, Why couldn't God have improved the world by replacing Hitler with a morally better individual, while leaving the excellences of more excellent individuals (such as Arnauld) unchanged? One answer that Leibniz seems to want to give to this sort of question is that God could not do that because Arnauld (with his actual excellences) is not compossible with any such Hitler substitute. But how are we to understand this incompossibility? Suppose that Hitler is replaced by a more virtuous substitute in some possible worlds that contain a man whose internal, nonrelational qualities and states are exactly the same as Arnauld actually has. Of course if Arnauld's individual concept includes the whole history of the actual world, Arnauld himself will be absent, by definition, from any possible world containing such a substitute in place of Hitler. In that case there will be a trivial sense in which Arnauld is incompossible with a Hitler substitute. But this sort of incompossibility does not answer the question why God could not have made a better world by replacing particularly vicious or unhappy creatures with better and happier ones while replacing his more excellent creatures with counterparts[33] that would have exactly the same excellences internally and would differ only in their extrinsic denominations. To this question, I suppose, Leibniz could reply that creatures that would be internally just like the excellent actual creatures, but in a world that is not just like the actual world, would thereby lack an important (relational) excellence of all actual creatures, in that they would not perceive their whole world just as it is. But in this reply it is not incompossibility but harmony that is called in to solve the fundamental problem.

Perhaps, indeed, the appeal to incompossibility is just a covert appeal to considerations of harmony. But it would be something more if Leibniz thought that the internal states of possible substances are perceptions that are conceptually connected with the existence and states of other substances, so that no individual in any possible world has exactly the same history of internal states as any individual in any other possible world. Then the internal histories of substances in one world would be incompossible with the internal histories of substances in any other world, and this incompossibility would put a constraint on God's options that would be quite independent of the constraints of harmony.

Despite these reasons for ascribing to Leibniz the view that God could not have actualized an individual substance without actualizing the whole possible world perceived by that substance, I know of no text in which Leibniz exactly asserts it,[34] and there are texts in which he explicitly contradicts it.[35] Indeed, it is hardly to be reconciled with his account of the pre-established harmony. Every student of Leibniz is familiar with his statement that the series of future perceptions that follows from his present nature "would not fail, and would happen to me just the same, if everything that is outside of me were destroyed, provided that there remained only God and I" (DM 14; cf. G I,382, IV,484/L 457). This strongly suggests that Leibniz thought that without creating any other substance, God could create a substance with qualitatively the same substantial form and series of perceptions as Leibniz actually has. But this is not the strongest evidence, for Leibniz might conceivably be using a counterfactual conditional with an impossible antecedent, as a rhetorical device to express the mutual causal independence of created substances.

More significant is the fact that in explaining the pre-established harmony Leibniz repeatedly says that only the action of God can cause created substances to correspond to each other's perceptions. "There is nothing but God . . . to be the cause of this correspondence of their phenomena, and to make what is particular to one to be public to all" (DM 14). The "ideal influence of one Monad on another . . . cannot have its effect except by the intervention of God. . . . For since one created Monad cannot have a physical influence on the interior of

[33]I am *not* using 'counterpart' here in the technical sense used in Lewis, "Counterpart Theory and Quantified Modal Logic."

[34]His statement that "we need other substances" (G IV,364/L 389), containing no explanation of why we need them, does not clearly imply the view.

[35]On this subject, cf. Sleigh, *Leibniz and Arnauld*, pp. 180–82.

another, it is only by this means that one can have any dependence on another" (Mon 51). Leibniz presents the difficulty of achieving this correspondence as a proof of the infinite knowledge and power of God.

> For since each of these Souls expresses in its way what goes on outside, and cannot have this through any influence of other particular Beings, or rather must draw this expression from the resources of its own nature, each one must necessarily have received this nature (or this internal reason of the expression of what is outside) from a universal cause on which all these Beings depend and which makes the one perfectly agree and correspond with the other. This is not possible without an infinite knowledge and power, and by so great an artifice, especially with respect to the spontaneous agreement of the machine with the actions of the reasonable soul, that [Bayle] doubted, as it were, whether it did not surpass all possible wisdom, saying that the wisdom of God did not seem to him too great for such an effect, and recognized at least that the feeble conceptions that we can have of the divine perfection had never been put in such high relief. (NE 440f.; cf. G IV,578, LC V,87)

But the harmony or correspondence of the perceptions of created substances with each other could hardly be such a powerful proof of God's infinite wisdom and power if no creator could have created a world that lacked such correspondence, as Des Bosses pointed out to Leibniz in 1715 (G II,493). The use of the pre-established harmony to prove the greatness of the creator seems therefore to presuppose that among the possible worlds that God could have actualized were some in which created substances fail to correspond with each other's perceptions. Accordingly, Leibniz responded flatly to Des Bosses that God "was able absolutely [to create one of those monads that now exist without creating all the others], but was not able hypothetically, given that he decided to do everything most wisely and harmoniously" (G II,496/L 611).[36]

4. *Conclusions*

We are left, I think, with the conclusion that, according to Leibniz,

(1) It is only by virtue of God's wisdom and goodness that there is no failure of correspondence of the primitive forces of created substances with what happens in the world.

We have identified two failures of correspondence that Leibniz seems to think are prevented only voluntarily by God—the failures that would be involved in God's annihilating a substance whose past did not "demand" annihilation, or

[36]The use of "absolutely" in this context is probably meant to suggest the famous Scholastic distinction between God's *absolute power* and God's *ordered power*. In Aquinas's version of this distinction, God's absolute power is God's power considered apart from the constraints of other divine attributes such as wisdom and goodness. So God is able absolutely to do whatever God could do were it not for the divine wisdom and goodness. God's ordered power is God's power considered in relation to the other attributes that actually determine its exercise—for Aquinas, indeed, in relation to the determination of its exercise by the plan God has actually chosen. See M. Adams, *William Ockham*, pp. 1186–90.

creating a substance without the external relations internally expressed by it. This may seem inconsistent with the thesis that:

(2) Nothing with qualitatively the same primitive forces as any actual substance has would have existed if anything at all in the world had gone differently.

The argument about the Genoese marble certainly commits Leibniz to thesis (2).

In fact, there is no inconsistency here. There is a strong connection between the primitive forces of each actual creature and absolutely everything that happens in the actual world, and this connection can be expressed in a counterfactual conditional such as (2). But connections do not have to have absolute metaphysical necessity in order to ground counterfactual conditionals. The connection in this case may depend on the wisdom and goodness of God. If God had created a world in any way different, God would not have created any substance with primitive forces qualitatively the same as those of any actual substance, because that would have produced a state of affairs too discordant for the divine wisdom and goodness even to consider it seriously as a candidate for creation. The demands of God's wisdom and goodness are more than strong enough to ground counterfactual conditionals.

This line of thought gives some support to the first hypothesis considered in Chapter 1, section 2.3, for explaining contingent connections between possibles—the hypothesis that alternative predicates for an individual created substance are "possible in themselves" if they are excluded by the substance's individual concept only in virtue of the laws of its universe. That is because the principal doubt about the viability of the hypothesis concerned the acceptability to Leibniz of the distinction between features of a substance that are particular to it, as embodied in its primitive forces, and the laws of its universe. And proposition (1) implies that there are indeed alternative predicates for a created substance which are not excluded by the substance's primitive forces all by themselves, but only in virtue of the decision of God's goodness to create a world conforming to at least minimally harmonious laws.

Proposition (2) is a claim about counterfactual *qualitative* identity. Leibniz was interested in it largely as a basis for defending his thesis of the completeness of individual concepts against Arnauld's claims of counterfactual *individual* identity. This may suggest to us that if the truth of (2) depends on God's wisdom and goodness, so do Leibniz's denials of counterfactual individual identity. Is this Leibniz's view? Assuming that only divine wisdom and goodness keep God from creating someone internally just like me, but in an externally different situation, would Leibniz say that such an individual, if God did create one, could be *me*? This is a difficult question. The possibility of such a discordant state of affairs, I suspect, held no more interest for Leibniz than for Leibniz's God. It is possible to deny counterfactual individual identity even where counterfactual qualitative identity of an individual's internal history, or an initial segment of its history, obtains, and some texts discussed in Chapters 1 and 2 (e.g., LA 42,52) might suggest that Leibniz would do this. So does his writing in the mid-1680s that "a concept that is still indeterminate even in the slightest circumstances . . . could be common to two different individuals" (Gr 311); for it seems to follow that an individual must be defined by a concept that is not undetermined in any way, even regarding external relations or duration of existence. On the other hand, where Leibniz does envisage the chaotic situation in which God creates a substance without creating the external relations that it expresses internally, he uses the language of individual identity, speaking freely of *himself* and God existing without anything else (DM 14), or of God creating "one of those Monads that now exist" without all the others (G II,496/L 611).

Let us assume for the sake of argument that Leibniz's claims of counterfactual individual nonidentity do depend on God's wisdom and goodness in the same way as his claims of counterfactual qualitative nonidentity. It might be thought that this conclusion would be inconsistent with the thesis for the sake of which Leibniz resisted Arnauld's claims of counterfactual identity, the thesis that

(3) All the predicates of each substance are contained in the individual concept of that substance.

Again there is in fact no inconsistency here. We have seen in Chapter 1 that a most important predicate of actual substances—their existence—is contained in their individual concepts, according to Leibniz, but only by virtue of God's wisdom and goodness. So being contained in an individual concept and depending on God's wisdom and goodness are not inconsistent modalities for Leibniz.[37] There are indeed texts in which it seems pretty explicit that in Leibniz's view the containment of an action in a created substance's individual concept, and hence the failure of counterfactual individual identity, like that of counterfactual qualitative identity, depends on God's wisdom and goodness, at least in some cases. Leibniz says that Caesar's decision to cross the Rubicon "presupposes the sequence of things that God has chosen freely, and that is founded on the first free decision of God, the import of which is to do always that which is most perfect" (DM 13). Likewise, in reading notes from about 1695, having stated that "when I ask what would have been if Peter had not denied Christ, what is asked is what would have been if Peter had not been Peter, for having denied is contained in the complete concept of Peter," Leibniz goes on to say that it can happen sometimes that a decision (presumably one like Peter's) "does not follow [from anything in the universe] unless a new divine decree occurs by reason of bestness" (Gr 358).

Does this interpretation lead to the conclusion that Leibniz does not deny transworld identity of individuals after all? He seems to deny it, couching his point in terms of possible worlds, in the *Theodicy* (T 414). In fact, he suggests a sense in which he can deny it without contradicting the conclusions proposed here. The suggestion comes in an explicit statement, from 1698, that God could have created substances that would not have corresponded with each other's perceptions: "God was able to give each substance its phenomena independent

[37]If I understand it, the sense of Sleigh's claim that Leibniz affirmed "superintrinsicalness" but not "superessentialism" is similar to the interpretation that I have offered thus far in this section. See Sleigh, *Leibniz and Arnauld*, pp. 57f., 69–72.

of those of the others, but in that way he would have made, so to speak, as many worlds without connection as there are substances" (G IV,519).[38] This suggests that a collection of substances that did not correspond with each other's perceptions would not be sufficiently connected to constitute a single "world." Perhaps Leibniz did not think that every state of affairs or set of creatures that God could (but for the divine goodness) have actualized should be counted as a "possible world" (or part of a possible world). Perhaps only complete sets of perfectly harmonious created substances are to count as possible worlds. Certainly Leibniz was so convinced of the supreme worth of harmony that he would not have expected God seriously to consider actualizing any state of affairs that did not satisfy this constraint, and I do not know of any passage in which Leibniz himself speaks of "possible worlds" that do not satisfy it. If Leibniz assumed that the notion of a "possible world" is subject to this requirement of harmony, he would have a clear reason to hold that substances with different relational properties, or different durations, in different *possible worlds* must have had different internal properties (different perceptions) from the very beginning; and this would support a denial of transworld identity, giving it a sense in which it would follow from his metaphysics of causality and perception. Of course it would also move him still farther from the conception of possible worlds in terms of which the question of transworld identity has been raised in our time.

Appendix: 'A Priori' and 'A Posteriori'

Proofs a priori and a posteriori, in the original sense of those terms, are proofs from the cause and from the effects, respectively, of the fact to be proved. This sense of the terms is still found in the *Port Royal Logic*, which speaks of matters in which our mind may be "capable of finding and comprehending the truth, either in proving the effects by the causes, which is called demonstrating a priori, or inversely in demonstrating the causes by the effects, which is called proving a posteriori."[39] The conception is clear, although the authors go on immediately to remark that "it is necessary to extend these terms a little in order to reduce all sorts of demonstrations to them."

There are many indications in Leibniz's writings that he understood 'a priori' in the older sense that I have indicated. He says, "Proof *a priori* or Apodeixis is explanation of the truth" (C 408). He equates knowledge a priori with knowledge through causes (C 272). A reason "would make known the reality [of a definition] *a priori* in exhibiting the cause or possible generation of the thing defined" (NE 294). Most telling, perhaps, is an early passage in which Leibniz treated indirect proof [*reductio ad absurdum*], which is not normally empirical, as a case of proof a posteriori—presumably because it does not explain *why* the proposition proved is true (C 154).[40]

[38]On this text, cf. Sleigh, *Leibniz and Arnauld*, pp. 150f.

[39]Arnauld and Nicole, *Port Royal Logic*, IV,1.

[40]Couturat's editorial commments (C 153f.) note internal evidence for dating this piece to 1677. The watermark also suggests approximately that date (VE 309).

Nonetheless, there are passages in which Leibniz could easily be read in the newer sense in which 'a priori' means simply 'nonempirical'. He regularly connects the a posteriori with experience, and can contrast "truths *a posteriori*, or of fact" with "truths *a priori*, or of Reason" (NE 434). I suspect, indeed, that Leibniz played a crucial role in the transformation of the meaning of 'a priori'. I believe that 'proof a priori' always meant for him 'proof that explains the reason for the fact that is proved'. But it follows from his epistemology and his conceptual containment theory of truth that a priori knowledge in this sense coincides with knowledge that is independent of experience and with knowledge by analysis of concepts. It was therefore easy for him to use the term 'a priori' when the idea that was foremost in his mind was not that of knowledge by causes but one of these other ideas that were, for him, coextensive with it.

By the same token, it was easy for a Leibnizian like Alexander Gottlieb Baumgarten to *define* the a priori as the nonempirical.[41] Christian August Crusius, on the other hand, who was more resistant to Leibnizian views about sufficient reason, was still using 'a priori' and 'a posteriori' in the old sense in the middle of the eighteenth century:

> A demonstration a posteriori is one from which is known only that a thing is—for example, by experience, or by reduction to absurdity, or by comparison with some other thing. A demonstration a priori is one from which is known why a thing is—for example, where we deduce the attributes of things from definitions, or draw out the effect from the causes and determining reasons.[42]

[41]Risse, *Die Logik der Neuzeit*, vol. 2, p. 649.

[42]Risse, *Die Logik der Neuzeit*, vol. 2, p. 690. A similar conception is found in Crusius, *Entwurf der nothwendigen Vernunft-Wahrheiten*, § 35.

II

Theism: God and Being

4

The *Ens Perfectissimum*

We begin here a sequence of five chapters on Leibniz's views and reasonings on the relation between God and ontology. Leibniz is (in my opinion) the most interesting writer on the ontological argument for the existence of God between St. Anselm and the twentieth century. This chapter is concerned with one of the key ideas in Leibniz's version of that argument, his conception of God as a "most perfect being," an *ens perfectissimum*, by which he meant a "subject of all perfections" (A VI,iii,579/L 167), a being that has all perfections, and whose essence, indeed, is the "aggregate" (cf. A VI,iii,574) or conjunction of all perfections. Leibniz seems to have worked hardest on the development of this conception during 1676, at the end of his years in Paris, but it still dominates his thought about God in the *Discourse on Metaphysics* and in the *Monadology* (DM 1, Mon 41–48). He bequeathed the conception to his successors. In slightly varying forms it appears in Christian Wolff and Alexander Gottlieb Baumgarten, and it provides the concept of God for the excessively famous discussion of the ontological argument in Immanuel Kant's *Critique of Pure Reason*.

What sort of thing a subject of all perfections would be obviously depends on what perfections are. Leibniz offered definitions of 'perfection' on more than one occasion. The one I have chosen as a starting point occurs in one of his more finished papers from 1676 and figures prominently in his attempt to prove the possibility of God's existence, which I will discuss at length in Chapter 5. He writes: "A *perfection* is what I call every simple quality that is positive and absolute, or [*seu* = that is] that expresses without any limits whatever it expresses" (A VI,iii,578/L 167).

Perfections are *qualities*. Not every predicate expresses a quality. In particular, only monadic predicates, predicates of a single subject, (and perhaps not all monadic predicates) express qualities. Leibniz does not adhere rigidly to Aristotle's scheme of categories, but he is certainly Aristotelian enough to refuse to count relations as qualities. The question whether existence is a quality will be important in connection with the ontological argument.

A *simple* quality here is one that is not analyzable as a conjunction of other properties; this becomes explicit in the next step of the argument. A *positive* quality is not the negation of another quality. The most durable feature of Leibniz's conception of perfections is that they involve no negation at all. I take the last clause of the definition to indicate that an *absolute* quality is not a limited degree of any quality, and indeed involves no limitation at all; I will shortly offer some justification for this interpretation.

There are many misgivings one could have about this conception of God. Norman Malcolm objected that he could not understand how any quality could be intrinsically simple or positive.[1] I have always wondered whether it is really a conception of *God*. It is not immediately obvious that the conjunction of all simple, purely positive qualities that express without limits whatever they express (assuming that there are such qualities) would constitute the God of traditional theism rather than a "Metaphysical something"—to borrow a phrase that Leibniz uses to characterize someone else's theology (A VI,iii,474f./L 158). Some have suspected that ascribing to God the sum of all purely positive attributes has Spinozistic or pantheistic implications. We may wonder, at any rate, whether the definition of a perfection includes and excludes, respectively, those properties that would and would not characterize a being that is recognizably God. Shades of color, which God is not supposed to possess, have seemed to some to be simple and positive, and perhaps they are not limited degrees of anything, but are only perfectly themselves; should we count them as perfections? And are knowledge and power, which God is supposed to possess in unlimited degree, really simple and purely positive? Argument seems to be needed on such points.

We will not find as much argument as is needed, but the publication of the critical edition of Leibniz's philosophical writings from the Paris period, 1672–76,[2] makes possible a more adequate understanding of the development and meaning of his conception of the *ens perfectissimum* and of the structure of the universe over which this being presides. In these writings we get clear indications of what qualities Leibniz thought of as perfections and attributes of God. They are not sensible qualities, but basic metaphysical categories. Or, rather, they are primal, unlimited, purely positive versions of metaphysical categories that are combined with limits in other beings. Specifically, they include immensity, eternity, omniscience, and omnipotence, all conceived as the absolute degrees of the qualities or categories of reality manifested, respectively, in spatial and temporal being, in thought or intelligence, and in agency [A VI,iii,391f.,520 (March–April 1676)]. If the simple, purely positive qualities are precisely the unlimited degrees of these categories, the Leibnizian deity is, or could be, the personal God of traditional theism.[3]

Several issues of metaphysical and theological importance will repay a closer investigation here. I will try in section 1 to develop more fully the meaning and motivation of Leibniz's definition of a perfection, beginning with the interpretation of the term 'absolute'. Section 2 will be devoted to the question whether his definition picks out the right properties as perfections, with specific reference to sensible qualities and to knowledge. Some passages of surprisingly Spinozistic appearance occur in Leibniz's papers on this subject from 1676, and I will try in section 3 to show both how far his thought about God was Spinozistic then, and how in the end it escapes from any Spinozistic implication.

[1]Malcolm, "Anselm's Ontological Arguments," p. 59.

[2]A VI,iii (1980). Leibniz's letters from that period were already included in A II,i (1926), but the newer volume is vastly superior in documentation and indexing and contains more on this topic.

[3]Later, in the *Theodicy*, Leibniz tries to fit moral perfection, or perfection of the will, into this scheme, claiming that "the will consists in the inclination to do something in proportion to the good that it contains" and moral perfection is the absolute degree of this inclination (T 22).

1. *Absolute Qualities as "Requirements" of Things*

'Absolute' has several meanings. Leibniz offers formal definitions of it as meaning "what is thought without anything else being thought" [A VI,ii,489 (1671–72?)], or as the opposite of 'relative' [C 475 (1702–4)].[4] Non-relativity might be relevant here, but I have not found in Leibniz's discussions of the *ens perfectissimum* anything that is unambiguously about the role of relational properties. More clearly relevant is another family of senses in which 'absolute' means something like 'unqualified' [cf. C 51/P 19 and C 60 (both of April 1679)]. This conception is expressed, almost in the form of a definition, in a memorandum of March or April 1676 in which Leibniz speaks of a thing "to which existence is ascribed absolutely, that is, without a determining addition" (A VI,iii,520/L 163). The "determining addition" might be a condition; and 'absolute', accordingly, can mean 'unconditional' [cf. A VI,ii,397 (1669–71?); C 26 (Nov. 1677); GI 137 (1686)]. Alternatively, the "determining addition" can be a limitation, and 'absolute' can mean 'unlimited'.[5] Since 'unlimited' is one of the available meanings, the explicative clause ("that expresses without any limits whatever it expresses") makes it the likeliest meaning of 'absolute' in the present context.

There is no sharp distinction between 'absolute', in this meaning, and 'positive', for a limitation is a sort of partial negation. A quality "circumscribed by limits" is "understood through negations of further progress" (A VI,iii,578/L 167). At least once Leibniz explained 'absolute' as meaning 'affirmative' [A VI,iii, 519/L 163 (March–April 1676)], and he singles out the purely positive character of perfections as incompatible with their being analyzed as having limits (A VI,iii,578/L 167). The absence of a "determining addition" also means that an absolute quality is a pure and noncomposite quality, and Leibniz can use 'absolute' to mean something like 'primitive', speaking of "something absolute, into which the objects of thoughts must be analyzed" (C 409). Thus the meaning of 'absolute' can include that of 'simple' as well as 'positive', and Leibniz can speak of "all absolute forms or possible perfections" without separate mention of simplicity and positiveness, saying that from their "conjunction in the same subject arises the most perfect Being [*Ens perfectissimum*]" [A VI,iii,521/L 163 (March–April 1676)].

Leibniz's conception of divine perfection is a conception of infinity, or unlimited reality. He gives it a negative expression, as "without any limits." In view of his insistence on the simple and purely positive character of perfections, however, he cannot regard the nature of this infinity as adequately expressed in negative terms. Essentially negative accounts of infinity in general, and of God's infinity in particular, abound. According to Locke, "when we would frame an *Idea* the most suitable we can to the supreme Being, we enlarge . . . with our

[4]Other places where Leibniz appears to use 'absolute' to mean nonrelative are A VI,ii,161 (from 1669); A VI,iii,518 (probably from April 1676), though that is not the only sense of 'absolute' in this text; and C 590 (probably from 1688).

[5]See A VI,iii,502 (April 1676) and Gr 371 (1695–97), where Leibniz explicitly opposes the absolute to the limited; cf. A VI,iii,520/L 163. In notes written probably in the last year or so of his life, Leibniz distinguished two senses of 'absolute': one in which "it is opposed to the limited," and one in which "it is opposed . . . to the relative" (VE 1087 = LH IV,8,60–61).

Idea of Infinity" all our ideas of qualities desirable in ourselves; and the idea of infinity is essentially negative, "the Negation of an end in any Quantity."[6] In present-day philosophical theology omnipotence or unlimited power is standardly defined (at least roughly) as the ability to bring about any possible state of affairs.[7] The idea of infinity in that definition is expressed by a universal quantifier ("any"), and, as any logician knows, universal quantifiers are equivalent to a sort of negation. So conceived, omnipotence is such power that there is *no* possible state of affairs that its possessor could not actualize.

Descartes firmly rejected such negative conceptions of the divine infinity or perfection; in the third of his *Meditations* he says:

> And I ought not to think that I do not perceive the infinite by a true idea, but only by negation of the finite, as I perceive rest and shadows by negation of motion and light; for on the contrary I clearly understand that there is more reality in infinite than in finite substance, and that hence the perception of the infinite is in some way prior in me to that of the finite; that is, the perception of God is prior to the perception of myself.[8]

Setting aside for the moment questions of priority of the *perception*, we can at least say that Leibniz's conception of divine perfection commits him to agree with Descartes that in its own nature the divine infinity or perfection is primitive—that it is unanalyzable and not a negation of the finite. For him, as for Descartes, the infinite, in properties capable of infinity, is the primary case, and the finite is formed by limitation, or partial negation, of the infinite (NE 157f.). "The absolute is prior to the limited," Leibniz states. "And just so the unbounded is prior to that which has a boundary [*terminus*], since a boundary is something added [*accessio quaedam*]" [A VI,iii,502 (April 1676); cf. A VI,iii,392 (18 March 1676); A II,i,313f. = G I,214f. (5 April 1677)].

The priority of the unlimited is first of all conceptual. Being purely positive and simple, according to Leibniz, the unlimited is unanalyzable. It is "conceived through itself," in the sense that it has no constituents in terms of which it might be understood. Rather, the perfections are primitive, in the sense that they are first or ultimate constituents in the analysis of other qualities. But the priority of the unlimited or absolute is not only conceptual for Leibniz. Unless we see that it is also causal, we will miss an important part of the motivation of his conception of the *ens perfectissimum*. Causal dependence tended to fuse with conceptual dependence in his thought; he held that "the effect is conceived through its cause" [A VI,iii,514 (April 1676)], and he always thought that a definition or analysis of anything ought ideally to exhibit the cause of its existence, or at least a reason why it is possible (G IV,425/AG 26). So, if all other things are causally dependent on God, their essences should be conceptually dependent on the divine essence. This is accomplished if the divine essence is a conjunction of all the simple, positive attributes out of which all other predicates are constructed.

[6]Locke, *Essay*, II,xxiii,33; II,xvii,15.

[7]Qualifications may be added to deal with problems about, for instance, the free will of creatures.

[8]AT VII,45. Cf. AT VII,113,365.

In a passage to be discussed more comprehensively in section 3, Leibniz expresses this double primacy of the absolute, unlimited attributes or divine perfections by calling them the "first requirements" of things (A VI, iii,573). The term 'requirement' [*requisitum*] is one of which Leibniz made heavy theoretical use, especially, but not exclusively, in his early writings.[9] We will have several occasions to attend to it. In 1671–72 Leibniz defined a requirement as "something such that if it is not posited the thing [of which it is a requirement] is not" (A VI,ii,483). This formula is used, in a more elaborate definition from 1702–4, to define the notion of a sustainer [*suspendens*]. "A *sustainer*," says Leibniz, "is something such that if it is not given, something else is not given; it is also called a condition." The sustaining relation, thus defined, could be reciprocal; two things could be sustainers of each other. The requirement relation, however, is asymmetrical, and is therefore defined with an additional proviso of natural priority: "A *requirement* [*requisitum*] is a sustainer that is naturally prior" (C 417).[10] An otherwise compressed definition from the mid-1680s explains "naturally prior" in this context as equivalent to "simpler in nature" (Schmidt 481).[11]

Notoriously, there is more than one kind of necessary condition. A "requirement," in the indicated sense, may be what we would ordinarily call a *cause*, or more precisely a *causally* necessary condition, particularly if it is what Leibniz calls a "requirement for existence" (A VI,iii,584,118). Requirements seem to function as causes in a proof of the principle of sufficient reason developed in the early 1670s (A VI,ii,483; iii,118) and repeated in 1716 in Leibniz's last letter to Samuel Clarke (LC V,18).[12]

There are also logically necessary conditions, however, and it is clear that Leibniz thought of the defining or essential properties of a thing as among its requirements, its *requisita*. After all, they too are such that if they are not posited, the thing is not. "A definition," Leibniz says, "is nothing else than an enumeration of requirements" (A VI,iii,133; cf. A VI,iii, 462f.,573; C 60; G III,247; G VII, 293). This sort of "requirement" is clearly in view in texts of 1676 (A VI,iii,670f. = G VII,83) and of April 1679. In the latter Leibniz speaks of treating things in his general characteristic or language for reasoning

> insofar as we have distinct notions of them—that is, insofar as we know some requirements of them, by which, when examined in detail, we can distinguish

[9]I have been particularly helped in tracing and understanding Leibniz's use of this term by the editor's note 31 in Saame, 146. An example of its persistence in Leibniz's later work is a *requisita*-based analysis from a publication of 1684 (G IV,425/AG 26) which reappears in a letter of January 1699 to Thomas Burnett (G III,247/AG 287).

[10]This asymmetry is indicated, more awkwardly, when Leibniz writes, in April 1676, "Connected are things of which one cannot be understood without the other. Requirements are things that are connected to another and not conversely" (A VI,iii,515/L 161). Unfortunately, 'connected' has not been assigned here the directionality that it needs for its use in explaining the asymmetry of requirement.

[11]For the date, which is based on the watermark in the paper, and is earlier than that proposed by Schmidt, see VE 1251. The account of natural priority in terms of simplicity is found also in VE 170 (= LH IV,7C,71–72) (assigned a preliminary dating of 1679–85 by the Academy editors, on grounds of content), but a problem about the account is discussed in notes probably dating from Leibniz's Italian journey in 1689–90 (VE 132 = LH IV,7B,47–48).

[12]This proof is quoted in Chapter 2, section 5.

> them from any other things—or insofar as we can specify their definition. For these requirements are nothing but the terms whose notions compose the notion that we have of the thing. (C 50/P 18)

In view of the fusion of causal and conceptual dependence in Leibniz's thought, however, it is misleading to speak of these as two different types of requirement. His calling something a "requirement" must normally be assumed to have implications about both causal and conceptual relations, of which one may be more prominent than the other in a particular context.

There is a problem about the relation between limited and unlimited degrees of a quality, to which Leibniz, so far as I know, devotes no discussion and offers no solution. One might assume that different degrees of the same quality should be structured logically in such a way as to contain a common part—namely, the quality of which they are degrees. Given that a perfection is simple, and thus has itself as its only "part," it appears to follow that the perfection itself must be a "part" of the limited degrees of the same quality. This conclusion also seems to be supported by the idea that the perfection is the pure case of the quality, and limitation is a sort of negation. It also seems to be confirmed when Leibniz speaks of the divine perfections as present "in" things that have limited degrees of them (A VI, iii,391f.). Suppose *P* is a perfection, and *Q* is a limited degree of the same quality of which *P* is the unlimited degree. The apparent implication is that *Q* is derived from *P* by adding the negation of some quality, or in other words that *Q* = (*P* + not-*X*). This seems to entail, however, that whatever possesses *Q*, the limited degree, also possesses *P*, the perfection, since *P* is a conjunct in (*P* + not-*X*). This consequence casts doubt on the analysis, for the terminology is devised to compare a being that has a perfection with beings that possess *only* a limited degree of the quality.

There are at least two possible ways of dealing with this difficulty. One would be to reject the inference from a thing's possessing (*P* + not-*X*) to its possessing the perfection. To possess the perfection, it might be said, is not just to possess *P* in any way whatever, but to possess *P* *without* any limitation. The difficulty with this is that it looks like a negative understanding of the nature of a perfection. If Leibniz chose this course, he would have to deny that it involves analyzing the perfection as (*P* + not-limited). To have the perfection is not to have *P* plus a double-negative property; it is just to have *P* and not have a negative property.

If that does not sufficiently guard the purely positive character of the perfections, then Leibniz might wish to deny that the sameness of a quality in different degrees is to be understood in terms of a part or element that is common to all the degrees. The conception of the ultimate degree of a quality as the pure case of the quality is Platonic, and maybe we can draw here on one of Plato's ideas about the relation of the forms to their mundane instances—namely, that the latter are *imitations* of the former. The analogue of Plato's idea for the present case would be that other degrees of any quality are (imperfect) imitations of the ultimate degree of it. Leibniz actually uses this language in the *Monadology*, saying that "in created Monads . . . there are only imitations" of the divine perfections, and specifically of God's power, knowledge, and will—imitations "to the degree [*à mesure*] that there is perfection" (Mon 48). On the view that this suggests, the fundamental relations of the lesser degrees to the unlimited degree of a quality would be similarity but also distinctness, and indeed incompatibility. Since (as we shall see) Leibniz understands all incompatibility of properties in terms of one containing a negation of the other, and since the perfections are unanalyzable and purely positive, Q, the limited degree, must be analyzable as a conjunction having not-P, the negation of the perfection, as a conjunct. Perhaps the similarity will also be a conjunct, in which case the analysis of Q will be, or include, (similar to P + not-P); or perhaps the similarity will simply supervene on the analysis of Q.

Leibniz might find this solution problematic, too. It invokes similarity as a fundamental logical relation of properties, whereas much in his philosophy of logic seems to imply that the only such relations are distinctness, identity, and construction by conjunction and negation. But I think Leibniz would want in any event to maintain that limited and unlimited degrees of a quality are incompatible in any one substance. As I will suggest at the end of this chapter, that thesis may be important to Leibniz in differentiating his views from those of Spinoza.

2. *Sensible Qualities, Knowledge, and Perfection*

In thinking about the question whether Leibniz's definition of a perfection includes and excludes the right properties, for purposes of theology, let us focus on a pair of examples closely related in his thought: on the one hand, the sensible qualities, which God is not supposed to possess, and which should therefore not be classed among the perfections; and on the other hand, knowledge, or more precisely, omniscience, which Leibniz certainly counts as a perfection and an attribute of God. Leibniz's writings afford adequate material for the construction of a reasonable answer to claims that he should count sensible qualities as perfections. Indeed, he may be said to have addressed a form of that problem himself. I will conclude, however, that it would be more difficult for him to vindicate the classification of omniscience as a purely positive attribute.

As long as Leibniz defines the perfections as *simple* qualities, he seems to have an answer to the question why sensible qualities do not count as perfections. He held that color, for example, "is analyzable in its own nature, since it has a cause" (G VII,293;[13] cf. C 190,360f./P 51f.), or (as he put it in April 1676) that "the perception of a sensible quality is not one perception but an aggregate of infinitely many" (A VI,iii,515/L 161).[14] It is true that in a text from perhaps as early as February 1676 Leibniz lists "sensible qualities, such as heat, cold, light, etc." along with "Existence, the Ego, perception, the same, change," as examples of things that "seem to be *conceived through themselves* by us, the terms or Words

[13]To be dated, probably, 1683–86, on the basis of watermark (VE 900).

[14]Leibniz seems to say here that this is "on account of the divisibility of space and time to infinity," but the context also suggests the idea that sensible qualities cannot be "conceived through themselves," and therefore cannot be simple, because they have causes. 'Conceived through themselves' must be understood here (and in a number of other passages) in the sense Leibniz assigns 'understood through themselves' in the next passage I shall quote in the text.

for which are indefinable, or the ideas of which are unanalyzable." But I think these are not all supposed to be examples of properties that are absolutely unanalyzable in their own nature. Leibniz goes on to distinguish what is conceived through itself from what is understood through itself; the latter is "only that all of whose requirements we conceive, without the concept of another thing—that is, that which is its own reason of existing" (A VI,iii,275 = G I,131). This distinction seems designed to allow that there may be things that we conceive through themselves, inasmuch as we do conceive them but cannot analyze them, but that we do not understand through themselves, because in their own nature they are analyzable into requirements that we are either unable to conceive or unable to discern in them. That sensible qualities are simple only in the sense that *we* are unable to analyze them is certainly a thesis of Leibniz's mature philosophy, and I think the evidence indicates it was his view in 1676 as well.

In April 1677, however, in a conversation with Arnold Eckhard about the ontological argument Leibniz himself did raise the question why pain, which can be considered a sensible quality, should not be considered a perfection. Leibniz reports that he demanded from Eckhard a definition of perfection.

> *He* [said] that a perfection is every attribute, or every reality. *I* [said] that therefore even pain is a perfection. *He* [said] that pain is not something positive, but a privation of tranquillity, as darkness is of light. *I* [said] that it seems to me that pain can no more be called a privation of pleasure, than pleasure a privation of pain. But pleasure as well as pain is something positive. And pain is related to pleasure quite otherwise than darkness to light. For darkness cannot be made more and less intense, once light has been excluded, nor is one darkness greater than another where all light is absent. But pain does not exist by the mere removal of pleasure, and one pain is stronger than another. Therefore it follows that the most perfect Being has pains too.

The discussion continued a little further; but on this occasion, Leibniz records, "we were stuck . . . here, and it was not adequately explained why pain is not as much a perfection as pleasure or satisfaction of mind is" (A II,i,313 = G I,214).

Leibniz's approach in this conversation was polemical, directed against Cartesianism. It was Eckhard's definition of a perfection he was criticizing, not his own. He could have offered his own definition, but did not. And Eckhard's definition omits the criterion of simplicity that is a main part of Leibniz's. But it emphatically includes positiveness, which is also a main part of Leibniz's definition (indeed the most important part, as we shall see). It is not clear, therefore, whether Leibniz was stumped on this occasion by a problem that affected his own views as well as Eckhard's.

Later in 1677, in correspondence with Eckhard, Leibniz articulates a solution that seems at least to come close to satisfying him:

> Some of my objections cease when you have explained that for you perfection is Being [*Entitas*], insofar as it is understood to depart from non-Being—or as I should prefer to define it, that *perfection* is degree or quantity of reality or essence, as *intensity* is degree of quality, and *force* degree of action. It is clear also that Existence is a perfection, or increases reality; that is, when *existing A* is conceived, more reality is conceived than when *possible A* is conceived.

> Nevertheless it still seems to follow from this that there is more perfection or reality in a mind that is hurting than in one that is indifferent, that is neither enjoying nor hurting; and thus that, metaphysically speaking, even pain is a perfection. But since pleasure is also a metaphysical perfection, the question seems to arise, whether pain or pleasure is the greater perfection, metaphysically speaking. And it seems that *pleasure* is the greater perfection, since it is consciousness of power, in the same way that pain is consciousness of weakness. Weakness, however, is an imperfection, metaphysically speaking, and consciousness of metaphysical imperfection is also less perfect, metaphysically speaking, than consciousness of metaphysical perfection. And so pain implies some imperfection in the being that is in pain; yet there remain some scruples even here, which I now pass over. (A II,i,363/L 177)

There is metaphysical perfection in pain as well as in pleasure, it is suggested here, insofar as both augment consciousness; but to be in pain is also to be imperfect, insofar as pain is consciousness of metaphysical imperfection.

It is noteworthy that this solution seems to involve a different notion of perfection from that with which we have been working. We began with a definition that yields a yes-or-no answer to the question whether any property is "a perfection." But here we are introduced to perfection as a measure of the *degree* of reality contained in a property. This is not only a transition from 'Perfect or not?' to 'More perfect or less?' Simplicity also drops out as a criterion, and only positiveness and perhaps absoluteness are left. For degree of "reality" is a measure of positiveness and unlimitedness of being.

Commenting on a long letter from Eckhard, moreover, Leibniz accepts this definition of perfection: "*Perfection* for me is quantity or degree of reality" (A II,i,327 = G I,225). There is reason to think that simplicity is in fact dispensable as a criterion of perfections for Leibniz. It is not really needed for his proof of the possibility of a most perfect being (as we shall see in Chapter 5, section 2.1). Leibniz's earliest and latest versions of the proof, in saying that God's attributes are "affirmative" (A VI,iii, 395f.) or include "no limits, no negation" (Mon 45), without mentioning simplicity, leave out nothing essential. Similarly in the *Discourse on Metaphysics* (1686), in the first section, which is mainly devoted to the divine perfections, unlimited degree is the only criterion offered to explain what a perfection is: "the forms or natures that are not susceptible of an ultimate degree are not among the perfections"; simplicity is not mentioned.

This is not to deny that Leibniz believed (probably throughout his career) that each simple positive property in fact characterizes God, and God alone (C 513[15]). The simplicity of the perfections is used, unnecessary as it may be, in his fullest versions of the possibility proof, which date from fall 1676. In sketching the proof for the Princess Elizabeth about two years later, he puts it in terms of the attributes of God being "all the simple forms, taken absolutely," without explicit mention of their positiveness (A II,i,437f./AG 240).

It is not clear whether our data represent change and development in Leibniz's conception of perfections, or simply variety in his choice of strategies of proof. It is clear that from some time in or after 1678, if not before, he doubted "whether

[15]The watermark suggests that this text comes from the period 1678–86 (VE 869).

any [primitive or simple] concept appears to humans distinctly, that is, in such a way that they may know that they have it" (C 513; cf. C 431,360/P 51; G VII,293).[16] This could have been a reason for Leibniz not to require simplicity of perfections, since he claimed to know some of the divine perfections, such as power and knowledge (DM 1, Mon 48).

To the extent that positiveness was Leibniz's primary criterion of perfection, and that he may in the end have wished to count among the divine perfections qualities that might not be absolutely simple, the sensible qualities might be seen as presenting a more difficult problem for his view. For his belief that the sensible qualities are not simple will not provide him with an adequate reason for not regarding them as perfections, or at any rate as compatible with the divine nature. His conception of perfection approaches Eckhard's, and may face some of the same problems. The solution he proposed to Eckhard for the issue about pain may indicate the lines along which he would relate the conception of perfection to sensible qualities in general. Leibniz thinks that our conceptions of sensible qualities are confused conceptions of aspects of the world that have in them some measure of reality and perfection, but also of limitation and imperfection. They are therefore not conceptions of any of the absolute perfections of God, and are not even compatible with the nature of a being of unlimited perfection.

This solution reflects what I take to be a persistent aspiration of Leibniz—to reduce all qualities to combinations and degrees of what would seem to most of us to be rather abstract metaphysical categories, such as consciousness and power. It is difficult to see how the differentiation and structure of a world can be accounted for in that way. The mature Leibniz seems to have maintained that it is precisely in degrees of perfection, in various respects, that finite substances differ from each other and from God; what they all share is perception of the structure of the same world. The phenomenal spatial array that constitutes that perception in us does not fit neatly within the conceptual framework of Leibniz's speculations about divine perfections. It is not readily understood either as a simple positive quality or as constructed out of such qualities by negation and conjunction. It therefore seems not to be a perfection, which is an advantage for Leibniz, inasmuch as it enables him not to ascribe a perfection to finite things. If he wishes to adhere rigorously to his conception of the *ens perfectissimum*, however, he is left with the problem of understanding how God's perception of an infinitely complex structure of limited things could be a simple, purely positive quality, or a conjunction of such qualities.

This problem is aggravated by the fact that perfect knowledge, for Leibniz, is an omniscience that includes knowledge of what is not, as well as what is. God knows the possibles that will never be actual, and knows that they are not actual. If this negative knowledge is reducible to anything more basic, it would be the knowledge that the non-actual systems of possibles are less perfect than the actual system; and that is still knowledge of a fact that essentially involves

[16]C 431 suggests the interesting idea that there are only two absolutely simple concepts, one positive (pure Being [*Ens*] or God), and one negative (nothing), and that all other concepts are somehow compounded of these.

limitation, and hence negation. If perfect knowledge thus, and indeed of its very nature, has an object that involves limitation and negation, it is hard to see how perfect knowledge can be a purely positive attribute.

3. *Is Leibniz's Conception of God Spinozistic?*

3.1 Leibniz's Views in 1676

A different approach to the relation between divine perfection and the structure of the universe of finite things is suggested in a paper of 18 March 1676 in which Leibniz gives one of his fullest indications of what attributes he counts as perfections:

> But there is something in space which remains amidst the changes, and which is eternal, and is nothing other than the immensity itself of God, that is, a single attribute at once indivisible and immense. Of this, space is only a consequence, as a property is of an Essence. It can easily be demonstrated that matter itself is perpetually extinguished or repeatedly becomes something different. In the same way it can be shown that the mind also is continuously changed, except for that which is Divine in us, or which arrives from outside; just as in space there is something divine, the immensity itself of God, so in the mind there is something divine, which Aristotle called the agent intellect, and this is identical with the omniscience of God, in the same way as that which is divine and eternal in space is identical with the immensity of God, and that which is divine and eternal in body or the movable being is identical with the omnipotence of God, and that which is divine in time is identical with eternity. (A VI,iii,391f.)

Two features of this account may seem problematic. One is that it ascribes to God a perfection, immensity, which is quasi-spatial and is said to be "that which is divine and eternal in space." This was not an extraordinary view in the seventeenth century, though it was not uncontroversial. On the assumption of a realistic conception of space, it provides (though without much articulation) a way in which the structure of a spatial universe can be directly related to a divine perfection. But it seems to be in disagreement with the mature philosophy of Leibniz, in which space and time are ideal entities, which we would not expect to be grounded directly in attributes of God.

It is true that we find the mature Leibniz writing, probably about 1688, that "whatever is real in space is God's omnipresence itself"; this is associated with the view that "the extension of space per se is absolute" whereas "the extension of a body is limited in every way" (VE 1603 = LH IV,7C,99f.). By the end of his life, however, Leibniz contrasts the divine immensity as absolute with space as "purely relative," though he still brings the immensity of God into close relation with the idea of space (LC III,3–4), as he had in the *New Essays* (NE 158).[17] The thought that space involves, and gets its reality from, the divine immensity did not, for Leibniz, imply that they are on the same level of reality. As he wrote about 1695, "space, time, and motion are, to some extent, beings of reason, and

[17]I am indebted to Ayval Ramati for calling my attention to this passage.

are true or real, not per se, but only insofar as they involve either the Divine attributes of immensity, eternity, and operation, or the force of created substances" (GM VI,247/L 445).

The way in which Newton connected space with God was one of Leibniz's initial points of attack in his correspondence with Clarke, and one of the continuing themes in this correspondence was Leibniz's objection to Clarke's identification of infinite space with the divine immensity (admittedly a simpler identification than Leibniz himself would have maintained even in 1676). In his last years, Leibniz understands God's immensity as omnipresence (LC V,45; RS 38/AG 276) and seems favorably disposed to the Scholastic reduction of God's presence in a place to "immediate operation" on things that are in that place (LC III,12; LC IV,35; cf. NE 221f.).[18] This suggests the view that immensity is not a divine perfection distinct from omnipotence.

The other surprising feature of the quotation with which I opened this section is the way in which Leibniz locates attributes of God, something "divine and eternal," *in* parts or aspects of the creation. The divine immensity is found in limited form in spatial things; the divine eternity, in temporal things; the divine and perfect knowledge, or omniscience, in the mind; and the divine power, interestingly, "in body or the movable being"—that is, in substantiality and action.[19] Such affirmation of divine immanence may arouse suspicions that the conception being expressed is pantheistic. Leibniz seems to have been sensitive to this possibility, for later in the same paper he tries to distance himself from a certain form of pantheism, saying:

> There is in matter, as also in space, something eternal and indivisible, which seems to have been understood by those who believed that God himself is the matter of things. It is not correct to say that, however, since God constitutes, not a part, but a principle of things. (A VI,iii,392)

Without knowing more about what he meant by calling God a "principle" [*principium*, "beginning" or "source"] of things we can hardly tell how effectively this distances Leibniz from pantheism in general. His statement here may remind us of his writing to Burcher De Volder, almost thirty years later, that "substantial unities are not parts, but foundations, of phenomena" (G II,268/L 536), where he certainly meant that the phenomena are metaphysically constructed out of the "unities." Denying that God is a *part* of (finite) things will not differentiate Leibniz from Spinoza, the most important "pantheist" in his intellectual environment. The most serious question about the theistic orthodoxy of Leibniz's 1676 conception of divine perfection is indeed whether it is pantheistic in a Spinozistic way.

[18]The reduction is not flatly asserted in these texts, but there is ample evidence that through most of his adult life Leibniz thought that all presence of any substance in a place should be reduced to operation; see Chapter 12, sections 2.2–2.3.

[19]On the relation of space and body to the divine attributes, cf. Kant, *Lectures on Philosophical Theology*, pp. 52f. (Ak XXVIII,1021f.). Particularly interesting in this context is Kant's statement that "from the concept of matter" we can retain for ascription to God, "after separating off everything negative and sensible that inheres in this concept, nothing but the concept of an externally and internally active force."

It has been claimed that it is. Wolfgang Janke, in an important article, characterizes the form of ontological argument used by Leibniz in 1676 as "Spinozistic."[20] "The sum of all positive constituents of things . . . stands under the pressing suspicion 'that it is identical with the world as an All of existing beings (regardless of all protestations against Spinozism)'," Janke says, quoting Kant.[21] There is evidence to support this suspicion. It is clear that Leibniz was thinking about Spinoza while he worked on his proof of the possibility of God's existence. He showed Spinoza the most finished form of it when he visited him in the Hague. In fact, there is a good deal in the texts of 1676 in which the proof was being developed that suggests a Spinozistic conception of the relation between God and the world.

The prevailing tendency in recent research holds that Leibniz was always fundamentally opposed to Spinoza's philosophy,[22] and there are already plenty of statements of disagreement with Spinoza in Leibniz's writings from 1676. But points of agreement and disagreement need to be distinguished here with much care. During this period Leibniz's knowledge of Spinoza's thought was increasing but still quite imperfect. He had studied the *Theologico-Political Treatise* but did not have an opportunity to study the *Ethics* until he received a copy after Spinoza's death. He was learning more about Spinoza's metaphysics in conversations with Ehrenfried Walther von Tschirnhaus, who was familiar with at least parts of the *Ethics*, and he was seeing fragments of Spinoza's thought in letters. He copied out three letters of Spinoza to Henry Oldenburg, which were probably shown him by Oldenburg in London in October 1676, shortly before his meeting with Spinoza. In his marginal comments on these letters Leibniz vigorously takes issue with Spinoza's treatment of miracles and rejection of the doctrine of the incarnation (A VI,iii,365–67,371 = G I,124–26,130). Leibniz agrees that "the existence of things is a consequence of the Nature of God," but only because the divine nature "brings it about that only the most perfect can be chosen"; he is careful to specify that finite things do not proceed from God "without any intervention of the will," and that some things are possible that do not exist (A VI,iii,370,364f. = G I,129,123f.)[23]

Leibniz's insistence on the role of God's will, and choice of the best, in the theological explanation of the existence of the created world would remain the chief point in his differentiation of his own version of determinism from Spinoza's (see Chapter 1, section 1.4). It is also, I believe, the point on which Leibniz can most easily be seen as defending the *personality* of God against Spinoza. Spinoza held that "if intellect and will belong to the eternal essence of God, something very different must be understood by both of these attributes from what people

[20]Janke, "Das ontologische Argument," esp. p. 259.

[21]Janke, "Das ontologische Argument," p. 269; Kant, *Preisschrift über die Fortschritte der Metaphysik*, Ak XX,302. Kant elsewhere rejects the suspicion: *Lectures on Philosophical Theology*, pp. 73–75 (Ak XXVIII,1041f.).

[22]See Friedmann, *Leibniz et Spinoza*, esp. ch. 3, and Parkinson, "Leibniz's Paris Writings in Relation to Spinoza." Stein, *Leibniz und Spinoza*, had argued for an early Spinozistic phase of Leibniz's thought.

[23]All these disagreements with Spinoza are emphasized by Friedmann, *Leibniz et Spinoza*, pp. 117–21.

are commonly accustomed [to understand]. For the intellect and will that would constitute the essence of God" would agree with ours only in name, as "the dog, the celestial sign" or constellation, agrees with "the dog, the barking animal."[24] This seems to present an impersonal conception of God, a result which Leibniz certainly wished to avoid. Commenting, probably in the spring of 1676, on Chapter 14 of Spinoza's *Theologico-Political Treatise*, Leibniz says, "Here he sufficiently intimates his opinion: that God is not a mind [*animus*], but the nature of things etc., which I do not approve" (A VI,iii,269f.).[25] More emphatically, but without explicit reference to Spinoza, Leibniz writes on 11 February 1676:

> God is not a Metaphysical something, imaginary, incapable of thought, will, action, as some make out, so that it would be the same as if you said that God is nature, fate, fortune, necessity, the World; but God is a Substance, Person, Mind. . . . It should be shown that God is a person or intelligent substance. (A VI,iii,474f./L 158)

The point in Leibniz's philosophy that does most to give substance to his ascription of intellect and will to God is his insistence that the creation of the world must be explained by God's understanding all the possible worlds, and their values, and choosing the best.[26] These, and above all the role of final causation (that is, purposiveness) in the works of God, form the centerpiece of his objection to a sect of "new Stoics," who hold that "properly speaking, God has neither understanding nor will, which are attributes of men." He names Spinoza as a prime examplar of this sect [G VII,334/AG 282 (1677–80)].

What Leibniz clearly rejects in Spinoza's theology, therefore, is Spinoza's *denial* of choice and optimific purpose, and of intellect and will, in any ordinary sense, in God. Even in objecting to suggestions that God is the matter, or a part, of things, or "is nature, fate, fortune, necessity, the World," Leibniz may be objecting only to any idea that God is nothing more than these things (which may not in fact have been Spinoza's view). It would not necessarily follow that Leibniz thought the world is something external or additional to God. Likewise, it is not so clear how much Leibniz rejects of what Spinoza *affirmed* about the ontological relationship between God and creatures. Specifically, it is not easy to discern Leibniz's attitude, in 1676, toward the Spinozistic idea that finite things are in God as "modes" or modifications of the divine attributes.

Commenting thirty years later on Spinoza's statement, to Oldenburg, that "All things are in God," Leibniz would deny that "all things are in God . . . as an accident is in a subject" (RS 38/AG 276). That approaches an explicit rejection of the mode/attribute relation between finite things and God. Commenting on the same text of Spinoza in 1676, Leibniz wrote:

[24]Spinoza, *Ethics*, I, prop. 17, schol.

[25]The editors suggest that Leibniz's perception of this intimation was due to knowledge of Spinoza's metaphysics obtained from Tschirnhaus (A VI,iii,248).

[26]In one of Leibniz's legal writings from 1676 we can find a definition of 'person' as "what has some will" (A VI,iii,592 = Gr 722), which might suggest that will was Leibniz's main or even sole criterion of personality. But this definition was probably meant only for legal purposes. Both a later note on it, from Leibniz's hand, and the passage I have just quoted in the text suggest that in metaphysical contexts he recognized intellect as at least as important a criterion of personality.

> It can be said at any rate that all things are one, that all things are in God, as an effect is contained in its full cause, and a property of any subject in the essence of that same subject. For it is certain that the existence of things is a consequence of the Nature of God, which brings it about that only the most perfect can be chosen. (A VI,iii,370 = G I,129)

At first glance Leibniz seems here to be proposing causal dependence *instead of* ontological inclusion as the acceptable meaning of "All things are in God." There is a question, however, to be asked before ascribing to Leibniz this somewhat strained interpretation. *How* is an effect contained in its full cause, according to Leibniz? Is 'contained' meant as lightly here as we might think? We might take some warning from the fact that Leibniz offers, as an apparently equivalent explanation, that "all things are in God . . . as a property of any subject [is contained] in the essence of that same subject." This explanation is puzzling, but it certainly breathes no obvious air of ontological externality. Indeed, we might naturally expect the property and the essence to be present in the same subject.

The relation of property to essence is used several times in Leibniz's papers of 1676 as a model for the relation of finite things to God; it merits some discussion. 'Property' is clearly meant here, not in the broad sense in which we customarily use it, but in an older and narrower sense. Leibniz distinguished an *accident*, as "a contingent predicate" of a thing, from several kinds of "necessary predicate":

> An *attribute* is a necessary predicate that is conceived through itself, or that cannot be analyzed into several others.
>
> An *affection* is a necessary predicate analyzable into attributes. . . .
>
> A *property* is a reciprocal affection, or an affection containing all the attributes of a subject, or from which all other predicates can be demonstrated.
>
> An *essence* is . . . the aggregate of all the attributes [of a thing]. [A VI,iii,574 (late 1676)]

In a paper of April 1676 Leibniz proposes an example of the relation that concerns us. "It seems to me," he says, "that the origin of things from God is like the origin of properties from an essence." The essence of 6, he proposes, is $1 + 1 + 1 + 1 + 1 + 1$; among its properties are $3 + 3$, 3×2, and $4 + 2$.[27] These properties are distinct, for without thinking of any one of them we can think of any other, or of the essence: "Therefore as these properties differ from each other and from the essence, so also things differ from each other and from God" (A VI,iii,518f.). This example does not suggest much ontological externality between the derivative "things" and God. Neither does the paper of 18 March 1676 when it says (as I have quoted it, above) that "space is only a consequence of [the immensity itself of God], as a property is of an Essence" (A VI,iii,391).

Perhaps the most suggestive of the passages in which Leibniz uses the relation of essence to property as a model for the relation of God to other things is in another paper of April 1676:

[27] I rely here on the context for the interpretation of some signs by which I take Leibniz to mean equality and the multiplication relation.

> The attributes of God are infinite, but none of them involves the whole essence of God; for the essence of God consists in the fact that he is the subject of all compatible attributes. But any property or affection of God involves his whole essence, as God's having produced a certain something that is constant to our sensation, however small it be, involves the whole nature of God, because it involves the whole series of things of that kind. An infinite series, moreover, results only from infinite attributes. When all the other attributes are related to any one of them, there result in it modifications, whence it happens that the same Essence of God is expressed as a whole in any kind of World, and so that God manifests himself in infinite modes. (A VI,iii,514)

Here a "kind of World," or a "whole series of things of that kind," is presumably a possible world.[28] Leibniz envisages a world as arising from the relation of each of the infinite attributes of God to all the others. Given his definition of 'property', that is of course also the way in which a property of God arises. This creative interaction of attributes follows from the divine essence, but it will be crucial for Leibniz that the perfection of God's will plays a part in it, as well as the perfection of God's power. It is God's "having produced" things that so results. But it is interesting for Leibniz's relation to Spinoza that he speaks of the result of the interaction as *modifications* "in" an attribute, and as God's self-manifestation "in infinite *modes*." It is natural enough to think of God's power, for example, as modified by God's will, inasmuch as it is determined by the choice of the best. What is striking here is that Leibniz is *not* moved to speak clearly of the world as an additional "result" *outside* the divine being.

The passage suggests that Leibniz was thinking of the existence of created things as being, in the last analysis, a fact *about* the thought, will, and power of God. That thought seems to recur in Leibniz's repeated flirtation with the idea of *defining* existence in terms of "what pleases God" (see Chapter 6, section 2). On this account, our existence, for example, would consist in the fact that the perfections of knowing, willing, and power in God converge in the choice of our world as the best possible. And this idea was certainly in Leibniz's mind in April 1676, when he wrote that a created mind "will be and will subsist by the will of God, that is, of the understanding of the good. For being [*esse*] itself is nothing but being understood to be good" (A VI,iii,512).

Similar implications can be found in yet another paper of April 1676 in which Leibniz says that "Modifications . . . resulting from all [the simple forms], related to individual [simple forms],[29] constitute the variety in them" (A VI,iii,522/L 162). In the same paragraph he also uses the example of the relation of the essence of the number six to its properties to support what appears to be a denial of independent essences to derivative things:

> There is the same variety in any kind of world, and it is nothing but the same essence related in diverse ways, as if you look at the same city from diverse places; or if you relate the essence of six to three, it will be 3 × 2 or 3 + 2 [*sic*],

[28]At A VI,iii,523 Leibniz explicitly identifies "kinds of Things" with "Worlds."

[29]Loemker translates this as "related to individuals," apparently overlooking the feminine, rather than neuter, form of *singulas*, which must therefore refer to *formas* (also feminine) rather than to indefinite entities.

> whereas if [you relate it] to four it will be 6/4 = 3/2 or 6 = (4 × 3/2). Hence it is not strange that things are produced that are in a certain way different. (A VI,iii,523)

The example of a city viewed from different places recurs, of course, in another role in Leibniz's mature writings. It also is found in another text of 1676, in an explicit assertion that all things have the same essence. (The paper is one that contains important work on Leibniz's proof for the possibility of a most perfect being.) Here Leibniz flatly affirms the Spinozistic idea that finite things are only modes.

> That all things are distinguished not as substances but as modes, can easily be demonstrated, from the fact that if things are radically distinct, one of them can be perfectly understood without the other; that is, all the requirements of the one can be understood without all the requirements of the other being understood. But it is not so in things; for since the Ultimate reason of things is unique, which alone contains the aggregate of all requirements of all things, it is manifest that the requirements of all things are the same. And thus the essence is too; on the assumption that the essence is the aggregate of all the first requirements, the essence of all things is therefore the same, and things do not differ except in mode, as a City viewed from the highest place differs from [the city] viewed from a field. If the only things that are really different are those that can be separated, or one of which can be perfectly understood without the other, it follows that nothing is really different from another thing, but all things are one, as Plato also explains in the *Parmenides*. (A VI,iii,573)

Here the "first requirements" of a thing are presumably the simplest, purest attributes occurring in the analysis of the thing.[30] Leibniz is supposing that the conjunction of all the simplest, purest attributes constitutes the essence of God, and apparently also that all such attributes occur in the analysis of the essence of every finite thing.

The argument is not persuasive. The monistic conclusion is built into the implausibly demanding criterion of distinctness that is used as a premise. And why should we grant that "the essence [of each thing] is the aggregate of all [its] first requirements"? For it would seem that different essences could be constructed out of the same fundamental attributes—one essence containing *P*, another containing not-*P*, different essences containing different degrees of *Q*, and so forth. Behind the argument, however, is clearly the idea that we saw in other passages, of derivative things resulting from the relations, or logical interactions, so to

[30]Leibniz's use of the term 'requirement' is discussed in section 1 of this chapter. The paper I have just quoted, however, contains in its next paragraph a somewhat eccentric expression of Leibniz's characteristic fusion of conceptual and causal dependence relations. The conceptual aspect of the requirement relation is indicated, though the causal aspect is not excluded, when Leibniz says, "The aggregate of sufficient requirements is the Essence." The causal role of requirements comes to the fore when he adds, almost immediately, "Requirements seem to indicate a relation to existence, attributes to essence" (A VI,iii, 573). In the latter statement I take 'requirements' and 'attributes' to refer, at least for the most part, to the same properties, viewed in the one case as required for existence, and in the other as defining the nature of the thing. This distinction between requirements and attributes does not seem to have been an enduring feature of Leibniz's thought, and the paragraph in which it is found looks rather experimental.

speak, of all the divine attributes. And this time, ontological externality of the resulting entities seems explicitly rejected.

This is not, I think, a conclusion with which Leibniz was entirely happy, and it was not a stable outcome in his thought. To the statement that "all things are distinguished not as substances but as modes," he added an interlinear qualification by writing in the adverb 'radically' over the word 'substances'. Moreover, one of the other papers from which I have quoted a rather monistic statement concludes with a paragraph that introduces an important pluralizing notion. Beginning with the observation that when a change is perceived, there is a change in the perceiver, Leibniz says:

> And in this way everything is contained in some way in everything. But clearly in another way in God than in Things; and in another way in kinds of Things, or Worlds, than in individuals. Things are made, not by the combination of forms alone, in God, but [by combination] with a subject too. The subject itself, or God, with its ubiquity yields the immense; this immense, combined with other subjects, causes all the possible Modes, or Things in it [*Res in ipso*], to follow. Various results from forms combined with a subject cause particulars to result.

Leibniz is still working with the same model of logical dependence as a basis for ontological dependence or causal generation, for he adds:

> How things result from forms I cannot explain except by the similitude of Numbers [resulting] from unities, but with this difference, that unities are all homogeneous, but forms are different. (A VI,iii,523)

What is new here is the distinction of "subjects." Combined with the single divine subject, the simple forms constitute God; "combined with other subjects," the forms constitute derivative things. This is exactly the way in which most of us would intuitively expect ontological externality to be maintained in a pluralistic metaphysics—though it is strangely combined in this passage with the surviving characterization of derivative things as "Modes, or Things in it," which presumably means things "in" the divine subject.

Was Leibniz's permanent view introduced in this passage, which he dated "April 1676"? Does it mark a decisive and irreversible step toward the conception of finite things as distinct substances? We can hardly see this passage as so decisive if we accept the date of November 1676 which the editors of A VI,iii assign to the paper in which Leibniz flatly asserts that all things have a single essence and are distinguished as modes rather than as substances. But the evidence for the later date in that case is not conclusive, as the editors note.

3.2 Leibniz's Later Views

Clearly there was change in Leibniz's thought on this point in the 1670s. The idea that finite things "are distinguished not as substances but as modes" was definitely rejected by 1678. And whereas on 15 April 1676 he wrote that "God . . . is everything. Creatures are some things" (A VI,iii, 512), he wrote to Eckhard on the 28th of the following April that "it seems to be impossible for there to be a Being that is everything; for it could be said of such a Being that it is you and it is also me, which I think you will not admit" (A II,i,323 = G I,222).[31] Moreover something like the idea of "other subjects" recurs in Leibniz's comments on the text of Spinoza's *Ethics*, which he finally received in 1678. To the third definition of Part I ("By substance I understand that which is in itself and is conceived through itself") Leibniz objects that "on the contrary, it seems rather that there are some things that are in themselves even if they are not conceived through themselves. And that is how people commonly conceive of substances" (G I,139/L 196).[32] The "things" to which Leibniz refers here are obviously derivative or finite things, and in saying that they "are in themselves" he means that they have or are distinct subjects of predication, and thus are distinct substances, even though they are conceived, not through themselves, but through the attributes of God.

But this too may not represent a stable position in Leibniz's thought. We do not find the mature Leibniz grounding the distinctness of substances on a primitive distinctness of subjects as such. Such a grounding might even be inconsistent with his doctrine of the identity of indiscernibles. As in the case of necessity and contingency (see Chapter 1, section 1.4), we must be careful to let Leibniz disagree with Spinoza in his own way, and not to import alien assumptions about how an ontological pluralist would conceive the relation between God and the world.

There is ample evidence that, in traditional theological terms, Leibniz saw God as "immanent" as well as "transcendent" in relation to the world, and that the distinctness of created things was in some ways precarious for him. The *Discourse on Metaphysics* suggests a substantial connection between God and finite things, describing creation as a kind of emanation:[33]

> Now it is . . . very evident that the created substances depend on God, who conserves them and even produces them continually by a kind of emanation, as we produce our thoughts. For as God turns on all sides, so to speak, and in all ways, the general system of phenomena that he finds good to produce to manifest his glory, and regards all the faces of the world in every possible manner, since there is no relation that escapes his omniscience, the result of each view of the universe, as regarded from a certain place, is a substance that expresses the universe in conformity with that view, if God finds it good to render his thought effective and produce that substance. (DM 14)[34]

[31]The context is interesting. Eckhard has offered a proof of the possibility of God's existence strikingly similar to Leibniz's own proof (which, so far as we know, he had not communicated to Eckhard). But Eckhard's proof turns on identifying "the concept of an *Ens perfectissimum*" with "the concept of a Being that does not participate in non-being." Such a being, Leibniz argues, would have to be "everything," because there is nothing it could be said *not* to be. His own account does not have this untoward consequence, because he does not deny that there are negative truths about God. He denies only that any negation is contained in any one of the defining *attributes* of God.

[32]Cf. Leibniz's comment on proposition 14 of part I (G I,145/L 201).

[33]For extensive documentation of Leibniz's use of the vocabulary of emanation, see Robinet, *Architectonique disjonctive*, pp. 431f.; see also p. 438.

[34]Strikingly similar to this text are VE 62/L 185 of 1677 ("When God calculates and exercizes [his] thought, the world is made") and VE 292 = LH IV,1,14C,10. In the latter, however, a substantial form or soul results "from the very fact [*eo ipso*]" that God regards the whole universe as if from a certain body; no mention is made of God rendering his thought effective. This is not the

A similar account of the creation is given in the *Monadology*, although 'fulguration' replaces 'emanation':

> Thus God alone is the Primitive Unity, or the originating simple substance, of which all the created or derivative Monads are productions and are born, so to speak, by continual Fulgurations of the Divinity from moment to moment, limited by the receptivity of the creature, to which it is essential to be limited. (Mon 47)

A particularly important indication of the tendencies of Leibniz's thought on this subject is found in his statement, published in 1698, that if, as Malebranche held, there were no enduring causally efficacious force in things,

> it would follow that no created substance, no soul, remains numerically the same, and so that nothing is conserved by God, and hence that all things are only some evanescent or fleeting modifications and phantasms, so to speak, of the one permanent divine substance. This amounts to the same thing as that doctrine of most evil repute, which a certain subtle and profane writer recently introduced into the world, or revived—that the very nature or substance of all things is God. (G IV,508f./L 502)

The "subtle and profane writer" mentioned here is obviously Spinoza, and Leibniz is saying that their possession of enduring force (closely connected in his mind with form and essence) is all that keeps created substances from being mere modifications of the divine substance, along the lines of Spinoza's theory. This is a dramatic expression of the tenuousness of the creatures' independence from God in the Leibnizian scheme of things. Here Leibniz is not prepared to assert the distinction between God and created substances as a simple, primitive distinction between different subjects of properties. At the same time, it is clear that Leibniz is affirming that created things are substances, and not mere modifications of the divine substance. Their distinctness is traced to a distinction of *powers*.

It is not hard to see how Leibniz might have thought the powers of creatures distinct from God's power. For the powers of creatures have limitations. It is part of Leibniz's theory of forces that limited powers can be modifications of broader, more fundamental powers in the same subject.[35] But it does not follow that such limitations can be present in *God*. Indeed, I take it to be part of Leibniz's conception of the *ens perfectissimum* that no limited perfection can be ascribed to it, because every limited perfection involves some negation of an absolute divine perfection. No doubt it follows that the limited powers of creatures exist in subjects distinct from the divine subject. But the distinction of subjects here is not primitive. Rather, it flows from the distinction of powers, or (more broadly speaking) of forms—as it should, for a proponent of the identity of indiscernibles.[36]

That this is the right basis for distinguishing Leibniz's conception of the relation between God and finite things from Spinoza's is confirmed by a paper

---

only way VE 292 diverges from Leibniz's mature thought. I incline therefore to think it is earlier than DM. Its watermark is attested from 1679 and 1690. Leibniz's views on what God does in conserving creatures are discussed in Chapter 3, section 2.2.

[35]See, e.g., G II,270/L 537. This is a main topic of Chapter 13 of this volume.

[36]This point is analogous to a point I will make in Chapter 11, section 3: Leibniz reveals in this text that for him it is form rather than matter that is crucial for realism in physics.

titled "On the Abstract and the Concrete" from about 1688 (VE 1603 = LH IV,7C,99–100).[37] The relevant passage begins with an attempt to define the notion of "being in [*inesse*] a subject" in terms of the notion of requirement, apparently in the sense discussed in section 1 of this chapter.

> And therefore what *is in* a subject appears to be that whose reality is part of the reality of the subject itself. Or, to speak in a way more suited for forming and demonstrating propositions, *A is in B* if every thing that is immediately required for *A* is also immediately required for *B*. What is immediately required for something, however, in such a way that nothing further is immediately, nor even mediately, required for it, can be called [its] *reality*.

This suggests to Leibniz a form of the problem that we have been discussing: "But since all the reality of creatures is in God, it seems to follow from this that all creatures are in God." The point, presumably, is that, given Leibniz's belief that the "requirements" of creatures are the divine attributes, from which, ultimately, all the attributes of other things are composed, it follows from the definitions given here that the divine attributes are the "reality" of creatures, and the creatures "are in" God—which seems at least close to a Spinozistic conclusion. "But we must reply," Leibniz goes on, "that the reality of creatures is not that very reality that in God is absolute, but a limited reality, for that is of the essence of a creature." Here the thought seems very clear that the limited and the absolute or unlimited reality are different, indeed incompatible, attributes and hence are not present in the same subject, so that the creatures are not "in" God after all.

A little further on a worry seems to occur to Leibniz. "But it still seems undeniable that . . . the absolute reality is immediately required for the limited"—no doubt because the limited attributes are in some way constructed from the unlimited. This leads Leibniz to replace requirements with "constituents" in the definition of "being in."

> Therefore it seems the definition should be corrected, namely, so that we say that *A is in B*, a thing in[38] a different thing, if all the constituents of *A* itself are constituents of *B* itself.

Unfortunately the definition he then offers of "constituents" does not make very clear the difference between constituents and requirements.

> But I understand constituents to be those things that in principle [*ex instituto*] make a thing, in such a way, namely, that when they are posited the thing is posited, and that this is assumed as a principle. The constituents of a constituent are constituents of the [thing] constituted.

Unclear as this is, the most plausible reading of the passage as a whole is surely one according to which, first, creatures are not "in" God because their limited attributes cannot be "in" God and, second, some "requirements" of creatures

[37]All quotations from here to the end of the present chapter are from this source. The watermark of the document is attested from the last three months of 1688, and the paper seems related to another whose watermark has the same attestation and which cannot have been written before 1685 because it cites a book published in that year (VE 1607).

[38]Reading "in" for VE's "im."

(particularly the absolute attributes of God) are not "constituents" of creatures because they are not attributes of creatures (though attributes of creatures are constructed from them by limitation) and they are not "in" creatures.

We are left, I think, with the following answer to the question whether Leibniz's conception of God as *ens perfectissimum* has, inescapably, Spinozistic implications: it does not. The relation of the limited attributes of creatures to the absolute attributes of God is not the relation of mode to attribute, since they exclude each other from any one subject, by virtue of the negation involved in the creaturely attributes.[39]

[39]In this chapter, in addition to sources cited above, I have been helped by Schneiders, "Deus Subjectum."

5

The Ontological Argument

During the later 1670s Leibniz was intensely engaged with the Cartesian version of the ontological argument. He developed a standard line on the subject that recurs in various places in his writings from then on. It has three main points. (1) The Cartesian argument is incomplete. It does show that *if* God's existence is possible, then God exists; but it assumes without proof that God's existence is possible, which can be doubted.[1] (2) The existence of God should be *presumed* possible unless it is proved impossible. This presumption, together with the Cartesian proof, provides a justification of theistic belief, though it falls far short of demonstration.[2] But (3) the demonstration can be completed: it can be proved that God's existence is possible.[3] When Leibniz offers an a priori proof in support of his third claim, he touches on fascinating and difficult issues about existence that go right to the heart of the logical structure of his philosophy. The first claim will be discussed in this chapter; the third claim will be discussed in this chapter and the next; the second claim will be discussed in Chapter 8.

[1]A II,i,250/L 165f. (28 December 1675); A VI,iii,510f. (15 April 1676); A VI,iii,579/L 168 (November 1676); A II,i,300,306,325,383f. (1676,1677); A II,i,312,401 = G I,213,198 (1677, 1678); A II,i,436 = G IV,294 (1678); A II,i,478/L 211 (22 June 1679); A II,i,529 (1682); G VII,294/ L 231 (1683–86); G IV,424/L 292f. (1684); A II,i,545f. (1685); VE 47 = LH I,20,160 (1678–85?); DM 23 (1686); G IV,358f./L 386 (1692); G VII,310; A VI,vi,8 = G V,18 (1695?–97); G IV,401ff.,405 (1700–1701); NE 437f. (1704); G VII,490 (1710). (In some of these texts Descartes is not mentioned, but the argument, which Leibniz did not regard as peculiarly or originally Cartesian, is clearly in view.) In 1671 Leibniz did not yet give this objection, but a quite different one, to the Cartesian argument (A VI,ii,306). In "*De Vita Beata*" of 1676, he presents the Cartesian argument without any criticism (A VI,iii,642), the probable explanation being that the work is a pastiche of Cartesian views rather than a development of Leibniz's own thought.

[2]A II,i,312f. = G I,213f. (5 April 1677); A II,i,388 = G I,188 (3 January 1678); A II,i,436 = G IV,294 (1678); G IV,404,405 (1700–1701); G III,444 (20 November 1702); NE 438 (1704); G VII,490 (1710); also in a memorandum, probably of 1677–78, published in pp. 286f. of Janke, "Das ontologische Argument." Janke's paper is one of the most important on this subject, and I am much indebted to it. It should be noted, however, that, unlike its appendix III, which I have just cited, its appendices I and II have appeared in the Academy edition, in A VI,iii,571–73 and A II,i,391–93, respectively (the latter unaccountably overlooked by Janke).

[3]A II,i,433–38/AG 235–40 (1678); G IV,401–4,405f. (1700–1701); and NE 437f. (1703–5) are noteworthy for containing all three of the main points. Except for the first of them, however, they do not support the third point with an a priori proof of possibility. That is attempted most fully in texts from 1676 (A VI,iii,395f., 571–79/L 167f.), and with almost cryptic brevity in Gr 325 (mid-1680s) and in the *Monadology* of 1714 (§ 45). Writing to Eckhard, 28 April 1677, Leibniz says he thinks the possibility can be proved, but adds, "no one has done it yet" (A II,i,324 = G

1. The Incomplete Proof

That the possibility of God's existence can be doubted and that it must be either an assumption or a premise of any a priori theistic proof are truths so familiar in contemporary philosophical theology as to call for little comment here. Even in the seventeenth century Leibniz's objection to the Cartesian argument was hardly original. It had been presented to Descartes, in the Second Objections to the *Meditations*, and Descartes had given a reply.[4] Whether his reply was adequate is more properly a question for Cartesian than for Leibnizian studies. What deserves discussion here is the question, On what grounds did Leibniz believe that the ontological argument shows that if a necessary being is possible, it actually exists?

He wrote an elaborate and illuminating proof of this thesis, dated January 1678. This document was probably connected with the extensive discussion about the Cartesian ontological argument that he carried on, both orally and by letter, beginning in 1677, with Arnold Eckhard.[5] I will quote extensively from it, as I believe there is no published English translation.

> *Proof of the existence of God from his essence*
>
> (1) The possible existence or Possibility of any thing and the essence of that same thing are inseparable (that is, if one of them is given in the region of ideas or truths or realities, the other is also given there. That is, if the truth of one of them exists so does the truth of the other; for the truths exist even if the things do not exist and are not thought of by anyone. . . .)
>
> *Therefore by subsumption*
>
> (2) The possible existence or possibility of God and the essence of God are inseparable (for the essence of a thing is the specific reason of its possibility),
>
> *but*
>
> (3) The essence of God and his actual existence are inseparable.
>
> *Therefore in conclusion*
>
> (4) The possible existence or Possibility of God and his actual existence are inseparable,

I,224)—which may not be inconsistent with his thinking that he himself had an unpublished proof of it. In another letter of 1677 he says that the possibility cannot be proved on Cartesian principles but can be proved by the method of "analyses continued to the end" which will lead to the rational language or "characteristic" projected by Leibniz (A II,i, 383f.). See also A II,i,401 = G I,198.

[4]AT VII,127,149–51. Leibniz must have known of this and been unsatisfied with Descartes's reply. He criticizes a related passage of the Second Replies (AT VII,139) in presenting his objection in a draft of a letter to Malebranche in June of 1679 (A II,i,476f. = G I,338f.).

[5]The connection is suggested in a letter of 3 January 1678 to Hermann Conring, in which Leibniz clearly alludes to his discussions with Eckhard (whom he identifies only as "a professor from a neighboring Academy, a Cartesian") and claims to have discovered a demonstration "that God necessarily exists, given only that it is possible that he exists" (A II,i,388 = G I,188). In A II,i,390 the editors suggest that Leibniz prepared this proof for Henning Huthman, but the only evidence they cite for this hypothesis is a letter of the same month, to Leibniz, in which Huthman objects to an "argument recently proposed" on the ground "that I can prove that Existence cannot be deduced from any concept of Essence" (A II,i,389). Given this opinion, Huthman can hardly be the Cartesian that Leibniz mentions to Conring.

or, what is the same,

(5) On the assumption that God is possible it follows that God actually exists (A II,i,390).[6]

Step (4) follows from steps (2) and (3) by the transitivity of the inseparability relation. Step (2) follows from step (1) by instantiation and is justified on the ground that "the essence of a thing is the specific reason of its possibility,"[7] so that there is an essence of a thing if and only if the existence of the thing is possible.[8] These steps must be admitted if we are to allow Leibniz to mean what he says he means by 'inseparable', and what he must mean by 'essence'. I believe that step (5) also follows from step (4), given Leibniz's stated conception of inseparability, but there is a doubt to be overcome there that I will discuss presently. Step (3) remains as the one Leibniz rightly regards as most in need of further justification.

He offers two proofs of it. The first is an argument, along Cartesian lines, from God's supreme perfection. Commenting, however, that "this reasoning can be abbreviated at this point and the mention of perfection can be eliminated from it," he proceeds to offer a second proof in which God is simply defined as a necessary being. Leibniz recommends this streamlining of the argument elsewhere, too.[9] Indeed, it is another persistent feature of his critique of the Cartesian proof, although consideration of the divine perfection certainly remained important to his thought about the necessity of God's existence. The simplification eliminates (for the time being, at any rate) possible grounds of objection pertaining to ideas about perfection. It also throws into higher relief the most solid part of Leibniz's modal version of the ontological argument. It distinguishes Leibniz's treatment of the argument not only from Descartes's, but also from those found in Anselm, for whom the argument is first and foremost about divine perfection.

The conclusion of this part of the argument is, in effect, that if the existence of a necessary God, the God of what the Germans call "ontotheology," is so much as possible, then such a deity actually (and also, of course, necessarily) exists. Recent work on the subject has established, I think, that this conclusion is correct.[10] It is worthwhile, however, to try to understand whether and how

[6]In quoting from this document I omit some marginal additions and some cross-references to other parts of it.

[7]Leibniz says this also at A VI,iii,583; cf. VE 47.

[8]Discussing the ontological argument in a letter of 1685, Leibniz says, "For there being an essence of a thing is the same as the thing being possible" (A II,i,545). For a casual endorsement of this equivalence, see G VII,294.

[9]A II,i,312 = G I,212f. (5 April 1677, a memorandum of Leibniz's first conversation with Eckhard); A II,i,323f. = G I,223 (28 April 1677); G IV,359,402,405f. (1692, 1700–1701). An even more abbreviated form of the argument is given in the first two sentences of a piece (assigned by the Academy editors to late 1676 or 1677) headed "*Definition of God or the Being-of-itself*": "God is a being whose existence follows from its possibility (or essence). If then God, defined in this way, is possible, it follows that he exists" (A VI,iii,582). A particularly elegant short form of the argument is given in a letter of 1710: "If a Being, from whose essence existence follows is possible (or if it has an essence), it exists (this is an identical or indemonstrable axiom). God is a Being from whose Essence existence follows (this is a definition): Therefore if God is possible, he exists. Q.E.D." (G VII,490).

[10]See Hartshorne, *Logic of Perfection*, pp. 50f.; R. Adams "Logical Structure of Anselm's Arguments"; and Plantinga, *Nature of Necessity*, ch. 10.

Leibniz succeeded in establishing it. Here is the conclusion of his argument, beginning with his second proof[11] of step (3):

> [6] The essence of God involves necessity of existence (for by the name of God we understand a necessary Being).
>
> [7] If the essence of anything involves necessity of existence, its essence is inseparable from existence (for otherwise it is a merely possible or contingent thing).
>
> *Therefore*
>
> The essence and existence of God are inseparable.
>
> Finally therefore we have concluded that
>
> If God is possible, he actually exists, and therefore it need only be proved that a most perfect Being [*Ens perfectissimum*], or at any rate a necessary Being, is possible. (A II,i,391)[12]

The pivot of Leibniz's reasoning here is his conception of *essence*. In an annotation to this proof, he makes clear that for him a necessary being is one "whose existence necessarily follows, or is inseparable, from its very essence" (A II,i,392).[13] He avoids a circular version of the ontological argument in which God's existence is illegitimately presupposed:

> In saying that the Essence of God involves existence, it must not be understood as meaning that, if God exists, he necessarily exists, but in this way, as meaning that on the part of the thing [*a parte rei*], even if no one thinks about it, it is unconditionally, absolutely and purely true in that region of essences or ideas that the essence and existence of God are inseparably connected. (A II,i,392)[14]

Leibniz thinks of an essence as a quasi-logical structure that grounds truths that need not be hypothetical, or conditional on the existence of something exemplifying the essence. This is implicit in the explanation that "the essence of a thing is the specific reason [*ratio*] of its possibility," which surely means that the essence is a quasi-logical structure that grounds the (unconditional) *truth* that the existence of the thing is possible.[15] Likewise, an essence that involves (necessary) existence is a quasi-logical structure that grounds the (unconditional) truth that the thing (necessarily) exists. Such an essence is "inseparable" from the existence of the thing in a sense indicated by Leibniz's initial explanation of inseparability: the essence cannot be "given in the region of ideas or truths" unless

[11]The first proof, which Leibniz himself says is superfluous, will receive some critical attention in Chapter 6, section 1.

[12]I have renumbered steps to avoid confusion with previous steps.

[13]Cf. A II,i,391, and a text published by Janke in "Das ontologische Argument," p. 286. Leibniz gave a similar definition in 1701: "God is a Being-from-itself or primitive *Ens a se*; that is to say, one that exists by its essence" (G IV,405). And in comments written in 1685 or later, he thinks "Being [*Ens*] whose essence involves existence" is "more accurate" than "Being that suffices for itself alone" as a definition of "cause of itself [*causa sui*]" (VE 2189 = LH IV,3,6,1).

[14]Leibniz also charged that Spinoza was guilty of the sort of circular argument he mentions (A II,i,393).

[15]Similarly, Leibniz would say more than twenty years later (in 1701), "the essence of the thing is nothing but that which makes its possibility in particular." Therefore, he would go on to say, "it is quite evident that [for a thing] to exist by its essence is to exist by its possibility" (G IV,406).

the truth that follows from it, that the thing exists, is given too. For a supposed essence that implied the existence of something that did not exist would imply something false, and would thus be defective as an essence. It is clear that nothing that is defective in this way counts as an essence for Leibniz.

There are therefore only two alternatives for Leibniz. Either (A) there is an essence of a necessary God, or (B) there is not. (A) If there is, it must involve necessary existence, and so must ground the truth that a necessary God (necessarily) exists—and that must indeed be a truth. In this case, therefore, God exists, and exists necessarily. Conversely, (B) if it is not a truth that a necessary God exists, then there is no essence that grounds such a truth—or in other words, no divine essence involving necessary existence. That is, there is in this case no essence of a necessary God. But if there is no essence of a necessary God, the existence of such a being is not possible. Leibniz describes this alternative as one in which "the necessary being is an impossible fiction [*figmentum*}" (A II,i,392f.). For according to the plausible assumption that seems to underlie steps (1) and (2) of Leibniz's argument, the possibility of any thing's existence must be grounded in a quasi-logical structure that constitutes a consistent, nondefective essence. In short, if (A) there is an essence of a necessary God, it follows that such a being necessarily, and hence actually, exists; on the other hand, if (B) there is no essence of a necessary God, then the existence of such a being is not even possible. Q.E.D.

I will discuss two possible objections to Leibniz's reasoning. Our first objector may grant that the essence, and therefore the possibility, of a necessary God are inseparable from existence, or even from necessary existence, "in the region of ideas or truths or realities," but will deny that anything about the *actual* existence of such a being therefore follows from its mere possibility. The transition from step (4) to step (5) in Leibniz's proof, it will be claimed, is an instance of the illegitimate inference "from concepts to reality" that many philosophers have seen in the ontological argument. Elsewhere I have criticized this type of objection to the ontological argument.[16] Here it suffices to observe that the objector's metaphysical views fit neatly within one of the alternatives admitted at this stage of Leibniz's argument. For if no essence can ground the actual existence of a thing, then there is no essence that involves (necessary) existence in Leibniz's sense, and therefore no essence of a necessary God, and no possibility of such a being.

A second objector might charge that Leibniz has overlooked an alternative in assuming that if there is no essence of a necessary God, then there is no possibility of such a being's existence. The new suggestion is that even if there is in fact no essence from which the necessary (and therefore actual) existence of a God follows, perhaps there could have been such an essence. The relevance of this objection is undeniable. It proposes a way in which it could allegedly be possible for God's existence to be necessary even if it is in fact neither necessary nor actual. In terms of modern modal logic the objector questions the following principles:

[16]R. Adams, "Divine Necessity." My target in that earlier paper is actually an objection to the idea of a being whose existence is necessary, or follows from its essence, rather than to the ontological argument as such; but the metaphysical issues raised by the objection are the same.

(8) If it is not necessary that *p*, then it is not possible for it to be necessary that *p*.

(9) If it is not actually the case that *p*, then it is not possible for it to be necessary that *p*.

The recently developed proofs of the thesis that the existence of a necessary God is actual if it is even possible, to which I have alluded, all depend on one or the other of these principles, which are characteristic axioms of widely discussed systems of modal logic. They are not uncontroversial, though I do not see any compelling reason to doubt their correctness as applied to the issue of necessary divine existence. The question to be considered here, however, is, How well grounded is Leibniz's commitment to them?

I have argued in Chapter 1, section 3, that principle (8) is not valid on the demonstrability conception of necessity connected with Leibniz's infinite analysis theory of contingency. Principle (9) is also invalid on that conception, for similar reasons. I think it is clear, however, that the conceptions of possibility and necessity connected with the theory of infinite analysis are not the conceptions employed in Leibniz's discussions of the necessary existence of God. There the relevant modal conceptions are those indicated by the theory of essences that figures in these discussions, and they are much closer to those involved in Leibniz's other main theory of contingency—the theory that insists that whatever has "some essence" is "possible in its own nature" (Gr 289f.) and that distinguishes what is "necessary through itself" from what is necessary only on account of its relation to something else.[17] The latter distinction is certainly not alien to Leibniz's discussions of the ontological argument, for the divine existence is supposed to be necessary through itself, with a necessity that is internal to the divine essence. Commenting in 1676 on Spinoza's definition of substance, Leibniz equates "that which is its own reason for existing" with "that, all of whose requirements we conceive without the concept of another thing" (A VI,iii,275 = G I,131).[18] A necessary being is one that has in its essence a reason for its existence that does not involve the essence (or the action) of another being.

Here, however, we are not so much concerned with the distinction between the two types of necessity as with the grounds of possibility. In the theory of essences possibility appears as something positive rather than negative. It is not just the absence of impossibility. As positive, it requires a ground or reason, which will be a quasi-logical structure, as I have called it, and indeed an essence or system of essences. In this context, what would it mean to say that there could

[17]See Chapter 1, section 1.2.

[18]This is not a point on which Leibniz disagrees with Spinoza. Spinoza has a distinction between what is necessary through itself (or through its own essence) and what is necessary only on account of its relation to something else, and needs the distinction in order to obtain a sense in which God (substance) is a necessary being and modes are not. In 1676 Leibniz copied out a passage in which Spinoza makes this distinction, and Leibniz's brief comment—"This [presumably what Spinoza ascribes to modes] is just what is commonly called contingent"—suggests that he got the point. In G I,147f./L 202f., from about 1678, however, it is not clear to me that Leibniz understood Spinoza on this point—though the text does confirm that Leibniz himself understood an essence's involving existence as constituting internal as distinct from external necessity.

have been an essence, or a possibility, that there isn't? To say that there could have been is to say there is a possibility, which must have its "specific reason." And what is to keep that specific reason, or something implied by it, from being the essence that supposedly there isn't? These assumptions about the grounding of possibilities can be doubted, of course, but they seem plausible enough. I conclude that Leibniz reasonably employs in this context principles that imply (8) and (9), and that this first stage of his argument about necessary divine existence is well supported.

2. *Proof of Possibility*

To complete his version of the ontological argument Leibniz offers two types of proof for the possibility of a necessary God. The one used in his writings in the 1690s and the first years of the next century[19] is derived from a cosmological argument. Leibniz claims that if the existence of contingent beings is possible (as is obvious since they actually exist), the existence of a necessary God must also be possible, since it is only through the action of such a deity that the existence of contingent things could be explained in accordance with the Principle of Sufficient Reason. On the "oblique approach" [*biais*] that Leibniz advocates, according to which it establishes the conditional, but very important, modal conclusion that "if the necessary Being is possible, it exists," the ontological argument

> appears to have some solidity, and those who will have it that from notions, ideas, definitions, or possible essences alone one can never infer actual existence fall back into . . . denying the possibility of the Being-from-itself. But note well, this oblique approach itself serves to make known that they are wrong, and ultimately fills the hole in the demonstration. For if the *Being-from-itself* is impossible, all the beings-by-another are too, for they are, ultimately, only by the *Being-from-itself*; thus nothing would be able to exist. This reasoning leads us to another important modal proposition, equal to the previous one, which together with it completes the demonstration. It can be expressed thus: *if the necessary Being is not, there is no possible Being*. It seems that this demonstration had not been carried so far until now; however, I have also labored elsewhere to prove that the perfect Being is possible. (G IV,406)

Even if successful, this argument does not yield everything that Leibniz wanted, as I take to be hinted in the last sentence of the quoted passage. Because

[19]The argument is explicit at G III,450 (1702) as well as at G IV,406 (1701). Notice of the gap in the Cartesian argument elicits an appeal to a proof from effects (G IV,404, about 1700), or "from the fact that contingent things exist" (G IV,359/L 386, about 1692); but these passages are not clear about the modal structure of the strategy. Cf. G VII,302–8/L 486–91; VE 1909 = LH IV,6,9,6. A similar argument for the possibility of an "absolutely necessary Being" is found in a marginal addition to a text of 11 February 1676 (A VI,iii, 472). And in a marginal addition to a text of 1678 (discussed at length in section 1 of this chapter), Leibniz employed a slightly different strategy, arguing that the Principle of Sufficient Reason cannot be maintained unless it is granted that a necessary being is (actual and therefore) possible; for "otherwise all things would be contingent" and would have no sufficient reason (A II,i,390). These marginal additions may of course be later than the texts to which they are attached.

the conception of a comprehensively and supremely perfect Being plays no essential part in it, it needs supplementation, as Leibniz remarked, if it is to "prove that the necessary Being must have all perfections" (G III,450). Furthermore, and probably more decisively for Leibniz, the argument from the possibility of contingent beings is a demonstration "*a posteriori*—that is to say, from the effects" (G IV,404).[20] As such, it does not give direct insight into the possibility of a necessary God or explain how or why such a being is possible. Therefore Leibniz still aspires, in this context, to complete "the demonstration *a priori*" (G IV,404).

Leibniz's principal attempts at a more direct, a priori, proof of the possibility of necessary divine existence all appear to be of a single type, and they do begin with the conception of a being that possesses all perfections. The line of argument receives its fullest development in papers dating from the year 1676 (A VI,iii,395f.,571–79), and is later sketched, with approval, in 1678 in a letter to the Princess Elizabeth (A II,i,437f./AG 240). Something like it appears to be endorsed in a paper (Gr 325) from the mid-1680s,[21] and again in 1714, near the end of Leibniz's life (Mon 45). In laying out the argument I shall follow the best known and most finished version of it, which Leibniz says he showed to Spinoza in November of 1676, obtaining the latter's opinion that it was "solid" (A VI,iii, 578f./L 167f.). I shall quote roughly in order, but only in fragments as needed for my exposition, since text and English translation are widely available, and I shall draw supplementary material from other versions in Leibniz's papers.

2.1 *The First Stage of the Proof*

The first step of the argument appears to be a definition of 'perfection':

> (1) "A *perfection* is what I call every simple quality that is positive and absolute, or [*seu* = that is] that expresses without any limits whatever it expresses."

A *simple* quality here is one that is unanalyzable; this will shortly become explicit. A *positive* quality is not the negation of another quality. The most durable feature of Leibniz's conception of perfections is that they involve no negation at all. I take the last clause of the definition to indicate that an *absolute* quality is not a limited degree of any quality, and indeed involves no limitation at all; this interpretation is justified, and amplified, in Chapter 4, section 1.

All perfections are unanalyzable.

> (2) "But a quality of this sort, since it is simple, is therefore unanalyzable, or indefinable . . ."

[20]This argument is a posteriori in both of the senses in which that term may be interpreted in Leibniz (see the appendix to Chapter 3). That is, (1) it proceeds from the effect to the cause (and therefore does not *explain* the truth that it purports to prove), and (2) it has an empirical premise (that contingent beings exist, from which the possibility of their existence is inferred). The first, and older, of these senses is undoubtedly the more important in this context.

[21]Its watermark is attested from 1685; see VE 1251.

Here Leibniz offers a disjunction of reasons to show that this follows from the definition of a perfection.

> [F]or otherwise either it will not be one simple quality but an aggregate of several; or if it is one, it will be circumscribed by limits, and to that extent it will be understood through negations of further progress, contrary to the hypothesis, for it was assumed to be purely positive.

We may wonder why the disjunction is needed, since he has defined perfections as simple, which seems to mean unanalyzable. Leibniz appears to be thinking of analyzable properties as having two possible basic types of construction. Analyzable properties of the first type are conjunctions or (as Leibniz puts it here) "aggregates" of properties. Being *A* is a property of this type if it is analyzable as being *B and* C. This is the type of construction that Leibniz takes to be ruled out by simplicity: a simple quality is not a conjunction of still simpler ones. Analyzable properties of the second type are not *conjunctions* of simpler properties but are in some way *negative*. Some philosophers would say that a property formed by negation of another property is therefore not simple, but Leibniz does not use that argument here to establish that negative properties are not perfections, choosing rather to appeal to the fact that he has defined perfections as positive.

At this point Leibniz announces one of the main conclusions he will try to prove:

(3) "From these [considerations] it is not difficult to show that all *perfections are compatible with each other*; that is, they can be in the same subject."

He proceeds, not exactly by indirect proof, but by proposing for refutation a putative counterexample to the thesis announced in step (3).

(4) "For suppose a proposition of this sort: *A and B are incompatible* (understanding by *A* and *B* two simple forms of this sort, or perfections . . .)."

Leibniz adds, without argument, that "it is the same if more [than two] are assumed at the same time." 'Incompatible' is a modal term; '*A* and *B* are incompatible' means the same as 'It is necessary that *A* and *B* are not in the same subject'.

He then begins a lemma with the following premise:

(5) "It is evident that [the proposition proposed as an example in step (4)] cannot be demonstrated without analysis of the terms *A* or *B*, either or both."

He gives a rather obscure reason for the claim: "for otherwise their nature would not enter into the reasoning, and the incompatibility could just as well be demonstrated about any other things as about them." I interpret this as a cryptic abbreviation of the following argument.

Assume that if a proposition is demonstrated, it must be by virtue of some feature of the logical form of the proposition. Assume further that if the demonstration is based on some aspect of logical form internal to a term of the proposition, it must depend on an analysis of the term. Hence, if '*A* and *B* are incompatible' can be demonstrated without any analysis of *A* or *B*, the demonstration must follow from the logical form that the proposition has apart from any form that is internal to the terms. Apart from any logical form that is internal to the terms, however, the logical form of the proposition would not be affected by the substitution of any other distinct terms for *A* and *B*. So if '*A* and *B* are incompatible' could be demonstrated without analysis of *A* or *B*, this demonstration would follow from a logical form that the proposition shares with '*C* and *D* are incompatible', and a similar demonstration could be given for the latter proposition. Thus it could be proved that *all* qualities are incompatible. Since that result would be absurd, we must conclude that '*A* and *B* are incompatible' cannot be demonstrated without analysis of *A* or *B*.

The rest of this lemma is easy.

> (6) "But [*A* and *B*] are unanalyzable [*ex hypothesi*]."

For they are perfections [as assumed in step (4)], and all perfections are unanalyzable [by step (2)].

> (7) "Therefore this proposition cannot be demonstrated about them."

That is, it follows from steps (5) and (6) that '*A* and *B* are incompatible' cannot be demonstrated.

The next sentence of the proof contains another whole lemma: "It could certainly be demonstrated about them, however, if it were true, since it is not known through itself, but all propositions that are necessarily true are either demonstrable or known through themselves." I will separate and reorder the three steps of this subproof.

> (8) "All propositions that are necessarily true are either demonstrable or known through themselves."

Here I think Leibniz's terminology is somewhat misleading. He appears to tie a logical or metaphysical modality ("necessarily true") to epistemological criteria ("demonstrable or known through themselves"). In fact (as I have argued in Chapter 1, section 2.2) demonstrability, for Leibniz, is a structural feature of propositions and is not relative to the capacities or opportunities of a knower. When Leibniz wrote this, moreover, he probably had not yet developed his theory of infinite analysis, according to which features of an essence that could be elicited only by an infinite analysis are not demonstrable. This restriction must be disregarded here, in accordance with what I said earlier in section 1 of this chapter about the modalities relevant to Leibniz's version of the ontological argument. In other words, I do not take Leibniz to be claiming here that any conceptual incompatibility must be discoverable by a finite analysis, if analysis is needed at all. To leave open a chance that the concept of God may contain an inconsistency, though one that could be discovered only by something more than finite analysis, is to abandon Leibniz's project, since genuine essences cannot contain even that sort of inconsistency.

Similarly 'known through themselves' [*per se nota*] must be understood here as meaning 'know*able* through themselves', in principle, whether or not we in fact know them in that or any other way. Leibniz expresses himself more clearly in another version of this proof, where he says that if the proposition in question is necessary, then it will be "either *identical* or demonstrable" (A VI,iii,572, italics added). A necessarily true proposition, for Leibniz, is one that is either identical or can be reduced to identities by a logical process that counts as a demonstration. This can be true of a proposition even if no human being has ever so much as thought of it.

This understanding of 'known through itself' is crucial for the other premise of this lemma, which Leibniz simply asserts, without proof.

> (9) The proposition, '*A* and *B* are incompatible', "is not known through itself."

Of all the steps in the whole argument, we might initially think this one the most in need of proof. For if some simple, purely positive qualities are incompatible (which is the hypothesis Leibniz is trying to refute), their incompatibility is presumably a primitive, indemonstrable necessity. Leibniz's confidence in this premise is based on his conviction that all primitive, indemonstrable necessities must be identities. That is, they must have such a form as '$A = A$', or perhaps '*A* is not non-*A*', or 'What has *A* and *B* has *A*'. And where *A* and *B* are distinct perfections, '*A* and *B* are incompatible' does not have such a form, nor does the underlying non-modal proposition, '*A* and *B* are not in the same subject', which it declares to be necessary. This reasoning is more explicit in the other version I have mentioned of the argument, where 'identical' takes the place of 'known through itself'. There he says:

> This proposition, 'Quality *A* and quality *B* cannot be in the same subject', . . . cannot be identical, for then 'Where *A* is, *B* cannot be' would be the same as '*A* is *A*' or '*A* is [not][22] *B*', and so one would express the exclusion of the other, and so one of them would be the negative of the other, which is contrary to the hypothesis, for we assumed that they are all affirmative. (A VI,iii,572)

In other words, '*A* and *B* are incompatible' cannot be primitively, indemonstrably necessary. For if it were, it would have to be an identity, which it cannot be unless $A = \text{not-}B$ or $B = \text{not-}A$. But that is impossible [by steps (1) and (4)], since *A* and *B*, as perfections, are purely positive.

At this point we can see (as I promised in Chapter 4, section 2) that Leibniz's argument need not depend on the simplicity of the perfections. Their purely positive character is sufficient for it. Even if the perfections were analyzable,

[22]Leibniz wrote '*A* is *B*', but that is the opposite of the sense required here; so I assume "not" was inadvertently omitted.

'*A* and *B* are incompatible' could not be demonstrable, according to Leibniz, unless it were reducible to an identity. That could not be unless the analysis of *A* or *B* contained the negation of a property contained in the analysis of the other. And that cannot be if *A* and *B* are purely positive.

Leibniz saw this point, and made it himself in one of his 1676 versions of the proof, saying that the possibility of a most perfect Being

> will be clear if I show that all (positive) attributes are compatible with each other. But attributes are either analyzable or unanalyzable. If they are analyzable, they will be the aggregate of those into which they are analyzed. Therefore it would be enough to have shown the compatibility of all the first, or unanalyzable, attributes, that is, those which are conceived through themselves. For if individual [attributes] are thus compatible, pluralities will be too, and therefore also composites. (A VI,iii,572)

In other words, if all simple positive attributes are compatible with each other, then even if some of the divine perfections are not simple, they will still be compatible with each other as long as the simple attributes of which they are composed are all positive (as they must be if the perfections are purely positive).

Moreover, in what may be Leibniz's earliest version of the possibility proof, dated 22 March 1676, he does not mention simplicity but speaks only of "affirmative attributes . . . absolute, pure, and unlimited," which are neither "modified by limits" nor "in [any] way negative" (A VI,iii,395f.). In a related study four days earlier he had written, "A perfection is an absolute affirmative attribute" (A VI,iii,392). Again in his last, brief version of the proof, in the *Monadology* (1714), only the positiveness of the divine attributes is mentioned: "nothing can prevent the possibility of that which includes no limits, no negation, and consequently no contradiction" (Mon 45). As the *Monadology* was the only work of Leibniz containing the proof that was generally accessible in the eighteenth century, it is not surprising that his successors, Christian Wolff and Alexander Gottlieb Baumgarten, give a version of the proof that relies exclusively on the positiveness of the perfections.[23]

From steps (8) and (9) Leibniz infers that

(10) The proposition '*A* and *B* are incompatible' "could . . . be demonstrated if it were true."

This inference requires a suppressed premise, however, applying what step (8) says about necessary truths, as such, to the case under discussion. Leibniz is assuming that

(8a) If '*A* and *B* are incompatible' is true (at all), it is necessarily true.

Since '*A* and *B* are incompatible' is equivalent, as I have noted, to 'It is necessary that *A* and *B* are not in the same subject', (8a) follows from the modal axiom,

[23] Wolff, *Theologiae Naturalis Pars II*, pp. 1–18, esp. 9f. (paragraphs 1–28, esp. 13); Baumgarten, *Metaphysica*, pp. 330–32 (paragraphs 803–11, esp. 808–9).

'If it is necessary that *p*, then it is necessary that it is necessary that *p*', which seems acceptable in relation to any conception of necessity that Leibniz would be likely to be using here.[24] From (8) and (8a) it evidently follows that what (8) says about "all propositions that are necessarily true" is true about '*A* and *B* are incompatible' if the latter is true at all. That is, from (8) and (8a) it follows that

> (8b) If '*A* and *B* are incompatible' is true, it is either demonstrable or known through itself (that is, an identical proposition).

Now from (8b) and (9), which says that '*A* and *B* are incompatible' is not known through itself (or an identical proposition), step (10) follows straightforwardly by *modus tollens*.

By another *modus tollens* Leibniz infers from steps (7) and (10) that since '*A* and *B* are incompatible' is not demonstrable, it is not true.

> (11) "Therefore this proposition is not . . . true;[25] that is, it is not necessary that *A* and *B* are not in the same subject."

In other words, *A* and *B* are compatible. "And since the reasoning is the same about any other qualities of this sort that may be assumed," Leibniz adds:

> (12) "Therefore all perfections are compatible."

This is the conclusion that was announced in step (3).

Strictly speaking, since the reasoning was carried through with a pair of perfections, the most that could have been proved is that all *pairs* of perfections are mutually compatible. And that indeed has been proved, if the argument is good to this point, for, as Leibniz says, nothing in the reasoning has depended on *which* perfections *A* and *B* are. But more argument is needed to get us to the conclusion asserted in (12). Leibniz claimed at step (4) that "it is the same if more [than two] are assumed at the same time," but he offered no argument for the claim. He could plausibly argue that nothing in steps (5) to (11) depended on the number of perfections in the example, and therefore that the conclusion, if justified for two, is justified for any number of perfections. That seems fair enough, as long as we are talking about a *finite* number of perfections, but arguments that work for any finite number of terms do not necessarily work for an infinite number of terms. And no reason has been given here for thinking the perfections finite in

[24] I have argued in Chapter 1, section 3 that a conception of necessity in terms of demonstrability (understood broadly enough for identities to be counted as demonstrable) supports this axiom. Under the likeliest alternative conception in this context, the necessary would be conceived here as what is determined by essences alone. But surely if something is determined by essences alone, it is determined by essences alone that that is so; so this conception sustains the axiom, too.

[25] Leibniz wrote, "Therefore this proposition is not necessarily true." I have eliminated the modal qualifier, as it is not part of the conclusion required by the argument at this point, nor is it required by the explicative clause following "that is" [*sive*]. It follows, of course, from (8a), which Leibniz must be assuming, that the conclusions with and without 'necessarily' here are equivalent. His sloppiness in the use of iterated modalities in this argument began with his unnecessary use of the modal term 'incompatible' in the proposition proposed as an example whose modal status he was going to discuss.

number. Indeed, in a paper of the same year as this proof (1676), Leibniz had written that "There are infinitely many simple forms," and I think that probably refers to the divine perfections, though the interpretation of the text is not unproblematic (A VI,iii,521). In any event, there seems to be a gap to be filled in the argument at this point, though I doubt it would be a fatal weakness.

A restatement of step (12) yields as a conclusion the possibility of a being possessing all perfections:

(13) "There is given, therefore, or can be understood, a subject of all perfections, or most perfect Being [*Ens perfectissimum*]."

Since Leibniz is obviously assuming that such a being would be God, this looks like the possibility premise that is needed to complete the ontological argument. But it is not, or at any rate, not yet, for it is crucial that Leibniz's version of the ontological argument is about a necessary God, a God that is a necessary being. A proof of the possibility of a most perfect being does not establish the possibility of a necessary God, however, unless it has been proved that a most perfect being would be a necessary being. Leibniz himself would later object to one of Descartes's versions of the ontological argument as "taking for granted that necessary existence and perfect existence are just the same thing" (A II,i,476). Similarly, in his conversation with Eckhard in April 1677, he said that

> in this demonstration of the divine existence there are two things to be considered. One is whether a most perfect Being does not imply a contradiction. The other is, given that a most perfect Being does not imply a contradiction, whether existence is among the perfections. (A II,i,313 = G I,214)

2.2 The Second Stage of the Proof: One Version

Leibniz's way of structuring the problem in this remark to Eckhard reflects the strategy of the proof he showed to Spinoza, which concludes with the statement, "Whence it is evident that [the subject of all perfections] also exists, since existence is included in the number of the perfections." Here again a subproof is compressed into a single sentence, and it is the least carefully handled part of Leibniz's argument, in the version that we have been following. The premise that existence is a perfection is asserted without proof:

(14) "Existence is included [among] the perfections."

Within a few months Leibniz himself would be raising doubts about it in his conversation and correspondence with Eckhard (e.g., A II,i,313 = G I,214). From (13) and (14) Leibniz infers that

(15) The subject of all perfections, which has been proved to be possible, "also exists."

Both the inference and the role of the conclusion in Leibniz's strategy are highly problematic, as we shall see. For one thing, we may ask how (15) is supposed to follow from (13) and (14). Certainly (14) entails the following:

(14a) Any subject of all perfections is a subject of (i.e., has) existence.

From this, however, and the possibility of a subject of all perfections, supposedly established at step (13), what follows? All that follows, according to many philosophers, is the *possibility* of an *existing* subject of all perfections. But this affords no inference to the *actual* existence of such a being, which is asserted in step (15). Since the possibility of a being of any sort is generally assumed to be the possibility of an *existing* being of that sort, steps (14) and (14a) seem not to have gotten us beyond a claim of possible existence that was already obviously implicit in step (13).

Alternatively, one might infer from (14) that

(14b) Existence is contained in the nature of a subject of all perfections.

Step (15) could then be inferred from (13) and (14b) with the aid of the Cartesian predication principle:

(14c) Whatever is contained in the nature of a possible thing can be (truly) asserted of that thing.[26]

These are probably the assumptions underlying Leibniz's inference. And this is not the only place in which his discussion of the ontological argument appears to rely on (14c).[27] It is a controversial principle, however, regarded by many as vitiating versions of the ontological argument that depend on it.[28] Indeed, by January 1678 Leibniz himself was beginning to object to its use in an ontological argument, as we shall see in Chapter 6, section 1.

It may be a mistake, however, to worry too much about whether (15) follows from (14). The larger strategy indicated by Leibniz's argument of January 1678, discussed in section 1, was apparently not yet so clear in his mind in November 1676 when he wrote out for Spinoza his proof of the possibility of God's existence. For (15) says both more and less than the larger strategy requires in a conclusion of the possibility proof: more, since (15) asserts actual existence where a proof of possibility is all that was needed, and less, since (15) fails to identify God, the perfect being, as a necessary being. The conclusion required by the strategy is something like the following:

(15a) A subject of all perfections, which would be a necessary being, is possible.

In order to reach this conclusion Leibniz needs a premise that says about *necessary* existence what (14) says only about *existence*:

[26]This is asserted and used by Descartes in a version of his ontological argument (AT VII,162,166). It also plays a leading role in Leibniz's account of the Cartesian ontological argument in 1684 at G IV,424/L 292, and about the same time at G VII,294/L 231. (On the dating of the latter text, see VE 900 and Couturat, *La logique de Leibniz*, pp. 189, n. 1, 323*n*.)

[27]Another is a memorandum, dating very likely from 1677–78, published in pp. 286f. of Janke, "Das ontologische Argument."

[28]I have discussed the principle, and its problematic role in both Anselmian and Cartesian versions of the argument, in "The Logical Structure of Anselm's Arguments."

(14d) Necessary existence is included among the perfections.

There can be little doubt of the acceptability of this premise to Leibniz in 1676. For the existence that he regarded as a perfection is surely not the limited, contingent sort of existence that we possess, but the unlimited, necessary existence that God possesses. From (14d) and the trivial

(14e) Any subject of necessary existence would be a necessary being,

we can infer

(14f) Any subject of all perfections would be a necessary being.

The desired conclusion (15a) clearly follows from (13) and (14f). Let us therefore consider Leibniz's possibility proof as amended by the substitution of (14d) and (15a) for (14) and (15), respectively.

One objection to the proof, even as amended, is that it can easily be parodied to prove the possibility, and hence the existence, of far too many necessary beings. This is a classic type of objection to ontological arguments; one thinks of Gaunilo's perfect island and Caterus's existing lion.[29] There is an obvious problem of this sort for the *un*amended proof that relies on the Cartesian predication principle and the premise that *existence* is a perfection: Existence can consistently be conjoined with the defining properties of any sort of thing that could possibly exist—that is, in Leibniz's view, with any consistent set of properties; in this way it seems we can produce new, existence-implying definitions. So, if we are to rely on the Cartesian predication principle, we must accept an assertion of the existence of every possible sort of thing.[30]

Even the amended proof faces a similar difficulty.[31] Leibniz claimed that "only the essence of God has this privilege," that existence follows from it [A II,i,391 (January 1678); similarly A II,i,436/AG 238 (1678–79); Mon 45 (1714)]. But how can he sustain this claim? If necessary existence is a perfection, in the sense of step (1) of the possibility proof, it is a simple, purely positive property of unlimited degree. The heart of the amended proof will be the claim that by virtue of their simple, purely positive character, necessary existence and all the other perfections are mutually consistent, because there is no way in which simple, purely positive qualities can be mutually inconsistent. But now suppose that a perfection *P* (other than necessary existence) is replaced by its negation, not-*P*. That is, consider a set *S* of properties, composed of not-*P*, *N* (necessary exis-

[29]Gaunilo, "On Behalf of the Fool," § 6; Caterus, in AT VII,99f.

[30]This is a generalization of Gaunilo's famous "perfect island" objection to Anselm's version of the ontological argument, or Caterus's "existent lion" objection to Descartes's version. I have discussed these, and some replies to them, in section II of "The Logical Structure of Anselm's Arguments." My argument there would support the claim that even if defenders of an ontological argument wish to rely on the Cartesian predication principle, they have reason to run their argument in terms of necessary existence, rather than simply existence, being a perfection.

[31]I am indebted to my students for much discussion of this point. Jeffrey Weisman first proposed the objection to me.

tence), and all the other perfections except *P*. It seems that on Leibnizian principles *S* must be consistent. For his argument depends on the assumption that the only way in which a set of properties can be inconsistent is if one of them is the negation of another member of the set, or is a conjunction having such a negation as a conjunct. But not-*P* is not a conjunction and is not the negation of any other member of *S*, but only of *P*, which is not a member of *S*. And no other member of *S* is a conjunction or a negation of anything. It seems to follow, on Leibnizian principles, that there is a possible subject of *S*, which must be a possible, and therefore actual, necessary but imperfect being. Indeed, it seems that for similar reasons Leibniz must admit indefinitely many necessary beings that are less than perfect, as some other perfection instead of *P*, or two perfections instead of one, could be replaced by their negations without affecting the structure of the argument. I believe that this objection will prove fatal to any version of Leibniz's argument that relies on the premise that necessary existence is a perfection.

2.3 The Second Stage: Another Version

Versions that do not rely on it are found in Leibniz's works or suggested by later developments in his thought. One of them belongs to the same year as the version he showed Spinoza. In another paper of 1676, having given an argument very similar to steps (1) to (13) above, Leibniz tries to connect the perfect being with necessary existence by a different subproof, which does not have it as a premise that either existence or necessary existence is a perfection.

> Hence now it seems to be proved, further, that a Being of this sort, which is most perfect, is necessary. For it cannot be unless it has a reason for existing from itself or from something else. It cannot have it from something else, because everything that can be understood in something else can already be understood in it—that is, because we conceive it through itself [*per se*], or because it has no requirements outside itself. Therefore either it cannot have any reason for existing, and so is impossible, contrary to what we have shown, or else it will have it from itself, and so will be necessary. (A VI,iii,572)[32]

The key to understanding this proof lies in the statement that a most perfect being (*ens perfectissimum*) cannot have a reason for existing from something else "because we conceive it through itself, or because it has no requirements outside itself." Such a being is conceived through itself because it has all the simple, purely positive attributes, and therefore all the attributes into which the concept of it is ultimately analyzable are attributes that it possesses. It has no requirements outside itself for the same reason, on the assumption that a being's "requirements" are all attributes or predicates that occur in the analysis of its essence,[33] and that if it has requirements "outside itself," these will be proper-

[32]A little later (p. 573) in this same paper is found the passage, discussed at length in Chapter 4, section 3.1 in this volume, in which Leibniz offers a demonstration for the rather Spinozistic thesis that "all things are distinguished not as substances but as modes." The question of Spinozistic influence on the present argument will be discussed later in this chapter.

[33]Leibniz's notion of "requirements" is discussed at length in Chapter 4, section 1.

ties that the being does not possess but that are involved in the logical construction of its essential properties.

Why is this feature of an *ens perfectissimum* a reason for thinking that it cannot have a reason for existing from something else?[34] Given that such a being has no "requirements" outside itself in the sense that the *logical* structure of its essence involves no properties that the being itself does not possess, to take that as meaning that it has no "requirements" outside itself in the sense of having no *causally* necessary conditions in another being would seem (at least to many philosophers) a very bad pun. But Leibniz was not punning. He believed that there is a connection between logical dependence and causal dependence,[35] and claimed [A VI,iii,514 (April 1676)] that

(16) "The effect is conceived through its cause."

This claim must be understood as made about *every* effect, and as meaning that the cause has an attribute or predicate that the effect does *not* possess but that is involved in the analysis of the concept of the effect. For Leibniz offered (16) as a reason for

(17) "Whatever is conceived through itself, a cause of it cannot be understood."

The inference is valid, if (16) is understood as I have indicated and 'cause' in (17) means an external cause, a cause distinct from the effect. For reasons that I have discussed, Leibniz held that

(18) An *ens perfectissimum* must be conceived through itself.

And from (17) and (18), under the interpretation of 'cause' I have assumed for (17), it follows that

(19) An *ens perfectissimum* cannot have a reason for existing from something else.

The key premise in this reasoning is (16). It is reminiscent of Spinoza's axiom that "The knowledge of the effect depends on the knowledge of the cause, and involves it."[36] We cannot exclude the possibility that Leibniz's belief in (19) was

[34]A similar argument from the notion of a requirement is found in a piece of uncertain date (VE 51 = LH IV,1,15,3). There the argument is that if a nature is completely simple, it will have only one requirement, with which it will be identical, and a thing of such a nature must therefore exist through itself, and hence necessarily, if it exists at all. Leibniz does not apply this to the existence of God, however, nor does he here affirm the traditional doctrine of the absolute simplicity of the divine nature, which generally does not appear to be his view. (Cf. Grua, *Jurisprudence*, p. 244.) Rather he uses the argument as part of a larger argument that volitions must have complex requirements and must therefore have reasons.

[35]See, again, Chapter 4, section 1.

[36]Spinoza, *Ethics*, I, axiom 4. Leibniz is commenting on an exposition of Spinoza's ideas when he indicates his belief in something like (16), in another text of 1676, by equating a thing "that is

rooted in the Spinozistic idea that beings that are caused to exist are modifications of an infinite attribute possessed by the being that causes them. An *ens perfectissimum*, of course, could not be caused in this way because its attributes are all absolute, unmodified. In support of this interpretation it could be urged that the argument in which (19) figures seems calculated to provide, for the case of God, what Leibniz had demanded, probably somewhat earlier in 1676, for Spinoza's view that existence pertains to the essence of substance. He said, "It should be shown that this follows from the fact that [substance] is conceived through itself" (A VI,iii, 277 = G I,132). The paper containing the argument we are studying, that an *ens perfectissimum* must be a necessary being, is one of the most Spinozistic in appearance of Leibniz's writings from 1676, containing a demonstration "that all things are distinguished, not as substances, but as modes" (A VI,iii,573).[37] Suggestions of this idea are also found in the paper in which (16) is found. (A VI,iii,514f.)

Nevertheless, both (16) and (19) could be held without this Spinozistic belief. It is clear that throughout his life Leibniz saw conceptual and causal relations as in some ways fused.[38] Moreover, a weaker premise about causality than (16) could support (19). Many philosophers, notably including Descartes, have believed that

(16a) If anything causes, or is the reason for, the existence of something else, any perfection found in the effect must be found in at least as high a degree in the cause.

Leibniz believed there cannot be two absolutely perfect beings. In an early sketch of his possibility proof, he claimed that "it is manifest that such a Being [one to which all affirmative attributes belong] is unique" (A VI,iii,396)—from which it follows that

(17a) There cannot be a being that possesses, in at least as high a degree, all the perfections found in an *ens perfectissimum* that is distinct from it.

Leibniz argued for the uniqueness of the *ens perfectissimum* on the basis of the principle of the identity of indiscernibles, or something like it: "For if two unlimited [beings] differ numerically, they will also differ in species, since they will certainly differ." This is not the most lucid formulation of the principle, but it is coupled with an affirmation (and Leibnizian qualification) of the Thomistic thesis about the angels that Leibniz would later cite as a partial precedent for his own thesis of the identity of indiscernibles: "And St. Thomas rightly held that substances separated from matter (as is God alone) would differ in species if there were many of them" (A VI,iii,396). Statements (16a) and (17a) jointly entail

its own reason of existing" with a thing "all of whose requirements we conceive without the concept of another thing" (A VI,iii,275 = G I,131).

[37]See note 32 above.

[38]Cf. Chapter 3, section 1.

(19) An *ens perfectissimum* cannot have a reason for existing from something else.

Such a reason could be found, according to (16a), only in a being that satisfies a condition that no being can satisfy, according to (17a).

Regardless of how Leibniz meant to justify (19), he is obviously right in inferring from it that

(20) Either an *ens perfectissimum* cannot have any reason at all for existing, or such a being can[39] have a reason for existing from itself.

He adds two further premises:

(21) If any sort of thing cannot have any reason at all for existing, then that sort of thing is impossible.

(22) Any being that has a reason for existing from itself must[40] be a necessary being.

Statements (20), (21), and (22) jointly imply

(23) Either an *ens perfectissimum* is impossible, or an *ens perfectissimum* can be a necessary being.

But, Leibniz claims, he has just proved that

(24) An *ens perfectissimum* is possible.

So it follows by *modus tollens* that

(25) An *ens perfectissimum* can be a necessary being.

In other words, a necessary God is possible, which is just the conclusion Leibniz needs to complete his ontological argument.

This argument rests on a premise about causality—whether (16) or (16a)—that would be questioned, and even rejected, by many philosophers. Here, however, we need not pause to consider the *truth* of these assumptions. It is enough to point out that the use of any of them in the present context, as a premise in a completion of Leibniz's proof for the possibility of a necessary God, undermines the strategy of the proof.

The first stage of the proof, which I have articulated in section 2.1 of this chapter and which is supposed to establish the possibility of an *ens perfectissimum*, depends crucially on the assumption that the only way in which any sort of thing can be impossible is by including both a property and its nega-

[39]Leibniz wrote "will" at this point, but "can" is what is warranted and required by the argument.

[40]As in step (20), I have corrected Leibniz's modality, this time from "will" to "must."

tion among its essential or defining properties, or among conjuncts that would appear in an analysis of its essential or defining properties. But in conjoining (21) with (16) [or (16a)] Leibniz would commit himself to another way in which it is at least thinkable that a supposed sort of being could be impossible—that is, by having an essence that does not involve existence though it is conceived through itself (or is not analyzable in terms of a perfection that some other being could possess in higher degree). The argument of section 2.1 does not show that an *ens perfectissimum* could not be impossible in *this* way; so if we try to complete the argument by showing that an *ens perfectissimum* must be impossible in this way unless it is a necessary being, we merely invite the suspicion that an *ens perfectissimum* may indeed be impossible in this way.

Perhaps Leibniz would reply that we do not really have here *another* way in which something could be impossible. Perhaps he thought it could be shown that a supposed non-necessary being whose essence is conceived though itself (or is not analyzable in terms of a perfection that some other being could possess in higher degree) must contain an explicit contradiction among its defining properties, or among conjuncts into which they could in principle be analyzed. But I do not see how this could be shown, and it does not seem particularly plausible.

Ideas about causality related to (16) or (16a) might also have been thought to provide Leibniz with a defense for the version of the second stage of his possibility proof presented in section 2.2 of this chapter. That version faces the objection that a similar proof seems to be available for the possibility, and hence the existence, of indefinitely many *im*perfect necessary beings. Perhaps Leibniz thought of the perfections as "requirements" of all possible things in such a way that he might have replied that any possible being that would be in any way imperfect must (i) have a limited degree of one of the perfections and (ii) be caused by a being that has the unlimited degree of that perfection. The reason for (ii) would be that since the unlimited is prior in nature to the limited, the limited degree of the perfection must be conceived through the unlimited degree of it, and causal dependence runs parallel to conceptual dependence. We may add (iii) that a being that must be caused by another being is not a necessary being in the sense intended by Leibniz, since its existence does not flow from its own nature alone, and thus it is not necessary in itself (regardless of whether it is necessarily produced by its cause). From these assumptions it follows that necessary existence is inconsistent with any imperfection, so that only the absolutely perfect being, which possesses all perfections, could be a necessary being.

This defense, however, confronts the same crucial difficulty as the version of the proof that relies on (21) and (16) or (16a). That is, it undermines the assumption that an impossible sort of thing must contain an explicit contradiction among its defining properties, which is crucial to the first stage of Leibniz's possibility proof. For the defense relies on (i) and (ii) as necessary conditions on imperfect beings to show that an imperfect necessary being is impossible, but without showing that an imperfect necessary being, as an imperfect being not caused by another being, must contain an explicit contradiction among its defining properties. Leibniz may have believed that (ii) expresses a necessary truth of causal metaphysics, but it is hard to see how he could show that a limited degree of any perfection is analyzable as a conjunction having as a conjunct the property of being caused by another being having the unlimited degree of the perfection.

Neither of the 1676 versions of Leibniz's proof of the possibility of a necessary God seems to have much likelihood of succeeding. Even if the first stage, leading to the conclusion that an *ens perfectissimum* is possible, were to be judged successful, there is no answer in sight to the objections that confront both versions of the concluding stage, in which Leibniz tries to show that an *ens perfectissimum* must be a necessary being. Leibniz's views on the relation of existence to perfection continued to develop after 1676, however. In the next chapter we will consider whether his later views provide a basis for a better version of the possibility proof.

6

Existence and Essence

In his conversation and correspondence with Arnold Eckhard, beginning less than six months after his visits with Spinoza, we seem to see Leibniz working his way out of the assumption that existence is "a perfection" in the sense of a "simple quality that is positive and absolute." As I noted at the end of section 2.1 of the previous chapter, Leibniz pointed out to Eckhard that one of the "two things to be considered" regarding the Cartesian ontological argument is "whether existence is among the perfections." Leibniz then proceeded to propose a reason for thinking that existence is not a perfection: "For perfections seem to be qualities, as existence is not" (A II,i,313 = G I,214).

That existence is not a quality may not have been a fixed point for Leibniz in this discussion, for in his next letter to Eckhard he appears to equate the question "whether existence can follow from essence" (as he surely believed that it can) with the question "whether . . . existence can be understood as an essential quality of some Being, namely of God" (A II,i,324 = G I,223). In the resolution ultimately reached on this point in the correspondence, however, the idea of perfections as the simple primitive qualities seems to be left behind, at least for the time being. Leibniz dropped his objection to the claim that existence is a perfection "after [Eckhard] explained that for [him] perfection is Being [*Entitas*], insofar as it is understood to depart from non-Being—or as [Leibniz would] prefer to define it, that *perfection* is degree or quantity of reality or essence" (A II,i,363/ L 177). Given this definition of perfection, which Leibniz himself approved (A II,i,327 = G I,225),[1] he says "it is plain also that Existence is a perfection, or increases reality; that is, when *existent A* is conceived, more reality is conceived than when *possible A* is conceived" (A II,i,363/L 177).

I pointed out in Chapter 4, section 2, that in this definition simplicity drops out as a criterion for perfection, leaving positiveness to stand alone. More important in the present context is the relation between perfection and essence. In defining perfection here as "degree or quantity of reality or essence," Leibniz takes it to be either a second-order property,[2] a property of properties, and spe-

[1]Similarly, in "Elements of True Piety," whose watermark is attested from 1677–78 (VE 233), 'perfection' is defined as "degree [*gradus*] or quantity of reality" ("or quantity" being an emendation by Leibniz), and in "On Affections," dated April 1679, 'perfection' is repeatedly defined as "degree of reality" (Gr 11,527,529).

[2]I do not use 'property' here in the technical Leibnizian sense explained in Chapter 4, section 3.1, but in a broad sense in which it signifies anything that may be predicated of an object of thought,

cifically of essences, or else a property of things that is defined in terms of a (second-order) property of their essences. Here perfection depends on the essence. This is quite different from the 1676 proofs of the possibility of God's existence, where perfections are first-order properties, on which essences depend, inasmuch as essences are composed of perfections and/or of properties derived in some way from perfections. We need not suppose that a fundamentally different metaphysical structure is envisaged in these different texts, but the attachment of the concept of perfection to a different part of the structure in the Eckhard correspondence may open the way for a reconception of the relation between existence and essence. The beginnings of such a reconception appear by January 1678 at the latest. We can approach it by way of the question *how* existence increases reality, as Leibniz acknowledged to Eckhard that it does.

1. *Is Existence an Essential Quality of God?*

Leibniz's acceptance of Eckhard's definition of perfection as a measure of the degree of positive reality contained in the essence of a thing would be consistent with his continuing to think of existence as a simple, purely positive quality of the sort that he had called perfections in his 1676 proofs of the possibility of God's existence. His assigning 'perfection' to signify another feature of the metaphysical structure certainly did not mean that he had ceased to believe that there are such qualities and that they essentially and distinctively characterize God. Since anything has more "reality," in the relevant sense, if it possesses any purely positive quality than if it lacks it, the identification of existence as such a quality would explain how existence increases reality. If existence is conceived in this way, it is natural to suppose that existence may be related to an essence in the same way as other simple, positive qualities—that is, as a constituent of the essence, and thus as an essential or defining quality of the thing that has the essence.

Leibniz came to object to this way of thinking of existence, however, for he wrote:

> If Existence were something other than an essence's demand [*exigentia*], it would follow that it has some essence or superadds something new to things, about which it could be asked again whether this essence exists, and why this one rather than another. (G VII,195)[3]

provided it is understood that what is signified is a feature of the object, rather than a feature of thought or speech about the object.

[3]This is a (possibly later) marginal annotation to a manuscript that may be dated with some probability, on the basis of watermark, to the period 1677–80 (see VE 115). I think both the note and the underlying text, which also contains the idea of "an essence's demand," should be dated after the document of January 1678, discussed later in this section, which shows no trace of that idea and treats existence as similar to "realities or forms or perfections" that are consituents of essences (A II,i,392), even while it strives to articulate a different relation of existence to essence. For similar reasons I would assign a date after January 1678 (though not very much later) to "Elements of True Piety," whose watermark is attested from 1677–78 (VE 233), and which contains a version of the idea of an essence's demand, though in terms of "propensity [*propensio*] to exist," rather than in the metaphorical terms of "demand [*exigentia*]" (Gr 16f.).

We will come in due course to the conception, implicitly affirmed here, of existence as "an essence's demand." Our present concern is with the idea that existence "has some essence or superadds something new to things." If this were true, Leibniz objects, we could ask whether existence exists, or whether existent things exist, and why they exist rather than something else. Granting him that these questions are absurd, we may wonder why he thinks they would arise.

A similar argument in Kant springs readily to mind, one in which Kant also objects to the idea of existence adding something new to things. "The actual," wrote Kant, "contains no more than the merely possible. A hundred actual dollars contain not the least [coin] more than a hundred possible dollars," although "a hundred actual dollars have more effect on my financial condition than the mere concept of them (that is, their possibility) does."[4] Kant takes this as a reason for denying that existence is a "real predicate" or "determination" [*Bestimmung*]—that is, "a predicate that is added to the concept of the subject and enlarges it."[5] Thus far, I think, Kant is in substantial agreement with Leibniz.

Kant's favored alternative is to say that the function of the verb 'to be' in its existential use is to posit [*setzen*] "the subject in itself with all its predicates, and indeed [to posit it] as the *object* in relation to my *concept*."[6] Modern logical theory has carried this suggestion in a direction that is certainly not in agreement with Leibniz's views or with his practice. In our logical symbolism we do not normally treat existence formally or grammatically as a predicate at all. Existence is allowed expression only indirectly, in fusion with quantity—specifically, with the "particular" quantity of a term, as traditional predicate logic would have called it. '$(\exists x)Fx$' is normally interpreted as meaning simultaneously 'For some thing, x, Fx' and 'There exists (at least one thing) x such that Fx.' Under this customary interpretation, following Kant's comment about positing an object for our concept, we do not in the first instance ascribe existence to an object, but rather say that a predicate is exemplified. (In this we go beyond Kant, who explicitly allowed that existence could be used as a "logical predicate," though it is not a "real predicate."[7])

How can we allow 'For some x, Fx' and 'There exists an x such that Fx' to coincide? Might we not think that 'For some x, x is (or was) a winged horse' is true (since Pegasus, for example, was a winged horse), but 'There exists (or existed) an x such that x is (or was) a winged horse' is false (since Pegasus, and winged horses generally, have never existed)? The usual answer involves the idea that 'For some x, $\emptyset(x)$' means that $\emptyset$ is true of at least one member of a set of things which is known as the "universe of discourse." And in interpreting our symbolic logic we normally assume that only things that actually exist (at some time, or timelessly) are in the universe of discourse. On this interpretation 'For some x, Fx' will be true if and only if there exists an x such that Fx. This set of ideas is even taken as an explication of the concept of existence in the influential Quinean dictum that "to be is to be a value of a bound variable." Moreover, if we add the usual assumption that 'Fa' (where a is a particular individual) entails

[4]Kant, *Critique of Pure Reason*, A 599/B 627.
[5]Kant, *Critique of Pure Reason*, A 598/B 626.
[6]Kant, *Critique of Pure Reason*, A 599/B 627.
[7]Kant, *Critique of Pure Reason*, A 598/B 626.

'For some *x*, *Fx*', it follows from these views that predicates can be ascribed with truth only to existing things, and that existence is not needed as a separate predicate because it is implied in the ascription of any predicate.

It is clear that Leibniz differs from more recent logical theory on these points. 'Existent' is used as a predicate in his logical apparatus (C 271f.,375f./P 65f.), and, as we shall see, his papers abound with definitions of it. In the intensional interpretation of predicate logic which he most often prefers, moreover, 'Some *A* is *B*' does not imply that any *A* or *B* actually exists,[8] and it is possibility rather than existence that is required of a being or entity (*ens*) to which predicates are to be ascribed.[9] These are mainly formal points, however, and the ascription of predicates to possible beings as such was regarded by Leibniz as reducible to more fundamental sorts of proposition, as we shall soon see.

If we are to understand the considerations that led Leibniz to reject the conception of existence as a quality, and, in the case of God, an essential quality, we must focus not on the relation of existence to predication, but on the relation of existence to essence. Leibniz expressed the rejected view in terms of existence having "some essence," and I take that to mean having *content* of the sort that is required to constitute, in whole or in part, an essence—content of the sort possessed or contributed by positive qualities in general. In this way existence would be, in Kant's terms, "a predicate that is added to the concept of the subject and enlarges it," though something important to Leibniz is left out in replacing 'essence' by 'concept'. If existence had "some essence" in this sense, it would be the essence, or (more plausibly) part of the essence, of existent things, and existent things would be a *kind* of things, or existent *F*s would be a kind of *F*s.

Leibniz suggests, however, that on this view it would seem to be an open question, whether and why it is things of this kind that actually exist, rather than things of some other kind. This suggestion may seem puzzling; why aren't these questions answered by the observation that the kind of things we are talking about is *existent* things? But the point Leibniz is trying to make is that the concept of existence has an essential use in asking questions that cannot be answered in that way, and, more broadly, that saying that (or asking whether) *F*s exist is quite different from saying or asking anything about what kind of thing *F*s are. In Leibniz's way of thinking this is a point about the relation of existence to essence, because it is the essence of a thing that determines the kinds to which it belongs.[10] Our concept of existence, therefore, is not the concept of a kind of thing, or of a content that an essence might have. It would be more accurate to say that it is the concept of a *status* that things have, and carries with it the concept of a correlated status that the essences of existent things have. As we shall see, much of Leibniz's discussion of existence is an effort to characterize such statuses.

[8]See Chapter 2, section 3.

[9]There is at least one text [G VII,214/P 118 (after 1690)] in which Leibniz acknowledges the possibility of using an alternative interpretation in which actual existence is required of a being (*ens*). See Mates, *Philosophy of Leibniz*, pp. 55–57, for an interesting discussion of this topic, with many references—though I think that the existential interpretation of *ens* is less prominent in Leibniz's work than Mates suggests.

[10]In Aristotelian thought, accidental as well as essential kinds are recognized. For Leibniz, however, any difference in kind constitutes a difference in the essence of an individual thing, and thus essence completely determines kind-membership; see DM 16.

An important document of the development of these ideas in Leibniz's thought dates from January 1678. In his annotations to his version of the incomplete or conditional ontological proof, discussed in Chapter 5, section 1, he says:

> Spinoza reasons thus, following Descartes: It is the same to say that something is contained in the nature or concept of some thing, as to say that that very [predication] is true about that thing (as it is contained in the concept of a Triangle, or follows from its essence, that its three angles are equal to two right angles). But necessary existence is contained in the same way in the concept of God. Therefore it is true about God to say that necessary existence is in him, or that he exists. To this reasoning, and others like it, it can be objected that all those propositions are conditional, for to say that three angles equal to two right angles are involved in the nature or concept of a triangle is to say only that if a triangle should exist, then it would have this property. So in the same way, even if it be granted that necessary existence belongs to the concept of God, still all that will be inferred from that is that if God should exist, then he would have this property (of necessary existence), or that if God should exist, he would exist necessarily. Our reasoning, however, is not liable to this difficulty, but proves something more, namely that if God is even possible, he necessarily exists in fact. (A II,i,393)

Leibniz ascribes to Spinoza what I have called (in Chapter 5, section 2.2) "the Cartesian predication principle":

> (14c) Whatever is contained in the nature of a possible thing can be (truly) asserted of that thing.

This principle is a candidate for the interpretation of the key final transition in the proof that Leibniz himself showed Spinoza in 1676. Here, however, in 1678, Leibniz offers what seems to be the usual Kantian and post-Kantian objection[11] to the use of the Cartesian predication principle in the ontological argument: that from the containment of a property F in the nature or concept of an X it follows only that *if* there should exist an X, it would be F. His own argument, Leibniz says, is not liable to this objection. It begins by establishing a proposition that is frankly acknowledged as conditional. But its conditional conclusion is more substantial: not merely "that if God should exist, he would exist necessarily," but "that if God is even possible, he necessarily exists in fact." All that remains is to prove the possibility of the existence of such a necessary God.

In saying that 'B is involved in the nature or concept of A' is equivalent to 'If an A should exist, it would be B', Leibniz might be taken to be rejecting (14c) in such a way as to imply, contrary to his own usual practice, that predicates are to be ascribed only to existent things. But I think that would be a misreading. Leibniz is indeed a reductionist, but not an eliminationist, with regard to the ascription of predicates to possible things as such. This is clear in a well-known passage of the *New Essays*. There he treats the proposition, 'The angles of every three-sided figure are equal to two right angles,' as ascribing a Euclidian predicate to each possible triangle. At the same time, he treats this proposition as reducible, indicating that it is "at bottom conditional" and equivalent to 'If a figure

[11]It was already Gassendi's objection, of course (AT VII,323).

has three sides, [that same figure's] angles are equal to two right angles.' The way in which a proposition "about a subject" that does not exist "can have a real truth" is "that the truth is only conditional, and says that in case the subject ever exists, it will be found to be of this sort" (NE 446f.).[12]

To be sure, this is not the only Leibnizian reduction of predications whose subjects are considered merely as possible. There is also a reduction to relations of conceptual inclusion, which he regards as always implicit, and foundational, in anything said about a possible subject as such. His criticism of Spinoza could be regarded as reducing conceptual containment claims to conditional propositions about the properties actual existents would have. But a reductive intent is neither clear nor crucial at this point. The main burden of the argument is that the corresponding propositions of the two types are equivalent, and hence that '*B* is involved in the nature or concept of *A*' says *no more* than 'If an *A* should exist, it would be *B*'.

But how could Leibniz have thought that this refuted Spinoza without also destroying his own argument? He is here annotating a proof that has as a premise that "The essence of God involves necessity of existence" (which is surely the same property as the "necessary existence" that figures in Leibniz's rendition of Spinoza's argument). And the proof, when supplemented with a possibility proof, is supposed to establish the existence of a necessary being whose necessity consists in the fact that its essence "involves existence." Leibniz surely thinks this involvement means more than that if this being should exist, it would exist.

Leibniz's argument requires a distinction between (at least) two ways in which a predicate can be involved or contained in the nature or concept of a thing. He is quite explicit that his own version of the ontological argument turns on a sort of involvement that means something unconditional:

> In this place the eternal truths are not to be considered as hypothetical, [as] assuming actual existence; for otherwise a circle would arise. That is, the existence of God being assumed, thence [God's] existence would be proved. Certainly, in saying that the Essence of God involves existence, it must not be understood as meaning that, if God exists, he necessarily exists, but in this way, [as meaning that] on the part of the thing [*a parte rei*], even if no one thinks about it, it is unconditionally, absolutely and purely true in that region of essences or ideas that the essence and existence of God are inseparably connected. (A II,i,392)

What is to keep Spinoza from replying that in his argument, too, the containment of necessary existence in the nature or concept of God means something unconditional? Leibniz neither raises nor answers this question here, but I believe the best answer is the following. In the argument that Leibniz quotes (word for word) from Spinoza's 1663 geometrical demonstration of Descartes's *Principles* it is clear that it is as an essential property that necessary existence is said

[12]Leibniz had already expressed the same view in 1670: approving Nizolius's statement that in "essential" predications, such as 'Man is an animal,' "the existence of the subjects is not required," Leibniz commented, "They are right in saying this. For whoever says 'Man is an animal' means 'If anything is a man, it is an animal.' And since the condition posits nothing, therefore it is not required for the truth of this proposition that there be any man, but that if there should be, he would necessarily also be an animal, which is most true" (A VI,ii,472).

to be contained in the concept of God. Spinoza supports the containment claim by appeal to an axiom that says that necessary existence is contained "in the concept of God, or of a supremely perfect being; for otherwise it would be conceived as imperfect, contrary to what is supposed to be conceived."[13] The reasoning here is evidently that necessary existence must be contained in the concept of God because a being that did not exist necessarily would not qualify as perfect, and therefore would not qualify as God. But the strongest containment claim that could be warranted by this reasoning (on the assumption that its premises are correct) says no more than the conditional thesis that *if* any being is God, that being must exist necessarily. And from such a conditional thesis, as Leibniz argues, it does not follow that there actually exists such a being.

This makes clear, I think, the crucial point about the relation of existence to essence. If the necessary existence of any being is to be explained in terms of the involvement of existence in the essence of that being, this involvement must not be of the sort that essential or defining properties have. For the involvement of *B* as a defining or essential property in the essence of *A* means no more than that *if* anything is *A*, it must have *B*. And from this it does not follow that such a thing actually exists. Thus nothing can be "defined into existence"; it cannot be "true by definition" that any being exists. If the essence of God involves existence in such a way as to render God's existence necessary, it must not be simply by saying that a being must exist necessarily in order to be God, but by virtue of some other feature of the divine essence. This may be expressed by saying that existence must be connected with the essence of a necessary being, not primarily as a part of the essence, but by virtue of a second-order, and probably holistic, property of the essence.

Not that Leibniz had seen all of this in January of 1678. The clearest evidence of the incompleteness of his grasp of the relevant points at that time is in his treatment of existence as "a perfection," apparently in the sense of his 1676 arguments. For he offers the following lemma (A II,i,391):

(1) The essence of God and supreme perfection are inseparable (*ex hypothesi*, for we suppose that the essence of God contains supreme perfection).

(2) Supreme perfection and every perfection in kind [*in specie*] are inseparable.

(3) Actual existence is a perfection in kind [*in specie*].

Therefore

The essence of God and his actual existence are inseparable.

This lemma plainly expresses the view that existence is contained as an essential property in the essence of God as a supremely perfect being, and is thus essentially similar to Spinoza's Cartesian proof that Leibniz would criticize later in the same document. The inseparability of essence and existence established in this way is simply the inclusion of existence as a part of the essence, and

[13]Spinoza, *Opera*, vol. 1, p. 155; cf. p. 158. Spinoza evidently relies on a previously stated definition of God as a supremely perfect substance (ibid., p. 150). The argument for the existence of God in Spinoza's *Ethics*, I, prop. 7, and the first demonstration of prop. 11, is not liable (in my opinion) to the objection Leibniz makes here, because necessary existence figures in the argument,

it can hardly mean more than that *if* any being is God, that being must actually exist.

Leibniz's larger argument still escapes this objection, however, because this lemma is superfluous for the larger argument. As Leibniz notes, "the mention of perfection can be eliminated from" the argument by defining 'God' as signifying a necessary being. The argument proceeding from this definition[14] still turns on an involvement of (necessary) existence in the divine essence. But the argument is no longer that a being that did not exist could not satisfy the essence, but that an essence that did not involve necessary existence could not qualify as the essence of a necessary being. Here the involvement relation between existence and the divine essence need not be understood in terms of the inclusion of existence as a part, or essential or defining property, in the essence, but can be understood in terms of the essence necessarily having, for some other reason, the status of being actually exemplified. The significance of the latter sort of involvement is not exhausted by the conclusion that if any being is God, that being must actually exist.

This can hardly have been clear to Leibniz when he formulated the argument. Even in the annotations to it he assimilates existence, as a "form," to the "perfections."

> As in the region of eternal truths, or in the field of ideas that exists objectively [*a parte rei*], there subsist Unity, the Circle, Potency, equality, heat, rose, and other realities or forms or perfections, even if no individual beings were to exist, and these universals were not to be thought about; so also there among other forms or objective realities is found *actual existence*, not as it is found in the World and in examples, but as a universal form. If in the field of ideas this form is inseparably connected with some other essence or form, there results thence a Being that necessarily exists in actuality." (A II,i,392)

This invites, though it does not entail, the defining-property construal of the relation of existence to the divine essence. In the annotations, however, he does see, first, that in some contexts the involvement or containment of a predicate in a nature or concept means no more than that *if* anything has the nature or satisfies the concept, it must have the predicate, and, second, that he is therefore asserting a different sort of involvement of existence in the divine essence. Within the next few years he would articulate a conception of the relation of existence to essence that might be seen as promising an explication of the sort of involvement required by the argument.

2. *Defining Existence*

One of the clearest presentations of the line of thought I wish now to explore is found in the following brief, undated memorandum:

---

not merely as an essential qualification for being God, but as a feature of the divine nature's causal role in the structure of reality. But Leibniz would not have the *Ethics* before him until the month after this critique was penned.

[14]Premises [6] and [7] and the conclusion drawn from them in the argument discussed in Chapter 5, section 1.

Existence

> It can be doubted very much whether existence is a perfection or degree of reality; for it can be doubted whether existence is one of those things that can be conceived—that is, one of the parts of essence; or whether it is only a certain imaginary concept, such as that of *heat* and *cold*, which is a denomination only of our perception, not of the nature of things. Yet if we consider more accurately, [we shall see] that we conceive something more when we think that a thing *A* exists, than when we think that it is possible. Therefore it seems to be true that existence is a certain degree of reality; or certainly that it is some relation to degrees of reality. Existence is not a degree of reality, however; for of every degree of reality it is possible to understand the existence as well as the possibility. Existence will therefore be the superiority of the degrees of reality of one thing over the degrees of reality of an opposed thing. That is, that which is more perfect than all things mutually incompatible *exists*, and conversely what exists is more perfect than the rest. Therefore it is true indeed that what exists is more perfect than the non-existent, but it is not true that existence itself is a perfection, since it is only a certain comparative relation [*comparatio*] of perfections among themselves. (VE 2016 = B 119f.)

Here Leibniz explicitly denies, not only that existence is a "perfection," such as can constitute "one of the parts of essence," but also that existence is a second-order property of essences of the sort that was identified with perfection in his correspondence with Eckhard—that is, a "degree of reality." Existence cannot be identified with any one degree of reality, for the existence of any degree of reality is possible. Indeed, Leibniz believed that (infinitely) many degrees of reality actually exist. Existence is closely related to degrees of reality. It is identified with the property of having more reality or perfection than any incompatible alternative. Degrees of reality or perfection, however, are equivalent, in this scheme of things, not to existence itself, but to degrees of *tendency* to exist. An essence's perfection is measured by the strength of its "demand" [*exigentia*] for existence. Degree of perfection is not existence but the principle or source [*principium*] of existence (G VII,194f.,303f./L 487f.).[15]

Similar definitions of existence are found in several other places in Leibniz's papers. For instance, he defines 'existent' as "compossible with the most perfect," and says, "*Existent* is that series of possibles which involves more of reality, and whatever enters into it" (Gr 325).[16] These formulations make clear that this account of existence applies in the first place to complete sets of compossible

[15]The formulation that "perfection or degree of Essence" is "the source of existence" comes from the essay "On the Radical Origination of Things," of 23 November 1697, which certainly uses and develops ideas belonging to this nexus. We shall have to question later how fully the 1697 paper accepts the definition of existence we are studying. But the basic idea of essences "demanding" existence in proportion to their perfection is found in papers belonging certainly or probably to the period 1678–85, to which I believe most of Leibniz's development of this line of argument can be dated. See VE 238f.,277 = Gr 16f.,288/AG 20; and see note 3.

[16]The first of these formulations is preliminarily dated 1679–85, on the basis of content, and the second 1683–85, on the basis of watermark, in VE 169,166. The first formulation occurs in the same document with an alternative definition: "*Entity* [*Ens*] is [something] distinctly thinkable. *Existent* [is] distinctly perceivable" (VE 171). On the significance of this pairing of definitions of existence, and for additional references, see note 23. For another occurrence of the definition from the same period, see G VII,194f.

things, rather than to individual substances. The essences of actually existing earthworms are less perfect than the essences of possible human beings that do not actually exist. What exists is that set of compossible substances that is more perfect than any alternative that is not compossible with it.

This analysis of existence readily suggests ways of completing or revising the ontological argument for the existence of God. One way is to argue that the essence of a supremely perfect being involves (necessary) existence, with the sort of unconditional involvement required by Leibniz's argument, on the ground that such an essence obviously contains more perfection or reality than the essence of any thing that would be incompatible with it. To this it may be objected that competitors for existence meet the test of perfection, not singly, but in complete sets of compossible beings. The existence of God therefore does not follow directly from the fact that the divine essence is more perfect than any other essence of an individual substance; it must be proved that no set of compossible beings that excludes God has a higher sum of perfection than all the sets that include God. But Leibniz would have a ready answer to this objection. He could maintain, as most theists would, that the divine perfection, all by itself, without any supplementation by the perfection of other beings, is greater than the sum of perfection of any aggregate of less perfect beings. He could also argue that the existence of God must be compossible with that of the most perfect possible set of finite things, because the choice and creation of that set follows from the perfection of the divine will and power. On these grounds Leibniz could hold that (necessary) existence is involved, in the relevant way, in the essence of a supremely perfect being. And if the possibility of a supremely perfect being is taken as proved by the argument discussed in section 2.1 of Chapter 5, this seems to complete an ontological proof of the existence of God.

The following objection might be raised against the argument that God's existence must be compossible with the maximum of finite perfection. Leibniz says that "if there were not a best [*optimum*] among all the possible worlds, God would not have produced any of them" (T 8). From this the objector might infer that if there were no best among possible worlds, the existence of God, according to Leibniz, would not be compossible with the existence of any possible world. But Leibniz could reply that, given the definition of existence that is assumed here, the existence of God would not be preventing the actualization of a perfection that might otherwise exist. For if, among the possible worlds, all *in*com-

---

According to a later statement: "Existence is conceived by us as a thing having nothing in common with Essence, which cannot be, however, since there must be more in the concept of the Existent than [in that] of the non-existent; that is, existence must be [a] perfection, since really nothing else is explicable in existence except entering into the most perfect series of things" (C 9). This text has been assigned a preliminary date of about 1700 by the Academy editors (personal communication, 1977). I think this statement does not imply a reductive definition of existence, however, but is consistent with supposing existence to be an unanalyzable primitive. Despite the beginning of the statement, I also do not take it to imply that existence might enter into essences as a defining property of things. What it says is rather that existent things as such must differ from nonexistent things in some way that is rooted in their essence, and the only such difference that can be explained is that all and only the existent things enter into the most perfect series of things. That is something that I think Leibniz believed to the end of his life (with some qualifications for the unique relation of God to the most perfect series of things).

possible with each other, there is none that is better than all the others, then there is none that satisfies the definition of existence. It might also be replied that, given that we experience that some finite things do exist, we can infer, both from the definition of existence and from Leibniz's philosophical theology, that there is a best among possible worlds. But this does not yield an a priori argument; moreover, as we shall see, the definition of existence involved in the argument calls into question any empirical justification of existential claims.

Leibniz never offers this proof. That may surprise us less when we reflect that the definition of existence on which it rests is liable to rather obvious objections. It seems to trivialize the Leibnizian doctrine that the best of all possible worlds actually exists. Is it still good news, if the actual existence of the best world consists simply in its being the best? And do we still have reason to believe that our world actually exists, and is the best, if actually existing, for worlds, just *is* being the best? If we had to prove the actual existence of our world from its superiority over other possible worlds, we might be left in some doubt of our own existence.[17] Surely by actual existence we mean something more than being part of the best possible aggregate of things. And if we did not, we might conclude that the best possible world needs no help from God to exist, but exists simply by necessity of its nature, as the best. This would eliminate the role of God's choice in explaining the existence of the world, contrary to the theory of creation espoused by Leibniz throughout his intellectual career.

The obviousness of these objections suggests that the account of existence as simply identical with inclusion in the best possible aggregate of things may be too simple-minded to represent adequately Leibniz's intentions. Certainly it is not an explicit part of the philosophy that he presented to the learned world, and it appears to be inconsistent with the theory of creation that is found, for instance, in the *Theodicy* and the well-known essay "On the Radical Origination of Things" (T 7; G VII,302ff./L 486ff.). We must therefore try to situate the texts that suggest it within a larger pattern and development of Leibniz's ideas.

There is considerable variety in the definitions of existence proposed in Leibniz's writings. Particularly interesting is a paragraph of "General Inquiries about the Analysis of Concepts and Truths" (1686), in which Leibniz pursues the question "what 'existent' means." "An Existent," he says, "is an Entity [*Ens*], that is, a possible, and something besides"; and we understand actual existence as "something superadded to possibility or Essence." But what is this something extra?

> I say therefore that an Existent is an Entity that is compatible with the most; that is, an Entity maximally possible, and so all coexistents are equally possible. Or, what comes to the same thing, an existent is what pleases an intelligent and powerful [being]; but thus Existence itself is presupposed. However, it can at least be defined that an Existent is what would please some Mind, and would not displease[18] another more powerful [mind], if any minds at all were assumed to exist. Therefore the matter comes to this, that that is said to Exist which would not displease the most powerful Mind, if a most powerful

[17]On these objections, cf. R. Adams, "Theories of Actuality," pp. 212–14.

[18]At this point in P, a usually reliable translation, "please" should be corrected to "displease."

> mind were assumed to exist. . . . But it pleases a mind that what has a reason should come to be rather than what does not have a reason. (GI 73)

We get here what looks like quite a different definition: an existent is what would please (or would not displease) the most powerful mind; and this is not the only place in Leibniz's works where existence is analyzed in approximately this way.[19]

It is noteworthy, however, that Leibniz says this alternative definition "comes to the same thing as" the definition in terms of perfection which we have been examining. This may perplex us, inasmuch as they do not seem to have by any means the same meaning. The conclusion to be drawn, I think, is that neither definition is intended as an analysis of our meaning. Both are intended as *real* definitions—that is, as intended to explicate the nature of existence in such a way as to exhibit the reason or cause that any existence would have.[20] If we confine our attention to finite existents, we can see that each of these definitions provides part of the explanation that Leibniz thought there must be for the existence of any existent thing. One part of the reason is that the thing is included in the best possible aggregate of things; the other part is that (because of its superiority) that aggregate pleases God, the most powerful mind—and is therefore chosen and actualized by God. Thus the two definitions are complementary, each encapsulating elliptically, with different omissions, the same causal account of the nature of existence.

When the matter is viewed in this light, however, a serious problem arises. In saying that "an existent is what pleases an intelligent and powerful [being] . . . Existence itself is presupposed," as Leibniz himself notes. It is of course the existence of *God* that is presupposed. The explanation of existence contained in this pair of definitions, understood as mutually complementary, is that the best possible aggregate of things is chosen and created by God. But God must exist in order to create. This yields what is certainly the correct interpretation of Leibniz's talk about the possibles "striving" for existence and having a tendency to exist that is proportioned to their perfection. It is in the mind of God that they strive, and it is the power of God that gives reality to their tendency to exist. That implies the existence of God—which is why the striving possibles can figure in an argument for the existence of God (G VII,302ff./L 486ff.; T 7).[21]

[19]See C 405, where the claim that "the notion of existence is such that [what is] existent is such a state of the universe as pleases GOD" is immediately followed by the observation, "But GOD is pleased, freely, by what is more perfect." Interestingly, Leibniz began to write, "existent is such a state of the universe as is superior" (and before that apparently, "as is [more] perfe[ct]"), and then changed it to present the analysis in terms of pleasing God (VE 165).

[20]For Leibniz's preference for real or causal definitions see, e.g., his "Meditations on Knowledge, Truth, and Ideas" of 1684 (G IV,424f./L 293). For a text in which the definition of existence in terms of perfection is explicitly called a "real definition," and motivated by the need to "give a reason of the existence of things" (specifically a reason that fits the conceptual containment theory of truth), see G VII,195. Note also that in "General Inquiries" (C 360/P 51) Leibniz has already connected the possibility of defining 'existent' as "what is compatible with more things than anything else that is incompatible with it" with the possibility of giving "a cause of existence."

[21]The question of interpretation is well and thoroughly argued in Blumenfeld, "Leibniz's Theory of the Striving Possibles." See also Gr 324 (= VE 189f., with a watermark attested from 1683–86): "Every essence or reality demands existence. . . . And every possible not only involves Possibility, but also an effort [*conatus*] to actually exist—not as if things that are not make an effort, but because

The difficulty this poses for Leibniz goes much deeper than any mere problem of formulation, for it appears to imply that the account of existence given by the pair of definitions applies only to the existence of finite things. It can hardly apply to the existence of God, since Leibniz never suggests that the divine existence itself is to be explained by God's having chosen and actualized it as part of the best possible aggregate of things. This suggestion is not only implausible but also inconsistent with Leibniz's firm insistence that the existence of God is a necessary truth and that necessary truths do not depend on the divine will. This implies that the pair of definitions do not give an adequate account of the nature of existence *in general*, since the divine existence is a case of existence—indeed the prime case of it.

"General Inquiries" might be read as proposing a definition of existence in general, including the existence of God, in its resort to counterfactual modalities. Existence, on this account, would consist in being such as *would* please a God if one existed. God's existence satisfies this criterion because the perfection of the divine nature does please God, according to traditional theology. But this view is liable to an objection that must be crushing from Leibniz's point of view: it renders the existence of creatures, as well as that of God, independent of the presupposition of God's existence. If our world is such as a God *would* choose, that constitutes its existence. God's existing and actually choosing this world are not needed to explain its existence. But the dependence of creatures on God's actual decisions is a persistent theme in Leibniz's philosophy. It is what he chiefly seizes on, for instance, to differentiate his brand of determinism from that of Spinoza.[22]

A better way of integrating the ideas of the pair of definitions into a completely general account of the nature of existence might be sought in a striking text from 1672, early in Leibniz's Paris period. He wrote:

> I seem to myself to have discovered that to Exist is nothing other than to be Sensed [*Sentiri*]—to be sensed however, if not by us, then at least by the Author of things, to be sensed by whom is nothing other than to please him, or to be Harmonious. (A VI,iii,56)

This is not the earliest text in which Leibniz anticipated Berkeley's famous thesis that to be is to be perceived (see A VI,i,285; A VI,ii,282f.,487), and it is certainly not the latest (see C 437, of 1702–4).[23] What is particularly interesting about this text is that the ideas of existence consisting in pleasing God, and in being harmonious (which plays here the part of perfection), are embedded in a more fundamental conception of existing as being perceived, principally by God. These conceptions are linked by Leibniz's version of the traditional Scholastic doctrine that the way in which God knows about the existence of finite things outside himself is by knowing his own will to create them. God senses finite things,

---

the ideas of essences, which actually exist in God, make such a demand, after God has freely decreed to choose what is most perfect. . . . [F]or they are able to obtain existence, not by their own force but by God's decision." Cf. Gr 286, from 1679; and VE 1141 (= LH IV,1,14C,6), probably from about 1689.

[22]See Chapter 1, section 1.4.

[23]For a fuller discussion, see Chapter 9, section 2.

says Leibniz, by perceiving that they are harmonious and therefore please him—that is, by perceiving that he chooses to create them.

This text presents more than one possibility of a quite general account of the nature of existence. The most obvious is the account with which the text begins—that to exist is to be perceived, at least by God. This applies to the existence of God as well as of finite things, since God's existence is surely perceived by God. What is said about being harmonious and pleasing God would serve then to explain how finite things come to be perceived.

A more daring alternative would be to identify existence, in general, with being recognized by God as superior in perfection, and thus pleasing God. Even God's existence, it might be claimed, is not distinct from the pleasure God takes in the divine perfection. For traditional philosophical theology, after all, the divine perfection is the most essential object of the divine knowledge and love. It would not be claimed that God exactly chooses to exist, or causes his own existence by loving it, but rather that existing, for God, consists most essentially in knowing and loving the perfection of his own nature.

Unfortunately, neither of these accounts of the nature of existence provides an explanation of the necessity of God's existence. Perhaps God must exist if anything at all is to be perceived. Certainly God must exist if anything is to please God. But this is no reason for regarding as impossible the state of affairs in which God does not exist and therefore nothing at all is perceived or pleases God or exists. In any event, there is no strong reason to believe that the mature Leibniz held either of these theories.

Another alternative would be to have separate definitions of divine and creaturely existence. For God, existence would be defined simply as being more perfect than any incompossible thing or set of things. For creatures, however, existence would be defined as entering into an aggregate of finite things that pleases God, or is chosen by God, by virtue of the superiority of its sum of perfection to that of alternatives. Perhaps Leibniz would have regarded these separate definitions as having one of the most important of the virtues he sought in a real definition, expressing the real reasons of the existence of God and of creatures, respectively, insofar as they can be known to us. But they can hardly be regarded as entirely satisfying. In addition to the obvious disadvantage of failing to present a unified account of the nature of existence, they give us no answer to the question, What is it that God decides to give to creatures when he chooses them? Indeed, the definition of creaturely existence seems to preclude an answer to that question: if their existence simply *is* being chosen by God, there is nothing left for God's choice to be a decision to do. This is a defect, indeed, of *all* the definitions of existence we have been considering, in their application to creatures. None of them is consistent with Leibniz's theory of creation.

3. *Existence Irreducible*

At this point, the hypothesis that existence is indefinable, or at least not reductively analyzable into simpler elements, might be found appealing. It was, in fact, a recurrent hypothesis in Leibniz's thought, despite the profusion of definitions of existence that he produced. A forceful early statement of it is found in a text dated September 1677:

> *Being* [*esse*] itself seems to be conceived through itself. For suppose it to be conceived through other things, say a and b; it seems that about these things too it can be conceived that they are, which is absurd. Existence [*existentia*] is therefore an uncompounded or unanalyzable notion. (G I,271)[24]

Here, however, the hypothesis appears to be based on the conception, soon to be rejected, of being or existence as an essence or part of an essence. The argument assumes that if existence is analyzable into other terms "through" which it is conceived, they will be parts of an essence, in the sense that they will signify *kinds* of thing that can be conceived as existing, introducing what Leibniz regards as a vicious circularity into the analysis of existence. This argument for the indefinability of existence is therefore not available to Leibniz after he has drawn the appropriate conclusion from the circularity problem, in 1678. And no such circularity seems to arise from a definition of existence as entering into the most perfect possible aggregate of things, since it does not treat existents as a kind of thing.

This is not the only argument for the irreducibility of existence that disappears from Leibniz's thought. The treatment of existence as a perfection, in texts of 1676 bearing on the ontological argument, implies a view of existence as a primitive, unanalyzable quality, for which no real definition can be given. But we have seen that this view of the relation of existence to perfection did not survive Leibniz's discussions with Eckhard; it can be seen in 1704, but only with the qualification "as M. Descartes puts it" (NE 437).

Nonetheless, we still find the indefinability of existence asserted in the following text from the mid-1680s[25]—this time without any argument that Leibniz would thereafter have reason to reject—indeed, without being based on any argument at all:

> *Existent* cannot be defined, any more than Entity [*Ens*] or the purely positive—that is, in such a way that some clearer notion might be shown to us. We should know, however, that every possible will exist if it can; but since not all possibles can exist, as some interfere with others, those exist that are more perfect. Therefore, whatever is most perfect, it is certainly established that it exists. There is, moreover, a certain most perfect Being [*Ens perfectissimum*]; that is, the supremely perfect is possible, since it is nothing other than the purely positive. (Gr 325)

It is interesting that the indefinability of existence is asserted here in conjunction with the doctrine that the most perfect is assured of existing. This might represent a conscious abandonment of the attempt to define existence in terms of that doctrine. To be sure, Leibniz denies only that existence can be analyzed in such a way as to show *us* a clearer notion, but the definition of existence as

[24]This begins a document of about one printed page included by Gerhardt, but not by the Academy edition, in Leibniz's correspondence with Eckhard. It lacks any indication of epistolary form.

[25]Its watermark is attested from 1685; see VE 1251. The text is published more completely in Schmidt 478–84 than in Gr.

inclusion in the best series of possibles surely was an attempt to give *us* a clearer notion.

I am inclined to think that if Leibniz had any stable position on the subject, this caution with regard to definition, and a certain agnosticism about the deepest nature of existence, must have been an important part of it. I interpret the indefinability thesis as denying only that existence is *reducible* to something more fundamental, in which existence *consists*. It is consistent with some, at least, of the definitions of existence that occur in his later papers (and perhaps even some of those in his earlier papers), provided that what they are construed as attempting to identify is not what existence consists in, but only how to recognize existence,[26] or what difference between existing and nonexisting things explains the existence of those that exist.[27] This construal of Leibniz's intent in offering definitions of existence is supported by the cases (quoted in Chapter 9, section 2) in which he offers different definitions for the latter two purposes (VE 404f.,1086).

The conclusion of the passage quoted above from Gr 325 reminds us, however, of an attendant problem. In saying that "the supremely perfect is possible, since it is nothing other than the purely positive," Leibniz seems to be offering, in the briefest possible form, the argument for the possibility of a supremely perfect being that he had shown Spinoza some years earlier. The questions then arise, Is he still entitled to this argument? If so, what use is he entitled to make of it? His indefinability thesis gives rise to the following difficulty.

If a proof of the possibility of an *ens perfectissimum* is to complete an ontological argument that begins with a proof that a necessary God is either actual or impossible, it must be proved that the *ens perfectissimum* would be a necessary being. By 1678 Leibniz seems to have come, rightly, to the conclusion that this cannot be proved by counting (necessary) existence among the perfections (in the sense of his 1676 arguments). It could be proved by a reductive definition of existence in terms of perfection, if that were acceptable, but he appears here to abandon such a definition—again rightly. So a gap may be thought to remain in the argument.

The passage before us suggests a somewhat different strategy of argument, however. It seems to contain an argument for the existence of God, for its brief argument for the possibility of an *ens perfectissimum* immediately follows the statement that it is certainly established that whatever is most perfect exists. The theistic argument this suggests is more modest in its pretensions to purely formal rigor than those of 1676. Leibniz articulates here no logical doctrines, and no definitions, that would justify his premises. He does offer a metaphysical doctrine, however—that "every possible will exist if it can" and "those exist that are more perfect." The existence of a possible being can be prevented only by its incompatibility with something more perfect. This is not a definition, and it applies in different ways to God and creatures. But it does apply to God, on the view that Leibniz seems to hold here. Since an *ens perfectissimum* cannot be incompatible with anything more perfect, it must exist, and will therefore be a

[26]It is hard to believe that more than this is intended by Leibniz's fairly numerous definitions of existence in terms of perceptibility, except perhaps some of the very earliest of them. See p. 169 and Chapter 9, section 2, for citations and fuller discussion.

[27]The definition of existence offered at C 360/P 51 (1686) can be regarded plausibly enough as offered only for the last of these purposes.

necessary being, if it is a possible being at all. The thesis of its possibility will perhaps be supported, not only by the logical argument that, as purely positive, it contains no formal contradiction but also by the metaphysical argument that, as purely positive, it cannot interfere with anything of greater reality.[28]

This metaphysical argument seems consistent with Leibniz's theory of creation. Thus far, however, it is unsatisfying at another important point: it does not explain *why* those possible things exist that are more perfect. Therefore it also fails to explain *how* (necessary) existence is involved in the essence of an *ens perfectissimum*. Moreover, we might suspect that Leibniz's answer to the former question must be a mere conjunction of principles about the necessary existence of the most perfect possible being, on the one hand, and that being's choice of the best possible world of beings of limited perfection, on the other hand. Such a conjunction, if not exactly ad hoc, offers too little insight into the nature of existence (or of anything) to have much persuasive force in this context. The metaphysical analysis must be deepened if it is to satisfy.

Such a deepening might begin with the observation that the principle of essence's demand for existence, in the general form 'Each essence will be exemplified unless there is some reason that prevents its exemplification', is a corollary of a version of the Principle of Sufficient Reason (PSR). Evidence that Leibniz understood it in this way is provided by a text (G VII,194) in which the principle "Every possible demands to exist" takes the place he usually assigns to PSR as the absolutely first among truths of fact. Since PSR, as such, applies equally to the existence of God and of finite things, so, in a general way, does the principle of essence's demand for existence.

Further development of the latter principle for God and creatures bifurcates, however, at the question, What sort of reason can prevent existence? What reasons can prevent a thing's existence depends on whether the thing, if it existed, would exist through itself or through an external cause. If it would exist through itself, its existence can be prevented only by inconsistency in its own essence. If it would exist (if at all) through the causal agency of another being, its existence can be prevented by a reason that would prevent the cause from acting to cause it.

These considerations can be related to Leibniz's views about the perfection of God and of creatures, by way of some of his views about *requirements* [*requisita*]. According to these views, causal dependence and independence are determined by the attributes involved in a thing's essence. The first requirements of any thing are the absolute degrees of the attributes involved in its essence. The line of argument I am developing depends on accepting as necessary truths two principles about requirements and the causation of existence.

First, the being whose essence contains the absolute degrees of all attributes has all its requirements in itself, that is, in its essence. Such a being exists, if at all, through itself. We have already (in Chapter 5, section 2.3) seen evidence that Leibniz held this, at least in 1676. Second, a being that has a limited degree of any attribute exists, if at all, through the causal agency of the being that has the absolute degree of all attributes (or of all that are involved in its essence, but I

[28]The metaphysical type of rationale I have presented in this paragraph could also be used to interpret the brief version of the ontological argument in § 45 of the *Monadology*.

suspect Leibniz thought that an empty qualification). That Leibniz believed this proposition, inasmuch as he believed that God has the absolute degree of all attributes, is clear. To ascribe it to him as a metaphysical principle of deep explanatory force is a more speculative interpretation, but he came close to asserting it as such in 1676, in equating "that which is its own reason for existing" with "that, all of whose requirements we conceive without the concept of another thing" (A VI,iii,275 = G I,131). For he certainly thought that the requirements of a limited being cannot be conceived without the concept of attributes that belong only to an unlimited being.

The second principle is narrower than the principle that he rejected in 1678 or 1679 in objecting to Spinoza that it is "false" that "that without which something cannot be conceived is its cause" (G I,147f./L 203). In this text Leibniz accepts the implication from 'A causes B' to 'The concept of B involves the concept of A', but rejects the converse implication. This is consistent with his maintaining the following: 'The essence of B involves an absolute attribute A which is not an attribute of B' entails 'The existence of B depends causally on the existence of something that does possess A.' It is noteworthy that what Leibniz is attacking is an argument of Spinoza's in support of the proposition that "God is the efficient cause not only of the existences, but also of the essences of things," and that his counterexamples to the inference that he rejects are drawn from relations between mathematical objects. Leibniz does not normally speak of essences as "caused,"[29] and it may be that he is only resisting the extension to essences of a principle that he accepts as applied to existences.

Given that the essence of the *ens perfectissimum*, as Leibniz understands it, is the essence that contains the absolute degrees of all attributes, it has all its requirements in itself and exists, if at all, through itself. Its existence could be prevented, therefore, only by an inconsistency in its essence. Given that, as Leibniz believes, the essence containing the absolute degrees of all attributes is consistent, it follows that nothing can prevent the existence of a being (God, the *ens perfectissimum*) that has the absolute degrees of all perfections; from that and from PSR it follows that the *ens perfectissimum* exists. If all the premises of this reasoning are necessary truths, then the essence of the *ens perfectissimum* involves (necessary) existence. And this indeed is *how* such an essence involves (necessary) existence, on this interpretation of Leibniz.

Finite beings, on the other hand, would exist (if at all) through the causal agency of the *ens perfectissimum*. Their existence therefore can be prevented by a reason that would prevent the *ens perfectissimum* from acting to create them. Given what Leibniz believes about the way the action of a most perfect being is governed by reasons, it follows that the existence of a finite being whose essence is internally consistent can be prevented only by the possibility of a more perfect series of things that excludes it, which is what would give God a reason to refrain from creating the less perfect series.

Thus all essence incorporates a tendency to exist, and the tendency can be

[29]Leibniz does speak of God in Mon 43 as "the source . . . of essences," and at G VII,305/L 488 as "the source [*fons*] of every essence," but in a way that does not depend on the particular content of the essences. I will discuss this subject in the next chapter.

said to be proportioned to the perfection of the essence. This is based on a general principle that applies both to God and to finite beings, though it applies to them in different ways. This reasoning rests on several potentially controversial metaphysical theses. A comprehensive assessment of them would overstep by far the bounds of our historical inquiry, but I think it will be appropriate to consider briefly three objections to the reasoning, as interpretation and as argument.

1. It assumes that the relevant version of PSR is a necessary truth, but it may be doubted whether that is consistent with Leibniz's treatment of PSR as the first principle of contingent truths (G VI,413; cf. T 44, Mon 31–32,36). It is difficult to determine Leibniz's views on the modal status of PSR,[30] but I do not think he is committed to its being contingent in any sense that undermines the argument before us. In the sense that most concerns us here, God has necessary existence if the divine existence follows from the divine essence, without essential reference to the essence of any other thing; moreover, finite things lack necessary existence inasmuch as the reason of their existence does involve the essence (and existence) of another being (God). The existence of finite things remains contingent in this sense even if it is a necessary truth that there must be a reason for their existence or nonexistence.

The question whether the truths involved can be proved by a finite analysis does not enter into this system of ideas, as originally worked out by Leibniz, as I argued at the end of section 1 of Chapter 5. But even if necessity is understood in terms of finite demonstrability, the contingency of finite existences is consistent with the necessary truth of PSR if, as Leibniz believed,[31] it is not finitely demonstrable which finite things have the strongest reasons for their existence. Whether Leibniz in fact thought that 'God always chooses the best' (an obvious and crucial corollary of PSR) is finitely demonstrable, and hence necessary, is a difficult interpretive question; I have argued earlier (Chapter 1, section 2.5) that an affirmative answer fits best with Leibniz's philosophy as a whole.

There is also a textual consideration that favors a reading of Leibniz as supposing that PSR plays a part in grounding the necessary existence of God. Leibniz claims, early and late, that the proof of the existence of God depends on PSR [Gr 268 (1679); NE 179 (1703–05); T 44 (1710)]. How can he have believed this? For he never ceased to believe that the existence of God can be proved by a priori argument, and therefore never believed that a cosmological argument is *required* to prove it (Mon 36–45). These positions can be reconciled, however, if Leibniz thought that even the a priori proofs involve PSR as a principle required to account for the necessity of the divine existence.

2. It is noteworthy that this account of the necessity of God's existence presupposes a version of PSR that requires a reason for the nonexistence as well as for the existence of anything.[32] Indeed, it may be said to demand a reason more stringently for nonexistence than for existence, treating existence rather than nonexistence as

[30]Cf. Parkinson, *Logic and Reality in Leibniz's Metaphysics*, pp. 62–69.

[31]See Chapter 1, sections 2.1–2.2.

[32]Thus far, Leibniz's argument is in agreement with Spinoza, *Ethics* I, prop. 11. Indeed much of the reasoning I am ascribing to Leibniz can be found in Spinoza's argument there, though Leibniz parts company with Spinoza emphatically in the role he assigns to God's will and choice of the good in the reason which explains the existence of those finite things that exist.

the default status, so to speak, for any possible thing. For it allows the absence of a sufficient reason for nonexistence to count as a sufficient reason for existence. This is a controversial feature of the theory, as it is common to demand a reason more stringently for existence than for nonexistence and to allow the absence of a sufficient reason for existence to count as a sufficient reason for nonexistence.[33]

Leibniz's defense on this point is both clear and interesting. He argues that we must suppose that a bias in favor of existence is built into the most fundamental truths of ontology, for otherwise nothing at all would exist, which is manifestly contrary to fact. "This proposition, 'Every possible demands to exist', can be proved a posteriori, given that something exists. . . . If there were not some inclination to existence in the very nature of Essence, nothing would exist" (G VII,194; cf. Gr 16f., G VII,303/L 487).[34] This is not a silly argument. The fact that something exists, rather than nothing, does indeed seem to be a reason for suspecting that there is a bias for existence in the most basic metaphysical truths.

3. It may be suspected that a vicious circle lurks in the very idea of a being that exists "through itself," or through its own essence. In such an explanation of the existence of a necessary being, isn't the existence of the being itself, or at least of its essence, already presupposed? And doesn't that leave either an unexplained existence or a vicious circle in explanation? Here it is significant that the idea that essences involve a "propensity to exist" (Gr 17) does not mean that essences are efficient causes that act to produce the existence of the thing. An efficient cause must already have a foothold in existence in order to act. But essences can be viewed as formal rather than efficient causes (Gr 269). They are not efficient causes of existence.[35] God is the efficient cause of the existence of finite things, and the power to cause their existence is in God. The essences of finite things are *reasons* that influence the creator's choice. Even the divine essence need not be understood as an efficient cause of God's existence. It is a *reason* that excludes the possibility of God's nonexistence.

This does not dispose of the issue of circularity, however, for Leibniz certainly believed that essences require a foothold in existence which depends on the divine existence. It seems that he explains God's existence by God's essence, and he explains the reality of all essences, including God's, as depending on God's existence. This presents an appearance of circularity that cannot be dismissed without a fuller discussion of the relation of the ontological status of essences and their relation to God in Leibniz's philosophy. That relation will be the subject of the next chapter.

[33]Cf. Rowe, *Cosmological Argument*, ch. 2. Rowe is uncertain of the truth of PSR, but proposes as the most defensible version one that demands a reason *only* for *existences*, arguing that some such limitation is necessary to avoid sweeping necessitarian implications of a sort that give rise to much of the discussion in Chapter 1 above.

[34]At PNG 7 (1714), in the course of developing a cosmological argument for the existence of God, Leibniz says that "nothing [*le rien*] is simpler and easier than something." This might seem difficult to reconcile with the doctrine of a fundamental metaphysical bias in favor of existence. I think it is probably something that Leibniz should not have said, but I doubt that it represents an intentional abandonment of the bias for existence, which played a part in his reasonings over a long period of time. For more discussion of this statement in PNG 7, see Chapter 8, pp. 210–11.

[35]Where operation rather than existence is to be explained, however, substantial forms, which are close kin to essences, and may even be viewed as concretized essences, are efficient causes for Leibniz; see Chapter 3, section 1, and Chapter 11, section 1.1.

7

The Root of Possibility

1. The Proof of the Existence of God from the Reality of Eternal Truths

"If there were no eternal substance," wrote Leibniz, "there would be no eternal truths; and from this too GOD can be proved, who is the root of possibility, for his mind is the very region of ideas or truths" (G VII,311/MP 77). Similarly, in the *Monadology* he claimed to have proved the existence of God "from the reality of eternal truths" (Mon 45).

> It is true . . . that in God is not only the source of existences, but also that of essences, insofar as they are real, or of what is real in possibility. That's because the Understanding of God is the region of eternal truths, or of the ideas on which they depend, and because without him there would be nothing real in the possibilities, and not only nothing existing, but also nothing possible.
>
> For if there is a reality in the Essences or possibilities, or indeed in the eternal truths, that reality must be founded in something existing and Actual; and consequently in the Existence of the necessary Being, in which Essence includes Existence, or in which being possible is sufficient for being Actual. (Mon 43–44)

To John Bernoulli, in May 1699, Leibniz wrote that the propositions, "God exists [*est*]" and "Two contradictories cannot be true at once" can be held to "coincide," on the ground that "the Divine essence is, so to speak, the region of eternal truths, so that it is through the existence of God that truths about non-existent possibles are made real, and they would otherwise lack a subject and support" (GM III,586).

This argument deserves attention in its own right. It is more persuasive, I think, than any of Leibniz's (or anyone else's) versions of the ontological argument, though in important ways less complete. It is also the main context[1] for major parts of Leibniz's theory of the ontology of logic.

According to Leibniz, the objects of logic exist in the mind of God. Among these objects are mentioned possibilities or possibles, necessary or "eternal" truths,[2] and essences or ideas. They are stratified. The essences are for Leibniz

[1]Not the only context, however. The theory appears without this argument in T 184, for instance, and in the context of a different, more cosmological argument for theism at G VII,305/L 488.

[2]"*The Eternal Truths* . . . are absolutely necessary, so that the opposite implies a contradiction" (T pd2).

the most fundamental objects of logic. Possibilities depend on essences, as discussed in Chapter 5, and the eternal truths are said to depend on "ideas" (Mon 43), by which I believe essences are meant. The essences can be identified with ideas in God's mind, ideas of possible individuals, which constitute the possibility of such individuals, and which are concatenated to constitute the ideas, and the possibility, of possible worlds. And the necessary truths express, or follow from, facts about the essences and their relations.

Analysis of the argument may begin with a thesis clearly presupposed, but not fully articulated, by Leibniz in the texts quoted above—that whatever is true (or possible), there must *be* something by virtue of which it is true (or possible). This is implied by Leibniz's claim that without the existence of God's mind for the possibilities to exist in, there would be nothing possible (Mon 43). In another context he flatly asserts a similar thesis about truth: "Now it is sure that every true predication has some foundation in the nature of things" (DM 8). And with regard to "the reality of eternal Truths" he says, "Every reality must be grounded in something existent" (T 184; cf. Gr 392f.). These theses have great intuitive appeal, and are by no means peculiarly Leibnizian. Michael Dummett has stated, "It is certainly part of the meaning of the word 'true' that if a statement is true, there must be something by virtue of which it is true."[3] Some may be less certain than Dummett that this is part of the meaning of 'true'; but it is at the very least a philosophically respectable premise.

What is there by virtue of which the truths of logic (and mathematics) are true? Modern thought on this subject has focused mainly on two answers. According to "Platonism,"[4] as it is called, the necessary truths themselves, or the essences, propositions, numbers, or whatever sort of "abstract object" it may be that they depend on, exist, or perhaps "subsist," independently of any other sort of reality—independently, in particular, of being either exemplified or thought of. The principal alternative to Platonism has been "anthropological," as I shall call it, holding that the truths of logic and mathematics are true in virtue of some feature of *human* thought, which might be ideas in our minds, our intentions regarding our use of language, or proofs we have actually constructed.

Leibniz rejected both Platonistic and anthropological theories in the ontology of logic, and he was conscious of this rejection as part of the grounds of his argument for the existence of God from the reality of eternal truths. This is clearer from a pair of early notes, one certainly and both probably from August of 1677, and completely unpublished until recently (VE 65–67 = LH IV,5,3,3–4), than from the later and sketchier formulations of the argument which are better known.

The notes seem to be closely connected with the "Dialogue" of August 1677, in which Leibniz attacks what I am calling an anthropological theory, a type of conventionalism that he ascribes to Hobbes, according to which truths of logic and mathematics are arbitrary because "definitions depend on our decision" (G VII,191/L 183). Leibniz grants that it is arbitrary or conventional what sounds or signs we use in what senses, but he argues that truths of logic and mathematics depend on something else, something more "permanent [*perpetuum*]," and

[3]Dummett, "Wittgenstein's Philosophy of Mathematics," p. 335.

[4]What is said about "Platonism" here is not meant as an interpretation of the historical Plato, though I also do not mean to exclude him from the class of Platonists.

independent of our wills, which appears to correspond to what we would call logical form (G VII,192f./L 184f.).

To say that logical form, and truths grounded in it, are independent of our wills, is not yet to say that they are independent of us in every way. This more sweeping point Leibniz attempted to establish in one of the notes to which I have referred.

> It is true, and even necessary, that the circle is the largest of isoperimetric figures.
>
> Even if no circle really existed.
>
> Likewise even if neither I nor you nor anyone else of us existed.
>
> Indeed even if none of those things existed which are contingent, or in which no necessity is understood, such as the visible world and other similar [things].
>
> Since, therefore, this truth does not depend on our thought, there must be something real in it.
>
> And since that truth is eternal or necessary, this reality too that is in it independent of our thought will be from eternity. (VE 65)

I think the last of these statements contains the main premise of this argument. Since the truths under consideration are eternal, in the sense of being necessary, whatever the reality is in which they are grounded must be eternal and necessary too. The whole argument proceeds on the assumption that there are indeed necessary truths, truths that would be truths no matter what. And since it is surely false that I or you or anyone else of us humans would exist no matter what, it follows that there would be the necessary truths even if we did not exist, and that whatever reality grounds them could be without us—from which in turn it follows that they do not depend on our thought.

Leibniz assumes here that since, trivially, the nonexistence of each contingent thing, considered singly, is possible, therefore a state of affairs is possible in which "none of those things [would exist] which are contingent." This inference is not trivial, and we shall return to it later. For the present, however, the possibility of a state of affairs in which no human beings at all would exist may readily be granted to Leibniz, and that suffices for the rejection of anthropological theories in the ontology of logic, if we assume with Leibniz that there would be necessary truths, and something grounding them, no matter what.

Here Leibniz makes a related point that the being of the necessary truths cannot depend on the existence of things instantiating or exemplifying the essences in which they are grounded, for there would be necessary truths about circles, for example, "even if no circle really existed." Leibniz obviously intends Bernoulli, in 1699, to make a similar inference from the assumption that the eternal truths include "truths about non-existent possibles" (GM III,586).

A Platonist ontology of logic seems no more acceptable to Leibniz. The objects of logic, in his opinion, are not the sort of thing that could subsist of themselves. "The objective realities of thinkable natures and truths . . . are not substances" (VE 66). "If no one[5] thought, there would still exist the impossibility of a square

[5]In the context, "no one [*nemo*]" cannot be intended to exclude God, but only human, or at most finite, thinkers. This is so clear in this text that when Leibniz writes, less than six months later, in a document of January 1678, that "even if no one thought about them, . . . it would still remain true in the region of ideas or truths" that the objects of logic "actually exist," I think we should assume he is not excluding dependence on *God's* thought, but only restating the claim he

larger than an isoperimetric circle. And since it is only a mode, there must be something that is its subject" (VE 67). An impossibility is "only a mode." Likewise "natures and truths are modes" (VE 67). (In these early notes "natures" seem to play the part of essences.) We may wonder whether "mode" is really the right category here, and we should not assume that Leibniz would have adhered to it in this context throughout his career. The basic idea is that impossibilities, truths, natures or essences, and other objects of logic are abstract objects in the original sense; that is, they can be conceived only by abstraction from a richer, more complete being or "subject." The connection of the idea of abstraction with that of modes is explicit in Leibniz's preface for the reprinting, in 1670, of a book by Marius Nizolius: "For concrete [objects] are truly things [*res*]; abstract [objects] are not things, but modes of things." Leibniz goes on to amplify his conception of modes in a way that makes it less surprising that he would treat abstract objects in general as modes of a (divine) mind: "most modes, however, are nothing but relations of a thing to the intellect, or capacities [*facultates*] for appearing" (A VI,ii,417/L 126).

The assumptions grounding Leibniz's rejection of anthropological and Platonist ontologies of logic are intuitively appealing, I think, on both sides. One might be reluctant to let oneself feel the strength of both sets of intuitions at once if one could see no other alternative ontology of logic. Leibniz has an alternative in store, however, a theistic modification of Platonism, sponsored in antiquity by Philo and Augustine, and generally accepted in the Middle Ages.[6] On this view, the reality in which necessary truths, and more generally the being of the objects of logic and mathematics, are grounded is the ensemble of ideas in the mind of God. These ideas take up in many ways the role of the self-subsistent Ideas of Plato's middle dialogues. They exist necessarily, since God's having and understanding them follows from the divine essence, but they can be regarded by Leibniz as modes of the divine being. In this way the implausibilities of both anthropological and Platonist ontologies of logic can be avoided. It seems to be a theoretical advantage of theism that it makes this possible, and Leibniz's proof from the reality of eternal truths is an attempt to exploit this advantage.

A theoretical advantage of any view is of course a reason in its favor, but the rejection of anthropological and Platonist theories, even combined with the assumption that truths of logic and mathematics must have some ground in reality, falls far short of a *proof* of theism. If it is concluded that there must eternally and necessarily exist thoughts of some non-human sort grounding the truths in question, this is a momentous conclusion for metaphysics, but it does not amount to the existence of *God*. For one thing, it is relevant at most to God's intellectual attributes. Nothing in the argument from the reality of eternal truths implies the existence of an omnipotent or perfectly good being, for example. In

has made in the previous clause, that "[e]ssences, truths, or the objective realities of concepts do not depend . . . on *our* thought" (A II,i,391f., italics added), even though in the text from January 1678 there is no explicit identification of "the region of ideas or truths" with the divine mind.

[6]On the medieval background of this aspect of Leibniz's thought, see Grua, *Jurisprudence*, pp. 262–67.

this way it is less complete than the ontological argument, which, if it were successful, would establish the existence of a being perfect in every way.

Still, if the argument could establish the necessary existence of a conceptually omniscient being, a being that eternally understands all essences, possibilities, and necessary truths, that would be a substantial achievement for philosophical theology, as well as for metaphysics in general. But even this requires more argument than we have explored previously. At most we have thus far been given reason to believe that there must necessarily exist thoughts sufficient to ground all those objects. A further inference is required to conclude that thoughts of all of them must necessarily exist in a single mind. Ockham's razor might favor a single omniscient necessary being, as ontologically more parsimonious than a plurality of knowers sufficient to keep the objects of logic in being, but a more rigorous argument would be desirable.

Leibniz attempts to provide such an argument in the two notes from 1677; I know of no other text in which he even takes note of the need for it. His argument of 1677 is based on the interrelations of necessary truths and other objects of logic.

> A plurality of truths joined with each other produce new truths. And there is no truth which does not produce a new truth when united with any other truth whatever. Therefore whatever in any truth exists from eternity with respect to the object [*a parte rei*] is united with any other truth whatever. And this is much more manifest from the fact that one nature joins [*concurrit*] in constituting another nature. Natures and truths are modes. The cause why a necessary proposition is true when no one is thinking must be in some subject with respect to the object [*a parte rei*]. The cause why the above-mentioned proposition about the circle and the square is true is not in the nature of the circle alone nor in the nature of the square alone, but also in other natures that enter into it—for instance, of the equal and of the perimeter. The proximate cause of one thing is single. And its cause must be in some [thing] [*in aliqua*]. Therefore [it must be] in that in which the nature of the circle, the square, and the others is; that is, in the subject of ideas, or God. (VE 67)

Take any plurality, *P*, of (necessary) truths or natures, we may say, to paraphrase Leibniz's argument. Some further necessary truth, *T*, will be based on a relation, *R*, among all the members of *P*, on "some real connection among themselves" that "all the realities in the eternal Truths" have (VE 66). As a necessary truth, *T* would be a truth no matter what. The crucial question for the argument is what must exist, eternally and necessarily, in order to sustain *T* in being.

The ultimate grounds of *T*, in Leibniz's view, are the natures or essences involved in it. They could exist, individually, each as an idea in the mind of a different intelligent being. But Leibniz argues that that would not be enough to sustain *T* in being. As a single thing, *T* must have a single proximate cause or (as it might be better to say in this context) reason or ground. The proximate ground of *T* is *R*.

Leibniz claims that in order to sustain *T* in being, "its [proximate] cause must be in some" thing; and he means, in some *one* thing. What justifies this assumption? Since the "cause" in question is *R*, a relation necessarily obtaining among the members of *P*, we might think that the existence of all the members of *P*, each in a different mind, would be enough to sustain *R*, and hence also *T*, in being. Leibniz's reasons for thinking that would not be enough are to be sought in his views about relations. It is a persistent theme in his philosophy that relations as such, at least insofar as they involve more than one substance, are mental entities, having their being only as objects of thought or perception.[7] A relation has foundations in its *relata*, the items that it relates; but without a mind that relates the *relata*, or regards them as related, the relation itself does not exist. So if all the members of *P* exist in different minds, but there is no one mind that perceives or understands the relation *R* among them, then foundations of *R* exist but *R* itself does not.

We might be tempted to express this view by saying that in such a case the members of *P*, in their isolated existence, are such that *if* some one mind understood them all adequately, then there *would* be the relation *R* among them. But Leibniz cannot accept even this. For the truth of such a counterfactual conditional about the members of *P* would be a relation among them; in fact, it would be equivalent to *R*. And so there can be no such truth if there is no mind with enough understanding to sustain *R* in being. Understood in this way, as it must be to support the theistic argument, Leibniz's thesis of the ideality of relations is very radical, and it is doubtless a point at which some philosophers will object to the argument.

According to Leibniz's argument, for any plurality, *P*, of (necessary) truths or natures, there necessarily exists a necessary truth, *T*, grounded in a relation, *R*, among all the members of *P*; in order to sustain *T* in being there must eternally and necessarily exist at least one mind that understands *R*. But a mind that understands *R* must be one that understands the members of *P*, a mind "in which [the idea of] the nature of the circle, the square, and the others is," if those are the natures in which *T* is grounded; understanding all that, it will presumably be a mind that understands *T* itself. The conclusion of this argument is that for any plurality, *P*, of (necessary) truths or natures, there eternally and necessarily exists at least one mind that understands all the members of *P*.

This may help explain why Leibniz does *not* offer the type of argument that Kant favored in his early (1763) treatise on *The Only Possible Ground of Proof for a Demonstration of the Existence of God*,[8] and still viewed with some favor in his "critical period." It is an argument that God's existence is required to account for the ontological status of possibilities, but it is based on God's *exemplifying* all perfections rather than on God's *understanding* all possibilities. It depends on the idea that "all things as partly real, partly negative, presuppose a being that contains all realities in itself, and that must have constituted these things through the limitation of these realities."[9] It should be clear from Chap-

[7]This theme, as applied to relations of unity among parts, plays an important part in Leibniz's argument that bodies, as aggregates, are merely phenomenal (see Chapter 9, section 3.2). I believe the theme is already present in that argument in 1687 (LA 100f.; cf. the later, more explicit NE 145f.). That relations are beings of reason, or ideal, or depend on the understanding, is frequently stated in Leibniz's works from after 1700 (NE 145,227,265; G II,438,486,517/AG 199,203, L 609; LC V,47). And as early as 1676 he called relations "imaginary ideas" (A VI,iii,399). Cf. Mates, *Philosophy of Leibniz*, ch. 12.

[8]Ak II,64–163; the argument itself is found in pp. 77–92.

[9]Ak XXVIII,1033f., translated in Kant, *Lectures on Philosophical Theology*, p. 66. This text, which ascribes real though limited value to the argument, not sufficing to establish the "objective

ter 4 that Leibniz had in his philosophy the material for such an argument; why didn't he use it? One possible reason is that because of his views about relations, Leibniz thought that it is not enough for the ontological ground of possibilities and necessary truths to contain the materials for their construction; it must also contain some correlate of the limitations and other relations by which they are constructed from those materials, and the latter can be found in the contents of God's understanding, but not in God's attributes as such.

One step remains to the conclusion that there eternally and necessarily exists a conceptually omniscient mind. It depends on the assumption that the *totality* of essences, possibilities, and necessary truths constitutes the sort of plurality I have discussed, that must have a necessary truth grounded in a relation among *all* its members. This is not a trivial assumption. Leibniz seems to rely on it without argument, though he knew well enough (if less well than twentieth-century logicians) that paradox can lurk in infinitizing or maximizing assumptions (see, e.g., G IV,424/L 293). The "classical" intuitions about logic and mathematics that impel Leibniz to reject anthropological theories provide some support for the view that there are necessary truths that depend on nothing less than the totality of all essences and possibilities, and perhaps on all necessary truths other than themselves. But if this view is too fraught with risks of paradox, one who shared Leibniz's other premises might seek to avoid paradox by stratifying the objects of logic into "logical types" and might maintain that for each logical type there is a necessary truth (of the next higher type) grounded in *all* the essences, possibilities, and necessary truths of that type and lower types—and hence that there eternally and necessarily exists at least one intelligent being that is conceptually omniscient with respect to that type and lower types. Thus the Leibnizian could have a proof of the necessary existence of conceptual omniscience up to as high a logical type as you please.

The conclusion of Leibniz's argument to this point is that it is necessary that there exists at least one being that is omniscient with respect to a vast realm of possibilities, necessities, and essences. Would this be a necessary being? It must be, if Leibniz was correct in assuming, as he seems to have done, at least in 1677,[10] that if each possible being of a certain type is contingent, it must be possible for *none* of them to exist. But this is not obviously correct. Why couldn't it be necessary that there is *some* conceptually omniscient being (for reasons indicated in the proof from the reality of eternal truths), but contingent *which* such being exists? Some may doubt that Leibniz has adequate reason for rejecting this hypothesis, but it is not likely to appeal to anyone as committed as he was to the Principle of Sufficient Reason: it is hard to see what the sufficient reason would be that would determine *which* of those individually contingent beings would exist, if there is not one of them that necessarily exists with the power to decide which contingent beings shall exist.

necessity" of God's existence, but only "the subjective necessity of supposing it," represents lectures given after the first edition of the *Critique of Pure Reason*.

[10]See the discussion of VE 65, p. 179 in this chapter.

2. Leibniz's Theory Examined

Having examined Leibniz's principal line of argument for it, we may further explore his theological theory of the ontology of logic by considering three objections to it, beginning with the charge of circularity that I mentioned at the end of Chapter 6.[11]

2.1 Circularity or Self-Existence?

The charge may be directed at Leibniz's account of the reality of essences. The thesis that God's existence is necessary plays a prominent part in Leibniz's account of the ontology of logic. Leibniz understands necessary existence in terms of a being's existence following from its essence, as we have seen in Chapters 5 and 6. But if Leibniz holds that the reality of all essences, presumably including the divine essence, depends on the existence of God, while also explaining God's existence as grounded in the divine essence, is he not involved in a vicious circle?

Alternatively, the charge may be directed at Leibniz's account of the reality of eternal truths, as it was by Bertrand Russell:

> Moreover, God's existence is deduced from the Law of Contradiction, to which it is therefore subsequent. . . . Again, without the law of identity or contradiction, as Leibniz truly says (G V,14), there would be no difference between truth and falsehood. Therefore, without this law, it could not be true, rather than false, that God exists. Hence, though God's existence may depend upon the law of contradiction, this law cannot in turn depend upon God's existence.[12]

An attempt might even be made to enlist Leibniz himself in support of this objection. He pressed a similar charge of circularity against the Cartesian doctrine that necessary truths depend on God's will: "For thus the necessity of the divine existence and the necessity of the divine will themselves will depend on the divine will; and thus something will be both prior and posterior in nature to itself" (A II,i,351 = G I,253). Leibniz sees Descartes as involved in a vicious circle that affects God's understanding as well as God's will: "For if the truth itself depends only on the will of God and not on the nature of things, and as the understanding is necessarily *prior* to the will (I speak of natural, not temporal, priority), God's understanding will be prior to the truth of things and consequently will not have the truth as its object" (A II,i,507 = G IV,285). Can Leibniz escape circularity in his own theory without renouncing either his theological ontology of logic or the necessity of God's existence?

A first point to be made in Leibniz's defense is that he normally seeks or postulates a *reason*, rather than an *efficient cause*, for the divine existence. In 1677 he wrote, "If [something] is through itself [*per se*], then its reason of existing is taken from its own nature. . . . But if something is through something else, then it has a reason of existing outside itself; that is, it has a cause" (VE 302 =

[11]Important discussions of Leibniz's views on the ontology of logic, including aspects of his views that I will not treat here, are found in Mates, *Philosophy of Leibniz*, ch. 10; Mondadori, "Nominalisms"; and Mugnai, "Leibniz's Nominalism."

[12]Russell, *Philosophy of Leibniz*, p. 180.

LH IV,4,3C,12–14), which seems to deny a cause to anything that exists per se. Leibniz does not usually even speak of God as *causa sui* [self-caused], except when discussing Spinoza.[13] This is an important difference between Leibniz's own position and Cartesian voluntarism, as I take him to have understood it in 1677. For the will seems to be an efficient cause, and one that presupposes alternatives in some sense possible.[14] There is a vicious circle in the idea of such a cause pushing itself into existence. But we are not to take Leibniz as thinking of the divine essence pushing itself, or God, into existence. Nor is such a push needed, for a main point of Leibniz's doctrine is that there is not, and cannot be, any state of affairs in which God does not exist. There is no problem of getting from divine nonexistence to divine existence, for there is no possible divine nonexistence to be a starting point for any transition. The only possible problem for explanation here is what reason there can be why the divine existence is necessary.

All of the key theses in this part of Leibniz's philosophy, indeed, are asserted as necessary truths. That God exists; that God's essence exists; for each essence, that it exists; for each of the eternal truths (including the principle of contradiction), that it is true; for each of the essences and eternal truths, that God understands it; that the reality of the essences and eternal truths consists in God's understanding them—all are necessary truths according to Leibniz. Whatever relations of explanation and metaphysical dependence Leibniz supposes to obtain among these theses, he cannot consistently suppose that any of them is independent of any of the others in the sense that there is a possibility of its obtaining without them, for he does not believe that there is any possibility of any of them not obtaining. All necessary truths are in this way inseparable from each other.

We must be careful therefore not to foist on Leibniz claims of priority to which he is not committed. His argument for theism from the reality of eternal truths does not imply that God's understanding is naturally prior to the necessary truths. It does imply that the truths could not exist without being understood by God, and that is supposed to explain what sort of being the truths have. But it is equally part of Leibniz's view that God could not exist without understanding exactly those necessary truths. Neither could exist without the other. They are two sides of a single fact.

God exists through himself [*per se*], according to Leibniz. Alternatively, God exists through his essence; but Leibniz affirms the traditional thesis that "In God existence does not differ from Essence" (Gr 302/AG 28; cf. Gr 354). Either way, God's existence is presented as *self*-explanatory. The existence of God, the real-

[13]See Grua, *Jurisprudence*, p. 244. Grua's point is presumably that in criticizing Spinoza for defining *causa sui* as "that whose essence involves existence" (B 104 & G I,147, cited by Grua, loc. cit.), Leibniz implies that an essence involving existence is not to be understood as a cause in the usual sense. The texts do not seem to me to imply that much, for in both Leibniz says rather that Spinoza needs to *prove* that *causa sui* so defined has the usual causal implications. The texts do at least imply, however, that Leibniz did not think the idea of a thing's existence being explained by its own essence can only be understood in terms that are in the ordinary sense causal.

[14]That it presupposes this seems to be implied by Leibniz in 1677; on the Cartesian view, since the nature of justice depends on the divine will, "there will be able to be a world in which the pious are damned, the impious saved" (A II,i,352 = G I,254). By 1710 Leibniz had not changed his own opinion, but was prepared to entertain an alternative interpretation of Descartes's voluntarism (T 186), which is discussed later in section 2.3.

ity of the divine essence, and of all other essences as contained in it, and the truth of all necessary truths as grounded therein, form in a sense a single indissoluble metaphysical reality, the first of all realities. There is no getting beyond it to anything metaphysically deeper. It must therefore have the reason of its existence within itself, in accordance with Leibniz's version of the Principle of Sufficient Reason. The standpoint from which such a reason can be given can only be one in which the existence rather than the nonexistence of this first, divine reality is the default value, so to speak—just as we can intelligibly speculate about the ontological status of the Principle of Contradiction only from a standpoint in which the truth rather than the falsity of that principle is the default value.

A reason given from this standpoint should not be seen as specifying something that *makes* God exist. It is more naturally understood as explaining why there is no alternative possibility to be opposed to the divine existence. One approach to this takes up an idea central to the tradition of the ontological argument: that the divine existence is too good to be false—that God is so perfect that God cannot fail to exist. It focuses, however, on the converse: that a supposed state of affairs in which God does not exist is too defective, metaphysically, to be possible. What would be the defects of such a state of affairs? An answer to this question suggested by the proof from the reality of eternal truths is that a supposed state of affairs in which God would not exist would not have the necessary structure of any state of affairs, inasmuch as there would be in it no necessary truths (indeed in a certain sense no truths at all), because there would be in it no ideas, possibles, essences, or relations among them.

Despite the metaphysical inseparability of all necessary truths from one another, it remains that in our reasonings we derive some necessary truths from others and explain some features of the system of necessary truths in terms of other features of it. Leibniz is clearly engaged in such an enterprise with regard to the essence and existence of God. But it is important that we can distinguish here two quite different questions: *Why* does God exist? *What kind of being* does God's essence have? The first question gets (in Leibniz's view) an answer in terms of the (character of) God's essence. The second gets the answer that God's essence exists as exemplified and understood by God—which of course cannot be unless God exists. But it is not *the same* question that gets answered in terms of God's essence as regards God's existence, and in terms of God's existence as regards God's essence. Similarly, the proposition 'God exists' depends for its *truth* on the truth of the Principle of Contradiction, while the Principle of Contradiction depends on the existence of God, not for its truth, but for its *reality*. In this way, I think, a vicious circle in explanation is avoided. To be sure, Leibniz has not explained God's existence in terms of something that could exist without God existing, but there cannot be any such thing if God's existence is necessary as Leibniz claims.

2.2 God and the Epistemology of Logic and Mathematics

The point that necessary truths depend on the existence of God, not for their truth, but for their reality,[15] has important implications for the epistemology of

[15]This thesis is emphasized, and ascribed to Duns Scotus as well as to Leibniz, in Mondadori, "Modalities, Representations, and Exemplars: the 'Region of Ideas'."

necessary truth. It explains why Leibniz can say, "Essences can in a certain way be conceived without God, but existences involve God" although "the very reality of the essences, by which indeed they flow into existences, is from God" (RS 24/AG 273). One can understand the contents and interrelations of essences without any attention to the fact that their reality consists in their being understood by God, whereas, according to Leibniz, one cannot understand why other things exist without reference to God. Leibniz held that "an Atheist can be a Geometer. But if there were no God, there would be no object of Geometry" (T 184). The atheist geometer does not necessarily make geometrical mistakes; she can understand the reasons for all necessary geometrical truths about, say, triangles. The reasons for these truths are found in the content and interrelations of the essence of triangle and other essences. One can understand them without inquiring what the reality of essences and necessary truths consists in, though not without in some sense recognizing that reality. To explain, correctly, why there is any essence of triangle at all, one must refer to God. But one can understand without reference to God why it follows from the essences of triangle, angle, side, and so on that a triangle has just as many sides as angles.

In another way, however, Leibniz can hardly regard knowledge of geometry or logic as completely independent of awareness of God. If the objects of logic and mathematics have their reality in God's mind, in being understood by God, it seems to follow that in knowing them we are aware of some of God's thoughts. And Leibniz does not reject this inference, though of course he denies that the atheist mathematician must recognize what she knows as thoughts of God. Like Augustine,[16] he links a theological ontology of logic with an epistemology of divine illumination:

> While what is true remains true even if it were known by no human being; and what is good retains its goodness even if no human being made use of it; on the other hand, if there were no God, there would not only be nothing actual, but also nothing possible, and thus the true and the good would be annihilated together, so that it can well be said that the *true* is what agrees with the understanding, and the *good* is what agrees with the will, of God, the first being [*Urwesen*].
>
> And this can also help us to distinguish the true from the false and the good from the evil. For there are found in us certain rays of the divine wisdom and of the eternal word, namely the first eternal truths which are a criterion [*maaß*] of the others that spring from them. In other words, just as he is an original source of all things, so also is all fundamental knowledge to be derived from God's knowledge, and in his light we see light. (G VII,111)

The continuation of this passage, on the good, need not concern us here. The remarks about the good in quoted text have a more voluntaristic flavor than is usual in Leibniz, who generally insists that God's understanding of the good is prior to God's will. The statement that "the good is what agrees with the will of God" can of course be read in a sense that is consistent with Leibniz's usual views, since he famously held that what is best is in fact always willed by God. But perhaps this text is anomalous on this point.

[16]Augustine, *De diversis quaestionibus LXXXIII*, xlvi, in PL vol. 40, cols. 30–31.

There is no reason, however, to suspect that its teaching about divine illumination is anomalous for Leibniz. He expresses similar views in other places. "God is the sun and light of souls, 'the light illuminating every human being who comes into this world'," he declares (DM 28), quoting the Bible (John 1:9). "Our Understanding comes from God, and should be considered as a ray from that sun" (G III,353).

The terminology of divine "illumination" and of rays from the divine sun is obviously metaphorical.[17] What relations between God and the human mind Leibniz regarded as justifying the metaphor may perhaps be seen more clearly in considering his reaction to Nicolas Malebranche's celebrated doctrine that we see all things in God. That doctrine, to be sure, is not concerned simply with the ontology and epistemology of logic and mathematics, but what Leibniz says about ideas in response to it certainly applies to his own views on those subjects.

Leibniz understood Malebranche to mean that "our ideas themselves are in God, and not at all in us." That view Leibniz regarded as irreconcilable with his own account of the nature of substance, according to which every substance must have in itself a ground of all its predicates. In particular, the human soul "includes everything that happens to it, and expresses God, and with him all possible and actual beings" (DM 29). That in our souls which grounds our being truly said to know the objects of logic and mathematics, and which expresses those objects as they are in God, is our idea of those objects; and it is indeed in us.

Nevertheless, Leibniz acknowledged a sense in which we "see in God" the possibilities which "subsist always as eternal truths of the possibles whose whole reality is grounded in something actual—that is to say, in God." Leibniz is

> persuaded that God is the only immediate external object of souls, since there is nothing but him outside the soul that acts immediately on the Soul. And our thoughts, with all that is in us, inasmuch as it includes some perfection, are produced without interruption by his continuous operation. So inasmuch as we receive our finite perfections from his which are infinite, we are immediately affected by them; and it is thus that our mind is immediately affected by the eternal ideas that are in God, when our mind has thoughts that are related to them and participate in them. And it is in this sense that we can say that our Mind sees everything in God. (G VI,593f./L 627)

The claim that God is the only immediate external object of our souls is found in writings from quite different periods of Leibniz's life.[18] The principal reason given for it in the text I have quoted is causal: God is the only external cause on which our existence and finite perfections, including our ideas, directly depend. "Because of the divine concurrence which continually confers on each creature whatever of perfection there is in it, it can be said that the external object of the soul is God alone, and that in this sense God is to the mind as light is to the eye" (Dutens II,224/L 593).

These causal claims must be understood, of course, in the context of the theory of pre-established harmony. The whole series of my thoughts is a consequence

[17]Leibniz could express the same thought in an altenative metaphor, appealing to the ear rather than the eye: "Reason is the natural voice of God" (Gr 138).

[18]G VI,593 is from 1712–15 (on the date, see RML 427f.). Dutens II,224 is from 1707, and DM 28 is from 1686. See also G III,561f., from 1714.

of my own nature. God does not intervene to cause any thoughts in me that do not follow from my nature. What God directly and continually causes is simply the existence of a unique being having my nature. But in so doing God also causes the ideas that are consequences of my nature. And as "every effect expresses its cause" (DM 28), my finite perfections, including my ideas, as aspects of my nature, are caused by the infinite perfections in God to which they correspond.

The causal relation is surely relevant to the claim that God is an object of our awareness in our understanding of logic and mathematics, but it is just as surely not enough to establish it. Leibniz sees the claim as grounded also in a relation of expression or resemblance, which in turn is grounded in the causal relation.

> Thus it is only in virtue of the continuous action of God on us that we have in our soul the ideas of all things; that is to say, because every effect expresses its cause, and because the essence of our soul is thus a certain expression, imitation, or image of the divine essence, thought, and will, and of all the ideas that are contained there. It can therefore be said that God alone is our immediate object outside us, and that we see all things through him. (DM 28)

Since God is our cause and "every effect expresses its cause," therefore the essence of our soul expresses or images, in its imperfect way, the divine essence. And because the divine essence includes the divine ideas of all things, therefore our essence, in expressing or imaging the divine essence, includes ideas that express or image the divine ideas. Inasmuch as our ideas of the objects of logic express the divine ideas and are caused by them, they can be said to have the divine ideas as their object, in Leibniz's view. This conclusion may be further confirmed by the reflection that we readily take ourselves, in logic and mathematics, to be thinking about something that is independent of our thought; that can be so, according to Leibniz, only if we are thinking about something that exists, whether we realize it or not, in God's mind.

An epistemology of divine illumination is not a silly theory. I think, in fact, it may be the best type of theory available to us for explaining the reliability of our supposed knowledge of logic and mathematics, since the alternative type of theory most salient for us, in terms of natural selection, does not obviously explain our aptitude for the higher reaches of those subjects, which was of no use to our ancestors on whom the selective pressures were supposedly operative. But this is not the place to develop that point; I have argued it elsewhere.[19]

2.3 Truth and Divine Understanding

Some of Bertrand Russell's objections to Leibniz's ontology of logic seem to be based on an interpretation of Leibniz as holding that God's knowing or understanding the necessary truths is "what makes them true."[20] This reading of Leibniz might be supported by a text I quoted in the previous section, according to which "it can well be said that the *true* is what agrees with the understanding . . . of God" (G VII,111). I believe this is not a correct interpretation, but the point is subtle and requires some examination.

[19] R. Adams, "Divine Necessity."
[20] Russell, *Philosophy of Leibniz*, p. 180.

Throughout his career, Leibniz was vehemently opposed to the Cartesian thesis that necessary truths depend on God's *will*.[21] This thesis, he argued, is contrary to the very nature of the will: "the will of God presupposes an understanding of the thing to be willed. This understanding involves the possibility of the thing understood. Therefore the will presupposes the possibility of the thing to be willed" (A II,i,354 = G I,256). Hence it is incoherent to suppose that the will of God determines what is possible. But possibilities are inseparable from essences and necessary truths, which must therefore also be presupposed by the divine will. The theological consequences of the Cartesian position, moreover, seemed to Leibniz appalling. If God's will did not presuppose essences and necessities independent of it, Leibniz argued—particularly if it did not presuppose the essences of justice and goodness, and necessary truths following from them—then God would be arbitrary in ways that would fatally undermine belief in divine goodness and justice (A II,i,298f.; Gr 433).

In the *Theodicy* Leibniz tries to put a more acceptable interpretation on Descartes's claims.

> I suspect that he had in view here another extraordinary way of speaking, of his own invention, which was to say that affirmations and negations, and internal judgments in general, are operations of the will. And by this artifice the eternal Truths, which had been, up until this writer, an object of the divine understanding, have become at one stroke an object of [God's] will. Now the acts of his will are free, so God is the free cause of the Truths. (T 186)

On this interpretation, however, "these actions would be nothing less than free, for there is nothing to choose." The account would "keep only the name of freedom" (T 186). The point of this criticism, of course, is that a free choice must be among a plurality of alternatives possible in themselves (see Chapter 1, section 1.4). That there is no such alternative to a necessary truth, even for the divine will, is perhaps the central thesis in Leibniz's critique of Cartesian voluntarism.

In this passage of the *Theodicy* Leibniz does not reject the thesis, ascribed to Descartes, that necessary truths depend on the affirmations or judgments by which God accepts them. Elsewhere, however, he does reject it, and I think the rejection expresses an authentically Leibnizian thought.

> It is thoroughly erroneous, however, [to think] that the eternal truths and the goodness of things depend on the divine will, since every volition presupposes a judgment of the understanding about goodness—unless someone by a change of names were to transfer all judgment from the understanding to the will—though even then it could not be said that the will is the cause of the truths, since the judgment also is not. The reason of the truths lurks in the ideas of things, which are involved in the divine essence itself. (G VII,311/MP 77)

No mental act, whether of the will or of the understanding, makes the necessary truths true, Leibniz implies here, because the necessary truths follow from the divine essence, which is presupposed by all God's mental acts.

[21]Important texts from the period of Leibniz's fullest development of the ontological argument and the proof from the reality of eternal truths are A II,i,298f.,351–55 (1676–77). From the middle years see DM 2 (1686) and Gr 365 (1695), and from his last years see T 186 (1710) and Mon 46 (1714). For other references see Grua, *Jurisprudence*, pp. 142f., 270–73.

Understanding and belief are not mental acts in the same way as judgment, however, and it seems to be through the divine understanding that "the ideas of things" in general "are involved in the divine essence." Could it still be God's understanding (and hence believing or accepting) them that makes the necessary truths true? Here I think we must return to a distinction very similar to one that was introduced earlier in section 2.1.

We can ask (1) Why are the necessary propositions *true*? Leibniz's answer seems to be that "the reason of the truths [why they are true rather than false] lurks in the ideas of things." That is, those propositions that are necessarily true are so because of the *content* of the (divine) ideas. "The sole principle of necessary truths is that the contrary implies [a contradiction] in terms" (A II,i,351 = G I,253; cf. Gr 365), as Leibniz says in criticizing Cartesian voluntarism. It is necessary, of course, that God believes or accepts the necessary truths; but that is necessary because of the reasons for their truth that are found "in the [divine] ideas of things." It is not because God accepts them that they are truths rather than falsehoods.

We can also ask (2) What sort of *being* do the necessary truths have? According to Leibniz, of course, their being depends on God's understanding. Does it depend on their being recognized in the divine intellect as truths, or simply on the presence there of the ideas on which they are based? That is a difficult distinction to make. Can one understand an idea, or can God perfectly understand an idea, without recognizing the necessary truths that flow from it? In section 1 of this chapter I argued that Leibniz's fullest version of the proof of God's existence from the reality of eternal truths depends on the theses that necessary truths typically depend on relations among ideas, and that the being of a relation depends on its being perceived or understood by some mind. But how can God perceive the relevant relations among ideas without recognizing the corresponding necessary truths? Such considerations should probably lead Leibniz to the conclusion that the being of necessary truths typically consists in their being recognized or accepted as true by God, though the reason why they are true (and hence accepted) rather than false (and hence rejected) is to be found in their content rather than in the divine acceptance as such.

8

Presumption of Possibility

Even if we have not found a compelling proof of the possibility of a necessary God, as long as such a being has not been proved impossible, Leibniz claims, it is to be *presumed* possible. Given that his modal version of the ontological argument shows at least that a necessary God does exist *if* the existence of such a being is possible, Leibniz is offering a presumptive proof of the existence of God.[1] This chapter is devoted to a study of this argument and its background in Leibniz's thought. We will begin with four statements of the argument from two quite different periods of his career.

1. In his initial conversation with Arnold Eckhard about the ontological argument, Leibniz records (5 April 1677), when he had said that Cartesians ought to prove the possibility of a most perfect Being, Eckhard called this a "hard demand," saying "that such a possibility need not be proved." After some discussion of geometrical examples, in which Leibniz seems to have obtained a concession that possibility proofs sometimes can and should be provided, Eckhard claimed "that it is otherwise with simpler things, which are understood to be possible." Leibniz describes the ensuing discussion:

> *I* [said] that their possibility is probable, but not certain, until it is proved. Certainly it is presumed until the contrary is proved. But this mode of proof is admitted only in the forum, not in philosophy. *He* [said] that it is admitted even in philosophy, for it is not the case that everyone is bound to prove everything. *I* [said] that if it concerns practice [*praxis*], I grant that the possibility of a necessary Being or most perfect Being is presumed. But where demonstration is concerned, it is incumbent on one who seeks perfect certainty or demonstration to prove all the propositions that he relies on. (A II,i,312f. = G I,213f.)

2. In a letter about the Cartesian ontological argument, probably written in the later part of 1678 to the Palatine Princess Elizabeth, Descartes's correspondent,[2] Leibniz says:

[1]On the background of this chapter in Leibniz's thought about probability, I have been helped by the classic discussion in Couturat, *La logique de Leibniz*, pp. 239–60; by Hacking, *Emergence of Probability*, esp. chs. 10, 14–15; and by Burkhardt, *Logik und Semiotic in der Philosophie von Leibniz*, pp. 422–34. A most helpful specialized study with considerable discussion of presumption is de Olaso, "Leibniz et l'art de disputer."

[2]The recipient is addressed simply as "Madame" and "Your Highness." Gerhardt (G IV,268) suggested that she was Elizabeth's sister Sophia, who in 1678 was sister-in-law to the Duke of

Moreover, I infer . . . that there is a presumption that God exists. For there is always presumption on the side of possibility; that is to say, everything is held to be possible until its impossibility is proved. Therefore there is also a presumption that God is possible—that is to say, that he exists, since in him existence is a consequence of possibility. That can suffice for the conduct of life [*la practique de la vie*], but it is not enough for a demonstration. (A II,i,436/ AG 238)

3. The fullest statement, and a more emphatically favorable evaluation, of a presumptive justification of theistic belief is found in a presentation that arose from Leibniz's discussions with Isaac Jaquelot in 1702:

This argument of Descartes, and before him of St. Anselm, Archbishop of Canterbury, is not a Sophism, as some claim; and in my opinion it is only an incomplete argument, or something must still be supplied. But if nothing would be supplied, there is already a very considerable usefulness, incomplete as the argument is, in that it shows that the divine Nature has the privilege that It needs, for its Existence, only its possibility or essence. And furthermore, this argument yields at least presumptively the Existence of God.

For every being ought to be judged possible until the contrary is proved, until it is shown that it is not possible at all.

This is what is called *presumption*, which is incomparably more than a simple *supposition*, since most suppositions ought not to be admitted unless they are proved, but everything that has presumption for it ought to pass for true until it is refuted.

Therefore the existence of God has presumption for it in virtue of this argument, since it needs nothing besides its possibility. And possibility is always presumed and ought to be held for true until the impossibility is proved.

So this Argument has the force to shift the burden of proof to the opponent, or to make the opponent responsible for the proof. And as that impossibility will never be proved, the existence of God ought to be held for true.

In order to complete the demonstration in an absolute and Geometric manner, however, it is to be wished that the proof of the possibility in question be given. (G III,443f.)

4. The latest of these texts is also the most familiar. A statement of the presumptive argument is found in the *New Essays* (1703–5):

And it is already something that by this remark [about the Cartesian argument] it is proved that *given that God is possible, he exists*, which is the privilege of Divinity alone. One has the right to presume the possibility of every Being, and above all that of God, until someone proves the contrary. So that

Hannover and would soon become Duchess of Hannover, and Leibniz's patroness. The editors of A II,i suggest the Princess Elizabeth (at that time Abbess of Herford) as the letter's addressee and propose 1678 as the date. They give no reasons, but I think they are probably right. The letter indicates that it was written to someone who had spoken briefly with Leibniz and asked for his views on the Cartesian argument. The Princess Elizabeth visited Hannover "in the winter of 1678" (Aiton, *Leibniz: A Biography*, p. 90; cf. A II,i,455). Beginning 5 December 1678, moreover, and continuing into 1680, one of Leibniz's correspondents, F. A. Hansen, repeatedly asked for a copy of a letter "touching the philosophy of Monsieur Descartes" that Leibniz had written to the Princess Elizabeth (A I,ii,389, 408,501; A I,iii,418f.). Hansen's reference is probably to the letter that concerns us here.

> this metaphysical argument already yields a moral demonstrative conclusion, which implies that in the present state of our knowledge we ought to judge that God exists, and act accordingly. (NE 438)

One is tempted to regard this argument, even in its fullest form, as a rather casual effort. Presumption is an inferior alternative to proof, and Leibniz always thought he could *prove* the existence of God in one way or another. Moreover, there seems to be an easy and obvious refutation of the presumptive argument in this case. For if "there is always presumption on the side of possibility," it would seem that presumption should favor the possibility of the nonexistence, as much as the possibility of the existence, of a necessary God. If the argument discussed in Chapter 5, section 1, is sound, however, either the existence or the nonexistence of a necessary God must be impossible. If the existence is not impossible, it is necessary; and if the existence is necessary, the nonexistence is impossible. Presuming either possibility therefore leads to rejection of the other, and the two opposing presumptions of possibility seem to cancel each other.

1. *Jurisprudence and Pragmatism in Theology*

This objection may indeed be conclusive, and we will return to discuss it more fully. But there is more to Leibniz's argument than meets the eye. Behind his appeals to presumption in connection with the ontological argument lies a large apparatus of definition and argument rooted in a particular intellectual tradition, a tradition of jurisprudence or legal theory. Most readers of this essay will be familiar with the rule of English common law according to which the defendant in a criminal case is "presumed innocent until proven guilty." Leibniz's voluminous writings in jurisprudence, oriented toward Roman law, also abound in discussions and cases of presumption. For instance, "a possessor is presumed to be an owner" (A VI, iii,608). When Leibniz says to Eckhard that presumption "is admitted only in the forum, not in philosophy," we are rightly reminded of the role of presumption in legal procedure and legal theory.

In thus calling attention to the fact that the concept of presumption has its home in the law rather than in "philosophy," Leibniz may strike us as disparaging the presumptive argument. This impression may be deepened by the related contrast between "practice" [*praxis*] or "the conduct of life" [*la pratique de la vie*] and "demonstration" in both of the first two passages I have quoted, for we know that what presumption governs in the legal system is *behavior*. Persons presumed innocent, for example, are not necessarily *believed* innocent. But surely (and particularly in the Lutheran tradition to which Leibniz belonged) religion requires belief or faith, and not just behavioral conformity. It might therefore seem natural to conclude that presumption could not be worth much in defense of a religious thesis, such as the existence of God, and that the assessment of the presumptive argument in the two earlier texts is widely at variance with the rather enthusiastic evaluation in the piece from 1702.

This interpretation is not totally mistaken. Certainly Leibniz meant to compare presumption unfavorably with demonstration. The theoretical insufficiency of presumption is most heavily emphasized in the earliest of these texts, and its apologetic usefulness is evident in the much later pair. But there is also an early text (probably of 1677–78) in which Leibniz offers the principle that "each thing is held to be possible until the contrary is proved" as a reason why a proof "that God either is impossible, or else actually exists" is "of great importance."[3] In the *New Essays*, moreover, a clear affirmation of the value of the presumptive argument seems to coexist happily with a characterization of its conclusion as "moral" and an emphasis on its relevance for action. A closer examination of Leibniz's conception of the relations among theology, jurisprudence, and the logic of probability will greatly mitigate the apparent disparagement of presumption in any of these texts and will show that all of them can be interpreted as expressing the same system of views, without any fundamental change from the earliest to the latest.

Leibniz clearly thought that jurisprudence is important for theology.[4] In his *New Method of Learning and Teaching Jurisprudence*, published in 1667, he states that "Theology is a certain species of Jurisprudence (the latter being taken universally); for it deals with the [system of] Justice [*Jus*] and Laws [*Leges*] obtaining in the Republic, or rather kingdom, of GOD over human beings." He justifies this claim by mapping a long list of topics of theology onto topics of legal theory. For instance: "infidels are like *rebels*; the Church like *good subjects*"; the doctrines of Scripture, the last judgment, and eternal damnation are like those of laws, judicial process, and capital punishment (A VI,i,294).[5] "In short," he adds, "almost all of Theology depends in large part on Jurisprudence. How often is a *testament*, how often *inheritance*, how often *slavery*, how often is *adoption* mentioned by St. Paul?" He goes on to give other examples of the use of legal concepts in theology (A VI,i,295). Leibniz cannot be said to have articulated here the idea, recently proposed in theology,[6] that the doctrines of religious bodies (as distinct from personal religious beliefs) are best understood as rules governing (verbal as well as nonverbal) behavior, but something of the sort may be implicit in his identification of the theological doctrine "of fundamental Errors" (heresies) as "like [the legal doctrine] of *Capital Crimes*" (A VI,i,294).

Thirty years later the same basic idea of theology as jurisprudence is expressed, though less fully and more cautiously, in a letter to Vincent Placcius: "practical theology is nothing but jurisprudence for the universal republic whose ruler is God, insofar as it describes our duties in it" (Dutens VI,i,84). 'Practical theology' here does not refer primarily, as it often does in modern theological curricula, to the arts of religious ministry and their specific theoretical background. Its sense is given by Leibniz's immediately preceding statement that

> God must be considered in two ways: *physically* and *morally*. *Physically*, that is, as the ultimate reason of things, with respect, of course, to every perfec-

[3]The text is printed on pp. 286f. of Janke, "Das ontologische Argument."

[4]In addition to texts cited below, see Gr 370. This point provides the title, and a leading idea, of one of our century's greatest works of Leibnizian scholarship, Gaston Grua's *Jurisprudence universelle et théodicée selon Leibniz*; see esp. ch. 4.

[5]Leibniz had also published these ideas, largely in the same words, the previous year in his *Dissertation on the Art of Combinations* (A VI,i,190f.).

[6]Lindbeck, *Nature of Doctrine*.

> tion that is in them; but *morally*, as the monarch of the most perfect republic, which is that political community [*civitas*], so to speak, of the minds of the whole universe. (Dutens VI,i,84)

"Practical" theology arises from the "moral" consideration of God, and takes as its field all the social or quasi-social relations between God and rational creatures. It is this part of theology that is a species of jurisprudence, and that was doubtless Leibniz's meaning in his youthful publications, too. Even in 1667 he would surely not have assigned to legal theory the "physical" consideration of God as the metaphysical first cause of things.

The portion of theology to which Leibniz was prepared to assign a practical character was very large, however.[7] The extent of his pragmatism regarding religious belief is perhaps nowhere more clearly revealed than in a paper, written about 1670, on the problem of a "judge" or criterion for resolving controversies (A VI,i,548–59).[8] The first half of it is devoted to religious controversies, and Leibniz avers that, at least from a Protestant point of view, theological questions that cannot be settled by recourse to explicit statements in Scripture "are not of faith, but of morals, not theoretical, but practical, which we are not commanded to believe, but to perform" (§§ 10–11). Even where there are explicit statements in Scripture, placing the issue in the theoretical category, pragmatic considerations may come in if there is doubt about the interpretation of the sacred text (as for instance of the statement, "This is my body," ascribed to Jesus at his last supper).

> In this case I think the duty of a Christian is this: hearing the words of the text, to appropriate them as true in a literal [*proprius*] sense, but with devout simplicity, which thinks that it could be mistaken, and that perhaps the proposition is true in a figurative [*tropicus*] sense, but that it is safer to act thus. And so this faith will be disjunctive, but inclining to one side. And this in fact, if you will notice, is what most Christians do in practice. (§ 24)

Here the acceptance of a disjunction of meanings is presumably theoretical, but the "inclining to one side" rather than the other looks like a behavioral response to the words of the text, defended as a "safer" way of "acting" (cf. Gr 32), and as "what most Christians do *in practice*."

Particularly striking, and interesting for our present discussion, is the fact that Leibniz was prepared to admit such a disjunctive faith, or something very like it, regarding the existence of God.

> Indeed it can be taught that the very faith of most Christians both now consists, and has always consisted, in the approval of propositions not understood. For see, if you ask a Peasant whether he believes there is a GOD, he will be indignant that you doubted it; but if you ask what he calls GOD, he will be amazed that you even ask this, and will finally confess that he has hardly ever paid any attention to what may be meant by the word [*vox*] GOD, [but] has been satisfied to recite this proposition, having conceived under the words some obscure sense, by which he has unstably imagined GOD, now as a large and wise man, now otherwise. (§ 30)

[7]On Leibniz's emphasis on the importance of the practical aspect of religion, see Le Brun, "Critique des abus et signifiance des pratiques," with ample documentation.

[8]Further reference to this text, in the present discussion, will be by section number.

The ordinary Christian's theoretical belief in God's existence is presented here as disjunctive, or perhaps simply vague. What is definite is the behavior of hearing and reciting (affirmatively) a form of words.

Some might think this theologically scandalous,[9] and the essay in which it is found was both youthful and never published by Leibniz. But a similarly pragmatic, though less fully developed, view of adherence to a religious position is found in the *New Essays*, written many years later and with a definite intention of publication. In terms not likely to be found scandalous in his own time, Leibniz writes of the deference due to expert opinion, and gives examples from the realm of religion.

> Thus a child, and any other person whose condition is hardly better in this respect, is obliged—even if he is quite highly placed—to follow the Religion of the country insofar as he sees nothing wrong with it, and insofar as he is not in a position to inquire whether there is a better one. And a governor of page-boys, whatever his own sect, will make each of them go to the Church that is attended by adherents of the belief professed by the young man. (NE 458)

Modern philosophical readers will naturally be reminded at this point of Descartes, for whom constant adherence to the religion in which he had been raised stood at the head of the code that he proposed to himself (and his readers) for guidance during a period of theoretical uncertainty. It is noteworthy that Descartes saw this code as a "morality" [*une morale*], and appealed to utility to defend adherence to the opinions of his own country in preference to those of the Persians and Chinese.[10]

For Leibniz as well as for Descartes, pragmatic considerations seem to have been in order wherever theoretical certainty was lacking. And Leibniz was quite willing to appeal to arguments of practical or moral force, specifically including presumption, in matters of basic religious belief.[11] For instance, in an essay written for Duke Johann Friedrich of Hannover in 1671, stressing the human and practical importance of a well-grounded belief in the immortality of the soul, Leibniz says:

> No philosopher has thus far been able to explain thought by the motions or shapes of bodies. I acknowledge that this yields a strong presumption of incorporeality, but not a demonstration. Therefore Digby's demonstration [which is based on this point], if you analyze it, is in the end a moral one, or establishes not a certainty but a presumption of immortality. I do not deny, however, that this is already something of great importance for motivating prudent people. (A II,i,113)

Likewise in an outline of his planned "Catholic Demonstrations," written slightly earlier, Leibniz thought it worthwhile to include, in addition to four theistic proofs of presumably stricter theoretical cogency, a "demonstration [of the existence

[9]See the attack on the idea of "implicit faith" in Calvin, *Institutes of the Christian Religion*, III,ii,2–5. Cf. NE 520f.

[10]Descartes, *Discourse on Method*, part 3 (AT VI,23).

[11]Leibniz also seems to have thought presumptive arguments quite in place in debates between Protestants and Roman Catholics; see Gr 198f. This text is cited by de Olaso ("Leibniz et l'art de disputer," p. 221f.), who also argues that Leibniz appeals often to considerations of burden of proof in his *Theodicy*.

of God] of infinite probability, or moral certainty" from "the beauty of the world" (A VI,i,494). And in his *Theodicy*, many years later, he declares that "the proofs of the truth of religion," meaning revealed religion, "can only give a *moral certainty*" (T pd5).

It may not be entirely obvious that in calling a certainty "moral" in these last texts Leibniz really meant to enter the sphere of practical considerations. Could he not be using 'moral certainty' simply as a name for the highest possible degree of probability? Certainly it did signify for him a degree of probability so high "that no noteworthy comparison can be made with [the probability of] the opposite" (G VII,44f.; cf. C 515; G VII,320/L 364; NE 68). But I doubt that Leibniz ever forgot the original point of speaking of a probability as a "moral" or "practical" certainty, which is that it is strong enough to *act* on without hedging one's bets in view of the theoretical possibility of error. This point is manifest in a particularly interesting discussion of empirical generalizations in science, published by Leibniz in 1670. For his justification for claiming a "practical or moral certainty" for the generalization that all fire (of the sort that we have observed) burns depends on premises about what "should be held in practice" (A VI,ii,431f./L 129f.).[12]

2. *Jurisprudence and the Logic of Probability*

There is reason, indeed, to think that Leibniz assigned all merely probable reasoning, all reasoning of less than fully demonstrative force, to the practical sphere.[13] This is suggested by texts from 1677–78 on the presumptive argument for theism, where "demonstration" is the sole alternative contrasted with "practice" or "the conduct of life" (A II,i,312f.,436). It is in this light that I would interpret the fact that, after discussing the presumption of the possibility of God's existence in his letter to the Princess Elizabeth, Leibniz goes on to say that "one has done nothing if one does not *prove* this possibility" (A II,i,436/AG 239, italics added). This is not a denial of the religious value, but only of the intellectual merit, of a presumption in favor of divine existence. The letter is very much concerned with intellectual merit, and breathes a spirit of competition with the Cartesians.

The assignment of probable reasoning to "practical philosophy" is not merely suggested but plainly implied in a letter of February 1697 to Thomas Burnett, which is especially interesting also for the connections it draws between jurisprudence and the logic of probability. Leibniz writes to Burnett that "Theological truths and inferences are of two kinds; some have a metaphysical certainty and others have a moral certainty." In order to deal properly with the latter sort, "one must also have recourse to the true Philosophy, and in part to natural Jurisprudence."

> For Philosophy has two parts, the theoretical and the practical. Theoretical Philosophy is founded on the true analysis, of which the Mathematicians give

[12]Some of the more important parts of this text, for my present purpose, are omitted in Loemker's translation.

[13]This point is not discussed, but background relevant to it is presented, in Schupp, "Theoria—Praxis—Poiesis."

> examples, but which ought also to be applied to Metaphysics and to natural theology, in giving good definitions and solid axioms. But practical Philosophy is founded on the true Topics[14] or Dialectics—that is to say, on the art of estimating the degrees of proofs, which is not yet found among the authors who are Logicians, but of which only the Jurists have given examples that are not to be despised and that can serve as a beginning for forming a science of proofs, suitable for verifying historical facts and for giving the meaning of texts. For it is the Jurists who are occupied ordinarily with the one and the other in [legal] processes. Thus before Theology can be treated by the method of Establishments, as I call it, a Metaphysics, or demonstrative natural Theology, is needed, and so is a moral Dialectic, and a natural Jurisprudence, by which the way to estimate the degrees of proofs may be learned demonstratively. For several probable arguments joined together sometimes make a moral certainty, and sometimes don't. There is therefore need of a sure method to be able to determine it. It is often said, with justice, that reasons should not be counted, but weighed; however no one has yet given us that balance that should serve to weigh the force of reasons. This is one of the greatest defects of our Logic; we feel the effects of it even in the most important and most serious matters of life, which concern justice, the peace and well-being of the State, human health, and even religion. It is almost thirty years since I made these remarks publicly, and since that time I have done a quantity of research, to lay the foundations of such work; but a thousand distractions have prevented me from giving final form to those Philosophical, Juridical, and Theological Elements that I had projected. If God still gives me life and health, I will make it my principal business. I still would not prove all that can be proved, but I would prove at least a very important part, in order to begin the method of Establishments, and to give others occasion to go further. (G III,193f.)

I know of no other text that unites all the points found in this programmatic statement, but it is by no means eccentric. Most of its ideas are found frequently in Leibniz's writings, and there is a plausible reference for his claim to have "made these remarks publicly" almost thirty years before this letter to Burnett. In his *Specimina Juris*, published in 1669, Leibniz remarks of a certain problem in legal theory that it "depends entirely on the Logical doctrine of degrees of probability; but it[15] has not been treated accurately by any Logician, so far as I know, although it would be of great use in practice, not only here, but also when presumptions are to be compared" (A VI,i,426).

The topic of probability was closely connected in his mind with legal theory. In a letter of 1697 to John Bernoulli, mentioning earlier meditations of his own on a "Doctrine of the degrees of probability," Leibniz says they were "especially for use in Jurisprudence and Politics" (GM III,377). And he often commends the legal theorists for their work on probability (A VI,i,280; NE 464f.; C 211f.; G VII,167,477,521; GM III,850; Dutens V,403; Dutens VI,i,36).[16]

[14]A science of dialectical or nondemonstrative reasoning is so named here after Aristotle's *Topics*. In 1667 Leibniz had identified Topics as "the art of discovery" [*ars inventiva*] (A VI,i,279).

[15]The sense here seems to me to require this 'it' to refer to the Logical doctrine of degrees of probability, and I cite the text on the assumption that this interpretation is correct; Leibniz's Latin is exactly as ambiguous as my English translation on this point, however.

[16]On legal theory as a source of ideas about probability, cf. Hacking, *Emergence of Probability*, ch. 10. At Gr 792f. the jurists are commended, but somewhat backhandedly.

Indeed, Leibniz's interests in the whole of logic and in jurisprudence were linked from the beginning. His *Dissertation on the Art of Combinations* (1666) is widely noted as the forerunner of the highly original researches in logic that have drawn so much attention in our century. It is less often noted that problems of legal theory figure prominently among the "uses" proposed for logic in this early work (A VI,i,177,189–91). Legal applications undoubtedly ranked high among the expected uses of the "general characteristic" of which Leibniz dreamed throughout his adult life, the quixotically massive proposed encyclopedia of definitions, axioms, and theorems that would facilitate accurate and relatively uncontroversial reasoning on every topic. And legal theory is one of the topics on which Leibniz was most assiduous, early and late, in compiling actual lists of definitions. To Antoine Arnauld, in 1688, Leibniz writes that his work on the "general Characteristic" includes "some essays in jurisprudence" (LA 134). It is undoubtedly his work on the general characteristic that Leibniz describes to Burnett as "a quantity of research" that he has done "to lay the foundations" of a "method of Establishments" having "Philosophical, Juridical, and Theological Elements" (G III,194).

Since the project under discussion in the letter to Burnett is the development of an adequate logical apparatus for *probable* reasoning, my interpretation of it as referring to the general characteristic may be questioned by students who have thought of the characteristic as a superrationalistic project for purely a priori reasoning to conclusions established on the basis of conceptual analysis and deductive logic alone. It is clear, however, that probable reasoning was in fact supposed to have an important place in the general characteristic.[17] Writing to Jean Gallois in 1677, for instance, Leibniz lists among the promised benefits of the characteristic that "we could estimate the degrees of probability, rather as [we do] the angles of a triangle" (A II,i,381 = G VII,22; cf. A II,i,384). Likewise, writing to Nicolas Rémond in 1714, Leibniz says that "this Language or Characteristic . . . would also serve for estimating the degrees of likelihood (when we do not have sufficient data to arrive at truths that are certain)" (G III,605). To these texts from the early and the final years of Leibniz's career can be added others from the intervening years confirming the partly probabilistic nature of the general characteristic (C 176,215; G III,259; G VII,26,125,167,188,201).

The comparison with estimating the angles of a triangle suggests that Leibniz's rationalism did extend to the view that even when merely probable reasoning must be employed, the probabilities themselves could be determined a priori with geometrical rigor, and this is strongly confirmed by most of the texts I have just mentioned. As early as 1678 Leibniz held that

> even in matters of fact that are contested with presumptions and conjectures on both sides, it can be accurately defined on which side there is greater probability from the given circumstances. Therefore probability itself can be demonstrated, and its degree admits of being estimated, although this argument is not much cultivated. (A II,i,387 = G I,187)

[17]The most extravagantly rationalistic interpretations of Leibniz are hardly compatible with his blunt statement, in a letter of 1680, that "It is ridiculous to expect universal knowledge (*pansophia*) from any characteristic, . . . as also from any analysis, for many things are known only by experience" (G VII,19).

Similarly, he says in another place:

> Even when dealing only with probabilities, one can always determine what is most likely from the data. . . . So when one hasn't enough conditions given to demonstrate certainty, as the matter is only probable, one can always at least give demonstrations touching the probability itself. (G VII,167)

These "demonstrations" presumably establish the probabilities of the relevant hypotheses "from the given circumstances" or "from the data"—that is, the *conditional probabilities* that measure how likely the hypotheses are to be true *if* these are the data (cf. G VII,44). The truth of the "data" may be given empirically, but the conditional probabilities are to be established a priori in the general characteristic: "One could say with Cardano that the Logic of probables has different inferences from the Logic of necessary truths. But the probability itself of these inferences must be demonstrated by the inferences of the Logic of necessary [truths]" (NE 484).

Why must this be so? In his preface to an edition of Nizolius, of 1670, Leibniz offers the following argument.

> It is evident that induction by itself produces nothing, not even a moral certainty, without the support of propositions that depend not on induction but on universal reason. For if the supports too were based on induction, they would need new supports and no moral certainty would be obtained [by following such a regress] to infinity. (A VI,ii,432/L 129f.)

As the context makes clear, the "supports" to which Leibniz refers are in effect propositions assigning conditional probabilities and thus determining how the (resulting) probability of general hypotheses is affected by empirical data. If we were to try to justify those "supports" themselves by induction or empirical evidence, we could not determine how their probability is established by such evidence without further "supports" to tell us the conditional probability; this, Leibniz argues, will lead to a vicious infinite regress unless we can rely at bottom on a priori determinations of conditional probability.

Leibniz says that the "supports," which I interpret as giving the conditional probabilities, are "universal propositions that depend . . . on the universal idea or definition of the terms" (A VI,ii,431/L 129). Ian Hacking has plausibly interpreted Leibniz as holding something like the view later adopted by Carnap, which has become known as the "logical" interpretation of the nature of probability.[18] On this view, the conditional probability of a hypothesis, *H*, on data, *D*, (the probability *H* would have if *D* were our data) is a *logical* relation that necessarily obtains between *H* and *D*. This could be true even if we were often unable to know these logical relations a priori. Commonly, however (as at G VII,167), Leibniz implies that the conditional probabilities can *always* be established demonstratively, "mathematically" (C 176), "with geometrical or metaphysical accuracy" (G III,259).

If we interpret these claims as applying only to *conditional* probabilities, we need not follow Hacking[19] in taking Leibniz to have changed his mind about the last of them when he says, in a letter of 1714 to Louis Bourguet: "Likeli-

[18]Hacking, *Emergence of Probability*, ch. 15.
[19]Hacking, *Emergence of Probability*, p. 128.

hoods are still estimated *a posteriori*, by experience, and one must have recourse to that in default of reasons *a priori*. For example, it is equally likely that a child to be born should be a boy or a girl, because the number of boys and of girls is found to be approximately equal in this World" (G III,570). Leibniz is indeed contrasting the probabilistic propensities of the human reproductive process, which can be known only empirically, with those of dice, which he seems to think can be known a priori. For all that is said here, however, he may still have assumed that it is known a priori that the *conditional* probability of a human fetus being female, on the assumption that 50 percent of observed human fetuses have been female, is 50 percent. For the observed past frequency of male and female human births may be taken as a major part of the data, which Leibniz (on my interpretation) always believed must often be given empirically. Hacking's further suggestion, that Leibniz's change of mind (if there was one) was due to persuasion by James Bernoulli, seems to me to have no ground in this text, which says about Bernoulli only that he had "cultivated [the study of probability] at [Leibniz's] encouragement" (G III,570).

3. *A Proof for the Presumption of Possibility*

Among the truths of probability that Leibniz explicitly claims are given by "reason" is the principle according to which "we presume that an idea is possible until the contrary is discovered by a more precise investigation" (NE 446).[20] This is precisely the principle to which Leibniz appeals in his presumptive argument for the existence of a necessary God. As we shall see, there is actually a proof of this principle in one of his early works.

The theory of presumptions is one of the more fully articulated parts of Leibniz's views on probabilities, and it is very often mentioned when he discusses the larger subject. Sometimes he seems to think of presumption as one of the higher grades of probability (NE 464), but other times he seems to distinguish it from probability as a closely related alternative (A VI,i,472; Gr 598). His definition of presumption exhibits some variation within a fairly constant pattern. In a particularly full statement of about 1671 he says, "To *presume* is to hold for certain until the opposite is proved," and adds, "*For certain* is what we follow in action as if it were certain. What is to be presumed is whatever is prudently presumed" (A VI,ii,567).[21] In 1676 he writes, "*Presumption* is what is held for true until the contrary is proved" (A VI,iii,631), and in the *New Essays* he says that presumption "is something more" than conjecture and "ought to pass for truth provisionally, until there is proof of the contrary" (NE 457; cf. NE 464, T pd33). There is some difference among these definitions as to whether what is presumed is held for certain or only held for true.[22] All the definitions

[20]Peter Remnant and Jonathan Bennett's generally reliable translation obscures the relevance of this passage to our concerns by translating *nous presumons* as "we assume."

[21]This is from a draft that Leibniz crossed out and replaced. I think the draft was abandoned for reasons not involving rejection of this definition, with which the revised text seems to agree.

[22]Ezequiel de Olaso, "Leibniz et l'art de diputer," n. 46, sees an oscillation in Leibniz's views about the relation of certainty to probability and presumption.

agree, however, that what is presumed is held until the contrary, or the opposite, is proved.

It is not always as explicit as it was in the 1671 passage that presumption is defined as governing *action*, but I believe that this is always implicit in Leibniz's talk of *holding* for true and *passing* for a complete proof. The definition in the *New Essays*, it may also be noted, is part of a series of explanations of legal standards of evidence, most of which are measured by the kinds of action they are accepted as warranting.[23] This is not to say, however, that presumption was for Leibniz exclusively a matter of overt behavior. There is at least one passage in which Leibniz seems to imply that presuming something to be true does not quite amount to believing it to be true (G VII,45). Normally, and especially in matters of religion, however, there is no sign that Leibniz does not assume that what is presumed to be true is also believed to be true (or at least to be probably true). And he clearly took a dim view of the sort of legal presumption *juris et de jure* which was supposed to hold despite any amount of contrary evidence, and which therefore did not imply a preponderance of probability (Gr 848; cf. A VI,iii,631*n*).[24]

Indeed, Leibniz insisted that presumption must have a foundation: "To *presume* is not . . . to *accept before* [*avant*] the proof, which is not permitted, but to *accept provisionally* [*par avance*], but with grounds [*fondement*], while waiting for a contrary proof" (NE 457). The grounds mentioned here are undoubtedly epistemological, but Leibniz believed that good epistemological grounds should also have a metaphysical foundation in the nature of things. He frequently connects the probability of an outcome or putative fact with the "ease" with which it could be produced, or, in other words, with the strength of the propensity in the nature of things to produce it (NE 372f.; C 515; G III,569f.).[25] "What is *easy* in reality [*facile in re*] is *probable* in the mind" (A VI,ii,492). That presumption is to be similarly grounded in ease or facility is affirmed in an early text. Leibniz had written, "For what we presume, we demonstrate from its nature to be easier, and hence we presume it to be more frequent" (A VI,ii,567). He crossed out the passage containing this statement; the final text of this (unpublished) paper contains a more complicated formulation:

> What is *easier*, however, and what is *to be presumed* differ as Less and part. For that is easier in which less or fewer [things] are required than the opposite; [whereas] that is to be presumed whose requirements are part of the requirements of the opposite. Therefore everything that is to be presumed is easier, but not conversely. (A VI,i,472, as corrected at A VI,ii,529)

This view about the proper foundation for presumption constitutes one of the key assumptions of Leibniz's proof that presumption favors possibility, which is found, indeed, in the text from which I have just quoted. A crucial notion for

[23]Presumption is also connected explicitly with action at NE 438, and with practice at A VI,ii, 431f./L 129f. (The cited translations of both texts fail to render *presumer/praesumere* as "presume.")

[24]On the subject of presumptions *juris et de jure*, see de Olaso, "Leibniz et l'art de disputer," p. 217f., and notes thereto.

[25]On this point see also de Olaso, "Leibniz et l'art de disputer," p. 218, and Hacking, *Emergence of Probability*, p. 127f., and "Leibniz-Carnap Program for Inductive Logic."

both the view and the proof is that of "requirements." As I have explained at length in Chapter 4, section 1, this term signified for Leibniz both conceptual constituents, such as defining properties, and causally necessary conditions, and he seems commonly to have used it with the assumption that the two significations would coincide.

Leibniz held persistently to the view that ease, and therefore inherent probability, varies inversely with quantity of requirements. In a list of definitions from 1702 to 1704 he still says, "*Easy*, that of which the requirements are few. *Difficult*, that of which they are many. Under many are included large; for the large have many parts" (C 474). There is obviously a question about the plausibility of Leibniz's position at this point. If we think of the number of requirements as a number of distinct efficient causes, it may be relatively plausible to suppose that the fewer are required, the easier the result will be. But if the requirements are defining properties, it may seem more doubtful to us whether something with more defining properties, or more complex logical requirements, must therefore be more difficult in such a way as to be intrinsically less likely to occur. Leibniz might reply that as we add properties or logical requirements to the definition, we close off ways in which the definition could be satisfied, so that if *A* has fewer defining properties than *B*, there will be more ways in which *A* could occur, and therefore *A* will be inherently more probable than *B*—just as the sum of points in a (fair) cast of dice is inherently likelier to be seven than twelve because there are more possible combinations that yield seven than twelve (cf. G III,569f.). We will need to be alert, however, to consider whether the differences in logical complexity that will concern us are indeed associated with differences in the number of possible ways of realizing the putative possibilities.

There are also difficulties in determining the number of properties contained as requirements in a definition. How do we individuate properties for this purpose? It may seem that Leibniz must count all individual substances, if possible at all, as having exactly the same number of essential requirements, since their concepts, as complete, must contain exactly one member of every pair of mutually contradictory properties (as explained in Chapter 2, above). We may be able to avoid these difficulties here, however. For the basis for presumption is to be the inclusion of the requirements of what is to be presumed as a proper part of the requirements of its opposite, and a proper part is necessarily less than the whole.

In the case of the proof that presumption favors possibility, we are not concerned with requirements for existence, but with requirements for possibility or impossibility. We are therefore primarily concerned with requirements as essential or defining features, rather than as (efficient) causes. The argument goes as follows:

> For it is easier for something to turn out to be possible than impossible. For nothing is required for the possible but that it be supposed; for the impossible, however, it is required that while it is supposed, its opposite be supposed at the same time. Therefore more things are required for the impossible than for the possible. . . . That is *presumed*, however, whose suppositions [*supposita*] are also suppositions of the opposite, and not conversely. (A VI,i,471)

From which it follows that anything is to be presumed possible unless and until there is weightier reason to believe it impossible.

The argument of this remarkably interesting passage deserves to be set out in a less compressed form than Leibniz has given it.

(1) "For nothing is required for the possible but that it be supposed."

This I take to mean that the requirements of a putative possibility are the essential or constitutive features of what would be possible.

(2) "For the impossible, however, it is required that while it is supposed, its opposite be supposed at the same time."

At first glance we might take Leibniz to be arguing that it is harder for something to be impossible than to be possible because, in order to think that it is impossible, we must hold contradictory suppositions at the same time. I think it is likelier that he means that, since impossibility is rooted in inconsistency, a putative impossibility not only has the requirements of the possibility denied (without which it would lack a subject matter) but also requires that they imply their opposites.

From this point the argument can go in two directions.

(3a) We can infer that *less* is required for a possibility than for the opposed impossibility.

And, as we have seen, Leibniz holds

(4a) That for which less is required is precisely that which is easier.

Therefore

(5a) "It is easier for something to turn out to be possible than impossible."

From (1) and (2) we can also infer

(3b) The requirements of a possibility are a *proper part* of the requirements of the corresponding impossibility.

But this is precisely the condition laid down in this text for presumption.

(4b) "That is to be presumed whose requirements are part of the requirements of the opposite," or "whose suppositions [*supposita*] are also suppositions of the opposite, and not conversely."

Therefore

(5b) Possibility is to be presumed unless and until the corresponding impossibility is proved.

4. *Presuming the Possibility of* Beings *as Such*

I doubt that we are in a position to know whether Leibniz had this early proof in mind, or even whether he would still have endorsed it, when he wrote in the *New Essays* that "reason yields" the principle by which "we presume that an idea is possible until the contrary is discovered by a more precise investigation" (NE 446). It will be worthwhile, however, to consider whether the proof yields a basis for a good reply to the obvious objection to his presumptive argument for theism. I will try to work out the sort of position that Leibniz would have to have held in order to have such a reply, drawing freely on texts that suggest such a position. Then I will discuss some objections both to the position itself and to the hypothesis that Leibniz held it.

In presenting the objection it is convenient to assume that when Leibniz says that "possibility is always presumed and ought to be held for true until the impossibility is proved" (G III,444), he means that the truth of any *proposition* ought to be presumed possible unless and until it is proved impossible. This rule, the objector points out, applies equally to the propositions, 'A necessary God exists' and 'No necessary God exists'. But Leibniz has argued that if 'A necessary God exists' is possibly true, it is necessarily true—from which it follows that if 'A necessary God exists' is possibly true, 'No necessary God exists' is not possibly true. Therefore we cannot consistently accept both of these propositions as possibly true. It may be plausible in most cases to presume, in the absence of proof, that a proposition is possibly true. But when we have two propositions of which we know that exactly one is possibly true, but we have not proved which one it is, the general rule of presuming propositions possibly true yields no consistent conclusion.

The only defensible general presumption in favor of possibility of propositions would really be a presumption in favor of *contingency*—a presumption that a proposition should be presumed contingent (possibly but not necessarily true) unless proved not to be. There are propositions that are known not to be contingent but about which it has not been proved whether it is they or their contradictories that are possibly (and hence necessarily) true. Goldbach's conjecture (that every even number greater than two is the sum of two primes) is a famous example. A general presumption in favor of contingency has no bearing on such cases, and that is as it should be. It would be absurd to suppose that we ought to decide about Goldbach's conjecture on the basis of a presumptive rule favoring possibility or contingency or any other modal status of propositions as such. The objector argues that this is also true of 'A necessary God exists'.

A general presumptive rule favoring possibility of *propositions* cannot tell us whether a given noncontingent proposition, rather than its contradictory, should be assumed possibly (and hence actually) true, because such a presumption fails to discriminate between the alternatives—that is, because no difference between the alternatives is relevant according to the rule. But perhaps Leibniz had a different rule in mind, one that would discriminate between 'A necessary God exists' and 'No necessary God exists'. It may be significant that some formulations of the rule of presumption given in his discussions of the presumptive argument for theism are explicitly about the possibility of *beings*: "Every being ought to be judged possible until the contrary is proved" (G III,444). "One has the right to presume the possibility of every Being, and above all of God, until someone proves the contrary" (NE 438). If Leibniz's rule of presumption does favor the possibility of beings as such, it will direct us to presume the possibility of (the existence of) a necessary God, and will not contradict its own advice by generating a countervailing presumption of the possibility of the nonexistence of a necessary God, since nonexistences are not beings.

Of course it might contradict its own advice in another way, by generating presumptions of possibility, and hence presumptive arguments, for the existence of two or more incompatible necessary beings. Perhaps these would be a necessary (personal) God and an impersonal Platonic Form of the Good, one conceived as necessarily independent of all other beings than itself, and the other conceived as necessarily a cause of all other beings than itself.[26] This would limit the applicability and usefulness of a rule of presumption favoring the possibility of beings as such. It could not help us to decide among hypotheses involving alternative and incompatible types of necessary being. So far as I can see, that task cannot be accomplished by a presumptive argument and must be dealt with in some other way. But this objection fails to show that such a rule could contradict its own advice in directing us to presume the possibility of there being a necessary being of some sort or other, a being whose existence follows from its essence. And since much of Leibniz's argument is simply about the existence of a necessary being as such, that rather general conclusion would surely still be of interest to him.

It is quite possible to interpret Leibniz's early proof that "presumption is . . . for possibility" (A VI,i,471) as an argument for presuming the possibility of *beings*. The proof turns on the concept of a "requirement." While Leibniz was certainly prepared to speak of the requirements of an event or of an impossibility, it is clear that in his mind it was primarily things, substances, that had requirements. The essential properties that enter into the definition of a thing are the prime case of requirements, particularly where we are concerned with requirements for possibility rather than for (actual) existence.

In Leibniz's view, the possibility of things is grounded in their essences, which are "the specific reason[s] of [their] possibility" (A II,i, 390), as we saw in Chapter 5, section 1. And the possibilities of events and states of affairs are grounded in the essences of the substances that enter into them. Certainly Leibniz held that the actuality of events and states of affairs, and even of the actual world as a whole, follows from, and is grounded in, the actualization of the essences of the individual substances that actually exist (DM 8–9,13–14). As possible worlds are collections of possible things in the same way that the actual world is a collection of actual things (G III, 573/L 662; cf. G VII,302ff./L 486ff.), it seems to follow that the possibility of a possible world, and of all that occurs in it, follows from, and is grounded in, the essences of the individual substances that

[26]See R. Adams, "Presumption and the Necessary Existence of God," pp. 22f., for a fuller presentation of this example and of this whole objection. I treated the objection there as showing conclusively that a rule of presumption favoring the possibility of beings as such is of no use in this context. I have come to think that too hasty a judgment, for reasons that will emerge in the present discussion.

would exist in it, and their compossibility. Given Leibniz's beliefs that all possible facts are about substances, and that the essence of every possible individual substance determines every fact that would be true about that substance, the essences of possible individual substances, in providing reasons for the possibility of the substances, must provide sufficient reasons for the possibility of all possible facts. In the structure of possibility, as seen by Leibniz, the foundations are the essences of substances. If anything could be more fundamental, it would be the general properties of which those essences are composed; but they, too, are properties of substances, and their possibility is the possibility of a kind of substance or being. The ultimate foundation of all possibility, of course, is the essence of God (Mon 43–46), which is composed of the simplest and most positive of general properties.

In light of these reflections we may interpret the first premise of Leibniz's argument for the presumption of possibility, that "nothing is required for the possible but that it be supposed" (A VI,i,471). I will take it as applying to the possibiity of an individual substance or a kind of substance. The context of the argument might be thought to tell against this interpretation. Leibniz is discussing the relation of legal modalities to logical modalities. Seeing the analogy between deontic logic and modal logic, he supports the thesis that it is easier for an act to be right [*justus*, permitted] than wrong [*injustus*] by arguing first that it is easier for something to be possible than impossible (A VI,i,470f.). This might be taken as suggesting that Leibniz was thinking of acts rather than substances as possible or impossible. But that is not required by his analogy between deontic and modal logic, and, in any event, I am here developing suggestions in Leibniz's work of a position that would have enabled him to reject the obvious objection to his presumptive argument for theism, reserving for later any doubts as to whether he did hold the position.

Applied to substances, Leibniz's premise implies that in that case the requirements of the possibility are simply the properties that constitute the essence of the substance or kind of substance itself. This is the simplest and therefore the easiest case, and, other things being equal, the most probable. For other cases there are additional requirements. For the impossibility of a thing, Leibniz implies, are required not only the properties that would constitute its essence if it were possible, but also their implying (inconsistently) their opposites.

Similarly, it may be suggested, both the existence and the nonexistence of a thing require something more than its simple possibility. The actual existence of a possible thing requires both its possibility, or its essence, and some reason why it is actual. And the requirements of a thing's nonexistence include both its essence (which defines what it is that does not exist) and some reason why it is not actual. The possibility of a thing's nonexistence, therefore, will require both the essence of the thing and the possibility of a reason why the thing would not actually exist. Thus the sum of the requirements of the possibility of the thing (that is, its essence) is a proper part of the requirements of the possibility of its nonexistence. The possibility of the thing is therefore easier, having fewer requirements, than the possibility of its nonexistence; and there is correspondingly less reason to presume the possibility of its nonexistence than to presume the possibility of the thing. This is an argument for accepting a rule of presumption that would favor the possibility of a necessary being in preference to the possibility of the nonexistence of such a being.

5. *Objections Considered*

It is not difficult to think of objections to this argument. It relies on some asymmetries, as yet undefended. One is already present in Leibniz's explicit argument for presuming possibility, as I understand it. The impossibility of a thing requires that the thing's defining properties, collectively, imply their opposites. The argument takes that to be a new requirement, over and above the defining properties themselves, but it does not take the mutual consistency of the defining properties as a new requirement, over and above the properties themselves, for the possibility of the thing. This asymmetry has some intuitive appeal: implying something may seem to be an additional requirement in a way that not implying something is not. But I would not know how to defend this intuition, and it seems to be a weak point of the argument. There is some intuitive appeal on the other side, for example, to the claim that inconsistency is not a more extraneous feature of the property set {spherical, pyramidal}, than consistency is of the set {triangular, equilateral}.

A similar asymmetry may be found in the argument I have suggested for regarding the possibility of a thing as having fewer requirements, and hence as preferable presumptively, in comparison with the possibility of its nonexistence. It supposes that a possible reason why it would not exist must be given as a requirement in addition to a thing's essence to yield a possibility of its nonexistence, but that the essence, without any corresponding addition, suffices as the sum of the requirements for the thing's possibility. This is questionable. Since Leibniz certainly supposes that the possibility of a thing involves the possibility of its existence, we may ask if a possible reason why the thing would exist shouldn't be considered an additional requirement for the possibility of the thing.

Here I imagine Leibniz would reply that a possible reason why a thing would exist is indeed a requirement of the thing's possibility, but not an additional requirement, as it is already included in the essence. (Except in the case of a necessary being, of course, the *actuality* of the reason for existence will not be included in the existence, and hence will be an *additional* requirement for the actual existence of the thing.) There are passages in Leibniz's writings that could be interpreted as supporting this view of the essences of things (LA 51; G III,572/L 661). We may ask, however, whether it is fair to rely on it at this point. If the essence includes a possible reason for the existence of the thing, ought we perhaps to exclude that part of the essence from the requirements for the possibility of the thing's nonexistence? That would enable us to avoid the conclusion that the possibility of a thing's nonexistence requires possible reasons both for its existence and its nonexistence, whereas the possibility of the thing requires a possible reason only for its existence. This asymmetry is crucial to the argument I have suggested for the preferential presumption in favor of the possibility of beings as such. The defensibility of that argument may depend on whether Leibniz could argue plausibly that a possible reason for a thing's existence is essential to the subject matter of both its existence and its nonexistence in a way that a possible reason for its nonexistence is not.

Another objection is related to both of these asymmetries. Suppose we grant Leibniz that the requirements of an impossibility, or of a possible nonexistence, include all the requirements of the corresponding possibility, or possible being, plus an additional requirement. We may still ask whether this additional requirement effects a reduction in the diversity of possible realizations. In both cases, I think, the answer is no. If the defining properties of a thing imply their opposites (which is the additional requirement for an impossibility), that is already implicit in the definition, even if it is not spelled out there. Likewise, if there is a possible reason for the nonexistence of a thing (which is the additional requirement for a possibility of nonexistence), that is presumably a necessary feature of the total logical or metaphysical setup, even if it is not part of the essence of the thing. So even if Leibniz could defend the classification of these requirements as "additional," their addition does not eliminate possibilities as the addition of equilaterality to the definition of a triangle as a closed, three-sided plane figure reduces the variety of ways in which the definition could possibly be satisfied. And where the "addition" of defining or essential requirements does not eliminate possibilities, I think there is little plausibility to Leibniz's thesis that what has more requirements is thereby metaphysically more difficult or inherently less likely. For this reason more than any other, the reason that Leibniz offered for presuming possibility, and the reason I have suggested he might have offered for presuming possibility of existence in preference, if need be, to possibility of nonexistence, both seem to me quite weak.

Leibniz seems to have always believed it a truth of reason that there is a presumption favoring possibility. There is an objection yet to be canvassed, however, to including in his philosophy the view that presumption favors preferentially the possibility of beings as such, or of existence. In "The Principles of Nature and of Grace" (§ 7), by way of motivating the question, why there is something rather than nothing, as a starting point for his cosmological argument for the existence of God, Leibniz says, "For nothing [*le rien*] is simpler and easier than something." This seems to mean that the existence of nothing is inherently easier than the existence of something—from which it would seem to follow, given Leibniz's other views, that if the rules of presumption have any systematic preference between existence and nonexistence, they would favor nonexistence. This apparent implication of a very late (1714) text seems to be confirmed by Leibniz's statement in 1670 that "the existence of a thing that is not perceived is not presumed," where "whatever is not presumed is in practice to be held for nothing" (A VI,ii,431/L 129).

For several reasons, however, I hesitate to regard these texts as decisive in the matter. In the first place, they concern the comparative ease or presumability of *actual* existence and nonexistence, whereas the argument we are considering is about the comparative ease and presumability of *possible* existence and nonexistence. If Leibniz embraced that argument he would say, as I have suggested, that a possible reason of nonexistence is, and a possible reason of existence is not, an additional requirement over and above the essence of the thing that is the subject of both putative possibilities. The actual existence of a thing, however, has the *actuality* of a reason for it as a requirement, and, except in the case of a necessary being, that is plainly an additional requirement over and above the essence of the thing. Leibniz might have thought that the actuality of a reason for nonexistence is in general easier than the actuality of a reason for existence, even if the requirements for the possible existence of a thing are a proper part of the requirements for its possible nonexistence.

In the second place, Leibniz's attempt to motivate the cosmological argument by saying that nothing is easier than something may be an ill-considered appeal to received opinion, and not really consistent with his philosophy. For he holds—indeed it is part of his fullest presentation of the cosmological argument—that "in possible things, or in possibility itself or essence, there is a demand [*exigentia*] for existence, or (so to speak) a claim [*praetensio*] on existence, and, to put it in a word, that essence of itself tends toward existence." This may at first seem to us far-fetched, but Leibniz has a reason for it that deserves careful reflection. He infers it "from the very fact that some thing exists rather than nothing" (G VII,303/L 487). If nonexistence is indeed inherently easier than existence, we might ask, How is it that anything exists at all? "If there were not in the very nature of Essence some inclination to exist, nothing would exist," Leibniz declares (G VII,194). How this demand or claim or inclination to existence is to be understood is a difficult issue in the interpretation of Leibniz, which I have discussed in Chapter 6. Here it is enough to remark that someone who thought that essence has of itself an inclination to exist might be expected to deny that nonexistence is easier than existence. Indeed, Leibniz wrote, at least once, in a context of this sort, that "everything is easier, the more it has of reality" (Gr 17)—that is, the more perfect its essence is.

It may also be remarked, in the third place, that the idea of Nothing, of a state of affairs in which nothing exists, as simple and easy does not fit very well in the Leibnizian structure of possibility. For in that structure, if I have understood it, every possibility is grounded in a reason, and the most basic reasons of possibility are the essences of things. But all essences are essences of possible things, and hence of realities. Although some essences contain or express more "reality" or perfection than others, there is no essence that contains or expresses no reality at all. Hence there is no essence of Nothing, no essence whose first task is to be the specific reason of the possibility of an empty universe. If such a state of affairs is possible at all, it cannot be for Leibniz a primitive possibility. Its possibility must be constructed or derived from the essences that are the specific reasons of more positive possibilities. It is not difficult to see how such a construction might go. I discussed earlier how the nonexistence of a thing might be constructed, having the essence of the thing among its requirements. A state of affairs in which nothing would exist might be constituted by the conjunction of the nonexistences of all possible things. This would be a very complex state of affairs, and not easy at all by Leibnizian standards, since the essences, and thus the requirements, of all possible things would be among its requirements. In the end, of course, Leibniz must say that it is not even a possible state of affairs, since something (namely, God) exists necessarily.

Although there is a rich system of thought behind Leibniz's talk about presumption, a system whose juridical aspects, particularly, I have hardly begun to explore, I do not think we are likely to find in it a compelling argument for the rational necessity of the rule that presumption favors possibility, let alone for a presumption preferentially favoring the possibility of beings as such. Certainly there are too many weak and doubtful points in the arguments presented earlier in sections 3 and 4. The opposite suggestion, that presumption favors the possible nonexistence, in preference to the possible existence, of a Necessary God, was not, to my knowledge, considered by Leibniz, and will therefore not be discussed here. As I have explained elsewhere, I think it can be made more plausible than Leibniz's presumptive argument, but I am not in the end persuaded by it.[27] Indeed, I not only doubt that the cliché that presumption favors possibility or contingency can be proved by a Leibnizian argument; I doubt its applicability to the case at hand. I think it does not in general provide a reasonable basis for deciding metaphysical issues that are modal in character, such as that of the existence or nonexistence of a necessary God.

No doubt there are cases in which it is plausible to presume possibility in the absence of proof. Or perhaps it would be more accurate to say that there are cases in which our failure to find a proof of impossibility is a good reason for assuming possibility. It seems to be metaphysically possible, for example, for Orel Hershiser to pitch thirty-five no-hit major league games in one year. One important reason for assuming this to be possible is that we can see no good reason why it would be impossible.

But that is because it is plausible to assume that if it were impossible we would see a good reason for thinking so. Incidental features aside, the supposed possibility differs only quantitatively from events (individual no-hitters) that we know to be possible because they are actual. There is therefore no reason to suspect that we are entering into an area of deep perplexity about modality in this case. The quantitative aspects of the case also seem fairly simple, so that if there were a mathematical impossibility we would probably have found it.

It is worth noting that we often have similar reasons for presuming *im*possibility. Can ideas sleep furiously? Most of us think not; why is that? I would not expect to find a strict proof in this matter, but I think we can reasonably reject any supposed possibility of ideas sleeping furiously, on the ground that we can't see how anything would count as ideas sleeping furiously. Here we assume that if there were a way in which ideas could do something that would count as sleeping furiously, we would see that that was so. Our inability to see any such possibility is a reason for thinking there is none.

Metaphysically interesting issues about possibility and necessity are more baffling. We cannot reasonably assume that if there are possible phenomenal colors, very different from orange, that would fall between red and yellow on a spectrum, we would see that that was so. And we cannot reasonably assume that if there is something that keeps travel to the past, or the nonexistence of God, from being possible, we would have discovered it. Therefore I think we should be very suspicious of any presumptive argument on these matters.

[27]R. Adams, "Presumption and the Necessary Existence of God," pp. 23–27. The subsequent paragraphs of the present section are drawn (in abbreviated form) from that paper.

A better approach for dealing with such issues is to look to broader theoretical considerations, asking whether there are attractive theories in metaphysics or any related subject that imply one position or the other on the modal issue, or that at least work best on the assumption of one position. This approach, in my opinion, offers the brightest prospects for justifying belief in a necessary God.[28] Leibniz pursued it, too, arguing that the existence of contingent beings, and the ontological status of possibilities and the objects of logic, could best be explained on the hypothesis of a necessary God (G IV, 406; NE 447, Mon 43–44). I have had a little to say about the former argument at the beginning of Chapter 5, section 2, and quite a lot about the latter in Chapter 7.

[28]For a fuller discussion of this point, see R. Adams, "Presumption and the Necessary Existence of God," pp. 30f.

III

Idealism: Monads and Bodies

9

Leibniz's Phenomenalism

The most fundamental principle of Leibniz's metaphysics is that "there is nothing in things except simple substances, and in them perception and appetite" (G II,270/L 537). It implies that bodies, which are not simple substances, can only be constructed out of simple substances and their properties of perception and appetition. ('Constructed' is our word for it. Leibniz commonly says that bodies or phenomena "result" from simple substances and their modifications, but resulting is not what we would call a causal relation in this context.)[1]

How are bodies constructed out of simple substances and their properties? In this chapter and the next I will present the main outlines of the complex answer given to this question in Leibniz's mature philosophy. Many of Leibniz's best interpreters[2] have seen in this complex structure irreconcilable theses, for which they have tried to account in terms of change of mind or one or another form of permanent tension. What I propose, by contrast, is a unitary interpretation, a metaphysical scheme to which, in its essentials, I believe Leibniz adhered throughout the last thirty years of his life. There were some variations and developments in detail and terminology during the period, but none, I believe, as substantial or revolutionary as others have argued. Some issues of change and development will be discussed in Chapters 9 and 10, but the most serious challenge to Leibniz's constancy in these matters, from 1686 to his death, will be examined principally in Chapters 11–13.

A construction of the whole of reality out of perceiving substances and their perceptions and appetites exemplifies a broadly idealist approach to metaphysics. Leibniz was the first of the great modern philosophers to develop an idealist metaphysics. Idealist strands appear very early in his thought (as early as 1670), though they keep company in the early years with less idealist strands. I will focus here mainly on the mature period of his thought (beginning about 1686); but

[1]"In actual realities the whole," for example, "is a result of the parts" (G VII,562), but that does not mean that the parts are (efficient) causes of the whole. I think the data from which something "results" in Leibniz's sense are jointly *sufficient* for the result, and the result adds nothing to them. (Cf. GM VII,21f./L 669—though the Latin *prosultare* is used there in place of the more usual *resultare*.) Perhaps the data will also be individually *necessary* for the result, but I doubt that that is implied in the notion of "result." Certainly the result need not be capable of definition in terms of the data, in a finite language, for the data will commonly be infinite.

[2]E.g., Hochstetter, "Von der wahren Wirklichkeit bei Leibniz"; Broad, *Leibniz: An Introduction*, pp. 49–92; Loeb, *From Descartes to Hume*, pp. 299–309; Garber, "Leibniz and the Foundations of Physics"; Robinet, *Architectonique disjonctive*; and C. Wilson, *Leibniz's Metaphysics*.

the most phenomenalist of these early strands will be the topic of section 2. It makes clear that Leibniz had articulated much of the structure of a phenomenalist theory of bodies long before reaching the mature period of his thought.[3]

It is also clear that phenomenalism retains an important place in Leibniz's mature philosophy, as stated for instance in two of his letters to Burcher De Volder:

> Matter and motion are not so much substances or things as the phenomena of perceivers, whose reality is located in the harmony of perceivers with themselves (at different times) and with the other perceivers. (G II,270/L 537)

> Therefore I feel that the bodies that are popularly regarded as substances are nothing but real phenomena, and are no more substances than parhelia and rainbows are. (G II,262)

The mature Leibniz tried to combine his phenomenalism with a theory of *corporeal substances*, but in a way that leaves intact the basic idealism of the system. I will discuss the theory of corporeal substance in Chapter 10, focusing in the present chapter on Leibniz's conception of a corporeal phenomenon. Another thesis of the mature Leibniz that might seem to be in conflict with his phenomenalism cannot wait so long for discussion. It is in fact so intimately bound up with his conception of bodies as phenomena that it must be taken up in this chapter. This is the thesis that bodies or masses of matter[4] as such are *aggregates* of substances.

How can bodies be both mere phenomena and aggregates of substances? In this connection interpreters have spoken of a vacillation in Leibniz or have tried to document a change of mind, assigning the different theories to different periods in his career.[5] I am convinced, however, that Leibniz did not vacillate or change his mind on this point. To be sure, he is often careless or imprecise, saying things in ways that ignore aspects of his views that he does not want to present at the moment. But Leibniz believed (rightly or wrongly) that the two theses, that bodies are phenomena and that they are aggregates of substances, are consistent, and he held both of them throughout the mature period of his thought (say, from 1686 on).

[3]Other early idealist strands may be noted. See A VI,i,509/L 116, a paper of 1670 on Eucharistic theology (discussed further in Chapter 12, section 2.3): "the Substance of a body is union with a sustaining mind." For another strand see A VI,ii,266/L 141, a treatise in physics of 1671, which exhibits what Daniel Garber has called a "mentalization of body," declaring that "every body is a momentary mind; that is, one lacking memory." However, the context of the latter strand in Leibniz's pre-Parisian physical theorizing, heavily influenced by Hobbes, may suggest that the mentalization of body is accompanied by a physicalization of mind. On this whole subject in the young Leibniz, see Garber, "Motion and Metaphysics in the Young Leibniz," esp. pp. 168–78 (this note quotes p. 168); Robinet, *Architectonique disjonctive*, esp. pp. 125–64; and C. Wilson, *Leibniz's Metaphysics*, pp. 45–70.

[4]To be more precise, masses of *secondary* matter, as we shall see in Chapter 10.

[5]For example, Hochstetter, "Von der wahren Wirklichkeit bei Leibniz," esp. the references to Leibniz's *Schwanken*, pp. 422 and 440; and Loeb, *From Descartes to Hume*, pp. 299–309—to mention two works that I hold in high regard. Nicholas Jolley, in his interesting paper, "Leibniz and Phenomenalism," also treats these theories as inconsistent, but claims that "Leibniz never did more than flirt with phenomenalism" (p. 51).

In this chapter I will try to show how these two theses belong, for Leibniz, to a single, phenomenalistic theory, which seems to me to be reasonably coherent. In section 2 I will trace the transition to this theory from an earlier, simpler conception of phenomenalism, and in section 3 I will try to explain why Leibniz thought that bodies are only phenomena precisely *because* they are aggregates of substances. In section 4 I will examine the distinction between real and imaginary bodies in his system, which is the principal point at which he might be suspected of using two or more mutually inconsistent constructions. Before that, however, I must try to explain what Leibniz does and does not mean by calling bodies "phenomena." Section 1 will be devoted to this topic, which contains (in my opinion) some of Leibniz's most valuable contributions to metaphysics.

1. *Phenomena*

1.1 *What Are Phenomena?*

Leibniz's phenomenalism is quite different from the sorts of phenomenalism with which English-speaking philosophers are likely to be most familiar, and I think it is superior to them in important respects. We need, therefore, to clear our minds of preconceptions when we consider what Leibniz meant by calling bodies phenomena. The word 'phenomenon' plays an important part in Leibniz's discussion of the nature of bodies, as it does not, for example, in Bishop Berkeley's. 'Phenomenon' is a Greek word that means 'appearance', or more literally 'thing that appears'. Things that appear are objects of awareness to someone to whom they appear. The first thing to be said about phenomena, as Leibniz conceives of them, is that they are *intentional objects*.[6] In this respect (though of course not in all respects) I believe that Leibniz's phenomenalism is a forerunner of the phenomenalism of Kant. Leibniz certainly did not devote as much attention to the relevant concept of "object" as Kant did, though he did at least once characterize "phenomena" as "*objects* of limited minds" (G VII,563, italics added). For present purposes, bodies, as phenomena, may be thought of as the objects of a story—a story told or approximated by perception, common sense, and science. In calling them phenomena Leibniz means that they have their being in perceptions that represent this story to perceiving beings.

Leibniz does not give us a well-developed account of the nature of the dependence of bodies, as phenomena, on perception. A simple identification of phenomena (and hence of bodies) with perceptions, or with collections of them, would position Leibniz's phenomenalism closer to the idealism of Berkeley. The interpretation of phenomena as intentional objects, which I favor, requires a more nuanced account of their relation to perceptions.[7]

[6]Cf. Furth, "Monadology," p. 172.

[7]This is a point on which it seems historically to have been difficult to attain clarity. We can find Kant tending to lapse into a simple identification of appearances with representations, even in a passage in which he is at least beginning to see that a more nuanced account of the relation between them is essential to his argument (*Critique of Pure Reason* A 190f. = B 235f.).

The texts that seem to tell us what phenomena are are of doubtful relevance to this issue. There are texts that could be read as simply identifying phenomena with perceptions, where Leibniz says that "phenomena are nothing but thoughts" (LA 70) and seems to favor the view that the "phenomena" that are always produced in us when we see bodies "are simply new transitory modifications of our souls" (RML 457/L 626).[8] It may be doubted, however, whether 'phenomena' is used in the same sense in these passages as in those in which bodies are said to be "phenomena."

There are also texts, most of them early, in which it is virtually explicit that 'phenomena' signifies intentional objects of perception, rather than the perceptions themselves as psychological states. Leibniz defines "phenomena" in 1672 as "what are certain by virtue of sensation" (A VI,iii,3) and in 1679 as "propositions that are proved by experience" (C 33). Here there is clearly no thought of identifying phenomena with mental images like the "ideas" of Berkeley's philosophy. Examples of "phenomena" that Leibniz mentions in the period 1671–72 include "*the light of the stars* (especially of the sun) and *the solidity and resistance of the earth*" (A VI,ii,329) and that fact that "the light of day is moved daily around the globe of the earth" (A VI,iii,69).[9] Writing about Nicolas Malebranche in 1697, Leibniz explicitly contrasts "the phenomena that take place in bodies" with what is "in us" in perception (RML 321f.). But these are not overtly phenomenalist texts, and are therefore of limited relevance to the meaning of 'phenomena' in phenomenalist contexts. A better text, perhaps, for my purposes is a list of definitions, related by watermark to the period 1683–86, which says that "a *thing* is a congruent phenomenon" (VE 180 = LH IV,7c,101). This certainly has a phenomenalist flavor, and "thing" can hardly be meant here to refer only to psychological states as such.

It is relevant that Leibniz says that different perceivers "all express the same phenomena" (DM 14). What they all express is presumably a common intentional object, but Leibniz certainly does not think they all express it by qualitatively the same psychological states. To be sure, he is also willing to speak, even in the same paragraph, of a perceiver's own phenomena, saying, that "all our phenomena . . . are only consequences of our being."[10] But *our own* phenomena can still be understood as the intentional objects or representational contents of our perceptions—what appears to us—the objective rather than the formal reality of our perceptions, in Cartesian terms.

In any event, it is difficult to accept that Leibniz simply identified bodies, as phenomena, with perceptions or aggregates of perceptions. One obvious reason

[8]Little weight, in such a subtle question, can be placed on such a casual equivalence as "perceptions or [*seu*] phenomena" (C 14/MP 176). (On the date of this text, see note 55 below.) *Seu* normally signifies an equivalence, but in a fairly vague way. It is noteworthy also that in the same paragraph Leibniz says that "every soul will represent proximately the phenomena of its own organic body," apparently taking the phenomena of the body as objects represented by the perceptions of the soul.

[9]Most of these texts, and others of related content (and early date) are noted in Robinet, *Architectonique disjonctive*, p. 154*n*.

[10]DM 14; cf. G II,444/L 602. Robert McRae, who calls attention to this terminological variation, in his *Leibniz: Perception, Apperception, and Thought*, p. 141f., takes it more seriously than I do as a sign of inconsistency.

for this judgment is that, as noted and as will be discussed in section 3, Leibniz identified bodies, as phenomena, with aggregates of *substances*. It is also clear that the properties he ascribes to bodies are different from those he ascribes to perceptual modifications of the mind. Perceptions, but not bodies, are distinct or confused. Bodies, but not modifications of the mind, have physical properties. Most important, as I shall argue, Leibniz shows no concern for some types of psychological analysis that are crucial for Berkeleyan reductions of bodies to perceptions.

One promising way of accounting for Leibniz's various utterances on this subject is to suppose that when he speaks of material things as phenomena, he normally thinks of those phenomena as perceptions, or as qualities or modifications of a perceiving substance, *considered only in a certain respect*. Specifically, corporeal phenomena are perceptions considered with regard to their objective reality or representational content, or insofar as they *express* some nature, form, or essence. Here I am extrapolating from things Leibniz says about "ideas." His notion of idea is by no means the same as his notion of phenomenon. The latter notion is more closely connected with perception than the former; and some phenomena are transitory, whereas ideas in general are not. But ideas, like phenomena, can be construed both as properties of the mind and as objects of the mind; and Leibniz gives much fuller discussion to the relation between ideas and the mind than I have found him to give to the relation between phenomena and the perceiving substance.

A famous controversy between Malebranche and Antoine Arnauld provides the starting point for much of what Leibniz says about ideas. Malebranche held that ideas of bodies are objects of awareness distinct from any modifications of our minds by which we are aware of them. He had to regard them as distinct, since he held that the ideas are in God's mind and not in ours. Arnauld maintained not only that we have ideas of bodies in our own minds, but also that they are modifications of our minds. Leibniz declared himself for Arnauld in this debate: "It suffices to consider ideas as Notions; that is to say, as modifications of our soul. That is how the School, M. Descartes, and M. Arnauld take them" (G III,659; cf. G IV,426/L 294).[11]

This declaration does not fully reflect the complexity of Leibniz's position, however. In the first place, he agreed with Malebranche that, *if* ideas are taken "as the immediate external object of our thoughts, it is true that they could only be placed in God, since there is nothing but God that can act immediately upon us" (RML 317). And in conciliatory moods he was prepared to say that "it can very well be maintained in this sense that we see everything in God" (RML 490). But Leibniz insists that we also have an immediate *internal* object of our thought (RML 317): "I hold, however, that there also is always something in us that corresponds to the ideas that are in God as well as to the phenomena that take place in bodies" (RML 321f.). In this sense we have our own ideas in our own minds (DM 28–29), and our ideas are modifications of our minds, or (RML 490)

[11]On Leibniz's relation to this controversy, see RML 133ff. Even before seeing the documents, Leibniz wrote in a letter that "Mons. Arnauld writes with more judgment" than Father Malebranche (RML 150).

relations of correspondence to God's ideas, which are included in modifications of our minds.

In the second place, Leibniz's calling ideas modifications of the soul should not lead us to suppose that he identified them with conscious episodes. In § 26 of the *Discourse on Metaphysics* he distinguishes two senses of 'idea':

> Some take the idea for the form or difference of our thoughts, and in this way we have the idea in our mind only insofar as we are thinking of it, and every time we think of it anew, we have other ideas of the same thing, although similar to those that went before. But it seems that others take the idea for an immediate object of thought or for some permanent form which remains when we are not contemplating it.

Leibniz prefers the second of these conceptions. An idea, properly speaking, is a "quality of our soul," but a permanent quality and not a transitory modification (DM 26). It manifests itself in distinct successive modifications when we think of it consciously, and even when we are not thinking of it, there remains in us a property [*habitudo*] that expresses the content of the idea (G VII,263/L 207). The concrete realization of the idea in our minds is thus quite different at different times.

In the third place, it is only considered in a certain respect that qualities of the soul are ideas. If we ask what it is that is permanent in an idea that takes such different forms as the conscious and the unconscious at different times, the answer is, first, that the representational content, or in Cartesian terms the objective reality, of the idea is constant and, second, that the mind always has in it a certain potentiality for making that content conscious, "the quality," as Leibniz puts it, "of representing to itself whatever nature or form it is, when the occasion arises for thinking of it" (DM 26). Leibniz himself, in the passage quoted, connects the permanence of the idea with its character as object of thought. We may say that the idea is a permanent quality of the mind considered with regard to its representational content. Leibniz says, "This quality of our soul *insofar as it expresses some nature, form, or essence,* is properly the idea of the thing, which is in us, and which is always in us, whether we are thinking of it or not" (DM 26, italics added). "An idea is that in which one perception or thought differs from another by reason of the object" (RML 73).

Similarly, when Leibniz speaks of bodies as phenomena, we may understand those phenomena as qualities or modifications of the perceiving substance considered with regard to their objective reality or representational content or insofar as they express some nature, form, or essence. Adapting Cartesian terms, one can say that in their objective reality or as phenomena, perceptions have properties that they do not have in their formal reality or as modifications of the mind, and vice versa. Among the most important of these properties, for Leibniz, are causal properties, for they are the basis of the pre-established harmony between body and soul. Students of Leibniz have sometimes wondered what the things are that need to be harmonized, if bodies are phenomena and phenomena are modifications of the soul. Leibniz holds that corporeal phenomena as such are caused mechanically by preceding corporeal phenomena, whereas modifications of the soul as such are to be explained teleologically by preceding appetites (Mon

79,87; G IV,391/L 409f.; C 12f./MP 173f.). God preestablishes a harmony between soul and body by so programming perceptions that, while their formal reality follows from the formal reality of previous perceptions and appetites of the same substance by laws of teleological explanation, their objective reality follows from the objective reality of previous perceptions by laws of mechanical explanation.

In spite of these fundamental differences between perceptions as phenomena and perceptions as modifications of the perceiving substance, Leibniz will resist any attempt to treat them as fully distinct entities. The point of his saying that phenomena are modifications of our souls is that as a conceptualist about all sorts of abstract entities and merely intentional objects, Leibniz does not believe that phenomena have any being except *in* the existence or occurrence of qualities or modifications of perceiving substances. The existence of a phenomenon must consist in the occurrence of certain perceptions: "Our Mind makes a phenomenon" (C 528).

Nonetheless, Leibniz distinguishes, among phenomena, between *real* and merely imaginary bodies and holds that some stories in which the real ones figure are *true*. The task of Leibnizian phenomenalist analysis is to explain what this reality and truth consist in. It is not to analyze the content of the true stories. Considered as phenomena, bodies still have the properties of *bodies*. I have found in Leibniz no attempt to reduce those properties to psychological properties of perceptions. This is a principal difference between Leibniz and many other phenomenalists.

I do not mean to deny that Leibniz may have thought that the objective reality of perceptions must *result*, in his sense, from their formal reality. I take him to be committed to the view that the objective reality of a perception must be expressed by the formal reality of the perception (cf. RML 321f.), where one thing expresses another if and only if there is a one-to-one mapping from elements of the latter to elements of the former according to appropriate rules (G VII,263f./L 207f.; LA 112). This is a *necessary* condition for a perception's having a certain objective reality. Leibniz seems also to have thought that expression of an objective reality in a simple substance is *sufficient* for a perception having that objective reality, though we may doubt that an adequate account of intentionality can really be provided in that way. "We could not say what the perception of plants consists in, and even that of animals we do not conceive well. For there to be a perception, however, it's enough that there be a variety in the unity" (G III,581/L 664; cf. Mon 14).

Even if Leibniz thought that there must *be* a reduction of the objective reality of perceptions to their formal reality, based on the notion of expression, it is no part of his philosophy of body to *give* such a reduction. Giving it would require identifying (without reference to objective reality or representational content) the formal, psychological features of perceptions that correspond with the corporeal features of represented objects, and Leibniz makes no attempt to do that. In his philosophy of body, the objective reality or representational content of a perception is treated for all working purposes as a primitive feature of that perception. Leibniz provides at least one analysis of the notion of the *reality* of a corporeal universe that appears to us (as we shall see later in sections 2 and 4).

But he provides no *analysis* of the notion of a corporeal universe's appearing to us (as opposed to something else appearing to us). He thus treats the notion of a corporeal universe's appearing to us as conceptually prior to the notion of such a universe's being real.

1.2 Leibniz and Berkeley

For further exploration of the distinctive features of Leibniz's conception of phenomena, let us turn to his explicit disagreements with Berkeley. His best-known comment on Berkeley, in a letter of 15 March 1715 to Bartholomew Des Bosses (G II,492/L 609), suggests that Leibniz failed to realize the strength of Berkeley's desire to be found in agreement with common sense and overlooked Berkeley's efforts to define a sense in which bodies can be called "real." Other evidence does not contradict these suggestions, but does make clear that Leibniz actually read Berkeley and saw more than he has commonly been thought to have seen of the similarities, as well as the differences, between Berkeley's views and his own. This evidence is provided by the following comments that Leibniz wrote on the last page of his copy of Berkeley's *Treatise Concerning the Principles of Human Knowledge*:

> Much here that's right and agrees with my views. But too paradoxically expressed. For we have no need to say that matter is nothing; but it suffices to say that it is a phenomenon like the rainbow; and that it is not a substance, but a result of substances; and that space is no more real than time, i.e., that it is nothing but an order of coexistences, as time is an order of subexistences. The true substances are Monads, or Perceivers. But the author ought to have gone on further, namely to infinite Monads, constituting all things, and to their preestablished harmony. He wrongly, or at least pointlessly, rejects abstract ideas, restricts ideas to imaginations, despises the subtleties of arithmetic and geometry. He most wrongly rejects the infinite division of the extended, even if he is right to reject infinitesimal quantities.[12]

Leibniz did not fail to see that he and Berkeley were fundamentally on the same side.[13] He thought much of their disagreement was in presentation, style, and tactics. Berkeley "expressed" their common beliefs "too paradoxically." Several substantial disagreements are reflected in Leibniz's critique, however. I will discuss three of these.

1. The perceptual atomism of Berkeley's construction of physical objects evokes Leibniz's strongest protest. Berkeley "most wrongly [*pessime*] rejects the infinite division of the extended." For Berkeley, extended things are ideas or col-

[12]The Latin original is published, with a full report of the discovery, by Willy Kabitz, "Leibniz und Berkeley"; the quoted text is on p. 636. It has been republished, and further annotated, by André Robinet, "Leibniz: Lecture du *Treatise* de Berkeley." An English translation has been published in AG 307.

[13]Margaret Wilson's valuable paper, "Leibniz and Berkeley," is to some extent a protest against this evaluation. She rightly points out a number of important differences between Leibniz and Berkeley, including some that I discuss here, as well as some that are not relevant to my present purpose, which is the exposition of Leibniz's conception of a phenomenon. So far as I can see, the disagreement between her reading of the texts and mine, though significant, is purely a matter of emphasis.

lections of ideas, and these ideas in turn are composed of parts that are only finitely small because they cannot be smaller than the mind in which they exist can discriminate (*Principles*, § 124). In dividing any extended thing, therefore, we come eventually to parts that are still extended but so small that they cannot be divided any further; Berkeley maintains that there are no distinct parts within these least discernible parts, on the ground that as an idea exists only in the mind, "consequently each part thereof must be perceived" (ibid.).

Leibniz accepts no such construction of extended things from extended but indivisible perceptions. He can be seen as constructing corporeal phenomena from indivisible, simple substances inasmuch as he regards the former as aggregates of the latter (as I will discuss in section 3). But this is a construction from substances, not from ideas or perceptions. Moreover, the simple substances must be *un*extended precisely because they are indivisible; divisibility is of the very essence of extension for Leibniz. This is one reason why Leibniz can view bodies as infinitely divided.

There is in Leibniz's view an extended but merely ideal object that enters into the construction of corporeal phenomena (as I will also argue in section 3.4). This is space. It has extended parts, but is not constructed from them. Leibniz regards it as prior to them:

> Indeed space is something continuous, but ideal. . . . In actual things, simple things are before aggregates; in ideal things the whole is prior to the part. (G II,379)

> In the ideal or continuous the whole is prior to the parts, as the Arithmetical unit is prior to the fractions that divide it, which can be assigned arbitrarily, the parts being only potential; but in the real the simple is prior to the groups, the parts are actual, are before the whole. (G III,622; cf. G VII,562f.)[14]

This is not to say that we have a very comprehensive spatial perception that is prior, in its "formal" reality, to other perceptions that are its psychological parts. Space is ideal for Leibniz in the sense that it is *merely* an object of thought or perception. His priority claim is that the *representing* of space by our thoughts or perceptions is prior to the *representing* of parts of space—and that there is nothing more to space or its parts, as such, than a representational content.

There are thus in the Leibnizian scheme of things no psychological entities that serve as building blocks in the construction of extended things in the way that ideas do for Berkeley.

2. Leibniz's insistence on "the infinite division of the extended" is based on the intellectual demands of his geometry and metaphysics, not on the phenomenology of sensation. This is related to his view that Berkeley is wrong to "restrict ideas to imaginations." Leibniz rejects the sensationalism of Berkeley's theory. If bodies are phenomena for Leibniz, the "perceptions" of which they are objects

[14]Bodies that are well-founded phenomena fall on the real rather than the ideal side of this contrast, and therefore are not prior to their parts or constituents in Leibniz's view (see sections 1.3.2 and 2.1 in this chapter). In "Phenomenalism and Corporeal Substance in Leibniz," pp. 222f., I mistakenly applied to corporeal phenomena as such what Leibniz says here about ideal things. Glenn A. Hartz and J. A. Cover, in their valuable paper on "Space and Time in the Leibnizian Metaphysic," showed me the error of my previous treatment of these texts—though I still disagree with them on some related points, as discussed in section 3.4 in this chapter.

are by no means only sensations, though he was certainly capable of putting a phenomenalist point in terms of "the phenomena of the senses" (NE 392). In Leibnizian terms, perceptions of bodies may be either too confused or too distinct to be sensations. Leibniz held, famously, that the largest part of our (and other creatures') perceptions of bodies are too confused to count as sensations, but he did speak of "phenomena" represented by them (G II,521/AG 206). We need not pause here to worry about the important and obvious difficulties of ascribing representational content to unconscious perceptions, for it is surely Leibniz's departure from sensationalism in the other direction, the direction of greater distinctness, that motivates his critical comment about Berkeley's "restrict[ing] ideas to imaginations."

Leibnizian corporeal "phenomena" are objects of the *intellect* as well as of sensation and unconscious perception. Writing to Arnauld in April 1687, Leibniz explicitly assigns reasoning a role in the construction of corporeal aggregates as phenomena (LA 101). The intellect's part in our perception of corporeal phenomena is particularly important and includes both mathematics and physics.

Among the features of phenomena that we perceive primarily by the intellect are *forces*. Force is characteristic of monads, but there are forces that are properties of phenomena:

> As I take bodies to be, so also [I take] corporeal forces [to be]: that is, in the phenomena.[15] (G II,276/AG 182)
>
> As matter itself is nothing but a phenomenon, but well founded, resulting from the monads, it is the same with inertia, which is a property of this phenomenon. (G III,636/L 659)

Certainly Leibniz did not think we have a sensory image of inertia. He regards "the essence of body" as constituted by a "force of acting and resisting, which we perceive, not by imagination, but by the intellect" (G VII,314f./MP 82).[16] It is by (rudimentary or sophisticated) scientific thinking that we perceive forces as such.

Indeed, I believe that for Leibniz the universe of corporeal phenomena is primarily the object, not of sense, but of science. This is another point of similarity between the phenomenalism of Leibniz and that of Kant, for whom the phenomenal world includes objects not perceptible by our senses but postulated on scientific grounds.[17] The *reality* of corporeal phenomena depends for Leibniz,

[15]At this point Leibniz adds, "that is, if they are understood as superadding anything to the simple substances or to their modifications," which I take to be a somewhat obscure way of underlining the corporeal character of the forces said to be phenomena. These forces are phenomenal insofar as they are understood as distinct from the forces internal to simple substances, which constitute the most fundamental properties of the simple substances.

[16]It could conceivably be argued that the reference here is to intramonadic rather than to corporeal forces. Given the place of "the essence of body" in the statement, however, it seems more plausible to take the remark about our perception of forces as directed either specifically at corporeal forces or else indiscriminately at all the forces that might be closely connected with bodies. The phenomenal character of corporeal forces may also not be in view in this text, which is much earlier than those in which Leibniz explicitly speaks of certain forces as phenomena; but I see no reason to suppose that he would have hesitated at any time to say that forces in general and as such are perceived "not by imagination, but by the intellect."

[17]Kant, *Critique of Pure Reason*, A 226 = B 273. Unfortunately, Kant's example of such an object, "a magnetic matter pervading all bodies," is one no longer postulated by our science. It

as we will see in section 4, on their finding a place in the story that would be told by a perfected physical science.

3. Part of Leibniz's point in saying that bodies are phenomena is to claim that they have their existence only in substances that perceive them, and in this he agrees with Berkeley.[18] But there is something else going on in Leibniz's talk of phenomena, something that is reflected in his comment that Berkeley "ought to have gone on further, namely to infinite Monads, constituting all things." 'Phenomenon' contrasts not only as 'intramental' with 'extramental'; it also contrasts as 'apparent' with 'real'. And while Leibniz's metaphysics is certainly a form of idealism, it also includes a sort of qualified realism about bodies and about physical science. Part of what is going on in Leibniz's mature thought is that he does assume that in our perception of bodies we are at least indirectly perceiving something that is primitively real independently of our minds, and he asks what sort of thing that may be.[19] His answer is that it is "infinite Monads," whose harmonious perceptions are the "foundation" of corporeal phenomena.

This answer, however, does not adequately represent the interplay of appearance and reality in Leibniz's thought. Like almost all modern philosophers, he believed that good science requires us to suppose that there are very considerable qualitative differences between bodies as they appear to naive sense perception and bodies as they should be seen by science. In the corporeal world as described by modern science there is, in a certain sense, no part for colors and the other so-called secondary qualities to play. On the other hand, modern science postulates vast numbers of motions of minute particles in portions of matter that appear to our senses to be perfectly quiescent internally. This was true of what Leibniz regarded as modern science, and it is true of what we think of as modern science.

Many among us respond to this situation by supposing that, whereas what we perceive naively by our senses is only an appearance, what is described by science—or what would be described by a perfected science—is reality. Leibniz has a fundamental reason for rejecting this strong form of scientific realism—a reason for not expecting science to give us knowledge of reality as it is in itself. Scientific knowledge, as Leibniz sees it, is relatively distinct, but buys its distinctness at the price of studying a mathematical idealization. "Abstractions are needed for the scientific explanation of things" (G II,252/L 531). The complexity of

---

should also be noted that because of Kant's distinction between intuitions and concepts, and his treatment of it, regarded by Kant himself as a main difference between his philosophy and that of Leibniz, it is important to Kant, that any phenomenon not in fact perceptible by our senses be such that "we would . . . also, in an experience, encounter the immediate empirical intuition of it, if our senses were more acute" (ibid.). (Leibniz would say that too, but for different reasons having to do with his own theories of universal harmony and perception.) It remains clear that something can be a phenomenon for Kant by virtue of its appearing to the intellect and not to sensation—though of course it must appear in such a way as to be placed by the intellect within the spatiotemporal "form" of sensation.

[18]M. Wilson ("Leibniz and Berkeley," p. 7) is unwilling to say that Leibniz and Berkeley "agree" on this point, because there is such a large difference in what they mean by 'perception'. I agree that the difference is large, but I think it is not large enough to keep the perception-dependence of bodies from being an important point of metaphysical agreement between the two philosophers.

[19]For a nice statement on this point, see Antonio Lamarra, "Leibniz on Locke on Infinity," p. 181.

reality, he thinks, is infinite, intensively as well as extensively. It is not just that there are infinitely many objects in infinite space. Even when we perceive a body of limited extension, such as the body of a human being, Leibniz believes that the reality represented by our perception is infinitely complex, and that all of that infinite complexity is relevant to the explanation of some of the salient features of the body's behavior. Human minds are finite, however, and the definitive mark of finite minds is that they cannot distinctly know an infinite complexity. So if science is distinct knowledge, the only sort of science that is possible, even in principle, for human beings will have as its immediate object a finitely complex representation of the infinitely complex reality. At least to this extent, the objects of scientific knowledge will be phenomena. Leibniz's opinion, that the object of scientific knowledge is not reality as it is in itself but a mathematical abstraction from its infinite complexity, is plausible enough in its own right, I think, but it is also rooted in other aspects of his philosophy, which need not be recounted in detail here—in his theory of free action and infinite analysis conception of contingency,[20] for example, and in his doctrine that each thing expresses the whole universe.

1.3 The Phenomenality of Physical Qualities

Leibniz's treatment of the relation of the different sensible qualities to reality can be understood in this light. It would be convenient to be able to discuss it in terms of the distinction between "primary" and "secondary" qualities of bodies which has been established in English-speaking philosophy by Boyle and Locke, but that terminology is not Leibnizian. Leibniz used it in discussing Locke, but with some reservations (NE 130–33). He thought that the only fundamental difference between the two sorts of sensible qualities is in the degree of confusion with which they express a deeper reality. He regarded the degree of that difference as large (NE 403f.),[21] but placed it within a spectrum in which no sensible quality occupies a sufficiently distinguished position to merit the designation of "primary quality." He thought that there are qualities (namely, forces) that belong to bodies in a more primary way than any strictly sensible quality does. In articulating his views I will therefore refer to size, shape, and motion simply as such, or as "the Cartesian modes of extension," and to the so-called "secondary qualities" simply as "the other sensible qualities."

In § 12 of the *Discourse on Metaphysics* Leibniz wrote:

> It can even be demonstrated that the notion of size, shape, and motion is not so distinct as one imagines, and that it includes something imaginary and relative to our perceptions, as are also (though much more so) color, heat, and other similar qualities of which it can be doubted whether they are truly found in the nature of things outside us.

[20]See Chapter 1, section 2.4.

[21]This is a point rightly emphasized by M. Wilson, "Leibniz and Berkeley," p. 12. More important, she points out a major difference in Leibniz's and Berkeley's treatments of sensible qualities. While they both criticize the metaphysics of primary qualities that was the standard "modern" view of their time, they develop their criticism "in completely opposite directions," Berkeley ascribing all the sensible qualities equally to "real" bodies, and Leibniz distancing all the sensible qualities, though not equally, from what he regards as real in bodies (ibid., p. 12f.).

Many similar statements are found in other places in his work. It seems to be implied here that the other sensible qualities are even less real than the Cartesian modes of extension, although both sorts are in some degree apparent rather than ultimately real.[22] Size, shape, and motion, I think, can be more real only in the sense that they represent reality more distinctly than the other sensible qualities. They "contain more of distinct knowledge" than the others, but they both "hold something of the phenomenal [*tiennent du phénomène*]" (LA 119).

According to Leibniz, the perception of other sensible qualities, as they appear to us, is a confused perception of minute motions or textures—a confused perception of sizes, shapes, and motions that are too small for us to perceive them by sense (NE 131–33). We might put this by saying that the other sensible qualities are appearances *of* sizes, shapes, and motions—and as such are appearances of appearances. I do not know that Leibniz ever said exactly that, but in the last letter that he wrote to Des Bosses (29 May 1716) he did suggest relating other sensible qualities to the corresponding sizes, shapes, and motions as "resultant phenomena" to "constitutive phenomena." Thus the "observed perception" of white and black results from bumps and depressions, too tiny to be (consciously) observed, which reflect and trap rays of light, respectively, but these geometrical textures themselves are still only phenomena (G II,521/AG 206; cf. C 489).

1.3.1 Shape

Even within the realm of Cartesian modes of extension there are veils behind veils of appearance between us and reality in the Leibnizian universe. Inspect the leg of a fly with the naked eye and under a microscope; you will see rather different shapes.[23] Yet Leibniz would surely say that what you see with the naked eye is a confused representation of the more complex shape that appears under the microscope, and that the latter is still not complex enough to be more than an appearance. This is indeed one of Leibniz's reasons for holding that shape is only a phenomenon.[24]

> For even shape, which is of the essence of a bounded extended mass, is never exact and strictly determined in nature, because of the actual division to infinity of the parts of matter. There is never a sphere without inequalities, nor a straight line without curvatures mingled in, nor a curve of a certain finite nature without mixture of any other—and that in the small parts as in the large—which brings it about that shape, far from being constitutive of bodies, is not even an entirely real and determined quality outside of thought. (LA 119)

One of the reasons, I take it, why Leibniz thought that finitely complex shapes cannot be "entirely real . . . outside of thought" is that they cannot express a

[22] I see only a verbal inconsistency with this when Leibniz writes that shape and motion "involve something of the imaginary, *no less than* heat and color and other sensible qualities" (G VII,314/MP 82, italics added). It is equally (that is, absolutely) true of both sorts of quality that they involve *something* of the imaginary, but the other sensible qualities involve *more* of the imaginary than the Cartesian modes of extension do.

[23] Cf. Berkeley, *Works*, vol. 2, p. 189.

[24] For a discussion of Leibniz's reasons for holding that *motion* is only a phenomenon, see Sleigh, *Leibniz and Arnauld* pp. 111f., and McGuire, "'Labyrinthus Continui'," esp. p. 323f.

relation to every event in an infinitely complex universe as the qualities of a real thing ought to. "*There is no actual determinate shape in things*" he wrote, "for none is able to satisfy infinite impressions" (C 522/L 270).

The shapes thus excluded from nature are finitely complex shapes; "there is no line or shape in nature that gives exactly and keeps uniformly for the least space and time the properties of a straight or circular line, or of any other line whose definition a finite mind can comprehend" (G VII,563). The conclusion that I think Leibniz draws is not that real shapes are infinitely complex, though some things he says (e.g., in DM 6) might leave us with that impression. Rather, he concludes that shape as such is only a phenomenon. I suppose that an infinitely complex shape would involve a line segment of finite length that changes not merely its curvature but also the direction of its change of curvature infinitely many times, and that Leibniz would have thought that an absurd and impossible monstrosity. What I assume he would say, instead of postulating infinitely complex shapes, is that for every finitely complex shape that might be ascribed to a body there is another still more complex that more adequately expresses reality.

This is suggested by his use of the idea of an infinite series in an interesting text that may have been written shortly before the *Discourse on Metaphysics*,[25] and which expresses what is probably the correct Leibnizian answer to the question, Does shape, as a phenomenal property, belong to bodies (since after all bodies themselves are only phenomena) or only appear to belong to them? "No determinate shape can be assigned to any body," Leibniz claims in this text, and then adds the qualification, "although even in an infinite series' departure from a path [*deviatio*] some rules are observed by nature" (G VII,314/MP 81), suggesting an infinite series of shapes more and more adequately expressing reality. Every shape in the series, however, will still be only finitely complex, and for that reason among others will still be only an appearance, qualitatively different from the reality expressed, which is infinitely complex and does not literally have a shape at all. Leibniz does not consistently adhere, however, to the doctrine that determinate shapes do not belong to bodies, considered as phenomena, for (even apart from casual and presumably unmetaphysical comments about the shapes of bodies) he states, in a much later document, that finitely complex shapes "are found in phenomena or in the objects of limited minds" (G VII,563).

Bodies—organic or living bodies in particular—are appearances of *monads*.[26] A monad is represented by its body; we perceive it by perceiving its body. This is possible because the monad and its body express each other; the body is the expression of the soul. We have just seen, however, that a body conceived as a phenomenon having a certain definite extension, shape, and motion is not complex enough to be an adequate expression of any real thing, according to Leibniz. It is not complex enough to express something that expresses the whole universe

[25]Robinet (*Architectonique disjonctive*, p. 34*n*) argues persuasively for this dating. I am indebted to Sleigh, (*Leibniz and Arnauld*, p. 114) for pointing out the "suggestion," which Sleigh indeed takes to be more than a suggestion.

[26]Here I disagree with Hochstetter, "Von der wahren Wirklichkeit bei Leibniz," p. 436. It must be granted to Hochstetter that Leibniz did not explicitly speak of phenomena as "appearances of monads."

as a monad does. It is a mathematical abstraction. Perhaps the body that adequately expresses a monad is an infinite series of such abstractions, each more complex than its predecessors.

It should be noted that the fullest development I have found in Leibniz of an argument against the reality of shape is based on a diachronic account of how bodies would express an infinitely complex universe, rather than on the synchronic considerations presented (rather sketchily) to Arnauld in 1687 and developed in my exposition above. It is open to serious objection, in my opinion, but it may be the argument that in fact lay behind Leibniz's statement of about 1689 that "*there is no actual determinate shape in things*, for none is able to satisfy infinite impressions" (C 522/L 270). The diachronically based argument is found in a document dated (on the basis of watermark) about 1686:

> There is no precise and fixed shape in bodies, because of the actual division of the parts to infinity.
>
> Suppose for example a straight line *ABC*; I say that it is not exact [i.e., not exactly straight]. For as each part of the universe sympathizes with all the others, it must necessarily be that if the point *A* tends [to move] in the straight line *AB*, the point *B* has another direction. For as each part *A* tries to carry with it every other, but particularly the nearest part *B*, the direction of *B* will be composed of that of *A* and of some others. It is not possible that *B*, indefinitely near to *A*, be exposed to the whole universe in precisely the same fashion as *A*, in such a way that *AB* would compose a whole without any subdivision. (VE 1478 = LH IV,3,5B,1)

Leibniz argues here that in order for the physical state of bodies to express adequately their relations to each other, the matter at any two points, *A* and *B*, however close, must be tending in different directions, at any given time. Presumably he would extend the argument to any three points supposed to lie in a straight line, as suggested by the introduction of his example, and argue that the matter at them must be tending in three different directions, and similarly for any *n* points and *n* directions.

In his next paragraph Leibniz explains why he thinks it follows from this that the supposed straight line is not physically real after all.

> It is true that it will always be possible to draw an imaginary line at each instant; but that line, with the same parts, will not endure beyond that instant, because each part has a different motion from every other because it expresses the whole universe differently. Thus there is no body that has any shape during a certain time, however short it may be. Now I believe that what is only in a moment has no existence, since it begins and ends at the same time. (VE 1478 = LH IV,3,5B,1)

Leibniz argues that if all the matter at all the points that might be thought to lie in a physically real shape is moving in different directions at every time, as he argued in the previous paragraph, it follows that no such shape endures beyond an instant. To get the conclusion that no physically real shape exists, he adds another key premise, that "what is only in a moment has no existence." This last is a large and dubious assumption, however. I think Leibniz himself must probably ascribe to monads perceptual states that do not endure, unchanged, beyond an instant. I am therefore reluctant to regard this argument as the principal support of Leibniz's thesis of the phenomenality of shape, though it may be his most fully developed argument on the subject.

1.3.2 Continuity

Leibniz's list of merely phenomenal physical qualities goes beyond even the Cartesian modes of extension. It extends to extension itself,[27] and the dynamic properties of bodies:

> With many ancient sages, however, I judge that extension and, in it, Mass [*Moles*[28]] or impenetrability with the other corporeal predicates arising thence, which seem to many to constitute corporeal substance, and by others are held to be absolute real qualities, are in fact nothing but phenomena— well founded, to be sure, and not deceptive, but having no other objective reality than that by which we distinguish dreaming from waking, a mutual metaphysico-mathematical agreement of everything that the souls or Entelechies perceive. [G VII,468 (1705)]

The physical qualities that are most real, in Leibniz's view, are forces; but even forces, as found in bodies, are phenomenal (G II,276/AG 182). The question of the relation of physical forces to appearance and to ultimately real qualities of substances will be a major topic of Chapter 13.

Another important quality to which Leibniz ascribes diminished reality is *continuity*.[29] Continuity is of fundamental importance to extension. Extension was traditionally conceived as a species of continuous quantity, and Leibniz frequently defines extension as "the simultaneous continuous repetition of position" and "*a plurality, continuity, and coexistence of the parts.*"[30] Repetition, says Leibniz, is either discrete or continuous. In continuous repetition "the parts are indeterminate and can be assumed in infinite ways" (G IV,394/AG 251). There are other necessary conditions of continuity, of course, but indeterminacy of the parts is the feature of continuity that diminishes its reality in Leibniz's eyes. Real things are discrete, and anything composed of real things is therefore not continuous, but has fixed and determinate divisions. It is "ideal" wholes, as Leibniz puts it, that are divisible in indefinitely various ways into merely possible parts.

> In matter and in actual realities the whole is a result of the parts; but in ideas or in possibles . . . the indeterminate whole is prior to the divisions. . . . The

[27]Leibniz thinks extension can be proved to "enter into the essence or nature of body" though it does not constitute the whole essence of body (RML 437/L 619). I will offer a lot of evidence that Leibniz regards, and must regard, extension as no more than a phenomenon. I am not sure what to make of his writing to Rémond in 1715 that extension "is an attribute of substances" (RML 480).

[28]*Moles* is the Latin term usually translated as 'mass' in dynamic contexts. In some contexts I follow AG in translating it as 'bulk', to distinguish it from the Latin *massa*, which has a different (nonquantitative) meaning for Leibniz.

[29]For helpful accounts of Leibniz's philosophical treatment of continuity in general, see Breger, "Das Kontinuum bei Leibniz," and Lamarra, " Leibniz on Locke on Infinity."

[30]G II,339; G IV,467/W 104; see also C 361; B 124; G IV,394,364f.; G II,169f.,183/P 52; AG 251; L 390,516,519—texts dating from 1686–1707.

> better to conceive the actual division of matter to infinity, and the exclusion that there is of all exact and indeterminate continuity, we must consider that God has already produced there as much order and variety as it was possible to introduce there until now, and thus nothing has remained indeterminate there, whereas the indeterminate is of the essence of continuity. (G VII,562f.)[31]

Continuity, therefore, is "an ideal thing" (GM IV,93/L 544), not a feature of the ultimately real. It might still be thought a feature of bodies, if bodies are only phenomena; and Leibniz can be quoted on both sides of the question whether bodies *are* continuous or only *appear* to be continuous. An important text of 1702 classifies body as continuous (G IV,394/AG 251). The other answer is given in texts of 1705, at least as regards "matter": "In fact matter is not a continuum, but is something discrete, actually divided to infinity" (G II,278). "Matter appears to us [to be] a continuum, but it only appears so" (G VII,564).[32] This issue is deeply involved with issues about Leibniz's conception of bodies as aggregates of substances, so I will have to return to it in section 3. For the time being, I will just say that as in section 1.3.1 I preferred the view that (determinate, finitely complex) shape only *appears* to belong to bodies, so here I think Leibniz probably ought to hold that bodies only *appear* to be continuous.[33]

This view, in both cases, is associated with an account in terms of an infinite series of better and better approximations, an account that is somewhat more explicitly developed for continuity than for shape. An important text rejecting continuity "in every aggregate that is sensible or corresponds to phenomena" goes on, "Meanwhile the knowledge of continua, that is of possibles, contains eternal truths, which are never violated by actual phenomena, since the difference is always less than any assignable given difference" (G II,282f./L 539).[34] The point presumably is that while in actual phenomena (bodies) the division into parts is given and determinate, there is some such actual, given division (or series of divisions) as close as you please to any arbitrary line that might be drawn

[31]For similar statements, see G IV,491f./AG 146f.; G II,379; G III,622f. In the last of these passages, Leibniz both denies that "the continuum is something real" and states that "continuity is not an ideal thing, but what's real in it is what is found in that order of continuity." The point of the latter statement seems to be that if an aggregate of real things is viewed as arrayed in a continuous order such as those of space and time, the continuous order inherits a measure of their reality (though it surely is not therefore real in the most fundamental sense). But Leibniz's consistency here may be doubted.

[32]It is interesting, and perhaps revealing, that the diminished reality of both shape and continuity are discussed together in G VII,562–64. Ironically, however, this text, which clearly states that matter "only appears" to be a continuum, seems to give the opposite answer to the analogous question about shape, allowing that determinate shapes "are found in phenomena or in the objects of limited minds," which presumably include bodies.

[33]This is a correction of my 1983 paper, "Phenomenalism and Corporeal Substance in Leibniz," p. 242, where I overlooked a lot of the material discussed here and tried to maintain the continuity of Leibnizian bodies, even where they are understood as aggregates of substances. In so doing, I allowed density to count as a sort of continuity, something that Leibniz himself may sometimes have done (as I will suggest below). I am indebted to the criticisms of Hartz, "Leibniz's Phenomenalisms," for forcing me to rethink the topic.

[34]The importance of this point is emphasized by the next sentence, which mentions agreement with eternal truths as a mark of the reality of phenomena. Agreement with mathematical truth figures similarly as a mark of reality, in connection with similar views about continuity, at G IV,569.

through the body, because the body is actually divided to infinity. This implies, in modern terminology, that the actual divisions in every body, though not continuous, are *dense*.

We may wonder whether Leibniz occasionally referred to the dense as "continuous." To Des Bosses, in 1707, he writes:

> When I say that Extension is the continuation of the resistant, you ask whether that continuation is only a mode. What I think is that it is related to the things continued or repeated as number is to the things numbered: that is, a simple substance, even though it does not have extension in itself, still has position, which is the foundation of extension, since extension is the simultaneous continuous repetition of position. (G II,339)

Number, conceived as related to things numbered, is surely discrete. Leibniz uses the composition of number "from unities" as an example of discrete structure, as contrasted with the composition of number "from fractions," which is continuous (G II,282/L 539; cf. G VII,562; G III,622). Moreover, he is speaking here of a repetition of simple substances, which must certainly be discrete. It appears therefore that the "continuation" that he discusses here must be a discrete operation or construction; and that is not problematic in itself, since continuation [*continuatio*] is not continuity. What is problematic in this passage is that Leibniz goes on to say that an extension which must, in the context, be formed by this discrete operation on the positions of simple substances, is "continuous." It is hard to see how 'continuous' can mean more here than that the repetition of the positions of simple substances is dense, as Leibniz surely believed it to be.

Defining extension in terms of such a weakened sense of continuity (that is, in terms of density) would avoid the implication that the extended must have indefinite parts. And that would eliminate one objection to the reality of the extended.[35] This consideration may have motivated a number of formulations in which Leibniz says that what is extended is continued, or continually repeated, but does not say that it is continuous.[36] But such treatment of the definition of extension does not leave Leibniz in a position to hold that extension is more than a phenomenon. For extension, as defined here, consists in a relation among the substances repeated, and Leibniz held that relations depend on perceivers who apprehend them, as we shall see in section 3.2. Writing to De Volder in 1704 or 1705, accordingly, Leibniz explicitly connects the relational character of extension with its being something intrinsically ideal [*res per se idealis*]. The next paragraph of the same letter, it may be added, suggests another ground of the phenomenality of extension: the repetition or diffusion involved in extension requires a homogeneity of that which is repeated or diffused;[37] this homogeneity is only apparent and "obtains only by an abstraction of the mind" (G II,277/AG 183).

[35]In some contexts, Leibniz may, of course, have wished to use this objection as an argument for the phenomenality or diminished reality of extension. Such an argument is developed by McRae, *Leibniz: Perception, Apperception, and Thought*, p. 40f.

[36]G IV,589 (1702); G II,269/L 536 (1704); RML 443/L 621 (1712).

[37]On this requirement, cf. C 542f.

2. *Esse* Is *Percipi*

The simplest and starkest version of phenomenalism to be found in Leibniz's writings belongs not to his mature philosophy, but to the years 1675–79. Many of its ideas persist in his thought. His later phenomenalism grows out of it much more by addition than by subtraction, and it provides an illuminating background to the complexities of his later thought.

This early phenomenalism is connected with a notable anticipation of Berkeley's famous doctrine that (for sensible things) "*esse* is *percipi*"—to be is to be perceived.[38] There is a long series of texts, running from Leibniz's youth to his old age, in which he identifies existence with being perceived or (in some texts) perceivable, and often connects this with the idea that what exists is what is best or most harmonious. In 1672, for example, early in Leibniz's stay in Paris, he writes:

> I seem to myself to have discovered that to Exist is nothing other than to be Sensed [*Sentiri*]—to be sensed however, if not by us, then at least by the Author of things, to be sensed by whom is nothing other than to please him, or to be Harmonious. (A VI,iii,56)

In most of these texts, concerned with defining existence, there is no clear phenomenalist intent, despite the striking resemblance to Berkeley. In some there is reason to doubt the presence of any sort of reductive intent. For instance, VE 171 (= LH IV,7C,71f.), which belongs, I think, to a family of texts from the early 1680s, has the interesting feature that the same document contains a definition of existence in terms of perfection. That both types of definition could be appropriate at once is explicit in VE 1086 (= LH IV,8,60–61), probably from the last year or so of Leibniz's life and certainly after 1706, where Leibniz says, "I once defined an Entity (*Ens*) as whatever is distinctly thinkable, Existent as what is distinctly sensible or perceivable. Explaining the matter a priori, an Entity is whatever is possible, but there actually exists whatever is in the best series of possible things." Explaining the matter a priori here clearly means explaining it from its causes or reasons (cf. the appendix to Chapter 3 of this volume); and a "real" definition of existence does that. But another sort of "definition" follows the order of knowledge rather than of causality, identifying existence in terms of a criterion (perceivability) by which it is recognized. VE 404f. (= LH IV,7C,73f.), of uncertain date, admits both types of definition in similar terms.[39]

There are two important manuscripts from the mid-to-late 1670s, however, in which the identification of existence with being *perceivable*, and *harmoniously* so, is clearly in the service of a phenomenalist argument. The relation between *perceivability* and existence lies at the heart of the argument in a fragment entitled by Leibniz "Body is not a Substance but only a mode of a Being or

[38]Berkeley, *Works*, vol. 2, p. 42 (*A Treatise concerning the Principles of Human Knowledge*, part I, § 3).

[39]There are at least four other passages in VE in which Leibniz offers a definition of existence in terms of perception or perceivability. The watermark of VE 1339 (= B 123f.) is attested for the early 1690s. There is some reason to date VE 146 (= LH IV,7C,47) in the late 1670s. VE 476f. (part of which = G VII,319/L363) and VE 180 (= LH IV,7C,101) have watermarks attested for the mid-1680s. See also see C 437, of 1702–4. In Chapter 6, section 2 I have discussed some passages of this sort in relation to issues about existence.

a coherent appearance," although the thought of offering a *definition* or account of the nature of existence (and, in this case, truth) does not emerge until the end of the text, and then in connection with harmony and pleasing God rather than with perceivability.

> I understand, however, by body, not what the Scholastics compose of matter and a certain intelligible form, but what the Democriteans [i.e., atomists], in another context, call mass [*moles*]. This I say is not a substance. For I shall demonstrate that if we consider mass as a substance we fall into [views] implying a contradiction, just because of the labyrinth of the continuum, where we must consider especially, first, that there cannot be Atoms, for they conflict with the divine wisdom. Next, that bodies are actually divided into infinite parts, yet not into points, and therefore that there is no way in which a single body can be marked out, but that any portion whatever of matter is a being by accident, and even in perpetual flux. But if we say only this, that bodies are coherent appearances, that puts an end to all inquiry about infinitely small things, which cannot be perceived. But here there is a place also for that Herculean argument of mine, that all those things about which it cannot be perceived by anyone whether they are or not, are nothing. Now that is the nature of bodies, for if God himself willed to create corporeal substances such as people imagine [*fingunt*], he would do nothing, and even he would not be able to perceive that he had done anything, since nothing is perceived, in the end, but appearances. The sign of truth, therefore, is coherence, but its cause is the will of God, and its formal definition [*formalis ratio*] is that God perceives that something is best or most harmonious, or that something pleases God. Therefore the divine will itself, so to speak, is the existence of things. (VE 1872 = LH IV,1,14B,1)

Several points in this remarkable text deserve comment here.

1. The Academy editors date it no earlier than 1677, after Leibniz first settled in Hannover. But the text contains no trace of the interest in finding something substantial in bodies, and in affirming the existence of some sort of corporeal substance, so evident in Leibniz's correspondence with Arnauld and other texts from 1686 and later. The only references to the idea of corporeal substance here are hostile. And while the "Scholastic" conception of corporeal substance as composed of matter and substantial form is explicitly excluded from the scope of this critical discussion, there is no positive indication here that Leibniz has decided to rehabilitate the notion of substantial form—a decision he apparently made in summer 1679.[40] This suggests that the text before us should be dated no later than the first half of 1679.

2. This dating is confirmed by the treatment of the first of the two arguments for phenomenalism offered in the text, which is an early version of Leibniz's argument (discussed more fully in Chapter 11, section 2.2) against the substantiality of extended things as such, from their infinite division into parts. While the presence of this argument links this text with Leibniz's mature philosophy, its employment here is notably different from its later use. Here it is simply an

[40]This pinpointing of the momentous decision is due to Robinet (*Architectonique disjonctive*, pp. 245–51). His argument is persuasive and strongly supported by a comparison of A II,i,469f. and 490. Given the date of death of Duke Johann Friedrich, its addressee, the latter text shows that Leibniz's decision can hardly have been made later than 1679.

argument for phenomenalism, and the hypothesis "that bodies are coherent appearances" is presented as a completely satisfying solution to the problem posed by the infinite division of extended things. In later texts this infinite division is indeed presented as a reason why extended things as such are merely phenomena (because merely aggregates). Indeed, as we shall see, this argument is a more crucial support of phenomenalism in Leibniz's later thought than it is here. But phenomenalism is rarely the whole point of the argument in the later texts. More stress is usually laid on the conclusion that if there is to be anything substantial in bodies (as there should be, in Leibniz's later view), there must be in bodies something indivisible, a substantial form, or soul, or monad (and indeed many such). This contrasting strategy of argument is evident in a passage from one of the earliest texts reflecting Leibniz's decision to try to rehabilitate substantial forms:

> Here we must treat of the soul, and show that all things are animated. If there were no soul or form, a body would not be any being, since no part of it can be marked out which will not consist in turn of many, and so nothing could be marked out in a body which could be called *this something* or *some one thing*. (VE 651 = LH XXXVII,3,9–10)[41]

3. The other phenomenalist argument in our text deserves several paragraphs. It is the one Leibniz calls his "Herculean argument," based on the principle that "all those things about which it cannot be perceived by anyone whether they are or not, are nothing." This of course expresses one half of the equivalence of existence with perceivability, the thesis that existence entails perceivability, though we are not told here whether it rests on a definition of existence. Claims of this sort in Leibniz have evoked the comment that "Leibniz comes close to employing what is now called the Verifiability criterion of meaning."[42] The comment is correct, as long as the "closeness" is not exaggerated, but we should be clear that Leibniz never offers a criterion of *meaning* in these terms. In the present case, the thesis is not about meaning but about *existence* and about the *reality of differences*.

As Leibniz begins this argument, we may expect it to be based also on the claim that "infinitely small things . . . cannot be perceived,"[43] but that claim drifts out of sight as the argument proceeds. The reason emphasized for thinking that even God could not perceive any difference between there being and there not being any bodies more substantial than mere appearances is that "nothing is perceived, in the end, but appearances." This must be understood, I think, as a claim that the object of perception, as such, is merely an appearance, whose existence is not distinct from its being perceived. Not only this claim but also its application to God's perceptions is echoed (independently, of course) by Berkeley,

[41]Cited by Robinet, *Architectonique disjonctive*, p. 246. The watermark of this text is attested from the period July 1678–June 1682.

[42]Mates, *Philosophy of Leibniz* p. 234. Mates is commenting on LC V,29.

[43]Leibniz here clearly rejects infinitely small things, as Berkeley would later. It is equally clear here, however, that he is not postulating finitely small indivisible objects of perception, as Berkeley would, but already affirms the infinite division of the extended, as he did eventually in his sharpest disagreement with Berkeley, as noted in section 1.2 in this chapter.

who, in the second of his *Three Dialogues between Hylas and Philonous*, argues that his idealism is superior to occasionalism by pointing out that

> it [is] not . . . easy to conceive how the external or absolute existence of an unthinking substance, distinct from its being perceived, can be inferred from my allowing that there are certain things perceived by the mind of God, which are to Him the occasion of producing ideas in us.[44]

This "Herculean argument" does not, to my knowledge, recur as an argument for phenomenalism in Leibniz's mature philosophy. He continued in other contexts to give favorable attention to definitions of existence in terms of perceivability (e.g., C 437), and to give arguments that seem to rest on the assumption that a difference not in principle perceivable is no real difference (G IV,514/L 505f.; LC V,29). But he no longer follows a direct route from that assumption to the phenomenality of bodies; the most prominent thought about the nature of existence in his later metaphysics of body is that *substantial* existence entails power to *act* (and, in finite, imperfect substances, to be acted on).[45]

The theme of *harmony* is not absent from this text of 1677–79. It emerges explicitly at the end, but is present more centrally in the identification of bodies, not merely with appearances, but with "coherent appearances." The emphasis of the text, nonetheless, falls on the relation of existence to perceivability, rather than to harmony. By way of contrast, the relation of existence to harmony, here conceived as "congruence," regularity, and "beauty," dominates a text written in Paris in 1676:

> Rightly considered, all that is certain is that we sense, and sense congruently, and that some rule is observed by us in sensing. To be sensed congruently is to be sensed in such a way that a reason can be given for everything, and everything can be predicted. And existence consists in this, in sensation keeping certain laws, for otherwise everything would be like dreams. Further that many sense the same thing, and sense things that agree. . . . Moreover sleep need not differ from waking by any intrinsic reality, but only by the form or order of sensations; wherefore there is no reason to ask whether there are any bodies outside us. . . . Hence it is clear that so far from material things being more real than others, on the contrary there can always be doubt of their existence—or rather their existence does not differ at all materially, or in itself, from the existence of dreams, even if they differ, of course, in beauty. (A VI,iii,511)[46]

This passage presents a theory of the nature of the distinction between real and unreal phenomena. Phenomena that really *exist* can be sensed. Leibniz frequently contrasted the existent, as something that can be sensed or perceived, with essence or entity [*ens*] as something that can be thought or conceived.[47] But the emphasis

[44]Berkeley, *Works*, vol. 2, p. 220.

[45]E.g., G IV,508/L 502. This thought is not absent from Leibniz's early thought about body; see, e.g., A VI,i,509/L 116.

[46]Castañeda, "Leibniz's Meditation on April 15, 1676," is an extended discussion of the passage from which this quotation is taken.

[47]A VI,i,285; A VI,ii,487; B 123f.; C 437; VE 146,171,404,180,1086 (= LH IV,7C, pp. 47, 71–74,101; LH IV,8,60–61).

falls here on a further thesis. Not only can really existent phenomena be sensed; they can be sensed harmoniously or "congruently," and that distinguishes them from dreams. These points will remain a part of Leibniz's mature account of the difference between real and imaginary phenomena, as we shall see in section 4. The most interesting thing, metaphysically, about the early form of this theory is that its strongly reductive character constitutes it a clearly phenomenalist theory, even though the only thing that receives a reductive analysis here is the difference between the really existent and the nonexistent (or not really existent) among ostensible bodies. It is striking how complete a phenomenalism can be constituted by a theory of the nature of this difference, and it is characteristic of Leibniz's phenomenalism that this is where the reductive analysis is done, as I argued in section 1.1.

Legitimate questions can be raised about the extent to which Leibniz was committed to phenomenalism in the mid-1670s. There seem to have been other, less idealistic strands in his thought during the period. Some texts of 1675 and 1676, growing out of Leibniz's relations with the skeptical philosopher Simon Foucher, suggest a view of material things as external causes of perception, "something other than that which thinks" (A II,i,246f./L 152; cf. A VI,iii,318f.). It is clear in these texts that Leibniz is quite conscious of the possibility of skepticism about the extramental existence of bodies, but phenomenalism is not proposed here as the only resolution of the problem. Catherine Wilson sees in these tendencies of the Paris period the groundwork of a permanent ambiguity in Leibniz's thought "on the question of the independent existence of 'external' things."[48] Clearly I reject the hypothesis of *permanent* ambiguity, but I do not pretend to offer a *comprehensive* account of Leibniz's philosophy of body at any stage of his career before the mid-1680s. For my present purpose, what is most significant about Leibniz's thought in the 1670s is that, whether or not he was committed to them, he had certainly articulated theories of a developed phenomenalist character.

The most fundamental differences of Leibniz's mature phenomenalism from the phenomenalism worked out in his writings of 1676–79 arise with his decision to try to rehabilitate the Scholastic notion of substantial form. Substantial forms are to be principles of unity, and Leibniz conceived of them on the model of souls (as will be discussed in Chapter 11, section 1). Two implications of their rehabilitation may be stressed here.

1. With the acceptance of substantial forms Leibniz "goes on to infinite monads," as he later thought Berkeley ought to have done. The only souls or perceiving beings whose existence is entailed in the phenomenalist writings of 1676–79 are minds.[49] But while all substantial forms are to carry powers of perception, most of them are not to count as minds, or even as souls, strictly speaking, because their powers of perception are too imperfect. Most substantial forms are to have only powers of *unconscious* perception. Thus there is to be added to the minds a multitude of inferior principles of unity and perception—an infinite

[48]C. Wilson, *Leibniz's Metaphysics*, p. 67).

[49]For a text of 1678 (though one in which phenomenalist issues are avoided) in which "minds" are clearly the only such beings that are allowed, see A II,i,400/L 189.

multitude, for substantial forms are to be found "in" every portion of matter, no matter how small, according to Leibniz's mature philosophy. This multiplication of perceiving beings is often emphasized in Leibniz's discussions of substantial forms, as in the following early endorsement of their rehabilitation:

> Therefore I judge that in every body there is some sensation and appetite, or soul, and accordingly it is as ridiculous to attribute a substantial form and perception, or a soul, to man alone, as to believe that everything was made for the sake of man alone and that the earth is the center of the universe. (VE 642 = LH XXXVII,3,1-6)

Leibniz seems never to have forgotten that this vast expansion of his ontology brought with it an increased vulnerability to skeptical doubts. For this reason, his earlier, more austere phenomenalism is sometimes visible behind the complex theory of his later years, as a rejected but respected alternative, or even as a fall-back position kept in reserve. This is particularly true of some of Leibniz's writings of the mid-1680s (e.g., G VII,319–22/L 363–65, which will be discussed in section 4). Robert Sleigh, Jr., notes that a theory like that which I have identified as Leibniz's earlier phenomenalism "is in the background, though not outright asserted at *DM* §§ 14 and 34," and claims that "a careful reading of [the original autograph] version [of the *Discourse*] indicates that no thesis asserted therein entails that there are" substances other than minds.[50] Sleigh also points out that Leibniz's letters and drafts of letters to Arnauld contain a number of indications that the question whether there are true substantial unities in nature other than (human) minds was regarded by Leibniz as a pivotal question in the philosophy of body, which he answered in the affirmative, but only with many expressions of caution.[51]

2. With the addition of an infinite multitude of inferior substantial unities "in" every portion of the corporeal universe, the relation of phenomena to substance becomes more complicated. In the phenomenalism articulated by Leibniz in 1676–79, most bodies (stones and trees, for example) had no substances "in" them; but in the mature view there is something substantial "in" every particle of matter. I think it is clear that the desire to find something substantial in bodies as such was a main motive for Leibniz's rehabilitation of substantial forms and his acceptance of a more expansive ontology.

In the earlier view, the relation of substance to phenomena was simply a perceptual one of subject to object. The phenomena were the (internal) objects of substances' perceptions. The substances were the subjects *to* which the phenomena appeared. This relation remains in Leibniz's mature phenomenalism, but is joined there by other relations. Since all bodies have substances "in" them, they can be regarded as appearances *of* substances as well as appearances *to* substances. They can even be treated as aggregates of substances. In order to maintain a phenomenalist position in his mature philosophy, therefore, Leibniz must argue that aggregates of substances are merely appearances. We shall see in section 3 that he does just that. From this point on we shall be concerned almost exclusively with Leibniz's mature philosophy.

[50] Sleigh, *Leibniz and Arnauld*, p. 98; see also pp. 101–3.
[51] See Sleigh, *Leibniz and Arnauld*, pp. 103–6, for much documentation.

3. *Aggregates*

The mature Leibniz holds that "the body is an aggregate of substances" (LA 135).[52] This applies not only to disorganized masses, but also to organic bodies: "the human body is an aggregate" (G VII,468*n*). We may be tempted to think this contradicts the thesis that bodies are phenomena, but Leibniz did not think these views inconsistent. He speaks of masses as "only beings by aggregation, and *therefore* phenomena."[53] Indeed, he frequently asserts that precisely as aggregates of substances, bodies are phenomena. In trying to understand this doctrine, it will be helpful to attend to three questions: Of what sort of substances are bodies aggregates? What is the ontological status of aggregates in general? What is the principle of aggregation that determines which individual substances are grouped together to form a particular corporeal aggregate? The next three subsections are devoted to these questions, and a fourth subsection will consider an objection to my answer to the third question.

3.1 *Aggregates of What?*

Leibniz is commonly read as holding that bodies are aggregates of *monads*. One might think that an aggregate of those ultimately real substances would be more than an appearance. But it may be questioned how far it is correct to say that Leibniz thought of bodies as aggregates of monads or simple substances. There are indeed places in his works where he speaks of a corporeal mass as aggregated from "unities" [G II,379 (1709)] or, more clearly, as "a result or assemblage of simple substances or indeed of a multitude of real unities" [G IV,491/AG 146 (1695)]. Other texts containing this idea were written in 1705 (G III,367; G VII,561), 1706 (G II,282/L 539), and 1714 (PNG 1; G III,622). There are also many texts, however, that support the view that "a mass is an aggregate of *corporeal* substances," where a corporeal substance "consists in a simple substance or monad . . . and an organic body united to it" [G VII,501f., italics added (1711)].[54] Other texts expressing this view were written in 1699 (G III,260/AG 289) or about then (G IV,572f.), in 1700 (G II,205f.), in 1705 or later (G VI,550), and in 1712 (G II,459/L 607; C 13f./MP 175).[55] The organic body, which is one of the constituents of a corporeal substance on this account, is a phenomenon according to Leibniz (G III,657). This might suggest to us that Leibniz thought corporeal masses are phenomena *because* they are aggregates of corporeal substances that are partly composed of phenomena.

[52]In arriving at the present form of this section (and also for section 1.3.2) I am indebted to discussion with Marianne Kooij, and to Glenn Hartz's paper on "Leibniz's Phenomenalisms." Neither of them, of course, is responsible for the views I express, and I remain in substantial disagreement with Hartz.

[53]G II,252/L 531, emphasis added. I take these phrases to apply, in the context, to masses. Literally, Leibniz says this about "the rest" [*reliqua*] by contrast with "simple things." Cf. G VII,344/AG 319, and, from as early as 1680–85, VE 1299 = LH IV,7C,105f.

[54]Of the arguably Leibnizian theories of corporeal substance to be discussed in Chapter 10, this text expresses the "two-substance" theory.

[55]On the date of C 13f., see MP 258. The use of the term *substantiatum* may indicate a relation between the document and correspondence of 1712 with Des Bosses. The document was dated about 1708 by Hochstetter, "Von der wahren Wirklichkeit bei Leibniz," p. 427*n*.

This explanation of Leibniz's belief in the phenomenality of bodies is unacceptable, however, for at least four reasons. (1) If bodies are phenomena because they are composed of corporeal substances that are partly composed of phenomena, the corporeal substances themselves should also be phenomena because they are partly composed of phenomena; Leibniz did not hold that corporeal substances are phenomena, however. (2) So far as I know, Leibniz never says that corporeal aggregates are phenomena because they are partly composed of phenomena, but he often says they are phenomena because they are aggregates. (3) Indeed, a vicious-looking circle would arise if Leibniz tried to explain the phenomenality of corporeal aggregates on the ground that they are partly composed of organic bodies that are phenomena, for he explains the phenomenality of organic bodies on the ground that they are (corporeal) aggregates. (4) In general, it seems that Leibniz's treatment of bodies as aggregates of *corporeal* substances is not meant to exclude the claim that at bottom they are entirely reducible to *simple* substances or monads, related in certain ways. Thus Leibniz can say that each body "is nothing but an aggregate of animals or other living and therefore organic things, or else of fragments or masses, but which also themselves are finally analyzed into living things"—where I take the "living things" to be corporeal substances. But he immediately adds that "the last thing in the analysis of substances is that there are simple substances, namely souls or, if you prefer a more general word, *Monads*, which lack parts" (C 13f./MP 175). For all of these reasons I think we must try to understand why Leibniz would have thought that aggregates as such cannot be more than phenomena even if they are aggregates of *simple* substances or monads.

This conclusion will survive examination of two texts in which Leibniz denies that body or matter is "composed of" monads, and which might seem to be evidence that Leibniz would deny that bodies are aggregates of monads. Both texts are related to the problem of the continuum, but I think they must be understood in rather different senses. I will begin with the later of the two texts, from a letter of 1712 to Bartholomew des Bosses, in which Leibniz had just introduced for the first time the theory of substantial bonds, an alternative to his purely monadological metaphysics, which will be discussed in Chapter 10, sections 5.3 and 5.4. Even if there are no substantial bonds, Leibniz states, "monads should not be said to be parts of bodies, to touch each other, or to compose bodies, any more than it is right to say that about points and souls" (G II,436/AG 199). Why, in this context, would it be wrong to say that "monads compose bodies"? We cannot be certain, but one possible rationale is related to the question discussed earlier, in section 1.3.2, whether bodies *are* continuous or only *appear* to be so. Leibniz held that aggregates of real substances are not continuous, because they are actually divided into discrete untities, whereas the continuous as such is only potentially divided into indeterminate parts. Hence, if bodies really are continuous, they cannot be aggregates of real substances, and in that sense they cannot be "composed of constitutive unities."

This train of thought is strongly suggested by a passage in Leibniz's last letter to Des Bosses, in 1716: "Besides, if monads alone were substances [and there were no substantial bonds], then either bodies would have to be mere phenomena or the continuum would have to arise from points, which is known to be absurd.

Real continuity cannot arise except from a substantial bond" (G II,517/AG 203). Why is it that, under the stated condition, "either bodies would have to be mere phenomena or the continuum would have to arise from points"? Presumably it is because, in order to be more than mere phenomena, in the relevant sense,[56] bodies would have to be composed, as aggregates, of monads, and then a mathematical continuum would have to arise from unextended, indivisible unities. But that presupposes that bodies are fully, mathematically continuous.

In the context of the Des Bosses correspondence, this presupposition can be viewed as a largely terminological accommodation to the concerns of the theory of substantial bonds. It appears from the 1716 passage quoted that obtaining "real continuity" is one of the aims of the theory. This may be seen as serving the main aim of the theory, which is obtaining real *unity* and, hence, substantiality for bodies. For, according to Leibniz, a continuous whole is prior to its parts, and its unity is thus original and not constituted merely by relations among the parts. It would therefore be natural for a substantial bond theorist to define bodies as continuous things and infer that bodies are less real even than aggregates of substances, unless there are substantial bonds to give rise to "real continuity."

It strains credulity, however, to suppose that during the period of the des Bosses correspondence Leibniz was really not willing to count discontinuous aggregates of substances as bodies. For in other texts from that period he affirms that bodies are aggregates of substances [C 13f./MP 175 (1712); PNG 1 (1714); G III,622,657 (1714,1715); cf. RML 447/L 623 (1712–15)], and Leibniz certainly did not think that aggregates of substances are continuous. These considerations support the view that Leibniz ought to say that bodies only *appear* to be continuous—and also the view that the theory of substantial bonds is not part of his philosophy.

In any event, the argument that bodies are continuous and therefore must not be aggregates of substances cannot motivate Leibniz's earlier statement, in a letter of 1704 to Burcher De Volder, that "accurately speaking, matter is not composed of constitutive unities, but results from them" (G II,268/L 536). I believe that "constitutive unities" refers here to simple substances or monads. The statement is certainly related to the problem of the continuuum, which Leibniz has just been discussing. But Leibniz has also just implied, unambiguously, that bodies lack one of the characteristics that define, for him, the continuous, declaring that "in real things, namely bodies, the parts are not indefinite (as [they are] in space, a mental thing), but are actually assigned in a certain way" (G II,268/L 536). The clue to the correct interpretation of the passage, I think, is given when Leibniz goes on to say, "Phenomena therefore can always be divided into smaller phenomena which could appear to more subtle animals, and one will never arrive at smallest phenomena. But substantial unities are not parts, but foundations, of phenomena" (G II,268/L 536). The *parts* of phenomena are smaller phenomena; "substantial unities" stand in some other relation to phenomena.

A related treatment of the part/whole relation is illuminating. In 1690 Leibniz wrote, "Furthermore even if an aggregate of these substances constitutes a body,

[56]A sense implying more distance from reality, obviously, than the sense in which an aggregate of substances, as an aggregate, is merely a phenomenon.

they still do not constitute it in the manner of a part, since a part is always homogeneous with the whole, in the same way that points are not parts of lines" (VE 2156/AG 105). A part of a line, on this view, must be homogeneous with the line, and therefore must be a line segment, and not a point.[57] Similarly, I suppose, a part of a phenomenon must be a phenomenon, and a part of an aggregate must be a subaggregate. Specifically, a part of a body must be a body. If a body is an aggregate of substances which are not aggregates, those substances will not be *parts* of the body, and the body will not be composed of them if being 'composed of' means having as parts.

But there is surely a broader sense in which an aggregate of substances is composed of those substances, and if they are not parts of it, they are some other sort of constituent of it. Leibniz used 'composed of' in both the narrower and the broader sense in the De Volder correspondence. When he wrote to De Volder that "matter is not composed of constitutive unities," I am arguing, he must have meant that the unities are not *parts* of the matter. But when he wrote to De Volder, less than eighteen months later, that "actual things are composed . . . of unities" (G II,282/L 539), he was presumably using 'composed of' in a broader sense and was not giving up the thesis that substantial unities are not *parts* of corporeal aggregates. In neither case, I believe, was he denying that bodies are aggregates of substances, or indeed of monads.

If not parts, what are the substances to the aggregates? Leibniz occasionally uses the word 'elements' in this context, saying that "it is necessary for all aggregates to result from simple substances as from the true elements" (G VII,502), or referring to "primitive unities" or "simple substances" as "the first elements of substantial things" (G IV,491/AG 146).[58] The picture that emerges is one in which bodies are aggregates of (infinitely many) simple substances. These substances are *elements*, but not parts, of the aggregates. The *parts* of the aggregates (or of the bodies) are subaggregates (or smaller bodies) which have simple substances as their first elements.[59] I believe that this, rather than anything belonging to the theory of substantial bonds, is the dominant scheme for these topics in Leibniz's philosophy.

3.2 The Ontological Status of Aggregates

The apparent conflict between the thesis that bodies are phenomena and the thesis that they are aggregates of substances springs from the assumption that an aggregate of *F*s must have the same ontological status as the *F*s. This is at best a controversial assumption. There is nothing at all odd about Leibniz's rejecting it.

[57]This was a traditional view, maintained in Aristotle's *Physics*, book VI, ch. 1.

[58]It is interesting that in this text of 1695 (as also in GM III,536 of 1698), Leibniz seems to deny that points are "the first elements of lines," thereby abandoning the close parallelism between the point/line and substance/body relations asserted in 1690 (VE 2156/AG 105). This may in fact reflect a change in his view of those relations; cf. Hartz and Cover, "Space and Time in the Leibnizian Metaphysic," pp. 493–97. Other texts of 1698–1705 (GM III,524; G II,276) in which 'element' seems to be used in the relevant sense, but not in reference to the relation of monads to corporeal aggregates, are quoted in Lamarra, "Leibniz on Locke on Infinity," p. 183*n*.

[59]For more discussion of the distinctions I have introduced here, and more evidence bearing on them, see Chapter 10, sections 3.1 and 3.2.

Aggregates are presumably close ontological kin to sets, and we are familiar with the fact that the assumption that a set of pencils must have the same ontological status as the pencils is highly controversial. We should not expect it to be assumed without argument that an army, one of Leibniz's favorite examples of an aggregate,[60] has the same ontological status as the soldiers that are its elements. In fact, Leibniz makes clear repeatedly that he believes that all aggregates, as such, are at most phenomena, and hence that an aggregate of substances does not have the same ontological status as the substances.

Another reason for finding this strange might arise from the fact that Leibniz thinks reality in some sense accrues to corporeal aggregates from the substances of which they are aggregates (as we shall see in section 4). Again, I think there is nothing really odd here. An aggregate of substances is for Leibniz a sort of logical or metaphysical construction out of substances, and thus out of ultimately real things. Such a construction has more reality than a construction out of things that are not real, but it is still not ultimately real in its own right. The "reality" of the constructed aggregate is not the same ontological status as the ultimate or original reality of the substances that are elements of the aggregate. Leibniz's theory of bodies is reductionist, and in a reductionist philosophy, being a logical or metaphysical construction out of ultimately real things is a different ontological status from that of the ultimately real things.

The reason Leibniz usually gives for thinking that aggregates as such are only phenomena is that they lack intrinsic [*per se*] unity. One reason why the idealistic character of Leibniz's philosophy may be less than obvious to us is that we expect idealism to be rooted primarily in the philosophy of perception, whereas for the mature Leibniz it is motivated largely by worries about the *unity* of bodies. Claims about perception played a more central role in the phenomenalism articulated in Leibniz's writings of 1676–79, discussed in section 2. But with the postulation of substantial forms "in" all bodies, so that the bodies can be regarded as aggregates of substances, the thesis of the phenomenality of bodies rests heavily on an argument that aggregates, by virtue of their disunity, are only phenomena.

"Finally," Leibniz writes, "bodies are nothing but aggregates, constituting something that is one accidentally [*per accidens*] or by an external denomination, and therefore they are well founded Phenomena" (G VII,344/AG 319). The unity of an aggregate comes to it by an "external denomination"—namely, by relation to a mind that perceives relationships among the things that are aggregated. Since Leibniz adhered to the Scholastic maxim that 'being' and 'one' are equivalent [*Ens et unum convertuntur*] (G II,304; cf. G II,300), he inferred that aggregates that have their unity only in the mind also have their being in the

[60]See, e.g., LA 97. In counting armies as aggregates, Leibniz ignores some distinctions found in Scholastic philosophy. For Francisco Suárez (*Metaphysical Disputations*, IV,iii,14), unity by aggregation is the weakest sort of accidental unity; the unity of an army, though still accidental, is stronger, because there is "some order" among the entities making up the army. For an even more elaborate array of Scholastic distinctions, see the Coimbra commentary on Aristotle's *Physics*, I,9,11,2, quoted in Gilson, *Index scolastico-cartésien*, pp. 304f. Leibniz does, however, recognize different "degrees of accidental unity," based on stronger and weaker relations among the constituents of an aggregate (LA 100).

mind. Historically, at least, this inference is not bizarre. A long Aristotelian tradition connects being and unity so closely that for Francisco Suárez an entity can be said to have *being per se* or *per accidens* on the basis of its having *unity per se* or *per accidens*.[61]

This reasoning is clearly expressed in Leibniz's long letter of 30 April 1687 to Antoine Arnauld.

> To be brief, I hold as an axiom this identical proposition which is diversified only by emphasis, namely that what is not truly *one* being [*un* estre] is not truly a *being* [un *estre*] either. It has always been believed that one and being are mutually convertible [*reciproques*] things. . . . I have believed therefore that I would be permitted to distinguish Beings of aggregation from substances, since those Beings have their unity only in our mind, which relies on the relations or modes of genuine substances. (LA 97)[62]

Leibniz's claim is that aggregates have their unity, and therefore their being, only in the mind, and that this is true even of aggregates of real things.

Why did Leibniz think that aggregates have their unity only in the mind? Another passage in the same letter to Arnauld reminds us that Leibniz was a conceptualist about abstract objects in general and also about relations (cf. NE 145; G II,438/AG 199), believing that they have their being only in the mind (especially in the divine mind). The same treatment is to be accorded to the unity of an aggregate and, hence, to the aggregate itself.

> Our mind notices or conceives some genuine substances that have certain modes. These modes contain relations to other substances. From this the mind takes the occasion to join them together in thought and to put one name in the accounting for all these things together, which serves for convenience in reasoning. But one must not let oneself be deceived thereby into making of them so many substances or truly real Beings. That is only for those who stop at appearances, or else for those who make realities of all the abstractions of the mind, and who conceive of number, time, place, motion, shape, sensible qualities as so many separate beings. (LA 101; cf. A I,ix,16)

In Leibniz's ontology, the only things that have being in their own right are particular "substances or complete Beings, endowed with a true unity, with their different successive states" (ibid.). Everything else, including universals, and also including aggregates, is logically or metaphysically constructed from the individual substances. This construction, in Leibniz's view, is a mental operation. The ontological status of entities logically or metaphysically constructed from substances, "being nothing but phenomena, abstractions, or relations" (ibid.), is therefore at least partly mental.[63] They exist in the mind and are dependent

[61]Suárez, *Metaphysical Disputations*, IV,iii,2–3.

[62]I have suppressed some unimportant emphases in the text, in order to let the emphases on "one" and "being" stand out more clearly. The last sentence in the quotation was not in the copy of the letter sent to Arnauld, but similar material at LA 101, which I will quote soon, was sent (see RL 69, 73f.). Similar ideas are found in G VI,516 (1702); NE 146,211 (1704); and RML 447/L 623 (1715).

[63]At NE 146 the mental or phenomenal character of beings by aggregation is grounded simply in the *relational* character of aggregation, as pointed out by McRae, *Leibniz: Perception, Apperception, and Thought*, p. 135f.

on being thought of. Doubts may remain, nevertheless, about the consistency of the view that bodies are aggregates and *therefore* phenomena. At least two questions arise here.

1. If bodies as phenomena are the objects of stories told by perception, by common sense, and especially by science, as I suggested in section 1, can they also be aggregates of substances? Certainly they can also be aggregates, for, according to Leibniz, it is part of the story told by science, and less distinctly also by common sense and perception, that every extended thing is composed of actual parts, and that is enough to make extended things aggregates in Leibniz's book. On the other hand, it does not seem to be part of the story told by perception, common sense, or science that extended things are composed of *monads*, nor perhaps even that they are composed of *substances* at all. To this I think Leibniz might say that those stories do not *exclude* the thesis that bodies are aggregates of substances. It is at least vaguely part of the stories told by common sense and science that the appearances of bodies have or may have some further foundation in reality. But no hypothesis of the nature of that foundation is part of the stories of Leibnizian science and common sense; it is left to metaphysics to consider what the foundation might be.

2. Can aggregates of substances possess the physical properties that bodies have in the story told by science? The most important, and most real, of those properties, for Leibniz, are *forces*, and he does ascribe physical forces to aggregates of substances (G II,251/L 530). The relation of forces to substances on the one hand and to phenomena on the other is too large a subject to be dealt with here, however. It will be a major topic of Chapter 13.

3.3 The Principle of Aggregation

Having examined Leibniz's reasons for holding that all aggregates, as such, are no more than phenomena, we should note that he has an additional reason for assigning the status of appearances to *corporeal* aggregates in particular. The rainbow provides Leibniz with a favorite example of a phenomenon, to which he frequently likens bodies (e.g., G II,262,390). His treatment of the example is not perfectly consistent. At least once (LA 58) he seems to contrast the rainbow with aggregates, but more often it is presented as something that is a phenomenon because it is an aggregate:

> The rainbow is an aggregate of drops which jointly produce certain colors that are apparent to us. . . . Hence the rainbow is of diminished reality under two headings, both because it is a Being by aggregation of drops, and because the qualities by which it is known are apparent or at least of that kind of real ones that are relative to our senses. (VE 188 = Gr 322)

The first of these reasons for the diminished reality of the rainbow corresponds to Leibniz's general thesis of the phenomenality of aggregates;[64] it is the second reason that I want to develop now.

[64]It may be significant that Leibniz speaks here of "diminished reality" rather than phenomenality. The next paragraph of this text is a rambling discussion of the question, "how a *Being by aggregation* . . . is one," in which Leibniz discusses more than one way in which an army has less

This reason has to do with the perceptual relativity of colors. Colors, Leibniz indicates in the same text, are "apparent qualities" in the sense that they "are not in things absolutely, but insofar as they act on us; thus the same water will seem cold or tepid or hot according to the disposition of my hands. Yet this is real in it, that it is naturally apt to produce this sensation in me when I am thus disposed." Colors in general are apparent qualities in this sense, according to Leibniz; but he neglects to emphasize that the colors of the rainbow are even more than ordinarily relative to perception. Any particular aggregate of drops of water in the air will be colored as a rainbow only relative to perceptions from a particular place. As I have noted in section 1.3, however, Leibniz thinks that even the more fundamental qualities of size, shape, and motion, have something of the phenomenal and are relative to perception; yet the aggregation of substances to form a body is based for Leibniz on such spatial properties of their bodies, as I shall argue. Because the aggregation of drops in a rainbow, and of substances in a body, is based on properties that are relative to perception in these ways, Leibniz infers that the rainbow and the body are phenomena and have diminished reality.

It is misleading, I think, that Leibniz says in presenting this argument that the qualities by which the rainbow is *known* or recognized [*noscitur*] are relative to our senses. What is crucial here is not that we know or recognize the rainbow by merely apparent qualities. Leibniz must say that in general we know or recognize even monads by properties of their bodies that are merely apparent, and the monads are none the less real for that. The crux of the argument is that the *existence* of the aggregate depends on properties that are relative to our perceptions. The relation to perception provides the principle of grouping that defines the aggregate. If we think of a rainbow as an aggregate of drops, what is it that picks them out from all the other drops of water in the sky and groups them as an object that we call a rainbow? It is their relation to the color perceptions that an observer (in one place but not in others) would have. It is thus only relative to appearances that there is more reason to aggregate these drops together than to form some other group from the drops in the sky. Likewise, the aggregation of substances as belonging to a single corporeal mass depends on largely phenomenal properties that their bodies *appear* to have.

Suppose through a cleverly contrived network of glass fibers the images of a thousand different people walking, talking, and gesturing on a thousand different streets of a hundred different cities were combined to give you an image of an angry mob. This "mob," we might say, is an aggregate of real human beings, but the reality of the individual persons does not keep the mob as such from being a mere phenomenon. This is because the existence of a mob depends on relations among its members in a way that the existence of a mathematical set does not, and I think the existence conditions for a Leibnizian aggregate are like those for a mob in this respect. If sets exist at all, the existence of all the mem-

---

unity than a soldier, but does *not* express the view that the unity of an aggregate is *mental*. The second reason for the diminished reality of the rainbow, which explicitly involves relativity to perception, may therefore be more important in this text than it would be in Leibniz's later work. The manuscript's watermark suggests a date in the period 1683–86, when Leibniz's mature philosophy was still in formation.

bers of a set suffices for the existence of the set. But that Leibnizian paradigm of an aggregate, a pile of wood, ceases to exist when the logs in it are scattered, even though the logs are not destroyed. A pile or mob exists only while its members are grouped by a certain proximity. In the case that I described, the mob is a mere phenomenon because its grouping is merely apparent and exists only in the image presented to you by the optical apparatus. This would be an apt example for Leibniz, because, on his view, the aggregation of substances to form bodies is no less dependent on perception, being based on the way that the substances, or their organic bodies, are spatially represented in our perceptions.

This argument rests on a premise whose Leibnizian character I have yet to establish, that the aggregation of substances to form bodies is indeed based on the way that the substances, or their bodies, are perceived. Leibniz seems to say as much, writing, in the last year of his life, that "the aggregates themselves are nothing but phenomena, since besides the monads that enter into them, the rest is added by perception alone, by the very fact that they are perceived together" (G II,517/AG 203).[65] The point is worth discussing, however, as it involves a basic issue about Leibniz's theory of corporeal aggregates, which we may call the question of the principle of aggregation: What determines which individual substances are grouped together to form a particular corporeal aggregate?

That Leibniz needs a principle of aggregation is intuitively obvious, I think, from what has been said above about rainbows and mobs and piles of wood. Not every randomly selected set of substances constitutes at any given time an aggregate, let alone a corporeal mass or body. Substances that constitute a body must stand in some mutual relation that distinguishes them from a set of substances not so aggregated, as logs that form a pile are distinguished from a random selection of the world's logs. Leibniz seems to assume this in presenting his account of corporeal aggregates to Arnauld, for he writes that relations between substances give the mind "the occasion to join them together in thought" (LA 101). In this construction our mind "relies on the relations or modes of genuine substances" (LA 97). It is true that Leibniz also says that "no ordered principle [*rien de reglé*] will ever be found for making a genuine substance of many beings by aggregation" (LA 101). But this is not a renunciation of principles of aggregation;[66] in the context it is rather a denial that any genuine *substance* can be formed by aggregation.

What, then, are the relations among substances, on the basis of which they are aggregated to form a body? Although Leibniz does not give much explanation on this point, I think it is fairly clear that a body will be an aggregate of all or most of the substances whose positions are within some continuous three-dimensional portion of space. This is the natural assumption, and, so far as I know, Leibniz never suggests any alternative to it. What portion of space the body occupies, and which substances are members of the aggregate, may change

[65]The Latin of the last phrase is *eo ipso dum simul percipiuntur*. *Simul* usually has a temporal meaning, and Roger Ariew and Daniel Garber (AG) have translated it, defensibly, as "at the same time." It can just mean "together," however, and I have translated it that way. *All* monads are perceived at the same time, after all; not just those belonging to the same body. I will argue that the togetherness involved at this point in Leibniz's theory is spatial, or based on spatial appearance.

[66]As claimed by Hartz, "Leibniz's Phenomenalisms," p. 538.

over time, of course. Spatial togetherness is a necessary condition for any corporeal aggregation, but it is presumably not a sufficient condition for even the accidental unity that Leibniz ascribes to a stone. For such unity, additional, quasi-causal conditions on the way in which the members of the aggregate change their positions relative to each other will also be necessary.[67]

If the aggregation of substances into bodies depends on the positions of the substances, the next thing we will want to know is what determines the positions of the substances in space. It is not hard to find an answer to this question if it is about *corporeal* substances. A corporeal substance is composed of a monad and the organic body of that monad (as we may assume for now, following G VII,501). The spatial position of the corporeal substance will surely be the spatial position of its organic body. The organic body is itself an aggregate, and hence a phenomenon; and spatial position is surely as merely phenomenal a property as size, shape, and motion. We may plausibly conclude that the spatial position of the organic body, and hence of the corporeal substance, is *given* in appearance, and is the one it appears to have, or perhaps the one it *would* appear to have in a sufficiently perfected science.

In section 3.1, however, I argued that we would do well to try to understand Leibniz's conception of bodies as aggregates on the assumption that he thought that the elements of the aggregates are *simple* substances or *monads*, rather than composite or corporeal substances. On this understanding we will need to associate the simple substances as well as the corporeal substances with spatial positions. This can be accomplished, even though monads per se do not have any location (G II,444,450f./L 602,604). We can assign to each simple substance the spatial position of its organic body, for, according to Leibniz, each simple substance has an organic body.[68] Spiritual, as well as material, change has "its place in the order of coexistences or in space," Leibniz writes to De Volder. "For even though monads are not extended, they still have some kind of position in extension—that is, some ordered relation of coexistence to other things—through the Machine, that is, over which they preside" (G II,253/L 531). "The Machine" is the organic body, as is clear in the context of this statement, and Leibniz is saying that monads "have some kind of position in extension" which they get through their relation to "their" organic bodies.

This construction of bodies as aggregates of either corporeal or simple substances has the metaphysical peculiarity that the grouping of substances into aggregates depends on the spatial appearance of the bodies. Those who seek a less phenomenalistic reading of Leibniz might wish to find a construction of corporeal aggregates that is independent of such phenomenal properties of bodies. One approach would be to suppose that monads are aggregated together on the basis of similarities among their perceptions. In a broad enough sense of 'similarity', this is surely correct, but the question is, Which similarities are relevant? The perceptions of *all* monads are precisely similar in that all perceive exactly the same universe, in all its infinite detail. They differ only in the distinctness or confusedness of perceptions. So if monads are to be aggregated on the basis of

[67]For this last point I am indebted to the late Wallace Anderson. Cf. LA 100.

[68]The relation between a simple substance and "its" body will be discussed in Chapter 10, section 4.

similarity of perceptions, the basis must be found in the distinctness or confusedness of their perceptions. In the most easily specifiable respect, the monads most similar to each other are those whose perceptions have approximately the same degree of distinctness. Thus the monads most similar to my soul are other human souls. But no grouping of human souls is a *corporeal* aggregate or body. More generally, every aggregate constituting a Leibnizian body will include substances that differ widely in the general distinctness of their perceptions. For whatever substances it includes, it will also include the substances contained in their bodies (GM III,542/AG 167f.); and the perceptions of the former will be more distinct than the perceptions of the latter, inasmuch as each monad perceives the universe more distinctly, in general, than those monads that are aggregated to form its organic body.

Reflection on this problem, I think, leads to the conclusion that if the aggregation of substances into corporeal masses is to be based on similarities among their perceptions, these must be similarities among their patterns of perceiving some things more distinctly than others. And the similarities must be relevant to assigning spatial positions to the substances, since we clearly will not count an aggregate of substances as a body if we do not assign them appropriately related spatial positions. Is there, then, a way of assigning spatial positions to substances on the basis of their perceptions, and thus of constructing corporeal aggregates, without presupposing phenomenal properties of bodies?

I once thought I had discovered a way of doing that. It starts with Bertrand Russell's statement that for Leibniz "places result from points of view, and points of view involve confused perception or *materia prima*."[69] In this construction all spatial relations are to be defined in terms of the points of view of monads. These points of view will be the positions of the monads, and will be conceptually prior to the positions of bodies. The points of view of monads will be positions determined by comparison of the degree of confusion of their perceptions of each other, in accordance with the principle that if monad A's perception of monad C is more confused than monad A's perception of monad B, then monad A is closer to monad B than to monad C.

William Irvine[70] has persuaded me that this construction is mathematically possible. That is, if we are given enough monads for them to be correlated one to one with every point of space, plus, for every triple of monads, A, B, and C, the information whether the distance AB is greater or less than, or equal to, the distance AC, that will suffice for the construction of all spatial relations. Furthermore, Leibniz often indicates that distance is correlated with confusion of perceptions. Nevertheless, I have not found this construction in Leibniz, and I have come to believe that it does not correspond to his intentions, for several reasons.

1. In order to make the points of view of the monads completely prior to bodies, I was trying to define them in terms of monads' perceptions *of each other*, rather than in terms of their perceptions of bodies. But it is not clear to me that

[69]Russell, *Philosophy of Leibniz*, p. 147.

[70]In an unpublished paper written at UCLA. A construction in some ways similar, but not claiming to be Leibniz's own and not making use of confusedness, or any other internal feature of perceptions suggested by Leibniz in this connection, is developed by Hacking, "A Leibnizian Space."

Leibniz thought that any monad, except God, ever perceives any other monad *directly*. In the *Monadology* (§ 62) he depicts the monad as representing "the whole universe in representing" its own organic body; and in Chapter 10, section 4.1, I will argue for an interpretation of Leibniz's system in which I perceive every other created monad by perceiving, more or less distinctly, its organic body.

This argument has limited force in the present context. The whole subject of directness of perception is very obscure (as we will also see in Chapter 10, section 4.1). There could be a question of the relevance of a passage I have already quoted (LA 101), in which Leibniz does speak of the mind's perception of "some genuine substances" and their modes and relations as prior to its construction of aggregates of substances (though the context is ambiguous at to whether these genuine substances are monads or corporeal substances). This of course does not exclude, but certainly does not convey, the idea that the mind's perception of the "genuine substances" is by way of an appearance of their organic bodies that precedes the interpretation of those bodies as aggregates. Two other arguments seem more conclusive.

2. It is not plausible to suppose that we always perceive nearer things more distinctly than anything that is farther away, and Leibniz does not seem to have believed it. In response to a related objection by Arnauld, he wrote that in distinctness of perception "the distance of some is compensated for by smallness or other obstacles in others, and Thales sees the stars without seeing the ditch in front of his feet" (LA 90). In other places he says that the things a monad perceives distinctly are "some that are nearer *or more prominent, accommodated to its organs*," or "the nearest, *or the largest* with respect to each of the Monads" (C 15/MP 177; Mon 50, italics added). Thus distance and confusion of perception are not always directly proportional to each other, and it is not clear that degrees of confusion of perception will provide enough usable data for a mathematically satisfactory construction of spatial relations.

3. The construction of all spatial relations, and therefore of bodies, from the points of view of monads depends on assigning to each monad a point in space as its precise position. Leibniz noted in 1709, however, that although he had once "located Souls in points," that was "many years [before], when [his] philosophy was not yet mature enough."[71] On more mature consideration, he did "not think it appropriate to consider souls as in points." A better approach would allow them to "be in a place" in such a way as to "be in the whole organic body that they animate" (G II,370-72/L 598f.). Similarly, in 1695, in a draft of the "New System," Leibniz referred to "the body that makes [or constitutes, *fait*] its [the soul's] point of view in the world" (G IV,477; cf. NE 221f.; G III,357).

I conclude that the construction of the spatial positions of substances in terms of a straightforward metric of comparative distinctness of their perceptions of

[71]The reference here to Leibniz's earlier views is pretty clearly to ideas present in his writings as far back as 1669–71 (A VI,i,496; A II,i,113). These ideas involved a much deeper metaphysical connection between souls and points than would be suggested in any of Leibniz's works of the 1680s or later. On this see the fascinating discussion in Robinet, *Architectonique disjonctive*, pp. 190–95. Though more than mere location is involved in the earlier writings, I think it is clear from the context that in 1709 Leibniz is denying that monads have any sort of location in points.

each other is not plausible as an interpretation either of experience or of Leibniz. Still, it may be argued, Leibniz is committed to the thesis that all the properties and relations of substances' bodies are represented by intrinsic features of the substances' perceptions. Why couldn't the aggregation of substances into bodies be grounded directly in those intrinsic perceptual features, and independent of the phenomenal representational content of the perceptions? This amounts to the suggestion that intrinsic features of substances' perceptions provide a *reason* for grouping them in corporeal aggregates, a reason that is independent of the phenomenal spatial positions represented by the perceptions. Those phenomenal positions provide the only reason *we* have for aggregating those substances, and the only reason that Leibniz makes clear. The possibility of an independent reason intrinsic to the perceptions of monads cannot be absolutely excluded, but it is surely not un-Leibnizian to see phenomenal features of the corporeal world as providing reasons of fundamental metaphysical importance. Leibniz thinks, for instance, that the pre-established harmony is prominent among God's reasons for choosing this world to actualize, and one of the main excellences of the pre-established harmony is that the corporeal world obeys mechanical laws (Mon 87; C 12f./MP 173f.) which concern physical properties that (as we have seen in section 1.3) are phenomenal rather than ultimately real.

On balance, I think the best construction of Leibnizian corporeal aggregates is the one I initially proposed, which begins with the spatial positions of substances' bodies. These positions, and therefore the aggregation of substances into bodies, depend on the apparent position of bodies as phenomena. And this is a reason for counting the bodies themselves as phenomena, since their constitution depends in this way on perceptual appearances.

3.4 Space

Glenn Hartz has objected to this argument on the ground that it depends on assigning positions in *space* to bodies, and at least derivatively to substances.[72] Hartz holds that Leibniz assigns space, bodies, and substances to three different metaphysical levels. Substances "are at the ground floor metaphysical level";[73] space is at the merely *ideal* level, farthest removed from ultimate reality; and bodies are at a *phenomenal* level between the other two.[74] There is some textual basis for this stratification. Hartz and J. A. Cover have rightly pointed out that whereas in 1687, writing to Arnauld, Leibniz classified space and time as (well-founded) phenomena (LA 118f.), from the mid-1690s on he usually classified space and time rather as "ideal" things.[75] It is ideal things, not usually phenomena, that are characterized from then on as continuous and having only indefi-

[72]Hartz, "Leibniz's Phenomenalisms," pp. 527–37.

[73]Hartz and Cover, "Space and Time in the Leibnizian Metaphysic," p. 503.

[74]Such a three-level interpretation is presented by McGuire, "Labyrinthus Continui," pp. 308–11, and by A. T. Winterbourne, "On the Metaphysics of Leibnizian Space and Time," as well as by Hartz and Cover, "Space and Time in the Leibnizian Metaphysic."

[75]Hartz and Cover, "Space and Time in the Leibnizian Metaphysic," pp. 493ff. Note, however, a text of 1712, in which Leibniz seems to classify space and time among "God's phenomena" and as having a certain "reality" (G II,438/AG 199).

nite, merely potential parts—and that are repeatedly contrasted in this respect with "real" or "actual" things.[76] Moreover, Leibniz sometimes places "matter" (G II,278; G IV,562) or "phenomena" (G II,282) on the real or actual side of this contrast—from which Hartz and Cover rightly infer, not that Leibniz is placing matter or phenomena at the ground floor metaphysical level, but that he ascribes *more* reality to them than to merely ideal things.

My disagreement with Hartz and Cover begins with their ascription to Leibniz of a "metaphysical apartheid beween ideal things and well-founded phenomena."[77] It is on account of this apartheid, I take it, that Hartz thinks it a mistaken mixture of levels to ascribe *spatial* properties, or a position *in space*, to corporeal phenomena in the Leibnizian system. I see no such "metaphysical apartheid" in the texts. It is true that Leibniz regards space, and other ideal entities, as purely mental, whereas he spoke at times of phenomena, particularly beings by aggregation, as "semi-mental" (e.g., G II,304). Semi-mental beings are also "semi-beings" (G II,506/L 617); they have their metaphysical place somewhere between the purely mental or merely ideal and the ultimately real. But that is not because they are metaphysically isolated from either; it is rather because they partake of both. In the case of beings by aggregation, being phenomenal [*de phénomène*] can be treated as equivalent to being "in some fashion mental" (NE 146). "The well-founded phenomenon," as Robert McRae puts it, "is part way between the real and the ideal or mental, a being which participates in both."[78] Both the ultimately real monads and merely ideal space are involved in the construction of such phenomena. I would add that Leibnizian phenomena are best seen, not as a single "level" between the monads and purely ideal objects, but as an infinite gradation of approximations to reality.

There are many places in Leibniz's later writings where he implies that bodies are located *in space*. Perhaps the clearest (acknowledged by Hartz[79]) is a letter of 1705 to De Volder in which Leibniz says that "no assignable part of space is empty of matter," while also affirming that "matter is not continuous but discrete" and that space is something "ideal" (G II,278). Hartz doubts that location in *space* is implied when Leibniz ascribes to unextended monads "some kind of position [*situs*] in extension, that is, some relation of coexistence to others" (G II,253/L 531), or when he seems to allow that a soul is in a place [*in loco*] through its relation to its organic body (G II,371/L 598).[80] But there are other types of text to be taken into account. In the last months of his life, discussing with Louis Bourguet his correspondence with Samuel Clarke, Leibniz wrote that "space is not an absolute being, but an order, or something relative, and which would be merely ideal if bodies did not exist in it [*y*]"—which seems by its counterfactual conditional form to imply that bodies do exist in space (G III,595). To Clarke himself Leibniz wrote that "space is the place of things,

[76]G IV,491f./AG 146f. (1695–96); G VII,562 (1705); G II,278f.,379 (1705,1709); G III,622 (1714).

[77]Hartz and Cover, "Space and Time in the Leibnizian Metaphysic," p. 512.

[78]McRae, *Leibniz: Perception, Apperception, and Thought*, p. 132.

[79]Hartz, "Leibniz's Phenomenalisms," p. 528.

[80]Hartz, "Leibniz's Phenomenalisms," pp. 528f. With regard to G II,253/L 531, I would point out that it ascribes to "spiritual changes" a "place in the order of coexistences or [*seu*] in space."

and not the place of God's ideas" (LC IV,29). If space is the place of things, presumably the things are in space; and what are these "things," if not bodies? Similarly Leibniz writes to Clarke of "the space occupied by a body" (LC V,37). Moreover, when Leibniz writes to Des Bosses in 1709 that "space, just like time, is a certain order, specifically (in the case of space) an order of coexisting, which embraces [*complectitur*] not only actuals but also possibles" (G II,379), he certainly seems to imply that *actuals* as well as possibles are ranged *in* the order that is space.

Hartz seems to suppose that if actual bodies were in space, they would have to be "indifferently divisible into an infinite variety of parts," as space is.[81] But I cannot see the grounds for this assumption, and Leibniz asserts the opposite: "Space can intelligibly be filled in infinite ways by matter actually divided into parts" (G II,279).[82] That is what we should expect. The claim that space is indifferently divisible, or has indefinite, merely potential parts, is most naturally understood as meaning that there are indefinitely various ways in which space *could* be occupied by things having *definite* parts.

It is certainly the dominant view of Leibniz's later years that space is something merely ideal, an order imposed by the mind, though grounded in relations of real things. There are no spatial facts at the ground floor level of Leibniz's metaphysics, except insofar as facts about monads' perceptions having spatial relations as part of their representational content may belong to that level. In themselves the monads have no spatial position and no other spatial properties. It is only by a mental construction that substances and aggregates of substances receive spatial properties. So if (as I claim) the aggregation of substances to form aggregates depends on (apparent) spatial properties of bodies, that will tend to infect the aggregates with mind-dependence, and diminish their reality. But that is not an objection to my interpretation of Leibniz. It is part of my interpretation, providing one of the reasons for the phenomenality of corporeal aggregates.

4. *The Reality of Phenomena*

Phenomenalists and idealists do not generally leave us without a systematic difference between the physical objects that appear to us in normal experience and those that appear to us in dreams and hallucinations. In Leibniz's thought there is a distinction between "real" phenomena and "imaginary" (G VII,319/L 363) or "false" or "apparent" phenomena (VE 188 = Gr 322). As I stated earlier in section 1.1, the analysis of this distinction is the main reductionistic analysis in Leibniz's phenomenalism. Indeed, a reductive analysis of this distinction can constitute a complete phenomenalism, as we saw in section 2, with reference to a text from 1676.

The analysis of the distinction given in that text is classically phenomenalistic in the sense that it is in terms of the contents of perception and their "harmony"

[81]Hartz, "Leibniz's Phenomenalisms," p. 533.

[82]Leibniz supports this claim with an argument, having to do with alternative geometrical constructions for filling a space. But the argument is difficult to follow. It is supplemented, in the manuscript, by a diagram, which Gerhardt does not print; but the visual aid does not help much.

or agreements with other perceptions. In 1704 Leibniz still gave De Volder recognizably the same analysis of what it is for phenomena to be "real": "Matter and motion are . . . the phenomena of perceivers, whose reality is located in the harmony of perceivers with themselves (at different times) and with the other perceivers" (G II,270/L 537). In Leibniz's mature thought, as we shall see, this account of the reality of phenomena in terms of their harmony is only the first layer of a more complex construction. But it remains a main feature of his phenomenalism and is found in his writings all through his mature years—in the early to mid-1680s (VE 188 = Gr 322, and DM 14), in criticisms of Descartes about 1692 (G IV,356/L 384), and in a sketch of his metaphysics prepared for Rémond in 1714 (G III,623), to mention only a few.

Leibniz's fullest discussion of criteria for the reality of phenomena is in an essay of 1683–86, "On the Method of Distinguishing Real from Imaginary Phenomena." He offers criteria similar to those proposed by other early modern philosophers. The *internal* marks of a real phenomenon are that it is *vivid*, *complex*, and *harmonious* [*congruum*].

> It will be vivid if qualities such as light, color, heat appear intense enough. It will be complex if they are varied, and suited for setting up many experiments and new observations; for example, if we experience in the phenomenon not only colors but also sounds, odors, tastes, tactile qualities; and that both in the whole and in various parts of it, which we can investigate again with various causes. (G VII,319f./L 363)

Vividness and complexity are not mentioned in most of Leibniz's formulations about the reality of phenomena. In the *New Essays* he disparages liveliness as a criterion for reality, on the ground that "although sensations are usually livelier than imaginations, one knows still that there are cases where imaginative persons are struck by their imaginations as much as, or perhaps more than, someone else is by the truth of things" (NE 374).[83]

Harmony is the criterion for reality that Leibniz mentions most often. *Internally*, "a phenomenon will be harmonious when it consists of several phenomena for which a reason can be given from each other or from some sufficiently simple common hypothesis" (G VII,320/L 364). The main *external* mark, and the most important mark, of the reality of a phenomenon is also a sort of harmony

> if it keeps the custom of other phenomena that have occurred to us frequently, so that the parts of the phenomena have the same position, order, and outcome that similar phenomena have had. . . . Likewise if a reason for this [phenomenon] can be given from those that precede, or if they all fit the same hypothesis as a common reason. The strongest evidence, however, is surely agreement with the whole series of life, especially if most other [people] affirm that the same thing agrees with their phenomena too. . . . But the most powerful evidence of the reality of phenomena, which even suffices by itself, is success

[83]Cf. Naert, *Mémoire et conscience de soi selon Leibniz*, p. 97. Naert suggests that concern about the imaginativeness "of the Visionaries and the Enthusiasts" led Leibniz to abandon vividness as a criterion of reality. She cites a letter of 1691 where Leibniz notes the fallibility of the vividness criterion in connection with the case of a visionary (A I,vii,34).

> in predicting future phenomena from past and present ones, whether that prediction is founded on reason or a hypothesis that has succeeded thus far, or on a custom that has been complied with thus far. (G VII,320/L 364)[84]

The notions of complexity and harmony are clearly connected in these statements with notions of explanatory and predictive order. Real phenomena are those that form part of a coherent, *scientifically* adequate story that appears all or most of the time, at least in a confused way, to all or most perceivers. That is the story that would be told, or approximated, by a perfected physical science. Imaginary phenomena are those that do not fit in this story.[85]

There is a problem about how Leibniz can admit imaginary phenomena in this sense at all, since he holds that every monad always perceives the whole universe. It follows that the true physical story appears at *all* times to *all* perceivers, not just to most of them at most times. How then can there be any false phenomena? He says that "as God's view is always true, our perceptions are also, but it is our judgments that are from us and that deceive us" (DM 14). This formulation corresponds accurately with the demands of Leibniz's philosophy in one respect, in that it postulates true and false mental contents at different levels, but it is hardly a complete solution to the problem.

Suppose I hallucinate a pink rat. Leibniz must say that this perception expresses, and is a perception of, some event in my body, to which it corresponds according to the pre-established harmony; but it is a confused perception of that event. "It is not that even dreams are not related to the organs and to the rest of the bodies, but [it is] in a less distinct manner" (G IV,519). Though confused, my perception of that event, as such, is a true, not a false, perception, and the event is a real, not an imaginary, phenomenon. What appears to me consciously, however, is not the event in my body, but a pink rat. In this case Leibniz has to say that my soul represents two different phenomena. The first, an event in my body, coheres with the story that would be told by an ideal physical science, and so it is real, but less distinctly perceived. The second, a pink rat, does not cohere with that story, and thus it is hallucinatory and false. What is less clear (to me, at any rate) is whether the process that produces the appearance of the pink rat is adequately characterized as "judgment" (as implied in DM 14). But that question could not be settled without a more extensive exploration of Leibniz's epistemology and theory of perception than I will attempt in this book.

The problem of error seems to play a part in some texts in which Leibniz proposes, not an ideal human science, but "God's view" (DM 14), as a standard of truth of phenomena. In 1712, in a study for a letter to Des Bosses, Leibniz wrote,

> If bodies are phenomena and are evaluated on the basis of our appearances, they will not be real, since they appear differently to different people. Therefore the reality of bodies, space, motion, [and] time seems to consist in their being God's phenomena, or the object of intuitive knowledge [*scientia visionis*]. (G II,438/AG 199)

[84]Cf. G II,270/L 537; VE 296 = LH IV,3,5E,2.

[85]This is a convenient way of talking. Leibniz's conceptualism might give rise to some problems about the ontological status of such a story, if we rely heavily on "would be told."

This passage raises an obvious interpretive problem: how can it be reconciled with the view that Leibniz seems to hold elsewhere (e.g., DM 14;G II,451f./L 605), that there is enough agreement among human perceivers for their phenomena to satisfy the intersubjective harmony condition for reality?

More than one answer to this question is possible.[86] Gregory Brown points out that in the quoted text of 1712, Leibniz goes on to say that "God views not only the individual monads and the modifications of each Monad, but also their relations, and in this consists the reality of relations and truths" (G II,438/AG 199). Brown argues that for Leibniz, only God sees the relations between created substances; and the reality of those relations, including the reality of the harmony among the perceptions of created monads, consists in God's perception of them. Brown argues further that the harmony among monads' perceptions depends on the divine mind inasmuch as the laws of nature determine for Leibniz the correct interpretation of what is expressed by each monad's perceptions, and what are the correct laws of nature depends on God's understanding, and choice, of which laws are best, an understanding that exceeds the power of any created mind.[87]

There is textual basis for Brown's interpretation. But I think there are also grounds for another interpretation in other things that Leibniz says to Des Bosses about God's phenomena. In 1713, offering his Jesuit friend a possible account of the Catholic doctrine of transubstantiation in purely monadological terms, without "substantial bonds," Leibniz says that on this account

> the substance of bodies should be said to consist in true phenomena, namely those that God himself perceives in them by intuitive knowledge, and the Angels and the Blessed likewise, to whom it is given to see things truly; and thus God, with the Blessed, perceives the Body of Christ, where bread and wine appear to us. (G II,474/L 607f.; cf. G II,482)

The phenomena that God is said here to perceive can hardly be intersubstantial relations that are perceived by God alone, since the angels and the blessed in heaven are also said to perceive them. Rather their perceiving "truly" is contrasted with what appears to us. This can be reconciled with the doctrine that we perceive, at least unconsciously, everything as it is, if we assume that truth in the distinct and conscious knowledge of the blessed is being contrasted with error in our conscious beliefs. Divine knowledge is thus the ideal to which the true physical story told by harmonious phenomena must approximate. On this interpretation, as on Brown's, the thought that the real phenomena are God's phenomena represents a development, not an abandonment, of the harmonious perceptions account of real phenomena.

There are many passages in which Leibniz seems to say that internal and external harmony, supplemented perhaps by vividness and complexity, or agree-

[86] This is contrary to my previous treatment of it in "Phenomenalism and Corporeal Substance in Leibniz," p. 245f., where I took the problem as grounds for regarding G II,438/AG 199 as an aberrant text in this respect.

[87] Brown, "God's Phenomena and the Pre-Established Harmony." Brown also provides there an illuminating discussion of the difficult question, what God's corporeal phenomena would be. I am indebted to Brown's interesting article for forcing me to think more about Leibniz's statements about God's phenomena.

ment with mathematical truth (a mark added in some later texts), is sufficient to constitute the reality of a phenomenon. In the essay "On the Method of Distinguishing Real from Imaginary Phenomena," however, he speaks more cautiously. There the marks of reality are presented as epistemic criteria by which we may tell when a phenomenon is real; it is not asserted that they define what the reality of a phenomenon consists in. Indeed, it is virtually implied that a phenomenon could possess the marks of reality and yet not be fully real: "It must be admitted that the proofs of real phenomena that have been adduced thus far, even taken in any combination whatever, are not demonstrative." They have "the greatest probability," or "moral certainty," but not "Metaphysical" certainty; there would be no contradiction in supposing them false:

> Therefore it cannot be absolutely demonstrated by any argument that there are bodies; and nothing prevents some well-ordered dreams from being objects to our Mind, which we would judge to be true and which would be equivalent for practical purposes to true things because of their mutual agreement.

Leibniz rejects Descartes's claim that in such a case God would be a deceiver:

> For what if our nature happened not to be capable of real phenomena? Surely God should be thanked rather than blamed in that case; for by causing those phenomena at least to agree, since they could not be real, he has furnished us with something equally as useful, for all of life, as real phenomena. (G VII,320f./ L 364)

Very similar ideas are found in Leibniz's writings as early as a letter of 1675 to Simon Foucher (A II,i,248f./L 153f.) and as late as the *New Essays* of 1704 (NE 379f.) and a letter of 1715 to Des Bosses (G II,496/L 611).

It has been thought that Leibniz vacillated or changed his mind about the sufficiency of the harmony and agreement of phenomena for their reality, but I think it is more accurate to see him as constantly aware of the epistemological vulnerability of the full ontology that he held throughout his mature years, and wanting therefore to maintain the availability of a starker phenomenalism as a fall-back position, as I suggested in section 2 of this chapter. For this purpose it was important to have a sense of 'real' in which bodies could be real, as opposed to imaginary, in the context of the starker phenomenalism; it seems to me probable that Leibniz used 'real' in stronger and weaker senses in expressing different aspects of a fairly constant, and consistent, system of thought.

A statement in the previous paragraph of "On the Method of Distinguishing Real from Imaginary Phenomena" is particularly revealing: "Indeed even if it were said that this whole life is nothing but a dream, and the visible world nothing but a phantasm, I would call this dream or phantasm real enough if we were never deceived by it when we used our reason well"—that is, if predictions reasonably based on past experience generally succeeded so far as future experience is concerned (G VII,320/L 364). To say that this whole life is a dream is presumably to say that its phenomena lack a kind of reality that phenomena could have; but Leibniz indicates a sense in which our phenomena would still be "real enough," provided only that our experience has all the *internal* marks of reality. A similar, weak sense of 'true' as applied to phenomena appears in the *Discourse on Metaphysics* when Leibniz says that if our phenomena are internally harmonious enough so that

> we can make observations that are useful for regulating our conduct and that are justified by the success of future phenomena, and that thus we can often judge of the future by the past without error, that would be enough to say that these phenomena are true, without worrying about whether they are outside us and whether others perceive them too. (DM 14)

This helps make sense of the fact that Leibniz seems to accept another account of what the reality of bodies consists in. This account, I suggest, should be seen as stating an additional condition that harmonious phenomena must satisfy in order to be real in the fullest sense, although their harmony is sufficient for their reality in a weaker sense that is enough for all practical purposes. It must be admitted, however, that both accounts are usually presented as if they were completely independent.

The additional account applies chiefly to aggregates as such and says that their reality consists in the reality of the substances that enter into them. Aggregates "have no other reality than that which belongs to the Unities that are in them" (G II,261). Given that Leibniz says that bodies *are* aggregates of substances, indeed, it is hard to see how he could fail to think that their reality consists at least partly in the reality of the substances that are aggregated in them. This thesis plays a part in the argument for monads. It is partly because an aggregate "has no reality unless it is borrowed from the things contained" in it that Leibniz "inferred, therefore there are in things indivisible unities, since otherwise there will be in things no true unity, and no reality not borrowed" (G II,267). There are several reasons for thinking that this is not a completely independent account of the reality of bodies—that it does not conflict with the account in terms of harmonious perceptions, but supplements it and even depends on it.

1. Leibniz seems to have regarded the two accounts as consistent. He sometimes gives both of them in the same document. I have quoted expressions of both of them from his letter of 30 June 1704 to De Volder (G II,267,270). And in a single two-page piece written in 1714 Leibniz says both that "what we call bodies" *are* assemblages of monads and that material things "have their reality from the agreement of the perceptions of apperceiving substances" (G III,622f.).

2. I think Leibniz believed that the two accounts are at least materially equivalent. He believed that there is a scientifically adequate story that is always at least unconsciously perceived by all monads, and therefore counts as "true," and that most of what appears consciously to conscious perceivers fits at least approximately into that story. He also believed that there are infinitely many monads whose internal properties are expressed by organic bodies that would figure in a sufficiently detailed extension of the true scientific story, and that aggregates of these monads (or of the corporeal substances that they form with their organic bodies) can therefore be regarded as the bodies that figure in the true scientific story. Thus the bodies of the true scientific story are real according to both accounts, both as coherent, harmonious phenomena and as aggregates of real things.

3. The claim that the reality of bodies consists in the reality of the substances that are aggregated in them presupposes that substances *are* aggregated in them, and this aggregation presupposes the harmony of perceptions. As I argued in section 3.3, the grouping of substances into corporeal aggregates depends on the spatial positions the substances' organic bodies appear to have. If a single system of aggregates of substances is to be real, as opposed to any others, which may be imaginary, it is surely not enough that the substances belonging to the real aggregates be real. We could doubtless dream up imaginary aggregates of real substances, which would still be unreal, despite the reality of their elements. Real aggregates must not only have real elements, but must be formed by a real or true grouping of those elements. And the true grouping of substances into corporeal aggregates can hardly depend on the positions the substances' organic bodies appear to have just a little of the time to just any perceiver. It must depend on something more definitive, and this for Leibniz involves the positions the bodies have in a coherent system of phenomena that is represented by all or most of the perceptions of all perceivers. In order for there to be corporeal aggregates that are real by virtue of the reality of the substances aggregated in them, they must appear as material masses in this coherent system of phenomena. Therefore they must satisfy the harmonious perceptions condition for reality.

Considering all these reasons, I think we find in Leibniz not two competing analyses of the reality of corporeal phenomena, but one analysis in two or three layers. Phenomena are real, in a weak sense, if and only if they fit into a single scientifically adequate system of harmonious phenomena of all perceivers. Those phenomena, and only those, that are real in this weaker sense are also real in a fuller sense to the extent that there exist real monads that are appropriately expressed by organic bodies belonging to the system of phenomena that is at least weakly real. And perhaps Leibniz also recognizes a still weaker sense in which phenomena are "real enough" if they belong to a scientifically adequate system of harmonious perceptions of a single perceiver.

10

Corporeal Substance

The rehabilitation of substantial forms, on which Leibniz seems to have resolved in 1679, as I noted in the last chapter, generally carried with it an affirmation of *corporeal substances*, composed, in Aristotelian terms, of form and matter. Indeed, as I also suggested there, the rehabilitation of the forms seems to have been motivated largely by a desire to accommodate realistic intuitions by finding something substantial in bodies. Some scholars have read Leibniz's account of corporeal substances as so realistic (and so Aristotelian) as to be inconsistent with the phenomenalism I have ascribed to him in Chapter 9. I think that exaggerates Leibniz's accommodation to realism. This chapter offers an interpretation of Leibnizian corporeal substance as a metaphysical construction from simple, perceiving substances, consistent with the idealistic foundations of his philosophy.

I would not deny, however, that a tension between the idealistic foundations and the accommodation of realism causes problems in Leibniz's theory of corporeal substance. As we shall see in section 5, there is some evidence that such problems may have weakened Leibniz's own adherence to his conception of corporeal substance in his last years, though he never really abandoned it.

1. Bodies and Corporeal Substances

It is not Leibniz's view that bodies in general are substances. The clearest reason for this is that only things that are, in some sense, *alive* are corporeal substances.

"I call that a corporeal substance," Leibniz wrote in 1711, "which consists in a simple substance or monad (that is, a soul or something analogous to a Soul) and an organic body united to it" (G VII,501). Corporeal substances are found where there are "bodies that are animated, or at least endowed with a primitive Entelechy or with a vital principle (if you allow the name 'life' to be used so generally)"; they can thus be called "living" (LA 118). But when Leibniz says that corporeal substances are living things and that "all nature is full of life" (PNG 1), he emphatically does not mean that every material object is a living thing. He rejects the view of "those who imagine that there is a substantial form of a piece of stone, or of another non-organic body; for principles of life belong only to organic bodies" (G VI,539/L 586; cf. LA 76). (Here, as in many other places, Leibniz uses the Aristotelian term 'substantial form' to signify the soul, or that which is analogous to a soul or principle of life, in any corporeal substance; this will be discussed much more fully in Chapter 11.) He adds that

> it is true (according to my System) that there is no portion of matter in which there is not an infinity of organic and animated bodies; among which I include not only animals and plants, but perhaps other sorts as well, which are entirely unknown to us. But it is not right to say, on account of that, that every portion of matter is animated—just as we do not say that a lake full of fish is an animated body, although the fish is. (G VI,539f./L 586)

Stones and lakes, then, are not corporeal substances. "Each animal and each plant too is a corporeal substance" (G III,260); I believe they are the only corporeal substances of which Leibniz claims empirical knowledge, if we include among animals and plants the tiny living things whose discovery under seventeenth-century microscopes so excited him (LA 122). In a lake full of fish the water between the fish is not a corporeal substance, but it is composed of corporeal substances, which may be very different from the things that we know as animals and plants (Mon 68). In particular, they may be even smaller than microscopic organisms; there is indeed no minimum size for corporeal substances.

Still, all corporeal substances are alive, in a broad sense. And Leibniz seems to have assumed that we can detect the presence or absence of life in bodies large enough to be distinctly perceived by our senses. He speaks of a study of nature that would enable us to "judge of the forms [of corporeal substances] by comparing their organs and operations" (LA 122).

The principal characteristic of living bodies that Leibniz mentions as distinguishing them from other portions of matter is that they are "organized" or "organic." "There is . . . no animated body without organs" (LA 124); "I restrict corporeal or composite substance to living things alone, or exclusively to organic machines of nature" (G II,520/AG 205f.). I have found little explanation in Leibniz of what distinguishes organic from inorganic bodies. It is not a radical difference in the kind of causality that operates in them. Leibniz always insists that everything can be explained mechanically in organic as well as in inorganic bodies. There is no need to refer to the substantial forms or souls of corporeal substances in explaining their physical behavior (e.g., LA 58,77f.): "And this body is organic when it forms a kind of Automaton or Machine of Nature, which is a machine not only as a whole but also in the smallest parts that can be noticed" (PNG 3; cf. G III, 356). Similarly, he speaks of "Organism, that is to say, order and artifice" (G III,340). Presumably, an organic body is one so organized mechanically that it continues over time to cohere and retain a sort of unity in physical interactions. But stones have that property, too, so it is not enough to distinguish organic bodies from others.

Perhaps the best account that can be given of the notion of organism here is that an organic body is a body so structured mechanically that it can be interpreted as always totally expressing and being expressed by the perceptions and appetites of a soul or something analogous to a soul. We recognize living things by observing that their behavior can be interpreted as a coordinated response to their environment on the basis of something like perception of the environment together with a tendency toward something like a goal—though Leibniz would insist that their behavior can *also* be explained mechanically. This account fits animals better than plants, but it is clear in any case that Leibniz's principal model of corporeal substance is the animal. He mentions plants only occasionally and seems favorably disposed toward the suggestion that they "can be included in the same genus with animals, and are imperfect animals" (LA 122).

So inorganic bodies, bodies in no sense alive, are not corporeal substances. But more than that—in the terms that Leibniz ultimately preferred—no bodies at all are substances, not even organic bodies. There are important texts from 1686 in which Leibniz frames the corporeal substance hypothesis in terms of "bodies" being substances (DM 34, LA 58,71), but in a more carefully regimented vocabulary usually (though not invariably[1]) employed from 1690 on, corporeal substances are not said to *be* bodies, but rather to be *endowed with* bodies.

This regimentation is manifested in very similar terms in two documents of March 1690, one of which is Leibniz's last letter to Antoine Arnauld: "The body is an aggregate of substances, and that is not a substance, properly speaking" (LA 135). "The body is not a substance, but substances or an aggregate of substances" (VE 2156 = FC 322/AG 105). These documents are not plausibly interpreted as abandoning the project of constructing a theory of corporeal substance. It is unlikely that Leibniz would have signaled such an abandonment to Arnauld, especially when their relations were as distant as they had become by 1690. There is still a corporeal substance, but it is not "the body." The change in Leibniz's position is merely verbal, or at most a clarification. The distinction marked by the later terminology is anticipated in letters of 1686–87 to Arnauld. Our body is not a substance really distinct from our soul:

> Our body in itself, setting aside the soul, or the *cadaver*, cannot be called *one* substance except by an abuse [of words], like a machine or a pile of stones, which are only beings by aggregation. (LA 75)
>
> As for corporeal substances, I hold that the mass, when one considers in it only what is divisible, is a pure phenomenon. (LA 126)

Insofar as the body is considered apart from the soul, the divisible from the indivisible, the body is not a substance. This nonsubstantial item is the "body in itself" or, in the terms Leibniz ultimately preferred, simply "the body." The corporeal substance is something more.

In some texts from the mid-1680s phenomenalism and the hypothesis of corporeal substance seem to be presented as mutually exclusive alternatives, as when Leibniz says, "if body is a substance and not a simple phenomenon like the rainbow" (LA 58; cf. LA 77, and DM 34 draft). But this is a misleading appearance, due to Leibniz's failure in these texts to distinguish the corporeal substance from its body as he eventually would when speaking carefully. When that distinction is made, the body as such is only an aggregate, and hence only a phenomenon—and that applies to both organic and inorganic bodies (G III,657). The substantiality of the corporeal substance is contributed by its indivisible, soul-like constituents. Thus the corporeal substance remains a metaphysical construction out of simple substances.

[1]In 1711, for example, we find him allowing the alternative: "A *body*, however, is either a corporeal substance, or a mass gathered from corporeal substances" (G VII,501).

"The body" appears as merely one ingredient in a fully developed account of Leibnizian corporeal substance. It is time to examine the complex structure implied in such an account.

2. *The Structure of a Corporeal Substance: Alternative Interpretations*

2.1 *The Two-Substance Conception*

Leibniz's fullest statement about the structure of a corporeal substance is in a letter of 20 June 1703 to Burcher De Volder:

> I distinguish therefore (1) the primitive Entelechy or Soul, (2) Matter, i.e. primary matter, or primitive passive power, (3) the Monad completed by these two, (4) the Mass [*Massa*] or secondary matter, or organic machine, for which countless subordinate Monads come together [*ad quam . . . concurrunt*], (5) the Animal or corporeal substance, which is made One by the Monad dominating the Machine. (G II,252/L 530f.)

The first three of these items, and their relation to each other, will occupy us intensively in Chapters 11–13; they can be discussed quite briefly here. The monad (3) is "a simple substance . . . ; *simple*, that is to say without parts" (Mon 1). The primitive entelechy (1) and primary matter (2) must not, therefore, be conceived as *parts* that compose the monad, but rather as aspects or properties of the monad. In particular, primary matter is not to be understood here as a substance or extended stuff. It is primitive passive power and is a fundamental property or aspect of the monad. 'Entelechy' is sometimes used by Leibniz (as in Mon 18,62–63) as a synonym for 'monad' or 'simple substance'; but here the entelechy clearly is not the complete monad, but a property or aspect of it. Since it goes together with primitive passive power to form the monad, the entelechy here is presumably the monad's primitive active power. In other passages the "substantial form" is given the role that is assigned here to the "entelechy." It is striking that the "soul" is not identified here with the monad, but with an aspect of it, and is presumably not a substance but something that can be considered as an entity only by abstraction from a complete substance or monad. This is one way in which Leibniz sometimes speaks of the "soul," though it appears in other texts as a simple substance or monad (e.g., Mon 19).

The *primitive forces* that combine thus to "complete" the monad are most fundamental features of the Leibnizian scheme of things. Leibniz held that "the very substance of things consists in the force of acting and being acted on" (G IV,508/L 502; cf. G II,248f./L 528). The properties possessed by monads as such are perceptions and appetites, or analogous to perceptions and appetites, as Leibniz wrote to De Volder on 30 June 1704 (G II,270/L 537). In his next letter, Leibniz drew the consequence that "primitive forces manifestly cannot be anything but internal tendencies of simple substances, by which according to a certain law of their nature they pass from perception to perception" (G II,275/AG 181).[2]

[2]The relation between forces as properties of monads and forces as properties of bodies will be discussed in Chapter 13.

My present purpose demands more attention to the mass, or secondary matter (4), which combines with the monad to form the complete corporeal substance. This is "the body," which is not itself a substance but belongs to the corporeal substance.

In speaking here of "seconday matter," and earlier of "primary matter," Leibniz picks up a Scholastic distinction. In relation to a statue, the bronze of which it is composed is matter; but as bronze it is not *pure* matter, for it must have a substantial form to constitute it as bronze. Something which in this way is matter *for* something else, but which has its own form or forms in it, is secondary matter. Primary or prime[3] matter is pure matter, matter considered apart from *all* forms that may inhere in it. The "mass" mentioned here is *secondary* matter insofar as it has substantial forms "in" it by virtue of the countless subordinate monads that "come together" to form it.

It is important, however, to note a major difference between the Scholastic conception of the relation between primary and secondary matter and the conception in the fivefold outline that Leibniz gave De Volder. For Scholasticism the primary matter of a substance is a substratum, and hence a constituent, of any secondary matter it has. But Leibniz describes them to De Volder as much more separate than that, presenting the primary matter of a corporeal substance as an aspect of its dominating monad, whereas its secondary matter is formed by the coming together of *other* (subordinate) monads.

The mass of secondary matter of a corporeal substance is an organic machine, as Leibniz says in his fivefold outline, or the organic body of the substance, as he more often says. Not every mass of secondary matter is an organic body; inorganic bodies are also masses of secondary matter. But only an organic body can be the body of a corporeal substance. No mass of secondary matter, organic or inorganic, is in itself a substance. The organic body, "taken separately (that is, apart, or isolated, from the soul) is not one substance but an aggregate of many" (G IV,396/AG 252f.). "And *secondary matter* (as for example the organic body) is not a substance" because "it is a mass of several substances, like a lake full of fish, or like a herd of sheep, and consequently it is what is called *One per accidens*—in a word, a phenomenon" (G III,657). A mass of secondary matter, as such, is thus merely a phenomenon *because* it is an aggregate of substances—and perhaps for other reasons as well.[4]

According to Leibniz, *every* created monad has an organic body of this sort, with which it forms a corporeal substance (G IV,395f./AG 252f.; G VII, 502,530; cf. Mon 62–63). The monad *always* has its body, and hence the organic body is an enduring, though constructed and merely phenomenal, object permanently attached to its dominant monad (G II,251/L 530). Even in death, it does not cease to exist, it does not cease to be organic; it just undergoes a sudden, drastic reduction in size and a change in its operations (e.g., PNG 6). The parts of an organic body do not belong to it permanently, however. "It is true that the whole which

[3]The terms, in Scholastic Latin, and in Leibniz's Latin and French, literally mean *first* matter and *second* matter; but I think it works out best to use 'primary' and 'secondary' in translating and discussing Leibniz.

[4]On the connection between being an aggregate and being a phenomenon, see Chapter 9, section 3.2.

has a true unity can remain strictly the same individual even though it loses or gains parts, as we experience in ourselves; thus the parts are immediate requisites only for a time" (LA 120). The substances that are included in an organic body can be replaced with other substances as long as the body retains the necessary organs and the same dominant monad (Mon 71–72).

The corporeal substance (5) formed in this way is not an aggregate, but one per se, according to Leibniz. Hence it is not a mere phenomenon; corporeal substance is regularly contrasted with the phenomenal (LA 77; G VII,314,322/MP 81, L 365; G II,435/L 600). But the corporeal substance appears to be composed of a monad and an organic body, and thus not to be simple in the way that monads are. How then can it be one per se? The answer given in this outline is that the corporeal substance "is made One by the Monad dominating the Machine." This statement gives rise to at least two questions: How does a monad "dominate" its organic body or "Machine"? How does this domination make the corporeal substance one per se? These questions will be the main topics of sections 4 and 5, respectively, in this chapter. But another issue will occupy us in the rest of section 2 and in section 3.

In the outline I have been following, Leibniz clearly distinguishes the corporeal substance (5) both from its organic machine and from its dominant monad. It is something formed by the combination of these two and can be described as "the Composite of" them (G III,657). Two different sorts of "substance" appear in the account when Leibniz says that a *corporeal* substance "consists in a *simple* substance . . . and an organic body united to it" (G VII,501). This "composite" or "two-substance" conception of the structure of a corporeal substance, as we may call it, clearly appears in a number of places in Leibniz's writings—unambiguously, for example, in a text dating very likely from about 1712 in which he says, "A substance is either simple, like a soul, which has no parts, or composite, like an animal, which is constituted of a soul and an organic body" (C 13/MP 175).[5] I know of no text that is flatly inconsistent with it, but all the clearest articulations I have found of it are in texts of 1703 or later. Some, though not all, earlier texts, may be more naturally interpreted as expressing alternative conceptions, which I want now to explore.

2.2 *One-Substance Conceptions*

In some of the most interesting passages from the 1680s and 1690s in which Leibniz presents a conception of corporeal substance, there is no unambiguous indication that he thinks of the corporeal substance as having a constituent, distinct from it, that is an individual substance of another sort. These texts seem to invite interpretation in terms of a *one-substance* conception of corporeal substance. But what is the one substance? In terms of the five-part outline of 1703, is it the monad? Or is it the composite substance of the two-substance conception? Both interpretations have some claim on our attention.

Those who emphasize the Aristotelian character of Leibniz's thought in the 1680s and 1690s might be tempted to embrace what could be called the *Aristo-*

[5]Another text for the two-substance conception is RML 451/AG 264 (1712 and 1715).

telian one-substance interpretation.[6] It recognizes nothing corresponding to the monad of the two-substance conception, because its one substance resembles the composite substance of the two-substance conception in having the organic body as a constituent. The distinctive feature of this view is that the substantial form or soul does not form a concrete individual substance at all except by uniting with the secondary matter that constitutes the organic body. That is arguably part of Aristotle's own conception of the relation of a substantial form to a body of which it is the form; and Leibniz sometimes speaks of the soul as the substantial form of the body. He does so, for instance, in the letter of November/December 1686 in which he first explains his conception of corporeal substance at length to Arnauld (LA 77), which is also a document that contains no explicit indication that Leibniz is talking about two different kinds of substance.

This is not a good argument for the Aristotelian one-substance interpretation, however. Leibniz was not generally scrupulous about interpreting according to their own intentions those philosophers with whom he claimed an agreement. In any event the Aristotelianism that he meant in some measure to revive was the Christian Aristotelianism of the later Middle Ages, for which at least one substantial form, the human rational soul, was certainly a concrete individual substance that could, and did, survive without its body. Since it is abundantly clear that the human rational soul was always regarded as the model for all substantial forms in Leibniz's rehabilitation project, his awareness of traditional antecedents would incline him to conceive of substantial forms as concrete individual substances.

Moreover, there is compelling evidence that in his letters to Arnauld, Leibniz recognized as a concrete individual substance something corresponding to the monad of the two-substance conception. This is explicit when he says of "a soul or substantial form after the example of that which is called *I* [*moi*]" that "these are the only genuine complete [*accompli*] beings" (LA 76). The soul or substantial form here is presumably the third item in the fivefold outline, the complete monad, as it is in a number of texts of Leibniz (e.g., G VI,550). It cannot be the first item, the primitive active force, which is not a complete being, but only an aspect of one. Moreover, in his last letter to Arnauld (23 March 1690), Leibniz says that "everywhere in body there are substances, indivisible, ingenerable, and incorruptible," which "have always been and always will be united to organic bodies, diversely transformable" (LA 135f.). Here Leibniz speaks explicitly of *substances* whose relation to organic bodies is being *united* to them, not having them as *constituents*.[7]

[6]Daniel Garber does not embrace it, but seems to favor the Aristotelian version of the two-substance interpretation discussed in section 2.3 in this chapter. See Garber, "Leibniz and the Foundations of Physics," p. 58.

[7]That a *complete* being or substance that can be identified with the soul or substantial form is present in Leibniz's view in his letters to Arnauld is convincingly, and more fully, argued by Robert Sleigh, *Leibniz and Arnauld*, pp. 109f. What I am calling the Aristotelian one-substance conception is roughly equivalent to the "unmodified corporeal substance theory" which Sleigh argues is *not* favored by the texts of DM and LA. The only other conception of corporeal substance that Sleigh considers, however, is a two-substance conception. He does not discuss the "qualified monad conception" that I am about to describe. The existence of Sleigh's illuminating and closely argued study is one reason why I have not selected these texts for more intensive treatment here.

If the Aristotelian interpretation is untenable, as I believe it to be, one might think that no one-substance interpretation could be accepted. We are concerned, after all, with texts in which Leibniz presents a conception of *corporeal* substance. So how could there be only one type of substance recognized in them if it is not the complete corporeal substance of the two-substance conception? There remains an alternative, however, which was suggested long ago by Ernst Cassirer. He identified corporeal substance with the monad itself "insofar as it is endowed with a particular organic body, according to which it represents and desires."[8] The monad can be called a *corporeal* substance inasmuch as it *has* a body. A corporeal substance, on this view, is not a monad *plus* a body, but a monad *as having* a body. We may therefore call this the "qualified monad conception" of corporeal substance.

It may be doubted that Leibniz would apply the label 'corporeal' to an entity that did not have a body as a constituent, but there is a passage from 1686 in which he says that "the reality of a corporeal substance consists in some individual nature, that is, not in mass [*moles*] but in the power of acting and being acted on" (G VII,314/MP 81). In 1696, likewise, he locates "the notion of corporeal substance . . . in the force of acting and resisting rather than in extension" (G IV,499/L 460). In each of these statements *corporeal* substance is said to consist in, be located in, or be completed by a dual power or a pair of entities in which we can unmistakably recognize the entelechy and primary matter by which, in the fivefold outline of the two-substance theory, the *monad*, not the composite substance, is completed.[9] The organic body or secondary matter is not mentioned as a constituent of corporeal substance in these statements.

Similar points could be made about a passage from 1702 in which Leibniz says that "the primitive active force, which is called the first entelechy by Aristotle, and popularly the substance's form, is the other natural principle which, with the matter or passive force, completes the corporeal substance." In this case, however, Leibniz goes on to say that the soul or entelechy "always naturally actuates some organic body, which itself, taken separately (that is, apart, or isolated, from the soul), is not one substance but an aggregate of several—in a word, a machine of nature" (G IV,395f./AG 252f.). "Actuates" [*actuat*] is Scholastic term, rarely used by Leibniz, for what a form does to matter whose potentiality it actualizes.[10] The clause in which Leibniz uses it here certainly seems to imply that by its relation to the soul or entelechy, the organic body enters (presumably as a constituent) into something more substantial than it could be by itself.

2.3 Complete and Incomplete Substances

There is a refinement in Scholastic Aristotelian accounts of corporeal substance that I have ignored thus far. According to Francisco Suárez, for example, both

[8]Cassirer, *Leibniz's System*, p. 408. In "Phenomenalism and Corporeal Substance in Leibniz," p. 229, I took a less favorable view of Cassirer's interpretation than I do now.

[9]Something similar could be said about a passage written in 1699 or 1700 and transmitted to Locke by Thomas Burnett, a mutual friend (A VI,vi,32 = G III,227). But a related letter of 1699 to Burnett (G III,260) is not so naturally interpreted in terms of the qualified monad conception.

[10]See, e.g., Suárez, *Metaphysical Disputations*, XV,vii,3.

the corporeal substance (such as a human being) and its substantial form (such as the human soul) are substances, but only the whole corporeal substance is a *complete* substance. Not that the substantial form is a mere abstraction; it too is a concrete, individual substance, as is clear in the case of the human soul. But it is an *incomplete* substance because it is "by its nature constructed [*institutus*] to inform matter," and thus to be completed by the matter. It has this natural "aptitude" even if it is able to exist without the matter; "and thus the rational soul is included [in the class of incomplete substances] even if it is separated from the body." A third type of concrete substance also enters the picture for Suárez; the matter, like the substantial form, is "a simple and incomplete substance"—incomplete because it has a natural aptitude to be completed by the form.[11]

Leibniz certainly does not share Suárez's view of matter. Matter for Leibniz is either secondary matter, which is not a simple substance but only a plurality or aggregate of substances, or primary matter, which for Leibniz (unlike Suárez) is never more than an abstraction, and thus not a concrete substance, as will be discussed more fully in Chapter 12. It might be thought that Leibniz and Suárez are as far apart on substantial forms as on matter, since Leibniz refers to substantial forms as "complete [*accompli*] beings" (LA 76). But such statements must be read in the light of other texts in which Leibniz seems to follow Scholastic precedent in viewing substantial forms as incomplete substances.

Writing to Damaris Cudworth Masham, for example, on 30 June 1704, Leibniz agrees with her that there are no "complete substances without extension . . . among creatures," and goes on to say that "souls or forms without bodies would be something incomplete, inasmuch as, in my opinion, the *soul* is *never without an animal* or some analogue" (G III,357). This seems to imply that the soul needs its (organic) body, and not just its primary matter, to form a complete substance, and thus that nothing like the "monad" of the two-substance conception could be a *complete* substance.

It is not plausible in this context, however, to see Leibniz as holding the Aristotelian one-substance conception, in which there is no concrete substance at all corresponding to the "monad" of the two-substance conception. For this text is dated on the very same day as the letter in which Leibniz said to De Volder that "there is nothing in things except simple substances, and in them perception and appetite" (G II, 270/L 537). These "simple substances" are surely the "monads" of the two-substance interpretation. In this letter to Lady Masham, moreover, Leibniz says, "I hold that it is not matter that thinks, but a Being that is simple and apart by itself or independent, joined to matter" (G III,355/AG 290). This simple and separate being is surely the "monad" of the two-substance conception, which appears to be present in this letter, but regarded as an incomplete substance, in line with Scholastic conceptions.

A fuller expression of Leibniz's interest in the distinction between complete and incomplete substances is found in a passage written probably about 1699.[12] In the course of arguing, against occasionalism, that the agreement of soul and body is not supernatural but natural, Leibniz says:

[11]Suárez, *Metaphysical Disputations*, XV,v,1–2; cf. XXXIII,i,11.

[12]The date is suggested by the fact that the text is a response to something that appeared in the *Journal des Savants* in September 1698.

> The opinion of the School, that the soul and matter are incomplete in a way [*ont quelque chose d'incomplet*], is not so absurd as is thought. For matter without souls and forms or entelechies is only passive, and souls without matter are only active, since the complete corporeal Substance, truly one, which the School calls *one per se* (as opposed to a Being by aggregation) must result from the principle of unity which is active and the mass [*masse*] which makes the multitude and which would be purely passive if it contained only primary matter. (G IV,572)

Leibniz purports here to be defending the Scholastic view of form and matter as incomplete beings. But the matter and forms of which he proceeds at once to speak are not the concrete but incomplete substances of Suárez, but rather the first two of the five items of the outline of 1703, the entelechy or soul which is merely active and the primary matter which is merely passive. These are mere abstractions (as I will show in Chapter 12, sections 2–3), and as such they are certainly incomplete, but with an incompleteness more radical than that of Suárez's matter and substantial form, which are particular concrete beings.

The one item of the five in the outline of 1703 that is not mentioned in the passage before us is the third, the "monad" of the two-substance theory. "The mass which makes the multitude" is plausibly taken to be the fourth item, secondary rather than primary matter, and this interpretation is confirmed by the statement that it *would* be purely passive if it contained only primary matter, which carries the implication that it in fact contains something more which makes it partly active. "The complete corporeal Substance" mentioned here is presumably the fifth item of the outline of 1703, the composite substance rather than the simple substance of the two-substance theory. The passage's silence about the latter suggests the question of whether the text expresses the Aristotelian one-substance conception of corporeal substance.

That conception is further suggested by the fact that Leibniz says here that the corporeal substance results from the active principle of unity and the mass that makes the multitude. This seems to imply that the organic body or multitudinous mass of secondary matter unites directly with the (abstract) soul or substantial form—that is, with the first rather than the third item in the outline. That is a distinctive feature of the Aristotelian one-substance conception. In both the two-substance and the qualified monad conception, the (abstract) soul or substantial form unites first with the primary matter to form the monad, and the monad as a whole relates to the organic body.

The Aristotelian one-substance reading of the document is not plausible, however. A direct union of the abstract substantial form or entelechy with secondary rather than primary matter does not fit the demands of the argument about incompleteness. For it is as merely active that the entelechy is incomplete, and it is primary matter that is the principle of passivity. Hence it should be a union with primary rather than secondary matter that is required to bring the soul or form to completion. The apparent implication of our text, that the soul or substantial form unites directly with the secondary matter or organic body, may perhaps best be accounted for as an ellipsis or metonymy that leaves the primary matter out of account, letting the soul or form stand for the complete monad. Leibniz was capable of this, I think, because he was always much more interested in the substantial form than in the primary matter.

Moreover, the concrete simple substance, the "monad" of the fivefold outline, is implicitly present in the continuation of our text. Leibniz says:

> Whereas the secondary matter or mass [*masse*] which constitutes our body has parts throughout which are complete substances themselves, while these are other animals or separately animated or actuated organic substances. But the mass [*amas*] of these organized corporeal substances which constitutes our body is not united with our Soul except by that relation which follows from the order of phenomena that are natural to each substance separately. And all of this shows how it can be said, on the one hand, that the soul and the body are independent of each other, and on the other hand, that the one is incomplete without the other since the one is never naturally without the other. (G IV,572f.)

Two features of what is said here about incompleteness distinguish it from Leibniz's statements on the same subject earlier in the document.

1. "The soul and the body" that are said here to be incomplete are not the first two items of the fivefold outline, but the third and fourth. That "the body" here is the fourth item, the organic body, is obvious. This of course is never a substance in Leibniz's mature writings, but at most an aggregate of substances. It is therefore not an incomplete *substance*, and Leibniz does not say that it is, but only that it is "incomplete."

"The soul," I think, is not only incomplete but an incomplete *substance* here, being the "monad" of the fivefold outline. This may be less obvious, but presence of the "monad" in this passage is implied by the statement that the soul is united to the secondary matter or organic body only by a harmony of the internal properties (the "phenomena") of separate substances. It follows that the soul must *have* some phenomena separately, and must have them prior, metaphysically, to its union with the mass of other substances that constitute its organic body. This it can do only if it is (or is a constituent of) a concrete individual substance that is constituted independently of the organic body. What would this substance be, if not the "monad" of the two-substance theory? And the ascription of incompleteness here surely applies to this substance.

What we seem to have in this passage, therefore, is not an Aristotelian one-substance conception of the structure of a corporeal substance, but a version of the two-substance conception in which the simple monad is an incomplete substance, and only the whole composite corporeal substance is a complete substance. We might think of this as an Aristotelian two-substance conception, as it is arguably more Aristotelian, or more Scholastic, than the simpler version of the two-substance conception presented earlier in section 2.1. Although he does not express it very fully or very often in his writings, I believe that this Aristotelian version of the two-substance conception is the view that most adequately realizes Leibniz's aims in trying to incorporate a version of the Scholastic theory of corporeal substance into his philosophy.

2. The other distinctive feature of the claim about the incompleteness of soul and body that concludes the quoted passage is the reason given for it: "since the one is never naturally without the other." The word 'naturally' is important here;

it is not an idle qualifier. Saying that the soul is never "naturally" without the body leaves open the possibility that the soul could exist without the body by the power of God, though that would be unnatural.[13] The Leibnizian reason for thinking it unnatural is that it would be inconsistent with the harmony of things, as suggested by the implication in our text that the soul is united with its body by the harmony of the perceptions of the substances involved.

This is important for Leibniz's conception of the unity of a corporeal substance, and in that connection I will return to this text in section 5. For the present I want rather to emphasize that the incompleteness that soul and body have by virtue of the fact that the harmony of perceptions demands that each be "completed" or complemented by the other is much less radical than the incompleteness that merely active and merely passive principles in a substance have by virtue of their being mere abstractions. The incompleteness of mere abstractions, asserted earlier in the text, is so radical that it may be doubted whether they could be made to exist separately even by the power of God.[14] It is thus more radical also than the incompleteness of incomplete substances for Suárez, since he held that substantial forms and (primary) matter can be made to exist separately from each other by the power of God.[15]

In this respect, indeed, even Leibniz's claim of "natural" inseparability seems stronger than Suárez would accept without qualification, for Suárez held that one substantial form, the rational soul, "is able even naturally to remain without matter,"[16] though it has a natural "aptitude" to inform matter. Comparison on this point is difficult, and perhaps dubious, however, because we cannot assume that Suárez and Leibniz had the same conception of the difference between what is natural and what is not.

Not only do we thus have more and less radical claims of incompleteness, but also, I believe, Leibniz uses the language of completeness and incompleteness in correspondingly different senses in different contexts. Thus body and soul are incomplete, because not "naturally" separable, in the context we have been discussing. The soul that is thus incomplete is a "complete [*accompli*] being" in another context (LA 76), however, and it is "completed," because rendered concrete, by the union of active and passive principles in it (G II,252).[17] In one sense

[13]We have seen in Chapter 3, section 3, that, while the textual evidence is not unambiguous, Leibniz seems to have believed that it was within the power of God to create a single substance without the others that are represented by its perceptions, and hence presumably to create a soul without the other substances that would form its organic body.

[14]Leibniz at least doubted it. About the same time as the text we have been studying he wrote a letter to John Bernoulli, discussed more fully in Chapter 12, section 3, in which he declined to answer the question (GM III,560/AG 169f.). But I think this expresses only a reverential caution rather than a real uncertainty. I can see no reason in his philosophy for accepting any possibility of separate existence for abstractions, and no evidence in the texts that he did accept it.

[15]Suárez, *Metaphysical Disputations*, XV,ix,1–3.

[16]Suárez, *Metaphysical Disputations*, XV,ix,1.

[17]This point is obscured at L 530f. and AG 177, because neither translation renders *completam* by "completed." Incompleteness seems likewise to be a matter of abstractness when Leibniz says that secondary matter is "a complete substance but not merely passive," whereas primary matter "is merely passive but is not a complete substance" (G IV,512/L 504), but the classification of secondary matter here as "a substance" of any sort is a piece of sloppiness, since Leibniz at the time (1698) was insisting that "secondary matter . . . is not a substance, but substances" (GM III,537/AG 167).

it is the abstract that is incomplete (see Chapter 12, sections 2–3); in the other sense "natural" inseparability is enough for incompleteness.[18]

I cannot claim, however, that Leibniz kept these senses clearly distinct in his writing. For example, in a passage written for another letter to Lady Masham, though apparently not sent to her, Leibniz writes that "the soul without the body or the body without souls" would be incomplete "as a number without numbered things, and a duration without enduring things" (G III,363). Now "a number without numbered things, and a duration without enduring things" would surely be regarded by Leibniz as *abstractions*, and incomplete on that account. And "the [organic] body without [any of the] souls [of the substances in it]" would also be an abstraction in Leibniz's view. But "the soul without the body" (as distinct from the soul without primary matter) is incomplete only as naturally inseparable, and not as an abstraction, except on an Aristotelian one-substance interpretation, which is clearly inadmissible here, inasmuch as this text, only a few lines later, explicitly acknowledges two meanings of 'substance' which are precisely the two types of substance of the two-substance conception. We must therefore suppose that Leibniz has carelessly mixed examples of things that are incomplete in quite different ways.

3. *The Structure of a Corporeal Substance: Some Texts*

An examination of some other sources from the years 1690–1704 will yield a richer sense of the difficulties, and the relevant factors, involved in interpreting Leibniz's views on the structure of a corporeal substance. Most of these texts have been cited, or might be, as evidencing a less idealistic view than I think should be ascribed to Leibniz.

3.1 *The Fardella Memo (1690)*

The first is a memorandum that Leibniz wrote in March 1690, in Venice, about some metaphysical discussions he had had, orally and in writing, with Michelangelo Fardella, an Italian Franciscan friar and priest. The passage most cited in discussions of Leibniz's views on substance is the following:

> I do not say that a body is composed of souls, nor that a body is constituted by an aggregate of souls, but of substances. Moreover the soul, properly and accurately speaking, is not a substance, but is a substantial form or primitive form existing in a substance; [it is] a first actualization [*actus*], a first active faculty. But the force of the argument consists in this, that a body is not a substance, but substances or an aggregate of substances. Therefore either there is no substance, and so no substances either, or there is something other than body. Furthermore even if an aggregate of these substances constitutes a body, they still do not constitute it in the manner of a part, since a part is always homogeneous with the whole, in the same way that points are not parts of

[18] Stronger and weaker senses of 'incomplete' are explicitly distinguished by Descartes in a closely related context, AT VII,222.

> lines. However the organic bodies of the substances included in any material mass are parts of that mass. . . . So there are substances everywhere in matter, as there are points in a line. And as there is no portion of a line in which there are not infinite points, so there is no portion of matter in which there are not infinite substances. But just as it is not a point that is part of a line, but a line in which the point is, so also it is not the soul that is part of matter, but the body in which it is. (VE 2156 = FC 322/AG 105)[19]

One might certainly be tempted to take the statement that the soul is not a substance, strictly speaking, because it is a substantial form, as expressing the Aristotelian one-substance theory, in which a corporeal substance has its organic body as a constituent and does *not* have a simpler substance as a constituent. The statement does not compel us to this interpretation, however. In saying that the soul is not a substance Leibniz certainly has in mind that it is only an aspect of, or abstraction from, a concrete substance.[20] The question is, What is that concrete substance of which it is an aspect? Is it a substance of which the organic body is a constituent, as in the Aristotelian one-substance conception? Or is it an unextended monad, as in the qualified monad and two-substance conceptions? In the two-substance conception as expressed in the fivefold outline of 1703, after all, the soul or substantial form is the first item, which is only an aspect, but an aspect of the third item, the monad, rather than of the fifth item, the composite substance. And in the qualified monad conception, as I have formulated it, the one "corporeal" substance is the third item of the fivefold outline, which may still have the soul or substantial form as an aspect of it. The statement of the Fardella memo—that the soul, as a substantial form, is not a substance—is therefore quite consistent with both the two-substance and the qualified monad conceptions.

Other features of the text seem to me to make the Aristotelian one-substance interpretation implausible and the qualified monad interpretation comparatively plausible. Most important here is the way in which the relation between "substances" and bodies or matter is likened to that between points and lines. This comparison is more obviously apt if the substances in question are unextended monads than if they incorporate extended bodies as constituents.

At the end of the quoted passage, moreover, "souls" take the place of "substances" in being related to matter as points are to lines. "Souls" and "substances" seem here to be equivalent. Either 'soul' has changed its meaning from the first two sentences of the quotation, and here refers to the whole monad, the third rather than the first item of the fivefold outline, or else 'substance' has changed its meaning from the beginning of the passage, and here refers to the first item of the five. Both these uses are attested in other writings of Leibniz. I have already noted a passage (LA 76) in which 'soul' must refer to a concrete simple substance. A bit later in the the Fardella memo also, "soul, mind, Ego" are given as terms for that in me, surely concrete, which survives death (VE 2157 = FC 323/AG 105). On the other hand, Leibniz elsewhere recognizes a sense in which 'substance' signifies "substance in the abstract," which is "the substance of," and as

[19]With respect to this text I depart from my usual practice and cite VE, from which I translate, in addition to the other references, because the text given in VE is so much more adequate.

[20]On the role of abstraction in Leibniz's views on these topics, see esp. A I,vii,248f., and Chapter 12, sections 2–3.

such an aspect of, a concrete substance (A I,vii,248f.). In the present context in the Fardella memo, however, I think the interpretation of "substance" as substance in the abstract is untenable. For in the text's first likening of substances to points, in the fifth sentence, "these substances" must surely refer to the (concrete) substances of the beginning of the quoted passage, which are contrasted with (abstract) souls. And if the substances that are likened to points are concrete, then the souls at the end of the quotation, which seem to be equivalent to those substances, are presumably also concrete substances, as no souls are in what I have been calling the Aristotelian one-substance conception.

The meaning of this passage turns on Leibniz's conception of the parts of bodies. The statement that "a part is always homogeneous with the whole" is a key to this. A body, according to the memo, is an aggregate. Its homogeneous parts, therefore, are subaggregates (and thus still bodies) rather than the indivisible nonaggregates "of" which it is an aggregate. The latter we might call "elements" as distinct from "parts" of the corporeal aggregate (as I have suggested in Chapter 9, section 3.1), and I think nothing is said here to preclude their being (concrete) souls or, as I put it, "qualified monads."

That something like the "monad" of the two-substance theory plays a part in the conception of corporeal substance in the Fardella memo is attested by another pair of paragraphs from it:

> Hence, since I am truly a single indivisible substance, not analyzable into several others, the permanent and constant subject of my actions and affections [*passiones*], there must be, besides the Organic body, a permanent individual substance, totally different in kind from the nature of body, which being placed [*positum*] in the continuous flux of its parts, never remains the same, but perpetually changes.
>
> In a human being, therefore, besides the body, there is some incorporeal substance, which is immortal, since it is not able to be analyzed into parts. (VE 2154 = FC 320/AG 104)

It is hard to believe that the substance discussed here, which is something "besides the organic body" and "totally different in kind from the nature of body" is a being partly composed of an organic body, like the composite substance of the two-substance conception. It seems rather to be the simple substance that appears as the "monad" in the two-substance conception.

If there is only one sort of substance in the Fardella memo, it is the latter sort, a monad or concrete soul. It is harder to decide between a two-substance and a qualified monad interpretation of the Fardella memo than to reject the Aristotelian one-substance interpretation. The principal evidence for the qualified monad interpretation is that the memo says nothing to suggest that there are two different sorts of substance, related to bodies in quite different ways, though such a distinction, if accepted, would be highly relevant to the discussion. I think the text is most naturally read as talking about a single kind of substance throughout, and that is a weighty consideration. It is still an argument from silence, however, and therefore far from conclusive.

There are at least a couple of points in the memo at which there may be some reason to doubt that the qualified monad conception gives the correct interpretation. One is in the passage last quoted, where Leibniz speaks of an "incorporeal" substance. If he was also prepared to speak of "corporeal" substances, as he did in other texts of the period, must not these be two different sorts of substance? Maybe; but maybe not. This variation could be merely verbal, the monad being counted as corporeal inasmuch as it *has* a body, and incorporeal inasmuch as it *is not* a body.

At another place in the memo Leibniz says it is probable that beasts and plants "are constituted not only by a corporeal principle [*corporea ratione*], but also by a soul, in accordance with which the beast or plant, a single indivisible substance, the permanent subject of its operations, is led" (VE 2155 = FC 321/AG 104). If we take this to mean that the beast or plant is a substance that is composed of a body and a soul, we will have to conclude that the composite substance, as well as the monad, of the two-substance conception is present in the text. But we do not have to take it that way: being constituted by a corporeal principle [*corporea ratio*] as well as a soul is not clearly the same as being composed of a *body* as well as a soul. The corporeal principle might be, not the body, but whatever it is in the monad by virtue of which it *has* a body.

Our discussion of the Fardella memo can hardly be complete without mention of the last sentence of a text that appears to be closely related to it (perhaps as a fragmentary draft). Leibniz wrote, "It should be considered whether there must not be something in matter besides those indivisible substances" (VE 2159 = FC 325). If this refers to the indivisible substances of the Fardella memo, as seems to me probable, it has a double bearing on the interpretation of the memo. That there must be "something in matter besides those indivisible substances" is certainly not in keeping with my interpretation of Leibniz's philosophy and of the memo. On the other hand, this sentence beginning "It should be considered" is surely not a summary of the view that has been presented in the memo. It raises rather a doubt about the adequacy of what is said in it. And it may be harder to see why such a doubt would be raised if Leibniz had been postulating corporeal substances less mind-like than the qualified monad conception allows. The sentence may therefore be evidence of the presence of that conception in the Fardella memo. It is certainly evidence that in 1690 Leibniz was not a stranger to the thought that perhaps the ontology of his philosophy of body was too parsimonious. In section 5 we shall see him entertaining that thought much more extensively at a later date.

3.2 Bernoulli's Questions (1698)

In fall 1698 there was an important series of metaphysical interchanges in the long correspondence, mostly devoted to technical subjects, between Leibniz and the famous mathematician and physicist John Bernoulli (1667–1748). In a letter of August or September Leibniz sent Bernoulli a summary of his views on the nature of body, containing the following statements:

> By a Monad I understand a substance truly one, that is, which is not an aggregate of substances. Matter itself, in itself [*per se*], or bulk [*moles*],[21] which

[21]There is no happy translation for *moles* in this context. I follow AG in rendering it as 'bulk', as it would certainly be confusing to use the same English translation for *moles* and *massa* here. But *moles* is in many contexts an ancestor of 'mass' in modern physics; it is not a synonym for 'volume'.

> you can call primary matter, is not a substance, and not even an aggregate of substances, but something incomplete. Secondary matter, or Mass [*Massa*], is not a substance, but substances; so not the flock but the animal, not the fish-pond but the fish, is one substance. But even if the body of an animal, or my organic body, is composed in turn of innumerable substances, those substances are still not parts of the animal or of me (GM III,537/AG 167)

What is said about "the animal" here (that it does not have other substances as parts) is similar to what is said about "the monad" (that it is not an aggregate of substances). This would support, though it does not prove, a one-substance reading, in which the animal (which is surely to be identified with the "corporeal substance") and the monad are the same substance. The definition of a monad given here is noteworthy, too. Verbally it is different from that of the *Monadology*. In 1714 Leibniz defined a monad as "a simple substance, which enters into composites; simple, that is to say, without parts" (Mon 1). But there may be no substantive difference between the definitions. Not every sort of internal complexity is denied to monads in the *Monadology*; they have many different perceptions, for instance. What they clearly must not have as parts is substances, and not being an aggregate of substances is precisely the mark of a monad (and not having substances as parts is the mark of an "animal"), according to this letter to Bernoulli.

It is therefore natural to construe the "monad" (and perhaps also the "animal") here as much the same sort of thing as the "monad" of the two-substance conception. But these considerations do not absolutely exclude the possibility that at least the "animal" (and perhaps also the "monad") is more like the complete corporeal substance of the two-substance conception. For the latter, though composite, was definitely regarded by Leibniz as one per se, and therefore not an aggregate; its unitary character might have given him some reason to deny that it has other substances as "parts," though not having parts seems to be given as a distinctive feature of the noncomposite type of substance where the two-substance conception is most clearly presented (C 13/MP 175).

Bernoulli responded with a set of inquiries, which, together with Leibniz's subsequent division of them into six questions, provided the framework for the ensuing discussion. I will let them provide the framework for my discussion, too, focusing mainly on the last four questions at present, as the first two will provide the main topic of section 3 of Chapter 12.

> I do not adequately grasp [1] what you understand by primary matter *in itself* [*per se*] or by *bulk* [*moles*] as distinct from secondary matter or mass [*massa*], nor, also, [2] what is incomplete for you. [3] If secondary matter or mass [*massa*] is not *a substance* but *substances*, if you are right to compare it with a flock or a fishpond, then divide for me a certain portion of matter into its separate, singular or individual substances, as a flock is divided into animals, an army into soldiers, etc. [4] And explain clearly, please, in what you think such a singular substance consists. [5] Let it be something analogous to the soul: you grant that no portion of matter is so small that there do not exist in it an infinity of such souls, such substances, such monads, or whatever you wish to call them; how far must I go then to arrive at a simple unity, singular and individual, to be able to say that this is a substance, not *substances*? [6]

> Surely matter will have to be divided not only into infinitely small parts, but into least parts, that is, into points or unquantified things [*non quanta*], which do not exist. (GM III,539f., numbering added)

All that need concern us now about the first two questions is found in Leibniz's initial replies to them:

> You ask (1) what I understand by matter in itself, or primary matter or bulk, as distinct from secondary [matter]. I answer: that which is merely passive, and separate from souls or forms.
>
> You ask (2) what is incomplete for me here. I answer: the passive without the active, and the active without the passive. (GM III, 541f./AG 167)

The "active" that is incomplete "without the passive" is certainly the substantial form or entelechy, considered as an aspect of a substance. And it is clearly implied here that what is needed to complete it is precisely the primary matter as principle of passivity. If "the active" and "the passive" here are the first two items of the fivefold outline, then their "completing" each other surely yields the third item of that outline, the simple monad, and an organic body (the fourth item in the outline) is not required for the completion of the substantial form, as would be demanded by an Aristotelian one-substance interpretation of the passage.

The third question is probably the easiest of the set, though it is basic to Bernoulli's concerns. In his initial response Leibniz wrote:

> (3) You ask me to divide for you a portion of the mass into the substances of which it is composed. I reply that there are as many individual substances in it as there are animals or living things or things analogous to living things. Therefore I divide it in the same way as a flock or a fishpond, except that I judge that the fluid interposed between the animals of the flock, and between the fish, and likewise the fluid (and indeed the remaining mass) contained in any fish or animal, must be divided again, as a new fishpond, and so on to infinity. (GM III,542/AG 167f.)

Bernoulli seems not to have felt any difficulty understanding this reply, for in his next letter, instead of requesting further clarification, he asked Leibniz how he would respond to a Cartesian objection to the Leibnizian multiplication of soul-like entities (GM III,546). We need not follow that objection through the remaining rounds of discussion.

The fourth question, in what Leibniz thinks "such a singular substance consists," is the one that most interests us here. For in the context, immediately following the third question, "*such* a singular substance" must mean a *corporeal* substance. Leibniz's initial (and, as it turned out, only) direct reply to this question is:

> (4) What I call a complete monad or singular substance is not so much the soul as the animal itself or analogous thing, endowed with a soul or form and an organic body. (GM III,542/AG 168)

This answer certainly does not seem to envisage any substance besides "the animal" which here, as usually for Leibniz, is clearly the corporeal substance; it therefore suggests a one-substance conception of the structure of corporeal substance. If we consider the quoted sentence alone, we might well be tempted to suppose that the one substance is a composite substance having an organic body as a constituent.

The text does not say, however, that "the animal" has an organic body as a *constituent*, only that it is "endowed" [*praeditum*] with one. This latter thesis belongs to the qualified monad conception as much as to the Aristotelian one-substance conception. It is also compatible with the qualified monad conception that "the soul" appears here as an aspect of a substance rather than as a substance. So Leibniz's explicit answer to question (4) is ambiguous with respect to our two one-substance conceptions.

We might seek further illumination in discussion of the question in succeeding letters, but, unfortunately, Bernoulli's interests were not ours, and the original question (4) is displaced or swallowed up by others, beginning with his next letter. We will have more luck with Leibniz's initial response to the fifth question.

> (5) You ask how far we must go in order to have something that is a substance and not substances. I reply that such are presented right away, even without subdivision, and every single animal is such. For neither are I, you, he composed of the parts of our body. (GM III,542/AG 168)

Can "qualified monads," as I have called them, be "presented" [*offerri*] in the way envisaged here? Certainly. For *as* having bodies, monads can be perceived since, as I shall argue in section 4.1, they are perceived by perceiving their bodies. And there is an indication here that the substances presented are not composites having organic bodies as constituents. For I, you, and he are surely mentioned as examples of the sort of substance in question, and it is said that we are not composed of the parts of our body. It is natural to take that as implying that the parts of the body are not constituents of the substance. And one might think that if the parts are not constituents of the substance, neither is the whole body, which is the sum or aggregate of the parts.

The likeliest way of avoiding this conclusion would be to suppose that by 'are composed of' here Leibniz meant 'have as parts' in a sense that is stronger than 'have as constituents', so that he need not be denying that we have our bodies, and their parts, as constituents of us. Leibniz seems to have used 'composed of' both in the broader sense, related to "constituents," and in the narrower sense, relating to "parts," in different places (as I have argued in Chapter 9, section 3.1). It is my intention to use 'composed of' in the broader sense in this book, except where otherwise indicated; but I will give reason for thinking that it has the narrower sense in Leibniz's first answer to question (6). So I would not claim to have proved that this letter expresses the qualified monad conception. But such an interpretation is hard to exclude, and in writing to Bernoulli, at any rate, Leibniz shows no anxiety to preserve the possibility of the organic body, or secondary matter, being properly a constituent of a substance, and not merely, as he says at the outset, a plurality of substances.

Bernoulli's sixth question is perhaps his most penetrating. Bernoulli's main interest in this whole discussion is in the divisibility of matter. He already knows that Leibniz thinks every extended portion of matter is divisible, and indeed actually divided (GM III,536). He foresees an argument that therefore, since substances are indivisible, they must be unextended. Assuming that extension, or volume, is the foundation of the quantitative treatment of matter, he wonders how Leibniz's conception of corporeal substance can be related to a quantitative physics. Leibniz's initial reply, in late September, was:

> (6) You are afraid that matter will be composed of unquantified things [*non quanta*]. I answer that it is no more composed of souls than of points. (GM III,542/AG 168)

This response is reminiscent of Leibniz's statement in the Fardella memo that "just as it is not a point that is part of a line, but a line in which the point is, so also it is not the soul that is part of matter, but the body in which it is" (VE 2156 = FC 322/AG 105). I argued in section 3.1 that in that statement the "soul" is a concrete substance, the "monad" of the fivefold outline, and suggested that a *part* of matter there is a subaggregate, but that souls were not precluded from being the elements "of" which matter is an aggregate.

Leibniz's answer to Bernoulli's sixth question differs from the statement of the Fardella memo, however, in denying, not that souls are "parts" of matter, but that matter is "composed of" souls. This would exclude the qualified monad conception of corporeal substance *if* we assume, first, that "souls" are concrete monads here, as in the memo, and, second, that, in the sense intended here, an aggregate is "composed of" its elements, though the elements are not "parts" of the aggregate. But we are not obliged to make either of these assumptions. I am inclined in fact to reject both of them. I think that 'soul' is to be understood in the abstract rather than the concrete sense throughout this set of answers. And the answer to the sixth question that Leibniz and Bernoulli ultimately agreed on is closely related to the idea that the *parts* of matter are subaggregates.

However it is to be understood, Leibniz's initial response to the sixth question did not satisfy Bernoulli. In his letter of November 8 he restated the question:

> (6) I was never afraid that matter (that is, secondary matter) would be composed of unquantified things [*non quanta*], but that it would be composed of points endowed with forms, since the least corpuscle, supposing it even to be infinitely small, does not constitute a substance, but substances. A singular substance therefore must be a point with a form, not something quantified [*quantum*] with a form; otherwise it would be divided into more substances. (GM III,546f.)

Bernoulli had in fact said what he denies having said in the first sentence of this response. Moreover, he says it again in the last sentence of the restatement. I suspect a slip of the pen; if we emend "unquantified things" in the first sentence to "souls," we get a good response to Leibniz. His initial response in terms of "souls" did not address Bernoulli's concern, especially if "souls" was meant here (as I believe) in the abstract sense. Whether or not my emendation is correct, Bernoulli's interpretation of Leibniz in terms of "points endowed with forms" shows that *he* took Leibniz to be thinking of corporeal substances as having a constituent located in space, and saw a problem about physical quantities if that constituent turned out to be unextended, lacking volume.

Replying on November 18, Leibniz did not address the question whether the body of a corporeal substance is a constituent of the substance, which of course had not been raised as an issue by Bernoulli. What Leibniz did is to deny that the body of a corporeal substance is a point, or indeed indivisible.

> As to (6). I think there is no smallest Animal or living thing, none without an organic body, none whose body is not divided again into more substances. Therefore we never come to living points or points endowed with forms. (GM III,552/AG 168)

Bernoulli evidently found this illuminating, for in his next letter he wrote:

> Because I judged that you were of the opinion that no corpuscle is so small that it can be called one substance rather than many, I believed that I rightly inferred that a singular substance is not extended but a mere point. But from the preceding article I have learned that you include substances in a substance. (GM III,556)[22]

Leibniz let the issue rest there, though the sense in which he includes substances in a substance deserved comment. Bernoulli was satisfied, and had grasped a point that seemed decisive for his concern—namely, that the corporeal presence of a Leibnizian substance is always an extended (and divisible) body, never a mere point. The division of (secondary) matter is therefore always into extended bodies, never into things that lack quantity. I do not think this resolves all issues about the relation of Leibniz's metaphysics to physical quantities. In particular, it does not answer questions, which will engage us in Chapter 13, about the relation of primary matter to physical quantities. But I think it does deal adequately with Bernoulli's immediate concern, which pertained, in Leibniz's terms, to the division of secondary matter.

3.3 To De Volder (Draft), June 1703

A text which could be read, in isolation, as suggesting the Aristotelian one-substance conception can be found, strikingly, in an earlier version of the very paragraph in which Leibniz gave De Volder, in 1703, the fivefold outline of the two-substance conception. The paragraph begins with the sentence, "If you take the mass [*massa*] as an aggregate containing many substances, you can still conceive in it one preeminent substance, if indeed that mass constitutes an organic body animated by its primary entelechy."[23] At the stage of composition I have in mind, the next sentence, a long one immediately preceding the outline, began with the statement, "For the rest, to form the Monad or complete simple substance, I conjoin with the Entelechy nothing but the primitive passive force of the whole mass" (LBr 967,69). This introduces to the paragraph the idea of the monad or complete substance constituted by the entelechy and the primitve passive force. It identifies the primitive passive force, however, as that "of the

[22]This response clearly addresses Leibniz's previous comment on question (6), though it is numbered "5" in Bernoulli's letter of 6 December 1698, and is in fact the fifth and last of a set of responses there. It follows a brief paragraph, numbered "4," in which Bernoulli has commingled his discussion of questions (4) and (5).

[23]LBr 967,69. Gerhardt, unaccountably, abbreviates *si quidem corpus organicum ea massa constituat, sua entelechia primaria animatum* to *seu entelechia primaria animatum* (G II,252). The resulting hash, understandably, has led to desperate expedients at L 530 and AG 177.

whole mass"—a mass that has been identified in the preceding sentence as "an aggregate containing many substances." This certainly suggests that Leibniz is thinking of the entelechy or substantial form as combining directly with an aspect of body or *secondary* matter to form the "monad" or complete substance, as the Aristotelian one-substance conception requires.

This suggestion is firmly excluded, however, in the final version of the sentence, for Leibniz crossed out "of the whole mass," replacing it with a more nuanced phrase, so as to refer instead to "the primitive passive force related to the whole mass of the organic body" (LBr 967,69 = G II,252). This is clearly correct from the point of view of the two-substance conception (or even the qualified monad conception), for Leibniz certainly thought that the primitive passive force in the monad is *related* to the whole mass of the monad's organic body. What the relation is will be discussed in more detail in Chapter 13, section 2. For the present it is enough to observe that the terminological shift from the force *of* the whole mass to a force *related* to the whole mass is most plausibly understood as intended to avoid any implication that the force is an aspect of the corporeal mass and dependent on it in that way.

Not that this correction marks a time at which Leibniz shifted from the Aristotelian conception to the two-substance conception. A sketch of the fivefold outline, containing two items, the "Monad" and the "Animal," which can only be understood as substances, is found at the end of this paragraph in the margin of a still earlier manuscript of the letter (LBr 967,66). It was in all probability written there before Leibniz wrote "the primitive passive force of the whole mass" in the later draft. I conclude that Leibniz held the two-substance conception throughout the drafting of this letter, but was led into a misleading formulation at one point by his undoubted desire for a strong relation between the primitive passive force and the corporeal mass.

3.4 To De Volder, January 1700

One of Leibniz's earlier letters to De Volder gives expression to one of the strongest reasons that could have commended the qualified monad conception of corporeal substance to Leibniz.

> When I say that the soul or entelechy cannot do anything to the body, then by the body I mean, not the corporeal substance whose entelechy it is, which is one substance, but the aggregate of other corporeal substances that constitute our organs; for one substance cannot influence another, and therefore not an aggregate of others. So I mean this: whatever happens in the mass [*massa*] or aggregate of substances according to Mechanical laws, the same thing is expressed in the soul or entelechy [or if you prefer, in the Monad itself or the one simple substance constituted by both activity and passivity[24]] by its own laws. But the force of change in any substance is from itself or its own entelechy—which is so true, that even in an aggregate, everything that will occur can be gathered from those things that are already in the aggregate. However, since there are so many separate [*privatae*] entelechies in the mass [*massa*] of our body, it is easy to judge that not everything that happens in

[24]These words are bracketed in the original, and were presumably not sent to De Volder.

> our body is to be derived from our Entelechy, even if it accords with it.[25] Entelechy or force or activity doubtless differs from resistance or passivity; you may take the former for the form and the latter for the primary matter. They are not so different, however, that they ought to be considered as two different substances; but [they ought to be considered] as constituting one substance, and the force that changes the primary matter is by no means its own force but the entelechy itself. (G II,205f.)

The emphasis of this passage falls on the point that, because of the mutual causal independence of substances on which Leibniz insists, the soul or entelechy or form does causally influence its primary matter but cannot causally influence its secondary matter, inasmuch as it is an "aggregate of other corporeal substances." This is given as a reason for considering the form and primary matter, not "as two different substances, but as constituting one substance." Here we see one of the reasons why in Leibniz's letters to De Volder, as I have already noted, the primary matter of a substance is not a substratum or constituent of its secondary matter, as it was for the Scholastics; if it were, it would have to belong at once to the one substance and to the *other* substances that constitute its secondary matter, and hence would have to be both influenced and uninfluenced by the form or entelechy of the one substance.

My present concern is with another implication, however. In the first sentence of the quoted passage Leibniz is at pains to explain that he does not mean that the soul or entelechy cannot influence the corporeal substance whose entelechy it is. He seems to assume that a substantial form must be able to influence the substance it informs. But he denies that the form can influence its organic body. So if the organic body is a constituent of the corporeal substance, the influence of the form on the corporeal substance must nonetheless be exhausted by its influence on the substantial core that is the "monad" of the two-substance theory. In what sense can the substantial form and the organic body be constituents of one substance if there is no real causal interaction between them? In the last sentence of the passage, after all, it seems to be assumed that the primary matter is accessible to influence from the form if they are constituents of the same substance. The supposed composite substance that has the organic body as a constituent cannot satisfy a conception of substance according to which the metaphysical boundaries of a substance must bound a system of real causal action. This consideration strongly favors the qualified monad conception according to which a corporeal substance *is* a monad—a monad *as having* an organic body, but not a monad *plus* an organic body.

It is not clear, however, that Leibniz was thinking in terms of the qualified monad conception when he wrote this letter to De Volder. The way in which he speaks in successive sentences of "the corporeal substance" and then of "the Monad itself or the one simple substance constituted by both activity and passivity" can easily suggest that he is thinking of them as two different things and thus has in mind the two-substance conception that he would lay out so fully for the same correspondent three and a half years later. Leibniz seems never to

[25]This sentence is a marginal addition in Leibniz's manuscript (LBr 967,38), omitted by Gerhardt—presumably by oversight, since there is no indication in the manuscript that Leibniz did not intend it to stand in the letter.

have been content with the qualified monad conception despite the excellent fit between it and his fundamental idea of substances in general as closed causal systems. I think his talk of "corporeal substance" was usually rooted in an interest in accommodating within his system, at least verbally, and if possible more than verbally, a common sense or traditional realism about bodies. Probably the qualified monad conception was not sufficiently "corporeal" to satisfy that interest, whose destabilizing effects on Leibniz's thought are documented at more than one place in this chapter.

Summing up these investigations into Leibniz's views on the structure of a corporeal substance, I would say that the two-substance conception is the only one that we can be certain that Leibniz held at any time. He at least sometimes envisaged an Aristotelian version of it distinguishing between incomplete and complete concrete substances. Some of his writings, especially before 1703, may have been influenced by something like the qualified monad conception, but it is improbable that he ever accepted the Aristotelian one-substance conception.

Crucial to both the two-substance and the qualified monad conceptions is the idea that monads *have* (organic) bodies. How do they have bodies? In the terms used in the fivefold outline of 1703, in what sense does a monad "dominate" or rule its organic body? And in what sense does it dominate or rule the subordinate monads "in" its body, as Leibniz more often says? These questions are the topic of the next section.

4. Monadic Domination

In a letter of 16 June 1712 to Des Bosses, Leibniz says, "The domination, however, and subordination of monads, considered in the monads themselves, consists in nothing but degrees of perfections" (G II,451/L 604f.).[26] Clearly it is the dominant monad that must be more perfect than the monads subordinate to it, and perfection of monads, for Leibniz, is measured by distinctness of perceptions. So the dominant monad must perceive some things more distinctly than the subordinate monads.

What must the dominant monad perceive more distinctly than the subordinate monads? Everything that happens within its body, suggested Bertrand Russell. But that does not adequately explain the sense in which Leibniz thought the dominant monad rules the body. In particular, the sufficient condition for domination that Russell seems to propose is not plausible. He says:

> If, then, in a certain volume, there is one monad with much clearer perceptions than the rest, this monad may perceive all that happens within that volume more clearly than do any of the others within that volume. And in this sense it may be dominant over all the monads in its immediate neighborhood. (Russell, p. 148)

[26]Note also that in the same place Leibniz says that between the dominant monad and the others "there is no intercourse, but only consensus." This text must be used with care, because the context is one in which Leibniz is expounding a theory of "substantial bonds" (see section 5.3), which, in this letter at any rate, he is clearly not endorsing. The passage as a whole, however, seems to me to indicate that Leibniz believes what he says here about monads in themselves is true whether or not there are substantial bonds.

But suppose that a certain volume of air immediately adjacent to my right eye contains no monad that perceives anything in that volume or in my body as distinctly as I do. By Russell's criterion, if I dominate as a monad over my body, I will dominate also over the monads in that adjacent volume of air, and it will presumably form part of my body. The incorporation of such volumes of air in my body would surely be an unacceptable consequence for Leibniz. He might try to avoid it by insisting that in any such space there would always be a monad that perceived something in the space as distinctly as I do. But I would expect him to base his strategy more directly on the offensive feature of the example, which is that the volume of air does not seem to be part of the organic structure of my body.

In a letter to De Volder, Leibniz says, "Nay rather the soul itself of the whole would be nothing but the soul of a separately animated part, were it not the dominant soul in the whole *on account of the structure of the whole*" (G II,194/ L 522, italics added). A correct understanding of Leibniz's conception of monadic domination depends on the relation of the dominant monad to the structure of its organic body no less than on the superior distinctness of the dominant monad's perceptions. There are two main points to be discussed here.

4.1 Directness of Mutual Expression

In a preliminary draft of his "New System," Leibniz says that the perceptions of a monad correspond "to the rest of the universe, but particularly to the organs of the body that constitutes its point of view in the world, and it is in this that their union consists" (G IV,477). Every monad expresses everything in the whole universe, according to Leibniz; but each monad expresses, and is expressed by, its own organic body in a special way. "The soul's job, in part, is to express its body" (G VI,570). A monad and its organic body both *contain* expressions of an infinity of things, but each *is*, as a whole, an expression of the other, and this relationship of mutual expression is peculiarly direct. An organic body stands in this relation to its dominant monad alone, not to the subordinate monads in it—though they do of course contain expressions of it. This is an important part of the structural relationship between a monad and its organic body by which monadic domination is constituted.

An organic body is an expression of its soul or dominant monad. Leibniz has less to say about this than about the soul's expressing its body, but expression as he understands it is a relation of one-to-one mapping, which will normally be symmetrical. So if each monad is an especially good expression of its body, the organic body will be, reciprocally, an especially good expression of its dominant monad. I believe that in the most natural development of Leibniz's system this explains how one perceives another monad. There is only indirect textual support for this interpretation, but how else would Leibniz think that we perceive other monads?

Suppose I see a kitten jumping off a chair to pounce on a piece of string. Leibniz will presumably say that I perceive certain internal properties of the kitten's soul: its seeing the string and intending to seize it. And how do I perceive those psychological properties? By far the most plausible answer is that I read them off certain properties of the kitten's body: its structure, spatial position, and movements.

According to Leibniz the subordinate monads in the kitten's body also have internal properties analogous to the seeing and intending in the kitten's soul. And since I perceive everything, at least unconsciously, I must perceive these perceptions and appetitions of the subordinate monads. But it would not be plausible to say that I perceive them by perceiving physical properties of the whole body of the kitten. Rather, I perceive the subordinate monads by perceiving *their* organic bodies, which most directly express their perceptions and appetitions. Perhaps I do not usually perceive them consciously; but with a suitable microscope, for example, I might observe one of the kitten's white blood cells reacting to a bacterium in its vicinity. In this case I may be taken as perceiving a perception of the bacterium and an appetite for its obliteration that are present (confusedly, no doubt) in the dominant monad of the white corpuscle. And I would be reading these internal properties of the monad off the movements and other physical properties of the cell. If I understand Leibniz correctly on this point, each monad is perceived by perceiving *its* organic body, and perception of an organic body as such directly yields perception of its dominant monad but not of its subordinate monads.

My claim that for Leibniz one perceives a monad by perceiving its body is somewhat speculative, but he explicitly holds that each created monad expresses and perceives everything else *by* expressing and perceiving its own organic body.

> Thus although each created Monad represents the whole universe, it represents more distinctly the body which is particularly assigned to it and of which it constitutes the Entelechy; and as this body expresses the whole universe by the connection of all matter in the *plenum*, the Soul also represents the whole universe in representing this body, which belongs to it in a particular way. (Mon 62)[27]

The Leibnizian harmony is a system of infinitely many models—or even a system of systems of models. Each model perfectly, if perhaps obscurely, expresses all the others, but some express each other with a special closeness or directness. Leibniz seems to explain this special closeness in terms of distinctness of perceptions (Mon 62); I find it a point of obscurity in his philosophy. One system of models occupies a peculiarly central role, although it does not have high status ontologically. This is the universe of organic bodies, considered as phenomena extended in space and time. They are involved in all of the modeling in the whole harmony. Each of the ultimately real models, the monads, stands in a direct modeling relationship only to its own organic body. The organic body, however, is also a model of the whole universe of organic bodies. Leibniz thought that in a physical universe with no empty space every physical event would have some mechanical effect (albeit no metaphysically real influence) on each infinitely divided organic body, and that each such body would therefore always bear in itself traces from which, in accordance with the mechanical laws of nature, an infinite mind could read off all past, present, and future events in the universe of bodies (cf. Mon 62). Since my organic body expresses in this way the

[27]Cf. LA 90f.,112f.; G II,253/L 531; G IV,530ff.,545; NE 132f.; G VII,567; C 14/MP 176.

whole corporeal universe, and also is expressed by me as its dominant monad, I perceive the whole corporeal universe in perceiving my own body. And since the other organic bodies in the universe express their own dominant monads, and since each finite monad is expressed by its own body, I perceive each monad by perceiving its organic body and I perceive the whole system of finite monads by perceiving the whole system of organic bodies. And I perceive all of this by perceiving my own organic body. (So far as I can see, the thesis that I perceive other monads by perceiving their bodies is needed here if the idea that I perceive *everything* by perceiving my body and the mechanical effects of other bodies on it is to be carried through.)

Obviously, I do not *consciously* perceive all these things. Because I am finite, I perceive most of them much too confusedly to be conscious of them, Leibniz would say. His scheme is at least initially less plausible if we attend mainly to conscious perceptions. When I am reading a page, do I really perceive the letters on the page by perceiving what is going on in my eye? it seems that I can see perfectly well what is on the page without being conscious at all of what is going on in my eye (and without even being able to become conscious of the inner workings of my eye by paying attention to them). If my perception models what is going on in my eye more *directly* than it models the surface of the page, and if conscious perceptions are always more distinct than perceptions that cannot even be brought to consciousness by attending to them,[28] then this case shows that Leibniz cannot consistently explain directness of the expression and perception relations wholly in terms of distinctness of perceptions. Perhaps directness and indirectness of perceptions in such a case are founded on explanatory relations rather than on degrees of distinctness. I perceive what is going on in my eye more directly than what is on the page because the psychological laws that correlate corporeal phenomena with what happens in monads relate visual perceptions more directly to events in the eye than to events at a distance. The distant events are related to visual perceptions by virtue of their connection, under mechanical laws, with events in the eye.

The task of providing a satisfactory account of the relation of directness of expression will not be pursued further here, but clearly it is an important problem. The idea that each monad and its organic body express each other with a unique directness plays a pivotal role in Leibniz's philosophy. As we have seen, it is used to explain how every monad perceives everything else. I think it plays an essential part in determining which monad has, or dominates, which organic body. That is my present concern; in addition, I have argued in Chapter 9, section 3.3, that the spatial position or "point of view" of a monad depends in turn on which organic body it has, while any aggregation of monads to form bodies depends on their spatial position. Thus a great deal depends directly or indirectly on the relation of directness of expression.

[28] I believe consciousness and distinctness were linked in this way in Leibniz's mind, but the question could be raised whether his theory of perception would not go better if distinctness and consciousness were allowed to be two dimensions in which perceptions can vary independently—distinctness being a feature of the structure of the perception and consciousness being, as it were, the light that is turned on it. (I am indebted to Jeremy Hyman for this image.) Separating these dimensions would give the theory more flexibility.

4.2 Domination and Organic Functions

Leibniz does imply that a dominant monad perceives some things more distinctly than the monads subordinated to it do. What remains to be explained here about monadic domination is how the greater distinctness of the dominant monad's perceptions is related to the structure of the organic body and why these relations should be expressed by an idea of domination—that is, of rule or control. The hypothesis I propose to answer these questions is that what the dominant monad as such perceives more distinctly than any other monad in its body is an appetite or tendency for perceptions of the normal organic functioning of the body.

In developing the hypothesis I begin with a passage of an early draft of § 14 of the *Discourse on Metaphysics*:

> It is sure above all that when we desire some phenomenon and it occurs at the designated time, and when this happens ordinarily, we say that we have acted and are the cause of it, as when I will that which is called moving my hand. Also when it appears to me that at my will something happens to that which I call another substance, and that that would have happened to it thereby even if it had not willed, as I judge by frequent experience, I say that that substance is acted on [*patit*], as I confess the same thing about myself when that happens to me following the will of another substance.

These statements reveal the intuitive origin of the idea that activity and passivity can be explained in terms of distinctness of perceptions. Voluntary agency provides the paradigm of activity. It is characterized by consciousness of a tendency or appetite that has a certain event as its goal. The goal is described by Leibniz here as a "phenomenon," a certain event as perceived by the voluntary agent. The whole passage is stated very much in terms of what appears to the agent; that Leibniz was thinking in those terms is confirmed by the fact that he initially wrote "perception" where "phenomenon" stands in the quoted text, and started to write "when I will that it appear to me" in describing the willing of a motion of his hand.

A substance that is conscious of an appetite for a perception of a certain event is active in producing the event, if the appetite does indeed produce the perception, whereas the other substances involved in the event are acted on if their perceptions of the event are not produced by a conscious appetite for such perceptions. According to Leibniz's philosophy they must have had appetites for those perceptions, but they were not conscious of them. That is, they were much less distinctly aware of them than the active substance was of its corresponding appetite. "Our involuntary internal motions do not cease to correspond to our confused and imperceptible appetites, but these motions depend as little on the empire of the will as these appetites depend on our understanding" (G III,510).[29]

[29]This text of 1710, together with one of 1704 (G III,347), suggests a view in which the soul's (voluntary) domination of its body depends on appetites, mainly confused and unconscious, for those internal motions of its body that are means to the end consciously willed. But this seems to contribute more to an account of the *will* than to the distinction between dominant and subordinate monads, since most dominant monads have no conscious ends, and all monads have appetites (at least confused ones) for means to those events that actually happen.

More generally, activity and passivity in the production of an event can be understood as consisting in more or less distinct perception of a monad's own appetite for perceptions of the event, although this distinctness does not amount to consciousness in most cases as it does in voluntary action.

My hypothesis is that Leibniz saw the dominant monad as active in this way in the normal functioning of its organic body, the functioning that fits the body constantly to be the direct expression of the dominant monad. This is connected with Leibniz's speaking of the monad as the "soul" or "substantial form" of the body or corporeal substance. He was consciously and professedly adopting or adapting Aristotelian and Scholastic terminology here, and he explicitly took a position, in the famous Scholastic dispute about the unity or plurality of substantial forms, for those who held that there is only one substantial form or soul in each substance.[30] He considered himself to be in agreement with theological authority on this point (Gr 552). To Queen Sophia Charlotte he wrote:

> I also recognize degrees in activities, such as life, perception, reason, and thus [recognize] that there can be more kinds of souls, which are called vegetative, sensitive, rational, [and] that there are kinds of bodies that have life without sensation, and others that have life and sensation without reason. However, I believe that the sensitive soul is vegetative at the same time, and that the rational soul is sensitive and vegetative, and that thus one single soul in us includes these three degrees, without its being necessary to conceive of three souls in us, of which the lower would be material in relation to the higher; and it seems that that would be multiplying beings without necessity. (G VI,521;[31] cf. G II,389)

Two points in this text are important for my present purpose: that I am the vegetative and sensitive soul of my body, as well as the rational soul; and that the functions of a vegetative and sensitive soul are the activities of life and sensation, respectively. If I am the vegetative soul of my body, that is presumably because I am active in the functions of my body that sustain life—for example, in particular events of sugar metabolism in the cells of my body. And if I am active in those events, that is because I perceive my preceding appetite for my perception of them and that perception, though unconscious, is comparatively distinct. Specifically, it is more distinct than the perception any other monad in my body has of its corresponding appetite, and that is what is crucial for my status as dominant monad in my body.

This hypothesis allows, but does not require, that the dominant monad perceives *all* events in its body more distinctly than any other monad in the body does. All that is required is that it have more distinct perceptions of its appetites for all events of *normal* functioning of the body. I see no reason why the soul must be similarly active with respect to traumas of disease or injury in the body. In fact, I suspect Leibniz would deny that it is. His fullest discussion of the soul's role in the production of such traumas is in response to a criticism by Pierre Bayle.

[30]Regarding this dispute, see M. Adams, *William Ockham*, vol. II, pp. 638f.,647–69.

[31]In light of this very explicit text, we cannot find Leibniz's own view in another text of the same period (also G VI,521) in which he is willing to exploit for theological purposes what appears to be another person's advocacy of the plurality of substantial forms in a single substance.

Bayle had asked how the theory of pre-established harmony could explain the sudden transition from pleasure to pain in a dog that is struck unexpectedly by a stick while eating (G IV,531). What is the previous state of the dog's soul from which the sudden pain results, according to Leibniz? Leibniz replies:

> Thus the causes that make the stick act (that is to say the man positioned behind the dog, who is getting ready while it eats, and everything in the course of bodies that contributes to dispose the man to this) are also represented from the first in the soul of the dog exactly in accordance with the truth, but weakly, by little, confused perceptions, without apperception, that is to say without the dog noticing it, because the dog's body also is only imperceptibly affected by it. And as in the course of bodies these dispositions finally produce the blow pressed hard on the dog's body, in the same way the representations of these dispositions in the dog's soul finally produce the representation of the blow of the stick. Since that representation is distinguished and strong, . . . the dog apperceives it very distinctly, and that is what makes its pain. (G IV,532)[32]

What I want to emphasize in this text is that the soul's prior tendency to have the pain that is its perception of the trauma in its body is based on its unconscious perception of events outside its body. It perceives these events indirectly by perceiving its own body. Presumably it may in some cases perceive external events more distinctly than it perceives its own "appetite" that is grounded in them, as when I perceive that I am falling and about to strike the ground with considerable force;[33] but where the perception of the external events is very confused, the perception of the corresponding appetite certainly can be too. I cannot see that Leibniz is committed to saying that the soul perceives either the appetite or the external events more distinctly than the subordinate monads do. At any rate, a more distinct perception of external events, or of the causes of traumas, is not obviously connected with the functions of a vegetative soul.

This hypothesis about the nature of the rule that the dominant monad bears in its body confirms and illuminates my interpretation of the nature of organism in Leibniz. An organic body is one many of whose operations, in its parts of all sizes, can be explained not only mechanically but also *teleologically*, as directed in accordance with the active appetites of a soul that is at least vegetative and may also be sensitive and rational. And the active appetites of a vegetative soul are for states that contribute to the maintenance of the body as a direct expression of a monad and a perfect expression of the whole corporeal universe, according to certain laws of nature.

5. *Principles of Unity*

There are many texts in which Leibniz says that corporeal substances are distinguished from mere aggregates by a profounder sort of unity. Writing to Arnauld

[32]This explanation, according to which perceptions produce one another in the soul by virtue of their representing corporeal events that follow from one another by laws of the corporeal universe, is reminiscent of Spinoza's version of psychophysical parallelism, as developed in Part Two of his *Ethics*. Cf. also LA 92; G IV,591.

[33]I owe this observation to Timothy Sheppard.

late in 1686, he says, "if there are no corporeal substances, such as I wish, it follows that bodies are nothing but true phenomena, like the rainbow," for on account of the infinite division of matter, "one will never come to anything of which one can say, 'Here is truly a being', except when one finds animated machines whose substantial unity, independent of the external union of contact, is made by the soul or substantial form" (LA 77). This statement implies, first, that there cannot be a corporeal substance without a "substantial unity" stronger than the unity that many aggregates have by the bodily contact of their members with each other, and second, that such a substantial unity is somehow provided by the substance's "soul or substantial form." And this is only one of a number of texts in which the dominant monad, or the active entelechy in the dominant monad, is characterized as the principle of unity in the corporeal substance: A corporeal substance is "actuated by one Entelechy, without which there would be in it no principle of true Unity" (G II,250/L 529); "the Animal or corporeal substance . . . is made One by the Monad dominating the Machine" (G II,252/L 530f.).[34]

Substantial unity is not a peripheral issue. As indicated in the quoted statement to Arnauld, Leibniz regarded it as the main point in the question whether there are corporeal substances. A linkage of substantiality with per se unity was characteristic of the Aristotelian conceptual framework whose partial rehabilitation Leibniz was attempting. Mid-seventeenth-century debate as to whether Cartesianism allowed a human being to be a true substance, as conservative philosophers demanded, focused on whether it allowed a more than accidental unity of body and soul. Descartes himself attempted to give the human being unity per se by treating the soul as the substantial form of the human being.[35] Arnauld was less conservative on this point, however, and resisted Leibniz's insistence on tying substantiality in bodies to per se unity (LA 86f.,106f.).

On what I have called the qualified monad conception of corporeal substance there is no great difficulty about the per se unity of a corporeal substance, since it is identical with a simple substance. There is a serious problem, however, on the two-substance conception, which seems to have been Leibniz's main conception and may well have been his only conception of corporeal substance. For it may be doubted whether on Leibniz's showing the dominant monad could give to a composite that it forms with the organic body a unity different in kind from the unity of an aggregate.

5.1 *The Middle Years*

There are several texts of the 1690s (e.g., LA 136; G IV,477; E 127/L 458; RML 315) in which the union of soul and body that constitutes a corporeal substance is explicitly explained by Leibniz as arising from relations of harmony among the perceptions of substances involved in the union:[36]

[34]For similar claims see VE 416 = LH IV,7C,111; LA 120; E 124f./L 454; G IV,492/AG 147; G III,260f./AG 289f.; PNG 3.

[35]See Hoffman, "Unity of Descartes's Man."

[36]The explicit texts cited in this paragraph are all from the 1690s. But the harmonious perceptions theory of the nature of substantial unity is implicit in DM 33, and strongly suggested by

> The mass [*amas*] of these organized corporeal substances which constitutes our body is not united with our Soul except by that relation which follows from the order of phenomena that are natural to each substance separately. (G IV,573)
>
> Furthermore the union of the soul with the body in a human being consists in that most perfect agreement by which the series of motions corresponds to the series of thoughts. (FC 320/AG 104)

This is what Leibniz's idealism should lead us to expect. Given his doctrine that "there is nothing in things except simple substances, and in them perception and appetite" (G II,270/L 537), there is no way for the unity of a corporeal substance to be anything over and above the system of relations among perceptions of simple substances. But aggregates, too, are united by relations among the perceptions of substances, according to Leibniz, as I argued in section 3.3 of Chapter 9. So on this line of thought it might seem that the unity of a corporeal substance is of the same kind as the merely accidental unity of an aggregate.

The Scholastic tradition affords Leibniz a way out of this difficulty, which he seems to have envisaged at least once. Scholastic philosophers were intensively concerned with the question of how a being composed of other beings could be one per se. One of the main ideas proposed for solving this problem was that a composite being can be one per se if the beings that compose it are *incomplete*, and completed by their union in the composite.[37] Suárez, for example, counts it a certainty "regarding composite being . . . that there can truly and properly be a being per se and [something] one per se, as all philosophers teach regarding the substantial nature, insofar as it consists of matter and form. . . . For since neither matter nor form per se are complete and whole entities in their kind, but are by their nature constructed to compose that [*composite*], that which is immediately [*proxime*] composed of them, the essence or nature, is rightly called, and is, one *per se*."[38] For Suárez the matter and substantial form are *substances* that could exist apart from each other, at least by divine power.[39] They are nonetheless incomplete by virtue of their natural aptitude to unite with each other (as discussed earlier in section 2.3).

This idea appears in Descartes,[40] and was certainly available to Leibniz. As I argued in section 2.3, there are passages in which Leibniz treats the simple substance and its organic body as incomplete beings, "since the one is never naturally without the other" (G IV,572f.). This opens the way for Leibniz to say that

Leibniz's statement to Arnauld that the soul is "the form of its body because it expresses the phenomena of all the other bodies according to [their] relation to its own" (LA 58)—both from 1686. On this subject see also Garber, "Leibniz and the Foundations of Physics," pp. 44f.

[37]This idea was already proposed in the thirteenth and fourteenth centuries; see M. Adams, *William Ockham*, pp. 664–69.

[38]Suárez, *Metaphysical Disputations*, IV,iii,8.

[39]Suárez, *Metaphysical Disputations*, XV,v,1–2;ix,1–3.

[40]AT III,459f.; VII,222. The former text is from Descartes's correspondence with Regius, which Leibniz cites with approval on the per se unity of a human being as composed of soul and body. The sincerity of Descartes's more Scholastic utterances in this correspondence was already questioned in the seventeenth century, but Leibniz was inclined to accept it, as he largely approved the content (NE 317f.). Cf. Hoffman, "Unity of Descartes's Man," pp. 345f., 364–69.

the composite, corporeal substance composed of the simple substance and its organic body is one per se by virtue of the incompleteness of its constituents without each other, and their natural aptitude for their relation to each other. He does not quite say it, but the most important text on this point does begin with the per se unity of "the complete corporeal Substance" being closely associated with the incompleteness of its constituents (G IV,572).

This explanation does not compete with an account of the unity of a corporeal substance in terms of the harmony of perceptions, but supplements and presupposes it. For the relation to each other for which the simple substance and its body have a natural aptitude is understood by Leibniz as a harmony of perceptions, and it is by virtue of the pre-established harmony of perceptions that they are "never naturally without [each] other." It is thus perfectly appropriate that Leibniz's clearest statement of the view that soul and body are incomplete without each other is immediately preceded by the statement that "the mass [*amas*] of these organized corporeal substances which constitutes our body is not united with our Soul except by that relation which follows from the order of phenomena that are natural to each substance separately" (G IV,573).

This seems to me the best account of the unity of a corporeal substance suggested by Leibniz's writings of the 1680s and 1690s. It fits elegantly both his own metaphysics and some important Scholastic accounts of per se unity. It is therefore puzzling that he does not make more use of it.

Did Leibniz fear that in the context of his philosophy the union of incomplete beings would not be a strong enough relation to satisfy Scholastic expectations? That would not be a plausible fear with regard to the role of the concept of *incomplete being* in the account I have suggested for Leibniz. In this account the incompleteness of the soul or dominant monad and its body strengthens their union because it signifies that their togetherness is demanded by the pre-established harmony. And the demands of pre-established harmony are very strong demands in Leibniz's philosophy, tantamount to demands of the goodness of God, and surely not weaker than the natural aptitude that matter and substantial form have for each other according to Suárez.

There may be more reason to fear weakness in the unitive role that *harmony of perceptions* plays in the Leibnizian account. The relation in which matter and the substantial form that actuates it stand, according to Suárez, is a broadly causal relation (specifically, the relation of formal causation),[41] which might be thought a stronger relation metaphysically than a harmony of perceptions. In his later years Leibniz was clearly concerned about some such perception of comparative weakness in the harmony of perceptions account. In the 1680s and 1690s, however, he seems to have had no qualms about explaining the union of soul and body in terms of a harmony of perceptions. If he had any doubts on that point, it is hard to see why he would not have wanted to strengthen his account by incorporating the idea of incomplete beings, with respect to which he does not seem to be in a weaker position than Suárez.

[41]See Chapter 11, section 1.1.

5.2 *From Tournemine to the* Theodicy

About 1706 a noticeably different stance begins to appear, especially but not exclusively in writings that Leibniz addressed to Jesuit theologians. He noticed, "quite late" as he says, an article that had appeared under the date of May 1703[42] in the so-called *Mémoires de Trévoux*, an influential journal published by the Jesuits. The article was by one of the editors, René-Joseph de Tournemine, and objected against Leibniz that the union of soul and body cannot be explained in terms of harmony (AG 196). In his response, probably sent to Tournemine in January 1706, and finally published in the *Mémoires de Trévoux* of March 1708,[43] Leibniz disavowed any such explanation.

The response to Tournemine contains both negative and positive themes; both recur in later texts. The positive hypothesis has received far more attention, both from Leibniz and from his interpreters, but I shall argue that it was never part of his philosophy, though it may reveal something about the modality of his metaphysical thinking. The negative concession is less obviously dramatic, but it may in fact represent an abandonment of part of Leibniz's theory of corporeal substance. The response begins with the negative:

> Father Tournemine has spoken so obligingly of me . . . that it would be wrong for me to complain that he attributes to me an objection against the Cartesians that I don't remember, and that can obviously be turned against me. I declare, however, that if I have ever used it, I renounce it from now on. . . . I must admit that I would be very wrong to object to the Cartesians that the agreement that God maintains immediately, according to them, between the Soul and the Body, does not constitute a true Union, since assuredly my pre-established Harmony could not do it any better. (G VI,595/AG 196f.)

It is remarkable Leibniz could not remember claiming that his pre-established harmony could explain the union of soul and body better than the Cartesians could. As Tournemine did remember (G VI,596), Leibniz had claimed exactly that, in print, in the "New System" of 1695, which was probably the most discussed public presentation of his metaphysical views (E 127/L 457f.; cf. also G VI,551, from 1705). We may be surprised that he now denies it. For his theory of pre-established harmony contains two features that seem to strengthen the relation between soul and body and that are not found in Cartesian and occasionalist theories. First, the soul and its organic body are complete and perfect and peculiarly direct expressions of each other, and, second, the pre-established harmony imposes a strong requirement that if either the soul or its body exists, the other should also exist, in correspondence with it. By virtue of this requirement, as we have seen, the soul and its body, without each other, can be called "incomplete" beings. The strength that these features impart to the relation is apparent in Leibniz's statment of about 1704 that "according to me the

[42]Leibniz dated it March 1704, corresponding, it has been suggested, to the time of its actual appearance (AG 196).

[43]The initial date of submission may be inferred from letters to De Volder and Des Bosses (G II,281,296/L 538f.). The letters make clear that what was sent then was at least close in content to the response ultimately published.

soul's job, in part, is to express its body. Without the body, without the organs, [the soul] would not be what it is" (G VI,570).

To this it might be objected that these advantages of the pre-established harmony are balanced by the fact that in interactionist versions of Cartesianism the relation between soul and body is strengthened by direct causal links not found in Leibniz's system. But Leibniz does not seem to be thinking of an interactionist version of Cartesianism here. The one advantage he does claim for the pre-established harmony in this context is by comparison with what is clearly an occasionalist version of Cartesianism. The claimed advantage serves to introduce by contrast what I have called the positive theme or positive hypothesis of the response:

> My design has been to explain naturally what they explain by perpetual miracles, and I have tried to give a reason only for the Phenomena, that is to say, for the relation that is perceived between the Soul and the Body. But as the Metaphysical Union that one adds to it is not a Phenomenon, and as an intelligible Notion has not even been given of it, I have not taken it upon myself to seek the reason of it. I do not deny, however, that there is something of that nature. (G VI,595/AG 197)

This is an ambiguous statement. Leibniz does not affirm that there is a metaphysical union of soul and body not explained by his theory of pre-established harmony. He says only that he does not deny it. And he does deny, in effect, that such a union is part of his philosophy. But is he tactfully muffling his belief that it is an unintelligible absurdity? Or is he more straightforwardly acknowledging that there may be something in the universe that cannot be understood in his philosophy?

The text provides additional material for the latter interpretation, in the form of remarks assimilating metaphysical union to mysteries, as they figure in theology.

> It is as in the *Mysteries* where we also try to *elevate* what we conceive in the ordinary course of Creatures to something more sublime that can correspond to it in relation to the Divine Nature and Power, without being able to conceive there anything distinct enough and suitable enough to form a totally intelligible definition. (G VI,596/AG 197)

We may see here a suggestion that as there are religious truths that exceed human understanding, about which faith may believe mysteries that we grasp only dimly, a metaphysical union of soul and body may be classed among them, if it seems religiously important to do so. (Leibniz does not imply that it is religiously important to him, but it presumably was to Tournemine.) This, I think, is the most probable official meaning of the text.

The more cynical reading of the text is supported, however, by Leibniz's last letter to De Volder (19 January 1706), in which he reports his interchange with Tournemine. What he wrote to De Volder agrees closely in substance with what he wrote for Tournemine but is noticeably less respectful and more ironic in tone. It is introduced with the remark, "The scholastics commonly seek things that are not so much beyond this world [*ultramundana*] as Utopian. An elegant example was recently supplied to me by the Jesuit Tournemine, an ingenious Frenchman" (G II,281/L 538). The "example" stigmatized as "Utopian" is Tournemine's desire for an account of a union, different from harmony, between body and soul. This may well lead us to doubt that Leibniz took the possible reality of such a union very seriously.

Others took it very seriously, however, and the idea crops up repeatedly, though still noncommittally, in Leibniz's writings thereafter, especially in his letters to Bartholomew Des Bosses, his best friend among his Jesuit correspondents of the period. On 20 August 1706 Des Bosses sent Leibniz a list of propositions "mostly drawn from Descartes and Malebranche" that were "recently condemned by our schools at Rome." One of the condemned propositions was the following:

> 22nd. The union of the Rational Soul with the body consists in this alone, that God has willed that certain perceptions be aroused in the soul at certain changes of the body, and [has willed] conversely, for certain thoughts or volitions of the soul, that certain motions follow in the body. (G II,312)[44]

This makes clear that some influential Catholics did think it religiously important to maintain the union of soul and body, and to maintain it in a stronger sense than occasionalism can explain.

Leibniz's reply, a few days later, was brief and cautious on this point. "To the 22nd: Since the Soul is the primitive Entelechy of the body, the Union will consist at least in that; but agreement between perceptions and corporeal motions is intelligibly explained by the pre-established harmony" (G II,314). Des Bosses, having seen Leibniz's response to Tournemine, would surely take him here as contrasting the phenomena of correlation, as explained by pre-established harmony, with the union. But how deep is the contrast? The union, Leibniz claims, can be explained by the soul's being the entelechy of the body; and that in turn is explained in terms of the pre-established harmony, on views that Leibniz had held hitherto. What Leibniz says here is perhaps compatible with the view that something over and above the harmony is required to make the soul the entelechy of the body; but what would that be? One might expect it to be a metaphysical union, but then the union would explain the soul's being the entelechy of the body, rather than the other way around.

Leibniz did not forget his interchange with Tournemine. Two years later, 3 September 1708, and again 24 April 1709, in letters to Des Bosses, he mentions and summarizes his response, with the metaphysical union still falling within the scope of the cautious "I do not deny" (G II,354f.,371/L 598). He comes closer to unqualified affirmation of the metaphysical union in a letter of 8 September 1709 to Des Bosses, stating, in a Eucharistic context, "I have already given Tournemine the answer that presence is something Metaphysical, as union is, which is not explained by phenomena" (G II,390). In this context, however, the mention of union is a pendant to the discussion of presence, whereas the reverse had been true in the original response to Tournemine. Leibniz's commitment to

[44]Only a selection of the propositions are given in this letter. Des Bosses sent a full list, at Leibniz's request, with his letter of 17 September 1706. Gerhardt did not print this list, but the additional propositions can be found in Robinet, *Architectonique disjonctive*, pp. 115f. The numbering of the propositions used in the correspondence, and here, is that of the complete list.

an inexplicable union is presumably no stronger here than his commitment to an inexplicable presence. And the latter seems weak enough, for a few months later, in January 1710, he reasserts, to Des Bosses, a more reductionistic theory of presence that he had used in his Eucharistic theology for forty years (G II,399; see also Chapter 12, sections 2.2–2.3).

In letters of 1710 to Des Bosses, in Eucharistic contexts, we find Leibniz saying, "Since the bread in fact is not a substance, but a being by aggregation or substantiated [being] resulting from innumerable monads by some superadded Union, its substantiality consists in this union," and "Since the bread in fact is a being by aggregation or substantiated [being], its substantiality will consist in the union of the monads" (G II,399,403). These statements seem pretty assertive, although the future tense in the second may serve to distance the author from what is said and the first begins a paragraph that ends with the disclaimer, "But we who reject transubstantiation do not need such things." It is not clear from the context of this latter statement whether the superadded union is one of the things that Leibniz therefore does not need. In any event, these statements fall outside the group of texts related to the response to Tournemine, for at least on the surface they are not about the union between a soul or dominant monad and its organic body. Rather they seem to be about a union of monads to form a piece of bread, which is not an organic body but a mere mass which has no dominant monad—though we cannot exclude the possibility that Leibniz was speaking carelessly and really had in mind a plurality of superadded unions for the different corporeal substances contained in the bread, rather than a single union for the bread as a whole.[45]

Leibniz recalls his response to Tournemine again in the *Theodicy* (1710). In the Preface he wants to make clear that

> in denying *physical influence* of the soul on the body or the body on the soul, . . . I do not deny the union of the one with the other that makes of them a *suppositum*;[46] but this union is something *metaphysical*, which changes nothing in the phenomena. This is what I already said in responding to what Father Tournemine . . . had objected to me in the *Mémoires de Trévoux*. (G VI,45)[47]

Again Leibniz says only that he does not deny the metaphysical union; he does not actually assert its reality. He is marginally more assertive in another passage of the *Theodicy*, but with a more ambiguous content.

> We understand something by union . . . when we speak of the union of the soul with the body to make a single person. For although I do not hold that the soul changes the laws of the body, nor that the body changes the laws of the soul, and although I have introduced the pre-established Harmony to avoid that disorder, I do not fail to admit a true union between the soul and the

[45]Robinet (*Architectonique disjonctive*, pp. 98,101) takes these texts at face value, as concerned with a union of an aggregate, the bread, as such, and contrasts them in this with the theory of substantial bonds developed later in the correspondence.

[46]I render the French *suppôt* with the Latin technical term that lies behind it. A (created) *suppositum* is, roughly, a complete individual substance; see Suárez, *Metaphysical Disputations*, XXXIV,i,9.

[47]Page 68f. in Huggard's English translation.

> body, which makes of them a *suppositum*. This union belongs to the metaphysical, whereas a union of influence would belong to the physical. (T pd55)

To admit [French *admettre*] is most naturally read as implying an (unenthusiastic) assertion, though it might just be possible to read it as merely granting others the permission to make the assertion. But if admission is a sort of assertion here, what is asserted? The passage has enough similarity to the statement in the preface to tempt the reader to assume that what Leibniz asserts here is what he did "not deny" there—which is also what he did "not deny" to Tournemine. But the more assertive passage is not itself tagged with a reference to Tournemine, and what it says about the union of soul and body contains nothing that Leibniz could not have said about it from the standpoint of his reductionistic theory. That there is a real union, making of body and soul a *suppositum* or complete individual substance, and that this union is metaphysical, are things he could certainly have said in the 1690s while he was maintaining that the union must be understood in terms of the harmony of perceptions. On the other hand, since the union is mentioned here as something that Leibniz admits *although* he has introduced the pre-established harmony, the reader might naturally take it that the source or nature of the union is not to be found in the harmony.

That the idea, if not the unambiguous affirmation, of an irreducible metaphysical union of soul and body appears in the *Theodicy* marks an escalation of its importance for Leibniz. For the *Theodicy* was the most public of his works, not wholly candid (as I have argued in Chapter 1, section 4), but central to the impression of himself that he wished to give the largest possible educated public. Leibniz's belief in the irreducible metaphysical union is not, in my opinion, established by his writings of the years 1706–10, among which we must not forget to include the sarcastic comments to De Volder. But he did say repeatedly, in public and private, that he did not deny such a union. He could offer no theory of it, as he stated to Tournemine, but he at least granted its admissibility for those who saw a religious or other need for it.

5.3 Letters to Des Bosses (1712–16)

Beginning in 1712, the idea of an irreducible metaphysical union, as a factor in the constitution of a corporeal substance, assumes a much more elaborate form in Leibniz's letters to Des Bosses. This is the perplexing concept of a *substantial bond* [*vinculum substantiale*]. The substantial bond is "a certain union, or rather a real unifier superadded to the monads by God"; it is "*something absolute* (and therefore substantial)" (G II,435/L 600). It "will not be a simple result, that is, it will not consist solely of true or real relations, but will add besides some new substantiality or substantial bond; and it will be an effect not only of the divine intellect but also of the divine will" (G II,438/AG 199)—or as we might say, it will not be a mere logical construction out of monads and the relations of their perceptions. At least naturally, a substantial bond does not unite spatially scattered monads; it unites "monads that are under the domination of one, or that make one organic body or one Machine of nature" (G II,438f./AG 199; cf. G II,486/L 609). And each substantial bond is permanently attached to a single dominant monad (G II,496/L 611).

It is only by the order of nature, however, and not by absolute necessity, that the substantial bond must have these relations with monads. Supernaturally and miraculously, God can separate the bond from the monads, and "can make it correspond to monads that were not previously its own" (G II,495f./L 610f.; cf. G II,516/AG 202). These supernatural effects may occur in transubstantiation, which Leibniz proposed to explain in terms of "the substantial bond of the body of Christ" coming to unite the monads of the bread and wine in place of the substantial bonds of bread and wine (G II,459/L 607), though groups of the monads thus united may be widely separated in space, and the phenomena of the bread and wine are unchanged.

The conception of the substantial bond includes some of the properties that Leibniz had previously ascribed to the dominant monad, or to its entelechy. Its presence in a subject is likened to that of a substantial form (G II,504/L 614). More accurately, no doubt, "the very substantial form of the composite, and the primary matter taken in the scholastic sense, that is, the primitive power, active and passive," are said to inhere in the substantial bond (G II,516/AG 202), which apparently "ought to consist in the primitive active and passive power of the composite" (G II,485f./L 609). "This bond will be the source [*principium*] of the actions of the composite substance" (G II,503/L 613). Above all, "the unity of a corporeal substance" arises "from a superadded substantial bond" (G II,451/L 604).

Unlike any monad, however, the substantial bond is metaphysically acted on by other finite things. It does not change anything in the monads (G II,451,517/L 604, AG 203), for that would be contrary to their nature. But it unites them by being influenced by them (G II,495f./L 610f.). Also "it will be necessary that the accidents of the composite be its [the substantial bond's] modifications" (G II,486/L 609).

"If that substantial bond of monads were absent, all bodies with all their qualities would be nothing but well-founded phenomena, like the rainbow or the image in a mirror" (G II,435/L 600). But if there were substantial bonds, then corporeal substance would be "something making phenomena real outside of Souls" (G II,451/L 604; cf. G II,519/AG 205). Among the phenomena made real are not only bodies but their properties of continuity and extension (G II,517/AG 203; cf. pp. 242–43).

The question of the extent to which Leibniz personally accepted this theory of substantial bonds is extremely controversial. Some interpreters have taken the theory straightforwardly as a part of his philosophy in its final form. The majority view, however, is typified by Russell's statement, "Thus the *vinculum substantiale* is rather the concession of a diplomatist than the creed of a philosopher."[48] Several reasons can be given for not taking the theory of substantial bonds very seriously as a part of Leibniz's thought.

1. The most important is that it is blatantly inconsistent with other parts of his philosophy. It postulates something ultimately real in things besides "simple substances, and in them perception and appetite" (cf. G II,270/L 537). It also grants a real, as opposed to ideal or phenomenal, existence to continuous exten-

[48]Russell, *Philosophy of Leibniz*, p. 152. For a useful survey of the history of interpretation to 1960, see Mathieu, *Leibniz e Des Bosses*, pp. 12–25.

sion. Both of these positions are emphatically rejected in many places in Leibniz's writings, late as well as early (e.g., in G III,622f. and E 745f., written in 1714 and 1716, respectively).[49]

2. Russell says that "nowhere does Leibniz himself assert that he believes" the doctrine of substantial bonds.[50] This could be disputed. In a letter of 16 January 1716 he says to Des Bosses:

> And in this I judge that I certainly agree with the Scholastics, and that their primary matter and substantial form [are] the primitive powers, passive and active respectively, of the composite; and the complete thing resulting from them I judge to be in fact that substantial bond that I am urging. (G II,511)

This can easily be read as an endorsement of the doctrine, but it need not be. The statement is about the relation of substantial bonds to Scholastic metaphysics, and does not address the question of the relation of that metaphysics to the real world. It does imply that he is "urging" the substantial bonds, but that could mean only that he is urging them as preferable to nonsubstantial, merely modal bonds. That preference is something that he certainly is urging on Des Bosses, whereas he usually speaks of the substantial bonds in a rather tentative way that seems to leave open the alternative hypothesis that there are no bonds at all and bodies are in fact only phenomena. He even explicitly expresses to Des Bosses some preference for the phenomenalistic view (G II,461; cf. G II,450/L 604).

3. A particularly important indication of Leibniz's intentions is found in a passage, cited by Russell, from Leibniz's letter of 30 June 1715 to Des Bosses:

> Whether my latest answer about Monads will have pleased you, I hardly know. I fear that the things I have written to you at different times about this subject may not cohere well enough among themselves, since, you know, I have not treated this theme, of Phenomena to be elevated to reality, or of composite substances, except on the occasion of your letters. (G II,499)

The theme [*argumentum*] mentioned in this text is certainly the theory of substantial bonds. Leibniz is telling Des Bosses, in effect, that he has not thought enough about it and does not have the ideas clearly enough in mind to be confident that he has been consistent in what he has said about it from one letter to another. Whatever may have seemed plausible to Leibniz in those hours that he spent writing to Des Bosses, a theory that he did not "treat" except in this correspondence, that he did not keep clearly in mind, and that is blatantly inconsistent with important doctrines that he asserted in many other places and continued to assert during this period of his life, cannot be counted as a part of his philosophy.[51]

[49]One text outside the Des Bosses correspondence from 1715, a letter to Nicolas Rémond, contains an ambiguous reference to "the metaphysical union of the soul and its body, which makes them compose *unum per se*, an animal, a living thing" (G III,658). But this must be balanced against the flat statement, "I believe that the whole universe of Creatures consists only in simple substances or Monads, and in Assemblages of them" (G III,622), in a document written for Rémond the previous year but not sent to him, clearly because (as suggested in the text, G III,624) Leibniz feared it might scandalize.

[50]Russell, *Philosophy of Leibniz*, p. 152.

[51]Something like the substantial bond is discussed briefly, but without clear commitment to its existence, in a document outside the Des Bosses correspondence, written probably a few months

There is quite a range of attitudes, however, that one can have as a philosopher toward ideas that are not a part of one's own philosophy. One may be sure they are false. One may be afraid they may be true or wish they were true. One may think they present an intriguing or perhaps even promising alternative to some of one's own views. One may play more or less seriously with the thought of trying to incorporate them into one's philosophy. One may be completely confident of the correctness of one's own theories; but if not, if one is worried about their adequacy in some respect, that will affect one's interest in alternative theories.

In trying to discover Leibniz's attitude toward the theory of substantial bonds, we must form some assessment of his motives in discussing it with Des Bosses. Russell's claim that the *vinculum substantiale* is "the concession of a diplomatist" reflects a cynical assessment. It is based on the idea that the theory "springs from Leibniz's endeavour to reconcile his philosophy with the dogma of Transubstantiation."[52] Not that he meant at this stage in his life to accept the dogma. As a Lutheran, he was quite frank with Des Bosses that he did not accept it (G II,399), but "he was extremely anxious to persuade Catholics that they might, without heresy, believe in his doctrine of monads," suggests Russell.[53]

Leibniz was certainly capable of concealing part of his position in order to make the rest of it more palatable to others. He even left behind some indication from his earlier years that he believed in doing so (A VI,iii,573f.). But there are at least three reasons for regarding Russell's explanation of Leibniz's motives as implausible.

First, I must record my own impression that Leibniz is comparatively candid, rather than cautious, in his letters to Des Bosses. It is worth noting that the more phenomenalistic aspects of Leibniz's thought find much fuller expression

after this letter (VE 1083f., 1086 = LH IV,8,60–61—a set of notes on a Jesuit metaphysical treatise). The Leipzig *Acta Eruditorum* for August 1715 (p. 376) contains a brief note interpreting Leibniz's intentions in what he said about Eucharistic theology in his *Theodicy*. It states that Leibniz "rejects some bond or third [thing] superadded to things . . . as a modification connecting the things to be united, whether a local modification of inclusion or adhesion, or a hypostatic one like that [connecting] soul and body, [or] the word and humanity [in Christ], or another modification analogous to these, since this would be to multiply Beings beyond necessity and involve oneself in Philosophical perplexities," and perhaps in conclusions contrary to Lutheran teaching. Louis Dutens, who reprinted it in his edition of Leibniz's works, held that this note was composed by Leibniz himself (Dutens I,32). Robinet (*Architectonique disjonctive*, p. 85) takes the document as revealing "Leibniz's hostility towards the '*vinculum*'." But the bond discussed in the note would be a "modification," and hence is hardly the substantial bond of the Des Bosses correspondence. The note was printed without indication of title or author. It begins in the voice of the journal's editors, who say that it is inserted at the request of the Lutheran theologian Christopher Matthäus Pfaff (except that they give his first name, erroneously, as "Christian"). Pfaff had charged in print that Leibniz misrepresented Lutheran Eucharistic theology. Now, "better instructed about the mind of the Illustrious Author," he wished a correction to be published. On the most natural reading of this note, it gives *Pfaff's* interpretation of Leibniz. No doubt it insinuates that the interpretation is based on conversation or correspondence with Leibniz, but we have reason to mistrust Pfaff's understanding of such communications (see Chapter 1, section 4). Still it is likely enough that Leibniz said to Pfaff that Lutheran Eucharistic theology has no need of superadded bonds.

[52]Russell, *Philosophy of Leibniz*, p. 151.

[53]Russell, *Philosophy of Leibniz*, p. 152.

in them than they do in his publications and his letters to most correspondents, though he gave a fuller endorsement of such views to some others than he did to Des Bosses. Second, the theory of substantial bonds was proposed by Leibniz, not forced on him by Des Bosses, though the term 'bond' [*vinculum*] in this context does have resonance with Jesuit metaphysics of the seventeenth century.[54] Indeed, Des Bosses showed a rather persistent preference for accidental or modal bonds, against which Leibniz had to defend his substantial bonds. And Des Bosses did not react with horror to the phenomenalistic alternatives offered by Leibniz. If the *vinculum substantiale* was a concession, it was not in any simple way a concession to Des Bosses. Third, except in one of Leibniz's letters, neither he nor Des Bosses seems to have believed that the doctrine of transubstantiation could not be accommodated without the substantial bonds. Leibniz did once say that he could hardly see how the dogma could be "sufficiently explained by mere monads and phenomena" (G II,460). But he subsequently proposed two different theories of transubstantiation based on the assumption that only monads and their phenomena exist (G II,474,520f./L 607f., AG 206), and the availability of these theories did not seem to diminish his interest in substantial bonds.

Des Bosses also proposed to Leibniz a theory of transubstantiation based on "the Hypothesis of bodies reduced to Phenomena" (G II,453-55). He did not endorse this theory, but he liked it better, in one way at least, than Leibniz's substantial bond theory of transubstantiation. In Leibniz's theory the substantial bonds of the sacramental bread and wine, or of the corporeal substances contained in them, are miraculously destroyed, but the monads of the bread and wine endure and are miraculously united to the substantial bonds of the body of Christ. Des Bosses objected to the survival of the monads of the bread and wine as inconsistent with "the dogma of the Church . . . that the whole substance of the bread and wine perish" (G II,463; cf. G II,474,480). In Des Bosses's theory based on monads and phenomena alone, the monads of the bread and wine are destroyed and the monads of the body of Christ take their place. Leibniz was averse, of course, to the destruction of monads, but Des Bosses forced him to admit in the end that the destruction of substantial bonds would be just as unnatural (G II,481f.).

5.4 *Conclusions*

There is more than one alternative, of course, to a cynical reading of Leibniz's discussion of substantial bonds. Was he simply playing with ideas in letters to a good friend? Was he seriously tempted by the idea of a superadded union, if not yet ready to accept it? I have come to believe that the *Theodicy*'s "Preliminary Discourse on the Conformity of Faith with Reason" provides an important key to understanding here. Using a traditional distinction, Leibniz there contrasts beliefs that are *above reason*, "which cannot be comprehended, and for which one cannot give a reason," with beliefs that are *against reason*, which are

[54]Boehm, *Le "vinculum substantiale"*—a very useful book, though Boehm takes remarkably little note of the reasons for denying that the doctrine of the *vinculum* was part of Leibniz's philosophy.

"opposed by invincible reasons, or whose contradictory can indeed be proved in an exact and solid way" (T pd60). Leibniz approves of the former and disapproves of the latter. More precisely, he grants that faith, or theology, may need to assert some things that are above reason.

This idea can be seen at work in Leibniz's response to Tournemine. A superadded union of soul and body is beyond our comprehension; "an intelligible Notion has not even been given of it" (G VI,595/AG 197). And Leibniz cannot give a reason for it because it "cannot be explained from Phenomena and does not change anything in them" (G II,371/L 598). It is thus metaphysical in a more nonempirical way than the substantial forms that Leibniz thinks we can understand on the model of our own soul, and for which he argues as providing the best (metaphysical) explanation of phenomena, though they are of no use in explaining the (physical) *detail* of phenomena. Nonetheless, Leibniz *does not deny* that there is such a thing as a superadded union. And he explicitly invokes here the religious concept of *mystery* (G VI,596/AG 197, quoted earlier in section 5.2), in a way that I take to imply that the belief in a superadded union of soul and body is above reason but not against reason. Similarly, in the letters to Des Bosses, the hypothesis of substantial bonds is introduced under the condition, "if faith drives us to corporeal substances" (G II,435/L 600), that is, as something that could be accepted if theologically required.

The ideas of mystery, and of beliefs that are above reason, introduce into Leibniz's thought a category of what might be called *problematic* concepts. I deliberately borrow this term from Kant,[55] because the concepts that Leibniz thus admits have three important features in common with Kant's problematic concepts. (1) Our understanding of them is limited by their comparative unrelatedness to our experience. (2) Their objective reality can be neither proved nor disproved by reason. And (3) they are particularly important for the philosophy of religion. Of course, there are also important differences. The way in which experience is important for understanding is different for Kant and Leibniz, and more of the concepts that are important for both philosophers are problematic for Kant than for Leibniz.

There is plenty of evidence that Leibniz thought such problematic concepts would have to be used in doctrines to which he was committed, as he was not committed to transubstantiation.[56] The most important of these is the doctrine of the incarnation, and the problematic concept involved there is a concept of union, the union of the divine and human natures in Christ. Leibniz wrote to Des Bosses, 10 October 1712:

> If an account could be thought out for explaining the possibility of your transubstantiation even with bodies reduced to phenomena alone, I would much prefer that. For that Hypothesis pleases in many ways. Nor do we need any other thing besides Monads and their modifications, for Philosophy as opposed to the supernatural. But I fear that we cannot explain the mystery of the Incarnation, and other things, unless real bonds or unions are added. (G II,461)

[55]Kant, *Critique of Pure Reason*, A 254 = B 310.

[56]I gave more emphasis to this point, and developed it more fully, with some citations and quotations not used here, in "Phenomenalism and Corporeal Substance in Leibniz," pp. 253f.

Here Leibniz seems quite clear that he would accept "real bonds and unions" over and above "Monads and their modifications" only to account for supernatural things. He also seems to think that such a problematic concept is more likely to be needed for the doctrine of the Incarnation, which he does accept, than for that of transubstantiation, which he does not accept. So far as I know, he never proposed to account for the union of the divine and human natures in Christ on the basis of the pre-established harmony or any other feature of his monadology. This gives him theologically compelling grounds for accepting a problematic conception of that union. It does not give him similarly compelling grounds for accepting the much less localized compromise of his monadology that would come with substantial bonds or superadded unions uniting monads to form ordinary organic bodies or corporeal substances.

Still, it might be argued, if one is forced to use a problematic conception of union in a theological special case, there would be a certain economy in using it to solve problems more widely. This thought seems to have occurred to Leibniz, as evidenced by a theological fragment, not addressed to anyone, in which he says that

> everything can be explained by adding one thing to those things that can be explained by phenomena: namely [by adding] the *union* of God with the creature in the incarnation; of the soul with the body to make the *suppositum* of the human being; of the monads among themselves to make the secondary substance or organic body. Hence also metaphysical action, by which the actions of this composite are the actions of the soul. Thus only the action of union is something inexplicable which, joined to inexplicable[57] things that are sufficient for the phenomena, is also suffient for revelation. (RML 414)

This is a relatively isolated text, however, and there is no evidence that Leibniz thought that the problematic conception of a superadded union forming a merely created body or corporeal substance was required for any theological doctrine to which he was committed. It was therefore open to him to deny, as I have noted that he did to the end of his life, that there is anything in the created world over and above monads and their modifications (G III,622f.; E 745f.). At the same time he seems to have wished to leave it open to others, particularly Catholics, to use such a conception in developing their theological doctrines.

At the beginning of section 5.2 I distinguished a negative concession and a positive hypothesis in Leibniz's response to Tournemine. Like Leibniz himself and most of his interpreters, I have devoted most attention to the positive hypothesis of superadded unions or bonds forming corporeal substances. But I actually believe that the negative concession, that the per se unity of a corporeal substance cannot be explained by monads and pre-established harmony, is more disturbing for our understanding of Leibniz's philosophy.

The concession is repeated several times in the letters to Des Bosses, in the form of statements that without substantial bonds there would be no corporeal (or, more often, "composite") substances because the monads and their subordination would not be enough to confer unity per se (G II,435f.,444,511/L 600,602). Had Leibniz therefore abandoned his oft-repeated claim that the

[57]I take this word to have been written by mistake in place of "explicable."

dominant monad is the principle of unity that makes a corporeal substance one per se? It is not clear that he had. Important evidence on the subject is found in § 3 of *The Principles of Nature and of Grace* (1714). It contains two statements which, as first drafted, unambiguously express Leibniz's earlier view of the unity of a corporeal substance, but which are both more ambiguous in their final form.

The first of them originally said of "each simple Substance or Monad" that it "constitutes the center of a composite substance (as, for example, an animal) and the principle of its unity [*unité*]." Leibniz then changed *unité* to *unicité* [unicity], a word very rare in French of that period, and underlined it. *Unicité* should mean "uniqueness," but it might also be read as implying unity;[58] there is no reason to expect a comment about uniqueness in the context. The first version clearly implies that the dominant monad is the principle of unity of a composite substance; the final version leaves it ambiguous whether that is so.

The other statement originally read, "But there is a perfect *harmony*, *pre-established* from the beginning, between the perceptions of the soul and the movements of the body; and that is what the union of the soul and the body consists in." In the final version the second clause reads, "and that is what the agreement and the physical union of the soul and the body consists in, without one being able to change the laws of the other." The first version clearly asserts a pre-established harmony theory of the union of soul and body; the insertion of "physical" in the final version leaves open the hypothesis that there is a further, metaphysical union that is not explained by the harmony, though there is no explicit suggestion of such a hypothesis in the text. A similar ambiguity is present in the *Monadology* when Leibniz says of the pre-established harmony, "These principles have given me the means of explaining naturally the union, or alternatively [*ou bien*] the agreement of the Soul and the organic body" (Mon 78).

The initial formulations of the statements in PNG 3 reflect Leibniz's old account in which the dominant monad is the principle of unity of a composite substance whose unity is explained in terms of the pre-established harmony. The likeliest explanation of his having begun to write in that way is that this view still prevailed in his own thinking about corporeal substance. The final text does not reject this view, but leaves open, for readers who may be so inclined, possibilities of a less reductionist metaphysics of union.

Unequivocal endorsements of the harmony account of the unity of a corporeal substances are certainly hard to find in the writings of Leibniz's last years, though the evidence we have surveyed suggests that he still preferred it to less reductionistic alternatives. Why did he not defend it more vigorously? I know of no evidence that he had encountered or constructed a developed refutation of it that would have been persuasive to him; and I have argued in section 5.1 that he could have given a fairly powerful defense of it, in Scholastic terms, using a distinction between complete and incomplete substances.

This puzzle must be linked with another. The concept of corporeal or composite substance, while by no means absent from Leibniz's later writings out-

[58]There is no entry for *unicité* in the 1694 dictionary of the French Academy. Seventeenth-century use of the corresponding English word 'unicity', as recorded in the *Oxford English Dictionary*, does suggest implications of unity.

side of the Des Bosses correspondence, is noticeably less prominent there than in his writings of the 1680s and 1690s about the philosophy of body. There is no mention of composite substance or corporeal substance, as such, in the *Monadology*, for instance. It is clear from PNG 3 that Leibniz had not totally abandoned the concept, but he was quite prepared to give an account of the corporeal world without using it.

I believe these puzzling facts are best explained in terms of a distinction between what is autonomous and what is heteronomous in Leibniz's rehabilitation of Scholastic Aristotelian ideas. Some of his views about substantial forms were certainly autonomous. He had real personal convictions favoring an infinite multitude of substantial unities, and the metaphysical centrality of perception and force, which we shall explore in the next chapter. But I think Leibniz never had a deep personal commitment to the view that there are corporeal substances, one per se. His attempt to find a place for that idea in his philosophy was heteronomous, an accommodation to traditionalist concerns of others, especially Roman Catholics. So when he found that those others did not feel their concerns satisfied by his account of corporeal substance, he had little reason to insist on it.

11

Form and Matter in Leibniz's Middle Years

In Chapters 9 and 10 I have presented an interpretation of Leibniz according to which bodies must be reducible, metaphysically, to simple, perceiving substances and their perceptions and appetites, in accordance with Leibniz's statement of 30 June 1704 to Burcher De Volder that "There is nothing in things except simple substances, and in them perception and appetite" (G II,270/L 537). According to an important current of modern Leibniz interpretation, however, this view is characteristic of *only* the last dozen years or so of Leibniz's life, and a view of the physical world that is more realistic, less idealistic, and specifically more Aristotelian than this is presented in the works of what Daniel Garber calls Leibniz's "middle years"—roughly from the mid-1680s to about 1704.

This interpretation goes at least as far back as C. D. Broad's posthumously published lectures on Leibniz.[1] It has been given its most powerful and influential presentation to date in a long and extremely interesting paper by Garber,[2] and Garber's version of the interpretation is the one I will discuss. He calls our attention to the fact that the writings of Leibniz's middle years look much more Aristotelian than those of his last years. Particularly in his letters to Arnauld, Leibniz says nothing about simple substances as such, but much about corporeal substances, which he concludes are found everywhere in bodies. He thinks that in order to understand the possibility of corporeal substances, it is necessary to rehabilitate the Scholastic notion of substantial form. He declares to Arnauld:

> If the body is a substance, and not a simple phenomenon like the rainbow, nor a being united by accident or by aggregation like a pile of stones, it cannot consist in extension and one must necessarily conceive of something there that is called substantial form and that corresponds in some way to the soul. (LA 58)

I disagree with Garber's interpretation. More precisely, I believe that the Aristotelian elements that are undeniably present in Leibniz's thought are not inconsistent with his monadological theories, but are part of them, and that there is no major change from his middle to his later years on this point. The present

[1] Broad, *Leibniz: An Introduction*, pp. 49–92.

[2] Garber, "Leibniz and the Foundations of Physics."

chapter is not the place for a review of all the texts that bear on the interpretive issue. Some of them have already been reviewed in Chapter 10, section 3, and more will be discussed in Chapter 12. Here I will offer a more general examination of the meaning and motives of Leibniz's treatment of the Aristotelian polarity of form and matter in the works of his middle years. I believe this investigation will show that in Leibniz's thought of that period the main features of physical reality could hardly have been identified with anything but what he would later call "simple substances, and in them perception and appetite." I hope it will also illuminate the fundamental problems of modern natural philosophy with which Leibniz was wrestling.

1. Form

1.1 Form as Force

What is it in the notion of substantial form that attracted Leibniz?[3] It is common to think about both Platonic and Aristotelian forms in the context of the problem of universals in the philosophy of logic. This may lead us to think of the forms as properties. That is not entirely wrong; the form of warmth, for example, is like a property inasmuch as having it, with certain qualifications, *is* being warm.[4] But that does not make it any easier for us to grasp something that was even more important for the seventeenth century, which is that *the forms were causes*, real beings that really contribute to determining and explaining what occurs in the world.

For Aristotle the form is one of the "four causes"—the others being matter, the agent or efficient cause, and the end or goal or final cause. In the thought of the leading sixteenth- and seventeenth-century Scholastic Aristotelian Francisco Suárez, however, strictly formal causation is only a part of the causal activity of the forms; they are also efficient causes. According to Suárez, the formal causality of a substantial form consists in its union with matter to form a composite substance. Formal causality is a form's informing, or being the form of, whatever it is the form of. The effect of this causality can be described either as the composite substance itself, or as the "actuation" of the matter by the form.[5] The concept of actuation is rooted in the idea that the form and the matter with which it unites, or is able to unite, are related as the actuality and the potentiality of the very same thing. The form "actuates" the matter, then, in the sense that it converts the potentiality of the matter into the corresponding actuality or "act." And the formal causality of an accidental form is to be understood in much the same way as that of a substantial form. A substantial form is the form that makes a substance or individual thing the kind of thing it is; my substantial form, for instance, makes me a human being. Accidental forms confer other less essential properties on things.

[3]Leibniz's decision to try to rehabilitate the notion of substantial form seems to have been made in 1679, before the middle years, and I offer no account of the event. An informative and richly documented account is presented in Robinet, *Architectonique disjonctive*, ch. 5.

[4]The converse, that properties are forms, certainly does not hold in general. Some properties (privations, for example, such as blindness) are not forms and have no directly corresponding forms.

[5]Suárez, *Metaphysical Disputations*, XV,vi,7 and vii,2–3.

Of this "formal" sort of causality I find little trace in the thought of Leibniz. He rarely uses the term 'actuate' [*actuare*].[6] He explicitly recognizes it as an Aristotelian term for the actualization of a potentiality or power [*puissance*], which is conceived as a mere capacity or receptivity, in contrast with his own more robust conception of powers or forces (NE 169f.). More important, while he contrasts matter ("primary" matter) as *passive* with form as active in various transactions, he does not contrast matter as *potentiality* with form as actuality and does not seem to conceive of the being of matter as consisting in a potentiality for the actuality represented by the form. Therefore, the union of form with matter, of which he does speak, can hardly have for him the causal structure that it had for typical Scholastic Aristotelians.

As I have noted, however, Suárez also ascribed *efficient* causality to forms. The substantial form "is the principal source [*principium*] of all the actions of the subject [*suppositum*]."[7] It cannot be excluded from such a role "since it is the fount of the whole being [*esse*] and all its properties."[8] It is the active and senior partner in constituting, with the matter, the total or comprehensive "principle of operation" of the substance.[9] Accidental forms also have a part in efficient causation according to Suárez; how their role relates to that of the substantial form is a complicated story that will not be told here, since it is only for substantial forms that Leibniz seems interested in reviving the concept of form.[10]

A rough and ready presentation of a standard example may help give an idea of the causality of a substantial form as a "principle of operation." The substantial form of an oak tree is like the *property* of being an oak, insofar as having it is what makes an oak an oak. But in other ways it functions more like a control mechanism (or like DNA in modern biology[11]) than like what we would usually think of as a property. In each oak tree it is the "soul" of that individual plant. It is already present in an oak seedling, and even in an acorn, though they

[6]He does use it at G IV,395f./AG 252f. (1702), where he says that the substantial form "always naturally actuates some organic body, which itself, taken separately (that is, apart, or isolated, from the soul), is not one substance but an aggregate of many—in a word, a machine of nature." It is interesting that what is said here to be "actuated" is the "organic body," which in Leibniz's view is not primary but secondary matter. If Leibniz could view any sort of matter as having its being in a potentiality for an actualization or completion to be imparted by form, one might expect it to be primary rather than secondary matter, inasmuch as primary matter is incomplete in a way that secondary matter is not (G IV,512/L 504). Leibniz did ascribe a relevant sort of incompleteness to the organic body, however (see Chapter 10, section 2.3). In a letter of 1703 to De Volder it is the corporeal substance, rather than its matter or body, that is said to be "actuated by one Entelechy" (G II,250/L 529). These contexts present no asymmetrical actuation of matter by form, for Leibniz seems to regard the form or soul as completed by the matter or body no less than the latter by the former.

[7] Suárez, *Metaphysical Disputations*, XVIII,v,1.

[8]Suárez, *Metaphysical Disputations*, XVIII,ii,3. 'Properties' may, however, be used here in a narrower sense than is usual with us; cf. pp. 127–28.

[9]Suárez, *Metaphysical Disputations*, XV,xi,4.

[10]It may be interesting to explore analogies between the relation of primitive and derivative forces in Leibniz's thought and the relation of the causalities of substantial and accidental forms in Scholastic thought, but the former is certainly no simple translation of the latter. It is also true for Leibniz as for Suárez that (primary) matter has a part in the total operation of a substance, but, for now, our focus is on form.

[11]Cf. Furth, *Substance, Form and Psyche*, p. 119.

lack many or most of the characteristic perceivable properties of an oak tree. It (directly or indirectly) causes the acorn to sprout, and roots to grow down and foliage up and out, and bark to cover the stem. It continues to work in the mature tree, controlling its vegetative processes, keeping it alive, and keeping its leaves, and all its other parts, oak-like.

The causality of the substantial form described in this example is *immanent*—that is, it is action on the substance to which the form belongs. Perhaps this can be regarded as the primary and most characteristic causal action of substantial forms, though Scholasticism also recognized a "transeunt" action of such forms on other substances (for instance, in the generation of new substances). At any rate, it is a well-known feature of Leibniz's system that immanent causality is the only metaphysically real causality he recognized in created substances (RML 315).

Other features of the example I gave are also relevant to Leibniz's thought. The action of the substantial form in the example is teleological, aimed at developing and maintaining the form of life characteristic of a mature oak tree. I shall have more to say below about the teleological character of the action of Leibnizian substantial forms. Most important in the present context is the relation of substantial form to active power. A substantial form is not an event. The role of the form in what Suárez calls efficient causality is therefore not that of a triggering event. It appears rather that the form has an "efficient" causal role insofar as having a substantial form is or involves having certain powers and tendencies.

The concept of power or force is particularly important for Leibniz. It is already quite explicit in works of his middle years that extension and its modes (the "primary qualities," as we are accustomed to call them) belong to the phenomenal realm rather than to the ultimately real, although they do express reality more distinctly than other sensible qualities (DM 12,18; LA 119). The one thing in what we know of the physical world that is more real than extension and its modes, according to Leibniz, is force. Hence it is as a science of forces, rather than as a science of motions and other modes of extension, that physics is a study of reality; dynamics, the theory of forces, takes pride of place in Leibnizian physics.[12]

There can be no doubt that part of what Leibniz liked about substantial forms was their connection with the notion of force. Stating in the "New System" of 1695 that he had had to rehabilitate substantial forms, he goes on to say, "I found then that their nature consists in force" (E 124f./L 454). Similarly, he wrote to Joachim Bouvet in 1697 that "the forms of the Ancients or *Entelechies* are nothing but forces" (E 146/W 104). Specifically, as we shall see, the substantial forms, in the strictest sense for Leibniz, are *primitive active* forces. In thinking of substances as constituted by what he called forces, and what Suárez called a principle of operation, Leibniz explicitly, and correctly, traced the idea to Aristotle's own definition of "natures."[13]

> So when it is said that primitive force constitutes the substance of bodies, their nature or essence is understood; thus Aristotle says that the nature is the prin-

[12]Cf. Garber, "Leibniz and the Foundations of Physics," p. 90.

[13]Aristotle, *Metaphysics*, 1015^a 13–19. See T 87 for a somewhat different way in which Leibniz traced to Aristotle the connection of force with form.

ciple of motion and rest; and the primitive force is nothing but that principle in each body from which all its actions and affections[14] are born. (A I,vii,248)[15]

One of the reasons that made me employ the term force to explain the nature, the substantial form, the essence of bodies, is that it is more intelligible, and gives a more distinct idea. (A I,vii,250)

The ascription of internal, primarily active force or power to created things, as constituting their substance, is the keynote of Leibniz's disagreement with the occasionalism of Nicolas Malebranche, who ascribed genuine power or causal efficacy to God alone. The significance of the idea of internal powers in this confrontation is nicely captured in a comment by Burcher De Volder, one of Leibniz's most acute correspondents, and one inclined to occasionalism.

But not to be longer about it, it is certain that either an internal principle of changes must be acknowledged in things themselves, or we must have recourse to God. But this does not keep it from being true that I do not understand this internal principle or the way in which it operates. This difficulty of understanding an internal principle causes most to have recourse to God; and it cannot, in my opinion, be solved as it needs to be unless this principle and its way of operating are thoroughly understood. (G II,274)

I think it is not a historical eccentricity that Leibniz and many of his contemporaries saw these issues in terms of forces, powers, or, more broadly, dispositional properties. Two features of the causal order of the world are easy to see: there are many regularities (of occurrent or nondispositional fact) among observable phenomena, describable by true conditional generalizations, and these regularities obtain over time. Humeans maintain that these observable facts are all there is to the causal order of the world. If one finds that implausible (as I do), what are the alternatives?

One might ascribe some sort of metaphysical reality to the laws of nature in their own right, seeing them as freestanding features of the world that really determine what happens in it. Such an ascription of reality would not necessarily imply that the laws are substances, or in any strong sense "things." It would be enough if it were a metaphysically objective fact that these regularities *must* obtain—a fact over and above the fact that they *do* obtain, and a fact that is not *about* any object or objects in particular. But I think this is neither a very plausible approach nor one that was very influential in the seventeenth century.[16]

[14]In French, *passions*. The sense is that of the plural, if we had one, of 'being-acted-on'.

[15]The quotation is from a letter of January 1692 to Paul Pellisson-Fontanier. We should note that in this statement Leibniz is speaking not only of the substantial form in his strictest sense, in which it is only the primitive *active* force, but of the primitive active *and passive* forces of a substance, or as he would also say, the primary matter as well as the substantial form. *Together* they are the principle from which "all the actions and affections" of the substance spring. Here he is in agreement with Suárez, who also identifies the "nature," as defined by Aristotle, with a complex, the "metaphysical" substantial form, or "form of the whole," including the matter as well as the substantial form in the narrower, "physical" sense (Suárez, *Metaphysical Disputations*, XV,xi,4). It is clear, however, that for both Suárez and Leibniz, the principal or active dynamic role belongs to the substantial form in the strict sense, and not to the matter.

[16]I read Spinoza as one of those who have thought that the laws of nature are absolutely necessary, no less necessary than the laws of logic. It might be thought easier to understand how the

The idea of laws of nature was certainly becoming more prominent then in thinking about science, but there was usually in the background some idea of intentions of God or natures of created things in which the reality or effectiveness of the laws would be located.

If there is more to the causal order of the world than just the observable regularities of nondispositional fact, and if the laws of nature are not freestanding features of the world, it remains that there must be a feature (or features) of one or more objects or substances by virtue of which the regularities of nature obtain. It is reasonable to suppose that this will be an enduring feature of enduring things, since the regularities obtain over time. On the most influential and, I think, the most plausible accounts, it is a dispositional property of the things to which it belongs—a power or tendency or perhaps a liability. The main alternative I can see for non-Humeans would be an occurrent, primitive, real relation of cause and effect; but this would help less in accounting for the regularities of nature and would provide no ground at all for facts, in which most of us believe, about what would have happened in circumstances somewhat different from those that are actual. It is not surprising that the idea of powers has a perennial appeal and seems now to be regaining popularity with philosophers who wish to be realists about causation.

If we can at least appreciate the appeal of such a realism about powers, we may also be able to gain some insight into Leibniz's reasons for holding that there must be real powers or forces not only in God but also in created substances. For if a thing does have enduring powers, and especially if the powers determine the characteristics of the thing over time in accordance with some rule, that can be seen as unifying the thing metaphysically over time, making it an enduring thing or substance. Leibniz seems indeed to have favored a criterion of identity that assigns states to the same individual substance if and only if they are caused by the same individual causal nexus (or the same substantial form, in the favored terminology of his middle years). Due to Leibniz's denial of real causal interaction between created substances, this criterion will not, in his system, assign the same state to two different created individuals.[17] There is evidence that Leibniz also believed (rightly or wrongly) that without such individual

---

laws of nature could be "free-standing" if they are absolutely necessary. In fact, however, Spinoza regarded the necessity of the laws of nature as grounded metaphysically in the nature of God (see, e.g., *Ethics* I, prop. 33).

Paul Hoffman has pointed out to me that Descartes calls some laws of nature "secondary and particular causes of the diverse motions we notice in individual bodies" (AT VIII-1,62: *Principles* II,37). But I think that is compatible with Descartes's not supposing the laws to have any reality outside the intentions and operations of God. The most fundamental law of the conservation of motion has been explained (AT VIII-1,61f.: *Principles* II,36) as an expression of the immutability of God's operation. The quoted statement seems not to apply to that law, but is explicitly about laws that are also said to be known "from the same immutability of God" (*Principles* II,37). Descartes states, moreover, that the cause of these laws is "the immutability and simplicity of the operation by which God conserves motion in matter" (AT VIII-1,63: *Principles* II,39). It must be granted that this interpretation pushes Descartes in an occasionalist direction in which he may not have wished to go. But I think it is fair to say at least that the idea that the laws of nature have metaphysical reality in their own right, as distinct from powers and properties of God and particular creatures, is neither unambiguously nor articulately present in Descartes.

[17]See Chapter 3, for sources and a fuller discussion of this criterion.

causal principles of transtemporal unity, created things could not be unified over time and, as he says, would be merely "evanescent or fleeting modifications and phantasms, so to speak, of the one permanent divine substance" (G IV,508/L 502; cf. G III,575).[18]

Thus Leibniz believed that any substance has to have within it an enduring power or powers, a continuing center of immanent causal activity that unifies it and constitutes it as the substance it is. This is an important part of the role that it had typically been supposed that substantial forms play. If we begin to speculate about *how* this immanent causal activity takes place, additional aspects of the notion of substantial form come to the fore.

1.2 Form as Law

Suppose that, as Leibniz believed, the laws of nature are not freestanding features of the world, but the regularities described by the laws are to be explained by real powers in created things, which Leibniz called substantial forms. Since it remains that the regularities are a major part of what is to be explained, it follows, I think, that the powers must be, at least in part, dispositions to act in accordance with laws that describe or predict the regularities. In this sense, the laws must be incorporated in the substantial forms, and having the form must involve at least the functional equivalent of a sensitivity to whatever logical and mathematical structures or relationships are involved in the satisfaction or nonsatisfaction of the laws. For instance, if a mathematical law of universal gravitational attraction is a *fundamental* law of nature (as Leibniz denied and even Newton would not affirm), then the substantial form or inherent powers of every material thing would have to involve a disposition to behave according to that law, with responsiveness to the relevant mathematical relationships (e.g., of mass and distance) in which it might stand.

At this point I think Leibniz picks up an important strand in Aristotle's conception of form. The form as cause, said Aristotle, "is the *logos* of what it is to be [the thing in question], and the kinds to which this belongs . . . and the parts that are in the *logos*."[19] *Logos* is difficult to translate, as is *ratio*, its usual equivalent in Scholastic Latin. It can signify a linguistic expression, a thought expressible in language, or the content intended by either. In some contexts it seems to mean an explanation or reason. "The *logos* of what it is to be"[20] something would normally mean a definition, and form is closely related to *logos* in this sense for

[18]This forms Leibniz's sharpest attack on occasionalism, explicitly suggesting (G IV,509/L 502) that it leads to the pantheism of Spinoza. It is interesting that a formulation of occasionalism in Malebranche's *Search after Truth* (VI,ii,3: p. 448) practically invites this charge. Malebranche claims that "the nature or force of each thing is nothing but the will of God" (OM II,312). Malebranche was not a pantheist, but there might seem to be a perilously short step from describing the divine will as the *nature* of all things to regarding God as the *substance* of all things.

[19]Aristotle, *Physics* 194^b26–29 = *Metaphysics* 1013^a26–29. Commenting on this passage in his *Metaphysical Disputations*, XV,v,2, Suárez thinks it must be understood with some qualification as to what the form is the *logos* or *ratio* of, but he does not question the close connection between the concepts of form and *logos* or *ratio*.

[20]"What it is to be" is a more literal translation of an expression very common in Aristotle that is usually rendered as "the essence [of]."

Aristotle.[21] The form thus incorporates what we could call, broadly speaking, a logical structure, or the sort of thing that is the object of rational thought; and it is indeed by receiving forms that the mind understands, according to Aristotle.[22]

Now a law of nature is not exactly a definition, but it is, broadly speaking, a *logos* or *ratio*, a rationally intelligible content. Leibniz recognized that for Aristotle the form is a *ratio* or *logos* (A VI,ii,189,247). And as a *logos* could be for Aristotle a causally efficacious feature of the forms in things, so for Leibniz laws of nature are incorporated in the substantial forms of things. Indeed, he is prepared to identify the forms with laws. In "On Nature Itself" he indicates that "the law established by God leaves some trace of itself expressed in things," and this is the "form or force" in things that is called "nature" (G IV,507/L 501). Further on he says there must be "a soul, or a form analogous to a soul, or the first entelechy; that is, a certain effort [*nisus*] or primitive force of action which is itself the implanted law impressed by divine decision [*decretum*]" (G IV,512/L 504). In letters to De Volder he speaks of "the primitive force" of a substance as a "law" (G II,262/L 533). The idea can be found in his work, though without mention of "form," as early as 1676: "The essence of substances consists in the primitive force to act, or in the law of the sequence of changes, like the nature of the *series* in numbers" (A VI,iii,326/L 155).[23]

One of the most interesting Leibnizian texts on this point is the *Discourse on Metaphysics*, even though the substantial forms are not explicitly called "laws" in it.[24] In DM 10, rather, Leibniz says that ancient and medieval philosophers introduced substantial forms because they "had some knowledge of" what he had just been saying, which is that each individual substance has a complete concept from which all its predicates follow and is therefore "like a whole world" and "expresses, albeit confusedly, everything that happens in the universe, past, present, or future" (DM 8–9). Thus the substantial forms are closely connected with the complete individual concept. They are, I think, that *in* the substance which is expressed by the concept, and which Leibniz in the *Discourse* does not trouble to distinguish from the concept of the individual. This is of interest here because the complete individual concept is clearly a *logos* or logical structure or rationally intelligible content, and it is a *logos* that is expressed in real causal relationships. In DM 8–9 and 14 Leibniz seems to be arguing that *because* all the predicates of an individual substance, and hence all the events in which that substance will ever be involved, follow *logically* from its complete concept, therefore each substance is "like a whole world" or "like a world apart, independent of every other thing except God," and everything that happens to it is only a

[21] See Aristotle, *De Anima* 414^a4–14; *Metaphysics* 996^b8, 1035^a21, 1044^b12ff. Also relevant is the association of form with essence (= what it is to be *x*) in *Metaphysics* 1032^b1, 1035^b32, 1044^a36, and of soul with *logos, De Anima* $412^{9ff.}$

[22] See especially Aristotle, *De Anima* 429^a10–29.

[23] This translation of the last phrase seems to me to make the most sense. Leroy Loemker's translation, "as the nature of the *series* consists in the numbers" (L 155), is also possible. Another text in which "the primitive force of acting" seems to be treated as equivalent to "the law of the sequence of changes" dates probably from 1685 or shortly thereafter (RML 75).

[24] In DM 14, however, the "certain reasons or laws" that each substance carefully follows are surely connected with the substantial form. The text leaves open the question whether they are to be *identified* with it.

consequence of its "being." In other words, a real causal connection is inferred from, and presumably explained by, a logical connection.

Interpreters have treated this reasoning primarily as an argument for Leibniz's thesis of the mutual causal independence of created substances, and hence for the preestablished harmony. It is that, of course, but Garber in a very illuminating note points out that it is also an argument against occasionalism. He suggests indeed that Leibniz's principal purpose in introducing his theory of complete individual concepts in DM 8 was "to refute occasionalism and establish that individuals are genuine sources of activity." The context supports Garber's reading, for "DM 1–7 deals with God as cause, and DM 8 is presented as dealing with how 'to distinguish the actions of God from those of creatures'."[25] All these considerations confirm that substantial forms are seen in the *Discourse* first of all as internal sources of (immanent) causal action in created substances, and that their action is seen there as based on their incorporating a *logos* or logical structure or intelligible content that can be identified with laws of nature.

1.3 Form as Soul

Another aspect of Aristotelian theories of substantial form is rich in suggestions as to how the immanent causal action of such forms works. For the substantial form of a living thing was identified with its soul. In some cases this may not help us much in understanding how substantial forms work. Speaking of the "soul" of a plant, though important to Aristotelian theories of life, will not have much point for Leibniz or other modern philosophers, apart from a more general theory of soul or substantial form. The major source of illumination here for Leibniz is that in our own case we are privileged to witness the operation of a substantial form "from the inside," so to speak, if our substantial form is indeed our soul.

This possibility for interpreting the action of substantial forms may not have been generally exploited by Aristotelians, but it clearly was seized upon by Leibniz. He regularly says that substantial forms are souls, or like souls. At his first mention of substantial form in his correspondence with Antoine Arnauld, for example, he says that it "corresponds in some way to the soul" (LA 58). Our own minds are the only substantial forms that we have experienced (LA 121). Particularly illuminating is his introduction of substantial forms in the "New System" (1695):

> I found then that their nature consists in force, and that from this there follows something analogous to sensation and appetite, so that they must be conceived on the model of the concept that we have of *Souls*. (E 124f./L 454)

The causal character of substantial forms, Leibniz seems to be saying, their nature as force, implies that they are like souls and have something like sensation and appetite. The suggestion, I think, is that our experience of perceptual and appetitive functions in our own conscious selves is our best clue for understanding how the immanent causal action of substantial forms works. "If you have a clear idea of the soul, you will have one also of form," as Leibniz wrote to John Bernoulli in 1698 (GM III,552).

[25]Garber, "Leibniz and the Foundations of Physics," pp. 122f. (n. 166).

There are many other indications that Leibniz believed this. The intent to use our own experience of perception to explicate the notion of substantial form is clear in 1703 when, in response to Lady Masham's complaint that she found "no positive idea" of the essence of "what you call a *Form*, *Soul*, or *Atome de Substance*," Leibniz wrote, "The *positive Idea* of that simple substance or primitive Force is completely discovered, since it must always have in it an ordered progression of perceptions, according to the Analogy that it must have with our soul" (G III,350,356).[26] To Arnauld he wrote that substantial unity requires an entity whose "concept contains everything that is to happen to it, which cannot be found either in shape or in motion . . . but rather in a soul or substantial form after the example of what one calls *self* [*moi*]" (LA 76; cf. LA 72,78).

Extension and its modes, such as shape and motion, Leibniz seems to be saying in this statement to Arnauld, cannot encode enough information to predict the future or retrodict the past. But how could he believe that? Surely he was enough of a mechanistic determinist in physics to think that from the sizes, shapes, positions, and motions of all bodies in any brief period of time, together with the laws of motion, all past and future states of the physical universe follow. The key point here involves the laws of motion. Extension and its modes do not encode the laws of motion, and the laws must be added in order to generate any reliable prediction or retrodiction. It is not enough, Leibniz thought, for a substance to have a present state; it must also contain or encode the laws that connect that state with past and future states.

The expressive capacity of souls is much greater than that of the modes of extension.[27] Leibniz held, of course, that souls are expressed by their bodies. But I take it he thought that whereas what is expressed can be read off the bodies only with the aid of a code of laws that are not contained in them, the laws are already in the souls. Souls express by their perceptions. Since thoughts are counted among perceptions for Leibniz, we know from our own experience that it is possible for perceptions to represent both laws of nature and past and future states of affairs. This is certainly suggested in the *Discourse on Metaphysics*. Leibniz says that every substance "expresses, albeit confusedly, everything that happens in the universe, past, present, or future," and that this "bears some resemblance to an infinite perception or knowledge" (DM 9). The model of intentional following of rules understood is used in explaining the preestablished harmony when he speaks of each substance "following carefully certain reasons or laws that it has observed" (DM 14). Later, in 1702, Leibniz explicitly invokes the soul's advantage of memory for encoding laws (G IV,543f.). This helps explain how he could think that a law of nature which is a *logos* or intelligible content is effectually incorporated in a concrete substance as its substantial form.

For further explanation of the efficacy or force of laws within substances, we may turn to the concept of appetite, which, as we have seen, is linked with sensation, in the "New System," as the sort of thing that substantial forms must

[26]On the use of psychological notions to explicate the idea of force, see also G II,270/L 537 (1704), quoted and discussed in section 2.1.1 in this chapter, and Leibniz's approval of a similar move in Locke (NE 170f.).

[27]On the thought developed in this paragraph, cf. Sleigh, *Leibniz and Arnauld* pp. 132–34.

have in order to have force. I take it that Leibniz thought of *perceptions* as encoding the laws of nature (as well as other data), and of *appetites* as tendencies to act in accordance with the laws and data encoded. Leibniz never said as much about appetite as about perceptions, but at the end of his life, he explained the function of appetite by saying that "Souls act according to the laws of final causes by appetitions, ends, and means," and that "the Action of the internal principle that makes the change or the passage from one perception to another can be called *Appetition*" (Mon 79, 15). Appetition, as the name suggests, is a *teleological* principle of action: The idea that substantial forms act for an end is present, along with the idea of appetite, in writings of Leibniz's middle years (VE 642f./L 289; G VII,451/L 472). This certainly picks up another theme of Aristotelian thought, in which the operation of substantial forms typically has a teleological character.

In one respect, however, the language of "appetite" and "ends and means" may be somewhat misleading. It suggests the pursuit of a desired future state of affairs, but the action of a Leibnizian substantial form is more like what is sometimes called "acting on principle." In Leibniz's view the "internal principle" governing "the passage [of a substance] from one perception to another" is not based on the desirability of the later perception in itself, but rather on the following of certain laws of nature.[28] If souls or substantial forms in general act for the sake of "the good" (cf. VE 643/L 289), the good principally in view, in the Leibnizian system, must be the harmony of the universe that is maintained by following the laws of nature.

Leibniz was by no means eccentric in supposing that substantial forms would have to be like souls. The view was in the air in the seventeenth century. There is evidence that Descartes thought the idea of a substantial form was essentially an idea of a soul, for in a letter of 1642 he appears to endorse the views that the soul "is the true substantial form of the human being" and that the human soul "is the only substantial form" (AT III, 503, 505). There are also places where he seems to be saying that the idea of immanent action by a form (either a substantial form or a real quality) is anthropomorphic.[29] I take Descartes to be suggesting that the soul, and nothing but the soul, does indeed have something like the immanent causal action ascribed by Scholasticism to forms.

[28]DM 14. The point that the succeeding perception may not be desired for its own sake, or desirable in itself, is emphasized at G IV, 532, (a text of 1702) discussed in Chapter 10, section 4.2; a similar example is treated in essentially the same way at LA 114.

[29]The most famous of these places is that in which he writes to the Princess Elizabeth that in thinking of gravity or weight as a "real quality" which is joined to a body in such a way as to be able to move it, one misapplies to gravity a concept that "was given to us for conceiving the way in which the soul moves the body" (AT III,667f./K 139). See also passages cited by Hoffman, "Unity of Descartes's Man," p. 350. I am largely following Hoffman in this interpretation of Descartes and am also indebted to him for illuminating discussions. See also Garber, "Understanding Interaction," pp. 19–22. It should be noted that the charge of anthropomorphism has to do specifically with the idea of causation *by a form*. As Hoffman has pointed out to me, there are also passages in which Descartes seems to ascribe immanent causation, or action on itself, to a body, but without invoking the concept of form (AT VII,367; III,428). For other Cartesian references to the soul as substantial form, see Gilson, *Index scolastico-cartésien*, p. 297 (s.v. *union*).

A similar explicit association of the notion of substantial form with that of soul is found in the works of the British scientist and philosopher Robert Boyle.[30] Boyle would also agree with Leibniz that identifying the nature of a thing with a law by which it acts implies that the thing has something like a soul. For he observes that "to speak properly, a law being but a *notional rule of acting according to the declared will of a superior*, it is plain, that nothing but an intellectual Being can be properly capable of receiving and acting by a law."[31]

Boyle's observation suggests a question that may confront those who would ground in the natures of created things the actuality of natural regularities or laws of nature. How can anything be inherently responsive to a law without having some analogue of intelligence? Leibniz would solve this problem by ascribing to all substances an analogue of mentality.

Boyle is not led, like Leibniz, to postulate souls or soul-like forms in all the bodies that participate in natural regularities. Rather, he concludes that it is improper or figurative "to say, that the nature of this or that body is but *the law of God prescribed to it*."[32] Like Descartes, Boyle seems to ascribe a substantial form to human beings alone, declaring, "I know not any thing in nature that is composed of matter, and a substance distinct from matter, except man, who alone is made up of an immaterial form and a human body."[33]

It is not surprising, therefore, that in a letter of 1669, published in 1670, in which he still rejected the idea that bodies in general have substantial forms,[34] Leibniz already argued that *if* one (falsely) ascribed substantial forms to "inanimate things," it would be "more correct" to ascribe to the forms "sensation, knowledge, imagination, will," as he says Tommaso Campanella (d. 1639) and Marcus Marci (d. 1667) did.

> Certainly all those who speak of those incorporeal substances of bodies cannot explain their meaning except in terms borrowed from Minds. For hence that *natural appetite* or instinct has been ascribed to them, from which also follows natural knowledge. (A VI,ii,442/L 101; cf. A II,i,20)

[30]Robert Boyle, *The Origin of Forms and Qualities* (1666), in his *Works*, vol. 3, p. 27, said that "when any body is referred to any particular species (as of a metal, a stone, or the like) . . . most of the writers of physicks have been apt to think, that besides the common matter of all bodies, there is but one thing that discriminates it from other kinds, and makes it what it is, and this, for brevity's sake, they call a form: which because all the qualities and other accidents of the body must depend on it, they also imagine to be a very substance, and indeed a kind of soul, which, united to the gross matter, composes with it a natural body, and acts in it by the several qualities found therein, which men are wont to ascribe to the creature so composed."

[31]Boyle, *A Free Inquiry into the Vulgarly Received Notion of Nature* (1682), in *Works*, vol. 5, p. 170.

[32]Boyle, *Notion of Nature*, in *Works*, vol. 5, p. 170.

[33]Boyle, *Origin of Forms and Qualities*, in *Works*, vol. 3, p. 40.

[34]There is a document about the doctrine of transubstantiation, probably from this same period, in which Leibniz does seem to ascribe substantial forms to all bodies, but identifies the substantial form of a body with its union with a "concurrent mind"—a human mind, in the case of human bodies; the divine mind, in the case of bodies lacking reason (A VI,i,508–13/L 115–18). Since the substantial form thus ascribed to most bodies is not an internal source of causal activity, we have here only a terminological accommodation and not yet a metaphysical rehabilitation of the Scholastic idea. The mentalism of the account that is offered also tends to confirm my present argument.

This background should help us understand what was distinctive in the mature Leibniz's rehabilitation of Scholastic views about substantial forms. It was not unusual to ascribe to human beings something that could be called a "substantial form" (though the term was not particularly popular with the modern philosophers), and the view that if there are substantial forms they must all be like souls was more modern than Scholastic. Leibniz's boldness was in not restricting substantial forms to the human realm, but postulating them in every portion of matter, and accepting the consequence that this meant an infinite proliferation of soul-like entities. This was also Leibniz's own view of his agreement and disagreement with Descartes regarding substantial forms (LA 113; NE 317f.; G VI,547).

1.4 Leibniz and Cudworth

This boldness was not unparalleled. Many sixteenth- and seventeenth-century thinkers, often drawing on precedents from ancient thought, speculated about soul-like beings pervading the entire material world, including the parts of it that seem inanimate. An instructive parallel to Leibniz's thought on this point can be found in *The True Intellectual System of the Universe* (1678) of the Cambridge Platonist Ralph Cudworth (1617–88).

Cudworth speaks of a "plastic nature" created by God and acting in all material things. The plastic nature is conceived on the model of a soul in the sense of a principle of life; Cudworth defines life as "Internal *Energy* and *Self-activity*) (p. 159)."[35] He holds that the plastic nature acts "*for the sake of Ends*," but without knowledge, understanding, or even "express Consciousness," and hence without fully "intending" its ends (pp. 156–59.). Nonetheless, "he that asserts a *Plastick Nature*, asserts *Mental Causality* in the World" (p. 155); and Cudworth says "it cannot be denied but that the *Plastick Nature* hath a certain *Dull* and *Obscure Idea* of that which it Stamps and Prints upon Matter," which can be called "a kind of *Drowsie*, *Unawakened*, or *Astonish'd Cogitation* (p. 160)." Cudworth's plastic nature thus appears to be conceived on the model of a mind, but of much diminished capacity for thought or perception, like the inferior forms or monads in Leibniz's system.[36] In support of this view, indeed, Cudworth appeals to examples of habit, instinct, and bodily motions that we control without understanding them, to prove that there can be teleologically effective psychological functioning without consciousness (pp. 157f., 160f.). This is similar, in a way, to arguments Leibniz would later use to show that there can be unconscious perceptions, although the unconscious psychological function in which Cudworth is most interested is not perception but "Vital Autokinesie" (self-motion) (p. 159). In Cudworth's conception of plastic nature, indeed, as in

[35]Cudworth, *True Intellectual System of the Universe*. Parenthetical page references in the present paragraph are to this work. There are two pages numbered 155; I will refer shortly to the first of them. I give here only a very incomplete sketch of Cudworth's theory of the plastic nature.

[36]In stating the matter thus, I ignore a further complication of Cudworth's theory, for he leaves it open whether the plastic nature is in every case "a *Lower* Faculty of some *Conscious Soul*," or in some cases "an Inferiour kind of Life or *Soul* by it self, but essentially depending upon an *Higher Intellect*"—that is, on God (*True Intellectual System*, p. 172).

Aristotelian, and more broadly ancient, conceptions of soul, the idea of life is at least as fundamental as that of mentality. Leibniz, on the other hand, in this respect more Cartesian as well as more modern, relies at bottom only on decidedly mental functions, subjectively apprehended in ourselves, as models for conceiving of the activity of souls or substantial forms.

Among the functions that Cudworth ascribes to the plastic nature is the execution of the laws of nature. His argument for plastic nature makes explicit important parts of the rationale that I have suggested for Leibniz's regarding substantial forms as soul-like and incorporating laws. We find in Cudworth two ideas important to that rationale: that the alternative to occasionalism,[37] if the created world is indeed governed by laws, is real created causes that give effect to the laws; and that only a purposive, somewhat soul-like agent can execute a law of nature.[38]

> For unless there be such a thing admitted as a Plastick Nature, that acts . . . *for the sake of something*, and *in order to Ends*, Regularly, Artificially and Methodically, it seems that one or other of these Two Things must be concluded, That Either in the Efformation and Organization of the Bodies of Animals, as well as the other Phenomena, every thing comes to pass *Fortuitously*, and happens to be as it is, without the Guidance and Direction of any *Mind* or *Understanding*; Or else, that God himself doth all *Immediately*. . . . As also, though it be true that the Works of Nature are dispensed by a *Divine Law* and *Command*, yet this is not to be understood in a *Vulgar Sence*, as if they were all effected by the mere Force of a *Verbal Law* or *Outward Command*, because Inanimate things are not *Commandable* nor *Governable* by such a *Law*; and therefore besides the Divine Will and Pleasure, there must needs be some other Immediate *Agent* and *Executioner* provided, for the producing of every Effect; since not so much as a Stone or other Heavy Body, could at any time fall downward, merely by the Force of a *Verbal Law*, without any other *Efficient Cause*; but either God himself must immediately impel it, or else there must be some other subordinate Cause in Nature for that Motion. Wherefore the *Divine Law* and *Command*, by which things of Nature are administered, must be conceived to be the Real Appointment of some *Energetick*, *Effectual*, and *Operative Cause* for the Production of every Effect.[39]
>
> Wherefore since neither all things are produced Fortuitously, or by the Unguided mechanism of Matter, nor God himself may reasonably be thought to

[37]The occasionalist hypothesis plainly figures as a rejected hypothesis in Cudworth's work, though presumably without any literary dependence on Malebranche, as his daughter testified to Leibniz that Cudworth did not read French and was ignorant of the French occasionalists (G III,372).

[38]A very clear statement of these points, especially the latter one, and similar to Cudworth's, comes from the naturalist John Ray (1627–1705): "an intelligent being seems to me requisite to execute the laws of motion. . . . And as for any external laws or established rules of motion, the stupid matter is not capable of observing or taking any notice of them . . . ; neither can those laws execute themselves. Therefore there must, besides matter and law, be some efficient, and that either a quality or power inherent in the matter itself, which is hard to conceive, or some external intelligent agent, either God himself immediately or some plastic nature" [John Ray, *The Wisdom of God Manifested in the Works of Creation* (1691), quoted in Westfall, *Science and Religion in Seventeenth-Century England*, pp. 94f.] Cudworth did not regard the plastic nature as *intelligent*, however.

[39]Cudworth, *True Intellectual System*, p. 147.

> do all things Immediately and Miraculously; it may well be concluded, that there is a *Plastick Nature* under him, which as an Inferior and Subordinate Instrument, doth Drudgingly Execute that Part of his Providence, which consists in the Regular and Orderly Motion of Matter.[40]

Cudworth explicitly rejects what I have called "freestanding laws of nature," but with no suggestion that anyone might seriously advocate such a view. Those theists who reject a plastic nature, but suppose that God causes the world to be governed by laws of nature,

> must of necessity, either suppose these their *Laws* of *Motion* to execute themselves, or else be forced perpetually to concern the Deity in the Immediate Motion of every Atom of Matter throughout the Universe, in order to the Execution and Observation of them. The Former of which being a Thing plainly Absurd and Ridiculous,

we must conclude that, if these philosophers are opposed to occasionalism, they are confused, and

> their *Laws* of *Nature* concerning *Motion*, are really nothing else, but a *Plastick Nature*, acting upon the Matter of the whole Corporeal Universe, both Maintaining the Same Quantity of Motion always in it, and also Dispensing it (by Transferring it out of one Body into another) according to such Laws, Fatally Impress upon it.[41]

It is not likely that Leibniz was much influenced by Cudworth. He did not see the *True Intellectual System* until 1689.[42] To Cudworth's daughter, Damaris Masham, who sent him a copy of the book in 1703, he expressed, I would say, only a moderate appreciation for it, passing quickly to the topic of the theory of pre-established harmony that he would add to the idea of an intellectual system of the universe (G III,336). In 1705, prompted by Jean le Clerc, who was engaged in controversy with Pierre Bayle on the subject, Leibniz took another look at Cudworth's theory of the plastic nature. This time he recognized specifically that he agreed with Cudworth in postulating "principles of life" in every body, and that in this respect "substantial form" played a role for him that "plastic nature" played for Cudworth (G VI,551–53).

He dwelt more, however, on a disagreement he had with Cudworth that especially concerned "the formation of plants and animals" (G VI,543f./L 589). The occasion for this disagreement was the fact that Cudworth did not restrict the operation of the plastic nature in matter to the execution of mechanical laws, but extended it to teleologically governed productions and behaviors that he thought could not be explained mechanically, notably including the formation of organic bodies, reasoning that

> if there be a *Plastick Nature*, that governs the *Motions* of *Matter*, every where according to *Laws*, there can be no Reason given, why the same might not

[40] Cudworth, *True Intellectual System*, p. 150.

[41] Cudworth, *True Intellectual System*, p. 151.

[42] When he was in Rome (G III,336). That establishes the date; cf. Aiton, *Leibniz: A Biography*, pp. 158–60, and Robinet, "G. W. Leibniz à Rome." Leibniz's reading notes on the book from that period (LH IV,3,3,1–2, on paper with a watermark attested for the summer of 1689) are printed in VE 1882–92; a very small part of them is in Gr 327–29.

> also extend further, to the Regular Disposal of that Matter, in the *Formation* of *Plants* and *Animals* and other things, in order to that Apt Coherent Frame and Harmony of the whole Universe.[43]

Indeed, the purposive formation of particular biological structures seems in places to be the operation of plastic nature that is foremost in Cudworth's mind.

Leibniz agreed with Cudworth "that the laws of Mechanism all alone could not form an animal where there is nothing already organized" (G VI,544/L 589), but in Leibniz's view there is not in fact any origination of living bodies except by divine creation, since what appears as birth or generation is really the transformation of a pre-existing animal or plant.[44] Given the pre-existing organic bodies, he claimed that he did not need or want immaterial plastic natures to explain the (trans)formation of living bodies, but would explain it by those pre-existing structures, and thus by material mechanisms. He also put this point by saying that the true plastic natures are these organic mechanical structures, and thus are material rather than immaterial (G VI,544/L 589; cf. G III,374; VI,478f.,553f.). In a way, this application of the term 'plastic nature' to the feature of Leibniz's system which explains the (trans)formation of organic bodies is reasonable enough, since 'plastic' originally meant *formative*; but it is also misleading, since in other ways, as he recognized, it is substantial form that corresponds in his system to Cudworth's plastic nature. It is clear that the plastic nature is conceived by Cudworth as a principle of life; but Leibniz, in expressing his own views, applies 'principle of life' to his substantial forms, signaling thereby a partial agreement with Cudworth, while restricting 'plastic nature' to material mechanisms, signaling thereby his disagreement with Cudworth's account of biological formation (G VI,551–55,539-46/L 586–91).

That disagreement was important to Leibniz because Cudworth's theory on this point conflicted with Leibniz's insistence that everything that happens in matter can be explained mechanically. Central to Leibniz's attempt to modernize the notion of substantial form is his insistence that substantial forms are not to be invoked to explain the details of physics (DM 10). They do ultimately explain the conformity of bodies to mechanical laws, but those laws provide a complete system of explanations of particular physical events, and since substantial forms are not mechanical causes, they have no place in such particular explanations. Leibniz makes this point explicitly in the clearest and fullest of his writings about Cudworth:

> I admit these principles of life, or these souls, but I grant them nothing but internal vital actions, which are also linked with each other by certain laws within the same Agent, and also harmonious from one Agent to another, but the actions of the corporeal mass are linked with each other by the laws of mechanism. (G VI,553)

Leibniz's unwillingness to call substantial forms "plastic" natures can plausibly be traced to an apprehension that that might suggest a role for them as particular causes of the formation of organic bodies, interrupting the chain of mechanical causes.

[43]Cudworth, *True Intellectual System*, p. 151.

[44]I leave aside here, as Leibniz also does in this context, the question of how this applies to human beings, which was a sensitive and complex issue for Leibniz; see T 397.

2. *Matter*

The Aristotelian conception of corporeal substance included more than form, of course. There was also the matter with which the substantial form unites to form the complete, or composite, substance. There seems to be something that plays the role of matter in Leibniz's conception of corporeal substance, too, and he speaks of it, from time to time, as "matter."

But what sort of matter? This question, as Garber sees, is crucial to his interpretation. If there is a basis for ascribing to Leibniz, in his middle years, a less idealistic metaphysics than that of the monadology, it will not be found in the soul-like substantial forms, but in the matter.

Garber notes that "the Scholastics drew a distinction between two conceptions of matter, primary (prime) and secondary."[45] In the stock Aristotelian example of a bronze statue, the form is the shape, and the matter is the bronze. But bronze is already a substance, or a mixture of substances, and is constituted as bronze by a form or forms inhering in it. Bronze is therefore only secondary matter; it is matter in relation to the statue, but it is not pure matter. Primary matter, pure matter, is postulated in the Scholastic scheme of things as the ultimate substratum in which all forms inhere, and therefore as distinct from all forms, something over and above all forms.

Leibniz makes use of the terminology of primary and secondary matter (GM VI,237/L 437). Considered apart from its substantial form, the body of a corporeal substance is secondary matter. It is an aggregate of smaller corporeal substances, each of which has its own substantial form uniting its own secondary matter. Considered in itself, as an aggregate, this secondary matter is a phenomenon. Garber agrees that this was already Leibniz's view in the middle years.[46]

Thus far we have nothing inconsistent with the monadology of Leibniz's last years. We have an infinite hierarchy of corporeal substances constituted by substantial forms uniting corporeal substances constituted by substantial forms uniting corporeal substances constituted by substantial forms, and so on. This construction does not imply that there is anything in a corporeal substance over and above its substantial form and the infinite hierarchy of substantial forms that are ranged under it. We will never finish peeling the layers off this ontological onion, but all the layers we will ever peel off are substantial forms. And the substantial forms can be identified with the simple, soul-like substances of the monadology.

Leibniz does talk about primary matter as well as secondary matter. He says primary matter is constituted by primitive passive force, "the *primitive force* of *suffering* or of *resisting*" (GM VI,236/L 437), complementing the primitive active force with which he identifies substantial form. What is this primary matter or primitive passive force? Is it, finally, something that is real in things over and above "simple substances, and in them perception and appetite"? Garber has claimed that in the middle years, though not later, it is. Garber grants that Leibniz, in his last years, conceived of primitive passive force, and hence of primary matter,

[45] Garber, "Leibniz and the Foundations of Physics," p. 42. I introduced this distinction in Chapter 10, section 2.1.

[46] Garber, "Leibniz and the Foundations of Physics," p. 43.

as merely an aspect, the passive aspect, of the monad or simple substance, a function of the degree of confusedness of its perceptions.[47] But Garber prefers a less mentalistic interpretation of primary matter for Leibniz's middle years—an interpretation according to which primary matter is not an internal aspect of soul-like substances at all, and certainly not merely a function of their manner of perceiving. On this interpretation, Leibniz thought that "the primary matter of the Scholastics" exists as a "non-mental, material component of reality"—"something over and above the immaterial substances he calls forms, something from which extension can arise."[48]

I disagree. I think the theory of Leibniz's last years provides the best interpretation for the middle years, too. To begin with, Garber's view confronts a text now dated, on the basis of physical evidence, to the beginning of the middle years, or just before, in which Leibniz seems to embrace the confused-perception conception of primary matter, stating that "substances have Metaphysical matter or passive power insofar as they express something confusedly; active, insofar as [they do so] distinctly" (G VII,322/L 365).[49]

One such text does not refute Garber, of course, especially since he does not deny that more idealistic thoughts sometimes appear in writings of Leibniz's middle years.[50] More important support for my position comes from the needs and implications of Leibniz's larger theoretical projects, particularly his critique of the Cartesian thesis that extension constitutes the essence of corporeal substance. His opposition to Descartes on this point was a constant that endured through changes in his own positive views on the subject. Naturally there were also changes in his arguments against Descartes. Two of the main lines of argument that he used in the middle years seem to me to show that Leibniz had reason for identifying confusedness of perceptions with the primitive passive force from which extension arises, and that there was no room in his philosophy for anything very like the Scholastic conception of primary matter. The better

[47]As noted in Garber, "Leibniz and the Foundations of Physics," p. 47 and n. 68, the confused-perception conception of primary matter is strongly suggested in some letters of Leibniz to Des Bosses, dated after the middle years (esp. G II,324f., dated 16 October 1706; cf. also G II,460/L 607, from 20 September 1712). Similar implications may be seen in other texts that Garber would assign to the "later" file (G II,275/AG 181; G III,636/L 659). Although I am inclined to believe that Leibniz held this conception of primary matter in both his middle and his later years, I should note that there are later letters (of 1715 and 1716) to Des Bosses in which Leibniz says of *composite* substance that it consists in primitive active and passive power [*potentia*] or force [*vis*] (G II,506,517f./L 617, AG 203f.). In the earlier of the two passages Leibniz explicitly offers the alternative formulation, "or consists in primary matter . . . and in substantial form." These statements, or at least the second of them, seem to be connected with the hypothesis of "substantial bonds" (see Chapter 10, section 5.3), and I count that as reason to doubt that they express Leibniz's own convictions.

[48]Garber, "Leibniz and the Foundations of Physics," p. 48.

[49]The staff of the Academy edition have provisionally dated this text to 1683–86 on the basis of the watermark in the paper on which it is written. See VE 476 (for the dating), 481 (for the quoted sentence). In another fragment, dated to 1683 (because it is written on the blank portions of a bill dated 29 March 1683), the nature of "*matter* or the principle of passivity [*passio*]" is explained at least partially in terms of manner of cognition (VE 294f. = LH IV,1,14C,11). But the explanation is obscure, and not obviously in agreement with the text I have quoted. In 1683 Leibniz may still have been experimenting with these ideas.

[50]Garber, "Leibniz and the Foundations of Physics," pp. 65f.

known of these arguments has to do with infinite divisibility. The other, which I will discuss first, is based on the relational character of extension and its modes.[51]

2.1 The Analysis of Extension

To be *extended* is to have parts that bear certain spatial relations to each other. The most obvious and easiest to state of these relations is that the parts are distant from each other in three dimensions. (Leibniz's definition, as we shall see, is even more abstract, but no less relational.) Of the modes of extension, *size* and *shape* are also a matter of relations among the parts of the thing, being determined by the distances and directions in which the parts lie from each other. *Position* is a mode of extension that is constituted by relations of the body to other bodies (according to Descartes and Leibniz) or to points of space (according to Newton). And *motion* and *rest* are constituted by relations among relations—that is, by relations among the positions of the thing at different times. Insofar as these properties constitute the corporeal world as seen by Cartesianism, that world would appear to be just a system of spatiotemporal relationships.

In a way, this is just what Descartes, and Galileo, wanted: they wanted as much of physics as possible to be reducible to geometry, and geometry is certainly a study of spatial relations. Intuitively, however, a system of spatiotemporal relationships seems too hollow, so to speak, to constitute a substance. Relations presuppose entities that are related, and entities seem to need constitutive properties. So how would a system of spatiotemporal relationships ever get started, if it does not relate entities that have constitutive properties over and above spatiotemporal relations (and, hence, over and above extension and its modes)? In a note published in the *Journal des Savants* in 1693, Leibniz argued forcefully along these lines.

> Those who would have it that extension itself is a substance reverse the order of words as well as that of thoughts. Besides extension there must be a subject that is extended—that is to say, a substance that can properly be repeated or continued. For *extension* signifies nothing but a repetition or continuous multiplicity of that which is spread out—*a plurality, continuity, and coexistence of the parts*; and consequently it does not suffice to explain the very nature of the substance that is spread out or repeated, whose notion is prior to that of its repetition. (G IV,467/W 104)[52]

[51] Another line of argument, much emphasized by Leibniz in publications of the 1690s (E 112–14/W 102–4; GM VI,240–42/L 440f.; also in DM 21), has received (I think) its best discussion in Garber, "Leibniz and the Foundations of Physics," pp. 78f. Leibniz argued that if extension and its modes were the only properties of bodies, as Descartes affirmed, bodies would obey quite different laws of motion in collisions from those that are actually observed to obtain, and that therefore there must also be forces in bodies to explain their behavior. It is difficult to understand why any conclusions at all about the laws of motion would follow from Cartesian assumptions about the constitutive properties of bodies, and Leibniz provides no explanation on this crucial point. Garber's solution to the puzzle seems to me the likeliest: "this argument works *only* if we assume that the laws that govern the behavior of bodies in motion derive from something *intrinsic* to body" (ibid., n. 174). In other words, Leibniz is presupposing his anti-occasionalist views with regard to bodies.

[52] A similar argument is found in G IV,364f./L 390 (1692 or earlier), in G II, 169f.,183/L 516,519 (1699), in G IV,589 (1702), in G VI,584, and in several texts cited in my next note.

What property, according to Leibniz, does constitute the nature of the substance whose repetition or spreading out constitutes extension? Resistance, or passive (as opposed to active) force, is the property most emphatically offered by Leibniz as an answer to this question,[53] and we have seen that he identified primitive passive force with primary matter. What then is the resistance or passive force of which Leibniz speaks here? He says it is that "by which body resists not only penetration but also motion" (G IV,395/AG 252). But is this supposed to express the whole nature of resistance? Or does it merely indicate some effects of resistance, effects sufficient to identify resistance for purposes of physics?

The idea that resistance consists simply in a tendency of bodies not to be penetrated or moved does not fit very well in the argument about the relative character of extension. For that is only a tendency to stability in certain spatial relationships, and a tendency to stability (or to change) in spatial relationships seems to be just an additional relational feature of a system of spatiotemporal relationships, which leaves the system as "hollow" as it was before.[54] The ontological grounding of a system of spatiotemporal relationships requires entities that stand in the relationships, and Leibniz seems to be assuming, very plausibly, that such entities must have some "nature" that is diffused throughout the system. I take it that, in order to do its ontological job, this nature must include more than spatiotemporal relations and tendencies to have such relations; it must include some intrinsic, nonrelational property. It is indeed one of Leibniz's beliefs, enunciated in a paper of about 1689[55] that "there are no purely extrinsic denominations" (C 520/L 268), which implies that in order to have extrinsic or relational properties a thing must have intrinsic, nonrelational properties.

If resistance or passive force must include intrinsic properties, what can they be? I think that for Leibniz they can only be qualities of *perception*, or tendencies to such qualities. Here the identification of passive force as a function of confusedness of perceptions satisfies Leibniz's conceptual needs. Resistance, insofar as it is a nature prior to the system of spatiotemporal relations and can ground extension by its repetition or diffusion, will be a tendency to have confused perceptions. The entities in which the system of spatiotemporal relations is grounded will be perceiving substances, as is implied in the later years (after 1706) by Leibniz's statement that extension is "nothing but repetition of perceivers" (RS 42/AG 276).

[53]See G IV,393f./AG 251. There are also passages (G IV,394f./AG 252f.; G II,170/L 516) in which this role seems to be assigned to the *dynamikon*, which could be interpreted as including active as well as passive force. Active force seems explicitly included in a letter of December 1693 to Gerhard Meier, in which Leibniz speaks of "something . . . that is said to be extended—that is, spread out by repetition—in which there will be the character of substance, namely to act or be acted on" (A I,ix,634). A similar implication is found in a later (and undoubtedly fully monadological) letter to De Volder (G II,269/L 536). But in Leibniz's next letter to De Volder only passivity seems to be involved in this spreading out (G II,277/AG 183). In any event, we are primarily concerned here with the implications of the argument regarding passive force or primary matter.

[54]This claim will be examined in the fourth objection considered in section 2.1.1 in this chapter.

[55]See VE 1998 for the dating, based on the watermark.

2.1.1 Survey of Objections to This Interpretation

This interpretation, and its grounds, can be further illuminated by considering four possible objections to it.

First objection: It might be claimed that Leibniz did not really believe that any quality of perception is diffused throughout the spatial system, because perceiving substances are not strictly speaking in space. This objection seems to me erroneous. Leibniz did in fact believe in ways of assigning monads or perceiving substances to spatial locations (as discussed in Chapters 9 and 10). Thus we find Leibniz writing to Bartholomew Des Bosses in 1707, a little after the middle years, that the "continuation" involved in extension "is related to the things continued or repeated as number is to the things numbered: that is, a simple substance, even though it does not have extension in itself, still has position, which is the foundation of extension, since extension is the simultaneous continuous repetition of position" (G II,339). I think the envisaged assignments of monads to positions must amount to a construction of spatial relations from intrinsic properties of the perceiving substances. But that fits well enough into Leibniz's argument about the relational character of extension, for there he defines extension as "simultaneous continuous repetition." And he did believe that a tendency to confused perception is simultaneously repeated in infinitely many substances. If this repetition is not exactly continuous, since the perceiving substances are discrete, it is at least dense, in such a way as to approximate continuity (see Chapter 9, section 1.3.2). Indeed, on the interpretation I am offering, the need to have a densely, if not continuously, repeated intrinsic nature in order to ground extension is one of Leibniz's reasons for postulating the dissemination of perceiving things everywhere in matter.

Second objection: The most that Leibniz actually says about the nature of resistance in direct connection with the argument we are studying is that it is that "by which body resists not only penetration but also motion." Likewise, it is natural to read him as offering an account of the whole nature of resistance, and of primary matter, when he says, in a letter of 1699 to Burcher De Volder, that "the resistance of Matter contains two things, impenetrability or antitypy and resistance or inertia, and since they are equal everywhere in body, or proportional to its extension, it is in these that I locate the nature of matter or the passive principle" (G II,171/L 517; cf. G IV,510/L 503). Nonetheless, I find it hard to believe that Leibniz did not intend to postulate the diffusion of an *intrinsic* property, and also hard to believe that he regarded a tendency to resist penetration and motion as an intrinsic rather than a relational property. Moreover, it is difficult to see what the alternative to a feature of the perceptual faculty would be for Leibniz if he was demanding an intrinsic property. Aside from perceptions and perceptual faculties, the only clearly identifiable properties he ascribes to corporeal things are the primary qualities, as we call them, and dispositions regarding the primary qualities, which I have argued are all relational.

Third objection: We might ask whether Leibniz needs to identify the intrinsic property that is diffused through matter. Some philosophers would be content to postulate one without being able to say what it is, except that it is the property that fills this role. Some would say that in fact many of the properties studied by physical science have an intrinsic nature, but are known to us only by their role. They would agree with Thomas Reid that there is not necessarily anything wrong with postulating an occult quality, if that means only "some unknown cause of a known effect."[56] Whatever the merits of this position, it is hardly one that Leibniz would embrace. Indeed, he indicates that his insistence on analyzing extension in terms of the nature of that which is extended is based on his refusal to accept occult qualities.

> But from these [considerations] it is evident that extension is not some absolute predicate, but is relative to that which is extended or diffused, and therefore it can no more be severed from the nature of that which is diffused than number from the thing numbered. And accordingly those who have assumed Extension as some absolute, primitive attribute in body, indefinable and unutterable, have erred by insufficient Analysis and have really taken refuge in occult qualities, which in other respects they so much despise—as if extension were something that cannot be explained. (G IV,394/AG 251)

This strongly suggests that Leibniz would insist that the intrinsic nature whose diffusion constitutes extension must be explainable in terms of qualities that are known to us. By the time he wrote the *Monadology* it seemed quite clear to Leibniz that the only intrinsic qualities known to us are those of perception (Mon 8–16), and I think it would be hard to find in works of the middle years any suggestion of other qualities satisfying these criteria.

Of course it does not follow that Leibniz saw clearly during the middle years that he had no other serious candidate for this role. I know of no text from the period in which he states that explicitly. In discussing the next objection (the fourth) in this series we will examine a text from 1704 in which Leibniz argues from the nonrelational character of forces to their quasi-mental character. Of course that leaves a possibility that this link is one that Leibniz recognized only near the end of the middle years. Even if that was so, however, the idea that the primary operations of forces, including primitive passive force, have to do with perception represents no sharp turn in Leibniz's thinking, but is a natural development of leading ideas of his middle years—not to mention that we have already seen it reflected in a text of the 1680s (G VII,322/L 365).

Fourth objection: This calls for the longest discussion. In arguing, above, that the argument about the relative character of extension requires something more in resistance or primary matter than a tendency of bodies not to be penetrated or moved, I relied on the premise that a tendency to stability (or to change) in spatial relationships is just an additional relational feature of a system of spatiotemporal relationships. This premise might be questioned; it might be suggested that a "force" or disposition can be an intrinsic, not essentially relational property of a thing even if it is only a power or tendency to have certain relational properties. This suggestion seems to me both counterintuitive and contrary in spirit to Leibniz's insistence on the causal isolation of created substances.

He did characterize force as something "absolute," in contrast with motion, which is something "relative" (LA 133). But this characterization may (and I

[56]Reid, *Essays on the Intellectual Powers of Man* (1785), essay 2, ch. 18, p. 255; in his *Works*, vol. 1, p. 321.

think does) presuppose that the force is something more than a tendency to have certain relational properties: that the force always and necessarily involves some *intrinsic* operation—in the case of active force, an intrinsic action or effort [*conatus*] (cf. G IV,469f./L 433). Leibniz explicitly saw something analogous to effort in passive forces. The passive force of resistance "which is in matter" is not a mere "capacity or receptivity for motion," but something "more particular and more charged with reality" (NE 169f.). I have therefore thought it reasonable to interpret Leibniz as committed to the assumption that, in order to be an intrinsic, nonrelational property, a disposition, force, or tendency, even a passive one, must have an intrinsic, nonrelational operation.

This interpretation seems to me to be confirmed by the train of thought that leads Leibniz, in 1704, to his avowal that "there is nothing in things except simple substances, and in them perception and appetite" (G II 270/L 537). He has just presented his argument that "the concept of extension is relative," and "the nature of that which is supposed to be spread out, repeated, continued" to constitute extension "cannot be found in anything but the principle of acting and being acted on" (G II,269/L 536)—that is, in primitive active and passive forces. Now Leibniz is responding to De Volder's puzzlement about his metaphysics of forces. De Volder said he had "always considered forces, regarded apart from the foundation from which they flow, as like an external denomination"—that is, as merely relational, in comparison with the foundation, "which would exist in reality" (G II,266). Since De Volder had gone on to suggest (correctly, as Leibniz attested) that this "foundation" would correspond to the "primitive forces" in Leibniz's system, his relationality thesis seems to apply specifically to the other sort of force, which Leibniz called "derivative." The relation of derivative to primitive forces will be a main topic of Chapter 13. What concerns us here is just that Leibniz refuses in this context to accept the classification of derivative forces as merely relational; he is speaking particularly about active forces, but there is no reason why the main line of his argument would not also apply to passive forces.

> You add, "I have always considered forces, regarded apart from the foundation from which they flow, as like an external denomination." I should prefer to consider derivative forces in relation to the *foundation*, as shape in relation to extension, that is as a modification. . . . And this is what I have often said, with no deviation that I remember, that unless there were some primitive active thing in us there could not be derivative forces and actions in us, because everything accidental or changeable must be a modification of something essential or perpetual, and cannot involve more of the positive than that which is modified, since every modification is only a limitation; shape [is a limitation] of what is changed, and derived force [is a limitation] of what causes change [*figura variati, vis derivata variantis*]. (G II,270/L 537)

The derivative force, Leibniz implies, escapes being merely relational by being a modification of something permanent and essential to a substance. A Leibnizian force does not get its essence or nature from the effect toward which it tends (as an Aristotelian potentiality might be thought to get its essence), but rather from the cause that produces the effect. And the cause is a substance of which the force is an aspect, primitive forces being essential principles, and derivative forces being current states, of the substance. Now if the derivative force is to escape being an "external denomination" by being a modification of a substance in this way, it must be an *internal* or intrinsic state of the substance. But what sort of internal state might it be?

This is not exactly the question that perplexed De Volder, but it is close to it. He rightly inferred that the "foundation," of which Leibniz now says the derivative forces are a modification, is what Leibniz called "primitive forces." "But of these," he said, "such is the feebleness of my intellect, I perceive nothing except that you assert that all the other changes flow from them" (G II,266).[57] Leibniz replies that De Volder unjustly denigrates his own mental powers. These forces are not the sort of thing that can be *imagined*; they must rather be *understood*. And De Volder does understand something about them—namely, that changes flow from them. In case that may seem not to be enough, however, and in order to confirm the intelligibility of his notion of force, Leibniz adds a paragraph that is surely one of the most important in all his works:

> It is worthwhile, however, to consider that there is maximum intelligibility in this principle of Action, because there is something in it analogous to what is in us, namely perception and appetite, since the nature of things is uniform, and our nature cannot differ infinitely from the other simple substances of which the whole Universe consists. Considering the matter accurately, moreover, it must be said that there is nothing in things except simple substances, and in them perception and appetite. Matter, on the other hand, and motion, are not so much substances or things as phenomena belonging to perceivers, whose reality is located in the harmony of the perceivers with themselves (at different times) and with the other perceivers. (G II,270/L 537)

Thus we see that in the course of trying to make intelligible to De Volder the view that Leibnizian forces, even the "derivative" forces, are not merely relational in character, but are internal features of substances, Leibniz is led to present his belief that "there is nothing in things except simple substances, and in them perception and appetite." In other words, precisely in order to account for the internal, nonrelational character of the forces that he regards as aspects of substance, Leibniz is led to affirm the quasi-mental character of all the operations of substances. It seems clear that at this point Leibniz had nothing nonmental in mind as a model for conceiving of intrinsic or nonrelational properties of substances.

[57]It may be questioned whether "these" forces of which De Volder speaks here are primitive or derivative. In the original context in De Volder's letter, it is ambiguous. On the strictly grammatical ground that "these," in Latin, normally refers to the alternative that is, verbally, most recently mentioned, it should refer to derivative forces. This may be confirmed by the reference to "the other changes" [*reliquas . . . mutationes*], which suggests that "these" forces are themselves viewed as changes, which derivative forces may be but primitive forces certainly are not, in Leibniz's view. These considerations may well be outweighed, however, by one's sense that the main topic under discussion, at the point where De Volder says, "but of these," is primitive forces, and that De Volder is likely to have found the notion of primitive force more obscure than the more physical notion of derivative force. Moreover, it is explicitly primitive force that De Volder still claims not to understand two letters later (G II,279). Leibniz, at any rate, seems to have taken De Volder to be referring here to primitive forces, and it is Leibniz's line of thought that I am trying to interpret.

Of course this text is from 1704, at the end of the middle years. Did it represent a new departure in Leibniz's thought? Had he discovered these ideas only in June of 1704, in reflecting on De Volder's objections? De Volder's next letter expressed astonishment, saying, "in your last letter I noticed many things that were entirely new and unexpected" (G II,272). Leibniz rejected the imputation of novelty, however, replying:

> But perhaps you will discover that the same things were already sufficiently insinuated in earlier [letters], and that only prejudices kept you from reaching this point some time ago, so as no longer to seek substance and the source of forces where it is not. Thus I was forced to insist on some things more explicitly, and to respond, if not to [the question] that was asked, at least to [one] that should be asked. (G II,275/AG 181)

How far back did Leibniz think the monadological views in question could be traced in his correspondence with De Volder? We can only speculate. The earliest date he could have had in mind was 1699, when he began corresponding with De Volder about the nature of forces, and the latest was January 1704, when he wrote his last letter before the one that surprised De Volder. The tone of his response to De Volder suggests, at least, that he was thinking further back than a single letter.

2.1.2 The Enduring Interest of This Argument

It is interesting to note that Kant saw Leibniz as having thought about matter and relationality along the lines I have proposed. As part of his account of the Leibnizian philosophy in the "Note to the Amphiboly of Concepts of Reflection" in the *Critique of Pure Reason*, he presents a very similar argument for the conclusion that all reality is reducible to simple monads.

> According to mere concepts the inner is the substratum of all relation or outer determinations. . . . From this it seems to follow that in every thing (substance) there is something that is absolutely internal and precedes all outer determinations, in that it is what first of all makes them possible; and hence that this substratum is something that no longer contains in itself any outer relations, and consequently is *simple*. (For corporeal things, on the other hand, are never anything but relations, at least of their parts external to each other.) And since we know of no absolutely inner determinations except those [known] through our inner sense, therefore this substratum is not only simple; but also (in analogy with our inner sense) determined through *representations*; that is, all things would really be *monads*, or simple beings endowed with representations. (A 282f. = B 338–40)

Kant rejects this argument, as regards bodies, holding that "a persisting appearance in space (impenetrable extension) can contain only relations and nothing at all that is absolutely internal, and yet be the primary substratum of all outer perception" (A 284 = B 340). Intuition (in the Kantian sense) yields this possibility, though concepts do not. This is connected, however, with Kant's view that bodies are merely phenomenal. Things can be "given in intuition with determinations that express mere relations, without having anything inner as their ground, because they are not things in themselves but merely appearances"

(A 284f. = B 341). In other words, bodies can be constituted by relations alone, and thus be ontologically incomplete, for much the same reason that there need be no date that is the date on which a given fictitious event occurs. The typical scientific realist will find cold comfort in Kant.[58]

It would be a mistake to dismiss this argument from the relational character of extension as a historical curiosity. Most philosophers today will be no readier than Leibniz was to ascribe secondary qualities to bodies as intrinsic, non-relational properties. If science would now ascribe any properties to physical objects other than spatiotemporal relations, they would be properties that are not known to us by direct acquaintance but only through their role in causal explanation of perceptions and spatiotemporal relations. I think it follows that the scientific realist must suppose either (1) that the physical world is a system of spatiotemporal relations (and dispositions to have such relations), obtaining among ultimately real entities that have no intrinsic constitutive properties, or (2) that the physical world is constituted by things having relational properties, many of them at least partly understood by us, and also intrinsic properties, which are either (a) similar to phenomenal qualities that we experience in our own minds or (b) such as we are not directly acquainted with at all (and probably never will be). Of these alternatives, (1) seems to me the least plausible, and (2b) leaves those who hold it with little grounds for confidence that the real things whose intrinsic properties they confess to be quite unknown to us are not after all of a somewhat psychological character.

2.2 *Infinite Divisibility*

Of Leibniz's arguments against the Cartesian conception of extended substance, the most important for the structure of his philosophy turns on the infinite divisibility of extended things as such. He used it often; it will be convenient to examine it in its first full-dress appearance in the Leibniz-Arnauld correspondence. This is a passage[59] from a draft of a letter to Arnauld. If bodies are substances, Leibniz says, "I believe it can be inferred that corporeal substance does not consist in extension or divisibility." For if two bodies are brought into contact, that is not enough to make them a substance (or one[60] substance).

> Now each extended mass can be considered as composed of two or a thousand others; there is only extension by a contact. Thus one will never find a body of which one can say that it is truly a [or one] substance. It will always be an aggregate of several. Or rather, it will not be a real being, since the parts that compose it are subject to the same difficulty, and since one never arrives at any real being, as beings by aggregation have only as much reality as there is in their components. From this it follows that the substance of a body, if they have one, must be indivisible; whether it is called soul or form does not matter to me. (LA 72)

[58]I do not mean to be taking any position on the complex interpretive issue of whether Kant's account of bodies is less realistic than Leibniz's.

[59]Also quoted in Garber, "Leibniz and the Foundations of Physics," p. 32.

[60]It affects the form of the argument that Leibniz is writing in French, in which the indefinite article also means 'one'.

One of the premises of this argument is that any extended mass is composed of extended parts. It does not matter whether the parts can be physically divided or separated, "since the invincible attachment of one part to another (if it could be rationally conceived or assumed) would not destroy their diversity," as Leibniz points out in the "New System" (E 126/L 456). What matters to the argument is that any extended thing has distinct (extended) parts. And since these parts are extended too, the same is true of them in turn. So any extended thing has distinct parts, which have distinct parts, which have distinct parts, . . . and so on to infinity.

That every extended thing is composed of parts, in some sense, is relatively uncontroversial. It is generally accepted in both medieval and modern philosophy. In Leibniz's predecessors it is connected with the conception of extension as a species of continuous quantity, and with Aristotle's argument that "everything continuous is divisible into [parts] that are always divisible."[61] Descartes explicitly affirmed it: "it is not possible to divide any body into so many parts that each of these parts cannot still be understood to be divisible."[62]

An important issue lies below the surface here, however. Suarez thought there are homogeneous continuous masses of material substance, for instance of fire or of water, which are indeed composed [*constare*] of parts, but which are intrinsically [*per se*] one. An important part of his grounds for ascribing per se unity to these bodies is that Suárez thought that their parts are not actually but only potentially many.[63] But it was Leibniz's view that every (actual) extended thing has not merely a potential but an actual partition into infinitely many determinate parts. "In the ideal or continuous the whole is prior to the parts, . . . the parts being only potential; but in the real the simple is prior to the groups, the parts are actual, are before the whole" (G III,622; cf. G II,268,282,379/L 536,539; and Chapter 9, sections 1.2 and 1.3.2 in this volume). Writing to Arnauld in 1686, Leibniz seems already certain that the parts of any extended mass as such are one only accidentally [*per accidens*, not *per se*], and are as distinct from each other actually as any two diamonds that might be set in the same ring (LA 76).

His confidence on this point may well be connected with the second premise of the passage I quoted from LA 72, a premise expressed in the words, "beings by aggregation have only as much reality as there is in their components." I take this to mean that beings that are divisible, or divided, into parts get their reality from their parts—that the reality of a being that has parts consists in the reality of the parts, and that the reality of the parts is metaphysically prior to that of the whole.[64] I think this is a plausible thesis, and plausible as an interpretation

[61]Aristotle, *Physics* 231^{b}16.

[62]Descartes, *Principles of Philosophy*, I,26 (AT VIII/1,15); see also II,20 (AT VIII/1,51f.).

[63]Suárez, *Metaphysical Disputations*, IV,iii,9.

[64]This thesis is specifically about *reality* (in a sense no weaker than the strongest sense of "reality" of phenomena discussed in Chapter 9, section 4). To the extent that a whole is merely "ideal," Leibniz is prepared to regard it as prior to its parts. As he wrote in 1705, "in matter and in actual realities the whole is a result of the parts, but in ideas and in possibles . . . the indeterminate whole is prior to the divisions" [G VII,562; cf. G II,379 (1709), G III,622 (1714)]. On the relation of this point about ideality to Leibniz's own constructive views about bodies, see Chapter 9, sections 1.3.2 and 3.4.

of Leibniz,[65] but it is more debatable than the first premise. The lines along which Leibniz would defend it are clear enough. It rests for him on the assumption that an extended mass is a *mere* aggregate in the sense that its parts do not bear a more strongly unifying relation to each other than that of contiguity. I take it that is what he means by saying that "there is only extension by a contact." He was fond of likening extended things as such to heaps and flocks. Now most people would agree that in a heap of sand and a flock of sheep the grains of sand are ontologically prior to the heap, and the sheep to the flock (even if the sheep are all huddled together, touching each other). So if the relation between an extended whole and its parts is the same as that between the heap and the grains, or the flock and the sheep, it is plausible to infer that in the extended thing the parts are ontologically prior to the whole.

From these premises Leibniz draws the conclusion that in an extended mass as such "one never arrives at any real being."[66] His reasoning, presumably, is that the infinite regress of parts composed of parts composed of parts and so on is vicious because it is an infinite regress of things that get their reality from their parts, which get their reality from their parts, which get their reality from their parts, and so on. As all the links in the chain possess only derivative reality, one will never arrive, in such a regress, at anything that has reality in itself, or that has "a reality not borrowed," as Leibniz put it to De Volder in 1704: "And where there is no reality that is not borrowed, there will never be any reality, since it must belong ultimately to some subject" (G II,267).[67]

It is an interesting and difficult question whether Leibniz is right in regarding this regress as vicious. The idea that the existence or reality of a thing composed of parts consists in the existence or reality of the parts is both plausible and an inspiration for many philosophical projects. An infinite regress of things whose reality consists in the reality of other things, whose reality consists in the reality of other things, whose reality consists in the reality of other things, and so on does look vicious. On the other hand, the idea that masses can be both real and infinitely divisible into parts has great intuitive appeal. One might try to preserve this idea by arguing, contrary to Leibniz, that as the parts are not outside the whole, they are not "other things" than the whole and do not have such an ontological priority with respect to the whole that the whole cannot "have reality in itself" in the relevant sense. Perhaps the whole and the parts have reality in themselves collectively, so that it is not necessary for them to "borrow" their reality from something that has it in a way that divisible things cannot have it. Nonetheless, I think there is some plausibility to Leibniz's view that the infinite regress here is vicious unless such reality as the mass possesses can be traced to components that lie outside the regress.

On that view Leibniz seems justified in concluding that, insofar as there is anything real in them, bodies must be composed ultimately of indivisible things that have no parts and that such indivisible things must constitute "the

[65]It is clearly his meaning in the version of the argument he sent to De Volder on 30 June 1704 (G II,267), though Garber would put that text in the "later" pile.

[66]For a similar three-step argument, more focused on the issue of borrowed reality, in a letter of 21 January 1704 to De Volder, see G II,261.

[67]This passage may be found in translation in Russell, *Philosophy of Leibniz*, p. 242.

substance of that" any body that has a substance. This indivisible entity he is willing to call either "soul" or "form."[68] Note that this conclusion is about what must be true of a body in order for it to be even an aggregate. Even an aggregate, in order to be an aggregate of real things, must be composed ultimately of indivisible elements. This is most obviously the point of the argument when it recurs about five months later in a letter to Arnauld, and much later in the *Monadology*:

> *I believe that where there are only beings by aggregation, there will not even be real beings.* For every being by aggregation presupposes beings endowed with a true unity, because it has its reality only from that of its components, so that it will have none at all if each being of which it is composed is again a being by aggregation; or else yet another foundation of its reality must be sought, which cannot ever be found in this way if one must always go on seeking. (LA 96)

> And there must be simple substances, because there are composites; for the composite is nothing but a collection or *aggregate* of simples. (Mon. 2)

This argument must therefore be distinguished from a related argument (discussed in Chapter 9, section 3.2) that Leibniz offers for the conclusion that aggregates as such are only phenomena. That argument has the premises that things have being only insofar as they have unity, and that aggregates have their unity only in the mind—from which Leibniz concludes that aggregates (as distinct from the elements of which they are composed) have their being only in the mind. The argument we are discussing in the present section, however, does not presuppose the equivalence of being and unity. And its conclusion is not that in order to have being as a substance, a corporeal substance must have a substantial form that unifies it (though that is indeed a Leibnizian thesis), but that in order to be composed of anything real, a body must be composed ultimately of things that are indivisible, partless, and hence not extended.

This conclusion is radical. Leibniz's argument amounts to an attack on any conception of infinitely divisible stuff as a fundamental constituent of reality. More precisely, he opposes any belief in a real thing or constituent of a real thing that is infinitely divisible (or infinitely divided) and not composed of indivisibles. Such belief is not a peculiarity of Cartesian or even of modern philosophy. In medieval theories, too, primary matter (at least in the state in which it actually exists) is infinitely divisible and not composed of indivisibles. The argument of his correspondence with Arnauld will therefore not allow Leibniz to hold, consistently, anything very like a Scholastic theory of primary matter.[69]

[68]LA 72. In a Scholastic context the concept of soul would be more apposite for signifying something indivisible. For forms, even substantial forms, are not all indivisible according to Scholastic theories. The substantial form of water, for example, is as infinitely divisible as the matter that it informs. It was even thought that the souls of some animals are divisible; Arnauld had Scholastic precedent in taking the movement of both severed halves of a worm as evidence that the soul of the worm was divided into two parts when the body was divided (LA 87). The clearest cases of indivisible substantial things in the world of our experience, for Scholasticism, are the souls of higher animals and the human rational soul.

[69]The closest to Leibniz of the Scholastics on this subject is probably St. Thomas Aquinas, but Leibniz diverges even from Aquinas's theories at this as well as other points. See p. 349.

Leibnizian primary matter[70] must be indivisible. For it is a constituent of a real thing, and I shall argue that it cannot be *composed of* indivisibles. In this it differs from secondary matter. Leibnizian secondary matter is an aggregate of infinitely many substances and is infinitely divisible into parts which are sub-aggregates; and if Leibniz allows it to be a constituent of a real composite substance, that is only on the assumption that it is ultimately composed of indivisible unities, which are the substances of which it is an aggregate.

Those Scholastics who held that a substance can have secondary as well as primary matter assumed that any part of a substance's secondary matter would have among its constituents a part of the substance's primary matter. But this cannot have been Leibniz's view. The primary matter of each substance cannot be partitioned, and composed of indivisible unities, in the same way as the secondary matter. For what would they be?

Could the indivisible unities of which the primary matter of a substance is ultimately composed, on this hypothesis, be identified with the primary matter of the substances aggregated to form its body or secondary matter? No. For every Leibnizian substance has a body of secondary matter that is composed of parts, and parts of those parts, to infinity. So if the primary matter of every substance is partitioned in the same way as the secondary, the primary matter of the smaller substances will be infinitely divisible, too, and cannot play the part of indivisible unities. Moreover, the idea that each smaller substance in the organic body of a corporeal substance has a part of the primary matter that is a constituent of the larger substance suits very ill with Leibniz's oft-repeated view [e.g., GM III,537/AG 167 (1698)] that smaller substances in a substance's body are not parts of the larger substance.

In fact, there is no room in the thought of Leibniz's middle years for indivisible unities of which a divisible primary matter could be composed. During the middle years he never speaks of anything but form as able to confer indivisible unity on anything in reality. (The situation in his later years is more complicated, but contains no suggestion of principles of unity intrinsic to primary matter as such; see Chapter 10, section 5.) And any matter composed of entities unified by forms would be, by definition, secondary rather than primary matter.

Another argument against ascribing to Leibniz the view that primary matter is partitioned in the same way as secondary is based on texts from 1687 and 1706 in which Leibniz says of what is clearly (and in 1706 explicitly) meant to be primary matter that it is "always essential to the same substance" (LA 120; cf. G II,324). This is inconsistent with the supposition that a corporeal substance shares portions of its primary matter with other substances on the basis of their membership in the aggregate that forms its organic body. For that membership is continually changing, according to Leibniz, so that primary matter shared on the basis of it would have to belong to different substances at different times.

I am tempted to think this argument is explicit in the 1706 text (a letter to Des Bosses), where Leibniz says, "Therefore the primary matter of any substance that exists in its organic body involves the primary matter of another substance,

[70] I speak here of "primary matter" in the sense in which I believe Leibniz most often used the term. An alternative sense of the term occurs at least once in the *New Essays*, though not everywhere in that work, and is discussed in Chapter 12, pp. 372–75.

not as an essential part, but as an immediate requirement, and only for a time, since one succeeds another" (G II,324). The one disturbing feature of this statement, for my interpretation, is the mention of "an immediate requirement." I suspect it has to do with relations that are "required" in view of the order of the world and the pre-established harmony. There is at least one text, however, from 1690, in which 'immediate requirements' refers to "principles" (but not "parts") of which some matter is "composed" (FC 324). Nevertheless, I think it is not likely that the immediate requirement in the letter to Des Bosses is a component, for that would be inconsistent with the argument I have given, and with its premises, to which Leibniz appears to be committed in this letter.

We are left with the conclusion that the primary matter of a substance, on Leibniz's view, is as indivisible—and hence as unextended—as the substantial form. In the text of 1687 that I mentioned in the previous paragraph he flatly states of matter, in the sense of "the primitive passive power of a substance," that it "would be neither extended nor divisible" (LA 120).[71] If a substantial form unites with such a primary matter to form a substance (a perceiving substance, on Garber's interpretation as well as on mine), it is hard to see why the primary matter would not be an internal aspect of an unextended, perceiving substance. In other words, the primary matter seems to be, thus far, an internal aspect of what Leibniz would ultimately call a "monad," contrary to what I take to be the intent of Garber's interpretation.

This primary matter can still be closely associated with extension in Leibniz's thought. Denying its divisibility, he adds the qualification that "it would be the principle of divisibility, or of what amounts to it for the substance" (LA 120).[72] It is from the repetition of primary matter (or passive force) that extension results, as I have explained in section 2.1. But this is not a closer association between primary matter and extension than obtains in the monadological account; I think it is precisely the association between them that obtains in the monadological account. Leibniz's argument about infinite divisibility leaves no room, even in the philosophy of his middle years, for anything very like the more usual conceptions of matter.

3. *Realism*

Garber points out that "Leibniz was a physicist of some note in his day" and that the middle years were the period of his life in which he made his main contributions to physics. Garber thinks these facts must be found perplexing on the usual understanding of Leibniz's thought. "What status could the science of physics possibly have," he asks, "for a philosopher who . . . seems to hold a metaphysics so distant [as the monadology] from our common sense conceptions of the world of physics?"[73] It is one of the explicit motives of Garber's interpreta-

[71]This is the passage in which primary matter makes its clearest appearance in the Arnauld correspondence. It was omitted from the letter actually sent to Arnauld on 9 October 1687; see Chapter 12, section 1, for a full discussion.

[72]On the translation of this statement, see Chapter 12, note 15.

[73]Garber, "Leibniz and the Foundations of Physics," p. 27.

tion to remove this paradox by ascribing to Leibniz in the middle years a more "realistic" metaphysical conception of the physical world. The concluding sentence of his paper states: "It is only later in Leibniz's life, after he has put aside his serious work in physics that his science loses its grip on reality."[74]

I am not moved by this reason for Garber's interpretation. The most obvious reply to it is that it is not impossible for an idealist to take a serious interest in the science of physics and that it is certainly not unheard of for a physicist of note to flirt with idealism. A more fundamental reply, however, will focus on the notion of "realism" and the "grip" of science on "reality."

In what way, if at all, is Leibniz's theory of the physical world in the middle years more "realistic" on Garber's interpretation than on the monadological interpretation? On any interpretation, after all, Leibniz grounded physics in metaphysical considerations about substantial forms and final causes, which he regarded as beyond the professional expertise of the physicist. Even on Garber's reading, extension and its modes, which are among the main properties studied by physics, are not fully real.[75] It is at most the *forces* studied by physics that belong to ultimate reality. And on either reading of Leibniz, physics measures those forces by their phenomenal effects, such as motion, which are expressions and results of facts about primitive active and passive forces that are ultimately real. So on either interpretation the physical measurement of forces is a mathematical treatment of a phenomenal expression of something ultimately real. Does it matter to the grip of physics on reality whether the something ultimately real is states of soul-like monads only, or states of soul-like substantial forms plus states of a primary matter that is distinct from the forms and from any internal or perceptual feature of a soul-like substance? Even on Garber's interpretation it is hard to see what physics could tell us about the nature of whatever it might be that primary matter adds over and above the perceptual features of reality.

I think Leibniz would have been surprised at the idea that the concept of primary *matter* would be the key to the realism of his physics. If there was any context in which he saw himself as a champion of realism in physics, it was in his critique of occasionalism. In that context, what he regarded as essential to realism about bodies is belief in the reality of forces, especially of the active forces that he identified with substantial forms. For Leibniz it is on the concept of form, not of matter, that realism in physics principally depends.

This may seem strange to us because so much modern debate about realism has been focused on the concept of matter. But reflection on Leibniz's ideas about matter, and their Scholastic and modern antecedents, should make clear that the notion of matter so often taken for granted in modern philosophy is not a timeless possession of the human mind. At the end of the thirteenth century, and even more in the fourteenth, ideas of matter begin to look much more "modern" than those of Thomas Aquinas. More fully modern conceptions of matter are found in typical seventeenth-century thinkers (though not in Leibniz) and are still with us, but they may be in the process of dissolution in twentieth-century physics.

[74]Garber, "Leibniz and the Foundations of Physics," p. 99.
[75]Garber, "Leibniz and the Foundations of Physics," p. 90.

Leibniz's opinion that, of the features of bodies studied by physics, the forces are the most real retains much plausibility. Perhaps it has even *gained* plausibility. The secondary qualities are not studied by modern physics in their own right, anyway, and if they give us access to anything regarded as physically real, it is to powers or forces or structures of primary qualities. As for the primary qualities, they are constituted by relations in space and time. In the physics of our century, "space and time" have been replaced by four-dimensional space-time, which is a mathematical structure that is at most analogous to space and time as presented, and perceptually represented, in our experience. In what is that mathematical structure realized? The most plausible "realistic" and nonoccasionalist answer is that it is realized in a system of entities constituted by properties, such as mass and electrical charge, known to physics only as forces or powers and liabilities of certain sorts. Perhaps that will give us more sympathy for a seventeenth-century view in which it is the reality of forces, and of form rather than matter, that is crucial for realism in physics.

12

Primary Matter

In Chapter 11 I have argued that the main lines of Leibniz's philosophy in his "middle years" (roughly, 1685–1704) leave no room for matter to add anything to the very austere, and rather mentalistic, fundamental furniture of the universe indicated by his statement (of 1704, to Burcher De Volder) that "there is nothing in things except simple substances, and in them perception and appetite" (G II,270/L 537). There are undoubtedly texts from that period, however, in which Leibniz speaks of *primary matter* as something with which the substantial forms or souls of creatures must be joined in order to constitute a complete substance. I have yet to deal with these texts, which are an important part of the basis of Daniel Garber's less monadological interpretation of Leibniz's thought in the middle years. That is the task of the present chapter—though I reserve for Chapter 13 a few relevant texts, in which what is said about primary matter is closely connected with the distinction between primitive and derivative forces. I presuppose the explanation of the distinction between primary and secondary matter given in Chapter 10.

1. *Three Senses of 'Matter' in a Letter to Arnauld*

It is appropriate to begin an investigation of Leibniz's conception of primary matter in the middle years with the one place in his correspondence with Antoine Arnauld where Leibniz discusses a distinction of senses of 'matter'. It is in the letter of 9 October 1687 (LA 118–20).[1] Only one sense of 'matter' is mentioned in the text sent to Arnauld, but two others, readily identifiable as secondary and primary matter, are discussed in a marginal addition to the copy retained by Leibniz. Physically, of course, this addition could have been written long after the original letter, and we know Leibniz was still thinking of publishing the correspondence as late as 1707 (RL 107).[2] But we also know now, from the manuscript of a preliminary draft of the letter, which has recently come to light,[3] that

[1]Date of the copy received by Arnauld (RL 78); Leibniz dated his own copy "September 1687" (G II,111).

[2]In late 1706, also, he wrote Des Bosses a letter (G II,324) containing statements about primary matter that were strikingly similar to part of the marginal addition at LA 120.

[3]See Sleigh, *Leibniz and Arnauld*, pp. 8, 208f. for a brief account of the textual evidence. In Leibniz's copy of the letter itself this addition is written around other, adjacent marginal additions in a way that shows that it was written after them.

the main ideas (and some of the wording) of the marginal addition were in Leibniz's mind in 1687, when the letter was written. That, and the fact that the addition itself, in Leibniz's copy of the letter, is enclosed in brackets, strongly suggest that the addition was already written, and deliberately excluded from Arnauld's copy, when the letter was sent. Whenever the marginal addition was written, the draft manuscript and Arnauld's copy are evidence enough that Leibniz had some hesitation about the addition—either about the truth or theoretical adequacy of its content or about the wisdom of sending it to Arnauld—though it is not crossed out, as many passages are, in his own copy of the letter. Detailed discussion of the text will afford occasion for some speculations about possible reasons for withholding this passage.

1.1 Cartesian Matter

Arnauld received, then, a discussion of matter in only one sense. It is a sense that has plainly nothing to contribute to a nonphenomenalistic account of the substance of things. "Matter taken for mass in itself is nothing but a pure phenomenon or well-founded appearance, as space and time are too," Leibniz declares (LA 118f.). Later on in the paragraph, in a marginal addition that Arnauld did receive, he makes the point in terms that make a bit clearer what he means by "the mass in itself": "the extended mass considered without the substantial form . . . is not the corporeal substance, but an entirely pure phenomenon like the rainbow" (RL 86).[4] In the final state of the passage in Leibniz's copy of the letter it is quite clear that this is a third sense of matter, distinct from secondary matter and from what he usually identifies as primary matter. I think this is also the correct interpretation of the version received by Arnauld, but since it is less obvious there, it will be well to begin with a separate reading of that document.

The "entirely pure phenomenon" of our text can hardly be the primary matter that plays such an important part in the realism that Garber sees in Leibniz's middle years.[5] Moreover, there is a stronger (and not merely phenomenal) candidate for the role of primary matter in the portion of the text that was not sent to Arnauld. I shall assign the role to that stronger candidate, both here and in almost all of the mature Leibniz's references to primary matter. It should be noted, however, that we will see in section 4.4 some much later texts, from Leibniz's discussion of the philosophy of Locke, in which the role of primary matter seems to be assigned to something like the sort of matter described in this passage sent to Arnauld—though the documents about Locke also contain evidence for ascribing the role to the same stronger candidate as is found in the passage withheld from Arnauld.

Should we interpret the matter discussed here as secondary matter, matter conceived as an aggregate of substances? That is what we might have expected

[4]This is the text received by Arnauld. Regarding an emendation in Leibniz's copy, see p. 344 below.

[5]Garber ("Leibniz and the Foundations of Physics," pp. 43, 47, 53) does interpret the "extended mass" in this passage as primary matter, though he recognizes that this causes a difficulty for his more comprehensive reading of Leibniz, in view of the pure phenomenality ascribed to this mass here.

in the context. Leibniz is responding to a problem raised by Arnauld about the unification that substantial form is supposed, by Leibniz, to accomplish in corporeal things. "If a parcel of matter is not one being, but many beings," Arnauld said, "I do not conceive that a substantial form, which could give it only an extrinsic denomination, since it is really distinct from it, can make it cease to be many beings and become one being by an intrinsic denomination" (LA 107). In short, how can a substantial form bestow (intrinsic) unity on a portion of matter that is distinct from it?

With what sort of matter is Arnauld's objection concerned? Clearly, with matter that is, in itself, an aggregate, "not one being, but many beings." Leibniz's response to the objection, therefore, should presumably deal with matter of that sort. Indeed, in the paragraph preceding his response, Leibniz acknowledges as his own a view of "matter or extended mass in itself never being anything but many Beings" (LA 118). This characterization of "extended mass" as "many Beings" may well suggest that Leibniz is speaking of secondary matter, matter as an aggregate of substances.

Leibniz's answer to Arnauld's objection disappoints expectations in more than one way. He says it is not the matter but the corporeal substance that is unified by the substantial form: "I respond that it is the animated substance to which this matter belongs that is truly one being, and the matter taken for the mass in itself is nothing but a pure phenomenon or well-founded appearance" (LA 118). Fair enough, as far as it goes, but by no means a fully satisfying answer.[6] How a substantial form unifies a corporeal substance remains a serious problem for Leibniz (as discussed in Chapter 10, section 5), but, instead of taking the occasion of Arnauld's objection to say something about that problem, Leibniz goes on to explain why the matter of which he speaks here is purely phenomenal.

The explanation to which he proceeds is not his usual explanation for the phenomenality of secondary matter—the explanation he has given Arnauld in a previous letter (LA 100f.)—that aggregates as such are only phenomena. That would seem to be an apposite explanation in this context, inasmuch as being an aggregate is the feature of matter that gives rise to Arnauld's objection; and Leibniz does allude to the phenomenality of aggregates at the end of this paragraph as Arnauld received it. But the priority in explaining the phenomenality of matter goes here to the claim that "it does not even have precise and fixed qualities that could make it pass for a determinate being" (LA 119). Leibniz begins by arguing at some length for the indeterminacy, and hence phenomenality, of shape as a quality of an extended mass,[7] claims that his argument can be extended to size and motion, and concludes, "consequently, the extended mass considered without the substantial form, since it consists only in these qualities, is not the corporeal substance, but an entirely pure phenomenon like the rainbow" (RL 86; cf. LA 119).

This conclusion contains the clearest indication in the letter received by Arnauld that the matter or "extended mass" discussed here is not secondary matter after all. For it cannot be said that secondary matter, as an aggregate of

[6]With some justice, Sleigh, *Leibniz and Arnauld*, p. 107, calls it "nitpicking."

[7]This argument is discussed in Chapter 9, section 1.3.1.

real substances, "consists only in these qualities" of shape, size, and motion. Another clear indication is added to this sentence in the final version in Leibniz's copy (LA 119), where "without the substantial form" is crossed out and replaced by "without the Entelechies." What is most important in this emendation, for our present purpose, is the change from singular to plural number. To consider an extended mass without its (single, dominant) substantial form (if it has one) could be to consider it as secondary matter. But to consider it without (all) the (many) entelechies (or substantial forms) in it could not be to consider it as secondary matter, since it is precisely the presence of forms that distinguishes secondary matter. Leibniz may have made this change much later than 1687; noting that, while 'entelechy' occurs in Leibniz's copies of several items of the correspondence, "it does not occur in any letter received by Arnauld," Robert Sleigh opines that "every occurrence is an addition made after completion of the correspondence with Arnauld."[8]

The focus on geometrical qualities and motion in this argument helps illuminate the sense of 'matter' in the passage as Arnauld received it. Like secondary matter, and unlike primary matter in what I think is its usual sense for Leibniz, this sort of matter is a phenomenon. Unlike secondary matter, however, it is not an aggregate of substances. Its phenomenality springs not merely from its divisibility, but from its being constituted by the (phenomenal) qualities of shape, size, and motion. It is best interpreted, I think, as a phenomenon constituted by the appearance of physical qualities perceivable by sense.

Leibniz does not usually distinguish so sharply between a phenomenon so constituted and the phenomenon that is an aggregate of substances. Even here, where they seem to be two different types of "matter," we probably should not construe them as really distinct things. For in speaking of "the extended mass *considered* without the substantial form [italics added]" Leibniz may well have been thinking of this mass as *abstracted* from something that does include substantial forms. In other words, we may suppose that the matter Leibniz describes to Arnauld (like primary matter[9] and much more fully than secondary matter) is an abstraction, and that it is *from* secondary matter (i.e., from an aggregate of substances) that it is abstracted. The moving, geometrical physical appearance is an appearance *of* an aggregate of substances, and Leibniz may be thinking of it here as an aspect of such an aggregate, abstracted from its substantial forms. On this point it is interesting to compare this text with a much later (and undoubtedly fully monadological) letter to De Volder, in which Leibniz says that "the homogeneity of matter" which is involved in the "spreading out" that constitutes extension "does not obtain except by a mental abstraction, insofar as things that are only passive and therefore incomplete are considered" (G II,277/ AG 183; AG overlooks the plural number of the Latin verb here). In this later text, however, there is no suggestion of a special sense of 'matter', besides the primary and the secondary.

As noted earlier, the statement from which I have drawn these inferences is found in a marginal addition in Leibniz's copy of the letter, though it was included in the text sent to Arnauld. Leibniz's copy, without all its marginal additions,

[8]Sleigh, *Leibniz and Arnauld*, p. 209, n. 6.

[9]On the status of primary matter as an abstraction, see section 2 in this chapter.

presents a state of the text in which there is less evidence that the type of matter under discussion is not secondary matter. Is it therefore likely that in writing that state of the text, responding to Arnauld's concerns about matter conceived as "many beings," Leibniz meant to be talking about secondary matter, and only shifted the reference to another sort of matter in the process of revising the text with his marginal additions? I would answer this question in the negative, for several reasons.

1. Even before all its marginal additions the text, in arguing for the phenomenality of the kind of matter under discussion, gives the priority to the argument from the phenomenality of shape, size, and motion, and states that shape "is of the essence of a bounded extended mass." This suggests, though it does not strictly imply, that Leibniz was already thinking of a matter that "consists only in these qualities," as he would write in the margin.

2. The conception of matter as a phenomenon constituted by the perceptual appearance of physical qualities is not incompatible with a conception of matter as "many beings." For such a phenomenon is, as Leibniz says, extended, and as such composed of parts; and as composed of parts, it can also be seen as "many beings," though all of those many beings will themselves be pure phenomena, unlike the substances whose aggregation constitutes secondary matter.

3. The preliminary draft of the letter provides evidence that Leibniz did *not* take Arnauld to be thinking of what Leibniz would call secondary matter, for he speaks there of matter "in the manner in which you take it—namely, as an extended mass composed of parts where there is only mass and extension."[10] In Leibnizian secondary matter, by contrast, there is more than mass and extension, for there are also the substantial forms of the aggregated substances. The draft thus shows that Leibniz took Arnauld to be thinking of a Cartesian matter, which differs from Leibnizian secondary matter precisely in not having any substantial forms in it, and which, according to Leibniz, would also be "many beings."

Perhaps we may therefore take this passage, as it was sent to Arnauld, as explaining what place in a Leibnizian scheme of things can be assigned to a Cartesian matter, a matter constituted solely by extension and its modes: it can only be "an entirely pure phenomenon like the rainbow."[11] This would would help explain why this third type of matter rarely finds a place in Leibniz's writings: it is not part of the native structure of the Leibnizian system, but the product of an attempt to relate that system to an alien conception. Conversely, the consideration that the other two senses of 'matter' were further from his correspondent's own thought may have been among Leibniz's reasons for not sending Arnauld his discussion of them.

1.2 *Secondary Matter*

Leibniz's own pattern of thinking emerges more clearly in the addition that Arnauld did not see. That text begins:

[10] I quote the translation of this unpublished text given by Sleigh, *Leibniz and Arnauld*, p. 108.

[11] Leibniz seems to be speaking of the same Cartesian sort of matter when he says, later in the same letter, "I hold that mass, when nothing is considered in it but what is divisible, is a pure phenomenon" (LA 126).

> But if one takes as matter [of the corporeal substance], not the mass without forms, but [a secondary matter, which is] the multitude of substances whose mass is that of the [whole] body, one can say that these substances are parts of that matter, as those that enter into our body make part of it. (LA 119)

The bracketed words are interlinear additions within the marginal addition.[12] Apart from them, neither 'primary matter' nor 'secondary matter' occurs anywhere in this passage or in the preliminary draft of it. But if the phrase 'secondary matter' was introduced here some time after 1687, it represented no substantive change in Leibniz's thinking. Here the "multitude of substances" is clearly what he would call secondary matter, which differs from other sorts of matter precisely by having (an aggregate of) substances, and their substantial forms, somehow included in it. It is explicitly contrasted with "the mass without forms," which in the context surely refers to "the extended mass . . . consisting only in [the] qualities" of shape, size, and motion, which is discussed in the previous portion of the paragraph, the portion sent to Arnauld.

The issue about secondary matter that principally engages Leibniz's attention here is the relation of part to whole. After commenting that what he has said can be applied as easily to other corporeal substances as to a human being, he continues:

> The difficulties that people make for themselves in these matters come, among others, from the fact that they commonly do not have a distinct enough notion of the whole and of the part, which at bottom is nothing but an immediate requirement of the whole, and in some fashion homogeneous. Thus parts can constitute a whole whether it has or does not have a true unity. It is true that the whole that has a true unity can remain rigorously the same individual, even though it loses or gains parts, as we experience in ourselves; thus the parts are immediate requirements only for a time. (LA 120)

While the relation of part to whole may seem to have some relevance to the issue raised by Arnauld, how the substantial form can impart an intrinsic unity to matter, this discussion fails to address that issue. On that point, it adds nothing to Leibniz's initial statement that it is the corporeal substance rather than the matter that is unified by the substantial form. The "true unity" mentioned here must be a corporeal substance, for the secondary matter that is the body of such a substance, considered without the form of the substance, is certainly not a true unity in Leibniz's view. The secondary matter as such is a mere aggregate, and the only unity he can ascribe to an aggregate is not intrinsic but phenomenal, as he says at the end of the part of the paragraph that he did send to Arnauld, agreeing "that one can give the name *one* to an assembly of inanimate bodies even though no substantial form binds them, . . . but it is a unity of phenomenon or of thought, which is not enough for what there is that is real in phenomena" (LA 119).

The discussion of the part/whole relation is the likeliest source of any misgivings Leibniz may have felt about the theoretical adequacy of the text he withheld from Arnauld. There is nothing in the rest of the passage that he would not

[12] I have bracketed only simple additions; otherwise I translate the final text, which embodies the results of a few changes of other sorts.

later assert in one context or another. But on two points what he says here about corporeal substances as parts and wholes disagrees with other things he wrote during the last years of his correspondence with Arnauld.

First, his initial statement about secondary matter here, that corporeal substances can be said to be parts of it, disagrees with his statement in 1690, in a memo arising from discussions with Michelangelo Fardella, that "an indivisible substance should not therefore be said to enter into the composition of a body as a part, but rather as an essential internal requirement" (FC 320/AG 103).[13] It is also in tension with his statement in this very passage that a part must be "in some fashion homogeneous" with its whole; for substances are in the most important respects not homogeneous with aggregates, and therefore not with secondary matter.

Second, the implication here that a "whole that has a true unity" (which I have argued must be a corporeal substance) can have parts and gain and lose them obviously conflicts with a statement in the preliminary draft of this letter, that "a substance can lose its modes, but not its parts."[14] I think it is also in tension with the Fardella memo of 1690, in which having parts that always have other parts, and so on to infinity, is treated as a mark of not being a substance (FC 319/AG 103), for the way in which parts of corporeal substances seem to be admitted in the text before us offers no means of blocking such an infinite regress. Later still, writing to John Bernoulli in 1698, Leibniz was particularly explicit that the parts of a substance's organic body are not parts of the substance (e.g., GM III,537/AG 167).

1.3 Primary Matter

Immediately following this discussion of the relation of whole and part, as it pertains to secondary matter, Leibniz introduces another sort of matter:

> But if one understood by the term *matter* something that is always essential to the same substance, one could understand by that, in the sense of certain Scholastics, the primitive passive power [French *puissance*] of a substance, and in that sense matter would be neither extended nor divisible, although it would be the principle of divisibility, or of what amounts to it for the substance. But I do not wish to dispute about the usage of terms. (LA 120)

Identified as "the primitive passive power of a substance," this is clearly something that Leibniz would later call primary matter, though it is not so named in this text. The first thing Leibniz says about it here is that it "is always essential to the same substance." The bond asserted here seems to be tight in both directions. First, the same primary matter cannot belong to any substance but the one it now in fact belongs to. This excludes Leibnizian primary matter from one of the main functions of Aristotelian primary matter—namely, the function of being the substratum of substantial change, in which it belongs successively to different substances. Second, if a substance's primary matter is essential to it, it

[13]The document of 1690 from which I quote in this paragraph is discussed in Chapter 10, section 3.1.

[14]Sleigh, *Leibniz and Arnauld*, p. 109.

cannot be lost while the substance exists. In this it contrasts with secondary matter, which, as Leibniz has just been explaining, is composed of parts that can be lost or gained by the body of a corporeal substance. Since the parts of a substance's body can be lost or changed, while its primary matter cannot, it follows, as I have argued (for this and other reasons) in Chapter 11, section 2.2, that its primary matter cannot be divided into parts that are the primary matter of substances that are parts of its body. That is presumably one reason why primary matter is "neither extended nor divisible."

Though not itself extended or divisible, Leibniz says, primary matter, conceived as the primitive passive power of a substance, is "the principle of divisibility, or of what amounts to it for the substance."[15] That means, presumably, that it is the principle from which it follows that the substance has a divisible (and hence extended) body. We may be tempted to connect this with Leibniz's view, documented in Chapter 11, section 2.1, that it is the repetition of passive force that constitutes extension. But if the extension of my body is constituted by the repetition of primitive passive force or primary matter, it is presumably by the repetition of the primitive passive forces of the many substances contained in my body, rather than by a repetition of the primary matter that is essential to me as a substance. Indeed, it is hard to see how there could be a *repetition* of my primary matter as such, since it is presumably as single as I am. If the extension or divisibility of my body is derived from *my* primary matter, it must be by a different route (about which I will offer suggestions in Chapter 13).

Another implication of Leibniz's statement about this sort of matter as principle of divisibility deserves our attention. 'Principle' [French *principe*, Latin *principium*] means *source*, not result, as Leibniz surely knew well enough. His statement therefore presumably means that a corporeal substance has a divisible body because of its primary matter—*not* that it has primary matter because of its divisible body. This implies, I think, that the union of a corporeal substance's substantial form with its primary matter is prior, in the order of explanation, to the relation between the substantial form and the extended body or secondary matter. The primary matter appears here to be closely related to the substantial form: both are unextended and indivisible; both are always essential to the same substance; and both work, presumably together, in grounding the substance's possession of an extended body. Together they form a unit prior, metaphysically though not temporally, to the possession of the body. This agrees strikingly with what I take to be Leibniz's fully developed monadological view of corporeal substance: that the substantial form, or entelechy, and the primary matter together constitute the complete monad, which joins with the secondary matter to constitute the corporeal substance (G II,252/L 530f.). And it disagrees with one way in which some might be tempted to read Leibniz's theory of corporeal

[15] *Le principe de la divisibilité ou de ce qui en revient à la substance*. My translation of this phrase agrees in the main with H. T. Mason's (LA 120), but I think any translation of it is questionable. Grammatically, so far as I can judge after consulting several dictionaries of seventeenth-century French, *ce qui en revient à la substance* should mean "what comes of it for the substance," but that makes no philosophical sense in this context. To give the meaning that I have translated, Leibniz should have written, *ce qui y revient pour la substance*. My hypothesis is that he confused two idioms in French, which, after all, was not his native language.

substance in the middle years as less monadological and more Aristotelian—namely, by reading him as supposing that a complete substance possessing both substantial form and (primary) matter arises only from the relation of the substantial form to the (secondary) matter of its body.[16]

It remains to comment on Leibniz's identification of this sort of matter with "the primitive passive power of a substance." He claims to say this "in the sense of certain Scholastics." Probably the best Scholastic precedent for the identification is St. Thomas Aquinas, who held that primary matter is pure potentiality, and indeed that primary matter (or its essence) *is* its potentiality [Latin *potentia*].[17] And potentiality is certainly a passive principle for Aquinas, by contrast with the actuality or act [Latin *actus*] that constitutes form. Moreover, St. Thomas's primary matter, like Leibniz's, is prior, metaphysically, to divisibility; it is not divisible of itself, but only by virtue of a quantitative form inhering in it (ST I,q.50,a.2). Considered in abstraction from such forms, Thomistic primary matter is very unlike most modern conceptions of matter, and can hardly even be called a sort of "stuff."[18]

Leibniz confines primary matter to the role of passive power more strictly than Aquinas did, however. For when informed by a quantitative form Thomistic primary matter is an extended, divisible stuff, which is its normal, natural state. And it is definitely not always essential to the same substance, but is a substratum of substantial change. Other Scholastics, such as Scotus and Ockham, held views of primary matter even further removed from anything Leibniz could have accepted.[19]

2. *Matter and the Eucharist*

2.1 To Pellisson (January 1692)

The metaphysics of the Christian sacrament of the Eucharist played a significant part in the philosophy of body in the seventeenth century (at least on the Continent), though doubtless less than in the Middle Ages. It is a recurrent topic in Leibniz's theological notes and correspondence from 1668 to the end of his

[16]This is the "Aristotelian one-substance conception" of the structure of a corporeal substance I rejected in Chapter 10, section 2.2.

[17]ST I,q.115,a.1,ad 2; q.54,a.3; q.77,a.1. That Leibniz, at least in his youth, was aware of St. Thomas's conception of matter, and of its thinness, is attested by a manuscript in which he says, "Matter, according to Thomas, is a non-Being" (A VI,i,497*n*). That may indeed exaggerate the thinness of the Thomistic conception; it would be more accurate to say that (primary) matter does not have for Thomas a being [*entitas*] of its own, as it does for many later Scholastics. (It seems to me most natural to assume that "Thomas" here is Aquinas; unnatural to suppose it is the Thomas Anglus discussed in the quite separate manuscript of A VI,i,501–7.)

[18]Another interesting parallel between Leibniz's and Aquinas's views about primary matter has been pointed out to me by Houston Smit. It is well known that St. Thomas held that primary matter (signed by quantity) is the principle of individuation for substances that have it (see, e.g., M. Adams, *William Ockham*, vol. II, pp. 672–74). In Leibniz's philosophy, in his later years at least and, on my interpretation, in his middle years too, primary matter is the principle of confusion of perceptions, and substances are individuated by differences in the confusion of their perceptions—making primary matter a principle of individuation for Leibniz, too.

[19]See M. Adams, *William Ockham*, vol. II, ch. 16.

life. The sacrament seems not to have played a large part in his personal piety, at least in his later years,[20] but his philosophy would have to provide a metaphysics for it in order to be a basis for reunion of the churches. The puzzling, exploratory treatment of this topic in terms of "substantial bonds" in his letters to Bartholomew Des Bosses has been discussed in Chapter 10, section 5.3 and comes after the "middle years" that primarily concern us here. One of Leibniz's most important discussions of primary matter from the middle years, however, is found in a Eucharistic context, in a letter he wrote in January 1692 to Paul Pellisson-Fontanier (1624–93), a noted French convert from Protestantism to Catholicism, with whom he was exploring theological and philosophical bases for reunion of the churches.

> The word substance can be taken in two ways, for the subject itself and for the essence of the subject. For the subject itself, when one says that the body or the bread is a substance; for the essence of the subject, when one says, the substance of the body, or the substance of the bread; and then it is something abstract. So when it is said that primitive force constitutes the substance of bodies, their nature or essence is understood; thus Aristotle says that the nature is the principle of motion and rest; and the primitive force is nothing but that principle in each body from which all its actions and affections[21] are born. I consider matter as the first internal principle of passivity and resistance, and it is by it that bodies are naturally impenetrable. And the substantial form is nothing but the first internal principle of action, the first entelechy. (A I,vii,248)

The conception of matter presented here is clearly Leibniz's conception of *primary* matter, and several points relevant to our investigation can be elicited from this passage and its context, even before we fill in the background in Eucharistic theology.

1. In the distinction between substance as subject and substance as the essence of (or "substance of") the subject, primitive force is classed here as essence rather than as subject. Since primary matter appears here as the passive principle in primitive force, it follows that primary matter is classed as a feature of essence rather than as a sort of subject. This is a major point of difference from Aristotelian conceptions of matter. For while Aristotelians could speak of the essence of a body as including matter, in the sense that it requires the body to have matter, matter remained for them always a subject, and primary matter the ultimate subject of inherence in material things.

2. Most important is Leibniz's statement here that the essence "is something abstract." In the context it follows at once that primitive forces are abstract, and hence that both primary matter and substantial form are abstract. In calling these things abstract, of course, Leibniz does not mean that they inhabit some sort of Platonic heaven rather than a real world of acting and perceivable substances. "Abstract" must be understood here in relation to the mental operation of abstraction—that is, of considering something apart from the context in which it occurs. "Something abstract" is something that can be viewed as a thing or subject only by considering it apart from the only sort of context in which it can

[20]See Aiton, *Leibniz: A Biography*, p. 349.

[21]In French, *passions*. The sense is that of the plural, if we had one, of 'being-acted-on'.

occur. To say that primitive forces are abstract is not to deny that they have real existence, but to say that they have it only as aspects, properties, or features of a concrete subject that is not just a force. This is the abstract status that Leibniz assigns to both primary matter and substantial form.[22] We are left with the question, from what sort of subject they are abstracted. Is it very like the "monad" of Leibniz's last years, or is it somehow more robustly corporeal?[23]

3. One piece of evidence for the fundamentally monadological character of the view expressed in this text is that the primary matter (like the substantial form) is described as an *internal* principle [*principe interieur*]. An internal principle in a substance is presumably a principle that the substance has independently of its "external" properties—that is, independently of its relations to other substances. If that is the correct interpretation, it is implied here that the primary matter, as well as the substantial form, of a corporeal substance is metaphysically independent of full embodiment, because independent of relations to the other substances that go together, in some sense, to constitute its organic body.

4. The independence of the primary matter from the organic body or secondary matter is further evidenced by the fact Leibniz goes on in this letter to say that the primitive force is "a higher principle of action and resistance, from which extension and impenetrability emanate when God does not prevent it by a superior order" (A I,vii,249). Inasmuch as action is a function of substantial form, and resistance is a function of primary matter, primary matter and substantial form are presented here as fused in a single "principle of action *and* resistance." It is a "higher" principle, in the context, by contrast with extension and impenetrability, of which it is the source. As their source, it is prior to them, and therefore presumably prior to the embodiment of the substance whose principle of action and resistance it is. Moreover, Leibniz explicitly allows the possibility that God might prevent a "higher principle" of this sort from having the extension and impenetrability that would naturally emanate from it. This raises the issues about divine interference with the operations of created substances that were discussed in Chapter 3, section 2, and it certainly seems to envisage the possibility of the higher principle constituting a substance without a body, perhaps by virtue of God's not creating the other substances that would be involved in its body. In this metaphysical independence the entity from which primary matter is abstracted looks very much like the "monad" of Leibniz's last years.

An interesting foreshadowing of such a "higher principle" is found in a set of reading notes from about 1668 on a passage about the Eucharist by one Thomas White ("Thomas Anglus"). White had written something that seemed to Leibniz to presuppose "that matter is really distinguished from quantity, or at least can be taken apart [*praescindere*] from it." Leibniz's complaint that no one had

[22]That in Leibniz's view "primary matter is an abstraction from substance taken in its entirety" is also a feature of the interpretation advocated in Garber, "Leibniz and the Foundations of Physics," p. 54.

[23]This is obviously related to issues about the structure of a corporeal substance discussed in Chapter 10, sections 2–3. In the "two-substance" and "qualified monad" conceptions, the substantial form and primary matter are aspects of the monad. It is in the "Aristotelian one-substance" conception (which I argued was never held by Leibniz) that they are abstracted directly from something "more robustly corporeal."

explained "what that matter, consisting in something indivisible, would ultimately be" is so forceful that one might well be tempted to take him, in this text, as preferring a more or less Cartesian identification of matter with quantity (that is, with extension). But then he adds something of a rather different flavor:

> To explain this difficulty clearly and make perspicuous [the notion] that there is something in body pertaining to substance, which consists, however, in something indivisible, and is partly active and can appropriately be called form in the Scholastic Style, and partly passive and will rightly be called matter in their sense, which is prior to all mass, quantity, and shape; this is a task, this is hard work, thus far no mortal has accomplished it. (A VI,i,502)

Did Leibniz already think it could be accomplished? And (what probably amounted to the same thing for his youthful ambition) did he himself aspire to accomplish it? The text does not tell us, but I am inclined to think he did. Here we glimpse a conception Leibniz had very early of what it would be to rehabilitate Scholastic conceptions of primary matter and substantial form. They would be inseparable aspects of an indivisible substantial core which is metaphysically prior to such physical features as mass and extension.

5. If primary matter is a principle internal to a corporeal substance, must its metaphysically fundamental operation be internal to that substance? And must that operation be an aspect of the *perceptual* operation of the substance? These inferences are not explicitly drawn in the letter to Pellisson, but I believe they were warranted by Leibniz's principles at the time.

The first inference gets some support from a statement, in a fragment that seems to belong with Leibniz's Fardella memo of 1690, that "In every substance there is nothing but that nature or primitive force from which follows the series of its internal operations" (VE 2158 = FC 324)—which implies that some, and suggests that all, of the operations of a substance's primitive force are internal to the substance. A line of argument to support both inferences is based on Leibniz's repeated contrast of matter with form as passive with active. If this is the most fundamental difference between them, as he seems to imply, then it is natural to assume they are passive and active, respectively, with respect to operations *of the same sort*. Otherwise, and specifically if the operations of the one were perceptual and the other's were nonperceptual in character, that would be another fundamental difference that would deserve to be mentioned at least as prominently as the active/passive difference. So if Leibniz speaks of "the internal action" of a substantial form, and presents it as perceptual in character, that would be evidence that a perceptual internal operation is to be assigned to primary matter as well. There is a text from October 1693, with some relation to the Pellisson correspondence, in which Leibniz does just that, contrasting matter and form as passive and active, and saying:

> It is not that this form makes its body act otherwise than according to the laws of mechanics. But with that, the internal action of this form, which is called sensation in animals, and thought in man, has its jurisdiction apart, although it has its parallelism with the actions of the body. (A I,ix,211)[24]

[24]These lines are from a short piece about the essence of body, written for Jacques-Bénigne Bossuet (1627–1704), who was associated with Pellisson on the Catholic side of a correspondence

A more solid line of argument, I think, draws support from the January 1692 letter to Pellisson. If primary matter is a principle internal to a corporeal substance, and can be conceived as an entity only by abstraction from the substance, then surely the operation of the primary matter is an operation of the substance itself. This conclusion is supported also by the thesis that matter in this sense "is always essential to the same substance" (LA 120), which is echoed in this letter by a statement that the primitive force "remains always the same in the same body" (A I,vii,249). But Leibniz denies that there is any metaphysically fundamental operation of one substance on another. Talk of interaction of substances can be given an acceptable sense only in terms of a harmony of the internal operations of the different substances. And there is no exception to this, even in this period of Leibniz's thought, for relations between a corporeal substance and the other substances that are "in" its organic body;[25] to suppose otherwise would be to make hash of the "system of pre-established harmony." As an operation, or an aspect of the operation, of a corporeal substance, therefore, the fundamental operation of the primary matter must be internal to that substance.

In giving rise to extension and resistance, moreover, as it naturally does, the primary matter must be involved in interaction, in the derivative sense, with other substances, which must be explained in terms of a harmony of internal operations. But harmony of the internal operations of one substance with others *is* perception, according to Leibniz (LA 112). Hence the metaphysically fundamental operation of primary matter by which it naturally gives rise to extension and resistance is an aspect of a perceptual operation of a corporeal substance. Q.E.D.

2.2 Leibniz's Solution to the Problem of Multipresence

The rather monadological interpretation I have given this passage seems to me to be confirmed by the way in which Leibniz proceeds to use its ideas for a metaphysics of the Eucharist. At this point I need to make clear what was (and was not) the theological issue under discussion. Leibniz's understanding of two of the main doctrines to be distinguished had been articulated as follows in a much earlier document, probably dating from fall 1671:

> I. One and the same Body of Christ (which suffered on the Cross for us) is really present, by its substance, wherever the Eucharistic sacrificial offering [*Hostia*] is. II. In the sacrificial offering of the Eucharist the substance of the Body of Christ is under the forms [*species*] of bread. (A, VI,i,515)

---

with Leibniz about reunion of the churches. The passage of interest was bracketed and not actually sent to Bossuet, but I think that is probably because it went deeper philosophically than Leibniz normally wished to go with the famous bishop, as he thought less highly of Bossuet's reasoning than of his rhetoric (A I,viii,125). When he went deeper, as we have seen, with Pellisson, it was not without apologies for his "prolixity" (A I,vii,250).

[25] Cf. LA 136. It should be noted that Garber agrees ("Leibniz and the Foundations of Physics," p. 55). This is one of the doctrines of the *Discourse on Metaphysics* about the nature of individual substance that he says apply to corporeal substances as he thinks Leibniz conceived of them in the middle years.

Following the terminology of the Council of Trent, Leibniz refers to these as the doctrines of real presence and transubstantiation, respectively. He notes (correctly) that "The Augsburg Confession [of the Lutherans[26]] admits only the first proposition; the second is added by the Roman Church and, with most cautious phrasing, by the Council of Trent" (A VI,i,515). His formulation of the second proposition does not make the distinction between the doctrines as clearly as it should. The doctrine of real presence is positive—that the substance of the body of Christ *is* present in the sacrament. The main point that the doctrine of transubstantiation adds to this is negative—that the substance of the bread is no longer present in the sacrament, although its *species* or perceptible accidents remain.[27]

Leibniz did not at this time think the rejection of transubstantiation essential to the Lutheran position. In 1671 he was prepared as a Lutheran to accept both doctrines (A VI,i,515f.; A II,i,175). In later years he was less ready to affirm transubstantiation, but in 1694 he could be quite cautious on the point: "It does not seem to follow that since Transubstantiation . . . can be affirmed without overturning any principle of the Protestants, therefore it ought to be affirmed. For it does not follow that whatever we are not able to refute is true" (A I,x,112). It is of capital importance for the understanding of Leibniz's letters to Pellisson that what Leibniz was trying to explain and to vindicate in them is only the doctrine of real presence, to which he was personally and ecclesiastically committed, and not that of transubstantiation, which by then he avoided affirming. Pellisson and Leibniz both acknowledge their fundamental agreement on the real presence (A I,vii,168,295). This gives to what he says about Eucharistic metaphysics in these letters a seriousness that we have less reason to ascribe to the discussion of "substantial bonds" in his letters to Des Bosses, where he is trying to account for transubstantiation, which he by then explicitly did not accept (G II,390,399; cf. Gr 220; T pd18–19).

Leibniz's priorities as a Lutheran are reflected in the fact that the central problem that he tries to solve in most of his writings about Eucharistic metaphysics is the problem of multipresence—that is, of how the one body of Christ could be present in the many different places where the sacrament might be observed at once—which is a problem for the doctrine of real presence. In drawing on Eucharistic theology for an objection to Descartes's philosophy of body, for example, he does not take up the well-known objection that had been raised by Arnauld and discussed at some length by Descartes (AT VII,217f.,247–56), which is based not on the real presence but on a version of the doctrine of transubstantiation. Instead, and even in the very first letter Leibniz wrote to Arnauld, in 1671 (A II,i,171), Leibniz offers an objection based on the problem of multipresence—that it would be impossible for any body to be in many places at once if the essence of body were extension, as Descartes claimed, for then the extension, or the filling, of each place, each bounded space, would constitute a different body

[26]Leibniz disapproved of the term 'Lutheran' (Schrecker 57,96; A I,vii,257), and normally referred to his own church as "Evangelical," or by mention of the Augsburg Confession. He was sometimes willing, however, perhaps out of courtesy, to follow a princely correspondent in using 'Lutheran' (A I,iii,282,333; iv,419).

[27]For a philosophical account of the doctrine of transubstantiation in its Scholastic context, see M. Adams, "Aristotle and the Sacrament of the Altar."

(A VI,iii,158/W 63; A I,vii,198; cf. *Systema* 127; A I,x,111; Dutens I,30). This argument presupposes that if extension constitutes the essence of body, then the extension of a given space constitutes a principle of individuation for an individual body. It can be argued that this was also presupposed by Descartes in his arguments about rarefaction in *Principles* II,5–8 (AT VIII-1,42–45). Nonetheless, the objection raised by Leibniz was one that Descartes had not addressed, as Leibniz notes (A I,x,144).

Having presented this objection to Pellisson, Leibniz claims that his own conception of corporeal substance provides a solution to the problem:

> Then it is by the application to several places of this [higher] principle [of action and resistance], which is nothing but the primitive force of which I have spoken, or (to speak in more ordinary terms) the particular nature of the thing, that the multipresence of a body is to be saved. It is true, however, that the substance *in concreto* is something other than the Force, for it is the subject taken with that force. Thus the subject itself is present, and its presence is real, because it[28] emanates immediately from its essence, as God determines its application to the places. . . . I would even say that it is not only in the Eucharist, but everywhere else, that bodies are present only by this application of the primitive force to the place; but this occurs naturally only in accordance with a certain extension, or size and shape, and in regard to a certain place, from which other bodies are excluded. (A I,vii,249)

The metaphysical center of these lines is obviously the statement that "not only in the Eucharist, but everywhere else," the presence of a corporeal substance in a place consists only in the "application of [its] primitive force to the place." The substance or "body" of which this is said is presumably the substance of which primary matter is an aspect, or from which it is an abstraction; for it is the whole primitive force or higher principle of action and resistance, which includes the primary matter as well as the substantial form, that is said here to be applied to a place to constitute the presence of a body in that place. It seems to be implied, then, that primary matter is an abstraction from a substance that is not so "physical" as to have any more primitive way of being in a place than by operating (immediately) on or at that place—a substance that in this way also resembles the monads of the *Monadology*.

This conclusion is all the more strongly established in that Leibniz is resisting considerable theological pressure from Pellisson to find a more primitive way for a corporeal substance to be in a place. Leibniz had given Pellisson a preliminary account of his theory of multipresence in a letter of November 1691. On December 30 Pellisson replied with a misgiving:

> I am somewhat afraid that the way in which you explain . . . substance as a kind [*espece*] of force that can be applied in different places may give occasion to someone to say that you are not genuinely of the Augsburg Confession on the Eucharist because you do not believe in a genuine real presence, but in a presence of force and power [*vertu*], which most of the Sacramentarians accept, and Calvin much more than the others.

[28]"It" here probably refers either to the presence or to the force. A reference to "the subject" is grammatically impossible on grounds of the gender in French.

Pellisson asked for further explanation, adding that he himself conceived of force "as an ordinary and almost necessary consequence of substance, but not as being substance itself" (A I,vii,227f.).

This question is aimed quite accurately at a theologically sensitive point. Calvin had affirmed that believers enjoy in the sacrament a "true and substantial partaking of the body and blood of the Lord,"[29] and this was certainly understood as a communication of spiritual benefits by Christ's power. For Calvin, however, this interaction took place spiritually between Christ and the believer and did not involve the presence of Christ's body at any *place* except in heaven. It was the most impassioned disagreement between Calvin and the Lutherans that he denied, and they affirmed, the presence of the body of Christ in the *place* of the consecrated bread and wine.[30] Leibniz of course is trying to explain the presence of Christ's body in many *places*, which was important to Catholics as well as Lutherans, but Pellisson fears that he means nothing more than what Calvin would accept—that in the sacrament Christ's power operates on believers wherever they may be.

The long discussion of the nature of substance in Leibniz's letter of January 1692 is a response to Pellisson's concern. The following statements address the objection directly:

> It is true, however, that the substance *in concreto* is something other than the Force, for it is the subject taken with that force. Thus the subject itself is present, and its presence is real, because it emanates immediately from its essence, as God determines its application to the places. A presence by power [*presence virtuelle*], as opposed to a real presence, must be without that immediate application of the essence or primitive force, and happens only by actions at a distance or by intermediate operations. Whereas there is no distance here. Those who follow Calvin admit a real distance, and the power of which they speak is (it seems to me) spiritual and related only to faith; that has nothing in common with the force I mean. (A I,vii,249)

This is not a very satisfying answer to the objection. Calvin would not say that in the sacrament Christ does not operate on believers directly, but only by intermediate operations [as we might act on a distant body by throwing a stone at it, to borrow an example Leibniz would use later (A I,vii,294)]. Calvin did say that Christ's body remains at a distance from ours, and Leibniz denies that; but Pellisson's worry is precisely that the local presence among us that Leibniz ascribes to Christ's body is nothing but an operation that Calvin ascribed to Christ in other terms. Leibniz does allude to a difference that may be more significant, that the Calvinists speak of a power that is "related only to faith," or that is applied only to the believing soul; whereas Leibniz seems to speak of a force that is "applied" to the place of the consecrated bread and wine, or to whatever is in that place. But this difference is not really developed here.

Pellisson was somewhat mollified—not, I think, by this answer, but by the more general metaphysical exposition in Leibniz's letter of January 1692. Reply-

[29]Calvin, *Institutes*, p. 1382 (IV, xvii,19). This passage is paraphrased almost verbatim, and with evident understanding, by Pellisson (A I,vii,276).

[30]Calvin, *Institutes*, IV,xvii,5–12,16–19.

ing a month later, Pellisson is prepared to accept Leibniz as holding a real presence of the body of Christ if what he says is present is the primitive force understood as a *principle* of action, and not merely "the action that is the effect of this principle" (A I,vii,276). Leibniz responded in March, making clear that he did indeed mean to be speaking of the presence of the principle of action itself. But he looked Pellisson's gift horse in the mouth, expressing a reservation about contrasting the presence of the principle with a mere presence of operation. "I answer that everything that operates immediately in several places also is in several places by a true presence of its essence, and that the immediate operation cannot be judged to be distant from the individual that operates, since it is a manner of being of it" (A I,vii,294). What particularly interests me about this response is that Leibniz was not able to accept as sharp a distinction as Pellisson wanted between presence of essence and presence of operation. Perhaps indeed he is not able to make a sharp enough distinction to distance himself from Calvin on this issue.[31] The reason for that, I take it, is that Leibniz saw nothing for the local presence of a substance or its essence to be, if it is not a presence by some sort of operation.

What sort of operation that would be is one of the things we would most like to know, but Leibniz's letters to Pellisson are quite uninformative on the point, speaking vaguely of the "application" of primitive forces to places. I have argued, however, that Leibniz's principles require it to be an internal operation in harmony with other substances and, therefore, in a broad Leibnizian sense, perceptual. It may also be relevant to note here a much later text in which Leibniz seems to have been aware of the considerations that press him in this direction. Speaking of the assignment of places to souls, in a letter written to Des Bosses in April 1709, he offers the alternatives—"that they *are not in a place except by operation*, that is, speaking according to the old system of influence, or rather (according to the new system of pre-established harmony) that they *are in a place by correspondence*, and thus are in the whole organic body that they animate" (G II,371). The way in which these alternatives are formulated seems to imply that Leibniz himself must reject the interpretation in terms of operation and embrace instead an interpretation in terms of correspondence. We have been examining texts from the 1690s, however, when he already rejected the system of influence in favor of that of pre-established harmony, but in which he nonetheless ascribed to primitive forces (doubtless including souls) a local presence by immediate operation. The obvious way of rendering this consistent is to suppose that no metaphysical influence is implied in the texts of the 1690s, but at most an action of one substance on another in the derivative sense explained in DM 15, which amounts to a sort of correspondence of their internal properties. In other words, being in a place by (immediate) operation, as affirmed in the 1690s, is reduced to being in a place by correspondence.

[31]By 1699 Leibniz was willing to say to a representative of the Reformed communion that Calvin's account of the matter was "most satisfying" (Gr 449). (There is an implicit contrast in the text with other Reformed theologians whose views on the sacrament differed more from Lutheran positions than Calvin's did.) And in NE 514 Leibniz explicitly minimizes the importance of any difference between Lutheran and Calvinist positions on the manner of Christ's presence in the sacrament (see also T pd 18).

The question may be raised whether this reduction compromises the immediacy of the presence. In the *New Essays* (1703–5) Leibniz compares the local presence of souls with the Thomistic view of angels as not being "in a place except by operation, which according to me is not immediate and is reduced to the preestablished harmony"—a mode of presence that Leibniz goes on to contrast with the presence that God has by operating "immediately" on creatures (NE 222). It is natural, though I think not logically compulsory, to read the denial of immediacy here as applying to souls as well as to angels, and as inferred from the reduction to preestablished harmony.

By 1709, Leibniz seems to have had some doubts as to whether his theory offered a conception of substantial presence robust enough for all the theological demands that might be placed on it. The most public evidence of these doubts is the fact that in 1710, discussing the Eucharist in the *Theodicy* (T pd 19), Leibniz does not claim more than an "analogy" between presence and immediate operation. The strongest evidence of doubt or change is in a letter of 1709 to Des Bosses, where Leibniz says, in a Eucharistic context, "I have already given Tournemine the answer that presence is something Metaphysical, as union is, which is not explained by phenomena" (G II,390; cf. G VI,595). These texts may suggest a rejection of Leibniz's old theory of the real presence in favor of the postulation of a metaphysically primitive local presence of substance, which he had rejected in the 1690s. With regard to the notion of union, however, in the *Theodicy* and the texts connected with his interchange with Tournemine, I argued in Chapter 10, section 5.2, that Leibniz had not personally abandoned his own more reductionistic theory, but allowed at least a problematic possibility of something more for those whose theology might demand it. A similar interpretation of his statements about presence in these texts seems to me the most plausible. It is supported by letters of 1710 to Des Bosses in which Leibniz still defends his old theory. "And in truth," he says, "if God brought it about that something operated immediately at a distance, by that very fact he would bring about its multi-presence without any penetration or replication" (G II,399; cf. G II,407).

2.3 "On Transubstantiation" (1670)

My interpretation of the letters to Pellisson is in keeping with the prior history of Leibniz's theory of the real presence in the Eucharist. The main idea of the Eucharistic theory that he offered Pellisson is that if the substance of a body is seen as consisting, not in extension, but in a force or principle of action (and being acted on), the substance will be present where it operates immediately, and that while in the natural order the immediate operation of a corporeal substance is confined to one place, by the power of God it can be made to operate immediately in many places. Leibniz used this strategy for solving the problem of multipresence for forty years, if not more. It recurs from his youthful theological work in Mainz about 1670, through his middle years, and at least as late as 1710.[32] In the earliest surviving full development of the idea it is clear that

[32]See, e.g., A VI,iii,158f./W 64f. (from 1672–76); A I,iii,272f. and *Systema* 127f. (from the 1680s); A I,x,143f. (to Bossuet, 1694); Dutens I,30f. and Schrecker 87f.,120 (from 1698–99 in the

the operation by which the substantial principle is present in any place is perceptual or cognitive in character.

The text to which I refer is entitled "On Transubstantiation," and was composed in Mainz, I think probably in spring 1670 (A VI,i,508–13/L 115–18).[33] This essay begins with an account of the nature of substance according to which substance requires a principle of action that can be found only in a mind. Leibniz concludes that "the Substance of a body, therefore, is union with a sustaining mind." More precisely, since Leibniz did not yet believe in internal mind-like principles in nonrational creatures, "the Substance of the human body is union with the human mind; the Substance of bodies that lack reason is union with the universal mind or God" (A VI,i,509/L 116).

In this early work Leibniz accepts the doctrine of transubstantiation, and offers a metaphysical account of it as taking place "insofar as the special concurrence of the mind of Christ, who assumes the bread and wine into [his][34] body, is substituted in place of the general concurrence which the universal or Divine mind imparts to all Bodies" (A VI,i,509/L 116).[35] We are more concerned here, however, with Leibniz's theory of the real presence, and of multipresence, which is developed as follows in "On Transubstantiation." Having argued that "the mind is not in a place through itself [*per se*]," he goes on:

23. The mind operates on a body which is in space.
24. To that extent therefore it can be said to be in space by [its] operation. St. Thomas.
25. Every operation of the mind is thought.

---

context of discussions between the Lutheran and Reformed communions); and G II,399 (to Des Bosses, 1710).

[33] I hope to discuss this fascinating document in more detail elsewhere. No one doubts that it was written during the Mainz period. No date is recorded in it, and unfortunately it has come down to us only in an eighteenth-century copy, so there is no relevant physical evidence of its date of composition. (See A VI,i,*xxv*; ii,572f.) We must therefore rely on the agreement and disagreement of its content with other, more securely dated texts. It seems to have been written to be read as a Catholic statement, though Leibniz was still, as he said at about that time, "committed to the Augsburg Confession" (A VI,i,516). But I think this is no reason to doubt the authentically Leibnizian character of the text, for his approach to reunion of the churches was based on a belief that Catholic and Protestant (or, at any rate, Catholic and Lutheran) theologies were not irreconcilably opposed on basic issues. Leibniz seems to have assumed that reunion would take place within the institutional framework of the Roman Catholic Church and would leave the doctrinal framework of that church almost entirely intact, though it would demand some further reforms of its practices. His effort was to find interpretations of Catholic doctrines that could be accepted by Protestants without any substantial compromise of Protestant convictions, and that would still be acceptable to Catholics; reunion should take place *salvis principiis utriusque partis* [preserving the principles of both parties] (a phrase used by Leibniz to express his own aspirations in 1685: A I,iv,386f., and, with variations, 380,389). For most of these points about Leibniz's project for church reunion, see A II,i,488/L 259. It seems fairly clear that until some time in middle age Leibniz himself was prepared to assent to virtually all Catholic dogmas about the Eucharist, and that he never regarded such assent as incompatible with adherence to the Augsburg Confession.

[34] Something seems to have been omitted here by the eighteenth-century copyist.

[35] Despite his anti-Cartesian polemic on this subject, Leibniz may here be taking up a Cartesian idea. In a letter of 9 February 1645 to the Jesuit Denis Mesland, Descartes suggested that transubstantiation may take place by union of the soul of Christ with the particles of the bread and wine (AT IV,165–70); cf. Watson, "Transubstantiation among the Cartesians," p. 170.

26. The mind can think many things at once.
27. The mind can therefore be in many places at once by [its] operation.
28. Therefore the mind of Christ can bestow operation, action, or subsistence both on the glorious body of Christ and at the same time on the species of consecrated bread and wine, and on numerically different instances of the latter in different places on the earth.
29. Therefore the mind of Christ can be present everywhere to the *species* of bread and wine.
30. The mind of Christ concurring with his glorious body that suffered for us is its Substance, by no. 9.[36]
31. Therefore the Substance of the glorious Body of Christ can be present everywhere to the *species* of bread and wine. Q.E.D. (A VI,i,510/L 116f.)

The mind, we are told, is present in places by operation; any other, more direct way of being spatially present is inapplicable to it. And such presence of the mind of Christ constitutes substantial presence of the body of Christ, the body with which Christ's mind concurs. This substantial presence by operation is essentially the central idea of the theory of the real presence that Leibniz would offer to Pellisson over twenty years later, subject to the qualification, in the later texts, that the operation must be immediate. "On Transubstantiation" gives us an explanation of what the operation is: "Every operation of the mind is thought."

For a mind to operate at a place is presumably for the mind to think that place, or to have as object of its thought what is at that place. That seems to be presupposed in Leibniz's inference of the mind's possible multipresence from its ability to think many things at once; this interpretation is confirmed by the fact that in this document Leibniz refers to the union or concurrence of God's mind with a body as God's "idea of" the body. This foreshadows Leibniz's later view in which the body *of* a monad is the body which that monad perceives most directly.[37] The qualification of special directness (or of immediateness of operation, as in the letters to Pellisson) is needed early as well as late, of course, to distinguish a mind's own body from others of which it thinks; but Leibniz obviously had not worked all this through in 1670.

It is noteworthy also that Leibniz says here both that "every operation of the mind is thought" and that the mind of Christ bestows "operation, action, or subsistence both on the glorious body of Christ and at the same time on the species of consecrated bread and wine." The obvious implication that the latter bestowal takes place by thinking suggests a rather phenomenalist view of what there is in bodies besides the sustaining or concurrent mind.

This of course does not prove that the operation by which primitive forces are present in places according to Leibniz's letters to Pellisson is cogitative or perceptual, like the operation by which minds were said to be in places, over twenty years earlier, in "On Transubstantiation." But I think it is significant for the interpretation of the later texts that their central idea is one that Leibniz originally worked out with a cogitative or perceptual operation in mind.

[36]No. 9 was "The Substance of a body, therefore, is union with a concurrent mind."
[37]See Chapter 10, section 4.1.

3. Bernoulli's Questions

In fall 1698 there was an illuminating series of interchanges on the nature of corporeal substance between Leibniz and John Bernoulli, as we have seen in Chapter 10, section 3.2. A group of questions were proposed by Bernoulli and numbered by Leibniz as six. The first two of them were about primary matter, and were followed with notable persistence through several rounds of discussion. They were inspired by a previous statement of Leibniz: "Matter itself, in itself [*per se*], or bulk [*moles*],[38] which you can call primary matter, is not a substance, and not even an aggregate of substances, but something incomplete" (GM III,537/AG 167). Bernoulli formulated his questions about this statement as follows: "I do not adequately grasp [1] what you understand by primary matter *in itself* [*per se*] or by *bulk* [*moles*] as distinct from secondary matter or mass [*massa*], nor, also, [2] what is incomplete for you." (GM III,539f., numbering added)

In his letter of late September Leibniz replied:

> You ask (1) what I understand by matter in itself, or primary matter or bulk, as distinct from secondary [matter]. I answer: that which is merely passive, and separate from souls or forms.
>
> You ask (2) what is incomplete for me here. I answer: the passive without the active, and the active without the passive. (GM III, 541f./AG 167)

'Incomplete' here is roughly equivalent to 'abstract'. Primary matter is not a substance because it is not complete enough to be a concrete subject. It is a "merely passive" principle, and it takes both passive and active principles to constitute a substance. Either without, or "separate from," the other is incomplete, an abstraction from the complete or concrete substance. In light of the January 1692 letter to Pellisson, this seems to me the natural interpretation of these lines from Leibniz's letters to Bernoulli.[39]

Bernoulli, however, had presumably not seen the letter to Pellisson and responded on 8 November 1698 with the complaint that Leibniz's answers were "too Laconic" (GM III,545). He posed objections to them from a Cartesian point of view:

> (1) By matter in itself, or primary matter or bulk, as distinct from secondary [matter] you say you understand that which is merely passive, and separate from souls or forms. But a Cartesian, who has no idea of forms, and who places the nature of body in extension alone, would reply to you here that he does not know what it is to be separate from forms.
>
> (2) You say that what is incomplete is the active without the passive and the passive without the active. You could have said that what is incomplete is primary matter without form, and form without primary matter. But the same difficulty as in the preceding [question] would arise for a Cartesian, who acknowledges no distinction between matter and form. (GM III,546)

Replying ten days later, Leibniz said:

[38] On the translation of *moles* here, see Chapter 10, note 21.

[39] On the incompleteness of primary matter, as purely passive, cf. G III,657.

> As to (1). When I said that *primary matter* is that which is merely passive and separate from souls or forms, I said the same thing twice; that is, it is just as if I had said that it is merely passive and separate from all activity. For *forms* are nothing for me but Activities or Entelechies; and substantial forms indeed are primitive Entelechies.
>
> As to (2). I preferred to say that what is *incomplete* is the active without the passive, and the passive without the active, rather than that it is matter without form, or the reverse. That was in order to posit what is explained rather than what is to be explained, and in order to follow your advice, in a way, before you gave it, since the crowd of Modernizers is less offended by the name of activities than of forms. (GM III,551/AG 168)

Here Leibniz seems to be saying that the nature of form and matter is *exhaustively* explained in terms of activity and passivity, respectively. He hopes to avoid the Cartesian objection to the matter/form distinction by reducing it to the passive/active distinction. This has some implications for our topic.

One implication is that there is no primitive content, over and above passivity, in Leibniz's conception of primary matter. And passivity is clearly an *aspect* of things—not a substance, and nothing at all like a stuff. Perhaps primary matter was no more than this for Aquinas, but it certainly was for most later Scholastics. Moreover, I have argued earlier (p. 352) that if it is exclusively in its passivity that primary matter differs from form, then it should follow that the operations with respect to which primary matter is passive should be the same as those with respect to which substantial form is active, which Leibniz says are perceptual or quasi-psychological in character (A I,ix,211; E 124f./L 454).

Furthermore, the human self certainly has a passive aspect, and Leibniz thought that all created minds are in some ways passive. This suggests that if primary matter is simply the principle of passivity, it is at least in some cases an aspect of selves, minds, and mind-like beings.[40] This very point is taken up, from a different direction, in Bernoulli's next response (6 December 1698). He is led to it by the recognition that seems to come to him at this point that in Leibniz's view matter and form cannot be separate from each other except by abstraction; but he seems still to assume that Leibniz would not ascribe primary matter to spirits.

> (1) You say that *primary matter* (which I would name *uniform*, or rather *unformed*, extension) is that which is merely passive and separate from souls or forms. And elsewhere you say that forces or forms are of the same age as primary matter, and that it cannot subsist without them. Therefore the passive is not and cannot be separate from the active really, but only by a mental abstraction, inasmuch as we can consider the former without the latter, as we do in Geometry. But I ask nevertheless whether God by his omnipotence could not create the passive wihout the active, or primary matter without souls or

[40]The possibility of an argument of this sort is acknowledged by Garber, "Leibniz and the Foundations of Physics," p. 111, n. 67. His response that when Leibniz spoke of the primary matter of *corporeal* substances, he must have had something more in mind than a matter that accrues to substances by virtue of their passivity with respect to perception does not convince me. A corporeal substance for Leibniz is just a substance endowed [*praedita*] with an organic body. The organic body, as such, is secondary matter, and its presence says nothing clear about the nature of primary matter.

> forms, if indeed he has created souls, namely Spirits and Angels, without matter, or the active without the passive. . . .
>
> (2) I grasp your thought about the *incomplete*. But if the active without the passive, or form without matter, is something incomplete, it seems to follow that Spirits, Angels, and God himself, who is the most complete Being, are nevertheless incomplete. I see what you are going to say, namely that here you mean something incomplete with respect to composition, not perfection. Be careful nonetheless, not to give the malevolent and envious any ground for quibbling and twisting [your words] in a worse sense. (GM III,555f.)

Leibniz's response (17 December 1698: GM III,560/AG 169f.) is interesting. First he says, "You rightly judge that the passive is never actually separate from the active in creatures," ascribing this view to his correspondent, whereas it is not clear to me that Bernoulli meant to say more than that the view follows from Leibniz's premises. Then Leibniz sidesteps a standard Scholastic issue by saying "what God can do, I should not venture to define. If something exclusively passive, and the vacuum, do not conflict with his power, at least they seem to conflict with his wisdom." The phrasing suggests that he sees that his position seems to imply the Thomistic view that God could not create matter without form, but is reluctant, on reverential grounds, to draw that conclusion. Most interesting to me is what follows. Leibniz does not acknowledge the solution of problem that Bernoulli proposed for him in terms of composition and perfection. Rather he says:

> it is not certain that there are any utterly separate Intelligences, except God. And most of the [Church] Fathers inclined to the contrary, attributing bodies even to Angels.
>
> God doubtless is pure act [*purus actus*], since he is most perfect. But imperfect things are passive, and if you conceive of them otherwise, they are taken incompletely.

I take this response to mean that minds and mind-like beings, except for God, are to some extent passive, and therefore have matter. Given the context, in which it is passivity that is under discussion, and passivity has been identified with primary matter, Leibniz must mean that *primary* matter is to be ascribed to the (finite) mind-like beings, though he does not say that here explicitly. The phrase "attributing bodies even to Angels" might suggest that it is (organic) bodies, and hence secondary matter, that is attributed to the mind-like beings, but I think the phrase must be explained otherwise—as reflecting the content of the precedent to which Leibniz is appealing, and also the fact that for Leibniz a substance's possession of primary matter is connected with its possession of an organic body. That Leibniz believed in this connection is clear. The nature of the connection is not explained in this document. I would explain it by saying that it is the pattern of more and less distinct perception (which involves confused perception, hence passivity, hence primary matter) that links a substance with a particular organic body.[41]

Leibniz here infers activity from perfection and passivity from imperfection. He does not say to Bernoulli that he means perfection and imperfection of *per-*

[41]For Leibniz's expression of essentially the same views about the materiality of angels (though in less developed contexts) in the period 1703–5 see G III,457, NE 307, G VI,548.

ception. But what he does say here certainly fits the pattern of the earlier statement that "[s]ubstances have Metaphysical matter or passive power insofar as they express something confusedly; active, insofar as [they do so] distinctly" (G VII,322/L 365, from 1683). Similarly, in 1686, in DM 15, Leibniz had characterized activity and passivity in terms of increase and decrease of perfection, and perfection as perfection of the substance's expression of the universe. For Leibniz, as I have already remarked, a substance's (internal) expression of other substances, or of the universe, *is* perception—and all the more obviously so where intelligent substances are under discussion, as in this letter to Bernoulli.

It is clear from Leibniz's response to Bernoulli that he thought the possession of primary matter is entailed by any imperfection or passivity in respect of the operations that spirits are assumed to have, which are surely perceptual or cogitative operations. This at least strongly suggests that he did not suppose the possession of primary matter requires any operation at a metaphysically fundamental level that is not perceptual or cogitative. And no such requirement is suggested in these letters.

4. *The Debate about Thinking Matter*

An important group of Leibniz's statements about matter from the years 1698–1704 arise in the context of his interest in the philosophy of John Locke, the interest that issued ultimately in Leibniz's *New Essays on Human Understanding*. Characterizing his aims in the *New Essays* in a letter of 28 April 1704 to Isaac Jaquelot, Leibniz began by saying, "I devote myself above all to vindicating the immateriality of the soul, which Mr. Locke leaves doubtful" (G III,473). This may seem a surprising statement to those who have been introduced to the *New Essays* primarily as a defense of Rationalist epistemology and innatism, but Nicholas Jolley, in a major recent study of Leibniz's relation to Locke, has argued persuasively that the immateriality of the soul was indeed Leibniz's main concern in the work.[42]

The principal way in which Locke seemed to leave doubt about the soul's immateriality was by arguing that we are not in a position to know "without revelation . . . whether Omnipotency has not given to some Systems of Matter fitly disposed, a power to perceive and think," as opposed to having "joined and fixed to Matter so disposed, a thinking immaterial Substance" (*Essay* IV,iii,6). As Jolley notes, "Locke devotes so little space to [this] issue that it seems to have escaped Leibniz's attention when he first read the *Essay*."[43] It is not mentioned in his first written "Remarks" on the *Essay*, as transmitted to Locke in 1697. There Leibniz seems to take Locke as an antimaterialist ally, noticing rather his claim, in his proof of the existence of God (*Essay* IV,x) that matter and motion of themselves cannot explain thought (A VI,vi,8). In 1697, however, began the controversy, in print, between Locke and Edward Stillingfleet, the Bishop of Worcester; Locke's argument for the (epistemic) possibility of thinking matter was one of the targets of the bishop's attack. This seems to have drawn Leibniz's

[42]This is the main thesis of Jolley's *Leibniz and Locke*.

[43]Jolley, *Leibniz and Locke*, pp. 17f.

attention to the issue. He began to read the published documents of the controversy in 1698 (A VI,vi,*xxi*), and by January 1699 he was beginning to ally himself with Stillingfleet's criticism regarding the incompatibility of thought with matter (G III,248f.).

In relation to Leibniz's own views about matter, as we have been exploring them, we may at first wonder why he would be so concerned about "the immateriality of the soul," or what indeed he would mean by it. Considered as a concrete substance, after all, the soul in his view has primary matter as an aspect or constituent and is never without an organic body of secondary matter. Indeed he explicitly acknowledges in the *New Essays* that his belief that souls are immaterial substances is not a belief in "substances separated from matter" (NE 68). There is no doubt that he thought the immateriality of the soul was important because of its bearing on immortality. As he wrote to Thomas Burnett, 6 July 1706, he believed that "the immortality of the soul would be very improbable if its immateriality were destroyed, and if sensation could be produced and destroyed in matter as one of its modifications" (G III,311). But this, in a way, only adds to our perplexity, for as Jolley points out, "one of [Leibniz's] doctrines is that the body as well as the soul is conserved after death."[44]

In resolving these puzzles we must remember first of all that Leibniz is criticizing Locke's position rather than presenting an independent development of his own position. Some of his formulations may therefore be as much influenced by Locke's conceptions of matter as by his own. On one point, at least, they agreed. The idea of matter for Locke, like that of primary matter for Leibniz, is abstract or "incomplete," seeming to Locke "to be used for the Substance and Solidity of Body, without taking in its Extension and Figure" (*Essay* III,x,15); curiously, Leibniz does not record or comment on this agreement (NE 344). For Locke, however, unlike Leibniz, there can in principle be a substance whose essence is constituted by matter, in this abstract sense, either alone or supplemented by principles that are all purely passive, as matter is. From such an essence, Locke agreed, indeed insisted, thought does not follow and could not have its first beginning in the universe (*Essay* IV,x,10). But he did not see any proof that God could not "superadd" to a substance so constituted a power of thinking (*Essay* IV,iii,6).

A power or force is of course just what Leibniz thinks must be added to matter to form a thinking substance, or indeed any substance at all. But this cannot in Leibniz's view be an addition over and above the essence of the substance. It must be a substantial form, and thus must constitute the essence (or at least the active aspect of the essence) of the substance. Most important in this context is that the active force or substantial form *unifies* the substance and makes it indivisible. This is the one point that Leibniz takes as a target in his intitial criticism of Locke's views on thinking matter in his letter of January 1699 to Burnett. "However," he says, "I believe that at bottom one could reach a demonstration that the substance that thinks has no parts, although I am in agreement that extension by itself does not constitute the essence of matter" (G III,249). He recognizes that Locke does not hold the Cartesian doctrine that extension is the

[44]Jolley, *Leibniz and Locke*, p. 22. Jolley's work is illuminating on this subject.

whole essence of a material substance, but he (rightly) sees in Locke's idea of a material substance to which a power of thinking has been superadded nothing to preclude such a substance's having parts. And he views that as a threat to belief in the natural immortality of the thinking substance, for he assumes that a thing that is composed of parts could be destroyed naturally by disintegration, by the separation of its parts from each other. Leibniz pursues these concerns with several types of argument against Locke.

4.1 The Impossibility of Purely Material Substance

The argument that articulates the most fundamental disagreement between the two philosophers is that the purely material substance envisaged by Locke is impossible because "an extended solid thing without a soul is only a result of several substances, and not a true substance at all," as Leibniz wrote in his last letter to Lady Masham before Locke's death (G III,363). This is the first argument that Leibniz presents in the passage of the *New Essays* that is his formal commentary on Locke's discussion of thinking matter in *Essay* IV,iii,6:

> One must consider that *matter* taken for a *complete Being* (that is to say, *secondary matter*, as opposed to *primary matter* which is something purely passive and therefore incomplete) is only an aggregate [*amas*], or what results from one,[45] and that every *real aggregate* presupposes *simple substances* or *real Unities*. And when one considers further what belongs to the nature of these real unities, that is to say *perception* and its consequences, one is transported, so to speak, into another world, that is to say into the *intelligible World of substances*, whereas previously one was only among the *phenomena of the senses*. And this knowledge of the interior of matter makes visible enough what it is naturally capable of, and that every time that God gives it appropriate organs for expressing reasoning, the immaterial substance that reasons will not fail to be given to it too, in virtue of that harmony which is also a natural consequence of the substances. Matter could not subsist without immaterial substances, that is to say without the Unities; this should put an end to the question whether God is free to give it any or not. And if these substances did not have the correspondence or harmony among them of which I just spoke, God would not be acting according to the natural order. (NE 378f.)

This is a complex and fascinating passage. Its contrast of the phenomenal and intelligible worlds, anticipating Kantian terminology, clearly expresses a monadological (and not Kantian) view. Leibniz here asserts, and distinguishes, a weaker and a stronger connection between matter and immaterial substances. The weaker connection, less fully argued, is that the harmony of things, and therefore "the natural order," requires a thinking immaterial substance corresponding to every body that is organized in such a way as to express thought. But it is not excluded that God might act miraculously, contrary to the natural order, to create one without the other. Even miraculously, however, God could not create real (secondary) matter with no immaterial substances at all, for an

[45]This suggestion of placing secondary matter at a stage of logical construction even farther removed from the metaphysical foundation of things than the aggregate as such, rather than simply identifying the secondary matter with the aggregate, is interesting, but unusual in Leibniz's work.

aggregate of real unities that are immaterial substances is precisely what secondary matter is. That is the stronger connection.

Behind it, of course, is the central argument of the monadology: that any real thing composed of parts must ultimately be an aggregate of substances that have no parts. To this argument Leibniz evidently adds here the assumption that these indivisible substances will be immaterial. How would he justify this assumption? I believe he thought it true virtually by definition—by definition, that is, of 'immaterial'. In calling his real Unities "immaterial" he clearly did not mean that they do not "have" bodies of secondary matter, and he presumably did not mean that they do not have a passive aspect and hence a passive principle or primary matter. What remains for him to mean is simply that, unlike Lockean "matter" and Leibnizian secondary matter, the real unities are not divisible into parts—which is precisely what he wanted of immateriality for the proof of the natural immortality of the soul.[46]

What may be most enduringly surprising in Leibniz's treatment of this topic is that he does not always rely on this argument, nor even always mention that he does not believe in the metaphysical possibility of such a merely material substance as Locke envisages. I suspect this is due to his desire, in combating the materialistic influences he feared from Locke's thought, to extend his influence to people who might not be prepared to accept so much of his own metaphysics. His other arguments against Locke on the possibility of thinking matter do have less distinctively Leibnizian premises.

4.2 The Argument from the Mechanical Nature of Matter

This is plainly true of the other argument that is prominent in the *New Essays*. It is both certain and recognized more than once by Locke, Leibniz declares, that thought "cannot be an intelligible modification of matter, that is to say, that the sentient or thinking being is not a mechanical thing, like a watch or a mill, as if sizes, shapes, and motions could be conceived whose mechanical conjunction could produce something thinking, or even sensing, in a mass where there was nothing of the sort" (NE 66f.). The claim that mechanism cannot explain thought is one that Leibniz ascribed to Locke (rightly, in my opinion[47]) on the basis of *Essay* IV,x,10 (see NE 439f.), and would later develop more fully himself, arguing that if we could enter a machine, such as a mill, all we would find there would be "pieces that push each other, and never anything to explain perception" (Mon 17). As indicated by his "that is to say" (NE 66), Leibniz takes Locke to assume that nothing is explained by the nature of matter that is not mechanically explained, and it was probably reasonable for him to assume that this assumption would be part of the materialism he saw most need to combat. There is something *ad hominem* in Leibniz's argument at this point, inasmuch as he himself did not believe in any *substance* that acts mechanically, machines (and even organic bodies considered in themselves) being in his view secondary matter and

[46]Cf. Jolley, *Leibniz and Locke*, p. 22, n. 29: "I think it possible that Leibniz took simplicity and immateriality to be equivalent."

[47]The ascription is not uncontroversial. I have said a little more about it in R. Adams, *Virtue of Faith*, pp. 249f. and p. 261, n. 11.

at best aggregates of substances. In relation to his polemical project, however, he has reason to insist on the point that the nature of matter, *as the materialist of his time is likely to conceive of it*, does not provide an explanation of thought.

If Leibniz agrees thus far with Locke, how is he criticizing Locke? His attack is based on his conception of miracle:

> So it is not something natural to matter to feel and to think, and this can happen in it in only two ways. One is if God joins to it a substance to which it is natural to think. The other is if God puts thought in it by a miracle. (NE 67)[48]

The first alternative, of course, is the one that Leibniz favors. The other, involving a perpetual miracle, seems objectionable to him, as the harmony or orderliness of the universe demands that miracles be kept to a minimum. But even apart from the objectionableness of a perpetual miracle, the disjunction yields Leibniz a clever argument that the extinction of the soul or thinking being would involve a miracle at one point or another:

> And it is enough that one cannot maintain that matter thinks without putting in it an imperishable soul or else a miracle, and so the immortality of our souls follows from what is natural, since their extinction cannot be maintained except by a miracle, either in exalting matter or in annihilating the soul. (NE 67)

The issue of miracle was crucial in the historical context. No denial or even questioning of the actuality of life after death is ascribed to any party in this discussion, though Leibniz obviously fears that it lies at the bottom of a slippery slope. What is at issue is the *natural* immortality of the soul, which would imply that the conscious being cannot be annihilated at death except by a miracle. Its denial was associated by Leibniz with the Socinian heresy, as Jolley has shown.[49] The Socinians believed in life after death (for those who are saved), but thought it requires a miracle of grace. This seems religiously acceptable to many twentieth-century theologians, and evidently seemed so to Locke (*Essay* IV,iii,6); but Leibniz and many of his contemporaries thought it very dangerous.

Locke would probably resist the claim that his conception of thinking matter involves a miracle. His suggestion, after all, was not that God may cause all our thoughts directly, without the intervention of any "second cause," but that God may have superadded to matter a *power* or "faculty" of thought, which would presumably be a created cause of thoughts. Leibniz's claim about the miraculous character of thinking matter depends on a Leibnizian conception of miracle. In his view, whatever is not natural in the created world is miraculous, and whatever is natural must be derivable from the natures of created substances "as explicable modifications" (NE 66). The emphasis falls here on "explicable." For "what is natural must be able to become distinctly conceivable if one were admitted into the secrets of things" (NE 66). And this means explicable or distinctly conceivable by a finite, created mind; for "creatures' conception is not the measure of the power of God, but . . . their conceptivity or power of con-

[48]The argument, to this point, is reproduced more briefly at NE 379. It is presented or suggested in other texts from the period in which Leibniz was occupied with Locke: G III,355f.,363/AG 290f.; G VI,507.

[49]Jolley, *Leibniz and Locke*, pp. 12–25.

ceiving is the measure of the power of nature; for everything that conforms to the natural order can be conceived or understood by some creature" (NE 65). This is essentially the view of miracle laid out almost twenty years before in § 16 of the *Discourse on Metaphysics* (cf. Chapter 3, section 2.2.2 in this volume). And given this view of the natural and the miraculous, a "power" of thought that could not be explained by the *nature* of the thing to which it belonged would not be natural but miraculous.

4.3 *The Argument from the Simplicity of Thinking Substance*

Another argument against thinking matter is indicated briefly in a letter of January 1699 to Thomas Burnett, who transmitted a copy to Locke in March of the same year (A VI,vi,*xxi*). Leibniz acknowledges that Locke's thesis that the substance of body and of mind are (equally) unknown to us prepares the way for an argument that we are not in a position to know that they are not "inwardly [*dans l'interieur*]" identical, "although they are distinct in appearance." Leibniz's response is:

> At bottom, however, I believe one could arrive at a demonstration that the substance that thinks has no parts, although I remain in agreement that extension alone does not constitute the essence of matter. Thus I am of the opinion of those who believe that it is by nature and not by grace that souls are immortal. (G III,248f./AG 288)

The point of acknowledging with an "although" that "extension alone does not constitute the essence of matter" is presumably that someone might take this point as a basis for claiming that that thinking, too, belongs to the essence of matter. Against such a claim Leibniz argues that "the substance that thinks has no parts." Both the proof of this premise and much of the rest of the argument are here suppressed. The point is presumably that whatever its essence may be, matter, as understood by Locke, has parts, and therefore cannot be identical with the substance that thinks, if the latter has no parts. And the natural immortality of the thinking substance is probably seen by Leibniz as following directly from its partlessness, which I have argued is therefore what is crucial for him in its "immateriality."

4.4 *The Argument from the Passivity of Matter*

I have saved until last the argument against thinking matter that has most to do with primary matter. This argument is not used in the *New Essays*,[50] but Leibniz rests on it his whole case against thinking matter in a piece that he sent to Locke, by way of Burnett, in February 1700:

> My opinion is therefore that as matter is nothing but an essentially passive thing, thought, and even action, cannot be modifications of it, but of the complete corporeal substance that receives its completion from two constituents [*constitutifs*], namely from the active principle and the passive principle, of

[50] Though it is the argument suggested by the way Leibniz mentions his attack on thinking matter in summarizing the *New Essays* to Isaac Jaquelot as late as 28 April 1704 (G III,474).

> which the first is called form, soul, entelechy, primitive force, and the second is called primary matter, solidity, resistance. Thus it must be said that action, life, feeling, thought are affections or differences of the first, and not modifications of the second. As for durability, it must also be said that every indivisible Entelechy, such as our mind [*esprit*] is, subsists always and cannot perish naturally. (A VI,vi,32 = G III,227)

We do not learn much here about primary matter, except that it is a passive principle that enters, with an active principle called form or soul, into the constitution of a corporeal substance. The focus of the argument is not on Leibniz's personal conception of primary matter, but on the idea, accepted by most of his contemporaries and predecessors, that the nature of matter as such is purely passive. But a purely passive thing cannot have an active modification, Leibniz claims; and thought, he evidently supposes, is active. In order to have thought as a property, therefore, a substance must have an active principle, and so must be something more than matter. And Leibniz asserts here, without argument, that this active principle will be indivisible and hence naturally imperishable.

This is an argument that anything that thinks must have what Leibniz calls a substantial form. It seems to be an adaptation of an argument that had used earlier to show, more broadly, that there must be substantial forms in matter. For instance, in writing to John Bernoulli in November 1698, he said:

> There cannot be any active modifications of that which is merely passive in its essence, since modifications limit rather than augment or add; therefore besides extension, which is the seat or principal of shapes, we must posit a seat or first subject [*proton dektikon*] of actions, namely a soul, form, life, first entelechy, as one may choose to call it. (GM III,552)

And in the eleventh paragraph of his important article "On Nature Itself," published in 1698, Leibniz argued, against the Cartesian physicist Johann Christopher Sturm, that the evidence of activity in the physical world requires the postulation of "a first subject [*proton dektikon*] of activity, that is, a primitive motive force" in bodies, "since these activities or entelechies certainly cannot be modifications of primary matter or *mass* [*moles*], which is an essentially passive thing, as the most judicious Sturm himself very clearly acknowledges." He went on to say that "this substantial principle itself is what is called *soul* in living things, and in other things *substantial form*" (G IV,511/L 503f.).

Particularly interesting in "On Nature Itself" is that Leibniz explicitly ascribes to his discussion partner the assumption of the passivity of matter and at the same time distances himself somewhat from it. He repeats in the next paragraph that according to Sturm, "matter is a substance that is passive by its nature and essentially, . . . but a modification of an essentially passive thing cannot make the thing active (which I acknowledge to be beautifully said)." Leibniz's response is that "*matter* is understood either as secondary or as primary; the secondary indeed is a complete substance, but not merely passive; the primary is merely passive, but is not a complete substance; and therefore a soul, or a form analogous to a soul, must be added" (G IV,511f./L 504). This is a somewhat imprecise response, since Leibniz was quite clear in his letters of the same year to John Bernoulli that "secondary matter . . . is not a substance, but substances" (GM

III,537), that is, an aggregate. The response does capture the point, however, that secondary matter, in Leibniz's view, is not purely passive because substantial form enters into its constitution—namely, the substantial forms of the substances of which it is an aggregate.

We may see here one reason for the disappearance of this argument from the attack on thinking matter in the *New Essays*. Locke did conceive of matter as purely passive. But in other respects his conception of matter as concrete, extended, and substantial is closer to Leibniz's conception of secondary than of primary matter. Therefore, though Leibniz could legitimately use this argument *ad hominem* against Locke, his doing so might obscure rather than illuminate his own thought about matter. Another consideration that might have influenced Leibniz in discarding this argument from the polemic against Locke is that its focus on the *active* nature of the soul is less relevant to Leibniz's underlying concern about immortality than the partlessness of the soul that is highlighted in some of his other arguments.

Whatever the reasons, Leibniz's interest in this argument against thinking matter seems to have peaked in the years 1699 and 1700. The fullest statement of it, and the most interesting in its implications about primary matter, is in a document from that period, a letter to Burnett that is not known to have been transmitted to Locke. It is only slightly more explicit than the text that Locke did see on such points as that "what is essentially passive cannot receive the modification of thought without receiving at the same time some active substantial principle that would be added to it," and a bit subtler, perhaps, in its conclusion: "Therefore, although matter in itself cannot think, nothing prevents the corporeal substance from thinking" (G III, 261/AG 290). But it opens with a strikingly systematic statement about the nature of matter:

> In bodies I distinguish corporeal substance from matter, and I distinguish primary matter from secondary. Secondary matter is an aggregate or composite of several corporeal substances, as a flock is composed of several animals. But each animal and each plant is also a corporeal substance, having in itself the principle of unity, which makes it truly a substance and not an aggregate. And this principle of unity is what is called Soul, or else something analogous to the soul. But besides the principle of unity the corporeal substance has its mass or secondary matter, which is in turn an aggregate of other, smaller corporeal substances, and so on to infinity. Primitive matter, however, or matter taken in itself, is what is conceived in bodies when all the principles of unity are set aside, that is to say, what is passive, from which spring two qualities: *resistance* [*resistentia*] *and holding back* [*restitantia*] *or inertia*. That is to say that a body does not allow itself to be penetrated, and rather gives way to another, but that it does not give way without difficulty and without weakening the total motion of the one that pushes it. Thus it can be said that matter in itself, besides extension, includes a primitive passive Power. But the principle of unity contains the primitive Active power, or the primitive force, which is never lost and always perseveres in an exact order of its internal modifications, which represent those that are outside it. (G III,260f./AG 289f.)

We can only assume that "primitive matter, or matter taken in itself," here is a synonym of "primary matter." It is introduced as "what is *conceived* in bodies when all the principles of unity are *set aside*" (my italics). One might take this to commit Leibniz only to the claim that some people "conceive" such a thing to be in bodies, not that it is really there. And certainly "conceive" and "set aside" indicate mental activity by which (alone) primary matter attains the status of a thing. But I think it likeliest that this activity is seen as *abstraction*, as suggested by "set aside," rather than as the creation of a fiction. Leibniz had recently written to Bernoulli, and in "On Nature Itself," that primary matter is "incomplete." He thought that there really are both active and passive aspects of substances, either of which can be viewed in abstraction from the other, but neither of which, by itself, constitutes a complete substance.

There are important questions about the way in which this abstraction is conceived here, and first of all, what are "the principles of unity" that are "set aside." If we take them to be complete monads or simple substances, then Leibniz would be speaking here about something that is "conceived" to be, and perhaps (contrary to my interpretation) really is, in bodies over and above all the monads. This reading might seem to be supported by the fact that Leibniz says that "the principle of unity *contains* the primitive Active power" (my italics); does that distinguish the principle of unity as concrete from the abstract power that it contains? I think not. "Matter in itself," which is certainly viewed here as an abstraction, is also said to "include" [*envelopper*], rather than to be, a primitive passive power. Here as elsewhere in Leibniz's work, "principles," including "principles of unity," can reasonably be assumed to be abstractions.

There is another respect, however, in which this text may not fit so neatly into my account of Leibniz's conception of primary matter. I have called attention to passages in which primary matter appears as an abstraction from a single substance, something "always essential to the same substance." Here, however, there may be some indication that it is abstracted rather from secondary matter or corporeal aggregates. This is suggested first by the fact that it is described as something conceived "in bodies," rather than in corporeal substances, and more strongly by the fact that its conception involves the setting aside of "all the principles of unity," in the plural, rather than of the single active principle that in other texts, as I have argued, joins with primary matter to constitute a complete, and unitary, substance.

This reading of the text is not absolutely inescapable. We cannot exclude the possibility that in speaking of the setting aside of "all the principles of unity" Leibniz is aggregating the results of an abstraction that he envisages as performed on one substance at a time, setting aside one principle of unity at a time. But the *New Essays* contain other strong indications of a conception of primary matter as abstracted from secondary matter rather than from a unitary substance. For example, Leibniz expresses the belief "that perfect fluidity, like [perfect] rest, is appropriate only to *primary matter*, that is to say, [matter] in abstraction, and as an original quality; but not to *secondary matter*, such as it is actually found, clothed in its derivative qualities" (NE 222).[51] What is most striking about this

[51]There are difficult questions of construction and translation about this passage. I agree with Peter Remnant and Jonathan Bennett that "in abstraction" here means "matter in the abstract." (See their translation of NE 222.) I also agree with them that "it" in the quotation refers to matter

statement is not the explicit indication (common to many texts) that primary matter is an abstraction, but the ascription of *fluidity* to it. For it is hard to see how anything but an extended mass could be fluid, and, in Leibniz's view, the only real extended masses are secondary matter. To be sure, he is denying that secondary matter is *perfectly* fluid. His point seems to be that perfect fluidity is an idealization obtained by abstracting from the patterns of motion that divide real secondary matter into smaller corpuscles, and indeed into smaller organized bodies. This means that it is not obtained by aggregating a quality abstracted from many unitary substances, but by abstracting a feature that belongs to masses of secondary matter as such.

A similar implication can be found where Leibniz speaks of "matter insofar as it is only a machine, that is to say, insofar as one considers by abstraction only the incomplete *Being* of primary matter, or the entirely purely passive" (NE 379).[52] It is implied here that the property of being a machine belongs to primary matter and that it can be isolated only in the same process of abstraction as primary matter. But the property of being a machine is a property that belongs, in Leibniz's opinion, only to masses of secondary matter, appropriately organized. The character that is ascribed to primary matter here is therefore not an aspect of single substances, and it seems to follow that primary matter is abstracted from whole masses of secondary matter rather than from single substances.

Against these texts we may set a passage of the *New Essays* in which something that must surely be primary matter appears as an aspect of a single substance. Leibniz commends Locke for not taking matter "for a true and perfect *Monad* or *Unity*; since it is only a *Mass* [*Amas*] of an infinite number of Beings." He goes on to say, "in effect I give perception to all this infinity of Beings, each one of which is like an animal, endowed with Soul (or with some Analogous active principle, which constitutes the true Unity of it), together with what this Being needs in order to be passive and endowed with an organic body" (NE 440). What the being needs in order to be passive is surely primary matter. What it needs in order to be endowed with an organic body might be secondary matter, but here I think it is still the primary matter, the thought being that a (simple)

---

in general, and is used to say that matter as it is actually found is secondary matter; but in this case I have preferred a translation that offers the same ambiguities for interpretation as Leibniz's French. Unlike Remnant and Bennett, however, I think it is fluidity rather than primary matter that is compared to rest. Grammatically, it is more natural to attach "as an original quality" to (primary) matter, but it is possible, and metaphysically more plausible, to suppose it is fluidity that is treated as a "quality." I cannot recall another text in which primary matter, even viewed as a principle, power, or abstraction, is described as a quality; and we get a better symmetry here if fluidity, as an original quality *of* primary matter, is contrasted with what are clearly, in the following clause, the derivative qualities *of* secondary matter. But none of these points is crucial for the issue I am discussing here.

[52]It may be worth noting that these words replaced the following incomplete, but in some ways fuller, formulation in Leibniz's first draft: "matter insofar as it is known [*se fait connoistre*] only by the phenomena of the senses, which are based on extension and resistance, or insofar as it is only a machine or insofar as one abstracts." This does not exactly say that this sort of matter is only phenomenal, but perhaps the close link with what is only phenomenal may be seen as a similarity with the conception of matter discussed in section 1.1 in this chapter; cf. p. 342.

substance "has" a body by virtue of its primary matter, being related to its secondary matter by its internal passivity as well as its activity.[53] And what it needs to be passive is clearly identified in the next sentence, not only as material but also as a passive aspect of the nature of the substance: "Now these Beings have received their nature, active as well as passive (that is to say, what they have of the immaterial and the material), from a general and supreme cause." This implies, I think, that a sort of matter, which Leibniz in many places calls primary, is a feature of the nature of individual substances and can be abstracted from them.

Thus far we have uncovered at most a terminological inconsistency in this group of texts. Sometimes (NE 222,379) Leibniz uses the term 'primary matter' to refer to one sort of thing, whereas in other places in his work it refers to something else. Both sorts of thing seem to be recognized in the *New Essays*, but there is no substantive inconsistency in that. Both arise by abstraction, and there is no reason why Leibniz should not permit himself both abstractions, so long as he believes, as he seems to, that the things abstracted from (masses of secondary matter in the one case and individual substances in the other) really have the relevant features.

The primary matter that seems to appear in some of these texts as an abstraction from masses of secondary matter is very similar to the (merely phenomenal) matter of which alone, in the end, Leibniz actually sent a description to Arnauld, a matter constituted solely by extension and its modes (LA 118f.). In both cases we have a sort of matter constituted by physical features of extended masses, considered in isolation from the substantial forms that Leibniz believes are present everywhere in matter. And in both cases we have a sort of matter reached by abstracting from a *plurality* of substantial forms or entelechies, if we consider the letter to Arnauld in the final form it assumed in Leibniz's own copy.[54] In section 1.1, I suggested that he selected this sort of matter in writing to Arnauld because it was what he could make of the Cartesian or quasi-Cartesian matter in which he took Arnauld to believe.[55] Similarly, I suspect it occurs in Leibniz's writings about Locke as a representation, from Leibniz's point of view, of Locke's conception of matter.

There would be a more substantial divergence of positions, however, if the idea of primary matter as abstracted from masses of secondary matter carried with it a different conception of the operation of passive principles in created

[53]If this interpretation is accepted, this text might be read as expressing what I called in Chapter 10, section 2.2, the "qualified monad conception" of the structure of a corporeal substance. In support of this reading we might note that the "animal" is here said to be endowed, not with soul and organic body, but with soul and "what [it] needs in order to be . . . endowed with an organic body." Despite the appearances of isolated passages, however, I am inclined to think that Leibniz's writings related to Locke predominantly reflect the two-substance conception (cf. pp. 269f.).

[54]See p. 344.

[55]Another text (G IV,511/AG 162) in which an abstraction from secondary matter may be treated as primary matter is similarly directed against a Cartesian, Sturm. Having identified primary matter with bulk [*moles*], Leibniz denies that there are "atoms of bulk, or of minimum extension," in a way that seems to imply that bulk (= primary matter) is extended, which it can be if it is an abstraction from secondary matter, but not if it is an aspect of or abstraction from an unextended simple substance.

things from that carried by the idea of primary matter as abstracted from individual substances. But such a divergence cannot be established from the texts presented here. The main characterization of the operation of the passive principle in the letter to Burnett is that from it "spring [literally, are born, *naissent*] two qualities: *resistance* [*resistentia*] *and holding back* [*restitantia*] *or inertia*" (G III,260/AG 289). These are indeed physical qualities of extended masses, but it is quite consistent with this text to suppose that they are derivative rather than primitive functions of the passive principle. What the text says can be accounted for on any viable interpretation of Leibniz.

The *New Essays* contains as explicit a statement as any of Leibniz's writings that the most fundamental operation of passivity is perceptual rather than physical.

> I have already said that in metaphysical rigor, taking action for what comes to the substance spontaneously and from its own ground, everything that is properly a substance does nothing but act, for everything comes to it from itself, after God. . . . But taking *Action* for an exercise of *perfection* and *being acted on* [*passion*] for the contrary, there is no *Action* in genuine substances except when their perception (for I give some of it to all substances) develops itself and becomes more distinct, as there is no *being acted on* except when their perception becomes more confused. (NE 210)

This of course is about the activity and passivity of "genuine substances." Does Leibniz mean to leave open the possibility of a different sort of activity, or at least of passivity, in bodies as such? No; for he adds that in bodies there is no more than "an image" of true activity and passivity.

> As for motion, it is nothing but a real phenomenon because the matter or mass to which motion belongs is not properly speaking a substance. However, there is an image of action in motion, as there is an image of substance in mass, and in this regard it can be said that the body *acts* when there is spontaneity in its change, and that it *suffers* when it is pushed or impeded by another. (NE 210f.)

5. *Conclusions*

Several conclusions emerge from this review of discussions of primary matter in Leibniz's middle years.

1. The most fundamental is that primary matter is an abstraction, as is substantial form. That is, they can be considered as entities only by abstraction from a complete substance, a subject, *of* which they constitute the substance or essence. This point is most fully developed in the letter of January 1692 to Pellisson, but is quite clear in other documents of the period. It is still repeated quite clearly in the "Conversation of Philarète and Ariste" in 1715 (RML 439f./L 620), and especially in 1712 in the first draft of that dialogue (RML 440). We find it also in November 1715, in the form of the claim that primary matter "is not a substance but something incomplete" (G III,657).

Leibniz is not consistent in his treatment of the concept of substantial form on this point. There are passages from the middle years in which he refers to complete substances (which presumably have passive as well as active aspects) as "substantial forms." I believe that this variation is merely terminological, and does not represent any vacillation in the entities recognized, or the characteristics ascribed to them, in Leibniz's metaphysical system.

Be that as it may, there is no similar variation in his treatment of the concept of primary matter. So far as I know, the mature Leibniz never refers to a complete substance as "primary matter." And, unlike the primary matter of Aristotelian systems, Leibnizian primary matter is not an ultimate subject of inherence or predication, but a conceptually abstractable aspect or feature of such a subject.

2. The primary matter is the passive principle, as the substantial form is the active principle, in the primitive force that constitutes the complete substance. Indeed, passivity constitutes the whole content of Leibniz's conception of primary matter. This is implied in his letters of 1698 to John Bernoulli.

This gives rise to a subtle question, to which I suspect Leibniz himself did not attend carefully. Is primary matter a positive constituent of a substance, something which must be *added* to a substantial form to constitute a complete substance? Or is it simply the set of limitations characteristic of a particular substantial form, and thus merely the expression of something that has *not* been added to (or included in) the form? We have certainly seen texts in which Leibniz seems to be thinking of primary matter as a positive addition to the nature of a substance. On the other hand, as his letters to Bernoulli make clear, Leibniz regarded primary matter as a principle of imperfection, because it is passive, whereas form is a principle of perfection, because it is active. Indeed perfection and imperfection seem to have been for him the more fundamental pair of concepts, in terms of which he sometimes explained activity and passivity (as in DM 15). And he also seems to have thought of imperfection as mere privation, contributing nothing positive.

The latter view is clearly present in a text of 1698 that Leibniz wrote about seven months before his most relevant letter to Bernoulli. Speaking of God as "the primitive unity, expressed by all the others according to their capacity," and obviously thinking of the properties of creatures as imperfect imitations of divine perfections, Leibniz characterized "the creature" as "varied according to the different combinations of unity with zero; or indeed of the positive with the privative, for the privative is nothing but the limits" (Gr 126). Here it appears that all that is positive in creatures is the extent to which they do imitate God, the extent to which they are perfect, and therefore active; their imperfection, and hence their passivity, is merely privative, nothing but the limits of their perfection or activity.

3. Primary matter is "always essential to the same substance" (LA 120; cf. A I,vii,249; ix,212). It is likely that Leibniz saw this third point as implied by the first two. For the primitive force constitutes the essence of a substance (A I,vii,248); how could an aspect (the passive principle) of this essence belong to the substance only sometimes? Nor are principles or abstractable aspects a sort of thing that could be seen as migrating from one substance to another in any period of Leibniz's thought. That the essential bond between a substance and its primary matter is implicit in the character of primary matter as primitive force is suggested in the letter of January 1692 to Pellisson, where Leibniz says that the primitive force "remains always the same in the same body" (A I,vii,249).

4. That primary matter is "always essential to the same [individual] substance" carries the implication that it is not divisible (LA 120). For if it were divisible, parts of it would belong successively to different substances (cf. Chapter 11, section 2.2). Philosophers who believed in divisible substances and thought of them as constituted by primitive forces would presumably have reason to doubt the assumption that such constitutive principles must be "always essential," in the relevant sense, to a single substance. But Leibniz had no such reason to question the assumption, since he held that any individual thing that is fully a substance must be indivisible; this is true even of *corporeal* substance in the middle years on Garber's interpretation.[56]

5. What sort of thing is the complete substance or concrete metaphysical subject from which the primary matter and substantial form can be abstracted? I have argued that it must be very like the monad of Leibniz's last years. In particular, the primary matter and its union with the substantial form do not arise out of the form's possessing, and uniting, an extended organic body. Rather, the primary matter and the substantial form together form a unit that is prior, metaphysically though not temporally, to the possession of an extended body, "a higher principle of action and resistance, from which extension and impenetrability emanate when God does not prevent it by a superior order" (A I,vii,249; cf. LA 120).

6. Not only is primary matter itself unextended (LA 120). The substance of which it is a constitutive principle is present in a place only by immediate operation. And I have argued, in section 2.2, that Leibniz's theory of pre-established harmony in the middle years already required him to regard such operation as constructed from a correspondence of internal, nonrelational and therefore nonspatial properties of the substance with those of other substances.

7. Primary matter, like substantial form, is an "internal principle" in a substance (A I,vii,248). Presumably, therefore, the substance's possession of it does not depend on relations with other substances, not even those that are in its organic body. I have argued (in section 2.1) that it follows that any fundamental operation of primary matter must be internal to the substance of which it is a constitutive principle, and must indeed be an aspect of the *perceptual* operation of that substance, given Leibnizian assumptions about the harmony of substances and the nature of perception. In Leibniz's letters of 1698 to Bernoulli it appears that spiritual operations are sufficient for primary matter, provided only there is some passivity or imperfection in them. And by 1704, in the *New Essays*, Leibniz seems to imply that the operations of primary matter are necessarily and exclusively perceptual, holding explicitly that there is no *passion*—that is, no operation of the passive principle—"in genuine substances . . . except when their perception becomes more confused" (NE 210).

8. We have found a few texts, from Leibniz's discussion of Locke, in which the title of "primary matter" is given to something that appears to have been abstracted from secondary matter rather than from an indivisible substance. I have argued that this is a terminological variation rather than a vacillation in metaphysical belief.

[56]Garber, "Leibniz and the Foundations of Physics," pp. 55f.

13

Primitive and Derivative Forces

When Leibniz characterizes substantial form as "primitive active force" and primary matter as "primitive passive force"[1] the word 'primitive' marks a contrast, sometimes explicit, with "derivative" active and passive forces. The forces studied in physics are classifed as derivative by Leibniz. And we confront grave difficulties in trying to understand what relationship he envisaged between the derivative physical forces and the primitive forces that constitute, metaphysically, the essence of substance. These difficulties are probably the largest obstacle to understanding the relation between Leibnizian physics and Leibnizian metaphysics. They are the topic of the present chapter.

1. The "Mixed" Character of Derivative Forces

1.1 How Are Physical and Intramonadic Forces Related?

Leibniz clearly thought, as his terminology indicates, that the derivative forces are *derived* from the primitive forces, and there are many texts from Leibniz's middle years in which he speaks of derivative forces more specifically as *modifications* of primitive forces.[2] In some of them he explicitly invokes the analogy of the relation of shape to extension, making it clear that he has in mind something like the relation that obtains between mode and attribute in Descartes's thought. On 22 March 1703, for example, he wrote to Isaac Jaquelot that

> the derivative or accidental force that cannot be denied to bodies in motion must be a modification of the primitive [force], as shape is a modification of extension. Accidental forces cannot occur in a substance without essential force, for accidents are nothing but modifications or limitations, and cannot contain more perfection or reality than the substance. (G III,457)[3]

[1]In Leibniz's writings 'power' [*potentia/puissance*] sometimes replaces 'force' [*vis/force*] in both of these phrases.

[2]For many references, and important discussion, see Garber, "Leibniz and the Foundations of Physics," pp. 83f. and notes 191–94, 213. An earlier text than those cited by Garber is A I,ix,212 (23 October 1693).

[3]Similar use of the analogy can be found at least as early as 18 November 1698, in a letter to John Bernoulli (GM III,552/AG 169), and at least as late as 30 June 1704, in a letter to De Volder (G II,270/L 537).

In this statement it is clear, also, that Leibniz saw the conception of physical forces as modifications of primitive forces as a fulcrum yielding leverage for one of his arguments that there must be primitive or "essential" forces.

But a major problem looms here. Physical forces seem to pertain essentially to relations among extended, divisible masses. It is hard to see how they could be modifications of internal principles of indivisible substances. It is especially hard if (as I have argued in Chapter 12, pp. 352f.) the primary operations of those internal principles are also internal to the indivisible substances.

Our closer examination of this problem may begin with another very important statement about the relation between primitive and derivative forces, found in Leibniz's letter of 21 January 1704 to Burcher De Volder:

> The derivative force, however, is the present state itself as long as it is tending toward, or pre-involves, the following state, as every present is pregnant with the future. But the persisting [thing] itself, insofar as it involves all events, has primitive force, so that the primitive force is like the law of the series, and the derivative force is like the determination that designates some term in the series. (G II,262/L 533)

Here the primitive and derivative forces are related as persisting subject and present state.

The content of the primitive force is temporally comprehensive. It is likened to the law that determines a whole series; the series we are meant to think of here is surely the whole temporal succession of states of a substance. What "has primitive force" is something "persisting"—indeed, we know from other contexts that the primitive force itself is something persisting, "something substantial" (LW 130f.; G II,269f./AG 180), inasmuch as it constitutes the essence of a substance. This is emphasized seven months earlier, in another letter to De Volder, where Leibniz says, "When I speak of the primitive force remaining, I do not mean the conservation of the total power to move . . . , but the Entelechy which always expresses that total force as well as other things" (G II,251/L 530). As Daniel Garber aptly remarks, "A thing doesn't have Leibnizian *primitive* force in the way in which a body in acceleration has Newtonian force, but rather, in the way in which one might talk about the Church as a *force* in society, or Mohammed Ali as a *force* to be reckoned with in the boxing ring."[4]

A derivative force is a "present state," the value of the series for the present time. But here I think a distinction is called for that Leibniz does not treat very clearly in the quoted passage. For the present state of a substance will presumably have some nondispositional aspects that cannot plausibly be regarded as forces, not even as derivative forces, but only as effects of forces. The derivative force will rather be the aspect of the present state that is the tendency that the substance has now to pass to its immediately future states. As the value of the primitive force for the present context, the derivative force is the primitive force itself, just insofar as the primitive force is, or involves, a tendency to do now, and in the present circumstances, what "the law of the series" determines that the substance will do now and in those cirumstances. It is "what is momentary in action" (G II,269/L 537), by contrast with both the primitive force, which

[4]Garber, "Leibniz and the Foundations of Physics," p. 84.

persists, and the motions or changes produced, which take time. This, I take it, is what Leibniz means when he identifies the derivative force with "the present state itself as long as it is tending toward, or pre-involves, the following state." (G II,262/L 533; cf. G IV,396/AG 253).

An example may help make this point clearer. Two letters later, Leibniz wrote to De Volder that "primitive forces cannot be anything but internal tendencies of simple substances, because of which, by a certain law of their nature, they pass from perception to perception" (G II,275/AG 181). If we think of the operation of primitive forces as being perceptual in this way, then it is not my present perceptions that will be derivative forces, but my present appetites. Derivative forces, that is, will be present tendencies to pass to the next perceptions in the series.

But did Leibniz already think of the operation of forces as perceptual in this way in his middle years? I will address this question as it applies to *active* forces; the present section will be mainly about them. Many of the relevant texts may apply to passive forces as well, but it can hardly be doubted that when Leibniz spoke simply of "primitive" and "derivative" forces, active forces were normally uppermost in his mind. Indeed he himself stated that "active force . . . is usually called force without qualification" (G IV,395/AG 252).

There is a text from 1693 in which Leibniz says that "the internal action" of a form identified as the active power contained in the nature of body "is called sensation in animals, and thought in man" (A I,ix,211).[5] Does this leave open the possibility that the active power of a corporeal substance has an *external* action of a quite different sort? Hardly. No such external action is allowed by Leibniz's doctrine of pre-established harmony. As is already clear in the "New System" of 1695, that doctrine excludes all influence of the soul even on its own body, for it is the "mutual relation" of harmony "that alone constitutes the *union* of *the soul and the body*." And it is clear enough in this discussion in the "New System" that what is said about soul and body is meant to apply to the relation of any substantial form to its body (E 127/L 457f.). In order to act, metaphysically speaking, on its body, which is an aggregate of other substances, a substantial form would have to act on those other substances; and the impossibility of any metaphysically real action of one created substance on another is already a fixture of Leibniz's thought from the 1680s on (e.g., DM 14; C 521/L 269). These considerations support an interpretation of the operation of primitive active forces as perceptual even in the writings of Leibniz's middle years.

Contrasting with these implications about the internal character of the operation of *primitive* active force are statements which imply that Leibniz regarded the operation of *derivative* active force as dependent on relations between substances. The latter, he says, "resulting from the conflicts of bodies with each other, as if by a limitation of primitive force, is exercised changeably" (GM VI,236/L 436). The derivative forces in bodies "depend also on the other bodies" (G III,457). That is to be expected insofar as "we understand by derivative force . . . no other force than that which is connected with motion (motion with respect to place,[6] that is) and which in turn tends further to produce motion with respect

[5]This text is quoted, and discussed, on p. 352.

[6]*Motus localis* [local motion, as some translations have it]. The point, which will not occur to modern readers, is to signify unambiguously a change of place, in view of the fact that in Aristotle's

to place," a force also identified as that "by which bodies actually act on each other or are acted on by each other" (GM VI,237/L 437).[7]

Given their role in physics, we might expect these derivative forces to belong to the corporeal, extended masses that physics studies, rather than to indivisible substances. Leibniz does not entirely disappoint this expectation, even in the middle years. In 1699 he wrote to De Volder that "the secondary or motive forces, and the motions themselves, must be ascribed to the secondary Matter or to the complete body itself, which results from the active and the passive" (G II,171/L 517). The secondary matter, of course, is for Leibniz an extended mass, an aggregate, and as such a phenomenon, though well founded in the substances of which it is an aggregate. This implication of phenomenality is reflected explicitly in a later letter to De Volder, written by Leibniz in 1704 or 1705, where he says:

> Derivative forces I relegate to the phenomena, but I think it is clear that primitive forces cannot be anything but internal tendencies of simple substances, because of which, by a certain law of their nature, they pass from perception to perception. (G II,275/AG 181)

Garber has argued that "this represents a fundamental change from the thought of Leibniz's middle years," and that until about 1704 Leibniz held a less phenomenalistic, more realistic view of physical forces.[8] I believe, however, that the relegation or ascription of derivative forces to phenomena is essentially the same in the letter of 1699 as in the later letter, and that there is therefore no fundamental change here. (We shall return, especially in section 1.3, to the issue of change in Leibniz's views.)

In view of all this, how can derivative active forces be modifications of primitive active forces? Can an internal force, whose operations are all internal to a single substance, have a modification that depends on other substances? Can an essential principle of a substance that does not interact metaphysically with other substances be "limited" as a result of "the conflict of bodies with each other"? Can a tendency to produce "local motion" (change of place) be a modification of a force whose operations are all perceptual? Can a modification of the essence of an indivisible substance belong to secondary matter—that is, to an extended mass or aggregate?

There may well be serious problems here, but there is little evidence that they troubled Leibniz. Indeed, there are texts in which it is clear that he saw no inconsistency in this set of views. In his letter of 20 June 1703 to De Volder he wrote:

> The forces that arise from mass [*massa*] and velocity are derivative and belong to aggregates or phenomena. When I speak of the primitive force remaining, I do not mean the conservation of the total power to move, which was

philosophy the word *kinesis*, rendered into Latin as *motus* and into English as 'motion', is used to signify a wide variety of changes, including, but by no means limited to, change of place. Leibniz takes explicit note of Aristotle's usage at NE 169.

[7]Another text in which Leibniz indicates particularly clearly that the forces studied by physics are derivative is his letter of 20 June 1703 to De Volder (G II,250f./L 529f.).

[8]Garber, "Leibniz and the Foundations of Physics," p. 91.

> discussed between us earlier, but the Entelechy which always expresses that total force as well as other things. And certainly derivative forces are nothing but modifications and results of the primitive [forces]. (G II,251/L 530)

In this passage, strikingly, all of the following are asserted. (1) The derivative forces of physics belong to aggregates or phenomena. (2) Primitive force is identified with the entelechy, which here is surely the soul or active principle of an indivisible substance. And yet (3) the derivative forces are modifications of the primitive forces. Similarly, in a letter of 11 March 1706 to Bartholomew Des Bosses, to be discussed in section 1.3 of this chapter, Leibniz both refers to derivative forces in the strongest terms as "semi-mental, like the Rainbow and other well-founded phenomena," and states that "derivative forces, with their actions, are modifications of primitive [forces]" (G II,306f.).

That Leibniz was capable of asserting this combination of views in 1703 and 1706 certainly argues against reading his "relegating" derivative forces to the phenomena in 1704 or 1705 as a fundamental change. So does the fact that his ascription of derivative forces to secondary matter in 1699 comes during a period when he frequently expressed the view that derivative forces are modifications of primitive forces. The apparently conflicting views seem to have kept each other company in his mind for many years.

1.2 Can the Problem Be Solved?

How can he have combined them? Once again we may think of a distinction that Leibniz does not emphasize. The active forces that he is committed to classifying as derivative are of two quite different sorts—at least if sorts of forces are differentiated by the effects that they are powers or tendencies to accomplish. And a Leibnizian might be tempted to say that only one of these sorts of force is a modification of primitive active force, and only the other belongs to phenomena. I have already noted that Leibniz identifies derivative force as (1) the value of primitive force for a given time, and that on the assumption that the fundamental operation of primitive active force is the generation of a series of perceptions, the derivative force seems to be identified with the substance's tendency at the given time to pass to its next perceptions. This sort of derivative force is easily viewed as a modification of the primitive force. It is not easily identified, however, with (2) the sort of active force studied by physics, which seems rather to consist in powers and tendencies to produce motion in bodies. The latter sort of force, however, is easily regarded as belonging to the corporeal masses that Leibniz classified as secondary matter and as phenomena.

This is too easy a solution to our problem, however. In saying that derivative forces are modifications of primitive forces, Leibniz does not suggest an exception for the forces studied by physics. And the "forces that arise from mass and velocity" are explicitly included among the derivative forces in our text of 1703 in which Leibniz writes to De Volder that "derivative forces are nothing but modifications and results of the primitive [forces]" (G II,251/L 530). Moreover, the view that forces are the most real of the objects studied by physics depends on a real connection between the inherent forces essential to genuine substances and the derivative forces studied by physics. Martial Gueroult seems right in saying that Leibniz's notion of derivative force "is a mixed concept, in which both phenomenal reality properly speaking and substantial reality appear intimately joined to each other in the phenomenon itself."[9] A solution corresponding more adequately to Leibniz's intentions will resist the bifurcation of derivative forces.

Leibniz discussed our problem with Christian Wolff, in letters exchanged in 1710 and 1711. Wolff raised the issue in a general form: "if derivative forces are to be regarded as modifications of primitive forces, an explanation [*ratio*], and an intelligible one, of this modification should still be given" (LW 128). Leibniz's initial reply was brief: "The explanation of the modifications of primitive force is just the same as the explanation of the laws of motion. And it is intelligible indeed, as I have said, but not from mere mathematical considerations" (LW 129). Wolff quite rightly wanted to be told more; in particular he did not understand "how it can happen through laws of collision that whatever is lost from the forces of one body is acquired by the other. There would indeed be room for this if [force] were conceived on the model of a being diffused through matter and rushing from one quantity of it into another." But that seemed incongruous to Wolff "since I conceive of primitive force as not different from the essence of matter" (LW 129f.).

This evoked a fuller response from Leibniz. He began in a way that shows he took the discussion to be exclusively about *active* force: "If the discussion is about primary Matter, or the merely passive, or about that which consists in bare resistance, primitive force is not of the essence of Matter, even if it is of the Essence of body." Conatus and impetus must be "modifications of something substantial or permanent that must itself be active, lest there be more in the modification than in what is modified. Therefore I call it primitive Entelechy, or even just Entelechy. Derivative forces, therefore, are modifications of this substantial Active thing, as shapes are modifications of a substantial passive thing, that is of matter" (LW 130). (I will defer to section 2 the question arising from the last clause of this statement, In what sense are shapes modifications of a passive matter, which seems to be a counterpart of the entelechy, and is presumably primary rather than secondary matter?)

Leibniz goes on to correct one of Wolff's assumptions, and the correction is important for an understanding of Leibniz's solution of the problem:

> It should be known, however, that forces do not cross from body into body, since any body whatever already has in itself the force that it exerts, even if it does not show it or convert it into motion of the whole prior to a new modification. For example, when a ball that is at rest is struck by another, it is moved by an implanted force, namely by elastic force, without which there would be no collision. Moreover, the Elastic force in the body arises from an internal motion invisible to us. And the Entelechy itself is modified corresponding to these mechanical or derivative [forces]. Therefore it can be said that force is already present in every body, and it is determined only by modification. (LW 131)

Wolff had assumed that force is transmitted from body to body in collisions, and Leibniz probably took him to assume that colliding bodies are moved by

[9]Gueroult, *Leibniz: dynamique et métaphysique*, p. 199.

forces of other bodies. But Leibniz does not hold those views. He holds that each body is moved only by its own (derivative) force, which is internal to it, although the force would not be manifested in motion of the whole body, but only in minute internal motions, if there were no collision with another body. Much earlier, in the "Specimen Dynamicum" of 1695, Leibniz had stated that "every passion of a body is spontaneous or arises from an internal force, though on the occasion of something external" (GM VI,251/L 448).

There he had tried to ground this view on a physical doctrine of the equality of action and reaction. Writing to Wolff in 1711, he suggests a more metaphysical explanation, for he says that without the implanted force in a body that is struck "there would be no collision" (LW 131). Why would there be no collision? Presumably because the pre-established harmony would prohibit it. It is a feature of the harmony that each organic body expresses the whole universe (Mon 62). It follows that each organic body has within itself an expression of all the external circumstances that affect it according to physical laws. And if this is true of every organic body, it is true of every body, since every body is exhaustively composed of organic bodies. By Leibniz's definition of expression, this expression must consist in a correspondence, *according to some laws*, between the states of the body and its external circumstances. With these laws, together with the physical laws governing the universe as a whole, every collision that happens to the body, and its own movements in response to the collision, must be predictable on the basis of its own previous states. Therefore no collision would happen if the body did not already have states from which the collision could be predicted. And by virtue of these states, and the laws by which the postcollision movements of the body follow from them, the body can be viewed as having internal tendencies or forces that produce those movements.

This doctrine that each body is moved by its own internal derivative forces prepares the way for an important suggestion about the relation of intramonadic and physical derivative forces that Leibniz makes in this letter to Wolff when he says that "the Entelechy itself is modified corresponding to these mechanical or derivative [forces]" (LW 131). What this "correspondence" suggests is that intramonadic and physical derivative forces *express* each other. A modification of the primitive force of a substance is in the first instance the present tendency to pass to certain immediately future perceptions. The successive perceptions of a substance, however, are expressed by the successive states of its organic body.[10] It follows that the changes in the substance's perceptions are expressed by the changes in the organic body, which are motions. Moreover the substance's successive tendencies to change will be expressed by whatever successive tendencies produce the motions of the organic body. But the latter tendencies, as we have just seen, are motive forces internal to the organic body. And the motions and motive forces of inorganic bodies are composed, in accordance with physical laws, from the motions and motive forces of the organic bodies of which (in Leibniz's view) the inorganic bodies are composed.[11] These motions and motive

[10]See Chapter 10, section 4.

[11]On the organic foundations of the inorganic in Leibnizian physics, see the very interesting discussion of a possible "reduction of physics to biology" in Garber, "Leibniz and the Foundations of Physics," pp. 88f.

forces, Leibniz insists, all conform to deterministic mechanical laws. Thus the forces studied by physics are expressions, or composed of expressions, of substances' successive internal tendencies to perceptual change.

A subsequent letter makes quite explicit the relation of expression between intramonadic and corporeal derivative forces. Wolff found himself still unable "to conceive distinctly enough how the primitive force is modified when, for example, motion is accelerated in a heavy falling [body]" (LW 136). Replying on 9 July 1711, Leibniz wrote:

> You ask how the primitive force is modified, for instance when the motion of heavy [bodies] is accelerated by falling. I reply that the modification of the primitive force that is in the Monad itself cannot be explained better than by expounding how the derivative force is changed in the phenomena. For what is exhibited in phenomena extensively and mechanically is in Monads in a concentrated and vital way. . . . And what is exhibited Mechanically or extensively through the reaction of what resists and the restoration of what was compressed is concentrated dynamically and monadically (as I have already said) in the Entelechy itself, in which is the source of the mechanism and the representation of [things] mechanical; for phenomena result from Monads (which are the sole true substances). And while [things] mechanical are determined by external circumstances, for that very reason [*eo ipso*], in the source itself, the primitive Entelechy is modified harmoniously through itself, since it can be said that the body has every derivative force of its own from itself. (LW 138f.)

Here the implication seems quite clear that the relation between the modifications of the primitive active force (the entelechy) and the derivative forces in phenomena is one of "representation" and "harmony," and thus of expression.

This may not be enough to get Leibniz to the conclusion that physical derivative forces, like the intramonadic derivative forces they express, are modifications of primitive forces. Expression, after all, is not identity. Expressions do not typically have all the properties of what they express. But Leibniz's letter of 9 July 1711 to Wolff suggests an important step beyond expression at this point. As I have quoted him, Leibniz characterized the entelechy not only as "the representation of [things] mechanical" but also as "the source of the mechanism . . . , for phenomena result from Monads" (LW 139). This causal relation may make possible a sort of identity of intramonadic and physical derivative forces. For whatever is true of *types* of force, Leibniz did not have to regard *particular* forces as differentiated by their effects. We must bear in mind that a Leibnizian force, active or passive, is not a mere emptiness, a capacity or receptivity looking to its *telos* for its definition. Leibnizian forces are more real than that; they are causes already in being, with a positive character of their own.[12] A single force of this sort can presumably have effects of different types. And if we ask Leibniz what, in reality, are the causes of the motions studied by physics, the answer he suggests here (and that I think he must give) is that the motions are phenomena caused, at bottom, metaphysically, by the current tendencies of substances to pass from current perceptions to future ones. So if we can say that the derivative

[12]See G IV,469f./L 433; NE 169f.; and Chapter 11, section 1.1.

forces of physics are by definition the causes of physical motions, we can conclude that they are identical with the intrasubstantial derivative forces that are modifications of primitive forces.[13] Thus one and the same derivative force would have both an intrasubstantial effect, the passage from current to future perceptions, and a phenomenal effect, the physical motions.

In this way we can explain the duality in Leibniz's ways of speaking of derivative forces. In physical contexts it may be convenient to treat physical forces as individuated by the physical effects to which they tend. So viewed, the physical force is a phenomenon and a property of a phenomenon, and depends on relations among bodies. Metaphysically, on the other hand, physical forces can be treated as individuated by the real causes that tend to produce the physical effects. So viewed, physical forces are modifications of primitive forces, and of indivisible substances. But the forces viewed in these different ways are in some sense (doubtless not the strictest) the same. The two views represent different ways of carving up, conceptually, the same facts.

I think this is probably a correct interpretation of Leibniz's views, at least from the latter part of the middle years. But it is attended with some difficulties that complicate the interpretation of his views on the subject in his later years.

1.3 Issues from the Later Years

One problem about the explanation I have offered for the mixed character of derivative forces is that it seems to require Leibniz to count the current perceptual tendencies of a substance as *the* cause of the motions of its organic body, and it may be doubted whether he can consistently and reasonably do this. For an organic body, as a phenomenon, exists in being perceived not only by the substance whose body it is, but by all other substances as well. Its motions might then be thought to be caused by the perceptual tendencies of *all* substances, and not only by those of its own substance.

I know of no text in which Leibniz addresses this argument, and he would surely resist its conclusion. We can hardly doubt that he meant to assign the intrinsic forces of each created substance a preeminent role in explaining the physical behavior of its organic body. He might try to substantiate this preeminence by pointing out that, in his view, everything in the world goes as it does because the world was so ordered by God, and God's preeminent aim in this for each organic body, considered as such, is that its physical behavior should be an expression of the successive perceptions and appetites of the substance whose body it is. In that way the organic body can be seen as behaving as it does *because of* the perceptual tendencies of that substance rather than the other substances.[14]

[13]Something of this sort seems to be intended in a discussion of force in 1695, when Leibniz says that "the efficient cause of physical actions belongs to the jurisdiction of metaphysics" (G IV,472). Something similar is also suggested regarding *passive* forces when Leibniz says, in a bracketed sentence withheld from De Volder in 1704 or 1705, that "Matter can be said to be Real insofar as there is in simple substances the *reason* of what is observed in phenomena that is passive" (G II,276/AG 182, my italics).

[14]Cf. LA 95f., where minds can be called "occasional and even real causes, in a certain way, of the motions of bodies" because God has ordered the motions of bodies with regard to the percep-

This may still seem a shaky support for the identification of physical with intrasubstantial derivative forces, for it remains equally true that in another way the physical behavior of the organic body can be seen as produced by the perceptual tendencies of all the substances that perceive it.

This is a problem about the unity of a corporeal substance with its organic body. We have seen, in Chapter 10, section 5, that in his last years Leibniz manifested some misgivings about the ability of his philosophy to account for this sort of unity. It would not be surprising, then, if his last years also saw some retreat from the identification of physical forces with modifications of primitive forces. It is not easy to find unambiguous evidence of such a retreat, however. And the identification is still affirmed, as we have just seen, in letters of 1710 and 1711 to Wolff (cf. also T 396).

It is true that in the elaborate table appended to Leibniz's letter of 19 August 1715 to Des Bosses, derivative forces occur in more than one place, as modifications of something else, but no attempt is made to identify them with modifications of monads (G II,506/L 617). But this text belongs to the development of the theory of "substantial bonds," which was not adopted as a part of Leibniz's own philosophy (as I have argued in Chapter 10, sections 5.3–5.4). The derivative forces can be seen here as modifications of primitive forces, but the latter would be the primitive forces of a composite substance rather than a simple substance, and they would indeed be identified with the substantial bond (cf. G II,485f./L 609).

Regarding passive physical force, another very late text, a letter of 11 February 1715 to Nicolas Rémond, seems quite uncompromising in its statement that "as matter itself is nothing but a phenomenon, though well founded, resulting from monads, it is the same with inertia, which is a property of this phenomenon." There is evidence that Leibniz still wanted to emphasize the connection between physical and intramonadic forces, however, for by the end of this paragraph about inertia, he is pointing out that because created monads have a passive as well as an active aspect, "they are the foundation not only of actions but also of resistances or passivities, and their passive states [*passions*] are in confused perceptions" (G III,636/L 659).[15]

Leibniz's last letter to De Volder (19 January 1706) is particularly interesting in connection with this issue. He begins by suggesting, politely, that De Volder is seeking from him an account of force that he has neither the ability nor the desire to give, since it concerns a notion of force that is "not so much beyond this world as Utopian," and unintelligible. In this connection he alludes to his engagement, about that time, with a paper of Tournemine's, an interaction in which we found some of the earliest evidence of his misgivings about the unity of composite substances. Indeed, in this letter to De Volder he mentions as an example of something "Utopian" the idea of a union of body and soul that would differ from their agreement (G II,281/L 538f.).

---

tions of the minds. In this text, however, the focus is on giving a sense to interaction of substances, rather than on a mind's "causing" the behavior of its own organic body.

[15]Both this text and G II,506/L 617 are cited as evidence of a change in Leibniz's views by Garber, "Leibniz and the Foundations of Physics," n. 213.

Leibniz then goes on to say, "I am afraid that that force which is conceived in Extension or mass [*moles*], as outside of perceivers or their phenomena, is of the same [utopian] nature." For forces can be understood to be real only in terms of the "perceptions or reasons of perceptions" of simple substances, which (with the addition of "aggregates resulting from them") are all that can be understood to be real in nature (G II,281f./L 539). In a first draft of this letter Leibniz was even more emphatic about the phenomenality of forces outside of perceivers, declaring:

> I judge that that primitive or derivative power [*virtus*] which is conceived in Extension and Mass [*moles*] as outside of perceivers is not a thing but a phenomenon, in the same way as Extension itself and Mass and Motion, which are things no more than an image in a mirror or a rainbow in a cloud. (G II,281/AG 184)

A striking feature of this statement is that a sort of force that has been conceived in material things is said to be no more real than extension, mass, and motion. This could easily be read as retracting the claim that physical forces are more real than other physical properties, and specifically more real than extension and motion.

It is not clear, however, that the forces whose reality is so vigorously disparaged here are Leibnizian physical forces. In both the first draft and the letter that was sent there is a qualifying clause: the forces whose reality is denied are those that are conceived to exist "outside of perceivers." But if the interpretation offered above is correct, Leibniz is able to regard physical forces as more real than other physical properties only by identifying them with forces that are internal to perceiving substances, and that are therefore not "outside of perceivers." So the disparagement in these passages seems not to touch his own conception of physical forces, and one might speculate that the qualifying clauses are there precisely because Leibniz did not wish to exclude the identification of physical forces with modifications of (perceiving) substances. Such a speculation seems even more strongly invited by a similar statement in Leibniz's letter of about a year earlier, in which the qualifying clause is more emphatically qualifying: "Where I put bodies, moreover, I also put corporeal forces, namely in the phenomena, that is, if they are understood as adding anything over and above simple substances or their modifications" (G II,276/AG 182).

Another problem, about the individuation of physical forces if they are modifications of indivisible substances, surfaces in the first year of the correspondence between Leibniz and Des Bosses. In a letter of 11 March 1706, Leibniz wrote:

> [We understand that] secondary matter results from many monads, along with derivative forces, actions, [and] passive states, which are nothing but beings by aggregation, and therefore semi-mental, like the Rainbow and other well-founded phenomena. (G II,306)

The special problem here lies in the fact that Leibniz identifies derivative forces not merely as "semi-mental" or phenomena, or even as *belonging to* aggregates, but as "beings by aggregation" themselves. However, in the same letter he says that "derivative forces, with their actions, are modifications of primitive [forces]"

(G II,307). The primitive forces, I take it, are not aggregates but essential principles of indivisible substances. So how can modifications of them be aggregates? And of what would they be aggregates?

Unfortunately, this problem is not taken up in the subsequent letters that have come down to us from this early period of the correspondence. The idea of a "derivative power" that is "one by aggregation" does emerge again in the table connected with Leibniz's letter of 19 August 1715 to Des Bosses. There it is stated that such an aggregate is "collected from the modifications of substances" (G II,506/L 617). In that context modifications of *composite* substances, and ultimately of "substantial bonds," must be meant. In my view, as stated above, the theory of substantial bonds was not a part of Leibniz's own philosophy, and it seems not to have been in view anyway in Leibniz's letters to Des Bosses in 1706.

It is possible, however, to give the 1706 text an interpretation in terms of forces that are aggregates "collected from the modifications of substances" without any involvement of the notion of substantial bonds. On this interpretation, Leibniz was thinking of a mass of secondary matter as having a physical derivative force that is an aggregate of the intrasubstantial, and indeed intramonadic, derivative forces belonging to the substances that are included in the secondary matter. Since the intramonadic derivative forces are unproblematically modifications of intramonadic primitive forces, the derivative force of the secondary matter, if not itself a modification of the primitive force of a single substance, will at least be an aggregate of modifications of intramonadic primitive forces. I think this is not a strained interpretation. How would secondary matter's derivative forces be "beings by aggregation" if they are not formed by aggregation from some feature of the substances of which the secondary matter is aggregated?

One more problem, from three years later in the Leibniz-Des Bosses correspondence, takes us to the brink of the theory of "substantial bonds," and perhaps outside Leibniz's own philosophy. Its root, however, can be found outside the Des Bosses correspondence, indeed at the beginning of the middle years. On 6 September 1709 Des Bosses, a Roman Catholic, asked how Leibniz would account for the real presence of the body of Christ in the Eucharist (G II,388). Two days later Leibniz returned a very short answer about the real presence, a doctrine common to Catholics and Lutherans, alluding to his response to Tournemine "that presence, like union, is something Metaphysical, which is not explained by phenomena." He continued with an unsolicited comment about transubstantiation, a Catholic, not a Lutheran doctrine, which Leibniz by this time in his life rejected.[16] Most of the comment is concerned with the "common opinion" of Catholic theologians, as Des Bosses called it (G II,396), that the physical qualities (accidents) of the sacramental bread remain in being, really and not just in appearance, but "without a subject," after the substance of the bread has been replaced by the presence of the substance of the body of Christ (since the qualities of the bread, though still perceived, are not supposed to become qualities of the body of Christ). Leibniz wrote:

[16]On the difference between these two doctrines, their context in Eucharistic theology, and Leibniz's thought on the subject, see Chapter 12, sections 2.2–2.3.

> Whether and how your transubstantiation can be explained in my Philosophy would be a [subject for] more profound investigation. If you want real accidents to remain without a subject, you must say that when the monads constituting the bread are removed, as to [their] primitive active and passive forces, and the presence of the Monads constituting the body of Christ is substituted, there remain only the derivative forces which were in the bread, presenting the same phenomena that the monads of the bread presented. (G II,390f.)

Des Bosses found this suggestion "nicely consonant" with Catholic opinion, but stated very crisply the obvious objection as to its consistency with Leibniz's philosophy:

> But since derivative forces, for you, are nothing but modifications of primitive forces, I do not understand how the derivative forces can remain when the primitive are removed, unless perhaps you are confusing modes with the accidents that we call absolute. (G II,396)

Leibniz can hardly have been confused on this point. It is quite clear that when he spoke of derivative forces as "modifications" of primitive forces, during the middle years and later, he means that they are not "absolute" accidents in the sense of being able to subsist without the subject of which they are modifications. This is precisely the point of his saying, as he does to Jaquelot in 1703, that "accidental forces cannot occur in a substance without essential force, for accidents are nothing but modifications or limitations" (G III,457).

It is less likely that Leibniz was confused than that he was repeating, rather unreflectively, an idea he had worked out many years before for accommodating Catholic views on this subject. This idea appears in the so-called *Theological System*, which I think was probably written in the period 1684–86,[17] and which is one of the few places in Leibniz's writings about the Eucharist where the persistence of accidents without a subject seems to be affirmed, and not merely entertained as a Catholic opinion.[18] The elaborate explanation that he offers there for the possibility of such persistence turns on the claim that physical forces are "real or absolute accidents, which differ not only modally from a substance" and "superadd something absolute and real to it" (*Systema* 137). Specifically:

> This resistance [*antitypia*] or mass [*moles*], and this effort to act, or motive force, are distinguished from matter or the primary power of being acted on or resisting, and from the substantial form or primary power of acting. (*Systema* 135)

And this distinction is a "real distinction," so that the physical forces can be caused by God to subsist without the primary forces; and that is how the persistence of the accidents in the Eucharist is to be explained (*Systema* 137f.).

[17] I use (an English translation of) the customary title, though Leibniz himself seems to have intended to call the work *Examen religionis christianae* (*An Examination of the Christian Religion*) (see B 4). For general background see the discussion of the work in Sleigh, *Leibniz and Arnauld*, pp. 21–23. Sleigh cites authority for dating the work in 1686. The *Theological System* deals with ideas that are particularly prominent in Leibniz's correspondence with Count Ernst von Hessen-Rheinfels in 1684, though he did not forget them quickly in any event.

[18] Other places are A VI,iii,157–59, probably from 1673–75, and VE 218 = G IV,345, from 1683–86, though the affirmation is less explicit there.

This is plainly the same explanation that Leibniz offered Des Bosses over twenty years later, in September 1709. But it is hard to see how it can ever have been consistent with Leibniz's philosophy. I doubt that the *Theological System* expressed his own views on this point even in the early to mid-1680s.[19] And by some time in the early 1690s he was certainly claiming that derivative forces, including physical forces, are modifications of primitive forces, in a sense clearly incompatible with the physical forces being "absolute accidents."

How then did Leibniz respond when confronted with Des Bosses's objection? In his next letter to Des Bosses the objection is not actually mentioned, but Leibniz offers a new account of the persistence of the physical qualities in the Eucharist.

> Since the bread is not really a substance, but a being by aggregation or substantiated thing [*substantiatum*] resulting from countless monads through a superadded Union, its substantiality consists in this union. Therefore it is not necessary on your view for God to destroy or change those monads, but only to take away that through which they produce a new being, namely that Union. Thus the substantiality consisting in it will cease, even though there remains the phenomenon which will not arise now from those monads, but from some equivalent divinely substituted for the union of those monads. Thus no substantial subject will really be present. But we who reject transubstantiation do not need such things. (G II,399)

Here the *substantial bond*, or something very like it, appears on the scene, under the name of "superadded Union." And the previous theory of persisting accidents as physical or derivative forces seems at first glance simply to have disappeared. But in fact it may still be present, disguised by the new terminology.

On the theory previously suggested, the primitive forces, as constituting the substance of the bread, are annihilated. On the new account it is rather the "superadded Union" which constitutes, not exactly the substance, but the "substantiality" of the bread, and is annihilated. But this may not avoid the annihilation of primitive forces. For Leibniz might say of the superadded union, as he later appears to say of the substantial bond, that it "consists in the primitive active and passive power of the composite" (G II,485f./L 609).

On the new theory, the Eucharistic accidents remain as a "phenomenon." Could this still be the derivative forces of the older theory? As we have seen, Leibniz sometimes describes derivative forces as phenomena; physical forces have at least a phenomenal aspect for him. His new account of the persisting accidents does not actually say that they are forces, but that is not decisive for the implications of the account, because he might well have thought that Catholic theology would demand that physical forces be included among the persisting accidents. And I think it is not a serious problem for Leibniz that the primitive

[19]This is not the place for a detailed examination of the *Theological System*. It is not a mere reporting of Roman Catholic theology, but bears many traces of Leibniz's own thinking and is closely connected with his letters to Count Ernst von Hessen-Rheinfels. On the other hand, it is clear from those letters that, when dealing with Protestant/Catholic relations, Leibniz was willing to write pieces that did not express his own views (A I,iv,389). And there are differences as well as similarities between positions taken in the *Theological System* and the treatment of the same topics in the letters. For instance, compare *Systema* 31–35 with A I,iv,420 on justification by faith; *Systema* 177f. with A I,iv,335f., ix,151f. on ordination; *Systema* 91–113 with A I,iii,310 on the cult of the saints.

forces of which the derivative forces were modifications have been annihilated, so that if they remain as modifications it must be as modifications of something *different*. Leibniz does not allow qualities to migrate from one subject to another, but no such migration would be necessary in this case. For derivative forces are momentary states, as we have seen. There is therefore no question of the persistence of *numerically* the same derivative force in any case, and qualitatively the same physical forces could perfectly well have different subjects.

What the new theory does imply is that if the persisting accidents are derivative forces they are not modifications of substances, and therefore presumably not modifications of primitive forces. According to the theory, the persisting accidents will "arise . . . from some equivalent divinely substituted for the union of those monads." Leibniz is reticent about the nature of this "substitute," but it is explicitly not to be a "substantial subject." This implies that the accidents will not be modifications of a *different* substance, since they will not be modifications of any substance at all.

It is most unlikely that in this interchange we see Leibniz personally abandoning the principle that derivative forces, including physical forces, are always modifications of primitive forces, and thus of substances. His *Theodicy*, in which derivative forces are still "modifications of the primitive Entelechy" (T 396)), was printed a few months after this letter to Des Bosses. About a year after that letter, the same position was still maintained in letters to Wolff, as we have seen. Even in the last sentence of the quoted paragraph of the letter to Des Bosses Leibniz indicates that he does not need the theoretical apparatus deployed in the paragraph because he rejects transubstantiation. That is surely reason enough to refuse to take the paragraph as evidence of a change in Leibniz's own views. At most, it is evidence of the sort of tentativeness regarding theological issues discussed in Chapter 10, section 5.4—evidence that he did not think it absurd for Roman Catholics to assent to derivative forces being, in some cases, something other than modifications of primitive forces if their theology required it.

Even that tentativeness or tolerance seems threatened by a hardening of Leibniz's position in later letters to Des Bosses. In 1712, in the letter in which he introduces the terminology of "substantial bonds," Leibniz proposes to account for the Eucharistic accidents as "sensible phenomena founded in" the monads that survive when the substantial bonds of the bread and wine are taken away in transubstantiation. He goes on to consider a couple of ways of allowing absolute accidents "if you are altogether unwilling for these Eucharistic Accidents to be mere phenomena"; but he concludes by saying, "All the same, to tell the truth, I should prefer the Eucharistic Accidents to be explained by phenomena; that way there will be no need of non-modal accidents, which I don't understand well enough" (G II,435f./L 600f.).

A subsequent letter, of 20 September 1712, bluntly questions the coherence of a theological position involving non-modal accidents:

> But it is a question whether there are not some accidents that are more than modifications. These seem plainly superfluous, however; and whatever is in them besides a modification seems to belong to the substantial thing itself. Nor do I see how we can distinguish the abstract from the concrete or from the subject in which it is, or explain intelligibly what it is to be in or inhere in

a subject, except by considering what inheres as a mode or state of the subject. . . . But if you know another way of explaining *inherence*, please explain it, for the matter depends on it. If that cannot be done, we must fear that in saying that real accidents are preserved, you really preserve the substance, and thus the whole substance is not really transmuted." (G II,458/L 606)

Here non-modal accidents are on the brink of being rejected as not merely above reason, but contrary to reason.

2. *Primary Matter and Quantity*

"Passive force is likewise of two kinds, either primitive or derivative," Leibniz wrote in 1695 in his "Specimen Dynamicum (GM VI,236/L 437). Primitive passive force is closely related to physical magnitudes. It is a principle (i.e., source) of extension (cf. G II,306), and, as we shall see, is in some sense measured by extension. It is also a principle of resistance (impenetrability) and inertia (a Keplerian inertia, understood as resistance to motion rather than to acceleration or deceleration).

> And indeed the *primitive force* of *being acted on* [*patiendi*] or of *resisting* constitutes the very thing that is called *primary matter* in the Schools, if rightly interpreted. It is of course the force by which it happens that one body is not penetrated by another but opposes an obstacle to it and is at the same time endowed with a certain laziness, so to speak—that is, an opposition to motion—and so does not allow itself to be set in motion without somewhat breaking the force of the body acting upon it. (GM VI,236f./L 437)

The derivative passive forces will be the observable, physical manifestations of this. As Leibniz says, "Hence afterwards the *derivative force* of *being acted on* shows itself changeably in *secondary matter*" (ibid.).

The explicit connection of derivative passive force with secondary matter in this text of 1695 is noteworthy, though it does not go quite so far as to say that the force "belongs to" the secondary matter. At the same time, the parallelism of active and passive forces in this text suggests that derivative passive forces, like their active counterparts, arise "as if by a limitation of primitive force" (GM VI,236/L 436). Active or passive, derivative forces are linked both with primitive forces and with corporeal aggregates.

How is primitive passive force, or primary matter, a source of extension, resistance, and inertia? This question is a natural starting point for an exploration of the relation between primary matter and physics in Leibniz's thought. I shall assume from the outset that the metaphysically fundamental operation of primitive passive force is internal to a single substance and must in some sense be perceptual in character, as I have argued in previous chapters. This complicates the task of explaining its relation to physics; but the main difficulties in this project, as we shall see, do not depend on the assumption about perception.

Primitive passive force is a principle of imperfection (GM III,560/AG 170), specifically of imperfection in expression or perception (DM 15). And in perception imperfection is confusedness (cf. G VII,322/L 365). Primitive passive force will thus be a substance's tendency *not* to perceive distinctly. It can be considered an antiperceptual principle, though at the same time it is an aspect of the substance's perceptual life. This way of putting it suggests a real opposition and struggle between a force of distinctness and a force of confusion in the substance. So does much of Leibniz's language, as when he says that the idea that "a substance opposes its own active power . . . should not seem absurd to" De Volder, since "surely there must be a principle of limitation in limited things, as [there must be a principle] of action in agents" (G II,257/L 532). But this language may be too vivid, as Leibniz also suggests that perfection and imperfection are related not as positive and negative magnitudes, but as unity and zero, and that imperfection is merely limitation or privation of perfection (Gr 126). On this account a substance's tendency to confused perception, its primitive passive force, would simply be a weakness of its primitive active force, a limitation in its tendency to perceive distinctly.

It is clear that the primitive passive force or principle of imperfection is connected in Leibniz's mind with the possession of a body (see, e.g., GM III,560/ AG 170). And we can see how they would be connected. For a substance's *having* an organic body, in the relevant sense, consists in their completely expressing each other with a unique directness. And it is the differences in *degrees* of distinctness of their perceptions of different objects that determine which simple substances are most directly expressed by which organic bodies, and which simple substances "dominate" which organic bodies (as discussed in Chapter 10, section 4). God, being absolutely perfect, perceives everything with perfect, and therefore equal, distinctness, and hence is no more expressed by one body than another, and is the only substance that has no distinctive "point of view" within the universe. Thus it is through lack of a "passive" principle of confused perception that God has no body.

There is a questionable simplification, to be sure, in ascribing this only to the primitive *passive* force. For the assignment of bodies to substances depends on the *combination* of distinctness and confusedness in the substances' perceptions, and therefore on their active as well as passive forces. But there is a similarly questionable simplification in ascribing the law of progression of a substance's perceptions to the primitive active force alone, as Leibniz typically does.[20] For that law must determine confusedness just as much as distinctness. In the present interpretation I will not try to correct these simplifications, since Leibniz seems to make them.

Given such a simplification, the primitive passive force is a principle of (limited) *extension*. For in assigning the substance an organic body, the substance's pattern of confusedness of perception also assigns it the extension of that body. We may say that, as a tendency *not* to distinctly perceive[21] bodies outside its own, the primitive passive force determines the extension of the substance's own

[20] This point is made by Garber, "Leibniz and the Foundations of Physics," p. 88.

[21] As discussed in Chapter 10, section 4.1, degrees of distinctness can hardly be the only relevant factor here. There must also be a relation which I have characterized as "directness" of expression between a substance's perceptions and its organic body. Because Leibniz never articulates this very clearly, however, I will not try to frame the present discussion in terms of it. Leibniz must clearly suppose, in any event, that differential directness of expression is dependent somehow on confused perception; God perceives all created things with equal directness.

organic body, and also defines alien bodies out of its own, thus constituting the *impenetrability* of the organic body. Thus the primitive passive force is a principle of *resistance*. Likewise, the primitive passive force may be seen as determining the *shape* that bounds its organic body; this thought may help explain Leibniz's saying to Wolff that "shapes are modifications of a substantial passive thing, that is of matter" (LW 130).

Perhaps we may also say that, as a tendency not to perceive the future distinctly, the primitive passive force is a principle of resistance to change, which is expressed corporeally as resistance to motion, and thus is a principle of *inertia*. More accurately, it is a principle of resistance to perceptual patterns, and hence to spatial patterns, that are different from the present one. It gives rise to a need for some positive, active force if the present pattern is to be changed. This line of thought, however, is somewhat speculative as interpretation of Leibniz; I do not know of a text in which he presents it.[22]

On this interpretation, a substance's *derivative* passive forces, at present, will be its present tendencies to confused perception, and hence its present tendencies to maintain its (organic body's) extension and position, in the immediate future. In their expression as physical forces, these tendencies can be assigned a quantitative measure, which for Leibniz would be based on the present volume of the organic body.[23] "Impenetrability or antitypy and resistence or inertia," says Leibniz to De Volder in 1699, "are equal everywhere in body, and proportional to its extension" (G II,171/L 517). What is more perplexing is that, in the important article "On Nature Itself" of 1698, Leibniz explicitly assigns that quantitative measure to primary matter itself, and hence presumably to *primitive* passive force, saying of "*primary matter* or mass [*moles*]," identified with "the passive force of resisting," that it "is the same everywhere in body, and proportional to its size" (G IV,510/L 503).[24]

It is understandable that Leibniz should want to assign quantities to matter, since conceptions of quantity of matter had long played an important role in physics. One of the problems that the physicist John Bernoulli raised with Leibniz, in letters written at almost exactly the same time that "On Nature Itself" appeared, was the possibility that Leibniz's philosophy might undermine the quantitative treatment of matter. It was explicitly secondary matter, however, that Bernoulli wanted to see treated quantitatively (GM III,540,546).[25] And there are indeed serious difficulties in the quantitative treatment of Leibnizian primary matter.

So far as I can see, such a treatment is possible at all only by characterizing the primitive passive force in terms of its physical, corporeal expression. How

[22]This generalization of the notion of inertia to apply to *intra*monadic as well as corporeal passive forces was suggested to me by David Tai Wai Wan.

[23]On the use of volume as a measure for such purposes, and Leibniz's treatment of density in this connection, see G IV,395/AG 252.

[24]The words "the same" are unfortunately omitted in Loemker's translation. The letter of 1699 to De Volder comes close to this claim about matter, since Leibniz says there that he locates "the nature of the passive principle or matter" in the forces thus measured (G II,171/L 517). There is also a text of 1702 (G IV,395/AG 252), which will be discussed below, in which Leibniz says the same thing in almost exactly the same words about a "passive force," but it is not clear from the context whether this force is primitive or derivative.

[25]These passages are translated, and discussed, in Chapter 10, section 3.2.

would Leibniz quantify a tendency to confused perception? He seems to have thought of substances as occupying places in a rank-ordering of degrees of perfection, based on how distinct their perceptions are. But he proposes no mathematical function to measure such ranking. Certainly he did not think that the degree of perfection is inversely proportional to body size. An elephant is not less perfect perceptually than a mosquito; so the degree of confusedness that a substance tends to have in its perceptions cannot be proportional to the size of its organic body.

In saying that primary matter is "the same everywhere in body," moreover, Leibniz cannot have meant that all corporeal substances tend to have perceptions that are confused to the same degree or in the same way, for he clearly did not believe that. What he meant, surely, is that the physical expression of primary matter is not to be assigned different quantities in different bodies of the same size. So perhaps he thought that the primitive passive force of each created substance should be assigned the size (volume) of its organic body as a quantitative measure. But this is problematic. One problem is that the size of a substance's organic body changes over time, and thus seems less well suited to express a primitive force, which is constant, than a derivative force which is the "value" of the primitive force for a given time.

Other problems arise when we think about the aggregation and division of bodies. In saying that primary matter is proportional to body size "everywhere in body," Leibniz presumably means that not only organic bodies, but also inorganic bodies, which he views as aggregates, are to be assigned a quantity of primary matter in proportion to their volume. But what will be measured thereby? On the assumption that primary matter belongs only to substances, an inorganic body which is a mere aggregate has no primary matter of its own. Will the quantity of its primary matter be the sum of the quantities of primary matter belonging to all the substances whose organic bodies are included in the inorganic body? That way lies paradox, for every organic body has other organic bodies as parts, in Leibniz's view. The space occupied by an organic body is also exhaustively occupied by smaller organic bodies that are parts of it, and, in turn, by still smaller organic bodies that are parts of them, and so on. In this way the volume of any body, for example a stone, will be used infinitely many times over by the organic bodies included in it. Therefore the sum of the volumes of all the organic bodies contained in the stone, which is supposed to be the sum of the quantities of primary matter of the substances whose bodies they are, will be infinitely larger than the volume of the stone, and therefore cannot be measured by the volume of the stone.

An obvious solution is to say that the volume of an inorganic body measures the sum of the quantities of primary matter of the substances having the *largest* organic bodies that together completely fill the space occupied by the inorganic body. This may work mathematically, but it is not very satisfying philosophically. Why do we want to measure the primary matter of that particular set of substances? So far as I can see, it is not a set that plays a distinguished role at any other point in Leibniz's philosophy.

This problem would largely disappear, of course, if Leibniz partitioned a substance's primary matter among the substances whose bodies are part of its organic body, so that *all* of the "larger" substance's primary matter would belong also to "smaller" substances, and each of the "smaller" substances would have *part* of it. In that case, we could work with any exhaustive partition of a corporeal aggregate into organic bodies. The sum of the volumes of those bodies would of course equal the volume of the whole aggregate. And the sum of the primary matter of the substances to which those organic bodies belong would be, in a straightforward sense, the sum of all the primary matter in the whole aggregate. There would still be infinitely many other substances having smaller bodies, and perhaps some having larger bodies, in the corporeal aggregate; but their primary matter would stand in a part/whole relation to the primary matter of substances already counted, and therefore would not be an addition to it. But in fact (as I have argued in Chapter 11, section 2.2) Leibniz does not and cannot partition a substance's primary matter in the way required for this solution.

Leibnizian primary matter is indivisible and "always essential to the same substance," and this poses a problem in relation to physicists' aspirations for a quantitative treatment of matter. Quantitatively, for purposes of physics, the primary matter of a substance must in some sense coincide with the sum of the primary matter of the substances whose (smaller) organic bodies are completely contained in its organic body. They clearly must not be summed together. Metaphysically, on the other hand, they are perfectly distinct.

Perhaps this need not disturb Leibniz, however. It would be disturbing if the quantitative measurement of primary matter were metaphysically fundamental for him. But it is not fundamental. What is directly measured by volume is the extension jointly occupied by a group of substances. This also is the principal measure of the present physical effect of their primary matter. It follows that the present physical effect of my primary matter coincides with that of the primary matter of all the substances present in my body, but that is as it should be for Leibniz. And maybe there is nothing else to be measured quantitatively in primary matter. Primary matter is primitive passive *force*, after all, and Leibniz held, at least "with regard to physics," that "force must be measured by the quantity of the effect" (LA 137). This suggests an answer to the question, What is measured by assigning to a corporeal aggregate a quantity of primary matter proportionate to its volume? We can reply that this quantity measures the present physical effect of the primary matter of all the substances "included" in the aggregate.

This does not resolve the question, Why shouldn't a measure of *present* physical expression be a measure of derivative rather than primitive passive force? That difficulty is not due to the indivisibility of primary matter. It might be avoided, however, by an alternative interpretation of Leibniz's statement that "*primary matter* or mass [*moles*] . . . is the same everywhere in body, and proportional to its size" (G IV,510/L 503). I have been assuming that "primary matter" here has its usual Leibnizian meaning and refers to the primitive passive force that is essential to an individual substance. In Chapter 12 (pp. 372–75), however, I have noted that there are a few passages (NE 222,379) in which Leibniz appears to characterize as "primary matter" something that must be abstracted from secondary matter rather than from an indivisible substance. Could it be this passive aspect of secondary matter as such that Leibniz means to say is proportional everywhere to the volume of a body? The primary matter of a mass of secondary matter, on this interpretation, would not be a *primitive* force; it is not explicitly classified as primitive force in this passage. It would simply be the sum of the present derivative passive force of the secondary matter, as measured by the physical manifestation of that force in extension and/or intertia.

I do not find this an attractive interpretation, inasmuch as primary matter seems in the context (G IV,510f./L 503f.) to be something that joins with an active principle to constitute an indivisible substance, and therefore should be an essential principle of an indivisible substance. But I think it is a possible interpretation. And it does not change anything important in the interpretation of Leibniz's philosophy as a whole. On any reading, all we can quantify directly with respect to passive forces are current physical magnitudes. Such magnitudes are the physical expression of the derivative passive forces which are the current tendencies of the primitive passive forces of indivisible substances. And substances whose bodies are related as parts and whole must coincide in the physical expression of their passive forces. What is more difficult to determine, and may vary somewhat from text to text, is how Leibniz meant to relate the terminology of "primary matter" to those implications of his system.

One other, related problem about the quantification of matter claims our attention. In May 1702 Leibniz said, "Contrary to Aristotle and with Democritus and Descartes, I affirm no Rarefaction or Condensation except [merely] apparent" (G IV,393/AG 250). "Rarefaction" and "condensation" mean the *same* matter coming to occupy, respectively, a larger or a smaller volume. How does Leibniz reject this type of change? He held, after all, that the volume occupied by an individual created substance can change, and often changes dramatically in such incidents as growth and death. And since the same primary matter is always essential to an individual substance, it seems to follow that the volume occupied by the same primary matter often changes. So it can hardly be with respect to the primary matter of an individual substance that Leibniz rejects rarefaction and condensation.

He can more plausibly be taken as denying the rarefaction and condensation of *secondary* matter. It seems entirely in keeping with his philosophy to hold that a corporeal aggregate never changes size except by the addition or subtraction of one or more bodies. If my body grows, it must be by the addition of cells (to put the matter in terms drawn from twentieth-century science), or of some other particles. If my body shrinks dramatically at death, it must be by the exclusion of large masses of tissue from the living organism.

More intrinsic to the text of 1702 is the thought that the physical measure of quantity of matter never remains constant through a change of volume. For the passive force of impenetrability and inertia "is the same everywhere in body, and proportional to its size" (G IV,395/AG 252). So our understanding of Leibniz's views about the quantity of matter may reasonably determine our interpretation of the sense in which he denies rarefaction and condensation.

It is noteworthy that the position Leibniz takes on this subject in 1702 seems in tension with a thesis that forms part of the account of persisting Eucharistic accidents in the *Theological System* of almost twenty years earlier. There, as part of the argument for a real distinction between physical forces and primitive forces, the claim is made that God could increase the mass [*moles*] and density of a body, by increasing certain of its physical forces, without increasing its volume, which seems at the same time to be taken as measuring the quantity of primary matter (*Systema* 135f.). As noted, I think we need not assume that the cited passage of the *Theological System* represented Leibniz's own views even at the time it was written. But a reconciliation of the two texts, at least in part, seems possible. For in the *System*, while examples are alleged in which quantities of *active* physical force are *naturally* changed without change of volume, it is not clear that any more is claimed regarding *passive* physical forces than that they can be changed without change of volume by the absolute power of God, as distinct from the natural order. And it may also be that in rejecting rarefaction and condensation in 1702 Leibniz did not mean to be saying anything about what God could do, but only about the ordinary course of nature. It is not clear that he thought that the constant proportionality of passive force to volume is more than a feature of the physical order that God has contingently chosen as the best.

Bibliography

Citations in the text and notes of this book are by abbreviation or short name and title, keyed to this bibliography. Works cited by abbreviation are cited by page number unless otherwise noted below. Entries separated by a slash refer to the original and an English translation of the same passage; but I give my own translations from Latin, French, and German (with a few exceptions, where only a translation is cited). Because VE is not fully published, is not available in bookstores and libraries, and will be superseded by A VI,iv, I have cited it only where necessary and have generally given another reference for identification, except when citing VE for the dating of a text. Because A is the most authoritative (though not the most accessible) edition, it is cited, where available, in preference to others. Because L is the most compendious English translation of Leibniz's philosophical writings, it is generally cited in preference to others, where it has the text, though I have occasionally given precedence to another translation that seemed to me importantly superior in the passage in question.

1. *Works of Leibniz*

A *Sämtliche Schriften und Briefe*. Darmstadt and Berlin: Berlin Academy, 1923–1. Cited by series, volume, and page.

AG *Philosophical Essays*. Ed. and trans. by Roger Ariew and Daniel Garber. Indianapolis: Hackett, 1989.

B *Die Leibniz-Handschriften der königlichen öffentlichen Bibliothek zu Hannover*. Ed. by Eduard Bodemann. Hannover and Leipzig: Hann'sche Buchhandlung, 1895. A descriptive catalogue, in which numerous fragments and excerpts from the manuscripts are also printed.

C *Opuscules et fragments inédits de Leibniz*. Ed. by Louis Couturat. Paris: Félix Alcan, 1903. Reprint, Hildesheim: Georg Olms, 1966.

DM *Discours de métaphysique* [*Discourse on Metaphysics*]. Ed. by Henri Lestienne. New edition. Paris: Vrin, 1975. Cited by section number.

Dutens *Opera Omnia*. Ed. by L. Dutens. Geneva: Fratres De Tournes, 1768. Cited by volume, part (if relevant), and page.

E *Opera Philosophica*. Ed. by J. E. Erdmann. Berlin: Eichler, 1840.

FC *Nouvelles lettres et opuscules inédits de Leibniz*. Ed. by A. Foucher de Careil. Paris: Auguste Durand, 1857.

G *Die philosophischen Schriften von Gottfried Wilhelm Leibniz*. Ed. by C. I. Gerhardt. Berlin: Weidman, 1875–90. Reprint, Hildesheim: Georg Olms, 1965, Cited by volume and page.

GI *General Inquiries about the Analysis of Concepts and Truths* (in C 356–399/P 47–87). Cited, where possible, by section number.

GM *Leibnizens mathematische Schriften*. Ed. by C. I. Gerhardt. Berlin: A. Asher, and Halle: H. W. Schmidt, 1849–63. Cited by volume and page.

Gr *Textes inédits*. Ed. by Gaston Grua. Paris: Presses Universitaires de France, 1948.

L *Philosophical Papers and Letters*. Trans. and ed. by Leroy E. Loemker. 2nd ed. Dordrecht and Boston: Reidel, 1969.

LA The correspondence between Leibniz and Antoine Arnauld. Cited by pages of G II, which are given marginally in *The Leibniz-Arnauld Correspondence*, ed. and trans. by H. T. Mason (Manchester: Manchester University Press, 1967).

LBr Manuscripts of correspondence, from the Leibniz *Nachlass* in Hannover. Cited by Bodemann's enumeration and pagination. The last number in a citation normally refers to a (two-sided) page.

LC Leibniz's letters to Samuel Clarke. From G VII,352–420, cited by letter and section number. Clarke published their correspondence, with his own excellent translation of Leibniz's letters, which is reprinted in *The Leibniz-Clarke Correspondence*, ed. by H.G. Alexander (Manchester: Manchester University Press, 1956).

Le Roy *Discours de métaphysique et correspondance avec Arnauld*. Ed. with introduction and commentary by Georges Le Roy. Paris: Vrin, 1957.

LG "La correspondance de Leibniz avec Goldbach." Ed. by A. P. Juschkewitsch and Ju. Ch. Kopelewitsch. In *Studia Leibnitiana*, 20 (1988): 175–89.

LH Manuscripts, other than correspondence, from the Leibniz *Nachlass* in Hannover. Cited by the classification in B. The last number in a citation normally refers to a (two-sided) page.

LW *Briefwechsel zwischen Leibniz und Christian Wolff*. Ed. by C. I. Gerhardt. Halle: H. W. Schmidt, 1860.

Mon *Monadology*. Cited by section number from *Principes de la nature et de la Grace* and *Principes de philosophie ou Monadologie*. Ed. in one volume by André Robinet. Paris: Presses Universitaires de France, 1954.

Monado 74 *Monado 74: Discours de métaphysique et Monadologie*. Texte définitif avec indexation automatisée. Ed. by André Robinet. Paris: Vrin, 1974.

MP *Philosophical Writings*. Ed. and trans. by Mary Morris and G. H. R. Parkinson. London: Dent (Everyman's Library), 1973.

NE *New Essays on Human Understanding*. Cited by pages of A VI,vi, which are given marginally in the English translation by Peter Remnant and Jonathan Bennett (Cambridge: Cambridge University Press, 1982). Supplementary documents, not part of the *New Essays* and not translated by Remnant and Bennett are cited from A VI,vi rather than from NE.

P *Leibniz: Logical Papers*. Trans. and ed. by G. H. R. Parkinson. Oxford: Clarendon Press, 1966.

PNG *The Principles of Nature and of Grace*. Cited by section number from the same edition as Mon.

RL *Lettres de Leibniz á Arnauld d'après un manuscrit inédit*. Ed. by Geneviève (Rodis-) Lewis. Paris: Presses Universitaires de France, 1952. Reprint, New York: Garland, 1985. Leibniz's letters as received by Arnauld.

RML *Malebranche et Leibniz: Relations personnelles*. Ed. by André Robinet. Paris: Vrin, 1955.

RS *Réfutation inédite de Spinoza par Leibniz*. Ed. by A. Foucher de Careil. Paris: 1854.

Saame *Confessio Philosophi*. Critical ed. with introduction, trans., and commentary by Otto Saame. Frankfurt am Main: Vittorio Klostermann, 1967.

Schmidt *Gottfried Wilhelm Leibniz: Fragmente zur Logik*. Ed. by Franz Schmidt. Berlin: Akademie Verlag, 1960.

Schrecker *G. W. Leibniz: Lettres et fragments inédits sur les problèmes philosophiques, théologiques, politiques de la réconciliation des doctrines protestantes (1669–1704)*. Ed. by Paul Schrecker. Paris: Félix Alcan, 1934.

Systema *Gottfried Wilhelm Leibniz: Theologisches System* (*Systema Theologicum*). Ed. by Carl Haas. Tübingen, 1860. Reprint, Hildesheim: Georg Olms, 1966. A critical text of *Systema* is due to be published in A VI,iv.

T *Theodicy* (1710). Cited from G VI by section number; 'pd', 'k', and 'cd' precede section numbers from the "Preliminary Discourse on the Conformity of Faith with Reason," the remarks on Archbishop King's book on *The Origin of Evil*, and the *Causa Dei*, respectively; 'a' refers to the "Summary (*Abrégé*) of the Controversy Reduced to Formal Arguments," as divided by objection numbers. There is an English translation by E. M. Huggard (London: Routledge & Kegan Paul, 1951; La Salle, Illinois: Open Court, 1985); it omits the *Causa Dei*.

VE *Vorausedition zur Reihe VI—Philosophische Schriften—in der Ausgabe der Akademie der Wissenschaften der DDR*. Fascicles 1–9. Münster: Leibniz-Forschungsstelle der Universität Münster. 1982–1990.

W *Leibniz Selections*. Ed. by Philip P. Wiener. New York: Scribners, 1951.

2. *Other Historic Sources*

Ak *Kant's gesammelte Schriften*. Ed. by the Königliche Preußische Akademie der Wissenchaften. Berlin: de Gruyter, 1902–. Cited by volume and page.

AT *Oeuvres de Descartes*. Ed. by C. Adam and P. Tannery. Paris: L. Cerf, 1897–1913. Cited by volume and page.

Essay John Locke. *An Essay Concerning Human Understanding*. Ed. by Peter H. Nidditch. Oxford: Clarendon Press, 1975. Cited by book, chapter, and section.

OM *Oeuvres de Malebranche*. Ed. by André Robinet. Paris: Vrin, 1958–84. Cited by volume and page.

PL *Patrologiae cursus completus, Series latina*. Ed. by J. P. Migne. Paris: Garnier, 1844–.

ST St. Thomas Aquinas. *Summa Theologiae*. 5 vols. Madrid: Biblioteca de Autores Christianos, 1955–58. Cited by part, question, and article.

Anselm, St. *Proslogion*, with *A Reply on Behalf of the Fool* by Gaunilo and *The Author's Reply to Gaunilo*. Ed. and trans. by M. J. Charlesworth. Oxford: Clarendon Press, 1965.

Aristotle. *The Basic Works of Aristotle*. Ed. by Richard McKeon. New York: Random House, 1941.

———. *De Anima*. Ed., with introduction and commentary, by Sir David Ross. Oxford: Clarendon Press, 1961. Trans. by J. A. Smith in Aristotle, *Basic Works*, pp. 533–603.

———. *Metaphysics*. Ed., with introduction and commentary, by Sir David Ross. Two vols. Oxford: Clarendon Press, 1958. Trans. by Sir David Ross in Aristotle, *Basic Works*, pp. 681–926.

———. *Physics*. Ed., with introduction and commentary, by Sir David Ross. Oxford: Clarendon Press, 1960. Trans. by R. P. Hardie and R. K. Gaye in Aristotle, *Basic Works*, pp. 213–394.

Arnauld, Antoine, and Pierre Nicole. *La logique, ou L'art de penser* [*The Port Royal Logic*]. Critical edition by Pierre Claire and François Girbal. Paris: Presses Universitaires de France, 1965. Cited by text divisions that can be found in standard translations.

Baumgarten, Alexander Gottlieb. *Metaphysica*. 7th ed. Halle: C. H. Hemmerde, 1779. Reprint, Hildesheim: Georg Olms, 1963.

Berkeley, George. *The Works of George Berkeley, Bishop of Cloyne*. 9 vols. Ed. by A. A. Luce and T. E. Jessop. London: Nelson, 1948–57.

Boyle, Robert. *The Works of the Honourable Robert Boyle*. 6 vols. London: J. and F. Rivington, 1772.

Calvin, John. *Institutes of the Christian Religion*. Ed. by John T. McNeill; trans. by Ford Lewis Battles. Philadelphia: Westminster, 1960.

Crusius, Christian August. *Entwurf der nothwendigen Vernunft-Wahrheiten*. Leipzig: Johann Friedrich Gleditsch, 1745. Reprinted as Crusius, *Die philosophischen Hauptwerke*, vol. 2, ed. G. Tonelli. Hildescheim: Georg Olms, 1964.

Cudworth, Ralph. *The True Intellectual System of the Universe*. London: Richard Royston, 1678. Reprinted in facsimile as vol. 1 of the *Collected Works of Ralph Cudworth*. Hildesheim: Georg Olms Verlag, 1977.

Descartes, René. *The Philosophical Writings of Descartes*. Trans. by John Cottingham, Robert Stoofhoff, Dugald Murdoch, and Anthony Kenny. 3 vols. Cambridge: Cambridge University Press, 1985, 1984, 1991. This (now standard) translation need not be cited separately because it gives marginal references to AT.

Gaunilo. *On Behalf of the Fool*. Latin text and English trans. in Anselm, *Proslogion*, pp. 156–67.

Kant, Immanuel. *Kritik der reinen Vernunft* [*Critique of Pure Reason*]. Ed. by Raymund Schmidt. Hamburg: Felix Meiner, 1956. References in standard form to the first two editions.

———. *Lectures on Philosophical Theology*. Trans. by Allen W. Wood and Gertrude M. Clark. Ithaca, N.Y.: Cornell University Press, 1978.

Malebranche, Nicolas. *Entretiens sur la Métaphysique* [*Dialogues on Metaphysics*]. Text and trans. by Willis Doney. New York: Abaris Books, 1980.

———. *The Search after Truth*. Trans. by Thomas M. Lennon and Paul J. Olscamp. Columbus: Ohio State University Press, 1980.

———. *Treatise on Nature and Grace*. Trans. Patrick Riley. Oxford: Clarendon Press, 1992.

Pfaff, Christopher Matthäus. "Fragmentum Epistolae a Cel. D. Christoph. Matthaeo Pfaffio." In the Leipzig journal, *Acta Eruditorum*, March 1728, pp. 125–27.

Reid, Thomas. *The Works of Thomas Reid, D.D. 8th edition*. Ed. by Sir William Hamilton. Edinburgh: James Thin, 1895. Reprint, Hildesheim: Georg Olms, 1983.

Spinoza, Baruch. *The Collected Works of Spinoza*: vol 1. Ed. and trans. by Edwin Curley. Princeton, N. J.: Princeton University Press, 1985.

———. *Ethics*. In Spinoza, *Opera*, vol. 2, pp. 41–308, and Spinoza, *Collected Works*, vol. 1, pp. 408–617. Cited by part and proposition (or other relevant subparts).

———. *Opera*. 4 vols. Ed. by Carl Gebhardt. Heidelberg: Carl Winters, 1972.

Suárez, Francisco. *Metaphysical Disputations*. Cited by disputation, chapter, and section from the Latin, *Disputationes Metaphysicae*. In Suárez, *Opera Omnia*, ed. Charles Berton, vols. 25–26. Paris: Vivès, 1866.

Wolff, Christian. *Theologiae Naturalis Pars II*. 2nd ed. Frankfurt and Leipzig: Renger, 1741. Reprint as Wolff, *Gesammelte Werke*, div. 2, vol. 8, ed. Jean École. Hildesheim: Georg Olms, 1981.

———. *Vernünftige Gedanken von Gott, der Welt, und der Seele des Menschen*. 11th ed. Halle: Renger, 1751. Reprint as Wolff, *Gesammelte Werke*, div. 1, vol. 2, ed. Charles A. Corr. Hildesheim: Georg Olms, 1983.

3. *Secondary Sources*

Abraham, William E. "Complete Concepts and Leibniz's Distinction between Necessary and Contingent Propositions." *Studia Leibnitiana* 1 (1969): 263–79.

Adams, Marilyn McCord. "Aristotle and the Sacrament of the Altar." *Canadian Journal of Philosophy*, Supplementary Vol. 17: 195–249.

———. *William Ockham*. 2 vols. Notre Dame, Ind.: University of Notre Dame Press, 1987.

Adams, Robert Merrihew. "Divine Necessity." *Journal of Philosophy* 80 (1983): 741–52.

———. "Existence, Self-Interest, and the Problem of Evil." *Noûs* 13 (1979): 53–65. Reprinted, with a very substantial misprint corrected, as Ch. 5 of Adams, *The Virtue of Faith*.

———. "The Logical Structure of Anselm's Arguments." *Philosophical Review* 80 (1971): 28–54.

———. "Middle Knowledge and the Problem of Evil" *American Philosophical Quarterly* 14 (1977): 109–17.

———. "Must God Create the Best?" *Philosophical Review* 81 (1972): 317–32.

———. "Phenomenalism and Corporeal Substance in Leibniz" *Midwest Studies in Philosophy* 8 (1983): 217–57.

———. "Presumption and the Necessary Existence of God" *Noûs* 22 (1988): 19–32.

———. "Primitive Thisness and Primitive Identity" *Journal of Philosophy* 76 (1979): 5–26.

———. Review of Benson Mates, *The Philosophy of Leibniz*. *Mind*, 97 (1988): 299–302.

———. Review of William L. Rowe, *The Cosmological Argument*, in *Philosophical Review*, 87 (1978): 445–450.

———. "Theories of Actuality." *Noûs* 8 (1974): 211–31.

———. *The Virtue of Faith and Other Essays in Philosophical Theology*. New York: Oxford University Press, 1987.

Aiton, E. J. *Leibniz: A Biography*. Bristol: Adam Hilger, 1985.

Barber, W. H. *Leibniz in France, from Arnauld to Voltaire: A Study in French Reactions to Leibnizianism, 1670–1760*. Oxford: Oxford University Press, 1955.

Belaval, Yvon. *Leibniz critique de Descartes*. Paris: Gallimard, 1960.

Blondel, Maurice. *Une énigme historique: Le "vinculum substantiale" d'après Leibniz et l'ébauche d'un réalisme supérieur*. Paris: Gabriel Beauchesne, 1930.

Blumenfeld, David. "Leibniz's Theory of the Striving Possibles." *Studia Leibnitiana* 5 (1973): 163–77.

———. "Superessentialism, Counterparts, and Freedom." In Hooker, ed., *Leibniz*, pp. 103–23.

Boehm, A. *Le "vinculum substantiale" chez Leibniz: Ses origines historiques*. Paris: Vrin, 1938.

Breger, Herbert. "Das Kontinuum bei Leibniz." In Lamarra, ed., *L'infinito in Leibniz*, pp. 53-67.

Broad, C. D. *Leibniz: An Introduction*. Ed. by C. Lewy. Cambridge: Cambridge University Press, 1975.

Brody, Baruch. "Leibniz's Metaphysical Logic." In Kulstad, ed., *Essays on the Philosophy of Leibniz*, pp. 43–55.

Brown, Gregory. "God's Phenomena and the Pre-Established Harmony." *Studia Leibnitiana* 19 (1987): 200–214.

Burkhardt, Hans. *Logik und Semiotic in der Philosophie von Leibniz*. Munich: Philosophia Verlag, 1980.

Capek, Milic. "Leibniz on Matter and Memory." In Leclerc, ed., *The Philosophy of Leibniz and the Modern World*, pp. 78–113.

Carriero, John. "Leibniz on Infinite Resolution and Intra-Mundane Contingency." Forthcoming, in two parts, in *Studia Leibnitiana*, 25 and 26 (1993 and 1994).

Cassirer, Ernst. *Leibniz's System in seinen wissenschaftlichen Grundlagen*. Marburg: N. G. Elwert'sche Verlagsbuchhandlung, 1902.

Castañeda, Hector-Neri. "Leibniz's Meditation on April 15, 1676 about Existence, Dreams, and Space." *Studia Leibnitiana Supplementa* 18 (1978): 91–129.

———. "Leibniz's View of Contingent Truth in the Late 1680's." In Heinekamp, Lenzen, and Schneider, eds., *Mathesis rationis*, pp. 255–72.

Centro Fiorentino di Storia e di Filosofia della Scienza. *The Leibniz Renaissance: International Workshop (Firenze, 2–5 giugno 1986)*. Florence: Leo S. Olschki, 1989.

Clatterbaugh, Kenneth C. *Leibniz's Doctrine of Individual Accidents. Studia Leibnitina*, Sonderheft 4 (1973).

Collingwood, R. G. *The Idea of History*. New York: Oxford University Press, 1956.

Copleston, Frederick, S. J. *A History of Philosophy*, vol. IV. Garden City, N.Y.: Doubleday Image, 1963.

Couturat, Louis. *La logique de Leibniz*. Paris: Alcan, 1901.

———. "On Leibniz's Metaphysics." In Frankfurt, ed., *Leibniz*, pp. 19–45. Translation of "Sur la métaphysique de Leibniz," *Revue de métaphysique et de morale* 10 (1902).

Curley, E. M. "Recent Work on 17th Century Continental Philosophy." *American Philosophical Quarterly* 11 (1974): 235–55.

———. "The Root of Contingency." In Frankfurt, ed., *Leibniz*, pp. 69–97.

Denzinger, Heinrich *Enchiridion symbolorum, definitionum et declarationum de rebus fidei et morum*. 11th ed. Freiburg-im-Breisgau: B. Herder, 1911.

de Olaso, Ezequiel. "Leibniz et l'art de disputer." *Studia Leibnitiana Supplementa* 15 (1975): 207–28.

Dummett, Michael. *Frege: Philosophy of Language*. 2nd ed. Cambridge, Mass.: Harvard University Press, 1981.

———. "Wittgenstein's Philosophy of Mathematics." *Philosophical Review* 68 (1959): 324–48.

Frankfurt, Harry, ed. *Leibniz: A Collection of Critical Essays*. Garden City, N.Y.: Doubleday Anchor, 1972.

Friedmann, Georges. *Leibniz et Spinoza*. Paris: Gallimard, 1962.

Furth, Montgomery. "Monadology." *Philosophical Review* 76 (1967): 169–200.

———. *Substance, Form and Psyche: An Aristotelian Metaphysics*. Cambridge: Cambridge University Press, 1988.

Garber, Daniel."Leibniz and the Foundations of Physics: The Middle Years." In Okruhlik and Brown, eds., *The Natural Philosophy of Leibniz*, pp. 27–130.

———. "Motion and Metaphysics in the Young Leibniz." In Hooker, ed., *Leibniz*, pp. 160–84.

———. "Understanding Interaction: What Descartes Should Have Told Elizabeth." *Southern Journal of Philosophy* 21, supplement (1983): 15–32.

Gilson, Étienne. *Index scolastico-cartésien*. 2nd rev. and exp. ed. Paris: Vrin, 1979.

Grua, Gaston. *Jurisprudence universelle et théodicée selon Leibniz*. Paris: Presses Universitaires de France, 1953.

———. *La justice humaine selon Leibniz*. Paris: Presses Universitaires de France, 1956.

Gueroult, Martial. *Leibniz: dynamique et métaphysique*. Paris: Aubier-Montaigne, 1967.

Hacking, Ian. *The Emergence of Probability*. London: Cambridge University Press, 1975.

———. "Infinite Analysis." *Studia Leibnitiana* 6 (1974): 126–30.

———. "The Leibniz-Carnap Program for Inductive Logic." *Journal of Philosophy* 68 (1971): 597–610.

———. "A Leibnizian Space." *Dialogue* 14 (1975): 89–100

Hartshorne, Charles. *The Logic of Perfection*. La Salle, Illinois: Open Court, 1962.

Hartz, Glenn A. "Leibniz's Phenomenalisms." *Philosophical Review* 101 (1992): 511–49.

Hartz, Glenn A., and J. A. Cover. "Space and Time in the Leibnizian Metaphysic." *Noûs* 22 (1988): 493–519.

Heinekamp, Albert, Wolfgang Lenzen, and Martin Schneider, eds. *Mathesis rationis: Festschrift für Heinrich Schepers*. Münster: Nodus, 1990.

Hochstetter, Erich. "Von der wahren Wirklichkeit bei Leibniz." *Zeitschrift für philosophische Forschung* 20 (1966): 421–46.

Hoffman, Paul. "The Unity of Descartes's Man." *Philosophical Review* 95 (1986): 339–70.

Hooker, Michael, ed. *Leibniz: Critical and Interpretive Essays*. Minneapolis: University of Minnesota Press, 1982.

Ishiguro, Hidé. *Leibniz's Philosophy of Logic and Language*. London: Duckworth, 1972.

Janke, Wolfgang. "Das ontologische Argument in der Frühzeit des leibnizschen Denkens (1676–78)." *Kantstudien* 54 (1963): 259–87.

Jarrett, Charles E. "Leibniz on Truth and Contingency." *Canadian Journal of Philosophy* supplementary vol. 4 (1978): 83–100.

Jolley, Nicholas. *Leibniz and Locke: A Study of the New Essays Concerning Human Understanding*. Oxford: Clarendon, 1984.

———. "Leibniz and Phenomenalism." *Studia Leibnitiana* 18 (1986): 38–51.

Kabitz, Willy. "Leibniz und Berkeley." *Sitzungsberichte der preußischen Akademie der Wissenschaften*. Philosophisch-historische Klasse, N. xxiv (Jahrgang 1932): 623–36.

———. *Die Philosophie des jungen Leibniz*. Heidelberg: Carl Winters, 1909.

Kauppi, Railli. *Über die leibnizsche Logik*. Fascicle 12 of *Acta Philosophica Fennica*. Helsinki: 1960.

Kripke, Saul. "Semantical Analysis of Modal Logic I: Normal Propositional Calculi." *Zeitschrift für mathematische Logik und Grundlagen der Mathematik* 9 (1963): 67–96.

Kulstad, Mark, ed. *Essays on the Philosophy of Leibniz. Rice University Studies*, vol. 63, no. 4. Houston: Rice University, 1977.

———. *Leibniz on Apperception, Consciousness, and Reflection*. Munich: Philosophia Verlag, 1991.

Labrousse, Elisabeth. *Pierre Bayle*. 2 vols. The Hague: Martinus Nijhoff, 1963.

Lamarra, Antonio, ed. *L'infinito in Leibniz: problemi e terminologia*. Rome: Edizioni dell'Ateneo, and Hannover: G.-W.-Leibniz-Gesellschaft, after 1986.

———. "Leibniz on Locke on Infinity." In Lamarra, ed., *L'infinito in Leibniz*, pp. 173–91.

Le Brun, Jacques. "Critique des abus et signifiance des pratiques (La controverse Leibniz-Bossuet)." *Studia Leibnitiana Supplementa* 21 (1980): 246–57.

Leclerc, Ivor, ed. *The Philosophy of Leibniz and the Modern World*. Nashville, Tenn.: Vanderbilt University Press, 1973.

Lennon, Thomas M., John M. Nicholas, and John W. Davis, eds. *Problems of Cartesianism*. Kingston and Montreal: McGill, Queen's University Press, 1982.

Lewis, David. "Counterpart Theory and Quantified Modal Logic." *Journal of Philosophy* 65 (1968): 113–26.

Lindbeck, George. *The Nature of Doctrine: Religion and Theology in a Postliberal Age*. Philadelphia: Westminster, 1984.

Loeb, Louis E. *From Descartes to Hume*. Ithaca, N.Y.: Cornell University Press, 1981.

Lovejoy, Arthur O. *The Great Chain of Being*. Cambridge, Mass.: Harvard University Press, 1936.

Machamer, Peter, and Robert Turnbull, eds. *Motion and Time, Space and Matter*. Columbus: Ohio State University Press, 1976.

Malcolm, Norman. "Anselm's Ontological Arguments." *Philosophical Review* 69 (1960): 41–62.

Mates, Benson. "Individuals and Modality in the Philosophy of Leibniz." *Studia Leibnitiana* 4 (1972): 81–118.

———. "Leibniz on Possible Worlds." In van Rootselaar and Staal, eds., *Logic, Methodology, and Philosophy of Science*, vol. 3, pp. 507–29.

———. *The Philosophy of Leibniz: Metaphysics and Language*. New York: Oxford University Press, 1986.

Mathieu, Vittorio. *Leibniz e Des Bosses (1706–1716)*. Università di Torino, *Pubblicazioni della Facoltà di Lettere e Filosofia*, Vol. XII, Fascicolo 1. Turin: G. Giappichelli, 1960.

McGuire, J. E. "'Labyrinthus Continui': Leibniz on Substance, Activity, and Matter." In Machamer and Turnbull, eds., *Motion and Time, Space and Matter*, pp. 290–326.

McRae, Robert. *Leibniz: Perception, Apperception, and Thought*. Toronto and Buffalo: University of Toronto Press, 1976.

Mondadori, Fabrizio. "Leibniz and the Doctrine of Inter-World Identity." *Studia Leibnitiana* 7 (1975): 22–57.

———. "The Leibnizian 'Circle'." In Kulstad, ed., *Essays on the Philosophy of Leibniz*, pp. 69–96.

———. "Modalities, Representations, and Exemplars: the 'Region of Ideas'." In Heinekamp, Lenzen, and Schneider, eds., *Mathesis rationis*, pp. 169–88.

———. "Necessity ex Hypothesi." In Centro Fiorentino, *The Leibniz Renaissance*, pp. 191–222.

———. "Nominalisms." Forthcoming in the Proceedings of the International Leibniz Congress, Madrid, 20–22 September 1989.

———. "Reference, Essentialism, and Modality in Leibniz's Metaphysics." *Studia Leibnitiana* 5 (1973): 73–101.

———. "Understanding Superessentialism." *Studia Leibnitiana* 17 (1985): 162–90.

Mugnai, Massimo. *Astrazione e realtà: Saggio su Leibniz*. Milan: Feltrinelli, 1976.

———. "Leibniz's Nominalism and the Reality of Ideas in the Mind of God." In Heinekamp, Lenzen, and Schneider, eds., *Mathesis rationis*, pp. 153–67.

———. "'Necessità *ex hypothesi*' e analisi infinita in Leibniz." In Lamarra, ed., *L'infinito in Leibniz*, pp. 143–55.

Naert, Émilienne. *Mémoire et conscience de soi selon Leibniz*. Paris: Vrin, 1961.

Okruhlik, Kathleen, and James Robert Brown, eds. *The Natural Philosophy of Leibniz*. Dordrecht: Reidel, 1985.

Parkinson, G. H. R. "Leibniz's Paris Writings in Relation to Spinoza." *Studia Leibnitiana Supplementa* 18 (1978): 73–89.

———. *Logic and Reality in Leibniz's Metaphysics*. Oxford: Clarendon, 1965.

Plantinga, Alvin. *The Nature of Necessity*. Oxford: Clarendon, 1974.

Rescher, Nicholas. *The Philosophy of Leibniz*. Englewood Cliffs, N. J.: Prentice-Hall, 1967.

Risse, Wilhelm. *Die Logik der Neuzeit*. 2 vols. Stuttgart-Bad Cannstatt: F. Fromann, 1964–1970.

Robinet, André. *Architectonique disjonctive, automates systémiques, et idéalité dans l'oeuvre de G. W. Leibniz*. Paris: Vrin, 1986.

———. "G. W. Leibniz à Rome." In Lamarra, ed., *L'infinito in Leibniz*, pp. 237–47.

———. "Leibniz: Lecture du *Treatise* de Berkeley." *Les études philosophiques* 1983: 217–23.

———. *Système et existence dans l'oeuvre de Malebranche*. Paris: Vrin, 1965.

Rowe, William L. *The Cosmological Argument*. Princeton, N. J.: Princeton University Press, 1975.

Russell, Bertrand. *A Critical Exposition of the Philosophy of Leibniz, with an Appendix of Leading Passages*. 2nd ed. London: Allen & Unwin, 1937.

———. "Recent Work on the Philosophy of Leibniz." *Mind* 12 (1903). Reprinted and cited from Frankfurt, ed., *Leibniz*, pp. 365–400.

Schepers, Heinrich. "Zum Problem der Kontingenz bei Leibniz: Die Beste der möglichen Welten." In Ernest-Wolfgang Böckenförde, et al., *Collegium Philosophicum: Studien Joachim Ritter zum 60. Geburtstag* (Basel and Stuttgart: Schwabe, 1965), pp. 326–50.

Schneiders, Werner. "Deus Subjectum: Zur Entwicklung der leibnizschen Metaphysik." *Studia Leibnitian Supplementa* 18 (1978): 20–31.

Schupp, Franz. "Theoria—Praxis—Poiesis: Zur systematischen Ortsbestimmung der Logik bei Jungius und Leibniz." *Studia Leibnitiana Supplementa* 21 (1980): 1–11.

Sleigh, Robert C., Jr. *Leibniz and Arnauld: A Commentary on Their Correspondence*. New Haven, Conn.: Yale University Press, 1990.

———. "Leibniz on the Simplicity of Substance." In Kulstad, ed., *Essays on the Philosophy of Leibniz*, pp. 107–21.

———. "Truth and Sufficient Reason in the Philosophy of Leibniz." In Hooker, ed., *Leibniz*, pp. 209–42.

Sosa, Ernest, ed. *Essays on the Philosophy of George Berkeley*. Dordrecht: Reidel, 1987.

Stein, Ludwig. *Leibniz und Spinoza*. Berlin: Georg Reimer, 1890.

Tarski, Alfred. "Einige Betrachtungen über die Begriffe der ω-Widerspruchsfreiheit und der ω-Vollständigkeit." *Monatshefte für Mathematik und Physik* 40 (1933): 97–112.

van Rootselaar, B., and J. F. Staal, eds. *Logic, Methodology, and Philosophy of Science*, vol. 3. Amsterdam: North Holland, 1968.

Watson, Richard A. "Transubstantiation among the Cartesians." In Lennon, Nicholas, and Davis, eds., *Problems of Cartesianism*, pp. 127–48.

Westfall, Richard S. *Science and Religion in Seventeenth-Century England*. Ann Arbor: University of Michigan Press, 1958.

Wilson, Catherine. "Critical and Constructive Aspects of Leibniz's Monadology." In Centro Fiorentino, *The Leibniz Renaissance*, pp. 291–303.

———. *Leibniz's Metaphysics*. Princeton, N. J.: Princeton University Press, 1989.

Wilson, Margaret. "The Phenomenalisms of Leibniz and Berkeley." In Sosa, ed., *Essays on the Philosophy of George Berkeley*, pp. 3–22.

———. "Leibniz's Dynamics and Contingency in Nature." In Machamer and Turnbull, eds. *Motion and Time, Space and Matter*, pp. 264–89.

———. "Possible Gods." *Review of Metaphysics* 32 (1979): 717–33.

Winterbourne, A. T. "On the Metaphysics of Leibnizian Space and Time." *Studies in History and Philosophy of Science* 13 (1982): 201–14.

Yost, Robert M., Jr. *Leibniz and Philosophical Analysis*. University of California Publications in Philosophy, vol. 27. Berkeley and Los Angeles, 1954.

Index of Leibniz Texts Cited

General Index

Printed in the United States
957400002B